F·I·R·S·T
FEMINISTS

Nine Living Muses by Richard Samuel, 1779, Catalog No. 4905. *Courtesy of the National Portrait Gallery*, London.

Left-hand group: top, left to right, Hannah More and Elizabeth Montague; bottom, Elizabeth Griffith. Center figure: Catherine Macaulay. Right-hand group: top, left to right, Elizabeth Carter and Anna Letitia Barbauld; bottom, left to right, Angelica Kauffman, Elizabeth Linley, and Charlotte Lenox.

F·I·R·S·T
FEMINISTS

BRITISH WOMEN WRITERS

1578 — 1799

EDITED and with an INTRODUCTION

By MOIRA FERGUSON

INDIANA UNIVERSITY PRESS · BLOOMINGTON

THE FEMINIST PRESS · OLD WESTBURY, NEW YORK

Library of Congress Cataloging in Publication Data

Main entry under title:

First feminists.

Bibliography: p.

1. Feminism—Literary collections.   2. Women—
Literary collections.   3. English literature—Women
authors.   4. English literature—Early modern, 1500–1700.
5. English literature—18th century.   I. Ferguson, Moira.
PR1111.F45F57   1985   820′.8′09287   84–42838
ISBN 0–253–32213–8
ISBN 0–253–28120–2 (pbk.)

1 2 3 4 5   89 88 87 86 85

For my beloved and indomitable mother, Elizabeth Smith Ferguson,
and for my mother-in-law, Clara Goodman Fraser, with love and
respect for her lifelong revolutionary struggle.

CONTENTS

PREFACE   xi

INTRODUCTION   1

MARGARET TYLER, *fl.* 1578   51
  FROM TRANSLATION BY TYLER OF *THE FIRST PART*
    OF THE MIRROUR OF PRINCELY DEEDES AND
    KNYGHTHOOD: DEDICATION AND EPISTLE TO
    THE READER, 1578

JANE ANGER, *fl.* 1589   58
  JANE ANGER HER PROTECTION FOR WOMEN, 1589

ESTER SOWERNAM, *fl.* 1617   74
  FROM *ESTER HATH HANG'D HAMAN:* ADDRESS;
    FROM CHAPTER 7, 1617

JOANE SHARP, *fl.* 1617   80
  "A DEFENCE OF WOMEN": POEM CONCLUDING
    ESTER SOWERNAM'S *ESTER HATH HANG'D*
    HAMAN, 1617

MARGARET LUCAS CAVENDISH,
  DUCHESS OF NEWCASTLE, 1623–1673   84
  FROM *PHILOSOPHICAL AND PHYSICAL OPINIONS:*
    PREFACE "TO THE TWO MOST FAMOUS
    UNIVERSITIES OF ENGLAND," 1655
  FROM *THE CONVENT OF PLEASURE*, 1668

KATHERINE FOWLER PHILIPS, 1631–1664   102
  FROM *POEMS BY THE MOST DESERVEDLY ADMIRED*
    MRS. KATHERINE PHILIPS, THE MATCHLESS
    ORINDA . . . , 1667

MARGARET ASKEW FELL FOX, 1614–1702   114
  FROM *WOMENS SPEAKING JUSTIFIED*, . . . , 1667

BATHSUA PELL MAKIN, 1608?–1675?   128
FROM *AN ESSAY TO REVIVE THE ANTIENT EDUCATION
OF GENTLEWOMEN, . . .* , 1673

APHRA BEHN, 1640–1689   143
FROM *THE DUTCH LOVER:* PREFACE, 1673
FROM *SIR PATIENT FANCY:* EPILOGUE, 1678
FROM *LYCIDUS; OR, THE LOVER IN FASHION,* 1688
FROM TRANSLATION BY BEHN OF *LA PLURALITÉ DES
DEUX MONDES (THE THEORY OR SYSTEM
OF SEVERAL NEW INHABITED WORLDS):*
"THE AUTHOR'S PREFACE," 1700

SARAH FYGE FIELD EGERTON,
1669/72–1722/23   152
FROM *THE FEMALE ADVOCATE,* 1686
FROM *POEMS ON SEVERAL OCCASIONS,* 1703

JANE BARKER, *fl.* 1688 *and* 1723   171
FROM *POETICAL RECREATIONS . . .* , 1688
FROM *A PATCH-WORK SCREEN FOR THE
LADIES, . . .* , 1723

MARY ASTELL, 1666–1731   180
FROM *A SERIOUS PROPOSAL TO THE LADIES, . . .* ,
PARTS 1 AND 2, 1694, 1697
FROM *SOME REFLECTIONS UPON MARRIAGE . . .* , 1700
FROM *THE COMPLETE LETTERS OF LADY MARY WORTLEY
MONTAGU,* VOL. 1: MARY ASTELL'S PREFACE TO THE
EMBASSY LETTERS, 1724

JUDITH DRAKE, *fl.* 1696   201
FROM *AN ESSAY IN DEFENCE OF THE FEMALE SEX,* 1696

MARY LEE, LADY CHUDLEIGH, 1656–1710   212
THE LADIES DEFENCE, INCLUDING PREFATORY
MATERIAL, 1701
FROM *POEMS ON SEVERAL OCCASIONS,* 1703

ELIZABETH ELSTOB, 1683–1756   239
FROM *AN ENGLISH-SAXON HOMILY, . . .* : PREFACE, 1709

ANNE KINGSMILL FINCH, COUNTESS OF
WINCHILSEA, 1661–1720   247
FROM *MISCELLANY POEMS, ON SEVERAL OCCASIONS,* 1713
FROM *THE POEMS OF ANNE, COUNTESS OF WINCHELSEA,*
1903

MARY COLLIER, 1689/90–*after* 1759   257
THE WOMAN'S LABOUR, 1739
FROM *POEMS, ON SEVERAL OCCASIONS*, INCLUDING
"SOME REMARKS OF THE AUTHOR'S LIFE DRAWN
BY HERSELF," 1762

SOPHIA, *fl.* 1739–1741   266
FROM *WOMAN NOT INFERIOR TO MAN*, . . . , 1739
FROM *WOMAN'S SUPERIOR EXCELLENCE OVER
MAN*, . . . , 1740

CHARLOTTE CIBBER CHARKE, ?–1760   284
FROM *A NARRATIVE OF THE LIFE OF MRS. CHARLOTTE
CHARKE*, INCLUDING "THE AUTHOR TO HERSELF,"
1755

SARAH ROBINSON SCOTT, 1723–1795   311
FROM *A DESCRIPTION OF MILLENIUM HALL* . . . , 1762

ELIZABETH CARTER, 1717–1806   327
FROM *A SERIES OF LETTERS BETWEEN MRS. ELIZABETH
CARTER AND MISS CATHERINE TALBOT*,
VOLS. 1 AND 2, 1809

MARY SCOTT (TAYLOR), 1752?–1793   349
FROM *THE FEMALE ADVOCATE*, 1774

ELEANOR BUTLER, 1737–1829   368
FROM *THE HAMWOOD PAPERS OF THE LADIES OF
LLANGOLLEN* . . . , 1785–1821

ANN CROMARTIE YEARSLEY, 1756–1806   380
FROM *POEMS ON VARIOUS SUBJECTS:* "AUTOBIOGRAPHICAL
NARRATIVE," 1787
A POEM ON THE INHUMANITY OF THE SLAVE-TRADE, 1788

CATHERINE SAWBRIDGE MACAULAY
GRAHAM, 1731–1791   398
FROM *LETTERS ON EDUCATION*, 1790

MARY HAYS, 1759/60–1843   412
FROM *MONTHLY MAGAZINE:* JULY 2, 1796;
MARCH 2, 1797

MARY WOLLSTONECRAFT, 1759–1797   420
FROM *A VINDICATION OF THE RIGHTS OF WOMAN*, 1792
FROM *THE WRONGS OF WOMAN, OR MARIA*, 1798

MARY ANNE RADCLIFFE, 1746?–*after* 1810   437
    FROM *THE FEMALE ADVOCATE*, 1799

SUPPLEMENTARY READINGS: WORKS NOT
    EXCERPTED   457

PREFACE

This anthology ends where many excellent modern anthologies start—at the end of the eighteenth century. It grows out of a search for origins. Beginning in 1578 it traces through the writings of twenty-eight British women the evolution and growth of feminist ideas and connections between and among women over two centuries. By feminist I mean those ideas and actions that advocate women's just demands and rights, or that counter or offset, at any level, the socio-cultural, sexual, and psychological oppression and economic exploitation of women. I recognize that what we would define as feminist is dependent upon and changes within different historical periods.

The writings in this volume range from Margaret Tyler's mild protest about restrictions on women in a 1578 preface, to Mary Anne Radcliffe's 1799 attack on male usurpation of female occupations and the prevalence of prostitution. While a tumultuous, fundamental reshaping of British, French, and North American society was occurring, over seventy women wrote explicitly feminist works in English. Many others wrote feminist "passages" which in some way eschewed prescribed female roles. Still others raised wider issues of social justice, such as the protest against slavery. I have selected (with some difficulty) twenty-eight authors, both obscure and well known, who helped develop "mainstream" British feminist literature before 1800. As a whole these writings are representative of women from diverse backgrounds and different historical times. The variety of genres is also representative of the period. In concentrating on British feminist writings, we must recognize the crucial role of such continental writers as Christine de Pisan (1364–1430?) in initiating the debate ("querelle") on women. Not until the middle of Queen Elizabeth's reign did British women begin to question their situation.

I address the struggle against slavery not because early British feminists viewed that struggle as integral to justice for women (as far as I have read, none did) but because in the twentieth-century women's movement, resistance to the oppression and exploitation of women (and,

A shortened version of part of this introduction entitled "Feminist Polemic, a Reflex to Misogyny: Another 'Lost' Genre of Women's Literature" was presented as a paper at the Modern Language Association, December 30, 1979, in San Francisco, at a forum on "Changing Genres." At Buena Vista College, Storm Lake, Iowa, March, 1980, in the annual guest lecturer series, I read an expanded version entitled, "The Development of British Feminism in the Seventeenth Century."

therefore, of all people) of color and the elimination of that injustice is now recognized as a necessary precondition of liberation. The origins of this awareness may be found in some of the writing by women in English during the seventeenth and eighteenth centuries. I am therefore arguing that resistance to slavery and the slave-trade (in Ann Yearsley's poem, for example) is ultimately part of a more fully developed feminist consciousness. It is also true that most pre–1800 feminists did not protest slavery. Few did. When the subject of slavery did appear in early feminist writings, aside from those of Aphra Behn and religious women, it frequently described women's condition. At the very least, this usage suggests that slavery was viewed negatively even if it were not actively opposed.

For each of the twenty-eight writers included in this collection I give a short biography, a tract, essay, letters, poems, or, more generally, an excerpt, excerpts, or selections from a collection or a longer work, followed by brief and by no means exhaustive bibliographies of primary and related sources. Under primary sources I have cited first editions (i.e., earliest issues) when I could. I have not cited all editions of each primary work. For reference purposes, full titles of works—usually excerpted works in this volume—appear in the primary bibliographies. Notes on the location of each selection may be found at the foot of the first page of text. Occasionally, as with *Millenium Hall,* I had available only the modern edition. In the case of Judith Drake, I have inserted the original publishers in the bibliographical entry, although excerpted portions follow the modern editions. (In this particular case, the modern edition is out-of-print.)

Generally, I kept sixteenth-, seventeenth-, and eighteenth-century capitalization, but no italics or underlinings except when they were specifically used for emphasis. Sixteenth, seventeenth, and eighteenth-century writers had routinely no consistency of spelling. Consequently readers should not be surprised to find that even titles and proper names were variously spelled in the same extract. Old spellings have been retained, obvious typographical errors and inconsistencies silently corrected, and translations or synonyms of the now unfamiliar word given. When I give the name of sub-headings found in the text such as "Introduction" or "To the Reader," I use quotation marks; when making a title for purposes of clarity, I omit quotation marks. In the last section entitled Supplementary Readings: Works Not Excerpted, I cite forty-three additional writers for whom I give unabbreviated titles. This list may be found at the back of the book.

Any reader wishing to pursue research on an individual writer should in most cases be able to find an entry under either the name or the title in the British Library catalogue. In the cases of writers not entered in the British Library catalogue, such as Jane Anger or Aemelia Lanier, the *National Union Catalogue* (Anger) and the *Dictionary of Na-*

tional Biography (Lanier) are likely sources. Readers may also consult the primary and secondary bibliographies for each writer provided herein.

I would like to acknowledge the splendid assistance of the staff of the inter-library loan office of Love Library (particularly Kitty McGinnis, Shirley Rockle, and Thomas McFarland) at the University of Nebraska-Lincoln, who made the acquisition of much of this material possible. I am also greatly indebted to my home institution: to the University of Nebraska Research Council for a summer fellowship and grants, to the Vice Chancellor for Research for research initiation grants, to the Dean of the College of Arts and Sciences, and to the Department of English for its financial support toward acquisition of materials and for travel that enabled me to obtain materials and visit libraries. A grant-in-aid from the American Council of Learned Societies also greatly benefited my research.

Since this volume has involved visits to and correspondence with libraries in the United States and Great Britain, I would like to extend my thanks to the staffs of the British Library; the Boston Public Library; the Crosby Library, Gonzaga University, Washington; the Detroit Public Library; the Houghton Special Collections Library and the Widener Library, Harvard University; the Henry E. Huntington Library and Art Gallery, San Marino, California; the Lilly Library, Indiana University; the Newberry Library, Chicago; the Pforzheimer Library, New York; the Suzzallo Library, University of Washington; the William Andrews Clark Library, University of California, Los Angeles; Humanities Research Center, The University of Texas at Austin; the Union Theological Seminary Library, New York; the Beinecke Library, Yale University; and The Library, Vassar College. They furnished photocopies, lent materials, expertly answered my queries, and opened up their collections to me. I also wish to thank The National Portrait Gallery in London, the Avon County Reference Library in Bristol, and The Huntington Library in California for permission to reproduce the illustrations used in this book.

Many people helped me very generously during the preparation of this collection of materials. With students, colleagues, and friends I was frequently rewarded by invigorating discussions. I would like to express particular gratitude to the following: Paula Bachscheider, Roberta Buchanan, Jeanine Brink, Nancy Cotton, Robert Haller, Robert Halsband, Allison Heisch, Shawn F. D. Hughes, Joyce Irwin, Jean Kern, Janet Krischke, Mary Lamb, Edith Larsen, Frederick Link, Felicity Nussbaum, Sherry O'Donnell, Dolores Palomo, Ann B. Schteir, and Hilda Smith. I owe a special debt of thanks to Elaine Hobby, Ruth Perry, and Barbara Brandon Schnorrenberg for their careful late readings of the manuscript and many beneficial suggestions. For their aid with the research: Linda Endres, Mary Ingle, Laura Marvel, Barbara Tentinger, Pamela Varner, and the invaluable Catherine Yamamoto. For first-rate help in typing the excerpts, Marian Salzman, and for excellent secretarial skills and general goodheartedness, Roma Rector and LeAnn Messing. For fine editorial advice and kind, steadfast attention, Jo Baird, Managing Editor, and Florence Howe, Publisher of The Feminist Press. For constructive criticism and readings and continuing encouragement and camaraderie: Kathleen Blake, the late Joan Kelly, Catharine Stimpson, and Amy Swerdlow.

Finally I want to acknowledge what has been so important to me throughout this project: the collective goodwill and loving support of my husband Marc Krasnowsky and my children Paul, Christopher, and Sarah.

F·I·R·S·T
FEMINISTS

Bathsua Makin as appears in Samuel Woodburn's GALLERY OF RARE PORTRAITS, 1816, 27888 Vol.2, p. 38. *Courtesy of The Huntington Library, San Marino, California.*

The Ladies of Llangollen, in Library, from Charles Penruddocke's THE LADIES OF LLANGOLLEN, Llangollen, 1897. *Courtesy of The Huntington Library, San Marino, California.*

Elizabeth Carter by Sir Thomas Lawrence, Catalog No. 28. *Courtesy of the National Portrait Gallery, London.*

Portrait of Catherine Macaulay by
Catherine Read, 1764. *Courtesy of
The Huntington Library, San Marino,
California.*

Mary Wollstonecraft by John Opie,
1797. *Courtesy of the National Portrait Gallery, London.*

Introduction

Background and History

The literature in this volume was written in Britain between 1578 and 1799 by women who were conscious of the inferior status ascribed to women, not only by the men and women they lived and worked with but by the whole fabric of culture and society around them. That cultural fabric had begun to change long before mid-Elizabethan England, but during the two hundred years under consideration, the nation's economic and political power moved out of the hands of land-owning aristocrats into those of rising merchant-manufacturing capitalists.[1] Thus, the period covered by the literature in this volume marks the period of transition in England from feudal-agricultural to bourgeois-industrial society.

In seventeenth-century emerging capitalist society, the enclosure of land and the needs of society based on new socio-economic relations meant that the ancient social phenomenon of shared home livelihoods and industries was being eroded and replaced by the separation of private from public labor.[2] Women working at home and men working outside the home became a standard arrangement. Cities grew and jobs became more specialized, often at the expense of such traditional women's work as midwifery, baking, and home-spinning. During the eighteenth century, men replaced women in such well-known female occupations as millinery, hairdressing, and mantua-making.[3] As the population exploded in the second half of the eighteenth century, and so long as jobs could not keep pace with the changing demography, the pressure increased to provide work, especially in agriculture and crafts, for surplus male laborers.[4] Cast out of large sectors of the labor market, many women sought marriage as one of the remaining viable legal options. It is not surprising, therefore, that this period of dramatic economic and political shifts should also contain the earliest signs of a rising feminist consciousness in Britain. The process had been a slow one. Negative views of women dated back to the Hebrew, Greek, and Roman Ancient World and to early Christian antifeminist attitudes expressed most forcibly in patristic literature. The first feminist response to misogynous literature, by Christine de Pisan, surfaced in the late Middle Ages in France and the ensuing debate was labelled the *Querelle des Femmes*.[5] The earliest polemics in English appeared in mid-

Elizabethan England in 1578 and 1589 in response to cultural restrictions and traditional womanhating assaults.

Before the 1640s and the outbreak of the Civil War in England, several polemical responses written by women in response to antifeminist diatribes by men were published. These diatribes expressed male fury at increasingly independent public displays by primarily aristocratic and wealthy women. Part of the literary debate in the early 1620s centered on tracts about the allegedly masculine woman, "Hic Mulier," and the feminized man, "Haec Vir."[6] James I, the misogynous son of Mary, Queen of Scots, put legislation in motion to curb these gestures of female defiance.[7]

This rise in women's aggressive self-expression in English received further support from ideas of religious equality propagated by nonconformist sects during and after the Civil War (1642–49). Many sectaries (members of nonconformist sects)—radical religious women—agitated for freedom of speech and action and the right to challenge royal, church, and, by extension, patriarchal authority.[8] Their collective forthrightness and creativity inaugurated the right of women to public assertion and action. Women writers had arrived in numbers and in earnest. Reaction to the restoration of the monarchy in 1660 and the callous attitudes of a dissolute court toward women further engendered female resistance. These protests about the treatment of women were connected in tone, spirit, and ideas to the feminist writings of women from Margaret Tyler and Jane Anger in 1578 and 1589 to the tracts that responded to Joseph Swetnam around 1617.

During the seventeenth century, midwives had agitated to keep men out of their profession. At the same time, the occupation of business accounting became somewhat available to women and allowed for the training of female apprentices. Women had also become almanac writers and in some guilds and trades (printing, for example), women's participation continued into the eighteenth century.[9] The profession of writing attracted only the most audacious of women, for being paid to write fell into the same category as writing at all: society frowned upon it and only those who were both bold and desperate dared, or those whose privileged status allowed them to dispense with society's sanction of their activities.[10]

Though not the first British woman to write to earn a livelihood, Aphra Behn (1640–1689) was probably the first to do so exclusively; certainly she was the first major female dramatist. Mary Griffith Pix (1666–1720) followed Behn in this practice. Delarivière Manley (1663–1724), Catherine Cockburn Trotter (1679–1749), possibly Jane Barker, (fl. 1688 and 1723), and Eliza Fowler Haywood (1693?–1756), who began as an actor, attempted the same with differing degrees of success. In the next generation Susanna Centlivre (1667?–1723) also acted to begin with but soon switched to writing plays. The Anglo-Saxon scholar Elizabeth Elstob (1683–1756) was aided by her brother, but after he died she disappeared (for fear of debts) and was "found" by chance over twenty years later. She never worked again on scholarly projects. At the turn of the eighteenth century, such aristocrats as Lady Chudleigh (1656–1710) probably published without expectation of payment. Several others later in the century—Sarah Robinson Scott (1723–1795) and Elizabeth Carter (1717–1760) among them—tried to earn a subsistence by writing or translating, but they had other means, either a family or helpful friends, to supplement their incomes. By the late eighteenth century several female polemicists (Catherine Sawbridge Macaulay Graham, 1731–1791, Mary Wollstonecraft, 1759–1797, and Mary Hays, 1759/60–1843, among them) had committed themselves to writing as a major profession. When Ann Cromartie Yearsley (1756–1806), originally a Bristol milkwoman, attempted to do so, class and circumstances defeated her.

As a profession, education also began to attract women. Bathsua Pell Makin (1608–1675?) wrote to advertise her school as well as to argue for female education. Hannah Woolley (1627–1670) began teaching school at fifteen and wrote a form of training manual for women in the domestic arts at a time when jobs were disappearing. After the Civil War, women still agitated to be preachers.

In general, women were losing ground in their efforts to retain space and their traditional functions in the workforce. The enclosure of cultivable and common land also affected working women although it was a gradual process. Some of the dispossessed stayed in the countryside and eked out a living while others moved to the cities and found themselves frequently excluded from the skilled jobs that urban reconstruction and capital investment were opening up. During this time, the old family structure based on kin gave way more and more to a family unit based on the married couple. Changing work patterns made many women look to marriage for economic survival, in part because a woman's wages tended to be two-thirds those of a man. Nonetheless, protests (such as one in *The Gentleman's Magazine* in 1739) about male usurpation of female jobs were relatively rare until the late eighteenth century, when tough-minded feminists attacked the issue of occupations directly.[11]

In the same general time frame, Lord Chancellor Hardwicke's Marriage Act of 1753 came into being. It acknowledged the right of the state to interfere in the right of citizens to marry or not, and it condoned interference in private morals and cultural traditions, especially those of the poor. While it helped, somewhat, to curb the kind of abuse endured by Pamela Andrews and Clarissa Harlowe at the hands of employers, parents, and suitors, it also made more overt the generally unspoken equation of women with private property.

The legal status of married women matched their social status, since they had no legal identity apart from men. Legally, women were classified with "wards, lunatics, idiots, and outlaws." In common law, married women possessed no civil rights: they could not own property, make wills, testify in courts, serve on juries, or obtain divorces. So great was their dependent status that even if they acquired large debts women could not be imprisoned. Their children, like their bodies and personal property, belonged to their husbands. Single women, however, could own property and a widow could usually regain one-third of the goods that had automatically been acquired by her husband upon marriage.[12]

MIDDLE-CLASS OCCUPATIONS

For eighteenth-century middle-class women who remained single and who were not independently wealthy, occupations were severely limited to those considered lady-like. By and large, business and trade were regarded as the province of male workers. Mary Wollstonecraft's career as an independent petty-bourgeois worker ran the gamut of acceptable options. She began as a chaperone to a widow, then, while living with the family of her friend, Fanny Blood, she helped to supplement their income by sewing (which brought her face-to-face with the realities of laboring-class existence), and after that, with borrowed capital, she administered and taught in a day school, which also solicited a few pupils as lodgers. She wrote a courtesy manual in 1786, and while she worked as a governess to a aristocratic Irish family, she wrote her first novel. After her dismissal from that work, Joseph Johnson, the radical publisher, hired her as an editorial assistant, translator (self-taught), and reviewer for his journal. She then branched out as a full-fledged author, writing a moral handbook for young people, polemics, history, a travel-book, more educational pieces, and fiction. These occupations (aside from sewing, which was considered déclassé) were the basic socially acceptable ones for middle-class women. Most of the jobs depended on a certain educational level.

During the eighteenth century, as men worked for the new economy in an environment divorced from their private lives, there was a new focus on marriage. Its appropriateness as a social arrangement was preached from the pulpit and publicized in tracts and courtesy literature, its economic advantages for parents and society often glossed over. The majority of middle-class women began (or rather learned) to view being a mother as a paramount priority. (Women who sought work and economic self-sufficiency were a definite minority and nunneries as an option had substantially disappeared with the dissolution of the monasteries, 1536–1539.) Marriage was one of the few fashionable entrées as well as the only profitable one into adult society, "recommended as an alliance of sense."[13] Consequently, many women's lives took on a more isolated and private character. In turn, motherhood was accorded a new respect that helped to counterbalance the lack of respect and sense of social unproductiveness engendered by women's exclusion from the marketplace. Wives of merchant-traders and of up-and-coming "businessmen" gradually became, in their finery and through their leisure, indicators of their husbands' wealth rather than wage earners in their own right. People from abroad frequently commented on middle-class women's (voluntary and involuntary) idleness. By the end of the eighteenth century, however, the idea of choice in partner gained greater currency; daughters of the professional and landed classes attained more freedom than they had formerly possessed in their selection of spouse.

The cult of motherhood guaranteed the married middle-class woman a unique identity and status, which compensated for her absence from the waged work force. The doctrine of separate spheres had become a living reality in eighteenth-century gender reconstruction. Chastity and modesty became essential female characteristics, being without waged work was an acceptable and eventually, for some, a desirable status. The centuries-old misogynous characterization of women as inconstant, power-hungry, immodest, wanton, and sexually fierce had appeared in an updated variation in Restoration drama. These images were gradually replaced by the increasingly popular images of the angel in the house, the virtuous maiden in distress, the prostitute in the street, and the all-but-swashbuckling proletarian adventurer represented by Daniel Defoe's Moll Flanders (1722). As gentility reigned, even fiction was pronounced too risqué for what were now regarded as delicate feminine constitutions. Pure in body and spirit, submissive damsels of delicacy heard no aspersions cast about their foul sexual natures. From a bourgeois male standpoint, it was no longer socially or economically expedient to label women as Eve-like tempters.

ARISTOCRATIC OCCUPATIONS

The four duties of a "lady in polite society," as Roy Porter describes them, were to obey her husband, bear heirs and discharge her duty to her children, run a household (itself a complex, multi-faceted task), and be "an ambassadress of grace."[14] That position, however, was changing. The aristocratic woman was no longer the domestic *chargée d'affaires* of the large manor. Consumer goods had begun to reduce the need for heavy domestic production and huge household staffs. Also, in mid-eighteenth century, when maternal breastfeeding became more favored (often for health reasons) and as household duties became increasingly delegated by aristocratic and upper middle-class women, so too did the cult of appearance come more into vogue. Decreased participation in domestic work also fostered benevolence toward society's poor in the aristocrats' search (and the leisured middle-class woman's search) for useful activity. Country aristocrats spent fashionable seasons in London.

LABORING-CLASS OCCUPATIONS

On the other hand, the lives of laboring (working-class) women remained a matter of survival. Earning considerably lower wages, women still worked with men in the fields and in some industries. Mary Collier's experiences as a washerwoman and her description of women fieldworkers were probably accurate for England in the late 1730s. The double and triple shift was not uncommon in the provinces and elsewhere. In the course of the century, women lost jobs they had long held; in the city, the high rate of prostitution spoke tellingly about the availability of jobs, especially for deracinated country women, and it was not unusual for women to starve to death; in agriculture, women in some regions were specifically relegated to weeding.[15] The visible liminality of working women made marriage a more attractive proposition, although total withdrawal into domesticity was scarcely financially feasible for laboring people who frequently viewed marriage as a joint economic venture, if not a necessity. Domestic service, often of a thoroughly exploitative nature, was always available. Probably the major economic blow for women was the development of textile production late in the eighteenth century (following a series of technological inventions beginning with the spinning jenny), which gradually rendered domestic spinning an outmoded system. Nonetheless, Eric Richards finds cause to praise the shift in women's roles at this time:

> The accelerated growth of the British economy in the last decades of the Eighteenth Century generated employment in both old and new sectors—for instance in handloom weaving and in cotton spinning factories . . . Moreover, in the most spectacular growth sector, cotton, there was a disproportionate expansion in jobs which were to become almost specific to women.[16]

Women had been extensively pressed out of agricultural production; then late eighteenth-century textile factories became the workplaces for large numbers of laboring women.

LABORING-CLASS EDUCATION

Just as the occupational options available to a woman varied according to her socio-economic status, so did the kind of education a woman received.[17] For the laboring poor, endowed charitable institutions administered by share-holders on joint stock principles—the Society for Promoting Christian Knowledge (1699) was one—offered two areas of concentration: religious instruction, which taught acceptance of social place as part of God's plan; and skills for domestic service or, at best, a trade. Job training was especially favored since the Society's backers reaped profits from that scheme. By the end of the eighteenth century, earlier educational ideas, fostered in part by the Evangelical movement, had blossomed into a Sunday School movement—1,086 schools with 69,000 pupils by 1797—and some short-lived "schools of industry," which were primarily workshops to train the unemployed poor.[18] (Lack of profits caused their closure.) All systems of educating the poor stressed the rigid maintenance of "keeping one's place," an ideology calculated to preempt any form of resistance to social standing by the disadvantaged. Literacy was doubly distrusted for it both increased understanding and fomented rebellion.[19] As eighteenth-century crime increased and stories of the French revolutionary overthrow of tyrannical power crossed the channel, suppression of the poor became a particular concern. Since many "philanthropic educators" held High Church and Tory beliefs, their conservative attitudes made them fearful that even Sunday Schools would prove subversive. In the end, though, teaching humility, a sense of duty, and obedience to God's will seemed more profitable in an age of rapidly growing productivity. Stephen Duck, the thresher-turned-poet, in his poem "On Poverty" (ca. 1730), expressed in a terse couplet the ideology that middle-class philanthropists strove to instill:

> Let poverty or want be what it will,
> It does proceed from God; therefore's no ill.

ARISTOCRATIC EDUCATION

At the other end of the social scale, aristocratic families occasionally engaged governesses, and perhaps dancing, drawing, or singing masters for their daughters, while some received instruction from their brother's tutors. Frequently these well-connected daughters had access to a richly stocked library, if their fathers and mothers considered female education important. Also available were a few highly selective and expensive boarding schools. According to prescriptive literature, the education of an aristocratic female had to equip her "to devote her time, her talents, and her fortune, to the improvement of public morals, and the increase of public happiness."[20] Queen Mary, for example, pursued a difficult course of self-education, while the impecunious Saxonist scholar, Elizabeth Elstob, was hired to tutor the Duchess of Portland's children. She taught them religion, the practice of virtue, reading, speaking, and understanding English, a program not unlike that recommended in middle-class readers by middle-class educators. In contrast, Jonathan Swift commented contemptuously on "the daughters of great and rich families [who are] left entirely to their mothers, or they are sent to boarding-schools, or put into the hands of English or French governesses, and generally the worst that can be gotten for money."[21] An unapologetic Lady Mary Wortley Montagu (1689–1762) explained "the forlorn state of matrimony" by saying that "we have nothing to excuse ourselves but that it was done a great while ago and we were very young when we did it."[22] With marriage and social position the most crucial factors in the lives of females "born to estates," their education was often grievously neglected or was merely superficial, a schooling in fashion and manners. At best, the education of upper-class females seemed to have been an erratic affair.

MIDDLE-CLASS EDUCATION AND THE RISE OF PHILANTHROPY

Between aristocratic and laboring-class daughters were the middle-class females, many of whom attended boarding and day schools that offered a curriculum designed to equip pupils with "accomplishments" for a highly competitive marriage market. These included embroidery, lace-making, drawing and painting, music, deportment, and light ("snippet") learning. Anxious parents viewed this fashionable, genteel preparation as a model of the education favored by the upper class, whose customs and practices they sought to emulate. Competent day schools, which varied in quality throughout the country, presented another avenue to education.[23]

Parental attitudes toward the female education of middle-class and aristocratic daughters alike largely determined its quality. Extant records indicate that some clerical fathers took a special interest in educating their daughters, even in intellectual fields generally deemed inappropriate for women. Several mid- to late eighteenth-century women known as Bluestockings, who gained reputations as cultural intellectuals, were encouraged by such fathers. Moreover, recent evidence suggests that the tenets of prescriptive literature were rarely practiced, or at least not universally followed, and that many middle-class females received a more rigorous and classical education than has been previously thought.[24]

In the salons organized and frequented by Bluestockings between 1740 and 1790, female intellect and wit helped to demolish old ideas about the inferior social place and mental capacities of women and opened the door to public acceptance of women as serious thinkers.[25] Several wrote about female education, and one acknowledged Bluestocking leader, Elizabeth Robinson Montagu (1720–1800), discussed its advantages with a dissenting friend. All women who wrote about education, however—Bluestockings (who were generally conservative), Dissenters, Quakers, and Evangelicals alike—held that education should be appropriate to socio-economic status. In 1797, the year that Wollstonecraft died, for example, she was drafting an essay about the role of educated middle-class females in functioning as leaders for poorer or economically disadvantaged females. Even for the enlightened middle-class, education was not part of the agenda for disadvantaged women.

The fact that daughters received less complete education and had considerably fewer occupations available than their brothers left time weighing heavily on the hands of women who were neither devotees of fashion nor fulltime childbearers and childrearers. Many—often as a result of their religious affiliations and beliefs—chose philanthropy as a rewarding and useful avocation to compensate for their perceived lack of productivity and as a means of acceptable self-fulfillment. Several aristocratic women, such as Selina, the Countess of Huntingdon, were also well-known philanthropists.

Tending the sick, helping the homeless and downtrodden, and simultaneously making women feel useful also obscured the social and educational privations of females in general. Philanthropy held ambiguous implications for women. While women's public activities contradicted the idea that feminine delicacy necessarily anchored women at home and separated them from the world of thought and action, philanthropy also reinforced the insidious doctrine of separate spheres (in male and female occupations as well as between the privileged and the underprivileged of society), and implicitly strengthened old biological determinist distortions and fantasies.[26]

Most importantly, however, the public acceptance of women as social reformers led to female resistance to prostitution and slavery. Radical and dissenting writers were similarly concerned. Shortly after the Abolition movement was formed in 1787, for instance, several women wrote antislavery poems, tracts, and fictional episodes.[27] Waged and unwaged, women were entering the public sphere in earnest.

WOMEN WRITERS AND THE GROWTH OF FEMINISM

Having suggested some key areas of discrimination against women in this rapidly altering society from the late 1600s to 1800, I want to sketch in chronological sequence the development of feminist ideas and perspectives that this unwarranted discrimination provoked, and at the same time connect the ideas to the writers who thought creatively about this discrimination.

THE EARLY SEVENTEENTH CENTURY

Of the writers who ushered in feminist demands and attacks in mid-Elizabethan England, Margaret Tyler (fl. 1578), a Roman Catholic member—possibly a servant—in the aristocratic Howard household, and Jane Anger (fl. 1589) (probably a pseudonym), head the list. Despite differences in style and focus, they possessed a similar sense of women's rights, fostered in part by the presence of a woman ruler and Renaissance humanist ideas about learning.

Margaret Tyler, who translated the popular works of a Roman Catholic Spaniard, Diego Ortuñez de Calahorra, used that opportunity to protest the view that women were intellectually unfit for anything but translation. Tyler contended that women could write on or translate any subject customarily commandeered by men, such as war. She foreshadowed Aphra Behn, who was the first female professional writer, and Mary Wollstonecraft, whose second *Vindication* challenged Jean-

Jacques Rousseau's misogyny and the patriarchal condescension of male courtesy writers. Tyler stressed that women should be free to exercise their intellectual faculties.[28]

In the first sustained reactive feminist polemic by a woman in English, Jane Anger vociferously demanded rights for women and registered serious opposition to the behavior of men (and apparently one in particular) toward women.[29] Like Tyler she revealed an awareness about women as a group and wrote consciously on their behalf. Vehement and vitriolic in her tirade in marked contrast to Tyler's calm exposition, Anger resolutely responded to a particular detractor (and any others) who dared call women sexually inappeasable. Contemptuously scorning men who toyed with women, Anger forged a path that led to Behn, who was first to maintain that women were legitimate heirs to their own sexuality.

Twenty years after Anger, during the reign of the misogynous James I, Joseph Swetnam tipped his cap to a popular tradition and deliberately insulted women in a work entitled *The araignment* [sic] *of lewd, idle, froward, and unconstant women* (1617).[30] Three women responded. One of them, a pseudonymous Ester Sowernam (fl. 1617), indicted Swetnam for "scurrilous effrontery" and lack of responsibility.[31] Her rebuttal was consonant with the irate feelings of women who had to contend with James I's attempts to repress their social behavior and dress.[32] As sweet in her refutation as he was sour in his accusation (Swetnam vs. Sowernam, and probably an intended pun), she suggested that he be tried and jailed unless he repented. Sowernam's counterpolemic refused to countenance male abuse; she accused male detractors of becoming obsessive if not downright irrational, as they felt increasingly threatened by the developing resilience and resistance of women, whom they customarily disrespected and abused.

At the prelude to the Civil War, in 1640, two pseudonymous spinsters, Mary Tattle-Well and Joane Hit-Him-Home, explain how they were goaded into answering a woman-hating diatribe by John Taylor. (Internal evidence in Taylor's pamphlet, *The Juniper Lecture* (1639), makes it possible that Taylor wrote the *Woman's Sharp Revenge.*) Certainly both pamphlets illustrate the presence of attack and counterattack in this era and a sustained continuance of the *Querelle.*[33] A particularly outspoken woman, Katherine Chidley, the Amazonian Brownist-Congregationalist, proclaimed in 1641 that women should be their own moral agents; that even though tradition dictated female obedience in marriage, men should not expect automatic control of women's consciences.[34] Her actions and the actions of other radical women sectaries evinced a growing sense of female independence, bred by unconventional and changing times. Ecstatic women prophets, world travellers spreading God's word, itinerant preachers in the 1640s and 50s, and a plethora of writers on unorthodox religious beliefs bespoke a personal and collective style of public female independence. One critic estimates conservatively that between 300 and 400 women wrote in the period from 1640 to 1700, that over one-half wrote religio-political tracts, and that these writings constituted about one percent of texts published.[35] The attempt by male writers to reduce certain women to laughingstocks in Restoration comedy partly stemmed from fear of female autonomy and the need to staunch it. Women had to know their place, the patriarchy intoned, but from this era on, despite intermittent and even long lulls, the taste of freedom and its recognition were never lost. This grouping of religious women protesters could be said to be the first feminist wave in British history if we allow "feminists in action" (in Joan Kelly's phrase) as part of our definition.

By the time the Stuart line resumed power in 1660, the idea of religious egalitarianism had taken root. The tract of Margaret Askew Fell Fox (1614–1702) in 1667, which promulgated a woman's right to preach and denied the inferiority of women by citing scripture, was philosophically allied to the new notions about equality before God and salvation for all.[36]

Prior to Fell's campaign for women preachers, Katherine Philips (1631–1664), a merchant's daughter from the Protestant middle class, organized a circle of friends whom she endowed with classical names (her own was Orinda). She wrote poems to celebrate friendship and love between women.[37] By founding this active yet informal literary group of women (many of whom never met), Philips offered female love, affection, and friendship a concrete and expressive literary shape, but only in semi-private, until a 1664 pirated edition of Philips's poems apparently provoked her into reluctant publication. Until that time, Philips's poetry circulated at court and in Irish circles. The positive public reception of Philips's work—even while it did not secure acceptance for the less conventional women writers who followed her—at least ensured a lasting respectability for seventeenth-century romantic friendship and gained visibility for women writers and for the literature of love between women.

Before Philips's coterie sprang up and for some time afterwards, Margaret Cavendish, Duchess of Newcastle (1623–1673), on her return from continental exile where she had been exposed to advanced ideas about women, wrote on behalf of women.[38] The shoddy reception she encountered adumbrated that of Behn, but her social status and wealth rendered her less vulnerable. Her husband shrewdly evaluated the public response; "Here's the crime," he stated in the epistle to her *Philosophical and Physical Opinions* (1665) (the subjects cited in the Duchess's title were already exceptional choices for a woman writer), "a lady writes them." A versatile author, she articulated feminist statements in various forms, but most extensively through the many independent-minded heroines in her dramas. In a formal address, she explained to the faculty of

Oxford and Cambridge the need to empower women politically and expatiated metaphorically on their exclusion from public life. On another occasion, in the popular orations form, she chose female equality as the subject for debate. In her play, *The Convent of Pleasure,* which resembled Katherine Philips's love poems in its philosophy of women's unity and community, the Duchess proposed that women effect an idyllic withdrawal to a convent—in the tradition of celebrating pastoral retirement—and described the affectional and sexual relationships that might ensue.

Specifically, the Duchess dramatized a lesbian relationship between Lady Happy and the "Princess," in which Lady Happy tried to resolve the love she felt for a woman. Even the fact that the "Princess" turned out to be a man did not detract from the joy in loving that was expressed by Lady Happy before her discovery of male chicanery. Despite the stagey machinations of the plot, the Duchess's sympathetic, tender, and natural portrayal of lesbian love was probably the first in English literature. This idea of voluntary withdrawal from society, which Mary Astell (1668–1731) was to become renowned for proposing in the two volumes of *A Serious Proposal for the Ladies* (1694, 1697), had earlier been voiced by religious women, and was precisely the point objected to by Bishop Burnet in Astell's project: Too much like a Roman Catholic idea, he was rumored to have said.

One striking feature of the Duchess's writings which differentiated the pre- from the post-Civil War writings by women was her exploration of new scientific language and discoveries. In attempting to understand natural phenomena rationally, the Duchess introduced the principles of the new science and Cartesian philosophy into women's literature.[39] Before long, Aphra Behn, Mary Astell, and Damaris Cudworth, Lady Masham, to name only three celebrated exponents, would be writing in a similar manner.[40]

These Commonwealth and early Restoration writers, then, explored the love of one woman for another, wrote on women's friendships and their private lives. They stressed the right to preach, the need for education and the expression of female intellect, as far as the new science. As feminist writers, their contribution was to recognize female capacity and the importance that unity among women might provide as a buffer against entrenched patriarchal values. Furthermore, women writing to other women portrayed alternative ways of living—even women like the Duchess, who was happily married—in contrast to traditional marriage and the focus on husband and children. Such literature written by women for women also encouraged the possibility of female communities and affectional and sexual life-long relationships with other women. The literature signified that women could and did make choices of their own. Alienated individual women, moreover, might be inspired to seek out women friends.

THE LATER SEVENTEENTH CENTURY

In the 1670s, the learned Bathsua Makin, who had tutored the daughter of the soon-to-be-beheaded Charles I, argued for the right of gentlewomen to an education. (Contemporary Eurocentric attitudes are also evident in her text.) She proposed a rigorous education that consisted of a thorough grounding in languages, arts, and the sciences.[41] As Makin indicates, her essay doubled as an advertisement for the school she had opened in Tottenham High Road. The working gentlewoman who promoted her wares in the marketplace had arrived. In the same decade, Hannah Woolley also earned a living by writing popular encyclopaedic handbooks in the domestic arts for a female readership, but unlike Makin she was catering to women in service jobs as well as middle-class women who wanted to improve their repertoire in household cuisine and medicine.[42] Other women who tried to survive at least partially by writing were the midwives Jane Sharpe (fl. 1671) and Elizabeth Cellier (fl. 1680), both of whom feared professional extinction.[43] All of them prepared the public for secular didactic writings by women and trailblazed for Aphra Behn, who earned her living solely through her writing.

In the sixteenth and seventeenth centuries, the *Querelle des Femmes,* the controversy about women's talents and worth, whose most notable exponent was Christine de Pisan, had waged intermittently on the continent and in Britain.[44] By 1659, Anna Maria van Schurman's translated Latin tract, *The Learned Maid; or, Whether a Maid may be a Scholar?* had inspired Bathsua Makin, a one-time correspondent with Schurman, to write an essay intended "to revive the Antient Education of gentlewomen."[45] The disruption of national life by the Civil War, the return of exiles, antipathy to a bawdy, woman-baiting, male-dominated court, and economic survival played their part in Makin's contention that gentlewomen deserved an education. Makin contrasted the neglect of intellectual and moral training in Britain with the situation in France where intelligent women were highly respected and had created their own salon society.[46] However, Makin's desire for female education extended only to those who could afford substantial school fees. Not until the advent of charity schools toward the end of the seventeenth century, largely motivated by high numbers of illiterate and unemployed country and town poor, did the question of a more widely based education arise. Furthermore, the growing popularity of Cartesian philosophy, which encouraged analysis rather than unexamined acceptance of the world, complemented the idea that female education was desirable and appropriate, just as the emergence of rationalist ideas also encouraged a growth in feminist consciousness.[47] Yet few or no practical changes in women's conditions resulted.

By the time Aphra Behn was writing for a living in the theatre throughout the 1670s and 80s, one way to economic independence for women had been sketchily mapped out. In her first play, *The Forced Marriage*

(1671), as the title proclaimed, she evinced a shrewd sense about women's economic survival, while rape and impotence were featured in some poems.[48] In later prose fiction, she continued to explore marital tribulations. She also advocated a woman's right to her own sexuality, particularly in one or perhaps two late lesbian poems written in the last decade of her life.[49]

In *Oroonoko: or, the Royal Slave,* a long prose fiction about a noble black West African man and woman who are enslaved in Surinam, South America (at the time a British colony, today Guyana), Behn outspokenly castigated the barbarous practices of European slave-owners.[50] Although Oroonoko himself looks European, is educated by Europeans, and is a prince (factors which probably satisfied Behn's Royalist sympathies and admirers), Behn presented an abolitionist stance in at least one major episode despite internal political contraditions in the narrative. In so doing, she inaugurated a concern (along with a few earlier Quaker women who had noted colonial prejudice) that punctuated feminist literature up to Wollstonecraft and beyond: namely, the battle against slavery and the slave trade. Based on personal experiences in South America, *Oroonoko* was an amazing exception to the near absence of protest against slavery in the seventeenth and early eighteenth centuries in Britain. Behn envisioned how future feminists might ally with other dominated peoples.

Behn also popularized the spread of rationalist philosophy and scientific ideas by translating Bernard le Bovier de Fontenelle's *La Pluralité des Deux Mondes* (commonly translated as *A Discovery of New Worlds)* (1688), especially tailored to offer women the "new science" in palatable form.[51] In her preface, Behn specifically contended that women disparaged themselves intellectually and emotionally and urged a more finely-honed sharpening of their mental faculties. Specifically, Fontenelle's tract opened discoveries in astronomy and physics to women, through a set of dialogues between a "Lady" and a male philosopher who instructs her in the Copernican system. Behn also presented the Marchioness (the "Lady") as an intellectual woman, although the Cartesian framework was scaled down to accommodate the "inferior female mind."

That same decade, Sarah Fyge (later Field Egerton, 1669/1672– 1722/1723), a fourteen-year-old girl incensed by Robert Gould's misogynous tract entitled . . . *The Pride, Lust, and Inconstancy, etc. of Woman* . . . , penned the only major polemic of the 1680s, probably the work of the youngest feminist on record.[52] For this she was banished from her parents' home. In *The Female Advocate* (1686), Fyge took issue point-by-point with the three qualities Gould attributed to women, and concluded by accusing men of insecurity based on jealousy, incompetence, and a selfish love of power.[53] Her response at such an early age and in her own name indicated that Behn's public stand and the general uncompromising attitudes of some women were influencing the literary climate. Gould's tract and Fyge's reactive or counterpolemic may also reflect England's unstable political situation with its violent controversies over the Stuart succession. Further, limited knowledge about the lives of early polemicists makes it difficult to estimate other political influences on their work.

Contemporaneously in 1688, Jane Barker introduced two feminist themes into her first volume of poetry—the desirability of the single life and close female friendship.[54] The poems also relate to the tradition of celebrating pastoral retirement. In fact Barker was rumored to have initiated a coterie in the North of England similar to that of Katherine Philips. Her inclusion of related themes in *A Patch-Work Screen . . .* in the 1720s indicated a thirty-year interest in if not commitment to these ideas and possibly the existence of social support which strengthened her choice not to marry.[55] As a political Roman Catholic exiled for some time on the continent, she might have felt more freedom to experiment. Both Fyge and Barker expanded the range of polemic and posited new alternatives for women.

From about the mid-1680s until 1713 or thereabouts, unprecedented numbers of women wrote on women's condition, of whom Mary Astell was the best known. It was the first sizable wave of British secular feminist protest in history. Many were inspired by the general philosophical shift toward a rational and empirical analysis of life that rejected tradition and encouraged self-confidence and independent thought.

Mary Astell had risen to the occasion by arguing in *A Serious Proposal to the Ladies* (1694, 1697) for female education and eschewing scriptural justifications for inequitable conditions. She put explicit feminist demands on a firm footing and with rational common sense helped dissolve preposterously unscientific notions about women.[56]

Between the first part of Astell's *Serious Proposal* and her other major feminist work, *Some Reflections upon Marriage* (1700),[57] Judith Drake (fl. 1696) inscribed *An Essay in Defence of the Female Sex,* which borrowed its format from the Greek writer Theophrastus (who had composed witty character sketches, often of political opponents), and at the same time added to an incisive feminist literature that had begun to root its arguments in rationalist thought. These tracts sought philosophically to change the course of education and marriage for women. Women should ponder important decisions and never act on impulse or surrender to pressure, Astell insistently exhorted. Although some women had made public statements before hers, Astell's was the most open and intellectual; in her time she was unrivalled as an irreproachable guardian of feminist ideas. The growth of the new science, the application of rationalist approaches to problems, and an emphasis on empirical data, along with a political situation that encouraged individual efforts, empowered the feminist argument, or rather changed its shape for good.

Unfortunately, the same set of beliefs which caused Astell to speak out also produced a society divided into gender-based public and private spheres. As newly domesticated women accommodated the emerging capital-based economy, the individualist stance and ethic tended to become a male prerogative. Defoe's exceptional Moll Flanders testified, by virtue of her rarity as an autonomous woman, to the increased subjugation and enforced protection of the majority of women who were discouraged from unilateral actions.

The Early Eighteenth Century

In 1701, another reactive polemic in verse-debate form appeared, this time a response by the Anglican Lady Chudleigh to a sermon preached at Sherbourn in Dorsetshire in 1699 by a nonconformist minister, the Reverend John Sprint.[58] Lady Chudleigh used the reasoned debate of Astell's logical argumentation in an unusual combination with the dialogue form of the Duchess of Newcastle's orations. Astell's advocacy of improved treatment of and self-education for women greatly influenced Lady Chudleigh who rejected out of hand Sprint's argument about women's mental inferiority. A previous respondent, the indignant Eugenia, had penned a more traditional, scripturally-studded attack. (Astell may also have referred to Sprint in *Some Reflections*.)[59]

The respondents to Sprint are important to consider because they reveal two different approaches, one old, one up-and-coming: a rational versus a Scripture-based opposition. Moreover, Sprint himself, instead of using an age-old, irrational argument about women as unworthy, Eve-tainted strumpets, stressed the need for absolute female obedience toward husbands, a much favored eighteenth-century form of subtle misogyny.[60] Equally negatively, and unlike Swetnam, Taylor, and Gould, Sprint advocated marriage as the sole or highly desirable option for women, another indication of changing times. He encouraged women to view monogamy as a social and political goal; rhetorically he enshrined it as a sacrosanct institution. Whereas men had been busy ridiculing women for "Eve-like" tendencies in the past, now such men of the cloth as Sprint (and a host of contemporary marriage manuals) promoted a more submissive, madonna-like image of women. Thus, by 1700, women were beginning to be viewed as dependent and weaker beings, scarcely competent to fend or think much for themselves. This new condescension appropriately served a society in which men employed out of the home needed a wife to care for house and children and to establish guaranteed heirs to hard-earned fortunes. Underpinned by science and rational-empirical beliefs, the new order was burying, at least ostensibly and without ceremony, unscientific myths about sexually insatiable, wanton, fickle, impudent women, and substituting a new view of women as property-in-need-of-protection.

Nonetheless, women's independent thinking was not to be denied and the feminist counterattacks on Sprint were a case in point. Lady Chudleigh's two early eighteenth-century volumes of moral-philosophical essays and poems on female friendship, inequalities within marriage, and the need for women to be educated, asserted in the most respectable tones the same kind of creative autonomy that had been initiated in mid- to late Restoration feminist writings.[61]

Sarah Fyge, who in 1686 resembled Lady Chudleigh in writing a major feminist polemic to launch herself publicly as a writer, published a volume of poems two decades or so later, after her polemic against Gould, in which she addressed women friends lovingly, attacked marriage and male power, applauded liberty, and advocated female education.[62] Fyge paid a great deal more attention to unconventional love affairs than almost any other woman poet except Aphra Behn (and the Ephelia of 1679 who wrote love poems to a slave trader, J. G.). Fyge's father (whom she loved dearly according to poems in the 1703 volume), was associated with circles that studied necromancy, alchemy, Rosicrucian philosophy, the significance of numbers, and other unscientific, even fanciful matters. Although her father objected to the spirited riposte to Gould—Fyge is the second *known* female reactive polemicist after Rachel Speght in 1617—possibly her upbringing contributed to her unorthodox behavior, subject matter, and images.

A third poet, the High Church Tory Royalist Anne Finch, later Lady Winchilsea (1661–1720), wrote poems that addressed the rights of women to their own creativity and autonomous thought.[63] In her volume of poems she especially stressed those ideas in "The Introduction," the first poem, and reiterated them throughout. During her life at Eastwell, which afforded her the kind of rural, solitary retreat so relished in the eighteenth century, and despite personal melancholy, Lady Winchilsea also composed tender poems to several women friends in the classical style employed by Philips. She chose the name of Ardelia for herself, and Arminda for her close friend, Catherine Cavendish. Analyzing sexual politics in a detached manner appropriate to one in a happy marriage, in other poems Lady Winchilsea scrutinized uneven power relationships in contemporary marriages.

During this productive period for women's poetry, Elizabeth Elstob contributed rigorous scholarly translation to women's literary output. As a sophisticated scholar, she knew at first hand the twin difficulties (if not the impossibilities) of becoming and earning a living as a female scholar. Her preface to *An English-Saxon Homily* exhorted her readership to learn their history.[64] Women's exclusion from the universities made Elstob's accomplishments even more remarkable. She was encouraged, as were several other intellectual women then and later by sympathetic males, in her case a brother and a divine. (Her pursuit of scholarship might have owed something to the fostering of female intellect by such women as her friend Mary Astell.)

As women slowly but firmly began to incorporate feminist themes into their poetry during what Christopher Hill has called the "century of revolution"—a period that witnessed some relaxation in the licensing laws—several writers also wrote on personal melancholy. (The licensing

law of 1662 that lapsed for six years in 1679 and expired in 1694 made
government regulation of the press more difficult.[65] Taxes on printed
matter did not effectively begin until 1710.) Lady Winchilsea, Lady Chudleigh, and the Duchess of Newcastle, the earlier Royalist and aristocratic
recluse who had found little outlet for her rich, probing intelligence,
intermittently despaired. The suffering of this trio of titled women was
matched by the high incidence of melancholy that characterized the
writings of substantial numbers of women (and men) throughout the
century. Elizabeth Carter's headaches are said to have intellectually
incapacitated her from time to time, while Mary Wollstonecraft's life was
punctuated by states of melancholy and agonizing "nerves."

The fact that these writers were able to transcend personally difficult
circumstances illuminated the reality of their independent spirits,
perseverance, and self-confidence. Whether they lauded liberty, female
friendship, and the right to write, or criticized male privilege and the
injustice of a woman's lot, they were fashioning a public self that adver-
tized female resistance to anything short of equality and full humanity.
As a political Royalist who assumed her title in 1712 when her husband
succeeded somewhat unexpectedly to the earldom, Lady Winchilsea
stressed a woman's right to her talents as much out of psychological and
personal needs as political persuasion.

While poetry had long been considered a dignified avocation among
noblewomen, English political events encouraged women of other social classes to freer expression. Queen Elizabeth herself, along with
Mary Sidney Herbert, Countess of Pembroke, Queen Mary Stuart, Anne
Boleyn, and Lady Elizabeth Cooke Russell, had been prominent as poets
in the sixteenth century; in the seventeenth century, the aristocrats Lady
Mary Wroth, Princess Elizabeth, and Margaret Cavendish, Duchess of
Newcastle were joined by such middle-class poets as Anna Hume, Katherine Philips, and Anne Killigrew. John Dryden wrote an elegy on the
death of the admired and creative Killigrew who had suffered at the
hands of plagiarists, a fate not uncommon among women writers. And
women poets from the middle class as well as the aristocracy elegized
Dryden.[66] Not surprisingly then, both middle-class and aristocratic
women—Jane Barker, Elizabeth Singer Rowe (1674–1737), Sarah Fyge
Field Egerton, Lady Mary Chudleigh, and Lady Winchilsea—wrote and
published during the less severely regulated decades on either side of
1700. Changing times also fostered new approaches in women's poetry
and prose: the rationalism that informed Lady Chudleigh's verse debate
with the Reverend John Sprint and Mary Astell's complex essays were
among several fine examples. The female dramatists who followed
Aphra Behn also reaffirmed that women were entitled to use forms
generally viewed as exclusively male. But they suffered for their courage.
Such female wits as Delarivière Manley, Catherine Cockburn Trotter, and
Mary Griffith Pix endured particularly cruel treatment as they launched
their plays during the 1694–96 season.[67] Fear of this literary triumvirate

loomed so large (it seems) that an "unknown" cruelly parodied them in a play entitled *The Female Wits* (1696).

Poetry also afforded an escape from endless "leisure" for many aristocratic and middle-class women, for whom self-expression was tacitly vetoed. From the vantage point of her country retreat, Lady Winchilsea explored the state of mind and level of awareness of women and her personal anguish about the treatment accorded women poets. In many poems and essays, these writers testified to earnest wrestlings with the fatigue of that very leisure. Nearly all of them praised female friendship as a haven of security, born of common bondage and resistance, as well as choice.

After this efflorescence in the first decade or so of the eighteenth century, reaction set in. Some, like Eliza Haywood, who were considered exceptional were also considered marginal (and ridiculous), and as a result few women writers mounted opposition or proposed solutions to women's degraded status. In the 1720s, Mary Davys was one of the few who sounded the feminist void.[68] Besides, even such female intellectuals as Astell had been mocked in print.[69] Certainly Manley concocted scandal chronicles that involved a daringly explicit sexuality and love relationships between women, but her main intention was to vilify the Whig opposition.[70] Jane Barker's tale about the two women who sloughed off the husband of one of them and lived harmoniously also joined this growing literature of female friendship. Eliza Haywood narrated love tales with vigorous and occasionally feminocentric heroines and Susanna Centlivre offered bold prefaces and comic plays to the public that featured similarly strong women.[71] Elizabeth Elstob's plea for a rigorous female education including Anglo-Saxon scholarship, made an equally forceful impact of a different sort.

What caused this comparative dearth of full-length feminist works after the early years of the eighteenth century, following the Astell cluster, until 1739? Some contributing factors included the consolidation of Whig power and capitalist enterprise, the domestication of women, the cultural preference for very moral or very salacious literature that tended to preclude genuinely reformist literature, and an earnest effort to stabilize the nation in its post-revolutionary phase. Aristocratic and well-placed middle-class women who drove around Hyde Park after mandatory hours of dalliance at their toilette and women at the other end of the social scale who scrabbled for a living lacked either inclination or time for realistic appraisals of the status of women, let alone for feminist reforms. With education mostly denied them and marriage elevated to a principle, how could they consider the implementation of reforms, let alone the idea?

THE LATER EIGHTEENTH CENTURY

From the late 1730s until the continental and transatlantic political explosions in the 1770s and 1780s, a handful of women hesitantly and

cautiously tendered a few feminist ideas. This new, somewhat under-
stated feminist period began after bourgeois relationships had somewhat entrenched themselves. Both Sarah Fielding (1710–1768) and
Eliza Haywood in roughly mid-century called in different ways for a
reconsideration of female education. But even before their appearance,
Sophia (fl. 1739–1741) and Mary Collier (1689/90–after 1759) urged
unique feminist statements on the public.

Sophia used the "Goddess of Wisdom" as a pen name when she
translated (or refurbished) "A.L." 's translation of François Poulain de la
Barre's French tract, *De l'Egalité des deux Sexes, Discours Physique et
Moral, Où l'on voit l'importance de se défaire des Préjuges, (The Woman
as Good as the Man)* (1673).[72] Poulain de la Barre, Cartesian and cleric,
argued rationally for an end to prejudice against women on the grounds
that the belief in female inferiority amounted to no more than an opinion.[73] Perceiving women to be mentally underdeveloped as a result of
differential, biased treatment, Sophia assertively proclaimed her fundamental message: women are superior to men.[74] Gone was the polite,
biblical argument of Makin, citing worthy, intelligent women of the past,
and gone were Astell's reasoned requests for a retirement where well-
bred women could pursue the pious, intellectual life. Adding contemporary touches to her paraphrase, Sophia petitioned loudly for education
on the basis of women's obvious equality. Her non-scriptural argument
and refusal to accept predetermined sex roles prefigured the stance of
such writers of the revolutionary era as Catherine Macaulay and Mary
Wollstonecraft. Sophia also sought female autonomy in society that
would include access to professions in medicine, law, and even the
military. Education, in a word, was key; withholding it was a self-
perpetuating malicious practice that caused mental distinctions between women and men.

Lady Mary Wortley Montagu and an anonymous reviewer in the *Gentleman's Magazine* also remonstrated on women's behalf around 1739.
Throughout her correspondence Lady Mary espoused feminist ideas and
in her life executed independent actions, not least her elopement, while
in her periodical, *The Nonsense of Commonsense,* she contributed
substantially to the contemporary feminist debate. Her voluntary exile
announced to the public that a woman with intellectual and economic
resources could lead an independent, unconventional life if she so
desired. The 1739 reviewer challenged the usurpation of female occupations by men, and predicted that the continuing lack of occupations
for women would become even more of a pressing issue.[75]

These voices were contrapuntally accompanied in the same year by
that of Mary Collier, the washerwoman. Stephen Duck's paean of praise
to working men in *The Thresher's Labor,* which failed to mention female
workers, provoked an outraged Collier to defend her sex and class, an
extraordinary combination and literary coup in an age that had only
recently begun an elementary charity program to educate the "poor."[76]

Her argument that the work and lives of laboring women deserved respect was unprecedented in feminist literature and displayed remarkable vision and compassion. Certainly those who seemed to have been from the laboring class—possibly Margaret Tyler before 1700, and Mary Leapor (1722–1746) and Ann Yearsley in the eighteenth century—wrote on feminist issues, but no one else had defended laboring women as laboring women.

After her public drubbing in Alexander Pope's first version of *The Dunciad* (1729), Eliza Haywood reappeared in the 1740s to call for female education.[77] In her volume entitled *The Governess,* Sarah Fielding did the same, and in *The Adventures of David Simple* Fielding introduced an independently minded woman.[78] Fielding also complained about the politics of female economic survival.[79] Aside from a handful of minor poets, little else of feminist interest appeared until Charlotte Charke's (?–1760) autobiography in 1755.[80] Her racy, transvestite, risk-taking life, as well as her father's disowning of her, meant that few wanted or would have dared to emulate her. Yet she compiled her adventures as dramatically as an actress could, sold them, and tried to survive. Like Behn and Manley, she exemplified the bold, autonomous self. Around this time, Bluestocking assemblies became à la mode and, in new and different ways, offered the following messages to women: be assertive, take the lead, wait for no man, write, create, be vocal, do not flinch from flouting custom.

Primarily from professional and upper middle-class families, the Bluestockings held gatherings that tended to include "kindred spirits"—certain desirable male and female friends and conversationalists. They opposed card-playing (as *Rambler* 10 by Hester Mulso Chapone (1727–1801) made plain), the social "round," education in frivolous accomplishments, and the cult of *bon ton:* Elizabeth Robinson Montagu's "Dialogues" specifically addressed such issues.[81] Elegantly, they substituted moral, intellectual, and philanthropic activities. Several tried to help women, such as Elizabeth Elstob, down on their luck. They spoke contemptuously of forced marriage. Elizabeth Carter and Hester Chapone praised the single life.[82] Wearing the virtuous mantle of social acceptance, unlike the daredevil Charke, they presented various models of independent womanhood—male-identified or not—that mattered more in the long run than their salons and conversations combined.

Elizabeth Carter stood out as the foremost intellectual in the circle. Self-taught and educated by her rector-father and a Huguenot minister in nine languages including Arabic, Carter studied mathematics and astronomy and published poems in *The Gentleman's Magazine* as early as 1735. Her father was a friend of the editor, Edward Cave.[83] By the mid-eighteenth century some male supporters, among them George Ballard and John Duncombe, had begun to pay written tribute to learned women.[84] Carter's intellectual triumphs also included a translation of Epictetus in 1758 which earned her a modest living. To mid-eighteenth-century society she offered concrete evidence that popular ideas about female inferiority were and always had been false and prejudicial. Nor was marriage for her. Rather she preferred the kind of life favored by Lady Eleanor Butler (1737–1829) and Sarah Ponsonby (1755–1831) after their elopement: a healthy daily regimen with good exercise and diet, an impressive, steady program of learning, and a respectful attention to religion and the moral code.[85] Like Mary Astell, one suspects, Carter cherished the classical way of life—*mens sana in corpore sano*—and would have taken it to include speaking out for one's beliefs. She conceded the need for insurrection against tyranny and subscribed to a humanitarian ideal that included an active opposition to slavery. Furthermore, Carter's contribution to the feminist cause extended to the personal, passionate, and frequent correspondence with her young friend, Catherine Talbot, earning her a prominent place in the literature of romantic friendships.[86] For three decades, she and Talbot maintained an intimate correspondence and relationship, united in their devotion to aging parents and a healthy mental and physical life. Elizabeth Robinson Montagu, later labelled Queen of the Blues, eagerly pursued a close relationship with Carter, whose capacities she deeply admired. Occasionally Carter and Montagu sojourned together (and often with men like Lord Bath), and Montagu saw to it that Carter received a small annuity upon her husband Edward Montagu's death to cover Carter's admittedly ascetic needs. Paradoxically the Bluestocking challenge to patriarchal values was neither recognized as a conscious threat (perhaps because of their generally conservative political views) nor did it serve to precipitate female revolt.

Elizabeth Montagu's sister, Sarah Robinson Scott, after a short-lived marriage, set up house just outside Bath with her life-long companion, Lady Barbara Montagu, and together they conducted one of the most successful, practical implementations of Astell's educational proposal yet effected. Scott (with Lady Barbara's assistance, according to Horace Walpole), fictionalized their experiences in establishing a primarily female community in a novel entitled *Millenium Hall* (1762).[87] In this work five affluent young women, of whom two pairs were romantic friends, retire to the country and pool their money to help the less advantaged. They hire physically impaired servants, train gentlewomen who had fallen on hard times for appropriate occupations, and launch a local carpet and rug factory to aid local employment. The novel indirectly illustrated what ill-educated, alienated, and abandoned lives many women led. Sarah Scott's carefully woven confessional narrative veiled a concerned social commentary. Elizabeth Montagu wrote admiringly about her sister's daily activities, possibly to quell any rumors that Sarah was dissolute because she left her husband:

> My sister rises early, and as soon as she has read prayers to
> their small family, she sets down to cut and prepare work for

12 poor girls, whose schooling they pay for; to those whom she finds more than ordinarily capable, she teaches writing and mathematics herself. The work these children are usually employed in is making child-bed linen and clothes for poor people in the neighborhood, which Lady Bab and she bestow as they see occasion. Very early on Sunday morning these girls, with 12 little boys whom they also send to school, come to my sister and repeat their catechism, read some chapters, have the principal articles of their religion explained to them, and then are sent to the parish church. These good works are often performed by the Methodist ladies in the heat of enthusiasm, but thank God, my sister's is a calm and rational piety. . . . Lady Bab Montagu concurs with her in all these things, and their convent, for by its regularity it resembles one, is really a cheerful place.[88]

Sarah Scott and Lady Barbara lived on the edges not only of the London Bluestocking circles, but also of the Batheaston assemblies, modeled by a Lady Miller along Bluestocking lines. Anna Seward (1747–1809), whose writings to Honora Sneyd revealed the same deep attachment displayed by Carter in her letters to Talbot, was often a guest of honor at these affairs.[89] So once was Fanny Burney, the author of *Evelina*. Women's social and cultural circles had also taken temporary root outside London. As more evidence is discovered about women's lives at this time, we may find connections between the women with whom Katherine Philips and Jane Barker were respectively acquainted and the female circles with which Mary Astell, Lady Mary Chudleigh, Elizabeth Rowe, Sarah Fyge Field Egerton, Delariviere Manley, and other early eighteenth-century writers associated. There may even have been links between the early informal groupings and the Bluestocking and Batheaston circles. Their lives exemplify and affirm, in Adrienne Rich's phrase, a lesbian continuum, "a range—through each woman's life and throughout history—of women—identified experience. . . ."[90]

After establishing a home at Plas Newydd in the wake of their acclaimed elopement, which caused much familial consternation, Lady Eleanor Butler and Sarah Ponsonby lived a studious, contented, lesbian existence, celebrities in their lifetimes who attracted national and international visitors eager to see two eighteenth-century *beaux idéals* in practice: nonthreatening (as it was then perceived) female friendship and rustic retirement. Lady Eleanor recorded their industrious happy life in such daily detail that to read it seems almost an invasion of intimacy. Unostentatiously they lived a couple-centered version of the pious educational retirement recommended by Astell. Sarah Scott and Lady Barbara Montagu did the same. Since Sarah Scott ordered her letters burned, and her sister's letters about why Scott left her husband so hurriedly are missing, there are gaps in our knowledge of their history. Nonetheless, the day-books and diaries of Lady Eleanor record a comfortable "romantic friendship," tender personal revelations and socio-political commentary that epitomize the best in that informal genre.

Perhaps most strikingly significant in Sarah Scott's *Millenium Hall* and the Butler diaries was the living *and* fictional articulation of the fundamental desirability (and necessity) of female unity. Its political message to the world in the case of Lady Eleanor and Sarah Ponsonby was that intimate female friends could publicly cohabit; in the case of Sarah Scott and Lady Barbara Montagu, their philanthropic activities exemplified public-political involvement.

As the Bluestockings raised the tone of polite society, a provincial Southwest England woman, Mary Scott (Taylor) (1752–1793), inspired by John Duncombe's celebration of women in *The Feminiad,* wrote her own celebratory version in 1774, entitled *The Female Advocate.*[91] Digging into women's history, she exalted many women, Phillis Wheatley, the African-born poet sold in 1761 to a Boston family, who had just then visited Britain the year before, being an especially notable example. (Wheatley wrote her first poem at age fourteen.)[92] Assuredly a committed abolitionist, Mary Scott set herself apart from the earlier feminists who had used historical models, and nothing more, to prove the worth of women. She narrated the contributions of women through history, but additionally, in copious footnotes filled with biographical and historical information, she supplied an historical "parallel" narrative or extra-text. Unlike Makin, Scott did not simply recite lists of illustrious women whose existence, valor, social class, and intellect could counteract some argument from male authority with one of female authority; rather she attempted a commendatory historical overview.

In impressive contrast on the feminist spectrum, Mary Collier's class counterpart in the latter half of the century, Anne Yearsley, the Bristol milkwoman-poet, wrote an autobiographical preface to the fourth edition of her first volume of poems to dispute the right of Hannah More (1745–1833) to expropriate Yearsley's poetic earnings.[93] The fact that her second volume of poems published without More's patronage sold only moderately well, and that after other literary experiments, including a novel and a historical play, she dropped out of literary sight, proved that access to successful publication depended on economics as much as talent. This was especially true for laboring people. Nonetheless, Yearsley and Collier, along with Margaret Tyler (probably a domestic servant), and Mary Leapor (a gardener's daughter), proved that laboring women significantly contributed to the emerging feminist canon.

Yearsley's poems ranged from touching tributes to her mother and her children to a long, poignant poem against the slave trade.[94] Automatically excluded from Bluestocking circles after the rift with More, she self-avowedly identified with the physical and economic exploitation of enslaved people. A proud woman, she spoke out forthrightly in her preface against Hannah More's conduct. In economic terms, Yearsley had gambled and lost, for More's withdrawal of patronage eventually made Yearsley's attempted career as a writer a much more difficult task. Eventually she opened a circulating library. Her quarrel, rather than her poems, entered feminist annals. Nonetheless historical hindsight credits Yearsley and Collier as models of the kind of resistance that workers in the next century (in a quite different context) would muster against those whom they identified as "oppressor-bosses."

Unlike Yearsley, Catherine Macaulay, a spokeswoman for the radical, Whig-republican cause in Britain between 1760 and 1775, was admired on three continents.[95] Like the Bluestockings, she held a salon, but one where conversation was dominated by national and international politics rather than cultural affairs. As an ardent controversialist as well as an intellectually vigorous, well-travelled, self-supporting woman, her example might well have counted for more than her feminist writings. In *Letters on Education* (1790), Macaulay deplored the differential education of the sexes based on the theory of "sexual character," and argued that environmental circumstances and conditioning, as well as impoverished education bred of backward thinking, kept women deprived and by and large intellectually undistinguished. Macaulay posited that men have traditionally used their preeminent physical strength to subjugate women. Men and women needed to mix at every level, she entreated, and to eschew the untenable claim of male superiority. She derided the notion that the sexes differed in reason and moral virtues. Since no difference beyond the physical existed, (a position held over a century earlier by Poulain de la Barre) education should be accessible to all. Eventually, if boys and girls were to grow up, share, and play together, their friendships would surely be devoid of coquetry and shallow thinking. Macaulay also proposed women's direct rather than indirect participation in politics.

Strongly influenced by Macaulay before her own untimely death in 1797, Mary Wollstonecraft synthesized many of the earlier feminist themes.[96] In her first tract, *Thoughts on the Education of Daughters* (1787), she deplored the fact that male (and some female) writers on education pictured women as weak and unsuitable for disciplined study; instead she advocated a Lockean-based education and "thinking," not an activity then generally associated with women. She castigated the treatment of women like herself who worked in subservient jobs as governesses, chaperones, and in allied service-based occupations. Her love-elegy in fiction to her friend and erstwhile mentor Fanny Blood, publicly fictionalized their complex emotional relationship. *Mary, a Fiction* (1788) ranks with distinction among the literature of female friendship.

By the time Wollstonecraft wrote her second *Vindication* in 1792, she was openly polemicizing on behalf of all women. Invoking the theory of natural rights in alignment with Enlightenment tenets and nonconformist beliefs, she rallied against slavery, particularly in *A Vindication of the Rights of Men,* and the divisions between the haves and have-nots; she called for jobs, open access to employment, the vote, national public education for children up to nine years of age, co-education for women, and even-handed treatment for Native American Indians.[97] Women needed independence, she insisted, but middle-class women would (must) lead the way: Her adherence to a bourgeois liberal politic, which bestowed political primacy on the middle class, snagged her in contradictions from which she was never philosophically able to extricate herself. She still saw wife/mother as the primary role for women, but not for herself. The draft of her last novel, *The Wrongs of Women,* revealed a tension between her avowed philosophy which favored middle-class eminence and her depiction in fiction of a potential laboring class victory. The washerwoman Jemima is a psychologically and physically battered laboring woman who refuses surrender on any terms, whose level-headedness will see the bourgeois heroine Maria and her new-born daughter through and out of their difficulties.

Another outspoken feminist and dissenter, Mary Hays, echoed the concerns of Macaulay and Wollstonecraft in the *Monthly Magazine* columns where she denied the theory of "sexual character," from a rationalist perspective.[98] In her *Appeal to the Men of Great Britain in Behalf of Women* (1798), Hays called for job opportunities, training, and better treatment if not equality for women, demands that became more popular as the industrial revolution advanced. This emphasis on jobs and economic independence persisted as a theme in the literature of the period, accelerating as the bourgeois revolution became entrenched and women saw themselves as wives and mothers, and little more. Hays further argued that women should have access to power, for their capacities warranted an improved position in society.

By the end of the eighteenth century not only was Charlotte Turner Smith (1769–1806) writing radical novels that attacked colonialism, slavery, and women's subjugation, but Mary Anne Radcliffe (1746?– after 1810) cautioned that both laboring and petty-bourgeois women without decent occupations would be economically forced into prostitution, that in fact they were already on the streets in ever-growing numbers.[99] Radcliffe's tract denounced male usurpation of female trades and occupations. She passionately declared that usurpation had caused destitution and prostitution among the country's females. She cited many examples of impoverished gentlewomen who were unable to sell their labor legally for a living wage, after which they could either be admitted to asylums or sell their bodies. Radcliffe's work sketched the consequences of a patriarchal protection system that omitted any professional training for women and allowed men to co-opt female professions for their own benefit. She challenged the state to care for its poor. Women need jobs, she continually insisted, and they have an equal right to the marketplace. Most importantly, Radcliffe's *The Female Advocate* disclosed that women like herself had begun to discern the close relationship between economic exploitation and patriarchal oppression; the problems of her life had seen to that.

Writers who supported the French Revolution, some from dissenting backgrounds and frequently in search of economic independence, fused feminist ideas with enlightenment and with radical tenets about human rights. Overt agitators for women's rights in tracts, novels, and poems, most of them led lives of sexual unorthodoxy. They remained single, proclaimed the right to and practised sexual autonomy, lived with female friends; or separated from husbands, cohabited with married men, and bore children "out of wedlock." The correlation between unorthodox socio-sexual behavior, economic independence, and progressive ideas was at its most cogent and illustrative in the post-1788 revolutionary decade.

FEMINIST POLEMIC:
A NEW POLITICAL FORM

Contrary to received wisdom, therefore, and as my survey indicates, a large number of women had launched written protests in public against their subjective and collective situation long before Wollstonecraft's second *Vindication*. Formally they wrote in a wide variety of traditional and non-traditional categories: poetry, prose, and drama, as well as journal entries, prefaces, and tracts. I am naming this rich body of writings "feminist polemic." Let me explain what I mean by feminist polemic by setting down the traditional definition of polemic as a controversy or argument, especially one that is a refutation of or an attack upon a specified opinion or doctrine. The feminist polemicist writes to urge or to defend a pro-woman point of view which includes resistance to patriarchal values, convention, and domination, or a challenge to misogynous ideas. As I have argued, I consider writings by women opposed to slavery and the slave trade as feminist polemic since opposition to the physical and psychological enslavement of people of color—whether the struggle is particularly waged on behalf of females or not—is a necessary condition for the liberation of women of color and, by extension, all women. One useful way to codify and survey the extent and diversity of these early British feminist writers is to place their writings in four categories or subsets of feminist polemic: one, reactive polemic; two, sustained polemic; three, intermittent polemic; and four, personal polemic or polemic of the heart. (Both sustained and intermittent polemic also tend to fall within a larger category of reasoned or rational polemic.) Although chronology is important, several of the categories defy time and leap across the centuries to make connections and to help form a feminist tradition hitherto invisible.

REACTIVE POLEMIC

I use the term reactive polemic to describe poems or tracts written to refute unsolicited misogynous attacks. (Most often, reactive polemics are part of the *Querelle des Femmes.*) Such works include Jane Anger's against an oppressively satiated lover; Ester Sowernam's against Joseph Swetnam; Sarah Fyge's against Robert Gould; Lady Mary Chudleigh's against John Sprint; and Mary Collier's against Stephen Duck. With the notable exception of Margaret Tyler's writing in 1578, reactive polemics were, not surprisingly, the earliest feminist writings to appear, since reaction presupposes abuse as justification for the writer's response. Injustice calls forth a response, despite the subordinate status which tends to keep the subjugated silent. These responses appeared when males either felt threatened or secure enough to vilify women in public, hoping thus to daunt "upstart" women, or to thwart any potential displays of assertion. The literary misogyny of the early sixteenth century tended to be determinedly insulting toward women sexually, or thoroughly condescending about women's place. In both cases, Scripture provided a quasi-theoretical base. Usually fierce in tone and intensity, feminist responses returned blow for blow, rebuffed arguments, and structured into their responses the need for rebuttal. The feminist writers adopted independent, no-nonsense stances and challenged not only the offending male writer but the behavior of men in general.

Since they also confronted detractors, the works of later writers— Anne Yearsley, Mary Hays, and Mary Wollstonecraft—may also be seen as reactive polemic. In the autobiographical preface to her poems, Ann Yearsley neither responded point by point nor even in spirit to anything Hannah More wrote. Instead, the milkwoman mounted a brief polemical attack against More's expropriation of profits that accrued from the sale of Yearsley's poems. In letters to her wealthy Bluestocking friend Elizabeth Montagu, More contended that since Yearsley was a milkwoman, she should show gratitude for charity.[100] More had decided to secure the money in a trust fund to prevent Yearsley's having access to it; More would permit personal loans to Yearsley, nothing else. Apparently More's distrust of people socially beneath her fostered this negative or suspicious attitude toward her protégée.[101]

In the *Monthly Magazine,* Mary Hays upbraided antifeminists for their strictures on female education, while Mary Wollstonecraft, in the fifth chapter of her second *Vindication* and elsewhere, expounded on the patriarchal biases in the writings on female education of Jean-Jacques Rousseau, James Fordyce, and John Gregory. But her polemic was by no means limited to the matter of response and reaction to traditional misogyny.

SUSTAINED POLEMIC

Sustained polemic offers full-scale feminist polemic, which customarily calls for a change in women's condition. These began to appear

when women had gained more self-confidence, greater access to printing and publishers, and more refined philosophical tools with which to
analyse their situation. In this category, I include the writings of Margaret
Fell on women's preaching; Bathsua Makin on education for "gentlewomen"; Mary Astell on education and marriage; Judith Drake, who
sought more just treatment and a better education for females; Elizabeth
Elstob on female scholarship and learning; Sophia, who argued the
superiority of and demanded justice for women; Mary Scott, who celebrated the accomplishments of women throughout history; Mary Wollstonecraft, who abhorred the denial of rights to women and suggested
reasons for and solutions to this state of affairs; and Mary Hays, Mary
Wollstonecraft, and Mary Anne Radcliffe, who deplored the lack of occupations open to women. Radcliffe particularly worried about the increased incidence of female prostitutes as a result of their economic
deprivation.

Charlotte Charke's autobiography, which recounts the difficulties she
experienced in forging a self-sufficient existence, is a sustained feminist
defense of a different, more subtle sort. (At the level of intimacy and
informality, it overlaps with much of polemic of the heart.) Charke
described with flair the dire consequences of nontraditional living in an
entrenched patriarchal society. Although Charke ended up destitute, her
example mattered, for the act of "I" brandishing, of "I" prioritizing,
of writing about the self in a society that treated women as decora-
tive or sexual objects asserted that very autonomy of self that society
denied.

The same call of self-assertion could describe Mary Astell's *Some
Reflections upon Marriage,* which aimed to defend the Duchess of
Mazarin against her husband-detractor, and Sophia's *Woman's Superior
Excellence . . .* , which spoke to a misogynous response to her *Woman
not Inferior . . . .* (in this sense, both these works were also reactive.)
(Sophia probably also penned the misogynous section, just as François
Poulain de la Barre penned the middle misogynous section of his three-
part work from which Sophia's work derived.) Mary Scott's advocacy of
female accomplishments in response to the *Feminiad* and her attempt to
evaluate historically these contributions in *The Female Advocate* made
her poem in a positive sense reactive as well as sustained.

Several works on slavery belong in this category. In *Oroonoko,* for
example, Aphra Behn focused on enslaved West Africans who were
transported to Guyana (then called Surinam). Her personal experiences
accounted for the fact that she was first to write a sustained work on
slavery and the slave trade. In the same time period, Judith Drake, in
discussing the bondage of women, contemptuously referred to plantation slavery.[102] As Enlightenment and evangelical ideas spread, abolition
received more public attention. The abolitionist William Wilberforce
frequented Bluestocking circles.[103] Hannah More wrote a long antislavery poem to support Wilberforce's introduction of the bill to abolish

the slave trade.[104] Ann Yearsley's poem, "On the Inhumanity of the Slave-Trade," appeared shortly thereafter.

INTERMITTENT POLEMIC

Intermittent polemic describes the work of writers who took issue with the condition of women's lives more briefly, in passages within tracts, prefaces to works, or simply in a few poems in a volume. The topics of such works ranged widely, suggesting the breadth of women's concerns throughout the period. The earliest example of intermittent polemic may be found in Margaret Tyler's preface to her Spanish translation of Diego Ortuñez de Calahorra, in which she argued for the right of women to write what they please. The Duchess of Newcastle, in a preface addressed to the Oxford-Cambridge faculty, stressed her displeasure about the powerlessness of women; in an early poem, Jane Barker praised the single life in preference to perilous marriage; in their poems, Sarah Fyge Field Egerton, Lady Chudleigh, and Lady Winchilsea denounced marriage, called for recognition of women's creativity, demanded the liberty denied women, and collectively asserted the right of women to autonomous existences.

On a different, more pragmatic note, Aphra Behn argued for the right of women to earn a living by *writing*. (Of course Bathsua Makin, when she declared at the end of her educational tract in 1673 that she desired pupils for her school, was only one of many women who were trying to earn an independent living; Behn's example was unprecedented only because it applied to writing.) In her plays Behn also attacked forced marriage and sought to make the "new learning" accessible to women by translating Bernard le Bovier de Fontenelle's *La Pluralité des Deux Mondes (A Discovery of New Worlds)*. Anne Yearsley's forceful autobiographical prefaces in which she defended herself as a milkwoman-turned-poet considered incompetent to handle her own financial affairs; Catherine Macaulay's letters on behalf of female education; and Mary Hays's spirited defenses of women in the pages of the *Monthly Magazine* likewise belong in this section. In 1799 Hays also orchestrated a full-length appeal on behalf of women, to British men. Her writings, therefore, qualify in more than one category—the case with several writers, notably the Duchess of Newcastle, Behn, and Wollstonecraft—perhaps the most diverse of all the writers because they were the most prolific. (Delarivière Manley and Eliza Haywood also displayed a rich versatility, but for reasons of length are not excerpted here.)

I would also categorize several works by feminist writers that address slavery, often one-of-a-kind poems or episodes in novels, as intermittent polemic. Lady Eleanor Butler and several members of the Bluestocking community condemned slavery in private writings. In her celebration of women, Mary Scott included Phillis Wheatley. After the revolutions of 1776 and 1789, feminist writers frequently raised the issues of race and slavery, and among the novelists who did so were Mary Hays and Charlotte Smith. Mary Wollstonecraft attacked the practice of slavery and the slave trade, especially in *A Vindication of the Rights of Men,* and asserted the equality of Native American Indians.

PERSONAL POLEMIC, OR POLEMIC OF THE HEART

The fourth category of feminist polemic I see present includes works about relationships and daily living that celebrate love and friendship between women. Hitherto called "romantic friendships," these relationships between women have recently been the subject of a compelling study by Lillian Faderman.

Unlike the other polemical categories, personal polemic has several unique characteristics. Reactive, sustained, and intermittent polemic all attack misogyny, educational deprivation, marital tyranny (and allied matters), and clearly target an audience that opposes maltreatment of women. Such polemic is overtly propagandistic and didactic and either implicitly or explicitly agitates for an end to disadvantage or abuse. It is frequently couched in recognizably persuasive rhetorical strategies. In personal polemic, writings about love and friendship attack or subvert patriarchal domination quite differently, through affirming women in their support and love for one another. Although some were intended for publication, the forms of secret polemic tend to be of a more personal nature—letters, diaries, memoirs, closet drama, and private love poems.

This category includes the poems of Katherine Philips; the Duchess of Newcastle's *The Convent of Pleasure,* which depicts with sensitivity and warmth a lesbian relationship; a short tale by Jane Barker about a triangle, the resolution of which is the living together of the wife and her maid, and two poems by Barker, one a celebration of female community, and the other a moving love-elegy to a friend; poems by Aphra Behn, Sarah Fyge Field Egerton, Lady Chudleigh, and Lady Winchilsea to women friends; the letters of Bluestocking Elizabeth Carter to her friend Catherine Talbot, and from Anna Seward to Honora Sneyd; the novel, *Millenium Hall,* by Sarah Robinson Scott, which extolls women's friendships and a cooperative female community among women of different classes; Lady Eleanor Butler's personal writings about her beloved Sarah Ponsonby; and Mary Wollstonecraft's first novel, *Mary, a Fiction,* which fictionally elaborated on her passion for her friend Fanny Blood.

Classifying these writings as feminist polemic not only names a new category of women's literature, but gives visibility to a very large body of writings hitherto regarded as unconnected or sub-literary. Viewed as an integrated literary category with common characteristics, feminist polemic reveals rich interconnections beneath the surface, and allows readers more reason for following the political development of feminist ideas in women's literature. This category can also offer another perspective on seemingly titillating and politically ambiguous writings (vis-à-vis the situation of women) as Delarivière Manley's *New Atalantis,* or Hannah More's conservative *Strictures,* which relegates many women to an inferior education based on their class. We can more easily probe beneath the surface of fiction's "harmless cover stories," expose political "subtexts," and identify the dual purposes of literary polemic that speaks softly, indistinctly, or disarmingly. Nor are the subsets of feminist polemic rigid, but open-ended, revealing what was previously hidden: two hundred years of complex and recorded protofeminist and feminist underground networks of resistance.

———————————————— • ————————————————

CONCLUSION

This survey reveals the long honorable history of battles over fundamental political issues that engage women today. Struggles in Britain against discrimination on the basis of ethnicity, class, sex, and sexual preference originated in early efforts by some seventy heroic women. The process of protest was a continuously interrupted one but continuous nonetheless. Over the two centuries a certain loose pattern emerged. Response to detractors was one essential element and concern with religious, then secular, egalitarianism was another. The first step on the road toward observable social reform was taken by Elizabeth Tanfield, Lady Cary in her play *The Tragedy of Mariam* (1605).[105] The presumed villain of the drama, Salome, advocates divorce and an end to subjugated womanhood. Although the play's text offers divorce as an undesirable goal, the unhappy circumstances of Lady Elizabeth's life permits another interpretation.

A half century later during the early Restoration, poems by Katherine Philips on female friendship were reluctantly published. At the same time, a host of requests crowded the pages of feminist works—for education, retention of midwifery as a specifically female occupation, and for greater expertise in traditional female arts, crafts, and skills; some works also extolled the pleasures of economic independence and the single life. By 1686, male detractors continued to wage war as Sarah Fyge defiantly responded to Robert Gould's savage barbs against women's alleged pride, lust, and inconstancy. After another hundred years had elapsed, this kind of melodramatic male attack on women had substantially been reformulated. Where Gould's diatribe was an acceptable phenomenon in 1686, the vitriolic Richard Polwhele with his *The Unsex'd Females* (1798) seemed more of an anomaly, although anti-Jacobin readers adulated him.[106] The polarities in Polwhele's poem of "good and bad" women pinpointed an attitudinal shift. He condemned such perverted women as the Wollstonecraftians—Mary Wollstonecraft herself, Mary Hays, Charlotte Smith, Helen Maria Williams, Ann Yearsley, Mary Darby Robinson, and even the Unitarian abolitionist, Anna Laetitia Barbauld, who disagreed with advanced ideas about female education. Against them (among others) he pitted Hannah More, Elizabeth Carter, Elizabeth Robinson Montagu, Hester Mulso Chapone, Anna Seward, Hester Thrale Piozzi, and Fanny Burney—all of them involved either in the more traditional (and often conservative) circles of the Blue-stockings, Lady Miller at Batheaston, Samuel Richardson, or Samuel Johnson. Polwhele's favorites all had impeccable reputations (Thrale only until she remarried), as well as talent and intellect. We could also look at his ossified polarities another way: outright misogyny in the form of irrational attacks on sexually rampaging unnatural women had been subtly converted to protective advice about maintaining proprieties and staying in a subordinate place. The popularity of conduct manuals, from the seventeenth-century Lord Halifax's *Advice to a Daughter,* to *A Father's Legacy* by Dr. John Gregory a century later, stands as the testimony. The ire that John Wilkes incurred for the lewd *Essay on Women* (1763) that he allegedly wrote also indicated that unscientific, pornographic misogyny was held in increasing ill-favor, at least overtly.[107] Misogyny never ceased, but it acquired a more protean shape, becoming, in its protective guise, less frontal and more deceptive. Because so few pierced the masks of patriarchal protectiveness before Wollstonecraft, misogyny's form had become insidious and consequently more dangerous and difficult to combat. Dr. Gregory's solicitude beguiled female readers as much as the Reverend John Sprint had incensed his readership three quarters of a century earlier. Now women were children or angels rather than whores, innocent rather than lewd, patronized rather than exploited, a more easily manageable commodity for men whose absolute control was not to be gainsaid.

Throughout the late Restoration, Aphra Behn gave public lie to the ideology that women were weak, economically and psychologically dependent, non-political, asexual, and unintellectual creatures. For personal as well as political reasons, she added slavery to her feminist agenda. Before 1800, however, slavery was not perceived as a feminist issue by writers who addressed discrimination against women. Only those women who had various ideological objections to slavery or to tyranny in general, as well as objections to the subjugation of women, wrote on both subjects. The treatment of *female* slaves was rarely addressed, and no writings on slavery or on any other issue by women of color in Britain in that time period has, as far as I am aware, yet been found.

After 1688, the influence of Cartesian, Lockean, and spiritual egalitarian views of the world fostered several sturdy defenses of women. Mary Astell and Judith Drake, despite traditional apologist stances about writing at all, launched forthright feminist essays on a surprised public, in which they vociferously scorned the treatment accorded women, and recommended as solutions withdrawal and education (and a tactful amount of confrontational scorn).

Simultaneously, an unprecedented number of women poets with feminist concerns appeared, among them Elizabeth Rowe, Sarah Fyge, Lady Mary Chudleigh, and the Countess of Winchilsea. With the example of Behn and Philips before them (according to antifeminists, the Eve and Mary models of women's literature) *choices* were finally possible. Women wrote to and about their women friends, concerned themselves with women's social lot, deplored the bondage of marriage, the denial of creativity, and a wholesale loss of liberty. They came as close as any British woman writer ever had to denouncing, in Adrienne Rich's phrase, compulsory heterosexuality. Not surprisingly, slavery was a favorite metaphor in their descriptions of women's lives. Protesting poets flourished, many of whom knew one another and certainly of one another, for the country was still very small. Loosely linked feminist communities sprang up. The Countess of Winchilsea argued that a woman's natural right to exercise her own talents had been illegitimately denied, a position already fought for and obtained, for economic reasons, by Aphra Behn.

The right to scholarship, an extension of the educational demands of women such as Makin and Astell, was voiced by the linguist-antiquarian, Elizabeth Elstob, who had been obliged to abandon a brilliant career as a scholar and drop out of sight probably around 1718 because of financial difficulties after her brother died. Furthermore, since formal scholarship was taught and nurtured in universities which excluded all women, and since scholarship was not profitable then or later, her chances of continuing as a scholar, either financially or intellectually, were slim. Elstob ended up decades later in an aristocratic household, economically dependent and socially protected, a situation far from ideal but preferable to her post-1718 situation when she had taught in a dame school. Elstob's life contrasts with the intrepid lives of Aphra Behn, Delarivière Manley, and Catherine Trotter, the latter two labelled female wits along with Mary Pix. This trio followed Behn as defiant public dramatists. Elstob aside, no precedent for women scholars challenging the public existed, and she had probably been anxious about the possibility of debtor's prison.

After about 1710 or so, the trail of feminist writers becomes harder to follow. What flowed from the presses? Lady Mary Wortley Montagu wrote revealing letters and a periodical that bedevilled societal norms; Manley outraged the public with her scandalous *romans à clef;* Centlivre wrote plays with independent women figures; Haywood churned out copious popular prose fictions on the theme of love, until Pope's caustic lines in *The Dunciad* silenced her (it seems) for over a decade; Jane Barker and Mary Davys published several volumes each in the 1720s and 30s. But not until the mid-1730s did feminist resistance resume. Then the aristocratic Anne Howard, Viscountess Irwin, counterattacked Pope's attack on her friend, Lady Mary Wortley Montagu; the washerwoman Mary Collier rebutted Stephen Duck's assessment of laboring women; and "Sophia," adding points of her own, reshaped François Poulain de la Barre's arguments for and against female superiority.[108]

By the mid-1740s, Haywood and Sarah Fielding were arguing for women's education, albeit obliquely and with a consummate gentleness, with Haywood also assessing the question of prejudice. Elizabeth Carter celebrated her friendship with Catherine Talbot in letters that began in 1741 and spanned three decades. Mary Jones and Mary Leapor also published poems and essays on a host of subjects, some of them specifically related to women.[109] By 1755 Charlotte Charke had mustered enough courage to publish what for that time was an exceedingly bold, even risqué (and possibly embellished) autobiography. In the 1760s Sarah Robinson Scott wrote a novel that fictionally depicted the project she and her friend Lady Barbara Montagu had coordinated for women who had fallen on hard times. Together they implemented Astell's proposal for female education, but broadened its scope to reach women of all classes. Scott also wrote a novel that included a hard-hitting attack on the treatment of slaves.

At this point also the Bluestockings inaugurated salon entertainment and facilitated female intellectual visibility, a social and literary phenomenon in their own right. Women and their lives were finally worthy of consideration; the Bluestockings vindicated and perpetuated the lineage of female worthies. To anyone historically informed, it was evident that a cluster of very learned women stretched from Bathsua Makin, Mary Astell, Catherine Trotter, Damaris Cudworth, Lady Masham, and Elizabeth Elstob to Elizabeth Carter and Catherine Macaulay. Men such as George Ballard in *Memoirs* (1752) and John Duncombe in *The Feminead* (1754) enhanced and confirmed this image of learned women, which the Bluestockings in their inimitable fashion carried aloft into society. (There were, of course, many learned women prior to Makin who did not write on Women's issues.) These writers collectively wrote, translated, gave charitably to and in all senses patronized the poor, encouraged ingénues, and attacked forced marriage and slavery. Several of them enjoyed a wholesome independence from men. Despite their political conservatism, the Bluestockings proved that women had publicly arrived. Undoubtedly, their presence indirectly aided the acceptance of the first fiction of resounding intellectual success by a woman: Fanny Burney's *Evelina* (1778).

Close female friendships became more openly visible in the eighteenth century—among them, those of Lady Eleanor Butler and Sarah Ponsonby, Elizabeth Carter and Catherine Talbot, Sarah Robinson Scott and Lady Barbara Montagu, Sarah Fielding and Jane Collier, Anna Seward and Honora Sneyd until Sneyd's marriage, Hannah More and Eva Maria Violetti Garrick, Mary Wollstonecraft and Fanny Blood. These friendships reflected a growing self-assurance among women and resistance to patriarchal values, physical isolation, and emotional alienation, and most importantly, the exercising of personal choice in friendship. Furthermore, the expanding recognition of women's writings, talents, intellect, and charitable public works—controversy notwithstanding—enhanced mutual respect and self-respect, and ensured continuity. In her poem *The Female Advocate,* Mary Scott was among the first to acknowledge that a literary and political tradition was under way.

By the time of the French Revolution, women had established firm precedents for taking up the pen on their own behalf. Influenced by the outspokenness of the revolutionary time and its philosophical probing, the women of that era responded in kind. First Macaulay, then Wollstonecraft, and afterward Hays, Wakefield, Radcliffe, and others of their generation spoke out vigorously on behalf of women, arguing a multitude of cases logically and commonsensically, but almost always tinged with a sense of righteous indignation. They matched their writing to their sense of a just social reality. Moreover, Ann Yearsley, Hannah More, Helen Maria Williams, Charlotte Smith, and like-minded women confronted slavery head-on. However, the political bankruptcy of female-rights-denied was a complex affair and since women wielded no political or legal power by definition, they were in no position to ameliorate, let alone fundamentally transform, the overall condition of women. The story of that struggle belongs to another epoch.

———————— • ————————

Throughout the period from the Renaissance to the French Revolution, feminists wrote about deprivations and demands. Resistance to their inequitable condition took a variety of forms: first, they counterattacked; then at a more advanced stage of development, they mounted a variety of assaults, that included for some the fight against slavery, to demand certain denied rights; third, they tried to shun the whole situation (while being consciously or unconsciously aware of it), and sought instead to create a better life in their own image. This took the form of love poems, love letters, informal female communities, and a conscious intellectual unity. Fourth, they rejected traditional roles of submission, willfully and voluntarily empowered themselves by engaging in professional, educational, and intellectual activities, and made self-confident claims about their right to the self-shaped, autonomous life of writing, to greater and lesser degrees, autobiographically. Finally after the Bastille fell and people thought the millennium was at hand, with a knowledge of women's historical awareness and a lucid grasp of injustice such women as Yearsley and Wollstonecraft began to synthesize the approaches to the liberation of women. Wollstonecraft countered the antifeminist ideas of Rousseau and the half-stepping, genteel writers of courtesy books. She drew up in several works a ground plan for women that included education and jobs; she agitated both for an end to slavery and inhuman tyrannies, recognizing differential oppression on the basis of class; she wrote about love for women friends and relatives; and she argued in public for a woman's right to personal and economic independence. Standing in the shoes of Margaret Tyler as she advocated a woman's right to write, in Jane Anger's as she resisted the false claims of detractors, and in Aphra Behn's as she addressed deeply ingrained institutionalized domination and economic exploitation *and* wrote lovingly to women, Wollstonecraft, Yearsley, and the women of their epoch raised feminist development to its most advanced historical stage. Perhaps more significantly for later generations, they collectively pointed the way out of political abyss and impasse by insisting on the importance of writing and action as paths to freedom.

NOTES

1. Many good accounts of the Civil War and the bourgeois revolution exist including Christopher Hill, *The Century of Revolution* (New York: W. W. Norton, 1968); "Base Impudent Kisses," in *The World Turned Upside Down: Radical Ideas During the English Revolution* (New York: Viking Press, 1972), pp. 247– 60; and "The Spiritualization of the Household," in *Society and Puritanism in Pre-Revolutionary England* (New York: Viking Press, 1968), pp. 100–150. For further information consult Lawrence Stone, "The Rise of the Nuclear Family," in *The Family in History*, ed. Charles E. Rosenberg (Philadelphia: University of Pennsylvania Press, 1975), pp. 13– 57; J. H. Plumb, *England Between 1675 and 1725: The Origins of Political Stability* (Boston: Houghton Mifflin, 1967); and *England in the Eighteenth Century, 1716–1815* (London: Pelican, 1950). Among historians who record this period with sensitivity to women are F. W. Tickner, *Women in English Economic History* (London and Toronto: J. D. Dent & Sons, 1923) and Walter L. Blease, *The Emancipation of English Women* (London: Constable & Co., 1910). A. L. Morton, *A People's History of England* (New York: International Publishers, 1938) and Eric Hobsbawm, *The Age of Revolution, 1789–1848* (New York: Mentor, 1962) also provide detailed historical backgrounds to the period. See also Immanuel Wallerstein, *The Modern World-System: Capitalist Agriculture and the Origins of the European World Economy in the Sixteenth Century* (New York and London: Academic Press, 1974) and W. A. Speck, *Stability and Strife in England, 1714–1762* (Cambridge: Harvard University Press, 1977).

2. For a concise account of what the enclosure of land meant particularly for women, see Ida O'Malley, *Women in Subjection: A Study of the Lives of English Women Before 1832* (London: Duckworth, 1933), pp. 15–53; Ruth Perry, "The Economic Status of Women," in *Women, Letters, and the Novel* (New York: AMS Press, 1980), pp. 27–62. For diverse views of women from feudal to pre-industrial capitalist society, see collected essays in Renate Bridenthal and Claudia Koonz, eds., *Becoming Visible: Women in European History* (New York: Houghton Mifflin, 1977).

3. In *Working Life of Women in the Seventeenth Century* (London: George Routledge & Sons, 1919; reprint ed., New York: Augustus M. Kelley, 1968), Alice Clark portrays the place of women in the economic organization of society. The

chapter headings read: "Capitalists," "Agriculture," "Textiles," "Crafts and Trades," and "Professions." Dorothy George, *London Life in the Eighteenth Century* (New York: Harper & Row, 1964) and Christopher Hill, *From Reformation to Revolution* (London: Penguin, 1962) record the changing nature of trade and workers' conditions throughout seventeenth- and eighteenth-century England. In "From Good Wife to Mistress: The Transformation of the Female in Bourgeois Culture," *Science & Society*, May 1973, pp. 152–77, Margaret George offers a politically informed account of these changes, while Ivy Pinchbeck, *Women Workers and the Industrial Revolution, 1750–1850* (New York: F. S. Crofts & Co., 1930) continues to some extent where Clark leaves off. For a brief discussion of the economic factors that affected women consider also the introduction (and bibliography) to the new edition of Alice Clark, *Working Life of Women in the Seventeenth Century* (New York: Routledge and Kegan Paul, 1982), introduction by Miranda Chaytor and Jane Lewis. The introduction sketches out a revised view of the analyses of Alice Clark, Georgianna Hill, Ivy Pinchbeck, and others on women's economic status in the seventeenth and eighteenth centuries. Note also that in "Women's History in Transition: The European Case," *Feminist Studies* 3 (1975–76):84–103, Natalie Zemon Davis traces the history of women from Plutarch and the gradual inclusion of women in the work of social historians. She delineates the shift in "vantage-point" on women's history and suggests how the work of Alice Clark (and Léon Abensour) might be approached by contemporary historians. She further discusses the new importance attached to demographic factors; to the issues of dowry, inheritance patterns, kinship, family affection, and cross-generative relationships; and to available statistics and issues of sexuality.

4. Roy Porter, *English Society in the Eighteenth Century* (London: Pelican, 1982), p. 47.

5. See Joan Kelly, "Early Feminist Theory and the *Querelle des Femmes*, 1400–1789," *Signs: Journal of Women in Culture and Society* 8, 1 (1982):4–28. A longer version of the *Querelle* essay is forthcoming in Joan Kelly's collected essays by the University of Chicago Press. See also Susan Groag Bell, "Christine de Pizan (1364–1430): Humanism and the Problem of the Studious Woman," *Feminist Studies* 3, 3–4 (Spring– Summer 1976):173–84.

6. Susan C. Shapiro, "Feminists in Elizabethan England," *History Today* 27, 11 (November 1977): 703–11.

7. For attempts by James I to curtail the activities of women, see Elizabeth McClure Thompson, ed., *The Chamberlain Letters: A Selection of the Letters of John Chamberlain Concerning Life in England from 1597–1626* (London: Capricorn Books, 1966), p. 271.

8. See K. V. Thomas, "Women and the Civil War Sects," *Past and Present,* no. 13 (1958), pp. 42–63; Ellen McArthur, "Women Petitioners and the Long Parliament," *English Historical Review* 24 (1909): 698–709; and E. M. Williams, "Women Preachers in the Civil War," *Journal of Modern History* 1 (1929): 561–69. Katherine Chidley is mentioned with other women preachers in Thomas, pp. 49–52 and Williams, pp. 564–69. See also Elaine Hobby, "Breaking the Silence: English Women in Print, 1640–1700" (unpublished paper read at the Berkshire Conference of Women Historians, Smith College, Mass., 1984).

9. For an account of the seventeenth-century situation of midwives, see J. H. Aveling, *The Chamberlens and the Midwifery Forceps* (London: J. & A. Churchill, 1882); Thomas R. Forbes, "The Regulation of English Midwives in the Six-

teenth and Seventeenth Centuries," *Medical History* 8 (1964): 235–43; Hilda L. Smith, "Gynecology and Ideology in Seventeenth-Century England," in *Liberating Women's History,* ed. Berenice A. Carroll (Urbana: Univ. of Illinois Press, 1976), 97–114. See also Elaine Hobby, "Women Writers 1642–1688," (Ph.D. diss., University of Birmingham, forthcoming.) Elaine Hobby drew my attention to *Advice to the Women and Maidens of London,* 1653, "which seeks to make accountancy understandable to women—even if only privately to make them useful to husbands and fathers in male businesses," and to Sarah Jinner, an almanac writer in 1658–1664 who describes herself as a "student of astrology." Schoolkeepers and teachers such as Hannah Woolley and Bathsua Makin also count as seventeenth-century professionals. Sarah Jinner is mentioned in Bernard S. Capp, *English Almanacs: 1500–1800: Astrology and the Popular Press* (Ithaca, N. Y.: Cornell University Press, 1979).

10. A checklist of women writers throughout the period may be found in Joyce Horner, *The English Novelists and Their Connection with the Feminist Movement, 1688–1797,* Smith College Studies in Modern Languages, vol. 2, nos. 1–3 (Northampton, Mass.: The Collegiate Press, 1929–1930), pp. 124–27; in Bridget G. McCarthy, *Women Writers: Their Contribution to the English Novel, 1621–1744* (Oxford: Cork University Press, 1944); and in Alison Adburgham, *Women in Print: Writing Women and Women's Magazines from the Restoration to the Accession of Victoria* (London: Allen and Unwin, 1972). For women and drama, consult Nancy Cotton, *Women Playwrights in England, c. 1363–1750* (Lewisberg, Penn.: Bucknell University Press, 1980), and Jean Gagen, *The New Woman: Her Emergence in English Drama, 1600–1730* (New York: Twayne, 1954). Myra Reynolds, *The Learned Lady in England, 1650–1760* (Boston: Houghton Mifflin, 1920), also indicates the extent of circulating library growth, pp. 414–15. More generally, Reynold's book offers a good biographical, socio-cultural, and intellectual history of learned women. See also J. M. S. Tompkins, *The Popular Novel in England, 1770–1800* (London, 1932; reprint ed., London: Methuen, 1961); Hilda L. Smith, *Reason's Disciples: Seventeenth-Century English Feminists* (Urbana: University of Illinois Press, 1982); and Katharine M. Rogers, *Feminism in Eighteenth-Century England* (Urbana: University of Illinois Press, 1982). One excellent bibliography that covers the entire period (in separate sections) is Barbara Kanner, ed., *The Women of England, From Anglo-Saxon Times to the Present* (Hamden, Conn.: Archon Books, 1979), especially pp. 138–258.

11. Among the protest writings are Priscilla Wakefield, *Reflections on the Present Conditions of the Female Sex; with suggestions for its improvement* (London: Joseph Johnson, 1798; reprint ed., New York: Garland Publishing, 1974); Mary Anne Radcliffe, *The Female Advocate: Or, An Attempt to Recover the Rights of Women from Male Usurpation* (Edinburgh: Manners and Miller, 1810; reprint ed., New York: Garland Publishing, 1974); and Mary Hays, *Appeal to the Men of Great Britain in Behalf of Women* (London: Joseph Johnson, 1798; reprint ed., New York: Garland Publishing, 1974).

12. For accounts of the legal status of women, see Leo Kanowitz, *Women and the Law* (Albuquerque: University of New Mexico Press, 1969), especially chaps. 1 and 2; L. P. Brockett, *Women: Her Rights, Wrongs, Privileges, and Responsibilities* (Freeport, N. Y.: Books for Libraries Press, 1869), chap. 4; Mary R. Beard, *Women as Force in History: A Study in Traditions and Realities* (New York: Collier MacMillan, 1946), pp. 87–115 (includes a good discussion of William Blackstone's *Commentaries on the Laws of England*); Janelle Greenberg, "The

Legal Status of English Women in Early Eighteenth Century Law and Equity,"
Studies in Eighteenth-Century Culture 4 (1975): 171–81; and T. E., *The Lawes
Resolutions of Womens Rights: or The Lawes Provision for Women* (London: by
the Assignees of John More, and sold by John Grove, 1632; Huntington Library
#59134). According to the preface, T. E. seems an incorrect attribution. I. L., who
wrote the first address, or someone else entirely is more likely.

13. Porter, *English Society*, p. 40. There is much debate about the role of
marriage and how it affected women. See Lawrence Stone, *The Family, Sex and
Marriage in England 1500–1800*, for an encyclopaedic account of these institu-
tions that tends to gloss over the lives of laboring women and men. (New York:
Harper and Row, 1977). See also the following responses to Stone's work for
other perspectives on the issue. Joseph Kett, "Review of the Family, Sex and
Marriage," *Chronicle of Higher Education*, February 6, 1978; Christopher Hill,
"Sex, Marriage and the Family in England," *Economic History Review* 31
(1978):4; Hobby, "Women Writers 1642–1688"; Alan Macfarland, "Lawrence
Stone: *The Family, Sex and Marriage in England,* " book review, *History & Theory*
17, 1, (1979): 103–25; Joan Thirsk, "The Family," *Past & Present* 27 (1964); J.
H. Plumb, "Review of *The Family, Sex and Marriage,*" *New York Review of
Books*, November 24, 1977; Keith Thomas, "Review of Lawrence Stone, *The
Family, Sex and Marriage,*" *Times Literary Supplement*, October 21, 1977; E. P.
Thompson, "Happy Families," *New Society* 8 (September 1977).

14. Porter, *English Society*, p. 42.

15. George, *London Life*, p. 172 and *passim*; Porter, *English Society*, p. 46.

16. Eric Richards, "Women in the British Economy Since About 1700: An
Interpretation," *The American Historical Review* 78, 3 (June 1973): 345.

17. General discussions and advocacy of class-tiered female education in the
period occur in Hannah More, *Strictures on the Modern System of Female
Education with a View of the Principles and Conduct Prevalent among Women
of Rank and Fortune*, 2 vols. (London: T. Cadell, 1799; reprint ed., New York:
Garland Publishing, 1976) and Wakefield, *Reflections*. I have benefited greatly
from discussions with Ann B. Schteir about Priscilla Wakefield.

18. For a short account of Methodism and the Evangelical Movement see
Gilbert Thomas, *William Cowper and the Eighteenth Century* (London: Allen
and Unwin, 1955), chap. 7, pp. 132–62; Robert F. Wearmouth, *Methodism and
the Common People of the Eighteenth Century* (London: The Epworth Press,
1945); and Elie Halévy, *The Birth of Methodism in England*, trans. and ed.
Bernard Semmel (Chicago: University of Chicago Press, 1971).

19. For the state of literacy and attitudes toward it, see David Cressy, *Literary
and the Social Order: Reading and Writing in Tudor and Stuart England* (Cambridge: University Press, 1980) and Margaret Spufford, *Contrasting Communities: English Villagers in the Sixteenth and Seventeenth Centuries* (New York:
Cambridge University Press, 1974).

20. Wakefield, *Reflections*, p. 97.

21. Temple Scott, ed., "Of the Education of Ladies," *The Prose Works of
Jonathan Swift, D. D.*, vol. 11 (London: George Bell and Sons, 1907), p. 64.

22. Quoted in Dorothy Gardiner, *English Girlhood at School: A Study of
Women's Education Through Twelve Centuries* (London: Oxford University
Press, 1929), p. 394.

23. Some of the most useful works on female education include: Barbara
Brandon Schnorrenberg, "Education for Women in Eighteenth Century England:

An Annotated Bibliography," *Women and Literature* 4 (1976): 49–55, a review of the major educational manuals, which generally concentrated on manners, morals, and fashion rather than an intellectually based curriculum; Ruth Kelso, *Doctrine for the Lady of the Renaissance* (Urbana: University of Illinois Press, 1956); Gardiner, *English Girlhood at School;* Doris M. Stenton, *The English Woman in History* (London: Allen and Unwin, 1957); Josephine Kamm, *Hope Deferred: Girls' Education in English History* (London: Methuen, 1965); and Phyllis Stock, *Better than Rubies: A History of Women's Education* (New York: Capricorn, 1978), a recent overview of female education. See also Kanner, *The Women of England,* O'Malley, *Women in Subjection,* Reynolds, *Learned Lady,* and Smith, *Reason's Disciples.*

24. These views were presented in a paper by Barbara Brandon Schnorrenberg entitled "Thoughts on the Education of Daughters: The Education of British Girls ca. 1750–1850" (Consortium on Revolutionary Europe, Athens, Georgia, February 1982, to be published in the proceedings).

25. The salonières across the channel also helped to make intellectual women acceptable. See Caroline Lougée, *Le Paradis des Femmes: Women, Salons, and Social Stratification in Seventeenth-Century France* (Princeton: Princeton University Press, 1976); Ian Maclean, *Women Triumphant: Feminism in French Literature, 1610–1652* (Oxford: Clarendon Press, 1977); Evelyn Gordon Bodek, "Salonières and Bluestockings: Educated Obsolescence and Germinating Feminism," *Feminist Studies* 3 (1976): 185–99; R. Brimley Johnson, ed., *Bluestocking Letters* (London and New York: John Lane, 1926); W. S. Scott, *The Bluestocking Ladies* (London: John Greene & Co., 1947); R. Huchon, *Mrs. Montagu and Her Friends* (London: John Murray, 1907); and Chauncey Brewster Tinker, *The Salon and English Letters* (New York: Macmillan, 1915).

26. For a discussion of philanthropy, see Betsy Rodgers, *Cloak of Charity: Studies in Eighteenth-Century Philanthropy* (London: Methuen, 1949) and F. K. Prochaska, *Women and Philanthropy in Nineteenth-Century England* (Oxford: Clarendon Press, 1980).

27. Many of Joseph Johnson's authors and frequenters of his social circle wrote about slavery, the slave trade, and abolition, including William Cowper, John Aikin, Anna Laetitia Barbauld, Joseph Priestley, Mary Wollstonecraft, Mary Hays, and Erasmus Darwin. John Newton, an ex-slaveship captain who was instrumental in William Wilberforce's conversion, authored and published the influential *Thoughts Upon the African Slave Trade* (London, 1788). See Gerald Tyson, *Joseph Johnson: A Liberal Publisher* (Iowa City: University of Iowa Press, 1979), pp. 90–91. Other abolitionists include Priscilla Wakefield, Charlotte Smith, Ann Yearsley, and Hannah More. Earlier, Granville Sharpe, Thomas Clarkson, James Ramsey, and Olaudah Equiano had campaigned against the slave trade and in 1787 the Society for the Abolition of the Slave Trade was founded. Events that led up to the anti-slavery debate in the House are described in Rodgers, *Cloak of Charity*, "The Abolition of the Slave Trade: Granville Sharp, Thomas Clarkson, William Wilberforce," pp. 158–80. Even earlier, Granville Sharp's memorandum to the chief lawyers at the Inns of Courts was published in the 1760s as *The Injustice of Tolerating Slavery in England.* The Quakers, however, were first on both sides of the Atlantic to pass resolutions condemning the slave-trade; by 1761 Quakers engaged in slave trading were banned from membership. In addition to More, many of the Bluestockings supported abolition. Elizabeth Montagu drew attention to the issue of abolition by inviting

William Wilberforce to her assemblies and referring to him intimately as "The
Red Cross Knight." See *A Lady of the Last Century by Dr. Doran* (London: R.
Bentley, 1873), p. 351. For a discussion of Hannah More's role in the abolition
movement, see Mary Alden Hopkins, *Hannah More and Her Circle* (New York:
Longmans, Green, 1947), pp. 153–61.

28. Margaret Tyler, "Epistle to the Reader," in *The First Part of the Mirrour of
Princely deedes and Knyghthood* (London: Thomas East, 1578). On the question
of Margaret Tyler's identity, as an intimate of the Howard family (apparently) she
was probably a Roman Catholic and therefore, possibly, a recusant masquer-
ading under a pseudonymous name. This happened occasionally. (See biography of Margaret Tyler.) This hypothesis about Tyler was suggested by Robert
Bellow, a student of recusant history at Cambridge University. Leslie Dunn of
Cambridge University corresponded with me on the matter and I thank both of
them.

29. The work mentioned is Jane Anger, *Jane Anger her protection for Women
To defend them against the Scandalous Reportes Of a late Surfeiting Lover, and
all other like Venerians that complaine so to bee overcloyed with women's
kindness* (London: Richard Jones and Thomas Orwin, 1589).

30. Joseph Swetnam, *The araignment [sic] of lewd, idle, froward, and unconstant women: or the vanitie of them, choose you whether* (London: T. Archer,
1615).

31. Ester Sowernam, *Ester hath hang'd Haman: or an Answere to a lewd
pamphlet, entituled, the Arraignment of Women* (London: Nicholas Bourne,
1617).

32. See Thompson, *The Chamberlain Letters.*

33. In the Juniper lecture in 1639 (pp. 95–97) to which Mary Tattle-Well and
Joane Hit-Him-Home are allegedly responding, John Taylor mentions that certain women are going to respond to his work. The fact that he mentions his
knowledge of respondents to his text while he is writing it makes the possibility
that he authored the response likely. His reference to *The Woman's Sharpe
Revenge* (1640) by name in 1639 makes it even more likely. However, a tradition
in polemical debate of fast response and word-of-mouth pre-publicity—
especially if Taylor knew the women—could similarly account for his textual
references to their pamphlet. This was not an uncommon practice. The title
reads as follows: Mary Tattle-Well and Joane Hit-Him-Home, *The Woman's
Sharpe Revenge: Or an answer to Sir Seldome Sober that Write those railing
pamphlets called the juniper and crabtree lectures, etc. Being a sound reply and
a full confutation of those books: with an Apology in this case for the defense
of us women* (London, J. O. [Kes] for J. Becket, 1640).

34. Katherine Chidley, *The Justification of the Independent Churches of
Christ. Being an answer to Mr. Edwards his booke, which hee hath written
against the government of Christs Church, and toleration of Christs publicke
worship; briefly declaring that the congregations of the Saints ought not to have
dependence in government upon any other, or direction in worship from any
other than Christ their head and law giver* (London: William Lahrner, 1641).

35. See Hobby, "Women Writers 1642–1688," which outlines the depth and
range of women writers in this period. For statistics mentioned in the text, see
Hobby, "Breaking the Silence."

36. Margaret Fell, *Womens Speaking Justified, Proved and Allowed of by the*

Scriptures... (London: 1667, 2nd ed.; reprint ed., Los Angeles: William Andrews Clark Memorial Library, University of California at Los Angeles, 1979), no. 196.

37. Katherine Philips, *Poems by the most deservedly Admired Mrs. Katherine Philips, The Matchless Orinda. To which is added Monsieur Corneille's Pompey and Horace, tragedies. With several other translations out of French* (London: T. N. for Henry Herringman, 1678). See also Lillian Faderman, *Surpassing the Love of Men: Romantic Friendship and Love Between Women from the Renaissance to the Present* (New York: William Morrow & Co., 1981) for an account of the rise of romantic friendship, especially (for the time period of this volume) pp. 65–143.

38. Margaret Cavendish's Preface to *Philosophical and Physical Opinions, written by her Excellency the Lady Marchioness of Newcastle* (London: J. Martin and J. Allestrye, 1655); Cavendish, *The Convent of Pleasure*, in *Plays, never before printed* (London: A. Maxwell, 1668).

39. A. Boyce Gibson, *The Philosophy of Descartes* (London: Methuen, 1932), presents a cogent account of Descartes' life and philosophy. Smith, *Reason's Disciples* (Champaign: University of Illinois Press, 1981), argues and illustrates the importance of the Cartesian influence and scientific ideas in general in the development of feminism. Ruth Perry, *The Life and Times of Mary Astell (1666–1731): An Early English Feminist* (forthcoming), discusses the influence of rationalist philosophy on women in chap. 3, "The Self-Respect of a Reasoning Creature," and throughout relates it particularly to Mary Astell and her contemporaries. Dolores Palomo also addresses the connection between feminism, science, and rationalism in her unpublished manuscript on Margaret Cavendish. I have benefited greatly from discussions and correspondence with Dolores Palomo, Ruth Perry, and Hilda Smith. For a study of women and science, see Gerald D. Meyer, *The Scientific Lady in England, 1650–1760; An Account of her Rise, with Emphasis on the Major Role of the Telescope and Microscope* (Berkeley: University of California Press, 1955), and K. V. Thomas, *Religion and the Decline of Magic* (London: Weidenfeld & Nicolson, 1971). In her article on feminist theory, "Early Feminist Theory and the *Querelle des Femmes*, 1400–1789," Joan Kelly factors in the emergence of Cartesianism to the development of feminist history.

40. Several well-known exponents of Cartesian rationalism among the feminist writers include Aphra Behn, Damaris Cudworth, Lady Masham (who, in *Occasional Thoughts in Reference to a Virtuous and Christian Life* (London, 1705), elaborates on the reasonableness of female education), and the Bluestocking Elizabeth Carter (who, in addition to Behn, translated Fontenelle's *A Discovery of New Worlds*). The most notable is Mary Astell, whose Cartesian influence is clear in the second half of *A Serious Proposal to the Ladies, for the advancement of their true and greatest interest* (London, 1694, 1697; reprint ed., New York: Source Book Press, 1970). See also Marjorie Hope Nicholson, ed., *The Correspondence of Anne, Viscountess Conway, Henry More, and their Friends, 1642–1684* . . . (New Haven: Yale University Press, 1930).

41. Bathsua Makin, *An Essay to revive the Antient Education of Gentlewomen, in religion, manners, arts and tongues with an Answer to the Objections against this Way of Education* (London: J. D. to be sold by Thomas Parkhurst, 1673).

42. Hannah Woolley, *The Queen-like Closet, or Rich Cabinet: Stored with all manner of Rare Receipts for Preserving, Candying and Cookery. Very pleasant*

and beneficial to all ingenious persons of the Female sex. To which is added a supplement presented to all ingenious Ladies and Gentlewomen, 4th ed. (London: for R. Chiswell and T. Sawbridge, 1681). Note that this supplement explains that Woolley did not write *The Gentlewomans Companion* (with its autobiographical beginning) commonly ascribed to her. I am indebted to Elaine Hobby for sharing her discovery with me.

43. Jane Sharp, *The Midwives Book. Or the whole art of Midwifery discovered. Directing Childbearing women how to behave themselves. In their conception, breeding, bearing, and nursing of children in 6 books. . . .* (London: for Simon Miller, 1671); and Elizabeth Cellier, *A Scheme for the Foundation of a Royal Hospital, and raising revenue of five or six-thousand pounds a year, by, and for the maintenance of a corporation of skilful midwives, and such foundlings or exposed children, as shall be admitted therein, etc.* (London, 1687; reprinted in *Harleian Miscellany* 4, 1745), pp. 142–47).

44. See n. 5.

45. Anna Maria van Schurman, *The Learned Maid; or, whether a Maid may be a Scholar?* (London: John Redmayne, 1659).

46. See Lougée, *Le Paradis des Femmes.*

47. See Smith, *Reason's Disciples.*

48. Aphra Behn, *The Forc'd Marriage; or, the Jealous Bridegroom; a tragicomedy* (London: H. L. and R. B., for James Magnus, 1671).

49. Aphra Behn, *Lycidus; or, The Lover in Fashion* (London, 1688), reprinted in *The Works of Aphra Behn,* vol. 6, ed. Montague Summers (London: William Heineman, 1915), pp. 363–389. See also Angeline Goreau, *Reconstructing Aphra: A Social Biography of Aphra Behn* (New York: Dial Press, 1980), pp. 205–06.

50. Aphra Behn, *Oroonoko: or, the Royal Slave* (London, 1688; reprint ed., New York: W. W. Norton, 1973).

51. Aphra Behn, the Author's Preface to her translation of Bernard le Bovier de Fontenelle, *Entretiens sur la Pluralité des Deux Mondes* [*The Theory or System of Several New Inhabited Worlds, lately discover'd and pleasantly describ'd, in five nights conversation with Madam the Marchioness of *****,* also known as *A Discovery of New Worlds*] (London: W. O. for Samuel Briscoe, 1700).

52. Robert Gould, *Love Given O're: or, A Satyr against the Pride, Lust, and Inconstancy, etc. of Woman* (London, 1682; reprint ed., Los Angeles: William Andrews Clark Memorial Library, University of California at Los Angeles, 1976), no. 180.

53. Sarah Fyge (Field Egerton), *The Female Advocate, or, an Answere to a Late Satyr against the Pride, Lust and Inconstancy, etc. of Woman* (London: John Raylor, 1686; reprint of the 1687 2d ed., Los Angeles: William Andrews Clark Memorial Library, University of California at Los Angeles, 1976), no. 180.

54. Jane Barker, *Poetical Recreations: consisting of Original Poems, Songs, Odes, etc. With Several New Translations* (London: printed for Benjamin Crayle, 1688).

55. Jane Barker, "The Unaccountable Wife," in *A Patch-Work Screen for the Ladies, or, Love and Virtue recommended: in a Collection of Instructive Novels* (London, 1723; reprint ed., New York: Garland Publishing, 1973).

56. Mary Astell, *A Serious Proposal* and *Some Reflections upon Marriage, occasion'd by the Duke and Duchess of Mazarine's case; which is also consid-*

ered, 4th ed. (London: William Parker, 1730; reprint ed., New York: Source Book Press, 1970). For Astell's circle, see note 87.

57. Judith Drake, *An Essay in Defence of the Female Sex. In which are inserted the Characters of a Pedant, a Squire, a Beau, a Vertuoso, a Poetaster, a City-critick, etc. . . . In a letter to a lady. Written by a lady* (London: A. Roper and E. Wilkinson, 1696; reprint ed., New York: Source Book Press, 1970). Regarding Judith Drake's identity, see biography of Judith Drake.

58. Lady Mary Chudleigh, *The Ladies Defence; or, "The Bride-Womans Counsellor" Answer'd: A Poem* (London: for John Deeve, 1701). For interesting commentary on Lady Chudleigh's poem, see Anthony Coleman, " 'The Provok'd Wife' and 'The Ladies Defence,' " *Notes and Queries,* March 1970, pp. 88–91.

59. Eugenia, *The Female Advocate; or a Plea for the just Liberty of the Tender Sex, and particularly of Married Women. Being Reflections on a late Rude and Disingenous Discourse, Delivered by Mr. John Sprint, in a Sermon at a Wedding, May 11th, at Sherburn, in Dorsetshire, 1699. By a Lady of Quality* (London: for Andrew Bell, 1700). I thank Ruth Perry for bringing Eugenia to my attention. For information about the strong connections between Lady Chudleigh and Mary Astell, about Astell's possible reference to Sprint (in *Reflections,* p. 38 in the modern reprint), and for biographical clarification on Lady Chudleigh, I am indebted to Joanna Lipking. The information was first presented in "The Vehemence of Lady Chudleigh," MLA talk, December, 1978.

60. John Sprint, *The Bride-Womans Counsellor, Being a Sermon Preach'd at a Wedding, May the 11th, 1699, at Sherbourn, in Dorsetshire* (London: H. Hills, 1699). (Hill's edition was probably pirated. The edition by J. Bowyer, 1700, is probably the authentic edition.

61. Lady Mary Chudleigh, *Essays upon Several Subjects in Prose and Verse* (London: T. H. for R. Bonwicke, W. Freeman, T. Goodwin, 1710).

62. Sarah Fyge Field Egerton, *Poems on Several Occasions, together with a pastoral* (London: J. Nutt, 1706); Lady Mary Chudleigh, *Poems on Several Occasions* (London: Bernard Lintott, 1703).

63. Anne Finch, Countess of Winchilsea, *Miscellany Poems, on Several Occasions. Written by a Lady* (London: printed for J. B., 1713).

64. Elizabeth Elstob, Preface to *An English-Saxon Homily, on the birth-day of St. Gregory,* (London: W. Bowyer, 1709), pp. iii–vi. Information about Elizabeth Elstob appears in Perry, *The Life and Times of Mary Astell,* especially chap. 2, entitled "The Coal of Newcastle." See also articles entitled "Elizabeth Elstob, the Saxonist," by Caroline A. White in Sharpe's *London Magazine for Entertainment and Instruction for General Reading* 50, n.s. 35 (1869): 180ff. These articles were obtained for me through the kindness of the University of Nebraska Interlibrary loan staff from the Detroit Public Library and the Boston Public Library.

65. For an account of the relationship between economics and authorship, see Geoffrey Alan Cranfield, *The Press and Society from Caxton to Northcliffe* (New York and London: Longman, 1978); Cyprian Blagden, *The Stationers' Company A History, 1403–1959* (London: Allen & Unwin, 1960). Timothy Crist "Government Control of the Press After the Expiration of the Printing Act in 1679," *Publishing History,* no. 5 (1979); Frank A. Mumby, *Publishing and Bookselling: A History from the Earliest Times to the Present Day* (London: Jonathan Cape, 1930, 1949); Frederick Seaton Siebert, *Freedom of the Press in England, 1476–1776: The Rise and Decline of Government Control* (Urbana: University of Illinois Press, 1965); and A. S. Collins, *Authorship in the Days of Johnson, Being*

a Study of the Relation between Author, Patron, Publisher, and Public, 1726–1780 (London: Robert Holden and Co., 1927).

66. *The Nine Muses, or, Poems Written by Nine Severall Ladies Upon the Death of the late Famous John Dryden, Esq.* (London: Richard Bassett, 1700).

67. Delarivière Manley, Preface to *The Royal Mischief, A tragedy* (London: R. Bentley, 1696); Preface to *The Lost Lover; or, the Jealous Husband, A comedy* (London: R. Bentley, 1696). Catherine Cockburn Trotter, Prefatory address to *Agnes de Castro, a tragedy* (London, 1696). Mary Griffith Pix, Preface to *Ibrahim, the thirteenth Emperor of the Turks: a tragedy* (London, 1696).

68. Mary Davys, Preface to *The Works of Mrs. Davys: consisting of plays, novels, poems, and familiar letters* (London: printed for the author, 1725).

69. Gardiner, *English Girlhood at School*, p. 334.

70. Delarivière Manley, *The New Atalantis* (London, 1709), reprinted in *The Novels of Mary Delarivière Manley*, ed. Patricia Koster, 2 vols. (Gainesville, Fla.: Scholars' Facsimiles and Reprints, 1971), vol. 2. See particularly the controversial lesbian section on the cabal.

71. Eliza Fowler Haywood, *The British Recluse: or, The Secret History of Cleomira, Suppos'd Dead* (London: J. Watts, 1724); Susanna Freeman Centlivre, Preface to *The Platonick Lady. A Comedy* (London, 1707); "Preface" and Address "To the World" to *The Works of the Celebrated Mrs. Centlivre* (London: J. Knapton, etc. 1761). Note also that the "strong women" of the period could include everyone who wrote about the condition of women. However, Delarivière Manley and Eliza Haywood, in particular, had to endure substantial criticisms of their writings and their lives.

72. Sophia, *Woman not Inferior to Man: or, a short and modest vindication of the natural right of the fair sex to a perfect equality of power, dignity and esteem, with the Men* (London: John Hawkins, 1739), reprinted in *Beauty's Triumph* (London: J. Robinson, 1751). *Woman's Superior Excellence over Man: or, a reply to the author of a late treatise, entitled, Man Superior to Woman. In which, the excessive weakness of that gentleman's answer to woman not inferior to man is exposed; with a plain demonstration of woman's natural right even to superiority over the men in head and heart; proving their minds as much more beautiful than the men's as their bodies are, and that, had they the same advantages of education, they would excel them as much in sense as they do in virtue. The whole interspersed with a variety of mannish characters, which some of the most noted heroes of the present age had the goodness to fight for* (London, 1740). Reprinted in *Beauty's Triumph* (London: J. Robinson, 1751). François Poulain de la Barre, *De l'Egalité des deux Sexes* (Paris, 1673), trans. "A. L.," *The Woman as Good as the Man* (London, 1677). For an account of François Poulain de la Barre, see Jacob Bouten, *Mary Wollstonecraft and the Beginning of Female Emancipation in France and England* (Amsterdam: H. J. Paris, 1922). Note also that Poulain de la Barre wrote in 1675 against the equality of women in *De l'Excellence des Hommes contre L'Egalité des Sexes*, 1675 (B. L. shelf no. 8403.bb 11).

73. See Michael A. Seidel, "Poulain de la Barre's *The Woman as Good as the Man*," *Journal of the History of Ideas* 35, 3 (1974): 499–508. (See also bibliography for Sophia.)

74. Sophia's identity has never been uncovered. Although Lady Mary Wortley Montagu's name is often suggested, Lady Mary's biographer Robert Halsband concludes that it is impossible to tender proof either way.

75. Lady Mary Wortley Montagu, *The Nonsense of Common-Sense,* Number VI, in *Essays and Poems and Simplicity, A Comedy,* ed. Robert Halsband and Isobel Grundy (Oxford: Clarendon Press, 1977); Anon., *The Gentlemen's Magazine* 9 (1739): 525–26.

76. Stephen Duck, *Poems on Several Occasions* (London: printed by Samuel Richardson, 1736). Mary Collier, *The Woman's Labour: an epistle to Mr. Stephen Duck; in answer to his late poem, called "The Thresher's Labour."* (London: printed for the author, 1739.)

77. Eliza Fowler Haywood, ed., *The Female Spectator* (London: T. Gardner, 1746), April 1744 – May 1746.

78. Sarah Fielding, *The Governess; or, the Little Female Academy: Being the History of Mrs. Teachum and Her Nine Girls* (London, 1749; reprint ed., London: Oxford University Press, 1968); and *The Adventures of David Simple in Search of a Faithful Friend,* 3 vols. (London: A. Millar, 1744; reprint ed., London: Oxford University Press, 1969).

79. See the Preface to the first edition of *David Simple* for Fielding's forthright declaration of writing as a financial necessity for herself.

80. Charlotte Charke, *A Narrative of the Life of Mrs. Charlotte Charke, youngest daughter of Colley Cibber,* 2d ed. (London, 1755; reprint ed., edited by Leonard R. N. Ashley, Gainesville, Fla.: Scholars' Facsimiles and Reprints, 1969).

81. Elizabeth Robinson Montagu, in *Dialogues of the Dead* by George Lyttelton (London: W. Sandy, 1760). See the last three dialogues, which were written by Montagu.

82. For commentary on the question of the single life, see the letters of Elizabeth Carter to Catherine Talbot, in Elizabeth Carter, *A Series of Letters between Mrs. Elizabeth Carter and Miss Catherine Talbot from the year 1741 to 1770, to which are added, letters from Mrs. Elizabeth Carter to Mrs. Vesey, between the years 1763 and 1787,* ed. Montagu Pennington, 4 vols. (London: F. C. and J. Rivington, 1809); Hester Mulso Chapone, *The Posthumous Works of Mrs. Chapone containing her correspondence with Mr. Richardson . . . ,* 2 vols. (London: John Murray, 1807). See especially first and third letters on "Filial Obedience," *1750–1751.* For a full discussion of female romantic friendship see Faderman, *Surpassing the Love of Men.*

83. C. Lennart Carlson, *The First Magazine: A History of The Gentleman's Magazine . . .* (Providence, R.I.: Brown University Press, 1938), pp. 228–29 and passim.

84. The male feminist defenses of women and collections of women poets that appeared in short succession began with George Ballard, *Memoirs of several Ladies of Great Britain, who have been celebrated for their writings or skill in learned languages, arts and sciences* (reprint ed., Oxford: W. Jackson, 1752) and John Duncombe's *The Feminiad. or, Female Genius. A Poem . . .* (London: R. & J. Dodsley, 1757). See also Frederic Rowton, ed., *The Female Poets of Great Britain* (London: Longman, et al., 1848; reprint ed. of 1851 second printing, introduction by Marilyn L. Williamson, Detroit: Wayne State University Press, 1981); George W. Bethune, ed., *The British Female Poets* (Philadelphia: Lindsay and Blakiston, 1848; reprint ed., Freeport, N. Y.: Books for Libraries Press, 1972); and Reynolds, *Learned Lady.*

85. See especially Elizabeth Mavor, *The Ladies of Llangollen, A Study in Romantic Friendship* (London: Michael Joseph, 1971); *The Hamwood Papers of*

the Ladies of Llangollen and Caroline Hamilton, ed. Eva Mary Bell (London: Macmillan & Co., 1930).

86. Elizabeth Carter, *A Series of Letters between Mrs. Elizabeth Carter and Miss Catherine Talbot* (London: F. C. and J. Rivington, 1809) and *Letters from Mrs. Elizabeth Carter to Mrs. Montagu . . . ,* ed. Montagu Pennington, 3 vols. (London: F. C. and J. Rivington, 1817). See also Faderman, *Surpassing the Love of Men.*

87. Sarah Robinson Scott, *A Description of Millenium Hall and the Country Adjacent: together with the Characters of the Inhabitants, and such historical anecdotes and Reflections, as may excite in the reader Proper Sentiments of Humanity, and lead the Mind to the Love of Virtue. By a Gentleman on his Travels* (London: for T. Carnan, 1762; reprint edition entitled *A Description of Millenium Hall,* ed. Walter M. Crittenden, New York: Bookman Associates, 1955). Female circles existed among these early feminists; the community around Astell is described in Ruth Perry's biography of Mary Astell. See n. 39. The Thynne "set" at Longleat, Somerset receives attention in Helen Sard Hughes, *The Gentle Hertford: Her Life and Letters* (New York: Macmillan, 1940) and in Henry F. Stecher, *Elizabeth Singer Rowe: The Poetess of Frome: A Study in Eighteenth-Century English Pietism* (Frankfurt: M. Peter Lang; Bern: Herbert Land, 1973). Joanna Lipking deduces that Eugenia may have been tied to the Longleat circle because of the dedication to Lady Worseley, while the textual references to dissenting circles, on the other hand, suggest connections with John Dunton and his associates. Female circles also emulated the Bluestockings in the provinces. (In the previous century, Jane Barker is said to have modelled a female group after Katherine Philips's group). An account of Lady Miller's Batheaston assembly, which Fanny Burney and Anna Seward visited, is found in Ruth Avaline Hesselgrave, *Lady Miller and the Batheaston Literary Circle* (New Haven: Yale University Press, 1927); Barbara Brandon Schnorrenberg calls attention to the fact that Catherine Macaulay's salon, essentially political in nature, is seldom mentioned in studies of the period in "The Brood Hen of Faction: Mrs. Macaulay and Radical Politics, 1765–1775," *Albion* 2, 1 (Spring 1979): 33–45. See also Tinker, *The Salon and English Letters,* and Stenton, *The English Woman in History.*

88. Elizabeth Robinson Montagu to Gilbert West, October 16, 1755; quoted in Sarah Robinson Scott, *Millenium Hall,* ed. Crittenden, p. 13.

89. Anna Seward, *The Poetical Works of Anna Seward; with Excerpts from her Literary Correspondence,* vol. 3, ed. Walter Scott (Edinburgh and London: James Ballantyne and Longman, et al., 1810).

90. See Adrienne Rich, "Compulsory Heterosexuality and Lesbian Existence," *Signs* 5, 4 (1980): 631–660. Other women mentioned later in the text, such as Lady Eleanor Butler and Sarah Robinson Scott, clearly exist on that same continuum.

91. Mary Scott, *The Female Advocate, a poem occasioned by reading Mr. Duncombe's* Feminiad (London: Joseph Johnson, 1774). John Duncombe, *The Feminiad.* see n. 84.

92. For an account of the poetry of Phillis Wheatley see Gloria Hull, "Black Women Poets from Wheatley to Walker," *Black American Literature Forum* 9 (Winter 1975): 91–96. See also *The Poems of Phillis Wheatley,* ed. Julian D. Mason, Jr. (Chapel Hill: University of North Carolina Press, 1966).

93. Ann Yearsley, *Poems on Several Occasions,* 4th ed. (London: T. Cadell, 1786). An "Autobiographical Narrative" was added, in which Yearsley defended herself against Hannah More. *Poems on Various Subjects* (London: printed for the Author, 1787). "Autobiographical Narrative" again printed, "The Deed of Trust" added.

94. Ann Yearsley, *A Poem on the Inhumanity of the Slave-Trade* (London: G. G. and J. Robinson, 1788).

95. Catherine Macaulay, *Letters on Education, with observations on religious and metaphysical subjects* (London, 1790; reprint ed., New York: Garland Publishing, 1974). Barbara Brandon Schnorrenberg is in the process of writing a full-scale biography of Catherine Macaulay. Note also that Natalie Zemon Davis has convincingly illustrated Macaulay's influence as an early woman historian in "Gender and Genre: Women as Historical Writers, 1400–1820," in *Beyond Their Sex: Learned Women of the European Past,* ed. Patricia H. Labalme (New York: New York University Press, 1980), pp. 153–82. The article by Florence Boos and William Boos, mentioned in Macaulay's bibliography herein, is particularly wide-ranging.

96. Mary Wollstonecraft, *Thoughts on the Education of Daughters with Reflections on Female Conduct, in the more important Duties of Life* (London: Joseph Johnson, 1787; reprint ed., New York: Garland Publishing, 1974); *Mary, a Fiction* (London: Joseph Johnson, 1788; reprint ed., New York: Schocken, 1977); *A Vindication of the Rights of Woman: With Strictures on Political and Moral Subjects* (London, 1792; reprint ed., New York, New York: W. W. Norton, 1967, 1975 Penguin, 1975.); *The Wrongs of Woman, or Maria* (London, 1798; reprint ed., New York: W. W. Norton, 1975; and with *Mary, a Fiction,* London: Oxford University Press, 1976).

97. Mary Wollstonecraft, *A Vindication of the Rights of Men* (London: Joseph Johnson, 1790; reprint ed., Gainesville, Fla.: Scholars' Facsimilies and Reprints, 1960); and the Preface to her translation of Christian Gotthilf Salzmann, *Elements of Morality for the Use of Children* (London: Joseph Johnson, 1790).

98. Mary Hays, in *Monthly Magazine,* July 2, 1796 and March 2, 1797; *Appeal to the Men of Great Britain in Behalf of Women.*

99. Charlotte Turner Smith, Preface to and *Desmond, a novel,* 3 vols. (London: G. G. and J. Robinson, 1792; reprint ed., New York: Garland Publishing, 1974). Mary Anne Radcliffe, *The Female Advocate.*

100. Hannah More, "Letters to Elizabeth Robinson Montagu," in *The Female Spectator: English Women Writers Before 1800,* ed. Mary Mahl and Helene Koon (Old Westbury, N. Y.: The Feminist Press, 1977), 277–86.

101. This point of view is very clear in Hannah More, *Strictures on the Modern System.*

102. See Judith Drake, *An Essay in Defence of the Female Sex,* p. 39.

103. See n. 27.

104. Hannah More, *Slavery, a poem* (London: T. Cadell, 1788).

105. Elizabeth Tanfield Cary, Viscountess Falkland, *The Tragedie of Mariam, the Faire Queene of Jewry* (London: printed by Thomas Creede for Richard Hawkins, 1613).

106. Richard Polwhele, *The Unsex'd Females: A Poem* (London, 1798; reprint ed., New York: Garland Publishing, 1974).

107. John Wilkes, *Essay on Women* (London: for private circulation, 1763).

108. Anne Howard, Viscountess Irwin, "Answer to Pope's 'Of the Character of Women' " (London, n.d.).

109. Mary Jones, "Letters to Lady Lovelace," *Miscellanies in prose and verse* (Oxford: R. and J. Dodsley, 1750) and "Letter to the Hon. Miss Lovelace" in *Poems by Eminent Ladies,* ed. G. Colman and B. Thornton (London, 1755); Mary Leapor, *Poems upon several occasions,* 2 vols. (London: J. Roberts, 1748, 1751).

MARGARET TYLER
fl. 1578

The identity of the writer of the first known feminist tract in English remains unclear to this day. The information that we do have derives mainly from the epistle dedicatory to the translation. Not surprisingly the feminist statements occur in a preface to a translation. In prefaces, writers could air their views and not be perceived as aggressive controversialists; translation, which tends not to depend on original thought, was also viewed as a suitable medium for the allegedly less finely honed intellects of women. This was especially true in sixteenth- and seventeenth-century Britain, when interest in foreign languages and affairs intensified. Nonetheless, since education was still largely a masculine preserve, translation was a privilege largely accessible only to rich females of noble birth or the daughters of Renaissance humanists. In this golden age of translation, Margaret Tyler translated *The First Part of the Mirrour of Princely deedes and Knyghthood* by the Spaniard, Diego Ortuñez de Calahorra.

From the epistle dedicating this translation, written by Tyler, it appears that she was a member of and possibly a servant in the household of the aristocratic and Roman Catholic Howard family. Since her employers met untimely deaths, according to remarks Tyler makes to their son, to whom she dedicates her work, it is possible they were executed for involvement in the Ridolfi assassination plot against the Protestant Queen Elizabeth I. In that case, the father of the dedicatee would be Thomas, Third Duke of Norfolk, who was executed in June 1572. Because Tyler is paying homage to the parents, pledging allegiance to their son, and relying on his protection against critical assaults on her work, chances are that she was a Roman Catholic herself.

There is a slim possibility also that Margaret Tyler's real name was Margaret Tyrrell. The Tyrrells were a prominent Roman Catholic family and there was a Margaret Tyrrell living at the time who was sister-in-law to the Howard family. (Information supplied by Robert Bellow, whom I thank.) It was quite common for recusants (Roman Catholics who dissented from the Anglican communion) to disguise their names in this way, or even to take the name of another recusant family as a pseudonym. Robert Southwell, for example, the recusant cleric-poet who was connected with the Howard family, occasionally went by the name of Cotton.

A search of the Howard and Tyrrell (Tirel, Tyrell) families in the *Dictionary of National Biography,* family histories, encyclopaedic biographical dictionaries, and in Southwell and other historical biographies has so far failed to yield anything specific about Tyler's identity.

The epistle contains the first explicitly feminist argument published by a woman that I have found in English. Tyler argued that women have the same capacity to research and write as men do, and that they should, therefore, have the prerogative to do so and to choose their subject. Despite this assertion, she apologized for her "unbecoming" subject matter, a stance that continued among women writers for at least two centuries. This practice of defending women in the apparatus to a work rather than in the work itself constituted not only a literature of necessity because controversy was rarely tolerated, but more crucially a literature of subversion and camouflage.

FROM THE TRANSLATION OF
THE FIRST PART OF THE MIRROUR OF PRINCELY DEEDES AND KNYGHTHOOD:

DEDICATION
TO THE RIGHT HONOURABLE
THE LORD THOMAS HOWARD

Not beeing greatly forward of mine owne inclination (right Honourable) but forced by the importunitie of my friends to make some triall of my selfe in this exercise of translation. I have adventured upon

---

SOURCE: This selection comes from a printed volume in the Henry E. Huntington Library, shelf no. 60627. It is listed in the short-title catalogue under Ortuñez, no. 18860.

a peece of work, not indeed the most profitablest, as intreating of armes, nor yet altogether fruitlesse, if example may serve, as being historicall, but the while, either to be borne withall for the delight, or not to be refused for the strangeness: farther I meane not to make boast of my travaile, for the matter was offred, not made choice of, as there appeared likewise little libertie in my first yeelding. The earnestnesse of my friends persuaded me that it was convenient to laie foorth my talent for increase, or to set my candle on a candlesticke, & the consideration of my sufficiencie drove me to thinke it better for my ease, either quite to burie my talent, thereby to avoide the breaking of thriftlesse debtes, or rather to put my candle cleane out, then that it should bewraie [bury] every unswept corner in my house, but the opinion of my friends judgement prevailed above mine own reason. So upon hope to please them, I first undertooke this labour, & I have gone through withall, the rather to acquaint my selfe with mine olde reading: whereto since the dispatch thereof, I have made, my friends privie, & upon good liking, with request thereto I have passed my graunt unto them for the publication, referring for my selfe the order for the dedication, so as I shuld think best, either for the defence of my worke or for some perticular merit towards mee. And heerein I tooke no long leasure to finde out a sufficient personage. For the manifold benefites received from your honourable parents, my good Lord and Ladie, quickly eased me of that doubt, and presented your honour unto my view: whome by good right I ought to love and honour in especiall, as being of them begotten, at whose hands I have reaped especiall benefit. The which benefit if I should not so gladly professe openly, as I willingly received being offered, I might well be challenged of unkindnesse, but were I as able to make good my part, as I am not ignorant what may bee required at my handes, I would hope not to be found ungratefull. In the meane time this my travaile I commend unto your Lordship, beseeching the same so to accept thereof, as a simple testimonie of that good will which I bare to your parents while they lived, then being their servant, & now doe owe unto their ofspring after their decease for their demerits. Under your honors protection I shall lesse feare the assault of the envious, & of your honours good acceptation, I have some hope in the mildnesse of your Lordshippes nature, not doubting but that as your Lordship hath given no small signification in this your noble youth of wisdome and courage to so many as know you, it being the onely support of your auncestors line: so the same likewise will maintaine your auncestours glorie, and the hope of your owne vertues with affabilitie & gentlenesse, which was the proper commendation of your parents. The almightie increase this hope with the other vertues before named, to the good hope of your Countries peace, your Princesse safetie, and your owne honour, with the joy of your kindred & friends, whom not a few your parents good deserving hath assured unto you, and of whose earnest praiers you shall not faile, to further your well dooing.

Amongst them, though last in worthinesse, yet with the formost in well
wishing and desire of well deserving, your honour shall finde me.

Your honours humblie most assured,
Margaret Tyler.

EPISTLE TO THE READER

M.T. TO THE READER

Thou hast heere gentle Reader, the historie of Trebatio, an Emperour
in Greece: whether a true historie of him in deed, or a fained fable,
I wot not, neither did I greatlye seeke after it in the translation, but by me
it is done into English for thy profit and delight. The chiefe matter therein
contained, is of exployts of warres, and the parties therein named, are
especially renowmed for their magnanimitie and courage. The authors
purpose appeareth to be this, to animate thereby, and to set on fire the
lustie courages of young Gentlemen, to the advauncement of their line,
by ensuing such like steps. The first tongue wherin it was penned was the
Spanish, in which nation by common report, the inheritaunce of all
worldly commendation hath to this day rested. The whole discourse in
respect of the ende not unnecessarie: for the varietie & continuall shifte
of fresh matter, verie delightfull: in the speaches short and sweete, wise
in sentence, and warie in the provision of contrarie accidents. For I take
the grace thereof to be rather in the reporters device, then in the truth of
this report, as I wold that I could so well impart with thee that delight,
which my selfe findeth in reading the Spanish: but seldome is the tale
carried cleane from anothers mouth. Such deliverie as I have made I
hope thou wilt friendly accept, the rather for that it is a womans worke,
though in a storye prophane, and a matter more manlike then becometh
my sexe. But as for any manlinesse of the matter, thou knowest that it is
not necessarie for every trumpetter or drumstare in the warre to be a
good fighter. They take wages onely to incite others, though themselves
have privie maymes, and are therby recurelesse. So gentle Reader if my
travell in Englishing this Authour, may bring thee to a liking of the vertues
heerein commended, and by example thereof in thy Princes and Countries quarrell to hazard thy person, and purchase good name, as for hope
of well deserving my selfe that way, I neither bend my selfe thereto, nor
yet feare the speach of people if I be found backward, I trust every man
holdes not the plough, which would the ground were tilled, and it is no

sinne to talke of Robinhood, though you never shot in his bowe: Or be
it that the attempt were bolde to intermeddle in armes, so as the auncient
Amazons did, and in this storie Claridiana doth, and in other stories not
a few, yet to report of armes is not so odious, but that it may be borne
withall, not onely in you men which your selves are fighters, but in us
women, to whome the benefit in equall part apperteineth of your victo-
ries, either for that the matter is so commendable that it carryeth no
discredit from the homelynesse of the speaker, or for that it is so generally knowen, that it fitteth everie man to speake thereof, or for any it
jumpeth with this common feare on all parts of warre and invasion. The
invention, disposition, trimming, and what else in this storie, is wholy
another mans, my part none therein but the translation, as it were onely
in giving enterteinment to a straunger, before this time unacquainted
with our countrie guise. Marie the worst perhaps is this, that among so
many straungers as dayly come over, some more auncient, and some but
new set forth, some penning matters of great weight and sadnesse in
divinitie, or other studies, if profession whereof more neerely beseemeth
my yeres, other some discoursing of matters more easie and ordinary in
common talke, wherin a Gentlewoman may honestly imploy her travaile.
I have not withstanding made countenance onely to this gentleman,
whom neither his personage might sufficiently commend it selfe unto my
sexe, nor his behaviour (being light and soldier like) might in good order
acquaint it selfe with my yeares. So if the question now ariseth of my
choice, not of my labour, wherefore I preferred this storie before matter
of more importance. For answere wherein gentle reader, the truth is, that
as the first notion to this kind of labour came not from my selfe, so was
this peece of worke put upon me by others, and they which first coun-
sailed me to fall to worke, tooke upon them also to bee my taskemasters
and overseers, least I should be idle, and yet because the refusall was in
my power, I must stand to answere for my easie yeelding, and may not
be unprovided of excuse, wherin if I should alledge for my selfe, that
matters of lesse worthinesse by as aged yeares have bene taken in hande,
and that dayly new devises are published, in songs, sonnets, enterludes,
and other discourses, and yet are borne out without reproch, onely to
please the humour of some men: I thinke I should make no good plea
therein, for besides that I should finde therby so many knowen enimies,
as knowen men have bene authors of such idle conceits, yet woulde my
other adversaries be never the rather quieted for they would say, if as well
the one as the other were all naught, and though peradventure I might
passe unknowen amongest a multitude, and not be the onely gaze or
odde partie in my ill doing, yet because there is lesse merit of pardon if
the fault be excused as common, I will not make that my defence which
cannot helpe me, and both hinder other men. But my defence is by
example of the best, amongst which, many have dedicated their labours,
some stories, some of warre, some Phisicke, some Lawe, some as concerning government, some divine matters, unto diverse Ladyes and Gen-

tlewoman. And if men may and do bestow such of their travailes upon Gentlewomen, then may we women read such of their workes as they dedicate unto us, and if wee may read them, why not farther wade in them to the search of a truth. And then much more why not deale by translation in such arguments, especially this kinde of exercise, beeing a matter of more heede then of deepe invention or exquisite learning, and they must needes leave this as confessed, that in their dedications, they minde not onely to borrowe names of worthie personages, but the testimonies also for their further credite, which neither the one may demaund without ambition, nor the other graunt with out overlightnesse: if women be excluded from the viewe of such workes, as appeare in their name, or if glorie onely be sought in our common inscriptions, it mattereth not whether the partyes be men or women, whether alive or dead. But to returne whatsomever the truth is, whether that women may not at all discourse in learning, for men late in their claime to be sole possessioners of knowledge, or whether they may in some manner, that is by limitation or appointment in some kinde of learning, my per-swasion hath bene thus, that it is all one for a woman to pen a storie, as for a man to addresse his storie to a woman. But amongst all my ill willers, some I hope are not so straight that they would enforce me necessarily either not to write or to write of divinitie. Wheras neither durst I trust mine owne judgment sufficiently, if matter of controversie were handled, nor yet could I finde any booke in any tongue, which would not breed offence to some, but I perceive some may be rather angrie to see their Spanish delight tourned to all English pastime: they could well allow the storie in Spanish, but they may not affoord it so cheape, or they woulde have it proper to themselves. What natures such men bee of, I list not greatly dispute, but my meaning hath bene to make other partners of my liking, as I doubt not gentle Reader, but if it shall please thee after serious matters to sport thy selfe with this *Spaniard,* that thou shalt finde in him the just reward of mallice and cowardise, with the good speede of honestie and courage, beeing able to furnish thee with sufficient store of foreine example to both purposes. And as in such matters which have bene rather devised to beguile time, then to breede matter of sad learning, he hath ever borne away any price, which could season such delights with some profitable reading: so shalt thou have this stranger an honest man when need serveth, and at other times either a good companion to drive out a wearie night, or a merrie jest at thy boord. And thus much concerning this present storie, that it is neither unseemely for a woman to deale in, neither greatly requiring a lesse staied age then mine is. But of these two poynts gentle Reader I thought to give thee warning, least perhaps understanding of my name and yeares, those mightest be carried into a wrong suspect of my bold-nesse and rashnesse, from which I wold gladly free my selfe by this plaine excuse, and if I may deserve thy good favour by like labour, when

the choyce is mine owne, I will have a speciall regard of thy liking. So
I wish thee well.

                                                      Thine to use M.T.

PRIMARY SOURCE

Dedication and Epistle to the Reader in Margaret Tyler's translation of Diego
    Ortuñez de Calahorra, *The First Part of the Mirrour of Princely deedes and
    Knyghthood: Wherein is shewed the worthinesse of the Knight of the
    Sunne, and his brother Rosicleer, sonnes to the great Emperour Trebatio,
    with the straunge love of the beautiful Princesse Briana, the valiant acts
    of other noble Princess and Knights.* London: Thomas East, 1578.

RELATED SOURCE

Mackerness, E. D. "Margaret Tyler: An Elizabethan Feminist." *Notes and
    Queries,* 23 March 1946:112– 13.

JANE ANGER
fl. 1589

The identity of Jane Anger, the first major female polemicist in English, remains a mystery. All that exists is the signature, "JA: A. Gent," on the title page of her tract. Although male defenders of women often countered misogynous attack, Anger's tract is the first known sustained defense by a woman. The provocation was *Boke his Surfeit in Love* (1588). In caustic language she insulted and cursed men, denying that women are lustful.

While a search of volumes on the history of surnames for this period reveals that Anger was not an uncommon surname and was probably derived from the anglicized French "Anjou," it seems more likely that the expressive surname was a reflection of the author's sentiments.

In *The Crooked Rib,* Francis Lee Utley suggests that the anonymous poem, "Ye are to yong to bryng me in: An old lover to a yong gentilwoman" from *Tottel's Miscellany* (1557 or earlier), might have provoked Anger's retort. Helen Andrews Kahin favors the view that Anger was replying to an article by John Lyly. Recently, Simon Shepherd has speculated that the target of Jane Anger's tract was false learning. While suggestive, this theory does not explain why she felt compelled to respond to "a late surfeiting lover" who had apparently made a verbal sexual assault on women. Whatever the provocation, Anger's vigorous tract suggests that the controversy surrounding women, the *Querelle des Femmes,* was a vital aspect of Elizabethan culture.

JANE ANGER

HER PROTECTION FOR WOMEN

To the Gentlewomen of ENGLAND, health.

Gentlewomen, though it is to be feared that your setled wits wil advisedly condemne that, which my cholloricke vaine hath rashly set downe, and so perchance, ANGER shal reape anger for not agreeing with

SOURCE: This selection comes from a printed volume in the Henry E. Huntington Library, shelf no. 49047.

diseased persons: Yet (if with indifferencie of censure, you consider of the head of the quarell) I hope you will rather shew your selves defendantes of the defenders title, then complainantes of the plaintifes wrong. I doubt judgement before trial, which were injurious to the Law, and I confesse that my rashnesse deserveth no lesse, which was a fit of my extremitie. I will not urge reasons because your wits are sharp and will soone conceive my meaning, ne will I be tedious least I proove too too troublesome, nor over darke in my writing, for feare of the name of a Ridler. But (in a worde) for my presumption I crave pardon, because it was ANGER that did write it: committing your protection, and my selfe, to the protection of your selves, and the judgement of the cause to the censures of your just mindes.

Yours ever at commandement,
Ja: A.

To all Women in genenerall, and gentle Reader whatsoever.

Fie on the falshoode of men, whose minds goe oft a madding, & whose tongues can not so soone bee wagging, but straight they fal a railing. Was there ever any so abused, so slaundered, so railed upon, or so wickedly handeled undeservedly, as are we women? Will the Gods permit it, the Goddesses stay there punishing judgments, and we ourselves not pursue their undoinges for such develish practices. O *Paules steeple* and *Charing Crosse*. A halter hold at such persons. Let the streames of the channels in *London* streates run so swiftly, as they may be able alone to carrie them from that sanctuarie. Let the stones be as Ice, the soales of their shooes as Glasse, the waies steep like AEtna, & every blast a Whyrl-wind puffed out of Boreas his long throat, that these may hasten their passage to the Devils haven. Shal surfeiters raile on our kindnes, you stand stil & say nought, and shall not *Anger* stretch the vaines of her braines, the stringes of her fingers, and the listes of her modestie, to answere their Surfeitings? Yes truely, And herein I conjure all you to aide assist me in defence of my willingnes, which shall make me rest at your commaundes. Fare you well.

Your friend,
Ja. A.

A Protection for Women, &c.

The desire that every man hath to shewe his true vaine in writing is unspeakable, and their mindes are so caried away with the manner, as no care at all is had of the matter: they run so into Rethorick, as often times they overrun the boundes of their own wits, and goe they knowe not whether. If they have stretched their invention so hard on a last, as it is at a stand, there remaines but one help, which is, to write of us women. If they may once encroach so far into our presence, as they may but see the lyning of our outermost garment, they straight think that Apollo honours them, in yeelding so good a supply to refresh their sore overburdened heads, through studying for matters to indite off. And therfore that the God may see how thankfully they receive his liberality, (their wits whetted, and their braines almost broken with botching his bountie) they fall straight to dispraising & slaundering our silly sex. But judge what the cause should be, of this their so great malice towards simple women. Doubtles the weaknesse of our wits, and our honest bashfulnesse, by reason whereof they suppose that there is not one amongst us who can, or dare reproove their slanders and false reproches: their slaunderous tongues are so short, and the time wherein they have lavished out their wordes fully, hath bene so long, that they know we cannot catch hold of them to pull them out, and they think we wil not write to reproove their lying lips: which conceites have already made them cockes & wolde (should they not be cravened) make themselves among themselves bee thought to be of the game. They have bene so daintely fed with our good natures, that like jades (their stomaches are grown so quesie) they surfeit of our kindnes. If we wil not suffer them to smell on our smockes, they will snatch at our peticotes: but if our honest natures cannot away with that uncivil kinde of jesting then we are coy: yet if we beare with their rudenes, and be som what modestly familiar with them, they will straight make matter of nothing, blazing abroad that they have surfeited with love, and then their wits must be showen in telling the maner how.

Among the innumerable number of bookes to that purpose, of late (unlooked for) the newe surfeit of an olde Lover (sent abroad to warn those which are of his own kind, from catching the like disease) came by chance to my handes: which, because as well women as men are desirous of novelties, I willinglie read over: neither did the ending there of lesse please me then the beginning, for I was so carried away with the conceit of the Gent. as that I was quite out of the booke before I thought I had bene in the middest thereof: So pithie were his sentences, so pure his wordes, and so pleasing his stile. The chiefe matters therein contained were of two sortes: the one in the dispraise of mans follie, and the other, invective against our sex, their folly proceeding of their own flatterie joined with fancie, & our faultes are through our follie, with which is some faith.

The bounteous wordes written over the lascivious kinge Ninus his head, set down in this olde Lover his Surfeit to be these (Demaund and have:) do plainly shew the flatterie of mens false hearts: for knowing that we women, are weake vessels soone overwhelmed, and that Bountie bendeth everie thing to his becke, they take him for their instrument (too too strong) to assay the pulling downe of us so weake. If we stand fast, they strive: if we totter (though but a little) they will never leave til they have overturned us. Semeramis demaunded: and who would not if courtesie should be so freely offered: Ninus gave all to his kingdome, and that at the last: the more foole he: and of him this shal be my censure (agreeing with the verdict of the surfaiting lover, save onely that he hath misplaced and mistaken certaine wordes) in this maner.

Fooles force such flatterie, and men of dull conceite:
Such phrensie oft doth hant the wife. (Nurse Wisedom once rejected)
Though love be sure and firme: yet Lust fraught with deceit,
And mens fair wordes do worke great wo, unlesse they be suspected,

Then foolish NINUS had but due, if I his judge might be,
Wilde are mens lustes, false are their lips, besmer'd with flatterie:
Himselfe and Crowne he brought to thrall which passed all the rest
His foot-stoole match he made his head, and therefore was a beast.
Then all such beastes such beastly endes, I wish the Gods to send,
And worser too if woorse may be: like his my censure end.

The youthful king Sardanapalus with his beastlike and licentious
    deedes
are so plainly disciphered, and his bad end well deserved, so truly
    set
down in that Surfeit, as both our judgments agree in one.

But that Menalaus was served with such sauce it is a wonder: yet truely
their Sex are so like to Buls, that it is no marvell though the Gods do
metamorphose some of them, to give warning to the rest, if they coulde
think so of it, for some of them wil follow the smocke as Tom Bull will
runne after a towne Cowe. But, least they should running slip and breake
their pates, the Gods provident of their welfare, set a paire of tooters on
their foreheades, to keep it from the ground, for doubtles so stood the
case with Menalaus, hee running abroade as a Smel-smocke, got the
habit of a Coockold, of whom thus shall go my verdicte.

> The Gods most just doe justly punish sinne
> with those same plagues which men do most forlorn,
> If filthy lust in men to spring begin,
> That monstrous sin he plagueth with the horne.
>   their wisdome great wherby they men forewarne,
>   to shun wild lust, lest they wil weare the horne.
>
> Deceitfull men with guile must be repaid,
> And blowes for blowes who renders not againe?
> The man that is of Coockolds lot affraid,
> From Lechery he ought for to refraine.
>   Els shall he have the plague he doth forlorne:
>   and ought (perforce constrain'd to wear the horne.
> The Greek, Acteons badge did weare, they say,
> And worthy too, he loved the smocke so wel,
> That everie man may be a Bull I pray,
> Which loves to follow lust (his game) so well.
>   For by that meanes poore women shall have peace
>   and want these jarres. Thus doth my censure cease.

The greatest fault that doth remaine in us women is, that we are too credulous, for could we flatter as they can dissemble, and use our wittes well, as they can their tongues ill, then never would any of them complaine of surfeiting. But if we women be so perillous cattell as they terme us, I marvell that the Gods made not *Fidelitie* as well a man, as they created her a woman, and all the morall vertues of their masculine sex, as of the feminine kinde, except their Deities knewe that there was some soverainty in us women, which could not be in them men. But least some snatching fellow should catch me before I fall to the grounde, (and say they will adorne my head with a feather, affirming that I rome beyond reason, seeing it is most manifest that the man is the head of the woman, and that therfore we ought to be guided by them,) I prevent them with this answere. The Gods knowing that the mindes of mankind would be aspiring, and having thoroughly viewed the wonderfull vertues wherewith women are inriched, least they should provoke us to pride, and so confound us with Lucifer, they bestowed the supremacy over us to man, that of that Cockscombe he might onely boast, and therfore for Gods sake let them keepe it. But wee returne to the Surfeit.

Having made a long discourse of the Gods censure concerning love, he leaves them (& I them with him) and comes to the principall object and generall foundation of love, which he affirmeth to be grounded on women: & now beginning to search his scroule, wherein are tauntes against us, he beginneth and saieth that we allure their hearts to us: wherin he saieth more truly then he is aware off: for we woo them with our vertues, & they wed us with vanities, and men being of wit sufficient to tonder [consider] of these vertues which are in us women, are ravished *with that* delight of those dainties, which allure & draw the sences of them to serve us, wherby they become ravenous haukes, who doe not onely seize upon us, but devour us. Our good toward them is the destruction of our selves, we being welformed, are by them fouly deformed: of our true meaning they make mockes, rewarding our loving follies with disdainful floutes: we are the griefe of man, in that wee take all the griefe from man: we languish when they laugh, we lie sighing when they sit singing, and sit sobbing when they lie slugging and sleeping. *Mulier est hominis confusio,* because her kinde heart cannot so sharply reproove their franticke fits, as those madde frensies deserve. *Aut amat, aut odit, non est in tertio:* she loveth good things, and hateth that which is evill: she loveth justice and hateth iniquitie: she loveth trueth and true dealing, and hateth lies and falshood: she loveth man for his vertues, & hateth him for his vices: to be short, there is no *Medium* between good and bad, and therefore she can be, *In nullo tertio.* Plato his answere to a Viccar of fooles which asked the question, being, that he knew not whether to place women among those creatures which were reasonable or unreasonable, did as much beautifie his devine knowledge, as all the bookes he did write: for knowing that women are the greatest help that men have, without whose aide & assistance it is as possible for them to live, as if they wanted meat, drinke, clothing, or any other necessary: and knowing also that even then in his age, much more in those ages which shold after follow, men were grown to be so unreasonable, as he could not discide whether men or bruite beastes were more unreasonable: their eies are so curious, as be not all women equall with Venus for beautie, they cannot abide the sight of them: their stomackes so queasie, as doe they tast but twise of one dish they straight surfeit, and needes must a new diet be provided for them. *Wee are contrary to men, because they are contrarie to that which is good:* because they are spurblind, they cannot see into our natures, and we too well (though we had but halfe an eie) into their conditions, because they are so bad: our behaviors alter daily, because mens vertues decay hourely. If Hesiodus had with equity as well looked into the life of man, as he did presisely search out the qualities of us women, he would have said, that if a woman trust unto a man, it shal fare as well with her, as if she had a waight of a thousand pounds tied about her neck, and then cast into the bottomles seas: for by men are we confounded though they by us are sometimes crossed. Our tongues are light, because earnest in reprooving mens filthy vices, and our good counsel is termed nipping injurie, in that it accordes not with their foolish fancies. Our boldnesse rash, for giving Boddies nipping answeres, our dispositions naughtie, for not agreeing with their wilde mindes, and our furie dangerous, because it will not beare with their knavish behaviors. If our frownes be so terrible, and our anger so deadly, men are too foolish in offering occasions of hatred, which shunned, a terrible death is prevented. There is a continuall deadly hatred betweene the wilde boare and tame hounds, I would there were the like betwixt women and men unles they amend their maners, for so strength should predominate, where now flattery and dissimulation hath the upper hand. The Lion rageth when he is hungrie, but man raileth when he is glutted. The Tyger is robbed of her young ones, when she is ranging abroad, but men rob women of their honour underservedlye under their noses. The Viper stormeth when his taile is trodden on, & may not we fret when al our bodie is a footstoole to their wild lust: Their unreasonable mindes which knowe not what reason is, make them nothing better than bruit beastes. But let us graunt that Cletemnestra, Ariadna, Dalila, and Jesabell were spotted with crimes: shal not Nero with others innumerable, (& therefore unnameable) joine handes with them and lead the daunce? yet it greeves me that faithful Deianira should be falsely accused of her husband Hercules death, seeing she was utterly guiltlesse (even of thought) concerning any such crime, for had not the Centaures falshood exceeded the simplicitie of her too too credulous heart, Hercules had not died so cruelly tormented, nor the monsters treason bene so unhappely executed. But we must beare with these faultes, and with grrater then these, especiallye seeing that hee which set it downe for a Maxime was driven into a mad mood through a surfeit, which made him run quite besides his booke, and mistake his case: for wher he accused Deianira falsely, he would have had condemned Hercules deservedly.

Marius's daughter indued with so many excellent vertues, was too good either for Metellus, or any man living: for thogh peradventure she had some smal fault, yet doubtles he had detestable crimes. On the same place were Doun is on the hens head, the Combe grows on the Cocks pate. If women breede woe to men, they bring care, povertie, griefe, and continual feare to women, which if they be not woes they are worser.

Euthydomus made sixe kinde of women, and I will approove that there are so many of men: which be, poore and rich, bad and good, foule and faire. The great Patrimonies that wealthy men leave their children after their death, make them rich: but dice and other marthriftes happening into their companies, never leave them til they bee at the beggers bush, wher I can assure you they become poore. Great eaters beeing kept at a slender diet never distemper their bodies but remaine in good case: but afterwards once turned foorth to Liberties pasture, they graze so greedilie, as they become surfeiting jades, and alwaies after are good for nothing. There are men which are snout-faire, whose faces looke like a creamepot, and yet those not the faire men I speake of, but I meane those whose conditions are free from knaverie, and I tearme those foule, that have neither civilitie nor honestie: of these sorts there are none good, none rich or faire long. But if wee doe desire to have them good, we must alwaies tie them to the manger and diet their greedy panches, otherwise they wil surfeit. What, shal I say? wealth makes them lavish, wit knavish, beautie effeminate, povertie deceitfull, and deformitie uglie. Therefore of me take this counsell

> Esteeme of men as of a broken Reed,
> Mistrust them still, and then you wel shall speede.

I pray you then (if this be true as it truely cannot bee denied) have not they reason who affirme that a goose standing before a ravenous fox, is in as good case, as the woman that trusteth to a mans fidelitie: for as the one is sure to loose his head, so the other is most certaine to be bereaved of her good name, if there be any small cause of suspition. The fellow that tooke his wife for his crosse, was an Asse, and so we wil leave him: for he loved well to sweare on an ale pot, and because his wife, keeping him from his dronken vain, put his nose out of his socket, he thereby was brought into a mad moode, in which he did he could not tell what.

When provender prickes, the jade will winch, but keepe him at a slender ordinarie, and he will be milde ynough. The Dictators sonne was cranke as long as his cocke was crowing, but prosuing a cravin, hee made his maister hang downe his head.

Thales was so maried to shamefull lust as hee cared not a straw for lawfull love, wherby he shewed himselfe to be indued with much vice and no vertue: for a man doth that often times standing, of which he repenteth sitting. The Romain coulde not (as now men cannot) abide to heare women praised, and themselves dispraised, and therfore it is best for men to follow Alphonso his rule: let them be deafe and mary wives, that are blind, so shall they not grieve to heare their wives commended nor their monstrous misdoing shall offend their wives eiesight.

Tibullus setting down a rule for women to follow, might have proportioned this platform for men to rest in. And might have said. Every honest man ought to shun that which detracteth both health and safety from his owne person, and strive to bridle his slanderous tongue. Then must he be modest, & shew his modestie by his vertuous and civil behaviours: and not display his beastlines through his wicked and filthy wordes, for lying lips and deceitful tongues are abhominable before God. It is an easie matter to intreate a Cat to catch a Mouse, and more easie to perswade a desperate man to kil him self. What *Nature* hath made, Art cannot marre, (and as this surfeiting lover saith) that which is tried in the bone, will not be brought out of the flesh. If we cloath our selves in sackcloth, and trusse up our haire in dish clouts, Venerians wil nevertheles pursue their pastime. If we hide our breastes, it must be with leather, for no cloath can keep their long nailes out of our bosomes.

We have rowling eies, and they railing tongues: our eies cause them to look lasciviously, & why? because they are geven to lecherie. It is an easie matter to find a staffe to beate a Dog, and a burnt finger giveth sound counsel. If men would as well imbrace counsel as they can give it, Socrates rule wold be better follewed. But let Socrates, heaven and earth say what they wil, *Mans face is worth a glasse of dissembling water:* and therfore to conclude with a proverbe, *write ever, and yet never write ynough of mans falshoode,* I meane those that use it. I would that ancient writers would as well have busied their heades about disciphering the deccites of their owne Sex, as they have about setting downe our follies: and I wold some would call in question that nowe, which hath ever bene questionlesse: but sithence all their wittes have bene bent to write of the contrarie. I leave them to a contrary vaine, and the surfaiting Lover, who returnes to his discourse of love.

Nowe while this greedye grazer is about his intreatie of love, which nothing belongeth to our matter: let us secrrtlye our selves with our selves, consider howe and in what, they that are our worst enemies, are both inferiour unto us, & most beholden unto our kindenes.

The creation of man and woman at the first, hee being formed *In principio* of drosse and filthy clay, did so remaine until God saw that in him his workmanship was good, and therfore by the transformation of the dust which was loathsome unto flesh, it became putrified. Then lacking a help for him, GOD making woman of mans fleshe, that she might bee purer then he, both evidently showe, how far we women are more excellent then men. Our bodies are fruitefuil, wherby the world encreaseth, and our care wonderful, by which man is preserved. From Woman sprang mans salvation. A woman was the first that beleeved, &

a woman like wise the first that reverd of him. In women is onely true *Fidelity:* (except in her) there is constancie, and without her *no Huswifery.* In the time of their sicknes we cannot be wanted, & when they are in health we for them are most necessary. They are comforted by our means: they nourished by the meats we messe: their bodies freed from diseases by our cleanlines, which otherwise would surfeit unreasonably through their own noisomnes. Without our care they lie in their beds as dogs in litter, & goe like lowsie Mackarell swimming in the heat of sommer. They love to go hansomly in their apparel, and rejoice in the pride thereof, yet who is the cause of it, but our carefulnes, to see that every thing about them be curious. Our virginitie makes us vertuous, our conditions curteous, & our chastitie maketh our truenesse of love manifest. They confesse we are necessarie, but they would have us likewise evil. That they cannot want us I grant: yet evill I denie: except onely in the respect of man, who hating all good things, is onely desirous of that which is ill, through whose desire, in estimation of conceit we are made ill. But least some shuld snarle on me, barking out this reason: that *none is good but God, and therfore women are ill.* I must yeeld that in that respect we are il, & affirm that men are no better, seeing we are so necessarie unto them. It is most certain, that if we be il, they are worse: for *Malum malo additum efficit malum peius:* & they that use il worse then it shold be, are worse then the il. And therefore if they wil correct *Magnificat,* they must first learn the signification therof. That we are liberal, they wil not deny sithence that many of them have (ex *confessio*) received more kindnes in one day at our hands, the [than] they can repay in a whole yeare: & some have so glutted themselves with our liberality as they cry *No more.* But if they shal avow that women are fooles, we may safely give them the lie: for my selfe have heard some of them confesse that we have more wisdome then need is, & therfore no fooles: & they lesse then they shold have, & therefore fooles. It hath bene affirmed by some of their sex, that to shun a shower of rain, & to know the way to our husbands bed is wisedome sufficient for us women: but in this yeare of 88, men are grown so fantastical, that unles we can make them fooles, we are accounted unwise. And now (seeing I speake to none but to you which are of mine owne Sex,) give me leave like a scoller to prove our wisdome more excellent then theirs, though I never knew what sophistry ment. Ther is no wisdome but it comes by grace, this is a principle, & *Contra principiu non est disputandu:* but grace was first given to a woman, because to our lady: which premises conclude that women are wise. Now *Primu est optimu,* & therefore women are wiser then men. That we are more witty which comes by nature, it canot better be proved, then that by our answers, men are often proven to *No plus,* & if their talk be of worldly affaires, with our resolutions they must either rest satisfied, or prove themselves fooles in the end.

It was my chance to hear a prety story of two wisemen who (being cosen germane to that town of *Gotam*) prooved themselves as very asses, as they wer fooles: & it was this. The stelth of a ring out of a wise mans chamber, afflicted that loosers mind, with so grievous passions, as he could take no rest, til he went to aske a friends counsel, how he might recover his losse. Into whose presence being once entered, his clothes unbuttened, made passage for his friends eiesight unto his bosome: who seeing him in such a taking, judging by his looks that some qualme had risen on his stomack, the extremity wherof might make his head to ake, offered him a kertcher. This distressed man halfe besides himselfe, howled bitterly that he did mistake his case, & falling into a raving vain, began to curse that day of his birth, & the *Destinies* for suffering him to live. His fellow wise-man, mistaking this fit, fearing that some devil had possessed him, began to betake him to his heeles: but being stopped from running by his copanion, did likewise ban that cause of this suddain change, & the motion that mooved the other to enter his presence: yet seing how daungerously he was disturbed, & knowing that by no meanes he could shun his company, calling his wittes together (which made him forget his passion) he demanded that cause of that others griefe: who taking a stoole & a cushion sate downe and declared that he was undon: through the losse of a ring which was stolen out of his window: further saying. Sir, is it not best for mee to goe to a Wise-woman to knowe of her what is become of my ring? The other answering affirmatively, asked this: if he knewe anye? betweene whom, many wise women reckoned, they both went together for company, wher we wil leave them.

Now I pray you tell me your fancie, were not these men very wise, but especially did they not cunningly display their wisedome by this practise: Sithence that they hope to finde that through the wisedome of a woman, which was lost by the folly of a man. Wel, seeing according to the old proverb: *The wit of a woman is a great matter:* let men learne to be wiser or account them selves fooles: for they know by practize that we are none.

Now sithence that this overcloied and surfeiting lover leaveth his love, and comes with a fresh assault against us women let us arm our selves with patience & see the end of his tongue which explaineth his surfeit. But it was so lately printed, as that I shold do the Printer injurie should I recite but one of them, and therfore referring you to *Boke his surfeit in love*. I come to my matter. If to injoy a woman be to catch the Devill by the foote, to obtaine the favour of a man is to holde fast his damme by the middle: whereby the one may easily breake away, and the other cannot go without he carries the man with him.

The properties of the Snake and of the Eele are, the one to sting, and the other not to be held: but mens tongues sting against nature, and therefore they are unnaturall. Let us bear with them as much as may be, and yeeld to their willes more then is convenient: yet if we cast our reckoning at the end of the yeare, wee shall finde that our losses exceede their gaines, which are innumerable. The propertie of the *Camelion* is to change himselfe: But man alwaies remaineth at one stay, and is never out of the predicamentes of *Dishonestie* and *unconstancie.* The stinging of the *Scorpion* is cured by the *Scorpion,* wherby it seemes that there is some good nature in them. But men never leave stinging till they see the death of *honestie.* The danger of prickes is shunned, by gathering roses glove fisted: and the stinging of *Bees* prevented through a close hood. But naked *Dishonestie* and bare inconstancie are alwaies plagued through their owne follie.

If mens folly be so unreasonable as it will strive against *Nature,* it is no matter though she rewardes them with crosses contrary to their expectations. For if *Tom foole* will presume to ride on *Alexanders* horse, he is not to be pittied thogh he get a foule knocke for his labour. But it seemes the Gentleman hath had great experience of Italian Curtizans, wherby his wisedome is shewed, for *Experientia praestantior arte:* and bee hee that hath *Experience* to proove his case, is in better case then they that have al unexperienced book cases to defend their titles.

The smooth speeches of men are nothing unlike the vanishing cloudes of the *Aire,* which glide by degrees from place to place, till they have filled themselves with raine, when breaking, they spit foorth terrible showers: so men gloze, till they have their answeres, which are the end of their travell, & then they bid *Modestie* adue, and entertaining *Rage,* fal a railing on us which never hurt them. The rancknesse of grasse causeth suspition of the serpents lurking, but his lying in the plaine path at the time when *Woodcockes* shoote, maketh the pacient passionate through his sting, because no such ill was suspected. When men protect secrecie most solemnly, beleeve them lest, for then surely there is a tricke of knavery to be discarded, for in a Friers habite an olde Fornicator is alwaies clothed.

It is a wonder to see how men can flatter themselves with their own conceites: For let us looke, they wil straight affirm that we love, and if then *Lust* pricketh them, they will sweare that *Love* stingeth us: which imagination onely is sufficient to make them assay the sealing of halfe a dozen of us in one night, when they will not stick to sweare that if they should be denied of their requestes, death must needes follow. Is it any marveil though they surfeit, when they are so greedy, but is it not pittie that any of them should perish, which will be so soon killed with un-kindnes? Yes truly. Well, the onset given, if we retire for a vantage, they will straight affirme that they have got the victorie. Nay, some of them are so carried away with conceite, that shameles they will blaze abroad among their companions, that they have obteined the love of a woman, unto whom they never spake above once, if that: Are not these froward fellowes, you must beare with them, because they dwell far from lying neighboures. They will say *Mentiri non est nostrum,* and yet you shall see true tales come from them, as wilde geese flie under *London* bridge. Their fawning is but flattery: their faith falshoode: their faire wordes allurements to destruction: and their large promises tokens of death, or of evils worse then death. Their singing is a bayte to catch us, and their playing es[?], plagues to torment us: & therfore take heede of them, and take this as an Axiom in Logick and a *Maxime* in the Law, *Nulla fides hominibus.* Ther are three accidents to men, which of al are most unseperable. *Lust, Deceit,* and *malice.* Their glozing tongues, the preface to the execution of their wilde mindes, and their pennes the bloody executioners of their barbarous maners. A little gaule maketh a great deale of sweet, sower: and a slaunderous tongue poysoneth all the good partes in man.

Was not the follie of Vulcan worthy of Venus floutes, when she tooke him with the maner, wooing Briceris? And was it not the flatterye of Paris which intysed Hellen to falshood? Yes trulie: and the late Surfeiter his remembrance in calling his pen from raging against reason: sheweth that he is not quite without flatterie, for he putteth the fault in his pen, when it was his passion that deserved reproofe. The love of Hipsicrates and Panthea, the zeale of Artemisia and Portia, the affection of Sulpitia and Aria, the true fancie of Hipparchia and Pisca, the loving passions of Macrina, & of the wife of Paudoerus (al manifested in his Surfeit) shal condemne the undiscreetnes of mens minds: whose hearts delight in nought, save that only which is contrary to good. Is it not a foolish thing to bee sorry for things unrecoverable? Why then shold Sigismundus answer be so descaned upon, seeing her husband was dead, & she therby free for any man. If that aboundance of the hart, that mouth speaketh, which is verified by [that] railing kind of mans writing. If al kind of voluptuousnes they affirm *Lechery* to be that felt, &. yet some of them are not ashamed to confesse publiquely, that they have surfeited therwith. It defileth the body, & makes it stink, & men use it: I marvel how we women can abide them but that they delude us, as (they say) we deceive them with perfumes.

Voluptuousnes is a strong beast, and hath many instruments to draw to *Lust:* but men are so forward of themselves thereto, as they neede none to haile them. Dis court is already so full with them, that he hath more neede to make stronger gates to keepe them out, then to set them open that they may come in, except he wil be pulled out by eares out of his kingdome. I woulde the abstinence of King Cyrus, Zenocrates, Caius Gracchus, Pompeius and of Francis Sforce Duke of Millaine, (recited in *Boke his Surfeit in love*) might be presidents for men to followe, and I warrant you then we should have no surfeiting. I pray God that they may mend: but in the meane time, let them be sure that rashnes breedes repentance, and treacherous hearts, tragical endes: False *Flattery* is the messenger of foule *Folly,* and a slaunderous tongue, the instrument of a dissembling heart.

I have set down unto you (which are of mine owne Sex) the subtil dealings of untrue meaning men: not that you should contemne al men, but to the end that you may take heed of the false hearts of al, & stil reprove the flattery which remaines in all: for as it is reason that the

Hennes should be served first, which both lay the egs, hatch the chickins: so it were unreasonable that the cockes which tread them, should be kept clean without meat. As men are valiant, so are they vertuous: and those that are borne honorably, cannot beare horrible dissembling heartes. But as there are some which cannot love hartely, so there are many who lust uncessantly, & as many of them wil deserve wel, so most care not how il they speed so they may get our company. Wherin they resemble *Envie*, who will be contented to loose one of his eies that another might have both his pulled out. And therefore thinke well of as many as you may, love them that you have cause, heare everything that they say (& affoord them noddes which make themselves noddies) but beleeve very little therof or nothing at all, and hate all those, who shall speake any thing in the disprasse or to the dishonor of our sex.

Let the luxurious life of Heliogabalus, the intemperate desires of Commodus and Proculus, the damnable lust of Chilperiens and Xerxces, Boleflaus violent ravishings, and the unnaturall carnall appetite of Sigismundus Malotesta, be examples sufficiently probable to perswade you, that the hearts of men are most desirous to excell in vice. There were many good lawes established by the *Romanes* and other good kinges yet they coulde not restraine men from lecherie: and there are terrible lawes alloted in *England* to the offenders therein, all which will not serve to restrain man.

The Surfeiters phisike is good could he and his companions follow it: but when the Fox preacheth, let the geese take heede, it is before an execution. *Fallere fallentem non est fraus,* and to kill that beast, whose propertie is onely to slay, is no sin: if you wil please men, you must follow their rule, which is to flatter: for *Fidelitie* and they are btter enemies. Things far fetched are excellent, and that experience is best which cost most: Crownes are costly, and that which cost many crownes is wel worth God thank you, or els I know who hath spent his labour and cost, foolishly. Then if any man geveth such deare counsell gratfuly, are not they fooles which will refuse his liberalitie. I know you long to heare what that counsel should be, which was bought at so hie a price: Wherefore if you listen, the Surfeitert his pen with my hande shall foorth with shew you.

At the end of mens faire promises there is a *Laberinth,* & therefore ever hereafter stoppe your eares when they protest friendship, lest they come to an end before you are aware wherby you fal without redemption. The path which leadeth therunto, is Mans wit, and the miles ends are marked with these trees, *Follie, Vice, Mischiefe, Lust, Deceite, & Pride.* Those to deceive you shall bee clothed in the raimentes of *Fancie, Vertue, Modestie, Love, Truemeaning,* and *Handsomnes, Folly* wil bid you welcome on your way, & tel you his fancie, concerning the profite which may come to you by this jorney, and direct you to *Vice* who is more craftie. He with a company of protestations will praise the vertues of women, shewing how many waies men are beholden unto us: but our backes once turned, he fals a railing. Then *Mischiefe* he pries into every corner of us, seeing if he can espy a cranny, that getting in his finger into it, he may make it wide enough for his tong to wag in. Now being come to *Lust:* he will fall a railing on lascivious lookes, & wil ban *Lecherie,* & with the Collier will say, the devill take him though he never means it. *Deceit* will geve you faire words, & pick your pockets: nay he will pluck out your hearts, if you be not wary. But when you heare one cry out against lawnes, drawn-works, Periwigs, against the attire of Curtizans, & generally of the pride of al women: then know him for a Wolfe clothed in sheepes raiment, and be sure you are fast by the lake of destruction. Therfore take heed of it, which you shall doe, if you shun mens flattery, the forerunner of our undoing. If a jade be galled, wil he not winch? and can you finde fault with a horse that springeth when he is spurred? The one will stand quietly when his backe is healed, and the other go wel when his smart ceaseth. You must beare with the olde Lover his surfeit, because hee was diseased when he did write it, and peradventure hereafter when he shal be well amended, he wil repent himselfe of his slanderous speaches against our sex, and curse the dead man which was the cause of it, and make a publique recantation: For the faltering in his speach at the latter end of his book affirmeth, that already he half repenteth of his bargaine, & why? because his melodie is past: but beleeve him not, thogh he shold out swear you, for althogh a jade may be still in a stable when his gall backe is healed, yet hee will showe himselfe in his kind when he is travelling: and mans flattery bites secretly, from which I pray God keepe you and me too. Amen.

FINIS.

A Soveraigne Salve, to cure the late Surfeiting Lover.

    If once the heat, did sore thee beat,
        of foolish love so blind:
    Somtime to sweat, somtime to freat
        as one bestraught of minde:

    If wits weare take, in such a brake,
        that reason was exilde:
    And woe did wake, but could not slake
        thus love had thee beguilde:

    If any wight, unto thy sight,
        all other did excell:
    whose beautie bright, constrained right
        thy heart with her to dwell:

    If thus thy foe, opprest thee so,
        that backe thou could not start:

But still with woe, did surfeit thoe,
   yet thankles was thy smart:

If nought but paine, in love remaine,
   at length this counsell win,
That thou refrain, this dangerous pain,
   and come no more therein.

And sith the blast, is overpast,
   it better were certaine;
From flesh to fast, whilst life doth last,
   then surfeit so againe.
                             Uiuendo disce.

       Eiusdem ad Lectorem de Authore.

Though, sharpe the seede, by Anger sowed,
   we all (almost) confesse;
And hard his hap we aye account,
   who Anger doth possesse:
Yet haplesse shalt thou (Reader) reape,
   such fruit from ANGERS soile,
As may thee please, and ANGER ease
   from long and wearie toile.
Whose paines were tooke for thy behoofe,
   to till that cloddye ground.
Where scarce no place, free from disgrace,
   of female Sex, was found.
If ought offend, which she doth send,
   impute it to her moode.
For ANGERS rage must that asswage,
   as wel is understoode.
If to delight, ought come in sight,
   then deeme it for the best.
So you your wil, may well fulfill,
   and she have her request.

                FINIS
                        Io. A.

PRIMARY SOURCE

*Jane Anger her protection for Women To defend them against the Scandalous
Reportes Of a late Surfeiting Lover, and all other like Venerians that
complaine so to bee overcloyed with women's kindness.* London: Richard
Jones and Thomas Orwin, 1589. The Stationers Registers reveal that the
book Anger appears to refer to was entered on the 27th of November, 1588,
by Thomas Orwin: "Entred for his Copie, Boke his Surfeit in love. with a

farewel to the folies of his own phantasie" (sic). No extant copy has yet been found.

RELATED SOURCES

Hughey, Ruth. "Cultural Interests of Women in England from 1526–1640 Indicated in the Writings of Women: A Survey." Ph.D. dissertation, Cornell University, 1932.

Kahin, Helen Andrews. "Jane Anger and John Lyly." *Modern Language Quarterly,* March 1947: 31–35. Kahin mentions Hughey's work; see Kahin, n. 2.

Kelso, Ruth. *Doctrine for the Lady of the Renaissance.* Urbana: University of Illinois Press, 1956.

Shepherd, Simon. *Amazons and Warrior Women: Varieties of Feminism in Seventeenth-Century Drama.* New York: St. Martins' Press, 1981.

Utley, Francis Lee. *The Crooked Rib. An Analytical Index to the Argument about Women in English and Scots Literature to the End of the Year 1568.* Columbus, Ohio: Ohio State University, 1944.

Ester Sowernam
fl. 1617

In 1615, Joseph Swetnam wrote a misogynous tract entitled *The araignment of lewd, idle, froward, and unconstant women . . . profitable to young men, and hurtful to none,* to which there were four respondents, three female: Ester Sowernam, Constantia Munda, Rachel Speght; and one male, a Daniel Tuvil. These exchanges constitute a significant episode in the *Querelle des Femmes.* The first is surely pseudonymous: Sowernam undoubtedly chosen in witty contrast to Swetnam, such response exhibiting a clear feminist consciousness as well as a classical education. Sowernam's response appeared in her volume, *Ester hath hang'd Haman* (1617), in which she described herself on the title page as "neither Maide, Wife nor Widdowe, yet really all, and therefore experienced to defend all." In the Address before Part Two, the author noted that a stay in the country prevented her from completing the work earlier, perhaps suggesting that she worked at managing a large house.

Sowernam begins by stating directly that she writes "in defence of our Sexe." Denouncing Swetnam for his slander of women, with evidence as unscientific as his she first describes how women were created to be equal to men. In the second part, she surveys "at what estimate Women were valued in ancient and former times." After a scan of female worthies, she concludes by arguing that women "fall" more heavily, when they do err, because they are superior. Swetnam is arraigned before the "Judgesses, Reason, and Experience" in chapter five, and afterwards indicted. Sowernam then counters "all objections which are materiall, made against women."

Signed Joane Sharp, a quick-paced, zestful poem entitled "A Defence of Women, against the Author of the Arraignment of Women" brings Sowernam's text to a close. The identity of the author of this concluding piece is unclear. (See biography of Joane Sharp.)

FROM

Ester hath hang'd Haman

ADDRESS

TO ALL RIGHT HONOURABLE, NOBLE, AND WORTHY LADIES, GENTLEWOMEN, AND OTHERS, VERTUOUSLY DISPOSED, OF THE FAEMININE SEXE.

Right Honourable, and all others of our Sexe, upon my repaire to *London* this last *Michaelmas* Terme; being at supper amongst friends, where the number of each sexe were equal: As nothing is more usual for table-talke; there fell out a discourse concerning women, some defending, others objecting against our Sex: Upon which occasion, there happened a mention of a Pamphlet entituled *The Arraignment of Women,* which I was desirous to see. The next day a Gentleman brought me the Booke, which when I had superficially runne over, I found the discourse as far off from performing what the Title promised, as I found it scandalous and blasphemous: for where the Authour pretended to write against lewd, idle, and unconstant women, hee doth most impudently rage and rayle generally against all the whole sexe of women. Whereupon, I in defence of our Sexe, began an answer to that shamefull Pamphlet. In which, after I had spent some small time, word was brought mee that an Apologie for women was already undertaken, and ready for the Presse, by a Ministers daughter: Upon this newes I stayed my pen, being as glad to be eased of my entended labour; as I did expect some fitting performance of what was undertaken: At last the Maidens Booke was brought me, which when I had likewise runne over, I did observe, that whereas the Maide doth many times excuse her tendernesse of yeares, I found it to be true in the slendernesse of her answer, for she undertaking to defend women, doth rather charge and condemne women, as in the ensuing discourse shall appeare: So that whereas I expected to be eased of what I began, I do now find my self double charged, as well to make reply to the one, as to adde supply to the other.

SOURCE: This selection comes from the microfilm B212 reel 1188 at Love Library, University of Nebraska-Lincoln, short-title catalogue no. 22974.

In this my Apologie, Right Honourable, Right Worshipfull, and all others of our Sexe, I doe in the first part of it plainely and resolutely deliver the worthinesse and worth of women; both in respect of their Creation, as in the worke of Redemption. Next I doe shew in examples out of both the Testaments: what blessed and happy choyse hath beene made of women, as gratious instruments to derive Gods blessings and benefits to mankinde.

In my second part I doe deliver of what estimate women have been valued in all ancient and moderne times, which I proove by authorities, customes, and daily experiences. Lastly, I doe answer all materiall objections which have or can be alledged against our Sexe: in which also I doe arraigne such kind of man, which correspond the humor and disposition of the Author; lewd, idle, furious and beastly disposed persons.

This being performed, I doubt not but such as heretofore have beene so forward and lavish against women, will hereafter pull in their hornes, and have as little desire, and lesse cause so scandalously and slanderously to write against us than formerly they have.

The ends for which I undertooke this enterprise, are these. First, to set out the glory of Almightie God, in so blessed a worke of his Creation. Secondly, to encourage all Noble, Honourable, and worthy Women, to expresse in their course of life and actions, that they are the same Creatures which they were designed to be by their Creator, and by their Redeemer: And to paralell those women, whose vertuous examples are collected briefly out of the Olde and New Testament. Lastly, I write for the shame and confusion of such as degenerate from woman-hoode, and disappoint the ends of Creation, and Redemption.

There can be no greater encouragement to true Nobility, then to know and stand upon the honour of Nobility, nor any greater confusion and shame, then for Nobility to dismount and abase it selfe to ignoble and degenerate courses.

You are women; in Creation, noble; in Redemption, gracious; in use most blessed; be not forgetfull of your selves, nor unthankefull to that Author from whom you receive all.

FROM CHAPTER VII

It is a shame for a man to complaine of a froward woman, in many respects all concerning himselfe. It is a shame he hath no more government over the weaker vessell. It is a shame he hath hardned her tender sides, and gentle heart with his boistrous & Northren blasts. It is a shame for a man to publish and proclaime houshold secrets, which is a common practice amongst men, especially Drunkards, Leachers, and prodigall spendthrifts: These when they come home drunke, or are called in question for their riotous misdemeanours, they presently shew themselves, the right children of *Adam.* They will excuse themselves by their wives, and say that their unquiteness and frowardnesse at home, is the cause that they runne abroad. An excuse more fitter for a beast then a man. If thou wert a man thou wouldest take away the cause which urgeth a woman to griefe and discontent, and not by thy frowardnesse encrease her distemperature: forbeare thy drinking, thy luxurious riot, thy gaming, and spending, and thou shall have thy wife give thee as little cause at home, as thou givest her great cause of disquiet abroad. Men which are men, if they chance to be matched with froward wives, either of their own making, or others marring, they would make a benefit of the discommodity, either try his skill to make her milde, or exercise his patience to endure her curstnesse: for all crosses are inflicted either for punishment of sinnes, or for exercise of vertues; but humorous men will sooner marre a thousand women, then out of an hundred make one good.

    May men complain of women without cause?

And this shall appeare in the imputation which our adversarie chargeth upon our sexe, to be lacivious, wanton and lustfull: He sayth, "Women tempt, alure, and promote men." How rare a thing is it for women to prostitute and offer themselves? how common a practise is it for men to seeke and solicite women to lewdnesse? what charge do they spare? what travell doe they bestow? what vowes, oathes and protestations doe they spend, to make them dishonest? They hyer Pandors, they write letters, they seale them with damnations, and execrations, to assure them of love, when the end proves but lust: They know the flexible disposition of Women and the sooner to overreach them, some will pretend they are so plunged in love that except they obtaine their desire they will seeme to drown'd, hang, stab, poyson, or banish themselves from friends and countrie: What motives are these to tender dispositions? Some will pretend marriage, another offer continuall maintenance, but when they have obtained their purpose, what shall a woman finde, just that which is her everlasting shame and griefe, shee hath made her selfe the unhappie subject to a lustfull bodie, and the shamefull stall of a lascivious tongue. Men may with foule shame charge women with this sinne which they had never committed if thee had not trusted, nor had ever trusted if thee had not beene deceived with vowes, oathes, and protestations. To bring a woman to offend in one sinne, how many damnable sinnes doe they commit? I appeale to their owne consciences. The lewd disposition of sundry men doth appeare in this: If a woman or maide will yeeld unto lewdnesse, what shall they want? But if they would live in honestie, what helpe shall they have? How much will they make of the lewd? how base account of the honest? how many pounds will they spend in bawdie houses? but when will they bestowe a penny upon an honest maide or woman, except it be to corrupt them?

    Men are the serpents

Our adversary bringeth many examples of men which have beene overthrowne by women. It is answered, before the fault is their owne. But

I would have him, or any one living, to shew any woman that offended in this sinne of lust, but that she was first sollicited by a man.

Helen was the cause of Troyes burning; first, Paris did sollicite her; next, how many knaves and fooles of the male kinde had Troy, which to maintaine whoredome would bring their Citie to confusion.

When you bring in examples of lewd women, and of men which have beene stained by women, you shew your selfe both franticke, and a prophane irreligious foole to mention Judith for cutting off Holofernes head; in that rancke.

You challenge women for untamed and unbrideled tongues; there was never woman was ever noted for so shamelesse, so brutish, so beastly a scold as you prove your selfe in this base and odious Pamphlet: You blaspheme God, you raile at his Creation, you abuse and slander his Creatures; and what immodest or impudent scurilitie is it, which you doe not expresse in this lewd and lying Pamphlet?

Hitherto I have so answered all your objections against Women, that as I have not defended the wickednesse of any; so I have set downe the true state of the question. As Eve did not offend without the temptation of a Serpent; so women doe seldome offend, but it is by provocation of men. Let not your impudencie, nor your consorts dishonestie, charge our sexe hereafter, with those sinnes of which you your selves were the first procurers. I have in my discourse, touched you, and all yours, to the quick. I have taxed you with bitter speaches; you will (perhaps) say I am a rayling scold. In this objection, Joseph Swetnam, I will teach you both wit and honestie: The difference betwixt a railing scold, and an honest accuser, is this, the first rageth upon passionate furie, without bringing cause or proofe; the other bringeth direct proofe for what she alleageth: you charge women with clamorous words, and bring no proofe; I charge you with blasphemie, with impudencie, scurilitie, foolery, and the like. I shew just and direct proofe for what I say; it is not my desire to speake so much, it is your desert to provoke me upon just cause so farre; it is no railing to call a Crow blacke, or a Wolfe a ravenour, or a drunkard a beast; the report of the truth is never to be blamed, the deserver of such a report, deserveth the shame.

Now, for this time, to draw to an end; let me aske according to the question of *Cassian, Cui bono?* what have you gotten by publishing your Pamphlet; good I know you can get none. You have (perhaps) pleased the humors of some giddy, idle conceited persons: But you have died your selfe in the colours of shame, lying, slandering, blasphemie, ignorance, and the like.

The shortnesse of time and the weight of businesse call me away, and urge me to leave off thus abruptly, but assure your selfe where I leave now, I will by Gods grace supply the next Terme, to your small content. You have exceeded in your furie against Widdowes, whose defence you shal heare of at the time aforesaide, in the meane space recollect your wits, write out of deliberation, not out of furie; write out of advice, not out of idlenesse; forbeare to charge women with faults which come from the contagion of Masculine serpents.

PRIMARY SOURCE

Ester hath hang'd Haman: Or An Answere To a lewd Pamphlet, entituled, The Arraignment of Women with the arraignment of lewd, idle, froward, and unconstant men, and Husbands. Divided into two Parts. The first proveth the dignity and worthiness of Women, out of divine Testimonies. The second shewing the estimation of the Faeminine Sexe, in ancient and Pagan times, all which is acknowledged by men themselves in their daily action. Written by Ester Sowernam, neither Maide, Wife nor Widdowe, yet really all, and therefore experienced to defend all. London: Nicholas Bourne, 1617.

RELATED SOURCES

Crandall, Coryl. *Swetnam the Woman-Hater: The Controversy and the Play.* Lafayette, Ind.: Purdue University Studies, 1969.

Munda, Constantia. *The Worming of a Mad Dogge: Or, a soppe for Cerberus, The Jayler of Hell.* London: printed for Laurence Hayes, 1617.

Rogers, Katherine. *The Troublesome Helpmate: A History of Misogyny in Literature.* Seattle, Wash.: University of Washington, 1966.

Joane Sharp
fl. 1617

The name "Joane Sharp" appears at the end of a spirited feminist poem, the eighth and last chapter of Ester Sowernam's tract. Nothing is known of Sharp aside from this poem. The anonymity reminds one of how difficult it was to defend women openly; and the poet's vehemence may reflect a more general indignation and growing self-confidence among women readers of misogynist texts. Certainly, the poem as well as the responses of Sowernam and others to Joseph Swetnam's attack on women indicate a willingness to continue the controversial debate about women. (For location of excerpt see biography of Ester Sowernam.)

FROM
Ester hath hang'd Haman

A DEFENSE OF WOMEN,
AGAINST THE AUTHOR OF THE
ARRAIGNMENT OF WOMEN.

Chapter VIII

An idle companion was raging of late,
Who in furie 'gainst Women expresseth his hate:
Hee writeth a Booke, an *Arraignment* he calleth,
In which against women he currishly bawleth.
He deserveth no answere but in Ballat or Ryme,
Upon idle fantastickes who would cast away time:
Any answere may serve an impudent lyar,
Any mangie scab'd horse doth fit a scal'd Squire:

See source note for Ester Sowernam.

In the ruffe of his furie, for so himselfe saith,
The blasphemous companion he shamefully playeth.
The woman for an Helper, God did make he doth say.
But to Helpe to consume and spend all away.
Thus, at Gods creation to flout and to rest,
Who but an Atheist would so play the beast?
The Scriptures doe prove that when Adam did fall,
And to death and damnation was thereby a thrall.
Then woman was an Helper, for by her blessed seed,
From Hell and damnation all mankinde was freed.
He saith, women are froward, which the rib doth declare,
For like as the Rib, so they crooked are:
The Rib was her Subject for body we finde,
But from God came her Soule, and dispose of
her minde.
Let no man thinke much if woman compare,
That in their creation they much better are:
More blessings therein to women doe fall,
Then unto mankinde have been given at all.
Women were the last worke, and therefore the best,
For what was the end, excelleth the rest.
For womans more honour, it was so assign'd,
She was made of the rib of mettall refin'd:
The Countrey doth also the woman more grace,
For Paradise is farre the more excellent place.
Yet women are mischievous, this Author doth say,
But Scriptures to that directly say nay:
God said, 'twixt the Woman and Serpent for ever,
Strong hatred he would put, to be qualified never.
The Woman being hatefull to the Serpents condition,
How excellent is she in her disposition?
The Serpent with men in their workes may agree,
But the Serpent with women that never may be.
If you aske how it happens some women prove naught,
By men turn'd to Serpents they are over-wrought.
What the Serpent began, men follow that still,
They tempt what they may to make women doe ill.
They will tempt, and provoke, and follow us long:
They deceive us with [oaths], and a flattering tongue.
To make a poore Maiden or woman a whore,
They care not how much they spend of their store.
But where is there a man that will any thing give
That woman or maide may with honestie live?
If they yeeld to lewd counsell they nothing shall want,
But for to be honest, then all things are scant.
It proves a bad nature in men doth remaine.

To make women lewd their purses they straine.
For a woman that's honest they care not a whit,
Theyle say she is honest because she lackes wit.
Theyle call women whores, but their stakes they might save,
There can be no-Whore, but there must be a Knave.
They say that our dressings, and that our attire
Are causes to move them to lustfull fire.
Of all things which are we evermore finde,
Such thoughts doe arise as are like to the minde.
Mens thoughts being wicked they wracke on us thus,
That scandall is taken, not given by us.
If their fight be so weake, and their frailtie be such,
Why doe they then gaze at our beauty so much?
Plucke away those ill roots where sinne doth arise,
Amend wicked thoughts, or plucke out the eyes.
The humors of men, see how froward they bee;
We know not to please them in any degree:
For if we goe plaine we are sluts they doe say,
They doubt of our honesty if we goe gay;
If we be honest and merrie, for giglots they take us,
If modest and sober, then proud they doe make us:
Be we housewifly quicke, then a shrew he doth keepe,
If patient and milde, then he scorneth a sheepe.
What can we devise to doe or to say,
But men doe wrest all things the contrary way.
'Tis not so uncertaine to follow the winde,
As to seeke to please men of so humerous minde.
Their humors are giddy, and never long lasting,
We know not to please them, neither full nor yet fasting.
Either we doe too little, or they doe too much:
They straine our poore wits, their humors are such.
They say, women are proud, whearin made they triall?
They moov'd some lewd suit, and had the deniall:
To be crost in such suites, men cannot abide,
And thereupon we are entitled with pride.
They say we are curst and froward by kinde,
Our mildnesse is changed, where raging we finde,
A good Jacke sayes the proverbe, doth make a good Gill,
A curst froward Husband doth change womans will.
They use us (they say) as necessary evils,
We have it from them, for they are our devils.
When they are in their rages and humerous fits,
They put us poore women halfe out of our wits.
Of all naughty women name one if you can,
If she proved bad, it came by a man.
Faire Helen forsooke her Husband of Greece,

A man called Paris, betrayed that peece.
Medea did rage, and did shamefully murther,
A Jason was cause, which her mischief did further.
A Cresside was false, and changed her love,
Diomedes her heart by constraint did remove.
In all like examples the world may see,
Where women prove bad, there men are not free.
But in those offences they have the most share,
Women would be good, if Serpents would spare.
Let Women and Maides, whatsoever they be,
Come follow my counsell, be warned by me.
Trust not mens suites, their love proveth lust,
Both hearts, tongues, and pens, doe all prove unjust.
How faire they will speake and write in their love,
But put them to tryall how false doe they prove?
They love hot at first, when the love is a stranger,
But they will not be tied to racke and to manger.
What love call you that when men are a wooing,
And seeke nothing else but shame and undoing.
As women in their faults I doe not commend,
So wish I all men their lewd suites they would end.
Let women alone, and seeke not their shame,
You shall have no cause then women to blame.
'Tis like that this Author against such doth bawle,
Who by his temptations have gotten a fall.
For he who of women so wickedly deemeth,
Hath made them dishonest, it probably seemeth.
He hath beene a Traveller, it may be well so,
By his tales and reports as much we doe know.
He promiseth more poyson against women to thrust,
He doth it for phisicke, or else he would brust! [burst]
Thus I bid him farewell till next we doe meete,
And then as cause moveth, so shall we greete.

Joane Sharp.

PRIMARY SOURCES
No information available about Joane Sharp. (It is conceivable that the same person wrote Sowernam's tract and Sharp's poem).

Sowernam, Ester. *Ester hath hang'd Haman.* (See Primary Source for Sowernam.)

Margaret Lucas Cavendish

Duchess of Newcastle

1623 – 1673

Born to Thomas Lucas, a wealthy landed gentleman, and Elizabeth Leighton, Margaret Lucas was reared by her mother in female proprieties and educated by tutors. She was maid of honor to Queen Henrietta Maria from 1643–1645. While travelling with the Queen to Paris in 1645 she met and married William Cavendish, an exiled leader of the Royalist army. During the Civil War they lived in Paris, Rotterdam, and Antwerp.

After their return at the Restoration, they retired from court life. At this point, the Duchess devoted herself almost exclusively to learning and writing. Her numerous works include scientific and philosophical treatises, science fiction, a biography, an autobiography, and among several plays, one, *The Convent of Pleasure,* which features a lesbian relationship. This list of the Duchess's writings only begins to suggest her formidable literary range and learning in an age that produced very few prominent woman writers, let alone one with forthright feminist ideas. (She did also, on occasion, deprecate female capacities.) She was the first aristocratic woman in England to defend women, and the first woman to dedicate her life to the pursuit of knowledge, scholarship, and writing. She had no previous equal as a prolific, engaged writer who achieved public attention.

In keeping with her class, the Duchess of Newcastle's primary motivation was the improvement of her own individual situation, although in her address to the Oxford-Cambridge faculty she made it plain that she was advocating improved treatment for women as a whole. An aristocrat, she desired the same lasting fame for her achievements as the men of her class. She viewed the promise of fame as an incentive to aristocratic women to assert themselves and assure themselves immortality. The Duchess of Newcastle's ability to flout public censure, to write prodigiously, and to act and dress unusually all were privileges of her class. She was regarded by many contemporaries as a Royalist eccentric whose forward-looking views and sense of autonomy could consequently be dismissed.

---------------------------------- • ----------------------------------

FROM
PHILOSOPHICAL AND PHYSICAL OPINIONS

TO THE TWO MOST FAMOUS UNIVERSITIES
OF ENGLAND

Most Famously Learned,

I Here Present to you this Philosophical Work, not that I can hope Wise School-men and Industrious Laborious Students should Value it for any Worth, but to Receive it without Scorn, for the good Encouragement of our Sex, lest in time we should grow Irrational as Idiots, by the Dejectedness of our Spirits, through the Careless Neglects and Despisements of the Masculine Sex to the Femal, thinking it Impossible we should have either Learning or Understanding, Wit or Judgement, as if we had not Rational Souls as well as Men, and we out of a Custom of Dejectedness think so too, which makes us Quit all Industry towards Profitable Knowledge, being imployed only in Low and Petty imployments, which take away not only our Abilities towards Arts, but higher Capacities in Speculations, so as we are become like Worms, that only Live in the Dull Earth of Ignorance, Winding our Selves sometimes out by the Help of some Refreshing Rain of good Education, which seldome is given us, for we are Kept like Birds in Cages, to Hop up and down in our Houses, not Suffer'd to Fly abroad, to see the several Changes of Fortune, and the Various Humors, Ordained and Created by Nature, and wanting the Experience of Nature, we must needs want the Understanding and Knowledge, and so consequently Prudence, and Invention of Men; Thus by an Opinion, which I hope is but an Erroneous one in Men, we are Shut out of all Power and Authority, by reason we are never Imployed either in Civil or Martial Affairs, our Counsels are De-

---

SOURCE: These selections come from the British Library. "To the Two Most Famous Universities of England," Preface to *Philosophical and Physical Opinions,* shelf no. 31.e.8. *The Convent of Pleasure,* in *Plays, never before printed,* shelf no. 644.1.17.

spised, and Laught at, the best of our Actions are Troden down with Scorn, by the Over-weening conceit, Men have of Themselves, and through a Despisement of Us.

But I Considering with my Self, that if a Right Judgement, and a True Understanding, and a Respectfull Civility Live any where, it must be in Learned Universities, where Nature is best Known, where Truth is oftnest Found, where Civility is most Practised, and if I find not a Resentment here, I am very Confident I shall find it no where, neither shall I think I Deserve it, if you Approve not of Me; but if I deserve not Praise, I am sure to receive so much Courtship from your Sage Society, as to Bury me in Silence, that thus I may have a Quiet Grave, since not Worthy a Famous Memory, for to Lye Intombed under the Dust of an University will be Honour enough for Me, and more than if I were Worshipped by the Vulgar as a Deity. Wherefore, if your Wisdoms cannot give me the Bays, let your Charity strew me with Cypress; and who knows, but, after my Honourable Burial, I may have a Glorious Resurrection in Following Ages, since Time brings Strange and Unusual things to pass, I mean Unusual to Men, though not in Nature; And I hope this Action of mine is not Unnatural, though Unusual for a Woman to Present a Book to the University, nor Impudent, for it is Honest, although it seem Vain-glorious; But if it be, I am to be Pardoned, since there is little Difference between Man and Beast, but what Ambition and Glory makes.

FROM

THE CONVENT OF PLEASURE

ACT I. SCENE I.

Enter Three Gentlemen.

FIRST GENTLEMAN.   Tom, Where have you been, you look so sadly of it?

2. GENT.   I have been at the Funeral of the Lord Fortunate; who has left his Daughter, the Lady Happy, very rich, having no other Daughter but her.

1. GENT.   If she be so rich, it will make us all Young Men, spend all our Wealth in fine Clothes, Coaches, and Lackies, to set out our Wooing hopes.

3. Gent.   If all her Wooers be younger Brothers, as most of us Gallants are, we shall undo our selves upon bare hopes, without Probability: But is she handsome, Tom?

2. Gent.   Yes, she is extream handsome, young, rich, and virtuous.

1. Gent.   Faith, that is too much for one Woman to possess.

2. Gent.   Not, if you were to have her.

1. Gent.   No, not for me; but in my Opinion too much for any other Man.

Exeunt.

Scene II.

Enter the Lady Happy, and one of her Attendants.

Servant.   Madam, you being young, handsome, rich, and virtuous, I hope you will not cast away those gifts of Nature, Fortune, and Heaven, upon a Person which cannot merit you?

L. Happy.   Let me tell you, that Riches ought to be bestowed on such as are poor, and want means to maintain themselves; and Youth, on those that are old; Beauty, on those that are ill-favoured; and Virtue, on those that are vicious: So that if I should place my gifts rightly, I must Marry one that's poor, old, ill-favoured, and debauch'd.

serv.   Heaven forbid.

L. Happy.   Nay, Heaven doth not only allow of it, but commands it; for we are commanded to give to those that want.

Enter Madam Mediator to the Lady Happy.

Mediat.   Surely, Madam, you do but talk, and intend not to go where you say.

L. Happy.   Yes, truly, my Words and Intentions go even together.

Mediat.   But surely you will not incloyster your self, as you say.

L. Happy.   Why, what is there in the publick World that should invite me to live in it?

Mediat.   More then if you should banish your self from it.

L. Happy.   Put the case I should Marry the best of Men, if any best there be; yet would a Marry'd life have more crosses and sorrows then pleasure, freedom, or hapiness: nay Marriage to those that are virtuous is a greater restraint than a Monastery. Or, should I take delight in Admirers? they might gaze on my Beauty, and praise my Wit, and I receive nothing from their eyes, nor lips; for Words vanish as soon as spoken, and Sights are not substantial. Besides, I should lose more of my Reputation by their Visits, then gain by their Praises. Or, should I quit Reputation and turn Courtizan, there would be more

lost in my Health, then gained by my Lovers, I should find more pain
then Pleasure; besides, the troubles and frights I should be put to,
with the Quarrels and Brouilleries that Jealous Rivals make, would
be a torment to me; and 'tis only for the sake of Men, when Women
retire not: And since there is so much folly, vanity and falshood in
Men, why should Women trouble and vex themselves for their sake;
for retiredness bars the life from nothing else but Men.

MEDIAT.   O yes, for those that incloister themselves bar themselves from
all other worldly Pleasures.

L. HAPPY.   The more Fools they.

MEDIAT.   Will you call those Fools that do it for the gods sake?

L. HAPPY.   No Madam, it is not for the gods sake, but for opinion's sake;
for, Can any Rational Creature think or believe, the gods take delight
in the Creature's uneasie life? or, Did they command or give leave to
Nature to make Senses for no use; or to cross, vex and pain them?
for, What profit or pleasure can it be to the gods to have Men or
Women wear coarse Linnen or rough Woollen, or to flea their skin
with Hair-cloth, or to eat or sawe thorow their flesh with Cords? or,
What profit or pleasure can it be to the gods to have Men eat more
Fish then Flesh, or to fast? unless the gods did feed on such meat
themselves; for then, for fear the gods should want it, it were fit for
Men to abstein from it: The like for Garments, for fear the gods
should want fine Clothes to adorn themselves, it were fit Men should
not wear them: Or, what profit or pleasure can it be to the gods to
have Men to lie uneasily on the hard ground, unless the gods and
Nature were at variance, strife and wars; as if what is displeasing
unto Nature, were pleasing to the gods, and to be enemies to her,
were to be friends to them.

MEDIAT.   But being done for the gods sake, it makes that which in Nature
seems to be bad, in Divinity to be good.

L. HAPPY.   It cannot be good, if it be neither pleasure, nor profit to the
gods; neither do Men anything for the gods but their own sake.

MEDIAT.   But when the Mind is not imployed with Vanities, nor the Senses
with Luxury; the Mind is more free, to offer its Adorations, Prayers
and Praises to the gods.

L. HAPPY.   I believe, the gods are better pleased with Praises then Fasting;
but when the Senses are dull'd with abstinency, the Body weakned
with fasting, the Spirits tir'd with watching, the Life made uneasie
with pain, the Soul can have but little will to worship: only the
Imagination doth frighten it into active zeal, which devotion is rather
forced then voluntary; so that their prayers rather flow out of their
mouth, then spring from their heart, like rainwater that runs thorow
Gutters, or like Water that's forced up a Hill by Artificial Pipes and
Cisterns. But those that pray not unto the gods, or praise them more
in prosperity then adversity, more in pleasures then pains, more in
liberty then restraint, deserve neither the happiness of ease, peace,

freedom, plenty and tranquillity in this World, nor the glory and blessedness of the next. And if the gods should take pleasure in nothing but in the torments of their Creatures, and would not prefer those prayers that are offer'd with ease and delight, I should believe, the gods were cruel: and, What Creature that had reason or rational understanding, would serve cruel Masters, when they might serve a kind Mistress, or would forsake the service of their kind Mistress, to serve cruel Masters? Wherefore, if the gods be cruel, I will serve Nature; but the gods are bountiful, and give all, that's good, and bid us freely please our selves in that which is best for us: and that is best, what is most temperately used, and longest may be enjoyed, for excess doth wast it self, and all it feeds upon.

MEDIAT. In my opinion your Doctrine, and your Intention do not agree together.

L. HAPPY. Why?

MEDIAT. You intend to live incloister'd and retired from the World.

L. HAPPY. 'Tis true, but not from pleasures; for, I intend to incloister my self from the World, to enjoy pleasure, and not to bury my self from it; but to incloister my self from the incumbred cares and vexations, troubles and perturbance of the World.

MEDIAT. But if you incloister your self, How will you enjoy the company of Men, whose conversation is thought the greatest Pleasure?

L. HAPPY. Men are the only troublers of Women; for they only cross and oppose their sweet delights, and peaceable life; they cause their pains, but not their pleasures. Wherefore those Women that are poor, and have not means to buy delights, and maintain pleasures, are only fit for Men; for having not means to please themselves, they must serve only to please others; but those Women, where Fortune, Nature, and the gods are joined to make them happy, were mad to live with Men, who make the Female sex their slaves; but I will not be so inslaved, but will live retired from their Company. Wherefore, in order thereto, I will take so many Noble Persons of my own Sex, as my Estate will plentifully maintain, such whose Births are greater then their Fortunes, and are resolv'd to live a single life, and vow Virginity: with these I mean to live incloister'd with all the delights and pleasures that are allowable and lawful; My Cloister shall not be a Cloister of restraint, but a place for freedom, not to vex the Senses but to please them.

> For every Sense shall pleasure take,
> And all our Lives shall merry make:
> Our Minds in full delight shall joy,
> Not vex'd with every idle Toy:
> Each Season shall our Caterers be,
> To search the Land, and Fish the Sea;
> To gather Fruit and reap the Corn,

That's brought to us in Plenty's Horn;
With which we'l feast and please our tast,
But not luxurious make a wast.
Wee'l Cloth our selves with softest Silk,
And Linnen fine as white as milk.
Wee'l please our Sight with Pictures rare;
Our Nostrils with perfumed Air.
Our Ears with sweet melodious Sound,
Whose Substance can be no where found;
Our Tast with sweet delicious Meat,
And savory Sauces we will eat:
Variety each Sense shall feed,
And Change in them new Appetites breed.
Thus will in Pleasure's Convent I
Live with delight, and with it die.

Exeunt.

(In Act II, Scene I, the men discuss Lady Happy's plans)

SCENE II.

Enter the Lady Happy, with her Ladies; as also Madam Mediator.

LADY HAPPY.   Ladies, give me leave to desire your Confession, whether or
no you repent your Retirement.

LADIES.   Most excellent Lady, it were as probable a repentance could be
in Heaven amongst Angels as amongst us.

L. HAPPY.   Now Madam Mediator, let me ask you, Do you condemn my act
of Retirement?

MEDIAT.   I approve of it with admiration and wonder, that one that is so
young should be so wise.

L. HAPPY.   Now give me leave to inform you, how I have order'd this our
Convent of Pleasure; first, I have such things as are for our Ease and
Conveniency; next for Pleasure, and Delight; as I have change of
Furniture, for my house; according to the four Seasons of the year,
especially our Chambers: As in the Spring, our Chambers are hung
with Silk-Damask, and all other things suitable to it; and a great

Looking-Glass in each Chamber, that we may view our selves and take pleasure in our own Beauties, whilst they are fresh and young; also, I have in each Chamber a Cupboard of such plate, as is useful, and whatsoever is to be used is there ready to be imployed; also, I have all the Floor strew'd with sweet Flowers: In the Summer I have all our Chambers hung with Taffety, and all other things suitable to it, and a Cup-board of Purseline, and of Plate, and all the Floore strew'd every day with green Rushes or Leaves, and Cisterns placed neer our Beds-heads, wherein Water may run out of small Pipes made for that purpose: To invite repose in the Autumn, all our Chambers are hung with Gilt Leather, or Franchipane; also, Beds and all other things suitable; and the Rooms Matted with very fine Mats: In the Winter our Chambers must be hung with Tapestry, and our Beds of Velvet, lined with Sattin, and all things suitable to it, and all the Floor spread over with Turkie Carpets, and a Cup-board of Gilt Plate; and all the Wood for Firing to be Cypress and Juniper; and all the Lights to be Perfumed Wax; also, the Bedding and Pillows are ordered according to each Season; viz. to be stuft with Feathers in the Spring and Autumn, and with Down in the Winter, but in the Summer to be only Quilts, either of Silk, or fine Holland; and our Sheets, Pillows, Table-Clothes and Towels, to be of pure fine Holland, and every day clean; also, the Rooms we eat in, and the Vessels we feed withal, I have according to each Season; and the Linnen we use to our Meat, to be pure fine Diaper, and Damask, and to change it fresh every course of Meat: As for our Galleries, Stair-Cases, and Passages, they shall be hung with various Pictures; and, all along the Wall of our Gallery, as long as the Summer lasts, do stand, upon Pedestals, Flower-pots, with various Flowers; and in the Winter Orange-Trees: and my Gardens to be kept curiously, and flourish, in every Season of all sorts of Flowers, sweet Herbs and Fruits, and kept so as not to have a Weed in it, and all the Groves, Wildernesses, Bowers and Arbours pruned, and kept free from dead Boughs Branches or Leaves; and all the Ponds, Rivolets, Fountains, and Springs, kept clear, pure and fresh: Also, we will have the choisest Meats every Season doth afford, and that every day our Meat, be drest several ways, and our drink cooler or hotter according to the several Seasons; and all our Drinks fresh and pleasing: Change of Garments are also provided, of the newest fashions for every Season, and rich Trimming; so as we may be accoutred properly, and according to our several pastimes: and our Shifts shall be of the finest and purest Linnen that can be bought or spun.

LADIES. None in this World can be happier.

L. HAPPY. Now Ladies, let us go to our several Pastimes, if you please.

Exeunt.

[In Act III, Scene I, Lady Happy meets the Princess who (she thinks) has "come from a Splendid Court to a retired Convent." The Princess asks Lady Happy if she can dress in "Masculine-Habits" and be her "loving Servant." This delights Lady Happy who wants to be the Princess's "loving Mistress."]

SCENE II.

Enter Two mean Women.

FIRST WOMAN.   O Neighbour well met, where have you been?

2. WOMAN.   I have been with my Neighbour the Cobler's Wife to comfort her for the loss of her Husband, who is run away with Goody Mettle the Tinker's Wife.

1. WOMAN.   I would to Heaven my Husband would run away with Goody Shred the Botcher's Wife, for he lies all day drinking in an Ale-house, like a drunken Rogue as he is, and when he comes home, he beats me all black and blew, when I and my Children are almost starved for want.

2. WOMAN.   Truly Neighbour, so doth my Husband; and spends not only what he gets, but what I earn with the sweat of my brows, the whilst my Children cry for bread, and he drinks that away, that should feed my small Children, which are too young to work for themselves.

1. WOMAN.   But I will go, and pull my Husband out of the Ale-house, or I'le break their Lattice-windows down.

2. WOMAN.   Come, I'le go and help; for my Husband is there too: but we shall be both beaten by them.

1. WOMAN.   I care not: for I will not suffer him to be drunk, and I and my Children starve; I had better be dead.

Exeunt.

SCENE III

Enter a Lady and her Maid.

LADY.   Oh, I am sick!

MAID.   You are breeding a Child, Madam.

LADY. I have not one minutes time of health.

Ex.

SCENE IV.

Enter Two Ladies.

FIRST LADY. Why weep you, Madam?

2. LADY. Have I not cause to weep when my Husband hath play'd all his Estate away at Dice and Cards, even to the Clothes on his back?

1. LADY. I have as much cause to weep then as you; for, though my Husband hath not lost his Estate at play, yet he hath spent it amongst his Whores; and is not content to keep Whores abroad, but in my house, under my roof, and they must rule as chief Mistresses.

2. LADY. But my Husband hath not only lost his own Estate, but also my Portion; and hath forced me with threats, to yield up my Jointure, so that I must beg for my living, for any thing I know as yet.

1. LADY. If all Married Women were as unhappy as I, Marriage were a curse.

2. LADY. No doubt of it.

Exeunt.

SCENE V.

Enter a Lady, as almost distracted, running about the Stage, and her Maid follows her.

LADY. Oh! my Child is dead, my Child is dead, what shall I do, what shall I do?

MAID. You must have patience, Madam.

LADY. Who can have patience to lose their only Child? who can! Oh I shall run mad, for I have no patience.

Runs off the Stage. Exit Maid after her.

Scene VI.

*Enter a Citizen's Wife, as into a Tavern, where a Bush is hung out,
and meets some Gentlemen there.*

CITIZEN'S WIFE.   Pray Gentlemen, is my Husband, Mr. Negligent here?

1. GENT.   He was, but he is gone some quarter of an hour since.

CIT. WIFE.   Could he go, Gentlemen?

2. GENT.   Yes, with a Supporter.

CIT. WIFE.   Out upon him! must he be supported? Upon my credit Gentlemen, he will undo himself and me too, with his drinking and care-
lessness, leaving his Shop and all his Commodities at six's and
seven's; and his Prentices and journey-men are as careless and idle
as he; besides, they cozen him of his Wares. But, was it a He or She
Supporter, my Husband was supported by?

1. GENT.   A She-supporter,; for it was one of the Maid-servants, which
belong to this Tavern.

CIT. WIFE.   Out upon him Knave, must he have a She-supporter, in the
Devil's name? but I'le go and seek them both out with a Vengeance.

2. GENT.   Pray, let us intreat your stay to drink a cup of Wine with us.

CIT. WIFE.   I will take your kind Offer; for Wine may chance to abate
Cholerick vapours, and pacifie the Spleen.

1. GENT.   That it will; for Wine and good Company are the only abaters of
Vapours.

2. GENT.   It doth not abate Vapours so much as cure Melancholy.

CIT. WIFE.   In truth, I find a cup of Wine doth comfort me sometimes.

1. GENT.   It will cheer the Heart.

2. GENT.   Yes, and enlighten the Understanding.

CIT. WIFE.   Indeed, and my understanding requires enlightening.

Exeunt.

Scene VII.

*Enter a Lady big with Child, groaning as in labour,
and a Company of Women with her.*

LADY.   Oh my back, my back will break, Oh! Oh! Oh!

1 WOMAN.   Is the Midwife sent for?

2 WOMAN.   Yes, but she is with another Lady.

LADY.   On my back! Oh! Oh! Oh! Juno, give me some ease.

Exeunt.

SCENE VIII.

Enter two Ancient Ladies.

LADY.   I have brought my Son into the World with great pains, bred him
with tender care, much pains and great cost; and must he now be
hang'd for killing a Man in a Quarrel? when he should be a comfort
and staff of my age, is he to be my ages affliction?

2. LADY.   I confess it is a great affliction; but I have had as great; having
had but two Daughters, and them fair ones, though I say it, and
might have matched them well: but one of them was got with Child
to my great disgrace; th' other run away with my Butler, not worth the
droppings of his Taps.

1. LADY.   Who would desire Children, since they come to such misfortunes?

Exeunt.

SCENE IX.

Enter one Woman meeting another.

1. WOMAN.   Is the Midwife come, for my Lady is in a strong labour?

2. WOMAN.   No, she cannot come, for she hath been with a Lady that hath
been in strong labour these three days of a dead child, and 'tis
thought she cannot be delivered.

Enter another Woman.

3. WOMAN.   Come away, the Midwife is come.

1. WOMAN.   Is the Lady deliver'd, she was withall?

3. WOMAN.   Yes, of life; for she could not be delivered, and so she died.

2. WOMAN.   Pray tell not our Lady so; for, the very fright of not being able
to bring forth a Child will kill her.

Exeunt.

SCENE X.

Enter a Gentleman who meets a fair Young Lady.

GENT.   Madam, my Lord desires you to command whatsoever you please,
and it shall be obey'd.

LADY.   I dare not command, but I humbly intreat, I may live quiet and free
from his Amours.

GENT.   He says he cannot live, and not love you.

LADY.   But he may live, and not lie with me.

GENT.   He cannot be happy, unless he enjoy you.

LADY.   And I must be unhappy, if he should.

GENT.   He commanded me to tell you that he will part from his Lady for
your sake.

LADY.   Heaven forbid, I should part Man and Wife.

GENT.   Lady, he will be divorced for your sake.

LADY.   Heaven forbid I should be the cause of a Divorce between a Noble
Pair.

GENT.   You had best consent; for, otherwise he will have you against your
will.

LADY.   I will send his Lordship an answer to morrow; pray him to give me
so much time.

GENT.   I shall, Lady.

Exit Gentleman. Lady Sola [alone].

Lady.   I must prevent my own ruin, and the sweet virtuous Ladies, by
going into a Nunnery; wherefore, I'le put my self into one to night:

> There will I live, and serve the Gods on high,
> And leave this wicked World and Vanity.

Exeunt.

One enters and speaks the Epilogue.

> Marriage is a Curse we find,
> Especially to Women kind:
> From the Cobler's Wife we see,
> To Ladies, they unhappie be.

L. HAPPY TO THE PRIN.   Pray Servant, how do you like this Play?

PRIN.   My sweet Mistress, I cannot in conscience approve of it; for
though some few be unhappy in Marriage, yet there are many
more that are so happy as they would not change their condition.

L. HAPPY.   O Servant, I fear you will become an Apostate.

PRIN.   Not to you sweet Mistress.

Exeunt.

Enter the Gentlemen.

1. GENT.   There is no hopes of dissolving this Convent of Pleasure.

2. GENT.   Faith, not as I can perceive.

3. GENT.   We may be sure, this Convent will never be dissolved, by reason it is ennobled with the company of great Princess, and glori-

fied with a great Fame; but the fear is, that all the rich Heirs will make Convents, and all the Young Beauties associate themselves in such Convents.

1 GENT.   You speak reason; wherefore, let us endeavour to get Wives, before they are Incloister'd.

Exeunt.

ACT IV. SCENE I.

Enter Lady Happy drest as a Shepherdess; She walks very Melancholy, then speaks as to her self.

My Name is Happy, and so was my Condition, before I saw this Princess; but now I am like to be the most unhappy Maid alive: But why may not I love a Woman with the same affection I could a Man?

No, no, Nature is Nature, and still will be
The same she was from all Eternity.

Enter the Princess in Masculine Shepherd's Clothes.

PRIN.   My dearest Mistress, do you shun my Company? is your Servant become an offence to your sight?

L. HAPPY.   No, Servant! your Presence is more acceptable to me then the Presence of our Goddess Nature, for which she, I fear will punish me, for loving you more than I ought to love you.

PRIN.   Can Lovers love too much?

L. HAPPY.   Yes, if they love not well.

PRIN.   Can any Love be more vertuous, innocent and harmless then ours?

L. HAPPY.   I hope not.

PRIN.   Then let us please our selves, as harmless Lovers use to do.

L. HAPPY.   How can harmless Lovers please themselves?

PRIN.   Why very well, as, to discourse, imbrace and kiss, so mingle souls together.

L. HAPPY.   But innocent Lovers do not use to kiss.

PRIN.   Not any act more frequent amongst us Women-kind; nay, it were a sin in friendship, should not we kiss: then let us not prove our selves Reprobates.

They imbrace and kiss, and hold each other in their Arms.

PRIN.   These my Imbraces though of Femal kind,
                    May be as fervent as a Masculine mind.

The Scene is open'd, the Princess and L. Happy go in.
A Pastoral within the Scene.

The Scene is changed into a Green, or Plain, where Sheep are feeding,
and a May-Pole in the middle.
L. Happy as a Shepherdess, and the Princess as a Shepherd
are sitting there.

Enter another Shepherd, and Wooes the Lady Happy.

SHEPHERD.   Fair Shepherdess do not my Suit deny,
            O grant my Suit, let me not for Love die:
            Pity my Flocks, Oh save their Shepherd's life;
            Grant you my Suit, be you their Shepherd's Wife.
L. HAPPY.   How can I grant to every ones request?
            Each Shepherd's Suit lets me not be at rest;
            For which I wish, the Winds might blow them far,
            That no Love-Suit might enter to my Ear.

Enter Madam Mediator in a Shepherdess dress, and another Shepherd.

SHEPH.   Good Dame unto your Daughter speak for me.
         Perswade her I your Son in Law may be:
         I'le serve your Swine, your Cows bring home to Milk.
         Attend your Sheep, whose Wool's as soft as Silk;
         I'le plow your Grounds, Corn I'le in Winter sow,
         Then reap your Harvest, and your Grass I'le mow;
         Gather your Fruits in Autumn from the Tree.
         All this and more I'le do, if y'speak for me.
SHEPHERDESS.   My Daughter vows a single life,
               And swears, she n're will be a Wife;
               But live a Maid, and Flocks will keep,
               And her chief Company shall be Sheep.

The Princess as a Shepherd, speaks to the Lady Happy.

PRIN.   May I live in your favour, and be possest with your Love and Person,
        is the height of my ambitions.
L. HAPPY.   I can neither deny you my Love nor Person.
PRIN.   In amorous Pastoral Verse we did not Woo. As other Pastoral
        Lovers use to doo.
L. HA.   Which doth express, we shall more constant be, And in a Married
         life better agree.
PRIN.   We shall agree, for we true Love inherit, Join as one Body and Soul,
        or Heav'nly Spirit.

Here come Rural Sports, as Country Dances about the May-Pole: that
Pair which Dances best is Crowned King and Queen of the Shepherds
that year; which happens to the Princess, and the Lady Happy.

L. Happy to the Princ.   Let me tell you, Servant, that our Custome is to dance
   about this May-Pole, and that Pair which Dances best is Crown'd
   King and Queen of all the Shepherds and Shepherdesses this year:
   Which Sport if it please you we will begin.

Prin.   Nothing, Sweetest Mistress, that pleases you, can displease me.

*They Dance; after the Dancing the Princess and Lady Happy are
   Crowned with a Garland of Flowers: a Shepherd speaks.*

> You've won the prize; and justly; so we all
>   Acknowledge it with joy, and offer here
> Our Hatchments up, our Sheep-hooks as your due,
> And Scrips of Corduant, and Oaten pipe;
> So all our Pastoral Ornaments we lay
> Here at your Feet, with Homage to obay
> All your Commands, and all these things we bring
> In honour of our dancing Queen and King;
> For Dancing heretofore has got more Riches
> Then we can find in all our Shepherds Breeches;
> Witness rich Holmby: Long then may you live,
> And for your Dancing what we have we give.

A Wassel is carried about and Syllibubs.
Another Shepherd speaks, or Sings this that follows.

> The Jolly Wassel now do bring,
>   With Apples drown'd in stronger Ale,
> And fresher Syllibubs, and sing;
> Then each to tell their Love-sick Tale:
> So home by Couples, and thus draw
> Our selves by holy Hymen's Law.

The Scene Vanishes.

*Enter the Princess Sola, and walks a turn or two in a Musing posture,
   then views her Self, and speaks.*

Prin.   What have I on a Petticoat, Oh Mars! thou God of War, pardon my
   sloth; but yet remember thou art a Lover, and so am I; but you will
   say, my Kingdom wants me, not only to rule, and govern it, but to
   defend it: But what is a Kingdom in comparison of a Beautiful
   Mistress? Base thoughts flie off, for I will not go; did not only a
   Kingdom, but the World want me.

Exeunt.

*Enter the Lady Happy Sola, and Melancholy,
   and after a short Musing speaks.*

L. Happy.   O Nature, O you gods above,
                       Suffer me not to fall in Love;

O strike me dead here in this place
Rather then fall into disgrace.

Enter Madam Mediator.

M. MEDIAT. What, Lady Happy, solitary alone! and Musing like a disconsolate Lover!

L. HAPPY. No, I was Meditating of Holy things.

M. MEDIAT. Holy things! what Holy things?

L. HAPPY. Why, such Holy things as the Gods are.

M. MEDIAT. By my truth, whether your Contemplation be of Gods or of
Men, you are become lean and pale since I was in the Convent last.

Enter the Princess.

PRIN. Come my sweet Mistress, shall we go to our Sports and Recreations?

M. MEDIAT. Beshrew me, your Highness hath sported too much I fear.

PRINC. Why, Madam Mediator, say you so?

M. MEDIAT. Because the Lady Happy looks not well, she is become pale
and lean.

PRINC. Madam Mediator, your eyes are become dim with Time; for my
sweet Mistress appears with greater splendor then the God of Light.

M. MEDIAT. For all you are a great Princess, give me leave to tell you,

I am not so old, nor yet so blind,
But that I see you are too kind.

PRIN. Well, Madam Mediator, when we return from our Recreations, I will
ask your pardon, for saying, your eyes are dim, conditionally you will
ask pardon for saying, my Mistress looks not well.

Exeunt.

[*After this Lady Happy and her court discover the foreign princess is a
prince in disguise. Lady Happy and the prince marry in a conventional
ending.*]

PRIMARY SOURCES

The Convent of Pleasure: A Comedy. In *Plays, never before printed.* London:
A. Maxwell, 1668.

"To the Two Most Famous Universities of England." Preface to *Philosophical
and Physical Opinions, written by her Excellency the Lady Marchioness of
Newcastle.* London: J. Martin and J. Allestrye, 1655.

A True Relation of My Birth, Breeding and Life. Originally published in *Natures
Pictures drawn by Fancies Pencil to the Life.* London: J. Martin and J.
Allestrye, 1656 (*A True Relation . . .* was omitted from the second edition.)

RELATED SOURCES

Cotton, Nancy. *Women Playwrights in England, c. 1363–1750.* Lewisburg, Penn.:
    Bucknell University Press, 1980.
Gagen, Jean. "Honor and Fame in the Works of the Duchess of Newcastle."
    Studies in Philology, July 1959: 519–38.
_____. *The New Woman: Her Emergence in English Drama, 1600–1730.* New
    York: Twayne, 1954.
Palomo, Dolores. "Margaret Cavendish: Defining the Female Self." *Women's
    Studies* 6 (1979): 411–22.
Smith, Hilda L. *Reason's Disciples: Seventeenth-Century English Feminists.*
    Urbana: University of Illinois, 1982.

KATHERINE FOWLER PHILIPS
1631 – 1664

Born in 1631 to Presbyterian parents—Katherine (the daughter of Daniel Oxenbridge, fellow of the Royal College of Physicians) and John Fowler (a prominent London Merchant and member of the clothworkers' company)—Katherine Fowler attended Miss Salmon's celebrated school for girls in Hackney, London. Her father died in 1642 and she joined her mother in Wales in 1646 after the latter's remarriage. At sixteen, she married fifty-four-year-old James Philips, also a Presbyterian, who held positions in Oliver Cromwell's government. She bore a son in 1655 who lived two months and a daughter the following year.

Renowned for modesty and piety throughout her short life, she published her first poems in 1651, and many circulated in manuscript from then on, mainly to a warm group of Royalist friends. Despite the fact that her family and husband were Parliamentarians, she eulogized Charles II's return. In 1662 she travelled to Ireland with her newly married friend Anne Owen, now Lady Dungannon, and her husband Colonel Trevor, the first Viscount Dungannon, prolonging her stay one year to settle her husband's property claims; her husband remained in semi-retirement in Cardigan, Wales because of his Commonwealth activities. She returned to Wales and then left Cardigan at the end of 1663 for London, where she died of smallpox in 1664.

Philips initiated a Society of Friendship in or before 1651 and gave classical names to the almost exclusively female members. For the most part, this coterie corresponded and exchanged poems, but rarely, if ever, met as a group. The Society flourished for approximately a decade. Having assumed the classical name of Orinda during her lifetime, Philips was dubbed the "Matchless Orinda," a phrase that entered the language after her death to symbolize peerless poetry. Orinda and Astraea (Aphra Behn's classical name) became models of women writers for women writers and readers, and were constantly referred to in prefaces, acknowledgments, and even literary texts.

Philips's poems to women friends, lively, poignant, and passionate by turn, solidified emotional and cultural bonds among the writers as much as the classical names with which she re-baptized them as participants in the Society of Friendship. This conscious connectiveness among women is a feminist landmark. For the first time in recorded British history, through Katherine Philips, we have a record of vital female friendships in art and in life.

———————————— • ————————————

FROM POEMS
BY THE MOST DESERVEDLY ADMIRED
MRS. KATHERINE PHILIPS,
The Matchless
ORINDA.

Friendships Mystery, To my dearest Lucasia.

Come, my Lucasia, since we see
   That Miracles Mens Faith do move,
By wonder and by prodigy
   To the dull angry World let's prove
   There's a Religion in our Love.
2.
For though we were design'd t' agree,
   That Fate no liberty destroys,
But our Election is as free
   As Angels, who with greedy choice
   Are yet determin'd to their joys.
3.
Our hearts are doubled by the loss,
   Here Mixture is Addition grown;
We both diffuse, and both ingross:
   And we whose minds are so much one,
   Never, yet ever are alone.
4.
We court our own Captivity
   Than Thrones more great and innocent:
'Twere banishment to be set free,

SOURCE: These selections come from *Poems by the most deservedly* ... London: T. N. for Henry Herringman, 1678, in the Special Collections at the University of Nebraska-Lincoln, no. 821.49 q. P53.

Since we wear fetters whose intent
    Not Bondage is but Ornament.
                5.
Divided joys are tedious found,
    And griefs united easier grow:
We are our selves but by rebound,
    And all our Titles shuffled so,
      Both Princes, and both Subjects too.
                6.
Our Hearts are mutual Victims laid,
    While they (such power in Friendship lies)
Are Altars, Priests, and Off'rings made:
    And each Heart which thus kindly dies,
    Grows deathless by the Sacrifice.

A retir'd Friendship. To Ardelia.

Come, my Ardelia, to this Bower,
    Where kindly mingling Souls awhile,
Let's innocently spend an hour;
    And at all serious follies smile.
                2.
Here is no quarrelling for Crowns,
    Nor fear of changes in our Fate;
No trembling at the Great Ones frowns,
    Nor any slavery of State.
                3.
Here's no disguise nor treachery,
    Nor any deep conceal'd design;
From Blood and Plots this Place is free,
    And calm as are those looks of thine.
                4.
Here let us sit and bless our Stars,
    Who did such happy quiet give,
As that remov'd from noise of Wars
    In one anothers hearts we live.
                5.
Why should we entertain a fear?
    Love cares not how the World is turn'd:
If crouds of dangers should appear,
    Yet Friendship can be unconcern'd.
                6.
We wear about us such a charm,
    No horrour can be our offence;
For mischiefs self can do no harm
    To Friendship or to Innocence.

7.

Let's mark how soon Apollo's beams
    Command the flocks to quit their meat,
And not entreat the neighbouring streams
    To quench their thirst, but cool their heat.

8.

In such a scorching Age as this,
    Who would not ever seek a shade,
Deserve their Happiness to miss,
    As having their own peace betray'd.

9.

But we (of one anothers mind
    Assur'd) the boisterous World disdain;
With quiet Souls and unconfin'd
    Enjoy what Princes wish in vain.

Rosania Shadowed whilst Mrs. Mary Awbrey.

If any could my dear Rosania hate,
    They only should her Character relate.
Truth shines so bright there, that an Enemy
Would be a better Orator than I.
Love stifles Language, and I must confess,
I had said more, if I had loved less.
Yet the most critical who that Face see,
Will ne'er suspect a partiality.
Others by time and by degrees perswade,
But her first look doth every heart invade.
She hath a Face so eminently bright,
Would make a Lover of an Anchorite:
A Face where conquest mixt with modesty,
Are both compleated in Divinity.
Not her least glance but sets a heart on fire,
And checks it if it should too much aspire.
Such is the Magick of her looks, the same
Beam doth both kindle and refine our flame.
If she doth smile, no Painter e'er would take
Another Rule when he would Mercy make.
And Heav'n to her such splendor hath allow'd,
That no one posture can her Beauty cloud:
For if she frown, none but would phansie then
Justice descended here to punish Men.
Her common looks I know not how to call
Any one Grace, they are compos'd of all.
And if we Mortals could the Doctrine reach,
Her Eyes have language, and her Looks do teach.

And as in Palaces the outmost, worst
Rooms entertain our wonder at the first;
But once within the Prefence-Chamber Door,
We do despise whate'er we saw before:
So when you with her Mind acquaintance get,
You'll hardly think upon the Cabinet.
Her Soul, that Ray shot from the Deity,
Doth still preserve its native purity;
Which Earth can neither threaten nor allure,
Nor by false joys defile it, or obscure.
The Innocence which in her heart doth dwell,
Angels themselves can only parallel.
More gently soft than is an Evening shower;
And in that sweetness there is coucht a Power,
Which scorning Pride, doth think it very hard
That Modesty should need so mean a Guard.
Her Honour is protected by her Eyes,
As the old Flaming Sword kept Paradise.
Such Constancy of Temper, Truth and Law,
Guides all her actions, that the World may draw
From her one Soul the noblest Precedent
Of the most safe, wise, vertuous Government.
And as the highest Element is clear
From all the Tempests which disturb the Air:
So she above the World and its rude noise,
Above our storms a quiet Calm enjoys.
Transcendent things her noble thoughts sublime,
Above the faults and trifles of the Time.
Unlike those Gallants which take far less care
To have their Souls, than make their Bodies fair;
Who (sick with too much leisure) time do pass
With these two Books, Pride, and a Looking-glass:
Plot to surprize Mens hearts, their pow'r to try,
And call that Love, which is meer Vanity.
But she, although the greatest Murtherer,
(For ev'ry glance commits a Massacre)
Yet glories not that slaves her power confess,
But wishes that her Monarchy were less.
And if she love, it is not thrown away,
As many do, only to spend the day;
But hers is serious, and enough alone
To make all Love become Religion.
And to her Friendship she so faithful is,
That 'tis her onely blot and prejudice:
For Envy's self could never errour see
Within that Soul, 'bating her love to me.

Now as I must confess the name of Friend
To her that all the World doth comprehend,
Is a most wild Ambition; so for me
To draw her Picture is flat Lunacy.
Oh! I must think the rest; for who can write,
Or into words confine what's Infinite?

Rosania's private Marriage.

It was a wise and kind design of Fate,
That none should this day's glory celebrate:
For 'twere in vain to keep a time which is
Above the reach of all Solemnities.
The greatest Actions pass without a noise,
And Tumults but prophane diviner Joys.
Silence with things transcendent nearest suits,
The greatest Emperours are serv'd by Mutes.
And as in ancient time the Deities
To their own Priests reveal'd no Mysteries
Until they were from all the World retir'd,
And in some Cave made fit to be inspir'd.
So when Rosania (who hath them out-vied,
And with more Justice might be Deified;
Who if she had their Rites and Altars, we
Should hardly think it were Idolatry)
Had found a breast that did deserve to be
Receptacle of her Divinity;
It was not fit the gazing World should know
When she convey'd her self to him, or how.
An Eagle safely may behold the Sun,
When weak Eyes are with too much Light undone.
Now as in Oracles were understood,
Not the Priest's only, but the common good:
So her great Soul would not imparted be,
But in design of general Charity.
She now is more diffusive than before;
And what men then admir'd, they now adore.
For this Exchange makes not her power less,
But only fitter for the World's Address.
May then that Mind (which, if we will admit
The Universe one Soul, must sure be it)
Inform this All, (which, till she shin'd out, lay
As drowsie men do in a cloudy day)
And Honour, Virtue, Reason so dispence,
That all may owe them to her influence:
And while this Age is thus imploy'd, may she
Scatter new Blessings for Posterity.

I dare not any other wish prefer,
For only her bestowing adds to her.
And to a Soul so in her self complete
As would be wrong'd by any Epithete,
Whose splendor's fix'd unto her chosen Sphere,
And fill'd with Love and Satisfaction there,
What can increase the Triumph, but to see
The World her Convert and her History?

Injuria Amicitiae.

Lovely Apostate! what was my offence?
   Or am I punish'd for Obedience?
Must thy strange Rigour find as strange a time?
The Act and Season are an equal Crime.
Of what thy most ingenious scorns could do,
Must I be Subject and Spectator too?
Or were the Sufferings and Sins too few
To be sustain'd by me, perform'd by you?
Unless (with Nero) your uncurb'd desire
Be to survey the Rome you set on fire.
While wounded for and by your Power, I
At once your Martyr and your Prospect die.
This is my doom, and such a ridling Fate
As all impossibles doth complicate.
For Obligation here is Injury,
Constancy Crime, Friendship a Heresie.
And you appear so much on Ruine bent,
Your own destruction gives you now Content:
For our twin-Spirits did so long agree,
You must undo your self to ruine me.
And, like some Frantick Goddess, you're inclin'd,
To raze the Temple where you are enshrin'd.
And, what's the Miracle of Cruelty,
Kill that which gave you Immortality.
While glorious Friendship, whence your Honour springs,
Lies gasping in the Crowd of common things;
And I'm so odious, that for being kind
Doubled and studied Murthers are design'd.
Thy sin's all Paradox, for shouldst thou be
Thy self again, th' wouldst be severe to me.
For thy Repentance coming now so late,
Would only change, and not relieve my Fate.
So dangerous is the consequence of ill,
Thy least of Crimes is to be cruel still.
For of thy Smiles I should yet more complain,
If I should live to be betray'd again.

Live then (fair Tyrant) in Security,
From both my Kindness and Revenge be free;
While I, who to the Swains had sung thy Fame,
And taught each Echo to repeat thy Name,
Will now my private Sorrow entertain,
To Rocks and Rivers, not to thee, complain.
And though before our Union cherish'd me,
'Tis now my pleasure that we disagree.
For from my passion your last Rigour grew,
And you kill'd me because I worshipp'd you.
But my worst Vows shall be your Happiness,
And not to be disturb'd by my distress.
And though it would my sacred flames pollute,
To make my heart a scorned prostitute;
Yet I'll adore the Author of my Death,
And kiss the Hand that robs me of my breath.

Parting with Lucasia, A Song.

1.
Well, we will do that rigid thing
  Which makes Spectators think we part;
Though Absence hath for none a sting
  But those who keep each others heart.
2.
And when our Sense is dispossest,
  Our labouring Souls will heave and pant,
And gasp for one anothers breast,
  Since their Conveyances they want.
3.
Nay, we have felt the tedious smart
  Of absent Friendship, and do know
That when we die we can but part;
  And who knows what we shall do now?
4.
Yet, I must go: we will submit,
  And so our own Disposers be;
For while we nobly suffer it,
  We triumph o'er Necessity.
5.
By this we shall be truly great,
  If having other things o'ercome,
To make our victory compleat
  We can be Conquerors at home.
6.
Nay then to meet we may conclude,
  And all Obstructions overthrow,

Since we our Passion have subdu'd,
   Which is the strongest thing I know.

To Mrs. M. A. at parting.

1.

I have examin'd and do find,
   Of all that favour me,
There's none I grieve to leave behind
   But only, only thee.
To part with thee I needs must die,
Could parting sep'rate thee and I.

2.

But neither Chance nor Complement
   did element our Love;
'Twas sacred Sympathy was lent
   Us from the Quire above.
That Friendship Fortune did create,
Still fears a wound from Time or Fate.

3.

Our chang'd and mingled Souls are grown
   To such acquaintance now,
That if each would resume their own,
   Alas! we know not how.
We have each other so engrost,
That each is in the Union lost.

4.

And thus we can no Absence know,
   Nor shall we be confin'd;
Our active Souls will daily go
   To learn each others mind.
Nay, should we never meet to Sense,
Our Souls would hold Intelligence.

5.

Inspired with a Flame Divine,
   I scorn to court a stay;
For from that noble Soul of thine
   I ne'er can be away.
But I shall weep when thou dost grieve;
Nor can I die whilst thou dost live.

6.

By my own temper I shall guess
   At thy felicity,
And only like my happiness
   Because it pleaseth thee.
Our hearts at any time will tell,
If thou, or I, be sick, or well.

7.

All Honour sure I must pretend,
    All that is Good or Great;
She that would be Rosania's Friend,
    Must be at least compleat.
If I have any bravery,
'Tis cause I have so much of thee.

8.

Thy Leiger Soul in me shall lie,
    And all thy thoughts reveal;
Then back again with mine shall flie,
    And thence to me shall steal.
Thus still to one another tend;
Such is the sacred Name of Friend.

9.

Thus our twin-Souls in one shall grow,
    And teach the World new Love,
Redeem the Age and Sex, and shew
    A Flame Fate dares not move:
And courting Death to be our friend,
Our Lives together too shall end.

10.

A Dew shall dwell upon our Tomb
    Of such a quality,
That fighting Armies, thither come,
    Shall reconciled be.
We'll ask no Epitaph, but say
ORINDA and ROSANIA.

Friendship.

Let the dull brutish World that know not Love,
    Continue Hereticks, and disapprove
That noble Flame; but the refined know,
'Tis all the Heaven we have here below.
Nature subsists by Love, and they do tie
Things to their Causes but by Sympathy.
Love chains the different Elements in one
Great Harmony, link'd to the Heav'nly Throne.
And as on Earth, so the blest Quire above
Of Saints and Angels are maintain'd by Love;
That is their Business and Felicity,
And will be so to all Eternity.
That is the Ocean, our Affections here
Are but streams borrow'd from the Fountain there.
And 'tis the noblest Argument to prove
A Beauteous Mind, that it knows how to Love.

Those kind Impressions which Fate can't controul,
Are Heaven's mintage on a worthy Soul.
For Love is all the Arts Epitome,
And is the Sum of all Divinity.
He's worse than Beast that cannot Love, and yet
It is not bought for Money, Pains or Wit;
For no chance or design can Spirits move,
But the Eternal destiny of Love:
And when two Souls are chang'd and mixed so,
It is what they and none but they can do.
This, this is Friendship, that abstracted flame
Which groveling Mortals know not how to name.
All Love is sacred, and the Marriage-tie
Hath much of Honour and Divinity.
But Lust, Design, or some unworthy Ends
May mingle there, which are despis'd by Friends.
Passion hath violent extreams, and thus
All oppositions are contiguous.
So when the end is serv'd their Love will bate,
If Friendship make it not more fortunate:
Friendship, that Love's Elixir, that pure fire
Which burns the clearer 'cause it burns the higher.
For Love, like earthy firest (which will decay
If the material fuel be away)
Is with offensive smoke accompanied,
And by resistance only is supplied:
But Friendship, like the fiery Element,
With its own Heat and Nourishment content,
Where neither hurt, nor smoke, nor noise is made,
Scorns the assistance of a foreign aid.
Friendship (like Heraldry) is hereby known,
Richest when plainest, bravest when alone;
Calm as a Virgin, and more Innocent
Than sleeping Doves are, and as much content
As Saints in Visions; quiet as the Night,
But clear and open as the Summer's light;
United more than Spirits Faculties,
Higher in thoughts than are the Eagle's eyes;
What shall I say? when we true friends are grown,
W'are like———Alas, w' are like our selves alone.

A Dialogue betwixt Lucasia and Rosania,
Imitating that of Gentle Thersis.

Ros.   My Lucasia, leave the Mountain tops,
       And like a nearer air.

Luc. How shall I then forsake my Lovely Flocks
     Bequeathed to my care?
Ros. Shepherdess, thy Flocks will not be less,
     Although thou should'st come hither.
Luc. But I fear, the World will be severe,
     Should I leave them to go thither.
Ros. O! my friend, if you on that depend,
     You'll never know content.
Luc. Rather I near thee would live and dye,
     Would Fortune but consent.
Ros. But did you ask leave to love me too,
     That others should deprive me?
Luc. Not all Mankind, a stratagem can find
     Which from that heart should drive me.
Ros. Better't had been, I thee had never seen,
     Than that content to lose.
Luc. Such are thy Charms, I'd dwell within thine arms.
     Could I my station chuse.
Ros. When Life is done, the World to us is gone,
     And all our cares do end.
Luc. Nay I know there's nothing sweet below
     Unless it be a Friend.
Ros. Then whilst we live, this Joy let's take and give,
     Since death us soon will sever.
Luc. But I trust, when crumbled into dust,
     We shall meet and love for ever.

PRIMARY SOURCE

Poems by the most deservedly Admired Mrs. Katherine Philips, The Matchless Orinda. To which is added Monsieur Corneille's Pompey and Horace, tragedies. With several other translations out of French. London: J. M. for Henry Herringman, 1667. The selected poems in this volume are taken from the 2d ed. London: T. N. for Henry Herringman, 1678.

RELATED SOURCES

Faderman, Lillian. *Surpassing the Love of Men: Romantic Friendship and Love Between Women from The Renaissance to The Present.* New York: William Morrow & Co., 1981.

Souers, Philip Webster. *The Matchless Orinda.* In vol. V of *Harvard Studies in English.* Cambridge: Harvard University Press, 1931.

MARGARET ASKEW FELL FOX
1614–1702

Margaret Askew married Judge Thomas Fell of Swarthmore Hall in 1632 and bore nine children. She was related to Anne Askew, a courageous Protestant martyr of Henry VIII's reign, through her father John Askew, a well-to-do landed gentleman. In 1652, after meeting George Fox, she joined the Quakers, probably drawn to tradition-violating ideas on women (including their support of female education), which were publicized and written about by Fox himself. In 1669, eleven years after the death of her first husband, she married Fox. Throughout this period, she frequently petitioned to have Quakers released from jail, was imprisoned herself in 1664, and in 1674 persuaded Charles II to release Fox from prison.

During her first imprisonment—for allowing illegal meetings at her home and refusing the oath of allegiance in 1663—Fell Fox wrote four tracts, including *Womens Speaking Justified, Proved and Allowed of by the Scriptures, all such as speak by the Spirit and Power of the Lord Jesus* (1667). Other women sectaries (members of nonconformist religious sects) had argued much more radically for the same issue in the 1640s and 1650s, but Fell Fox was the first to do so at considerable length. Released from another prison term in 1668 by Society of Friends' efforts in London, she later visited all the prisons in which Quakers were confined. Reincarcerated in 1670, she was released under a patent in 1671.

Fell Fox responded to protests against women's church involvement by reinterpreting the Pauline injunctions against women preaching. She proffered examples of "female worthiness" and proclaimed women's capacity for divine inspiration and their divine connection. She used the Quaker concept of Inner Light (the Indwelling Spirit) to prove a *prima facie* case for female equality. Her sustained argument in favor of women's preaching (excerpted here) makes her one of a significant group of feminist religious polemicists. Suffused with Scriptural references, her work is largely a feminist revision of conventional Biblical interpretations.

FROM
WOMENS SPEAKING JUSTIFIED

Whereas it hath been an Objection in the minds of many, and several times hath been objected by the Clergy, or Ministers, and others, against Womens speaking in the Church; and so consequently may be taken, that they are condemned for medling in the things of God; the ground of which Objection, is taken from the Apostles words, which he writ in his first Epistle to the *Corinthians,* chap. 14. vers. 34, 35. And also what he writ to *Timothy* in the first Epistle; chap. 2. vers. 11, 12. But how far they wrong the Apostles intentions in these Scriptures, we shall shew clearly when we come to them in their course and order. But first let me lay down how God himself hath manifested his Will and Mind concerning women, and unto women.

And first, when God created Man in his owne Image: in the Image of God created he them, Male and Female: and God blessed them, and God said unto them, Be fruitful, and multiply: And God said, Behold, I have given you of every Herb, &c. Gen. I. Here *God* joyns them together in his own Image, and makes no such distinctions and differences as men do; for though they be *weak,* he is strong; and as he said to the Apostle, His Grace is sufficient, and his strength is made manifest in weakness, 2 Cor. 12.9. And such hath the Lord chosen, even the weak things of the world, to confound the things which are mighty; and things which are despised, hath God chosen, to bring to nought things that are, I Cor. I. And God hath put no such difference between the Male and Female as men would make.

It is true, The Serpent that was more subtile than any other Beast of the Field, came unto the Woman, with his Temptations, and with a lie: his subtilty discerning her to be more inclinable to hearken to him, when he said, If ye eat, your eyes shall be opened: and the woman saw that the Fruit was good to make one wise, there the temptation got into her, and she did eat, and gave to her Husband, and he did eat also, and so they were both tempted into the transgression and disobedience; and therefore God said unto Adam, when that he hid himself when he heard his voice, "Hast thou eaten of the Tree which I commanded thee that thou shouldest not eat?" And Adam said "The Woman which thou gavest me, she gave me of the Tree, and I did eat." And the Lord said unto the Woman, "What is this that thou hast done?" and the Woman said, "The

SOURCE: This selection is taken from the second edition printed in 1667 with "A Further Addition" and a "Postscript" from a photoreprint by the William Andrews Clark Memorial Library, University of California, Los Angeles, 1979, pub. no. 196.

Serpent beguiled me, and I did eat." Here the Woman spoke the truth unto the Lord: See what the Lord saith, vers. 15. after he had pronounced Sentence on the Serpent; "I will put enmity between thee and the Woman, and between thy Seed and her Seed; it shall bruise thy head, and thou shalt bruise his heel," Gen. 3.

Let this Word of the Lord, which was from the beginning, stop the mouths of all that oppose Womens Speaking in the Power of the Lord; for he hath put enmity between the Woman and the Serpent; and if the Seed of the Woman speak not, the Seed of the Serpent speaks; for God hath put enmity between the two Seeds, and it is manifest, that those that speak against the Woman and her Seeds Speaking, speak out of the enmity of the old Serpents Seeds; and God hath fulfilled his Word and his Promise, "When the fulness of time was come, he hath sent forth his Son, made of a woman, made under the Law, that we might receive the adoption of Sons," Gal. 4.4,5.

Moreover, the Lord is pleased, when he mentions his Church, to call her by the name of Woman, by his Prophets, saying, "I have called thee as a Woman forsaken, and grieved in Spirit, and as a wife of Youth," Isa. 54. Again, "How long wilt thou go about, thou back-sliding Daughter? For the Lord hath created a new thing in the earth, a woman shall compass a Man," Jer. 31.22. And David, when he was speaking of Christ and his Church, he saith, "The Kings Daughter is all glorious within, her cloathing is of wrought Gold; she shall be brought unto the King: with gladness and rejoycing shall they be brought; they shall enter into the Kings Pallace." Psal. 45. And also King Solomon in his Song, where he speaks of Christ and his Church, where she is complaining and calling for Christ, he saith, "If thou knowest not, O thou fairest among women, go thy way by the footsteps of the Flock," Cant. 1.8.c.5.9. And John, when he saw the wonder that was in Heaven, he saw "a woman clothed with the Sun, and the Moon under her feet, and upon her head a Crown of twelve Stars; and there appeared another wonder in Heaven, a great red Dragon stood ready to devour her Child": here the enmity appears that God put between the woman and the Dragon, Revelations 12.

Thus much may prove that the Church of Christ is a woman, and those that speak against the womans speaking, speak against the Church of Christ, and the Seed of the woman, which Seed is Christ; that is to say, Those that speak against the Power of the Lord, and the Spirit of the Lord speaking in a woman, simply, by reason of her Sex, or because she is a Woman, not regarding the Seed, and Spirit, and Power that speaks in her; such speak against Christ, and his Church, and are of the Seed of the Serpent, wherein lodgeth the enmity. And as God the Father made no such difference in the first Creation, nor never since between the Male and the Female, but alwayes out of his Mercy and loving kindness, had regard unto the weak. So also, his Son, Christ Jesus, confirms the same thing: when the Pharisees came to him, and asked him, if it were lawful for a man to put away his Wife? he answered and said unto them, "Have you not read, That he that made them in the beginning, made them Male and Female," and said, "For this cause shall a Man leave Father and Mother, and shall cleave unto his Wife, and they twain shall be one flesh, wherefore they are no more twain but one flesh; What therefore God hath joyned together, let no man put asunder." Mat. 19.

Again, Christ Jesus, when he came to the City of Samaria, where Jacobs Well was, where the Woman of Samaria was; you may read, in John 4. how he was pleased to preach the Everlasting Gospel to her; and when the Woman said unto him, "I know that when the Messiah cometh, (which is called Christ) when he cometh, he will tell us all things"; Jesus saith unto her, "I that speak unto thee am he"; this is more than ever he said in plain words to Man or Woman (that we read of) before he suffered. Also he said unto Martha, when she said, she knew that her Brother should rise again in the last day, Jesus said unto her, "I am the Resurrection and the Life: he that believeth on me, though he were dead, yet shall he live; and whosoever liveth and believeth shall never die. Believest thou this"? she answered, "Yea Lord, I believe thou art the Christ, the Son of God." Here she manifested her true and saving Faith, which few at that day believed so on him, John 11.25, 26.

Also that Woman that came unto Jesus with an Alabaster Box of very precious Oyntment, and poured it on his Head as he sat at meat; it's manifested that this Woman knew more of the secret Power and Wisdom of God, then his Disciples did, that were filled with indignation against her; and therefore Jesus saith, "Why do ye trouble the Woman? for she hath wrought a good work upon me; Verily, I say unto you, Wheresoever this Gospel shall be preached in the whole World, there shall also this, that this Woman hath done, be told for a memorial of her," Matt. 26 Mark 14.3. Luke saith further, "She was a sinner," and that "she stood at his feet behind him weeping, and began to wash his feet with her tears and did wipe them with the hair of her head, and kissed his feet, and annointed them with Oyntment." And when Jesus saw the Heart of the Pharisee that hath bidden him to his house, he took occasion to speak unto Simon, as you may read in Luke 7. and he turned to the woman, and said, Simon, "seest thou this Woman? Thou gavest me no water to my feet, but she hath washed my feet with tears, and wiped them with the hair of her head: Thou gavest me no kiss, but this Woman, since I came in, hath not ceased to kiss my Feet: My Head with Oyl thou didst not annoint, but the Woman hath annointed my Feet with Oyntment: Wherefore I say unto thee, her sins, which are many, are forgiven her, for she hath loved much." Luke 7. 37, to the end.

Also there was many women which followed Jesus from Galilee, ministring unto him, and stood a far off when he was Crucified, 28.55. Mark 15. Yea even the women of Jerusalem wept for him insomuch that he said unto them, "Weep not for me, ye Daughters of Jerusalem, but weep for your selves, and for your Children." Luke 28.

"And certain Women which had been healed of evil Spirits and Infirmities Mary Magdalen, and Joanna the Wife of Chuza, Herods Stewards Wife, and many others which ministred unto him of their substance," Luke 8.2,3.

Thus we see that Jesus owned the Love and Grace that appeared [in] Women, and did not despise it, and by what is recorded in the Scriptures, he received as much love, kindness, compassion, and [tender] dealing towards him from Women, as he did from any others, both [in] his life time, and also after they had exercised their cruelty upon him for Mary Magdalene, and Mary the Mother of Joses, beheld where he was laid: "And when the Sabbath was past, Mary Magdalen, and Mary the Mother of James, and Salom, had brought sweet spices that they might annoint him: And very early in the morning, the first day of the week, they came unto the Sepulchre at the rising of the Sun, And they said among themselves who shall roll us away the stone from the door of the Sepulchre? And when they looked, the stone was rolled away for it was very great." Mark 16.1, 2, 3, 4. Luke 24.1,2. "And they went down into the sepulchre," and as Matthew saith, "The Angel rolled away the stone, and said unto the Women, Fear not, I know whom ye seek, Jesus which was Crucified: he is not here, he is risen," Mat. 28. Now Luke said thus "That there stood two men by them in shining apparel, and as they were perplexed and afraid, the men said unto them, He is not here; remember how he said unto you when he was in Galilee, That the Son of Man must be delivered into the hands of sinful men, and be crucified, and the third day rise again, and they remembered his words, and returned from the Sepulchre, and told all these things to the eleven, and to all the rest."

It was Mary Magdalene and Joanna, and Mary the Mother of James, and the other Women that were with them, which told these things to the Apostles, "And their words seemed unto them as idle tales, and they believed them not." Mark this, ye despisers of the weakness of Women, and look upon your selves to be so wise: but Christ Jesus doth not so, for he makes use of the weak: For when he met the women after he was risen, he said unto them, "All Hail," and they came and held him by the Feet, and worshipped him, then said Jesus unto them, "Be not afraid, go tell my Brethren that they go into Gallilee, and there they shall find me," Mat. 28.10. Mark 16.9. And John saith, when Mary was weeping at the Sepulchre, that Jesus said unto her, "Woman, why weepest thou? What seekest thou? And when she supposed him to be the Gardiner, Jesus saith unto her, Mary; she turned herself, and saith unto him, Rabboni, which is to say master: Jesus saith unto her, touch me not, for I am not yet ascended to my Father, but go to my Brethren, and say unto them I ascend unto my Father, and your Father, and to my God, and your God," John 20. 16, 17.

Mark this, you that despise and oppose the Message of the Lord God that he sends by women, what had become of the Redemption of the whole Body of Man-kind, if they had not believed the Message that the Lord Jesus sent by these women, of and concerning his Resurrection?

And if these women had not thus, out of their tenderness and bowels of love, who had received Mercy, and Grace, and fo[r]giveness of sins, and Virtue, and Healing from him, which many men also had received the like, if their hearts had not been so united and knit into him in love, that they could not depart as the men did, but sat watching, and waiting, and weeping about the Sepulchre untill the time of his: Resurrection, and so were ready to carry his Message, as is manifested, else how should his Disciples have known, who were not there?

Oh! blessed and glorified be the Glorious Lord, for this may all the whole body of mankind say, though the wisdom of men, that never knew God, is alwayes ready to except against the weak; but the weakness of God is stronger than men, and the foolishness of God is wiser then men.

And in Act. 18. you may read how Aquila and Priscilla took unto them Apollos, and expounded unto him the way of God more perfectly; who was an eloquent man, and mighty in Scriptures: yet we do not read that he despised what Priscilla said, because she was a Woman as many now do.

And now to the Apostles words, which is the ground of the great Objection against Womens speaking: And first, 1 Cor. 14. let the Reader seriously read that Chapter, and see the end and drift of the Apostle in speaking these words: for the Apostle is their exhorting the Corinthians unto charity, and to desire Spiritual gifts, and not to speak in an unknown tongue, and not to be Children in understanding, but to be Children in malice, but in understanding to be men; and that the Spirits of the Prophets should be subject to the Prophets, for God is not the Author of Confusion, but of Peace: And then he saith, "Let your Women keep silence in the Church, &c."

Where it doth plainly appear that the women, as well as others, that were among them, were in confusion, for he saith, "How is it Brethren? when ye come together, every one of you hath a Psalm, hath a Doctrine, hath a Tongue, hath a Revelation, hath an Interpretation? let all things be done to edifying." Here was no edifying, but all was in confusion speaking together: Therefore he saith, "If any man speak in an unknown Tongue let it be by two, or at most by three, and that by course, and let one Interpret, but if there be no Interpreter, let him keep silence in the Church." Here the Man is commanded to keep silence as well as the woman, when they are in confusion and out of order.

But the Apostle saith further, "They are commanded to be in Obedience," as also saith the Law; and "if they will learn anything, let them ask their Husbands at home, for it is a shame for a Woman to speak in the Church."

Here the Apostle clearly manifests his intent: for he speaks of women that were under the Law, and in that Transgression as Eve was, and such as were to learn, and not to speak publickly, but they must first ask their Husbands at home, and it was a shame for such to speak in the Church: And it appears clearly, that such women were speaking among the Corinthians, by the Apostles exhorting them from malice and strife, and confusion, and he preacheth the Law unto them, and he saith, in the Law it is written, "With men of other tongues, and other lips, will I speak unto this people," verse 21.

And what is all this to Womens Speaking? that have the Everlasting Gospel to preach, and upon whom the Promise of the Lord is fulfilled, and his Spirit poured upon them according to his word, Acts. 2, 16, 17, 18. And if the Apostle would have stopped such as had the Spirit of the Lord poured upon them, why did he say just before, "If any thing be revealed to another that sitteth by, let the first hold his peace? and you may all prophesie one by one." Here he did not say that such Women should not Prophesie as had the Revelation and Spirit of God poured upon them, but their Women that were under the Law, and in the Transgression, and were in strife, confusion and malice in their speaking, for if he had stopt Womens praying or prophesying, why doth he say: "Every man praying or prophesying having his head covered, dishonoureth his head; but every Woman that prayeth or prophesieth with her head uncovered, dishonoureth her head? Judge in your selves, Is it comely that a Woman pray or prophesie uncovered? For the Woman is not without the Man, neither is the Man without the Woman, in the Lord," 1 Cor. 11. 3, 4, 13.

Also that other scripture, in I Tim. 2. where he is exhorting that Prayer and Supplication be made every where, lifting up holy Hands without wrath and doubting; he saith in the like manner also, That "Women must adorn themselves in modest apparel, with shamefastness and sobriety, not with broidered hair, or gold, or pearl, or costly array;" He saith, "Let Women learn in silence with all subjection, but I suffer not a Woman to teach, nor to usurp authority over the Man, but to be in silence; for Adam was first formed, then Eve; and Adam was not deceived, but the Woman being deceived was in the transgression."

Here the Apostle speaks particularly to a Woman in Relation to her Husband, to be in subjection to him, and not to teach, nor usurp authority over him, and therefore he mentions Adam and Eve: But let it be strained to the utmost, as the opposers of Womens Speaking would have it, that is, That they should not preach nor speak in the Church, of which there is nothing here: Yet the Apostle is speaking to such as he is teaching to wear their apparel, what to wear, ard what not to wear; such as were not come to wear modest apparel, and such as were not to come to shamefastness and sobriety, but he was exhorting them from broidered hair, gold, and pearls, and costly array; and such art not to usurp authority over the Man, but to learn in silence with all subjection, as it becometh Women professing Godliness with good works.

And what is all this to such as have the Power and Spirit of the Lord Jesus poured upon them, and have the Message of the Lord Jesus given unto them? must not they speak the Word of the Lord because of these undecent and unreverent Women that the Apostle speaks of, and to, in these two Scriptures? And how are the men of this Generation blinded, that bring these Scriptures, and pervert the Apostles Words, and corrupt his intent in speaking of them? and by these Scriptures, endeavour to stop the Message and Word of the Lord God in Women, by contemning and despising of them. If the Apostle would have had Womens speaking stopt, and did not allow of them, why did he entreat his true Yoak-fellow to help those Women who laboured with him in the Gospel? Phil. 4.3. And why did the Apostles joyn together in Prayer and Supplication with the Women, and Mary the Mother of Jesus, and with his Brethren, Acts. 1. 14. if they had not allowed, and had union and fellowship with the Spirit of God, wherever it was revealed in Women as well as others? But all this opposing and gain-saying of Womens Speaking hath risen out of the bottomless Pit, and spirit of Darkness that hath spoken for these many hundred years together in this night of Apostacy, since the Revelations have ceased and been bid, and so that spirit hath limited and bound all up within its bond and compass, and so would suffer none to speak, but such as that spirit of Darkness, approved of, Man or Woman.

And so let this serve to stop that opposing Spirit that would limit the Power and Spirit of the Lord Jesus, whose Spirit is poured upon all flesh, both Sons and Daughters, now in his Resurrection; and since that the Lord God in the Creation, when he made man in his own Image, he made them *male* and *female;* and since that Christ Jesus, as the Apostle saith, was made of a Woman, and the power of the Highest overshadowed her, and the holy Ghost came upon her, and the holy thing that was born of her, was called "the Son of God," and when he was upon the Earth, he manifested his *love,* and his *will,* and his *mind,* both to the Woman of *Samaria,* and *Martha,* and *Mary* her Sister, and several others, as hath been shewed; and after his Resurrection also manifested himself unto them first of all, even before he ascended unto his Father. "Now when Jesus was risen, the first day of the week, he appeared first unto Mary Magdalene." *Mark* 16.9. And thus the Lord Jesus hath manifested himself and his Power, without respect of Persons; and so let all mouths be stopt that would limit him, whose Power and Spirit is infinite, that is pouring it upon all flesh.

And thus much in answer to these two Scriptures, which have been such a stumbling block, that the ministers of Darkness have made such a mountain of; but the Lord is removing all this, and taking it out of the way.

M.F.

A further Addition in Answer to the Objection concerning Women keeping silent in the Church; For it is not permitted for them to speak, but to be under obedience: as also saith the Law, If they will learn any thing, let them ask their Husbands at home, for it is a shame for a Woman to speak in the Church: Now this as Paul writeth in 1. Cor. 14:34 is one with that of I Tim. 2.11. "Let women learn in silence, with all subjection."

To which I say, If you tie this to all outward Women, then there where [were] many Women that were Widows which had no Husbands to learn of, and many were Virgins which had no Husbands; and *Philip* had four Daughters that were Prophets; such would be despised, which the Apostle did not forbid: And if it were to all Women, that no Woman might speak, then *Paul* would have contradicted himself; but they were such Women that the Apostle mentions in *Timothy,* That "grew wanton, and were busie-bodies, and tatlers, and kicked against Christ": For Christ in the Male and in the Female is one, and he is the Husband, and his Wife is the Church, and God hath said, that his *Daughters* should Prophesie as well as his *Sons:* And where he hath poured forth his Spirit upon them, they must prophesie, though blind Priests say to the contrary, and will not permit holy Women to speak.

And whereas it is said, "I permit not a Woman to speak, as saith the Law": but where Women are led by the Spirit of God, they are not under the Law, for Christ in the Male and in the Female is one; and where he is made manifest in Male and Female, he may speak, for "he is the end of the Law for Righteousness to all them that believe." So here you ought to make a distinction what sort of Women are forbidden to speak, such as were under the Law, who were not come to Christ, nor to the Spirit of Prophesie: For *Hulda, Miriam,* and *Hanna,* were Prophets, who were not forbidden in the time of the Law, for they all prophesied in the time of the Law: as you may read, in 2 *Kings* 22 what *Hulda* said unto the Priest, and to the Ambassadors that were sent to her from the King, "Go," saith she, "and tell the Man that sent you to me, Thus saith the Lord God of Israel, Behold, I will bring evil upon this place, and on the Inhabitants thereof, even all the words of the Book which the King of Judah hath read, because they have forsaken me, and have burnt Incence to other Gods, to anger me with all the works of their hands: Therefore my wrath shall be kindled against this place, and shall not be quenched. But to the King of Judah, that sent you to me to ask counsel of the Lord, so shall you say to him, Thus saith the Lord God of Israel, Because thy heart did melt, and thou humblest thy self before the Lord, when thou heardest what I spake against this place, and against the Inhabitants of the same, how they should be destroyed; Behold I will receive thee to thy Father, and thou shalt be put into thy Grave in peace, and thine eyes shall not see all the evil which I will bring upon this place." Now let us see if any of you blind Priests can speak after this manner, and see if it be not a better Sermon than any you can make, who are against Womens speaking? And *Isaiah,* that went to the Prophetess, did not forbid her Speaking or Prophesying, *Isa.* 8. And was it not prophesied in *Joel* 2. that "Hand maids should Propesie"? And are not Hand-maids Women? Consider this, ye that are against Womens Speaking, how in the *Acts* the Spirit of the Lord was poured forth upon Daughters as well as Sons. In the time of the Gospel, when *Mary* came to salute *Elizabeth in the Hill* Country in Judea, "and when Elizabeth heard the salutation of Mary, the Babe leaped in her

Womb, and she was filled with the Holy Spirit; and Elizabeth spoke with
a loud voice, Blessed art thou amongst Women, blessed is the fruit of thy
Womb; whence is this to me, that the Mother of my Lord should come
to me? for lo, as soon as thy Salutation came to my ear, the Babe leaped
in my Womb for joy, for blessed is she that believes, for there shall be a
performance of those things which were told her from the Lord." And this
was *Elizabeths* Sermon concerning Christ, which at this day stands upon
Record: And then *Mary* said, "My soul doth magnifie the Lord, and my
Spirit rejoyceth in God my Saviour, for he hath regarded the low estate of
his Hand-maid: for behold, from henceforth all Generations shall call me
blessed; for he that is mighty, hath done to me great things, and holy is
his Name; and his Mercy is on them that fear him, from Generation to
Generation; he hath shewed strength with his Arm; he hath scattered the
proud in the imaginations of their own hearts; he hath put down the
mighty from their Seats, and exalted them of low degree; he hath filled
the hungry with good things, and the rich he hath sent empty away: He
hat[h] holpen his Servant *Israel,* in remembrance of his mercy, as he
spake to his Father, to *Abraham,* and to his Seed for ever." Are you not
here beholding to the Woman for her Sermon, to use her words to put
into your Common Prayer? and yet you forbid Womens Speaking. Now
here you may see how these two women prophesied of Christ, and
Preached better then all the blind Priests did in that Age, and better then
this Age also, who are beholding to women to make use of their words.
And see in the Book of *Ruth,* how the women blessed her in the Gate of
the City, of whose stock came Christ. "The Lord make the woman that is
come into thy House like Rachel and Leah which built the house of
Israel; and that thou mayest do worthily in *Ephrata,* and be famous in
Bethlehem: let thy house be like the house of *Pharez,* whom *Tamer* bare
unto *Judah,* of the Seed which the Lord shall give thee of this young
woman. And blessed be the Lord, which hath not left thee this day
without a Kinsman, and his Name shall be continued in Israel." And also
see in the first Chapter of *Samuel,* how *Hannah* prayed and spake in the
Temple of the Lord, "Oh Lord of Hosts, if thou wilt look on the trouble
of thy Hand maid, and remember me, and not forget thy Hand-maid."
And read in the second Chapter of *Samuel,* How she rejoyced in God,
and said, "My heart rejoyceth in the Lord; my Horn is exalted in the Lord
and my mouth is enlarged over my enemies, because I rejoyce in thy
Salvation, there is none holy as the Lord, yea, there is none besides thee;
and there is no God like our God: Speak no more presumptously, let not
arrogancy come out of your mouths, for the Lord is a God of knowledge,
and by him enterprises are established; the Bow, and the mighty Men are
broken, and the weak hath girded to themselves strength; they that were
full, are hired forth for bread, and the hungry are no more hired: so that
the barren hath born seven, and she that had many Children, is feeble;
the Lord killeth, and maketh alive; bringeth down to the Grave, and
raiseth up: the Lord maketh poor, and maketh rich, bringeth low and

exalteth, he raiseth up the poor out of the dust, and lifteth up the Beggar from the dunghil to set them among Princes, to make them inherit the seat of Glory; for the Pillars of the earth are the Lords, and he hath set the world upon them; he will keep the feet of his Saints, and the wicked shall keep silence in darkness, for in his own might shall no man be strong; the Lords Adversaries shall be destroyed, and out of Heaven shall he thunder upon them; the Lord shall judge the ends of the World, and shall give power to his King; and exalt the Horn of his Anointed." Thus you may see what a woman hath said, when old *Ely* the Priest thought she had been drunk, and see if any of you blind Priests that speak against Womens Speaking, can Preach after this manner? who cannot make such a Sermon as this woman did, and yet will make a trade of this Woman and other womens words. And did not the Queen of *Sheba* speak, that came to *Solomon,* and received the *Law of God,* and *preached* it in her own Kingdom, and "blessed the Lord God that loved *Solomon,* and set him on the throne of *Israel,* because the Lord loved *Israel* for ever; and made the King to do Equity and Righteousness?" And this was the language of the Queen of *Sheba.* And see what glorious expressions Queen *Hester* used to comfort the People of God, which was the Church of God, as you may read in the book of *Hester,* which caused joy and gladness of heart among all the *Jews,* who prayed and worshipped the Lord in all places, who jeoparded her life contrary to the Kings command, went and spoke to the King, in the wisdom and fear of the Lord, by which means she saved the lives of the People of God; and righteous *Mordecai* did not forbid her speaking, but said "If she held her peace, her and her Fathers house should be destroyed"; and herein you blind Priests are contrary to Righteous *Mordecai.*

Likewise you may read how *Judith* spoke, and what noble acts she did, and how she spoke to the Elders of *Israel,* and said, "Dear Brethren, seeing ye are the honorable and elders of the People of God, call to remembrance how our Fathers in time past were tempted, that they might be proved if they would worship God aright; they ought also to remember how our Father *Abraham,* being tryed through manifold tribulations, was found a friend of God; so was *Isaac, Jacob,* and *Moses,* and all they pleased God, and were stedfast in Faith through manifold troubles." And read also her prayer in the Book of *Judith,* and how the Elders commended her, and said, "All that thou speakest is true, and no man can reprove thy words, pray therefore for me, for thou art an holy Woman, and fearest God." So these elders of *Israel* did not forbid her speaking, as you blind Priests do; yet you will make a Trade of Womens words to get money by, and take Texts; and Preach Sermons upon Womens words, and still cry out, Women must not speak, Women must be silent; so you are far from the minds of the Elders of *Israel,* who praised God for a Womans speaking. But the *Jezebel,* and the Woman, the false Church, the great Whore, and tatling women, and busie-bodies, which are forbidden to Preach, which have a long time spoke and tatled, which are forbidden to speak by the True Church, which Christ is the Head of; such Women as were in transgression under the Law, which are called a Woman in the *Revelations*. And see further how the wife Woman cryed to *Joab* over the Wall, and saved the City of *Abel,* as you may read, 2 *Sam.* 20. how in her wisdom she spoke to Joab, saying, "I am one of them that are peaceable and faithful in *Israel,* and thou goest about to destroy a city and Mother in *Israel;* Why wilt thou destroy the Inheritance of the Lord? Then went the woman to the people in her wisdom, and smote off the head of *Sheba,* that rose up against *David,* the Lords Anointed: Then *Joab* blew the Trumpet, and all the People departed in peace," And this deliverance was by the means of a Womans speaking; but tatlers, and busie-bodies, are forbidden to preach by the True Woman, whom Christ is the Husband, to the Woman as well as the Man, all being compre-hended to be the Church; and so in this True Church, Sons and Daugh-ters do Prophesie, Women labour in the Gospel; but the Apostle permits not tatlers, busie-bodies, and such as usurp authority over the Man would not have Christ Reign, nor speak neither in the Male nor Female; Such the Law permits not to speak, such must learn of their Husbands: But what Husbands have Widows to learn of, but Christ? And was not Christ the Husband of *Philips* four Daughters? And may not they that learn of their Husbands speak then? But *Jezebel,* and Tatlers, and the Whore that denies Revelation and Prophesie, are not permitted, which will not learn of Christ; and they that be out of the Spirit and Power of Christ, that the Prophets were in, who are in the Transgression, are ignorant of the Scriptures; and such are against Womens speaking, and Mens too, who Preach that which they have received of the Lord God; but that which they have preached, and do preach, will come over all your heads, yea, over the head of the false Church, the Pope; for the Pope is the Head of the False Church, and the False Church is the Popes Wife: and so he and they that be of him, and come from him, are against Womens speaking in the True Church, when both he and the false Church are called "Woman", in *Revel.* 17. and so are in the Trans-gression that would usurp authority over the Man Christ Jesus, and his Wife too, and would not have him to Reign; but the Judgment of the great Whore is come. But Christ, who is the Head of the Church, the True Woman which is his Wife, in it do Daughters Prophesie, who are above the Pope and his Wife and a top of them; And here Christ is the Head of the Male and Female, who may speak; and the Church is called "a Royal Priesthood"; so the Woman must offer as well as the Man, *Rev.* 22.17. "The Spirit saith, Come, and the Bride saith, Come": and so is not the Bride the Church? and doth the Church only consist of Men? you that deny Womens speaking, answer: Doth it not consist of Women as well as men? Is not the Bride compared to the whole Church? And doth not the Bride say, "Come"? Doth not the Woman speak then? the Husband

Christ Jesus, the "Amen," and doth not the false Church go about to stop the Brides Mouth? But it is not possible for the Bridegroom is with his Bride, and he opens her Mouth. Christ Jesus, who goes on Conquering, and to Conquer, who kill and slayes with the Sword, which is the words of his Mouth; the Lamb and the Saints shall have the Victory, the true Speakers of Men and Women over the false Speaker.

The End.

POSTSCRIPT

And you dark Priests, that are so mad against Womens speak[ing] and it's so grevious to you, did not God say to Abraham, let it not be grevious in thy sight, because of the lad, and because of thy bond-woman? In all that Sarah hath said to thee, hearken to her voice (Mark here) the Husband must learn of the Woman, and Abraham did so, and this was concerning the things of God, for he saith in Isaac shall thy seed be called, and so Abraham [did] obey the voice of Sarah, as you may read in Genesis 21 and so he did not squench the good that was in his wife, for that which he spoke to Abraham was concerning the Church.

And you may read Deborah and Barack, and so how a woman Preacht and sung Judges 5. what glorious triumphing expressions there was from a Woman, beyond all the Priests Servants, whom Barack did not bid be silent, for she Sung and Praised God, and declared to the Church of Israel, which now the hungry Priest that denyes Womens Speaking makes a trade of her words for a livelyhood.

And in Judges 13. There you may see, how the Angel appeared to a Woman, and how the Woman came to her Husband and told him, saying, a man of God came to me, whose Countenance was like the Countenance of a Man of God, and said that she should Conceive and bare a Son, and again the Angel of the Lord appeared to the woman, and she made hast and ran, and shewed her Husband and said unto him, behold, he hath appeared unto me that came unto me the other day, and when the Angel of the Lord was gon, the Womans Husband said, we should surely dye because we had seen God, and then you may read how the Woman comforted her Husband again, and said, if the Lord were pleased to kill us he would not have shewed us all these things, nor would this time have told us such things as these, and this was a Woman that taught.

PRIMARY SOURCE
Womens Speaking Justified, Proved and Allowed of by the Scriptures. All such speak by the Spirit and Power of the Lord Jesus. And how Women were the first that preached the Tidings of the Resurrection of Jesus, and were sent

by Christ's Own Command, before He ascended to the Father, John 20.17. 2d ed. London, 1667. Photo-reprint with an introduction by David J. Latt. William Andrews Clark Memorial Library, Univ. of California, Los Angeles, 1979.

RELATED SOURCES

Braithwaite, William. *The Beginnings of Quakerism.* London: Macmillan & Co., 1912.

Hobby, Elaine. *Women Writers, 1642–1688.* Ph.D. dissertation, University of Birmingham, forthcoming.

Mack, Phyllis. "Women as Prophets During the English Civil War." *Feminist Studies* 8, 1 (Spring 1982):19–45.

Ross, Isabel. *Margaret Fell, Mother of Quakerism.* London: Routledge and Kegan Paul, 1949.

Williams, E. M. "Women Preachers in the Civil War." *Journal of Modern History* 1 (1929):561–69.

BATHSUA PELL MAKIN
1608?–1675?

Daughter of Mary Holland and John Pell, rector of Southwick, Sussex, and sister of the prominent mathematician John Pell, Bathsua Pell Makin was orphaned when her parents died in 1617 and 1616 respectively. Her birth and death dates are uncertain, given usually as 1608 and 1612, and 1674 or 1675. Nevertheless, she was reputed to be the most learned Englishwoman by the 1640s, when she became royal tutor to Princess Elizabeth, who was conversant in five languages by the time she was nine. In 1646 Makin wrote a tract against imprisonment for debt, which may be linked to the fact that she had trouble receiving the pension of £40 per annum that King Charles I had awarded her. (Ironically, her brother John was imprisoned twice for debt, but not until the 1670s and 1680s.) Her petition to the Council of State for payment of arrears was dismissed in 1655.

Very little else is known about Makin until 1673 when she wrote an essay on female education and a prospectus for a school at Tottenham High Cross "within four miles of London, in the Road to Ware: where Mris. Makin is Governess." The work is entitled, *An Essay to revive the Antient Education of Gentlewomen, in religion, manners, arts and tongues. . . .* The prospectus is the postscript to the *Essay.*

An Essay doubled as an advertisement for Makin's school. In part, it was inspired by the Dutch scholar, Anna Maria van Schurman, who had also advocated female education and with whom Makin corresponded. (Two of Makin's Greek letters to Schurman are included in Schurman's *Opuscula.*) Both women viewed leisured, probably rich, and socially well-connected females as their constituency. They also assumed they could appeal to such women's eagerness and aptitude for learning.

Makin was the first Englishwoman to recommend a systematic program of advanced education for females. As the title of her *Essay* indicates, Makin placed religion first. She wanted her pupils to have a sense of past "female worthies." She advocated an intensified program in learning classical and modern languages and rejected frivolous "accomplishments" in favor of a sound practical education, such as the buying of wool. Elizabeth Drake—mother of Elizabeth Robinson (Montagu), known as queen of the Bluestockings, and Sarah Robinson (Scott), the novelist—is said to have been educated at Bathsua Makin's academy.

FROM

AN ESSAY TO REVIVE THE

ANTIENT EDUCATION OF

GENTLEWOMEN

DEDICATION

TO all Ingenious and Vertuous Ladies,
more especially to her Highness the Lady MARY,
Eldest Daughter to his Royal Highness the Duke of YORK.

Custom, when it is inveterate, hath a mighty influence: it hath the force of Nature it self. The Barbarous custom to breed Women low, is grown general amongst us, and hath prevailed so far, that it is verily believed (especially amongst a sort of debauched Sots) that Women are not endued with such Reason, as Men; nor capable of improvement by Education, as they are. It is lookt upon as a monstrous thing, to pretend the contrary. A Learned Woman is thought to be a Comet, that bodes Mischief, when ever it appears. To offer to the World the liberal Education of Women is to deface the Image of God in Man, it will make Women so high, and men so low, like Fire in the House-top, it will set the whole world in a Flame.

These things and worse than these, are commonly talked of, and verily believed by many, who think themselves wise Men: to contradict these is a bold attempt; where the Attempter must expect to meet with much opposition. Therefore, Ladyes, I beg the candid Opinion of your Sex, whose Interest I assert. More especially I implore the Favour of your Royal Highness, a Person most Eminent amongst them, whose Patronage alone will be a sufficient Protection. What I have written is not out of humour to shew how much may be said of a trivial thing to little purpose. I verily think, Women were formerly Educated in the knowledge of Arts and Tongues, and by their Education, many did rise to a great height in Learning. Were Women thus Educated now, I am confident the advantage would be very great: The Women would have Honour and Pleasure, their Relations Profit, and the whole Nation Advantage. I am very sensible it is an ill time to set on sort this Design: wherein not only Learning but Vertue it self is scorn'd and neglected, as pedantick things, fit only for the Vulgar. I know no better way to reform these Exorbitancies, than to perswade Women to scorn those Toyes and Trifles, they now spend their time about, and to attempt higher things, here offered: This will either reclaim the Men; or make them ashamed to claim the Sovereignty over such as are more Wise and Vertuous than themselves.

Were a competent number of Schools erected to Educate Ladyes ingenuously, methinks I see how asham'd Men would be of their Ignorance, and how industrious the next Generation would be to wipe off their Reproach.

I expect to meet with many Scoffes and Taunts from inconsiderate and illiterate Men, that prize their own Lusts and Pleasure more than your Profit and Content. I shall be the less concern'd at these, so long as I am in your favour; and this discourse may be a Weapon in your hands to defend your selves, whilst you endeavour to polish your Souls, that you may glorify God, and answer the end of your Creation, to be meet helps to your Husbands. Let not your Ladiships be offended, that I do not (as some have wittily done) plead for Female Preeminence. To ask too much is the way to be denied all. God hath made the Man the Head, if you be educated and instructed, as I propose, I am sure you will acknowledge it, and be satisfied that you are helps, that your Husbands do consult and advise with you (which if you be wise they will be glad of) and that your Husbands have the casting-Voice, in whose determinations you will acquiesce. That this may be the effect of this Education in all Ladyes that shall attempt it, is the desire of

Your Servant.

[Prefatory material and text]

SIR,

It should be the earnest Endeavour of all men, to imploy their Lives to those noble, and excellent Ends, for which the Omnipotent and all-wise Creatour made them, which are, the Glory of God, the Eternal Happiness of their immortal Souls, and to be useful in their Places. One generation passeth away, and an other cometh: But the Earth, the Theatre on which we act, abideth for ever. All the Works of the Children of Men do remain, not only in respect of the present and future Emolument or Detriment, caused by them; But also in Reference to the Influence they have as examples on succeeding Ages. The harvest of Bliss or Woe, will be according to the Seed-time of this Life. This Life proceeds ordinarily, as it begins,

Quo   est imbuta recens servabit Odorem
Testa diu ———

So great is the Force of the first Tincture any thing takes, whether good, or bad. As Plants in Gardens excel those, that grow wild; or as Brutes, by due Management (Witness the Philosophers Dogs) are much altered: So Men; by liberal Education, are much betterid, as to intellectuals and morals. All conclude great Care ought to be taken of the Males: But your doubt in your Letter is concerning the Females. I think the greater Care ought to be taken of Them: Because Evil seems to be begun here, as in *Eve,* and to be propagated by her Daughters. When the Sons of God took unto themselves the Daughters of Men, Wickedness multiplied apace. It was the cursed Counsel of Balaam to debauch Israel by Balack's Idolatrous Women. Wretched Jezebel excites Ahab to greater Wickedness, than he could ever have thought of. God gave strict Command to the Israelites, not to marry with heathenish Women. When Solomon himself (the wisest of Men) did this, they soon drew his Heart from God. Bad Women, weak to make Resistance, are strong to tempt to evil: Therefore without all Doubt great Care ought to be taken, timely to season them with Piety and Virtue. Your great Question is, Whether to breed up Women in Arts and Tongues, is not a mere new Device, never before practised in the World. This you doubt the more: Because Women are of low Parts, and not capable of Improvement by this Education. If they could be improved, you doubt, whether it would benefit them? If it would benefit them, you enquire where such Education may be had? or, whether they must go to School with Boys? to be made twice more impudent than learned. At last you muster up a Legion of Objections.

I shall speak distinctly to your Questions, and then answer your Objections.

Women have formerly been educated in Arts and Tongues.

Little is recorded concerning the manner, how Women were educated formerly: You can expect my Proof to be only topical and by Circumstances.

It doth appear out of Sacred Writ, that Women were imployed in most of the great Transactions that happened in the World, even in reference to Religion. Miriam seems to be next to Moses and Aaron, she was a great Poet, and Philosopher: For both Learning, and Religion were generally in former times wrapt up in Verse.

The Women met David, singing triumphant Songs, composed (it's like by themselves) a great Specimen of liberal Education.

Deborah, the Deliverer of Israel, was without all doubt a learned Woman, that understood the Law. Huldah the Prophetess, dwelt in a Colledge, (we may suppose) where Women were trained up in good Literature. We may be sure she was a very wise Woman: For King Josiah sends Hilkiah the Priest, and the Nobles of his Court, in a Case of Difficulty and Danger, to consult with her. 2 Chro. 34.20.21 etc.

In the New Testament we find Anna a Prophetess.

Paul, Rom. 16.1. Commends unto them Phebe, who was not only a Servant of Christ: But a Servant of the Church at Cencrea. Ver. 12. He tells us Triphena, Triphosa and Persis laboured much in the Lord. Priscilla instructed Apollos.

Timothy's Grandmother called Lois, and his Mother Eunice were not only Gracious Women, but learned Women; for from a Child they instructed him in the holy Scriptures. 2 Tim. 1. 5. compared with Chap. 3.15. The Children of the Elect Lady, found walking in the Truth, were instructed by her. Philips four Daughters were Prophetesses, Acts 21. Though Women may not speak in the Church; yet those extraordinarily inabled, to whom Paul speaks, 1 Cor. 11.5. might: For Paul directs them they should not pray nor prophesie with their Heads uncovered, which supposes they might do the things. I shall not dispute these Texts what this praying and prophesying was; it serves my Turn, that Women extraordinarily inabled, were publickly imployed. . . .

There was a Contest between twenty Grecian and twenty Roman Ladies, which were most excellent in Learning. The Romane Dames were the best Oratours: But the Grecian Ladies the best Philosophers. This plainly shews they both were instructed in all kind of good Literature.

Women Educated in Arts and Tongues, have been eminent in them.

I should be too tedious, if I should commemorate all upon Record, that have been Smatterers in Learning. I shall only mention some few Ladies that have been equal to most Men.

It is reported of Zenobia Queen of Palmeria, that she was not only excellent her self in Arts and Arms: But Learning in her (like light in the Sun) influenced her whole People, only famous in her Daies.

Olympia Fulvia Maurata, Tutress to the Empress of Germany, understood French, Latin, Dutch; she was so good a Grecian, that she read publick Lectures in that Language. She was also reputed to be well skilled in Divinity.

The Lady Jane Grey excelled Maurata in this, she understood the Hebrew also. There is a large Discourse of her Learning (in which she took great delight) and Piety, in the Book of Martyrs.

The present Dutchess of New-Castle, by her own Genius, rather than any timely Instruction, over-tops many grave Gown-Men.

I am forbidden to mention the Countess Dowager of Huntington (instructed sometimes by Mrs. Makin) how well she understands Latin, Greek, Hebrew, French and Spanish; or what a proficient she is in Arts, subservient to Divinity, in which (if I durst I would tell you) she excels.

The Princess Elizabeth, daughter to King Charles the first, to whom Mrs. Makin was Tutress, at nine Years old could write, read, and in some measure understand, Latin, Greek, Hebrew, French and Italian. Had she lived, what a Miracle would She have been of her Sex!

The Princess Elizabeth, eldest Daughter to the Queen of Bohemia, yet living, is versed in all sorts of choice Literature.

Mrs. Thorold, Daughter of the Lady Car in Lincolnshire, was excellent in Philosophy, and all sorts of Learning.

I cannot without Injury forget the Lady Mildmay, and Dr. Loves Daughters; Their Worth and Excellency in Learning is yet fresh in the Memory of many Men.

Cornelia read publick Philosophy-Lectures at Rome, she brought up her Sons, the Gracchi, so, that they were the only Men famous in their Dayes. She was admired by Cicero for diverse of her Works. . . .

I cannot omit Constantia the Wife of Alexander Sforza; She was so Learned, that upon the suddain and without any premeditation She was able sufficiently to discourse upon any Argument, either Theological, or Philosophical: Besides, She was very frequent in the works of St. Hierome, Ambrose, Gregory, Cicero, and Lactantius. She was much admired for her Extempory vaine in Verse. Her Daughter Baptista was equal to Her in Fame and Merit, and was reckoned among the best Learned, and most Illustrious Women.

Christina late Queen of Sweden understood several Languages, and was well versed in Politicks, and acquainted with most Arts and Sciences.

I thought of Queen Elizabeth first, but purposely mention Her last, as the Crown of all. How learned She was, the World can testifie. It was usual for her to discourse with Forraign Agents in their own Languages. Mr. Ascam, her Tutor, used to say, She read more Greek in a day then many of the Doctors of her time did Latin in a week. You see some Women have been good Proficients in most kinds of Learning. I shall now shew you how they have been excellent in some particular parts of it, as the Tongues, Oratory, Philosophy, Divinity, and lastly Poetry.

Women have been good Linguists.

It is objected against Women, as a reproach, that they have too much Tongue: But it's no crime they have many Tongues; if it be, many Men would be glad to be guilty of that fault. The Tongue is the only Weapon Women have to defend themselves with, and they had need to use it dextrously. Many say one tongue is enough for a Woman: it is but a quibble upon the word. Several Languages, understood by a Woman, will do our Gentlemen little hurt, who have little more than their Mother-Wit, and understand only their Mother-Tongue: these most usually make this Objection, to hide their own Ignorance. Tongues are learnt in order to Things. As things were, and yet are in the World, its requisite we learn Tongues to understand Arts; It's therefore a Commendation to these Women after mentioned, that they were Mistresses of Tongues. . . .

It may now be demanded, by those studious of Antiquity, why the Vertues, the Disciplines, the Nine Muses, the Devisers, and Patrons of all good Arts, the Three Graces; should rather be represented under the Feminine Sex, and their Pictures be drawn to the Portraictures of Damosels, and not have Masculine Denominations, and the Effigies of Men? Yea, why Christians themselves, in all their Books and Writings which they commit to Posterity, still continue the same practice? Why Wisdom is said to be the Daughter of the Highest, and not the Son? Why Faith, Hope, and Charity, her Daughters, are represented as Women? Why should the seven Liberal Arts be expressed in Womens Shapes? Doubt-less this is one reason; Women were the Inventors of many of these Arts, and the promoters of them, and since have studyed them, and attained to an excellency in them: And being thus adorned and beautified with these Arts, as a testimony of our gratitude for their Invention, and as a token of honour for their Proficiency; we make Women the emblems of these things, having no fitter Hieroglyphick to express them by. I shall add this one thing, worthy observation, to the great honour and com-mendation of the Feminine Sex.

The parts of the World have their denomination from Women, Asia is so called from the Nymph Asia, the Mother of Japethus and Prometheus. Europe, from Europa the Daughter of Agenor. Lybia (which is Africa) from Libia the Daughter of Epaphus. America (lately discoverd) bears the same Female Figure.

It is usual for men to pride and boast themselves in the Wisdom, Valour, and Riches of their Ancestors; what wise Men their Fore-fathers have been, what great things they have done, and what large possessions they have had, when they themselves are degenerated and become Igno-rant, Cowardly, beggarly, debauched Sots.

I hope Women will make another use of what I have said, instead of claiming honour from what Women have formerly been, they will labour to imitate them in learning those Arts their Sex hath invented, in studying those Tongues they have understood, and in practising those Virtues shadowed under their Shapes; the knowledge of Arts and Tongues, the exercise of Virtue and Piety, will certainly (let men say what they will) make them honourable.

---·---

Care ought to be taken by us to Educate Women in Learning.

That I may be more distinct in what I intend, I shall distinguish of Women,

Women are of two sorts,   (RICH,) (Of good natural Parts.
                          (POOR,) (Of low Parts.

I do not mean, that it is necessary to the esse [essential being], to the subsistence, or to the Salvation of Women, to be thus educated. Those that are mean in the World, have not an opportunity for this Education: Those that are of low Parts, though they have opportunity, cannot reach this; Ex quovis ligno non sit Minerva: My meaning is, Persons that God hath blessed with the things of this World, that have competent natural Parts, ought to be educated in Knowledge; That is, it is much better they should spend the time of their Youth, to be competently instructed in those things usually taught to Gentlewoman at Schools, and the overplus of their time to be spent in gaining Arts, and Tongues, and useful Knowledge, rather than to trifle away so many precious minutes meerly to polish their Hands and Feet, to curl their Locks, to dress and trim their Bodies; and in the mean time to neglect their Souls, and not at all, or very little to endeavour to know God, Jesus Christ, Themselves, and the things of Nature, Arts and Tongues, subservient to these. I do not deny but Women ought to be brought up to a comely and decent carriage, to their Needle, to Neatness, to understand all those things that do particularly belong to their Sex. But when these things are competently cared for, and where there are Endowments of Nature and leasure, then higher things ought to be endeavoured after. Meerly to teach Gentlewomen to Frisk and Dance, to paint their Faces, to curl their Hair, to put on a Whisk, to wear gay Clothes, is not truly to adorn, but to adulterate their Bodies; yea, (what is worse) to defile their Souls. This (like Circes Cup) turns them to Beasts; whilst their Belly is their Godd, they become Swine; whilst Lust, they become Goats; and whilst Pride is their God, they become very Devils. Doubtless this under-breeding of Woman began amongst Heathen and Barbarous People; it continues with the Indians, where they make their Women meer slaves, and wear them out in drudgery. It is practised amongst degenerate and Apostate Christians, upon the same score, and now is a part of their Religion; it would therefore be a piece of Reformation to correct it; and it would notably countermine them who fight against us, as Satan against Adam, by seducing our Women, who then easily seduce their Husbands.

Had God intended Women onely as a finer sort of Cattle, he would not have made them reasonable. Bruits, a few degrees higher than Drils [baboons] or Monkies, (which the Indians use to do many Offices) might have better fitted some mens Lust, Pride, and Pleasure; especially those that desire to keep them ignorant to be tyrannized over.

God intended Woman as a help-meet to Man, in his constant conversation, and in the concerns of his Family and Estate, when he should most need, in sickness, weakness, absence, death, etc. Whilst we neglect to fit them for these things, we renounce God's Blessing, he hath appointed Women for, are ungrateful to him, cruel to them, and injurious to our selves.

I remember a discourse in Erasmus, between an Abbot and a learned Woman. She gives many good Reasons why Women should be learned, that they might know God, their Saviour, understand his Sacred Word, and admire him in his wonderful Works; that they might also better administer their Household Affairs amongst a multitude of Servants, who would have more reverence towards them, because they were above them in understanding. Further, she found a great content in reading good Authors at spare times. He gives her one Answer to all this, That Women would never be kept in subjection if they were learned; as he found by experience amongst his Monks, of all things in the World, he hated nothing so much as a learned Monk, who would alwayes be contradicting his Superior, from the Decretals out of Peter and Paul. He cared not if all his Monks were turned into Swine, so long as they would be obedient, and not disturb him in his Pleasures. Doubtless if that generation of Sots (who deny more Polite Learning to Women) would speak out, they would tell you, If Women should be permitted Arts, they would be wiser than themselves (a thing not to be endured) then they would never be such tame fools and very slaves as now they make them; therefore it is a wicked mischievous thing to revive the Ancient Custom of Educating them.

Seeing Nature produces Women of such excellent Parts, that they do often equalize, some-times excel men, in what ever they attempt; what reason can be given why they should not be improved? . . .

This kind of Education will be very useful to Women.

1. The profit will be to themselves. In the general they will be able to understand, read, write, and speak their Mother-Tongue, which they cannot well do without this. They will have something to exercise their thoughts about, which are busie and active. Their quality ties them at home; if Learning be their Companion, Delight and Pleasure will be their Attendants: for there is no pleasure greater, nor more sutable to an ingenious mind, than what is founded in Knowledge; it is the first Fruits of Heaven, and a glymps of that Glory we afterwards expect. There is in all an innate desire of knowing, and the satisfying this is the greatest pleasure. Men are very cruel that give them leave to look at a distance, only to know they do not know; to make any thus to tantalize, is a great torment.

This will be a Hedge against Heresies. Men are furnished with Arts and Tongues for this purpose, that they may stop the mouths of their Adversaries. And Women ought to be Learned, that they may stop their ears against Seducers. It cannot be imagined so many Persons of Quality would be so easily carried aside with every wind of Doctrine, had they been furnished with these defensive Arms; I mean, had they been instructed in the plain rules of artificial reasoning, so as to distinguish a true and forcible Argument, from a vain and captious Fallacy. Had they been furnished with Examples of the most frequent illusions of erronious Seducers. Heresiarks creep into Houses, and lead silly Women captive, then they lead their Husbands, both their Children; as the Devil did Eve, she her Husband, they their Posterity.

It is none of the least considerations, that a Woman thus educated, who modestly uses her Learning, is, in despight of envy, honoured by most, especially wise and good men; such a one is admired and even adored by the vulgar and illiterate.

More particularly, persons of higher quality, for want of this Education, have nothing to imploy themselves in, but are forced to Cards, Dice, Playes, and frothy Romances, meerly to drive away the time; whereas knowledge in Arts and Tongues would pleasantly imploy them, and upon occasion benefit others.

Seneca endeavouring to comfort his Mother Helvigia in her Affliction, when he was under Banishment, suggests to her, that she had been liberally brought up, and might now have an opportunity to be farther improved, and might comfort her self in the study of Philosophy.

We cannot be so stupid as to imagine, that God gives Ladies great Estates, meerly that they may Eat, Drink, Sleep, and rise up to Play. Doubtless they ought not to live thus. God, that will take an account for every idle thought, will certainly reckon with those Persons that shall spend their whole lives in idle play and chat. Poor Women will make but a lame excuse at the last day for their vain lives; it will be something to say, that they were educated no better. But what Answer Men will make, that do industriously deny them better improvement, lest they should be wiser than themselves, I cannot imagine.

$$\text{More particularly, Women are} \quad \left\{ \begin{array}{l} \text{Unmarried.} \\ \text{Married.} \\ \text{Widows.} \end{array} \right.$$

As for Unmarried Persons, who are able to subsist without a de-pendance, they have a fairer opportunity than Men, if they continue long in that estate, to improve the Principles they have sucked in, and to ripen the Seeds of Learning which have been sown in their minds in their tender years. Besides, this will be an honest and profitable diversion to possess their minds, to keep out worse thoughts. Maids that cannot subsist without depending, as Servants, may chuse their places, to at-tend upon honourable Persons, or to be imployed in Nurseries; by their Conversation, to teach Tongues to Children, whilst carried in Arms; who perhaps, when they find their own feet, will not abide the tedium of a School.

The famous Lord Mountagu was thus improved, to the amazement of all, which made him ever after hate all Pedantick Education.

Julius Cesar also received such a tincture, whilst he was in the Nurs-ery, that he was the reviver of the purity of the Latin Tongue in his dayes.

Married Persons, by vertue of this Education, may be very useful to their Husbands in their Trades, as the Women are in Holland; and to their Children, by timely instructing them, before they are fit to be sent to School; as was the case of Cesar and the Lord Mountagu.

I need not shew how any Persons, thus brought up, if they happen to be Widows, will be able to understand and manage their own Affairs.

2. Women thus educated, will be beneficial to their Relations. It is a great blessing of God to a Family, to provide a good Wife for the Head,

if it be eminent; and a presage of ruine, when he sends a ranting Jezebel to a soft Ahab.

One Athaliah, married to Joram, plucks ruine upon the House of Jehosaphat. How many Families have been ruined by this one thing, the bad education of Women? Because the Men find no satisfactory converse or entertainment at home, out of meer weariness they seek abroad; hence they neglect their Business, spend their Estates, destroy their Bodies, and oftentimes damn their Souls.

The Italians slight their Wives, because all necessary knowledge, that may make them serviceable (attainable by institution) is denyed them: but they court, adore, and glory in their Curtezans, though common Whores; because they are polished with more generous breeding.

Many learned Men, having married Wives of excellent Parts, have themselves instructed them in all kinds of Learning, the more to fit them for their Converse, and to indear them and their society to them, and to make them admired by others. The Woman is the glory of the Man; we joy in our Children when eminent, and in our Wives when excellent, either in Body or Mind.

I have said before how they may improve their Children in Learning, especially the Tongues; I mention it again, because it is a reason of so great weight, that it is sufficient (if there was nothing else) to turn the Scale. Tullia had never been so eloquent, had not she had so learned a Mother as Hortensia.

The Gracchi, Baptista, Damar, Aristippus, Eustochium (before mentioned) had never been so famous in Arts and Tongues, had they not been timely taught by their Mothers, Cornelia, Constantia, Arete, and Paula.

King Lemuel's Wisdom was extraordinary, yet he acknowledges the Seeds were sown by the timely instruction of his Mother, Prov. 31. Therefore Solomon charges Children to mind the Instruction of their Mothers; having found so much good by it himself.

Besides, none have so great an advantage of making most deep impression on their Children, as Mothers. What a prudent and virtuous Mother commends by Precept and Example, sticks long; witness Lemuel and his Proverbs, many of which he suckt in with his Mothers Milk.

Timothy was taught the Holy Scriptures from a Child, by his Grandmother Lois, and by his Mother Eunice.

We may presume the Children of the Elect Lady, were found walking in the Truth from their Mothers Instructions. For they seldom speake the Language of Canaan, whose Mothers are of Ashdod.

3. Women thus instructed will be beneficial to the Nation. Look into all History, those Nations ever were, now are, and always shall be, the worst of Nations, where Women are most undervalued; as in Russia, Ethiopia, and all the Barbarous Nations of the World. One great Reason why our Neighbours the Dutch have thriven to admiration, is the great care they take in the Education of their Women, from whence they are to

be accounted more vertuous, and to be sure more useful than any Women in the World. We cannot expect otherwise to prevail against the Ignorance, Atheism, Prophaneness, Superstition, Idolatry, Lust, that reigns in the Nation, than by a Prudent, Sober, Pious, Vertuous Education of our Daughters. Their Learning would stir up our Sons, whom God and Nature hath made superior, to a just emulation. . . .

My intention is not to equalize Women to Men, much less to make them superior. They are the weaker Sex, yet capable of impressions of great things, something like to the best of Men.

Hercules and Theseus were very valiant; Manalippe and Hyppolite were little inferior to them. Zeuxes and Timanthes were brave Painters. So were Timarete, Irene, Lala, Martia, and many others.

For Poetry, Sappho may be compared with Anacreon; Corinna with Pindar. Tullia was eloquent like Cicero. Cato's Daughter little inferior to himself in the Theory and Practice of Philosophy. Semiramis was like Alexander in magnificence. The Tanaquils as politick as Servius Tullius. The Porcea's were as mangnanimous as Brutus.

The inference I make from hence is, that Women are not such silly giddy creatures, as many proud ignorant men would make them; as if they were uncapable of all improvement by Learning, and unable to digest Arts, that require any solidity of Judgment. Many men will tell you, they are so unstable and unconstant, born down upon all occasions with such a torrent of Fear, Love, Hatred, Lust, Pride, and all manner of exorbitant Passions, that they are uncapable to practice any Vertues, that require greatness of Spirit, or firmness of Resolution. Let such but look into History, they will find Examples enow of illustrious Women to confute them.

Before I mention the Objections, I shall state the Propositions I have endeavoured to prove; That which I intend is this, That Persons of competent natural parts, indifferently inclin'd and disposed to Learning, whom God hath blessed with Estates, that they are not cumbred in the World, but have liberty and opportunity in their Childhood; and afterwards, being competently instructed in all things now useful that concern them as Women, may and ought to be improved in more Polite Learning, in Religion, Arts, and the knowledge of things, in Tongues also as subservient to these, rather then to spend the over-plus time of their youth, in making Points for Bravery, in dressing and trimming themselves like Bartholomew-Babies, in Painting and Dancing, in making Flowers of Coloured Straw, and building Houses of stained Paper, and such like vanities.

Object. No Body means Gentlewomen should be thus educated in matters of meer vanity; but in practicing their Needle, in knowing and doing those things that concern good Housewifery, which is Womens particular qualification.

Answ. I know not what may be meant, but I see what is generally done. In most Schools for educating this Sex, little more is proposed by the

Undertakers, or expected by the Parents. As far as I can observe, the less any thing of solidity is taught, the more such places are frequented. I do acknowledge, in the state of the Question, that Women should be accomplished in all those things that concern them as Women. My meaning is, The over-plus time may be imployed in polishing their minds with the knowledge of such things as may be honourable, pleasant and profitable to them, and their Relations afterwards.

Before I proceed further to Answer the remaining Objections, I desire this may be taken notice of, That what-ever is said against this manner of Educating Women, may commonly be urged against the Education of Men.

Object. If we bring up our Daughters to Learning, no Persons will adventure to Marry them.

Answ. 1. Many men, silly enough, (God knows) think themselves wise, and will not dare to marry a wise Woman, lest they should be over-topt.

2. As some Husbands, debauched themselves, desire their Wives should be chast, and their Children vertuous: So some men, sensible of their own want, (caused by their Parents neglect) will chuse a learned Woman, in whom they may glory, and by whose prudence their defect may be supplyed.

3. Learned men, to be sure, will chuse such the rather, because they are sutable. Some Men marrying Wives of good natural parts, have improved themselves in Arts and Tongues, the more to fit them for their converse. . . .

If all I have said may conveniently be done, I expect many will deride this Design. I am contented, let them abound in their own sense, and have Wives as silly as themselves desire, over whom they may tyrannize.

I hope I shall by this Discourse perswade some Parents to be more careful for the future of the Breeding of their Daughters. You cark and care to get great Portions for them, which sometimes occasions their ruine. Here is a sure Portion, an easie way to make them excellent. How many born to good Fortunes, when their Wealth hath been wasted, have supported themselves and Families too by their Wisdom?

I hope some of these Considerations will at least move some of this abused Sex to set a right value upon themselves, according to the dignity of their Creation, that they might, with an honest pride and magnanimity, scorn to be bowed down and made to stoop to such Follies and Vanities, Trifles and Nothings, so far below them, and unportionable to their noble Souls, nothing inferior to those of Men, and equally precious to God in Christ, in whom there is neither Male nor Female.

Let a generous resolution possess your minds, seeing Men in this Age have invaded Womens Vices, in a noble revenge, reassume those Vertues, which Men sometimes unjustly usurped to themselves, but ought to have left them in common to both Sexes.

POSTSCRIPT.

If any enquire where this Education may be performed; such may be informed, That a School is lately erected for Gentlewomen at Tottenham-high-cross, within four miles of London, in the Road to Ware; where Mrs. Makin is Governess, who was sometimes Tutoress to the Princess Elisabeth, Daughter to King Charles the First; Where, by the blessing of God, Gentlewomen may be instructed in the Principles of Religion; and in all manner of Sober and Vertuous Education: More particularly, in all things ordinarily taught in other Schools:

As
- Works of all Sorts,
- Dancing,
- Musick,
- Singing,
- Writing,
- Keeping Accompts

{ Half the time to be spent in these Things.

The other half to be imployed in gaining the Latin and French Tongues; and those that please, may learn Greek and Hebrew, the Italian and Spanish: In all which this Gentlewomen hath a competent knowledge.

Gentlewomen of eight or nine years old, that can read well, may be instructed in a year or two (according to their Parts) in the Latin and French Tongues; by such plain and short Rules, accommodated to the Grammar of the English Tongue, that they may easily keep what they have learned, and recover what they shall lose; as those that learn Musick by Notes.

Those that will bestow longer time, may learn the other Languages, afore-mentioned, as they please.

Repositories also for Visibles shall be prepared; by which, from beholding the things, Gentlewomen may learn the Names, Natures, Values Use of Herbs, Shrubs, Trees, Mineral-Juices, Metals and Stones.

Those that please, may learn Limning, Preserving, Pastry and Cookery.

Those that will allow longer time, may attain some general Knowledge in Astronomy, Geography; but especially in Arithmetick and History.

Those that think one Language enough for a Woman, may forbear the Languages, and learn onely Experimental Philosophy; and more, or fewer of the other things aforementioned, as they incline.

The Rate certain shall be 20 l. per annum: But if a competent improvement be made in the Tongues, and the other things aforementioned, as shall be agreed upon, then something more will be expected. But the Parents shall judge what shall be deserved by the Undertaker.

Those that think these Things Improbable or Impracticable, may have further account every Tuesday at Mr. Masons Coffe-House in Cornhil, near the Royal Exchange; and Thursdayes at the Bolt and Tun in Fleet-street, between the hours of three and six in the Afternoons, by some Person whom Mris. Makin shall appoint.

FINIS.

PRIMARY SOURCE

An Essay to revive the Antient Education of Gentlewomen, in religion, manners, arts and tongues with an Answer to the Objections against this Way of Education. London: J.D. to be sold by Thomas Parkhurst, 1673.

RELATED SOURCES

Ballard, George. *Memoirs of several ladies of Great Britain who have been celebrated for their writings or skill in the learned languages, arts and sciences.* Oxford: W. Jackson, 1752. Reprint. Edited by Ruth Perry. New York: AMS Press, forthcoming.

Brink, J. R. "Bathsua Makin: Scholar and Educator of the Seventeenth Century." *International Journal of Women's Studies,* July/August 1978: 417–26.

————. "Bathsua Makin: Educator and Linguist (English, 1608?–1675)." In *Female Scholars: A Tradition of Learned Women before 1800,* edited by J. R. Brink, 86–100. Montreal: Eden Press, 1980. (Also includes an essay on Elizabeth Elstob by Mary Elizabeth Green.)

Gardiner, Dorothy. *English Girlhood at School: A Study of Women's Education Through Twelve Centuries.* London: Oxford University Press, 1929.

Irwin, Joyce L. "Anna Maria van Schurman: The Star of Utrecht (Dutch, 1607–1678)." In *Female Scholars,* edited by J. R. Brink, 68–85.

van Schuman, Anna Maria. *Opuscula hebraea, latina, graeca, gallica, prosaica et metrica . . .* (Leydon 1648, rpt. Lipsiae: M. C. F. Mulleri, 1749. Makin's letters are on pp. 126–27 of Mulleri edition.)

Smith, Hilda L. *Reason's Disciples: Seventeenth-Century English Feminists.* Urbana: University of Illinois Press, 1982.

APHRA BEHN
1640 – 1689

Aphra Behn's recent biographer, Angeline Goreau, convincingly speculates (using circumstantial evidence) that most likely she was born Aphra Johnson and was the (so-called) "illegitimate" daughter of Lady Willoughby, the wife of Lord Willoughby, founder and Governor of the colony of Surinam in South America. This set of circumstances could explain the unusual adventures in Surinam from the autumn of 1663 until early 1664, recorded in *Oroonoko* (1688). On her return she apparently married a city merchant of Dutch extraction and after his death became a spy in Antwerp for Charles II. The problems she encountered in obtaining payment for espionage resulted in her being committed to Debtor's Prison. After her release she began to write in 1670 for the theatre, with the title of her first play, *The Forc'd Marriage,* an appropriate challenge to societal values.

After the popularity of play-going waned in the late 1670s, Behn turned somewhat unsuccessfully to translation, then around 1683, in financial straits, she negotiated for an increased advance for the publication of her collected poems, "I want extreamly or I wo'd not urge this." In her last few years, uninterruptedly ill and penurious, she made remarkable contributions to the rise of the novel with a series of prose narratives. This included what many contend is the first novel in English, *Oroonoko: or, the Royal Slave,* and the first fiction to include condemnation of slavery. She continued to write popular plays, including *The Lucky Chance,* in the apparatus of which she upbraided society for its treatment of women writers.

In 1688, Behn translated Bernard le Bovier de Fontenelle's *La Pluralité des Deux Mondes* in order to introduce women readers to rationalist philosophy and scientific ideas. In the preface to this simplified guide to Cartesian thought, Behn gently suggests that women should abandon frivolity and modishness in favor of learning and thinking. Acknowledging the obstacles placed in a woman's path to knowledge, Behn sees her translation as contributing to the effort to gain educational opportunities for women.

In 1688 she also published another volume of poems, *Lycidus,* the title poem a translation from the French of Tallemant. Their autobiographical content clear, several poems speak of her women friends and, particulary in the emphatically placed final poem, of lesbian love. As the first woman of letters in English to earn her living by writing, the first female dramatist to forge a niche in the theatre, and one of the first to violate traditional expectations about women's secondary status and sexual inactivity or reticence, she has earned a permanent place in the feminist pantheon. For almost three centuries, her persistence in writing has served as a positive model for creative, working women because she not only endured the ridicule meted out to women writers, but also had to suffer continual scrutiny of her private life. The excerpts illustrate her attentiveness to feminist themes and education, her refusal to be intimidated by those who scorned women writers, and the expression of her love for women. Aphra Behn was buried in Poet's Corner in Westminster Abbey.

———————————————————— • ————————————————————

FROM
THE DUTCH LOVER

PREFACE

Indeed that day 'twas acted first, there comes me into the pit a long, lithe, phlegmatic, white, ill-favored, wretched fop, an officer in masquerade newly transported with a scarf and feather out of France, a sorry animal that has nought else to shield it from the uttermost contempt of all mankind, but that respect which we afford to rats and toads, which though we do not well allow to live, yet when considered as a part of God's creation, we make honorable mention of them. A thing, reader—but no more of such a smelt: this thing, I tell you, opening that which serves it for a mouth, out issued such a noise as this to those that sat about it, that they were to expect a woeful play, God damn him, for it was a woman's. Now how this came about I am not sure, but I suppose he brought it piping hot from some who had with him the reputation of a villainous wit: for creatures of his size of sense talk without all imagination, such scraps as they pick up from other folks. I would not for a world be taken arguing with such a property as this; but if I thought there were a man of any tolerable parts, who could upon mature deliberation distinguish well his right hand from his left, and justly state the difference between the number of sixteen and two, yet had this prejudice upon him; I would take a little pains to make him know how much he errs. For

SOURCE: "The Author's Preface" to *La Pluralité des Deux Mondes* comes from the Houghton Library, Harvard University. The other selections come from Aphra Behn, *The Works of Aphra Behn,* ed. Montague Summers. A copy of *Lycidus,* reissued as *The Land of Love* (1717), is at the Henry E. Huntington Library, shelf no. 112081. See also *Lycidus; or, The Lover in Fashion* (1688) in *Works.*

waiving the examination why women having equal education with men, were not as capable of knowledge, of whatsoever sort as well as they: I'll only say as I have touched before, that plays have no great room for that which is men's great advantage over women, that is learning; we all well know that the immortal Shakespeare's plays (who was not guilty of much more of this than often falls to women's share) have better pleased the world than Jonson's works, though by the way 'tis said that Benjamin was no such rabbi neither, for I am informed that his learning was but grammar high; (sufficient indeed to rob poor Salust of his best orations) and it has been observed that they are apt to admire him most confoundedly, who have just such a scantling of it as he had; and I have seen a man the most severe of Jonson's sect, sit with his hat removed less than a hair's breadth from one sullen posture for almost three hours at the *The Alchymist;* who at that excellent play of *Harry the Fourth* (which yet I hope is far enough from farce) has very hardly kept his doublet whole; but affectation has always had a greater share both in the action and discourse of men than truth and judgment have; and for our modern ones, except our most inimitable laureate, I dare to say I know of none that write at such a formidable rate, but that a woman may well hope to reach their greatest heights. Then for their musty rules of unity, and God knows what besides, if they meant anything, they are enough intelligible and as practicable by a woman; but really methinks they that disturb their heads with any other rule of plays besides the making them pleasant, and avoiding of scurrility, might much better be employed in studying how to improve men's too imperfect knowledge of that ancient English game which hight [is called] long Laurence: and if comedy should be the picture of ridiculous mankind I wonder anyone should think it such a sturdy task, whilst we are furnished with such precious originals as him I lately told you of; if at least that character do not dwindle into farce, and so become too mean an entertainment for those persons who are used to think. Reader, I have a complaint or two to make to you and I have done.

FROM

SIR PATIENT FANCY

EPILOGUE

Spoken by Mrs. Gwin.

I here and there o'erheard a Coxcomb cry,
   Ah, Rot it—'tis a Woman's Comedy,
One, who because she lately chanc'd to please us,

With her damn'd Stuff, will never cease to teeze us.
What has poor Woman done, that she must be
Debar'd from Sense, and sacred Poetry?
Why in this Age has Heaven allow'd you more,
And Women less of Wit than heretofore?
We once were fam'd in story, and could write
Equal to Men; cou'd govern, nay, cou'd fight.
We still have passive Valour, and can show, ⎤
Wou'd Custom give us leave, the active too, ⎬
Since we no Provocations want from you. ⎦
For who but we cou'd your dull Fopperies bear,
Your saucy Love, and your brisk Nonsense hear;
Indure your worse than womanish Affectation,
Which renders you the Nusance of the Nation;
Scorn'd even by all the Misses of the Town,
A Jest to Vizard Mask, the Pit-Buffoon;
A Glass by which the admiring Country Fool
May learn to dress himself en Ridicule:
Both striving who shall most ingenious grow
In Leudness, Foppery, Nonsense, Noise and Show.
And yet to those fine things we must submit
Our Reason, Arms, our Laurels, and our Wit.
Because we do not laugh at you, when leud,
And scorn and cudgel ye when you are rude.
That we have nobler Souls than you, we prove,
By how much more we're sensible of Love;
Quickest in finding all the subtlest ways
To make your Joys, why not to make you Plays?
We best can find your Foibles, know our own,
And Jilts and Cuckolds now best please the Town;
Your way of Writing's out of fashion grown.
Method, and Rule—you only understand;
Pursue that way of Fooling, and be damn'd.
Your learned Cant of Action, Time and Place,
Must all give way to the unlabour'd Farce.
To all the Men of Wit we will subscribe:
But for your half Wits, you unthinking Tribe,
We'll let you see, whate'er besides we do,
How artfully we copy some of you:
And if you're drawn to th' Life, pray tell me then,
Why Women should not write as well as Men.

FROM

LYCIDUS;

OR THE LOVER IN FASHION

To the Fair Clarinda,
Who Made Love to Me,
imagin'd more than Woman.

Fair lovely Maid, or if that Title be
   Too weak, too Feminine for Nobler thee,
Permit a Name that more Approaches Truth:
And let me call thee, Lovely Charming Youth.
This last will justifie my soft complaint,
While that may serve to lessen my contraint;
And without Blushes I the Youth persue,
When so much beauteous Woman is in view.
Against thy Charms we struggle but in vain
With thy deluding Form thou giv'st pain,
While the bright Nymph betrays us to the Swain.
In pity to our Sex sure thou wer't sent,
That we might Love, and yet be Innocent:
For sure no Crime with thee we can commit;
Or if we shou'd—thy Form excuses it.
For who, that gathers fairest Flowers believes
A Snake lies hid beneath the Fragrant Leaves.

Thou beauteous Wonder of a different kind,
Soft Cloris with the dear Alexis join'd;
When e'r the Manly part of thee, wou'd plead
Thou tempts us with the Image of the Maid,
Whil we the noblest Passions do extend
The Love to Hermes, Aphrodite the Friend.

———————————— • ————————————

FROM THE TRANSLATION OF
La Pluralité des Deux Mondes
[The Theory or System of Several
New Inhabited Worlds]

"THE AUTHOR'S PREFACE."

I Find my self reduced almost to the same Condition in which Cicero was, when he undertook to put Matters of Philosophy into Latin; which, till that time, had never been treated of, but in Greek. He tells us, it would be said, his Works would be unprofitable, since those who loved Philosophy, having already taken the pains to find it in the Greek, would neglect, after that, to read it again in Latin (that not being the Original;) and that those who did not care for Philosophy, would not seek it, either in the Latin, or the Greek. But to this, Cicero himself answers, and says, That those who were not Philosophers would be tempted to the Reading of it, by the Facility they would find in its being in the Latin Tongue; and that those, who were Philosophers, would be curious enough to see how it had been turned from the Greek to the Latin.

Cicero has reason to answer in this manner; the Excellency of his Genius, and the great Reputation he had already acquired sufficiently defend this new Undertaking of his, which he had dedicated to the Benefit of the Publick. For my part, I am far from offering at any Defence for this of mine, tho' the Enterprize be the same; for I would treat of Philosophy in a manner altogether Unphilosophical, and have endeavoured to bring it to a Point not too rough and harsh for the Capacity of the Numbers, nor too light and trival for the Learned. But if they should say to me as they did to Cicero, that this Work is not at all proper for the Learned, nor would it instruct the rest of the World, who are careless of Knowledge; far be it from me to answer as Cicero did, who, perhaps, in searching for a middle Way to Philosophy, such as would improve every Understanding, I have taken that which possibly will be advantageous to none: It is very hard to keep to a Medium, and I believe I shall scarce take the pains to search a second Method to please. And if it happen that this Book should be read, I advertise those that have some Knowledge in Philosophy, that I have not pretended to Instruct, but to Divert them, in presenting them in a more agreeable manner, that which they already known solidly: And I also advertise those to whom this Subject is new, that I believe it will at once Instruct and Please them: The Knowing will act, contrary to my Intentions, if they seek only Profit; and the rest, if they seek only Pleasure.

I will not amuse my self in telling you, that I have taken out of Philosophy the Matter the most capable of inspiring a Curiosity; for in my Opinion, we ought to seek no greater Interest, than to know how this World which we inhabit, is made, and that there are other Worlds that resemble it, and that are inhabited as well as this: After all, let those that please, give themselves the trouble of finding out this Truth, but I am sure they will not do it in Complaisance to my Book: Those that have any Thoughts to lose, may cast them away here; but all People are not in a Condition, you will say, to make such an unprofitable Expence of Time.

In this Discourse I have introduced a fair Lady to be instructed in Philosophy, which, till now, never heard any speak of it; imagining, by this Fiction, I shall render my Work more agreeable, and to encourage the fair Sex (who lose so much time at their Toylets in a less charming Study) by the Example of a Lady who had no supernatural Character, and who never goes beyond the Bounds of a Person who has no Tincture of Learning, and yet understands all that is told her, and retains all the Notions of Tourbillions[?] and Worlds, without Confusion: And why should this imaginary Lady have the Precedency of all the rest of her delicate Sex? Or do they believe they are not as capable of conceiving that which she learned with so much Facility?

The Truth is, Madam the Marquiese applies herself to this Knowledge; But what is this Application? It is not to penetrate by force of Meditation, into a thing that is obscure in itself, or any thing that is obscurately explained; 'tis only to read, and to represent to yourselves at the same time what you read, and to form some Image of it that may be clear and free from perplexing Difficulties. I ask of the Ladies (for this System) but the same Attention that they must give the Princess of Cleve, if they would follow the Intrigue, and find out the Beauties of it; though the truth is, that the Idea's of this Book are not so familiar to the most part of Ladies, as those of the Princess of Cleve; but they are not more obscure, than those of that Novel, and yet they need not think above twice at most, and they will be capable of taking a true Measure, and having a just Sence of the whole.

I do not pretend to take a System in the Air, without a Foundation, but I have made use of true Philosophical Reasons; and of those, employed as many as are necessary; and, as it happily falls out, the Notions of Philosophy upon this Subject are pleasant; and at the same that they satisfie the Reason, they content the Imagination with a Prospect as agreeable, as if they had been made on purpose to entertain it.

Where I found some Pieces not altogether so diverting as I wish'd, I gave them Foreign Ornaments: Virgil made use of the same Method in his Georgicks, where he adorned his Subject (of itself altogether dull) with several Digressions, and very often agreeably. Ovid too has done as much in his Art of Loving, though the Foundation of his Theme was infinitely more agreeable than any thing that could be mixed with it; therefore it is to be supposed, he imagined it would be tiresome, always to treat of one and the same thing, though it was of Gallantry: But for my part, I, who have much more need of the Assistance of Digression, have, notwithstanding, made use of them very frugally: I have authorized them by Liberty of Natural Conversation, and have put them but to those places where I thought Every-body would be glad to find them; I have put the greatest part of them in the beginning of my Work, because the Mind will not be then so well accustomed to the principal Idea's that I present. In fine, I have taken them from the Subject itself, or, at least, approaching to it.

I would not have any Imagination of the Inhabitants of the Worlds that are entirely fabulous, but have endeavoured to relate only that which might be thought most reasonable; and the Visions themselves that I have added, something of a real Foundation in them; the True and the False are here mixed, but they always are very easie to be distinguished; yet I do not undertake to justifie a Composure so fantastical: This is the most important Point of this Work, and 'tis this only that I cannot give a Reason for; but the Publick Censure will inform me, what I ought to think of this Design.

There remains no more for me to say in this Preface, but to speak to one sort of People, who, perhaps, will be the most difficult to content (and yet I have very good Reasons to give them, but, possibly, such as they will not take for current Pay, unless they appear to them to be good;) and these are the scrupulous Persons, who may imagine, that in regard to Religion, there may be danger in placing Inhabitants any where, but on this Earth; but I have had a Respect even to the most delicate Niceties of Religion, and would not be guilty of any thing that should shock it in a publick Work, though that Care were contrary to my Opinion. But that which will surprize you is, that Religion is not at all concerned in this System, where I fill an infinite number of Worlds with Inhabitants; and you need only reform and clear one Error of the Imagination: But when I shall tell you the Moon is inhabited, you presently represent to your Fancy Men made as we are; and if you are a little of the Theologician, you will then be presently full of Difficulties: The Posterity of Adam could not possibly extend to the Moon, nor send Colonies into that Country; then they are not the Sons of Adam: And that would be a great perplexing Point in Theology, to imagine there should be Men, and those not to descend from Adam; there is no need of saying any more, all the Difficulties are reduced to that, and the Arguments we ought to employ in a tedious Explanation, are too worthy of Gravity to be put into this Book, though perhaps I could answer solidly enough to their Objections, if I undertook it; but 'tis certain, I have no need of answering them; let the Men in the Moon do it, who are only concern'd; for 'tis they that put the Men there, I only put Inhabitants, which, perhaps, are not Men. What are they then? 'Tis not that I have seen them, that I speak of them; yet do not imagine that I design, (by saying there are no Men in the Moon) to evade your Objections, but you shall see, that 'tis impossible (according to the

Idea's that I have of the infinite Diversity that Nature ought to use in her Works) that there can be none. This Idea governs all the Book, and it cannot be confuted by any Philosopher; therefore I believe I shall meet with no Objection from any but those who speak of these Entertainments, without having read them. But is this Reason enough for me to depend on? No; 'tis rather a sufficient Reason for me to fear, that this Objection will be often urged in several places.

——————————————— • ———————————————

PRIMARY SOURCES

The Author's Preface to her translation of *Entretiens sur la Pluralité des Deux Mondes.* (*The Theory or System of Several New Inhabited Worlds, lately discover'd and pleasantly describ'd, in five nights conversation with Madam the Marchioness of *****.*) London: W.O. for Samuel Briscoe, 1700. (Also known as *A Discovery of New Worlds.*)

The Dutch Lover. A Comedy. London: Thomas Dring, 1673.

The Forc'd Marriage; or, The Jealous Bridegroom; a tragi-comedy. London: H.L. and R.B., for James Magnus, 1671.

The Lucky Chance, or, an Alderman's Bargain. London: R.H. for W. Canning, 1687.

Lycidus; or, The Lover in Fashion. London, 1688. Reprinted in *The Works of Aphra Behn,* vol. 6. Edited by Montague Summers. London: William Heineman, 1915.

Oroonoko: or, The Royal Slave. London, 1688. Reprint. New York, 1973. Edited by K.A. Sey. Legon, Ghana: Ghana Publishing Co., 1977.

Sir Patient Fancy: A Comedy. London: E. Flesher for Richard Tonson, 1678.

The Works of Aphra Behn. Edited by Montague Summers. 6 vols. London: William Heineman, 1915.

RELATED SOURCES

Cotton, Nancy. *Women Playwrights in England, c. 1363–1750.* Lewisberg, Penn.: Bucknell University Press, 1980.

Gagen, Jean. *The New Woman: Her Emergence in English Drama, 1600–1730.* New York: Twayne, 1954.

Goreau, Angeline. *Reconstructing Aphra: A Social Biography of Aphra Behn.* New York: Dial Press, 1980.

SARAH FYGE FIELD EGERTON
1669/72 – 1722/23

A recent article by Jeslyn Medoff explains that Sarah Fyge's father, Thomas Fyge, was an apothecary, and her so far unidentified mother died in 1704. She was descended on her father's side from the Fyge family of Winslow, Buckinghamshire, landowners in the sixteenth and seventeenth centuries. She had five sisters. Revealing himself as a competent occasional poet, Thomas Fyge wrote commendatory verse to at least two works by the physician John Heydon, one of which described the ascent and descent of the spirits from earth to heaven, the harmony of the heavens, and of the human body and soul. In his commendatory poem to the second work entitled *The English Physicians Guide,* Thomas Fyge addressed "his Ingenuous Friend Mr. John Heydon, on his Book Intituled The Holy Guide" from "Myself your Friend and Servant." Thomas Fyge's friendship with John Heydon suggests that he knew people involved in Rosicrucianism and allied Hermeticism. Rosicrucians believed in the prolongation of life, the transmutation of metals, and occultism, all central ideas in Heydon's work. A hermeticist, Heydon also believed in alchemy and that salt, sulphur, and mercury caused all diseases. Much of Sarah Fyge's arcane learnedness in her poems came from these early associations.

According to Sarah Fyge's autobiographical verse, she was banished in 1686 from her parents' home and estranged from her father because of *The Female Advocate,* a long polemical poem published in 1686, which she seems to have written when she was fourteen. Fyge's refutation of Robert Gould's attack on women entitled *A Late Satyr Against the Pride, Lust and Inconstancy of Women* (1683) satirizes a particularly *ad feminam* example of misogynous Restoration verse. These works testify to the persistence of the controversy about women initiated in 1399 by Christine de Pisan. According to an exchange of correspondence in 1780 and 1781 volumes of *The Gentleman's Magazine* by someone who uses "M.J." as a signature and claims to have possession of 120 letters and notes by Sarah Fyge Field Egerton to a lover—"the poet" was born Sarah Fyge or Fyges, she "disobliged" her father, and had to leave his house. In the late 1680s or 90s, still according to "M.J.," she married Mr. Field, an attorney, and during this marriage she wrote one of the elegies to John Dryden in *The Nine Muses.* Her knowledge of the law, also evident in her poetry, probably dates from this time. After Mr. Field died, she married Reverend Thomas Egerton, rector of Adstock and a widower with grown children, who was her second cousin. It may have been an arranged marriage. In 1703, the year that her volume of poems was published, according to documents in the Lambeth Palace Library, she and Thomas Egerton were involved in a divorce petition on the grounds of cruelty. In his testimony, Thomas Egerton claimed he had been cuckolded, and offered extraordinary detail about his wife's behavior toward him and his daughter, as well as his violent response which he seeks to justify. She resoundingly countercharged. A later account in *The New Atalantis* (1707) by Delarivière Manley describing Egerton as someone unhappily married and rather hot-tempered matched these divorce testimonies.

With their continual references to occult matters, minerals, necromancy, mythology, magic, and metaphysical excursions, Egerton's poems are in the Rosicrucian discourse. "The Exstasy" and "The Liberty" are two examples. Unlike many poets, she is also frank about sexual passion, another index to her Behn-like risk-taking, independent spirit. Several of her poems of friendship address women friends. The inclusion of one of her poems in the elegiac tribute to John Dryden suggests she may have known other women writers, as does her friendship with Manley and the commendatory poems by other writers that introduce her 1703 volume. Jeslyn Medoff convincingly argues that she may have been professionally acquainted with Elizabeth Thomas (of *Pylades and Corinna*), John Froud, and perhaps Thomas Creech.

Egerton's excerpts exemplify a fine early example of feminist polemic while her poems highlight her unflagging will and opposition to the tyranny of many women's lives.

FROM

THE FEMALE ADVOCATE,

OR,

AN ANSWERE TO A LATE SATYR AGAINST THE PRIDE, LUST AND INCONSTANCY, ETC. OF WOMAN.

WRITTEN BY A LADY IN VINDICATION OF HER SEX.

TO THE READER.

That which makes many Books come abroad into the World without Prefaces, is the only reason that incites me to one, viz. the Smalness of them; being willing to let my Reader know why this is so: For as one great Commendation of our Sex, is *to know much,* and *speak little,* so an Intelligent Modesty informs my Soul, I ought to put a Period to the intended Length of the insuing Lines, lest censuring Criticks should measure my Tongue by my Pen, and condemn me for a Talkative by the Length of my Poem. Tho' I confess the Illustrious Subject requires (nay commands) an Enlargement from any other Pen than mine, (or those under the same Circumstances;) but I think it is good Frugality for young Beginners to send forth a small Venture at first, and see how that passes the merciless Ocean of Criticks, and what Returns it makes, and so accordingly adventure the next time. I might, if I pleas'd, make an excuse for the Publication of my Book, as many others do; but then, perhaps, the World might think 'twas only a feign'd Unwillingness: But when I found I could not hinder the Publication, I set a resolution to bear patiently the

SOURCE: This abridgement of *The Female Advocate* is taken from the second edition photo-reprint by the William Andrews Clark Memorial Library, University of California, Los Angeles, pub. no. 180. Selections from *Poems on Several Occasions* are taken from the microfilm of a manuscript at the University of Texas, Austin.

Censures of the World, for I expected its Severity, the first Copy being so ill writ, and so much blotted, that it could scarce be read; and they that had the Charge of it, in the room of blots, writ what they pleas'd, and much different from my Intention. I find the main Objection is, That I should Answer so rude a Book, when, if it had not been against our Sex, I should not have Read it, much less have Answer'd it; but I think its being so, required the sharper Answer, and severer Contradictions. I suppose some will think the Alterations occasion'd by their dislike of the former: If that had been intended for the Press, some things there inserted, had been left out; which I have now done, tho' they might pass well enough in Private, they were not fit to be exposed to every eye; but I think, when a Man is so extravagant as to Damn all Womankind for the Crimes of a few, he ought to be corrected: But in his Second Edition he hath been more favourable, yet there he goes beyond the bounds of Modesty and Civility, and exclaims not only against Vertue, but moral Honesty too, and supposes he hath banish'd all Goodness out of them; but it will be an impossible thing, because they are more essentially Good than Men; for 'tis observed in all Religions, that Women are the truest Devotionists, and the most Pious, and more Heavenly than those who pretend to be the most perfect and rational Creatures; for many Men, with Conceit of their own Perfections, neglect that which should make them so; as some mistaken Persons, who think if they are of the right Church they shall be infallibly saved, when they never follow the Rules which lead to Salvation: And when Persons with this Inscription pass currant in Heaven, then should it be according to my Antagonist's Fancy, that all Men are Good, and fitting for Heaven, because they are Men; and Women irreversibly Damn'd, because they are Women: But that Heaven should make a Male and Female, both of the same Species, both indued with the like rational Souls, for two such differing Ends, is the most notorious Principle, and the most unlikely of any that ever was maintain'd by any rational Man; and I shall never take it for an Article of my Faith, being assured that Heaven is for all those whose Purity and Obedience to its Law, qualifies them for it, whether Male or Female; to which Place the latter seem to have the justest Claim, is the Opinion of one of its Votaries.

S. F.

THE FEMALE ADVOCATE,

OR,

AN ANSWER TO A LATE SATYR AGAINST THE PRIDE, LUST AND INCONSTANCY, &C. OF WOMAN.

Blasphemous Wretch! How canst thou think or say
Some Curst or Banisht Fiend Usurpt the Sway
When Eve was Form'd? For then's deny'd by you
God's Omnipresence and Omniscience too:
Without which Attributes he could not be
The greatest and supreamest Deity:
Nor can Heav'n sleep, tho' it may mourn to see
Degen'rate Man speak such vile Blasphemy.

When from dark Chaos Heav'n the World did make,
And all was Glorious it did undertake;
Then were in Eden's Garden freely plac'd
Each thing that's pleasant to the Sight or Taste,
'T was fill'd with Beasts & Birds, Trees hung with Fruit,
That might with Man's Coelestial Nature suit:
The World being made thus spacious and compleat,
Then Man was form'd, who seemed nobly Great.
When Heav'n survey'd the Works that it had done,
Saw Male and Female, but found Man alone,
A barren Sex, and insignificant,
Then Heav'n made Woman to supply the want,
And to make perfect what before was scant:
Surely then she a Noble Creature is,
Whom Heav'n thus made to consummate all Bliss.
Tho' Man had Being first, yet methinks She
In Nature should have the Supremacy;
For Man was form'd out of dull senceless Earth,
But Woman had a much more Noble Birth:
For when the Dust was purify'd by Heaven,
Made into Man, and Life unto it given,
Then the Almighty and All-wise God said,
That Woman of that Species should be made;

Which was no sooner said, but it was done,
'Cause 'twas not fit for Man to be alone.

Thus have I prov'd Woman's Creation good,
And not inferiour, when right understood,
To that of Man's; for both one Maker had,
Which made all good; then how could Eve be bad?
But then you'l say, tho' she at first was pure,
Yet in that State she did not long endure.
'Tis true; but yet her Fall examine right;
We find most Men have banish'd Truth for spight:
Nor is she quite so guilty as some make,
For Adam most did of the Guilt partake;
While he from God's own Mouth had the Command,
But Woman had it at the second hand:
The Devil's Strength weak Woman might deceive,
But Adam only tempted was by Eve:
She had the strongest Tempter, and least Charge;
Man's knowing most, doth make his Sin more large.
But tho' that Woman Man to Sin did lead,
Yet since her Seed hath bruis'd the Serpent's Head:
Why should she thus be made a publick scorn,
Of whom the Great Almighty God was born?
Surely to speak one slighting word, must be
A kind of murmuring Impiety:
But yet their greatest Haters still prove such
Who formerly have loved them too much;
And from the Proverb they are not exempt,
Too much Familiarity has bred Contempt.
And as in Adam all Mankind did die,
They make all Base for one's Immodesty;
Nay, make the Name a kind of Magick Spell,
As if 'twould conjure married Men to Hell.

Woman! By Heaven, the very Name's a Charm,
And will my Verse against all Criticks arm.
The Muses or Apollo doth inspire
Heroick Poets; but yours is a Fire
Pluto from Hell did send by Incubus,
Because we make their Hell less populous,
Or else you ne'er had Damn'd the Females thus:
But if so universally they are
Dispos'd to Mischief, what need you declare
Peculiar Faults? when all the World might see
With each approaching Morn a Prodigy.
Man Curse bad Woman! I could here as well

The black infernal Devils Curse their Hell;
When there had bin no such damn'd Place we know,
If they themselves had not first made it so.
In Lust perhaps you others have excell'd,
And made all Whores that possibly would yield;
And courted all the Females in your way,
Then did design at last to make a Prey
Of some pure Virgins; or what's almost worse,
Make some chaste Wives to merit a Divorce:
But 'cause they hated your insatiate Mind,
Therefore you call what's Vertuous, Unkind;
And Disappointments did you Soul perplex,
So in meer spight you curse the Female Sex.
I would not judge you thus, only I find
You would adult'rate all Womankind,
Not only with your Pen; you higher soar,
You'd exclude Marriage, make the World a Whore.
But if all Men should of your humour be,
And should rob Hymen of his Deity,
They soon would find the Inconveniency.
Then hostile Spirits would be forc'd to Peace,
Because the World so slowly would encrease.
They would be glad to keep their Men at home,
And ev'ry King want more t'attend his Throne:
Nay, should an English Prince resolve that he
Would keep the number of's Nobility;
And this dull Custom some few years maintain'd,
There would be none less than a Peer ith' Land;
And I do fancy 'twould be pretty sport,
To see a Kingdom cram'd into a Court.
Sure a strange world, when one shall nothing see,
Unless a Bawdy-house or Nunnery.
For should this Act e'er pass, Woman would fly
Unto dark Caves to save her Chastity.
She only in a Marriage-Bed delights,
The very Name of Whore her Soul affrights:
And when that Sacred Ceremony's gone,
Woman I'm sure will chuse to live alone.

Ther's none can number all those vertuous Dames
Which chose cold death before their Lovers flames.
The chaste Lucretia, whom proud Tarquin lov'd,
Her self she flew; her Chastity she prov'd.
But I've gone further than I need have done,
Since we have got Examples nearer home:
Witness those Saxon Ladies who did fear

The loss of Honour when the Danes were here;
And cut their Lips and Noses, that they might
Not pleasing seem, or give the Danes delight:
Thus having done what they could justly do,
At last they fell their sacrifices too.
I could say more, but History will tell
Many Examples that do these excel.

In Constancy they often Men excel,
That steady Vertue in their Souls do dwell;
She's not so fickle and frail as Men pretend,
But can keep constant to a faithful Friend;
And tho' Man's always alt'ring of his mind,
He says, Inconstancy's in Womankind;
And would perswade us that we engross all
That's either fickle, vain or whimsical.
Man's fancy'd Truth small Vertue doth express;
Our's is Constancy, their's is Stubborness.
In faithful Love our Sex do them out-shine,
And is more constant than the Masculine:
For where is there that Husband that e'er dy'd,
Or ever suffer'd with his loving bride?
But num'rous trains of chast Wives oft expire
With their dear Husbands, wrapt in flaming fire
We'd to the same if Custom did require.
But this is done by Indian Women, who
Do make their Constancy immortal too,
As is their Fame; while happy India yields
More glorious Phoenix than th' Arabian Fields.
The German Women Constancy did show
When Wensberg was Besieg'd, begg'd they might go
Out of the City, with no bigger Packs
Than each of them could carry on their Backs.
The wond'ring world expected they'd have gone
Laded with Treasures from their Native home;
But crossing expectation, each did take
Her Husband, as her burden, on her back;
so sav'd him from intended Death, and she
At once gave him both Life and Liberty.
How many loving Wives have often dy'd
Thro' extreme Grief by their cold Husbands side?
If this ben't Constancy, why then the Sun
Or Earth do not a constant progress run.

. . . .

But hold, I think I should be silent now,
Because a Woman's Soul you do allow.
But had we none, you'd say we had, else you
Could never Damn us at the rate you do.
What, dost thou think thou hast a priv'ledge given,
That those whom thou dost bless, shall mount to heaven?
And those thou cursest, unto hell must go?
And so dost think to fill th' Abyss below
Quite full of Females, hoping there may be
No room for Souls as big with Vice as thee.
But if that thou with such vain hopes should'st die,
I'th' fluid Air thou must not think to fly;
Or enter into Heav'n, thy weight of Sin
Would crush the Damn'd, and so thou'dst enter in.

But hold, I am uncharitable here,
Thou may'st repent, tho' that's a thing I fear.
But if thou should'st repent, why then again,
It would, at best, but mitigate thy pain;
Because thou hast been vile to that degree,
That thy repentance must eternal be.
For wer't thou guilty of no other crime
Than what thou lately puttest into Rhime,
Why that, were there no more offences given,
Were crime enough to shut the gate of Heav'n:
But, put together all that thou dost do,
It will not only shut, but barr it too.

When wise Heav'n made Woman, it design'd
Her for the charming object of Mankind:
And surely Man degen'rate must be,
That doth deny our Native purity.
Nor is there scarce a thing that can be worse,
Than turning of a Blessing to a Curse.
'Tis to make Heav'n mistaken when you say
It meant, at first, what proves another way:
For Woman was created good, and she
Was thought the best of frail Mortality:
An help for man, his greatest good on Earth,
Made for to sympathize his Grief and Mirth;
Then why should man pretend she's worse than hell,
The only plague ot'h world, and in her dwell
All that is base or ill; no, she's not so,
Rather she is the greatest good below;
Most real vertue and true happiness,
His only steady and most constant bliss,

. . . .

Had my Antagonist but spent his time
Making true Verse instead of spightful Rhime,
As a small Poet, he had gain'd some praise,
But now his malice blasts his twig of Bays.
I do not wish you had, for I believe
It is impossible for to deceive
Any with what you write, because that you
Do only insert things supposed true:
And if by supposition I may go,
Then I'll suppose all Men are wicked too,
Since I am sure there are so many so.
And 'cause you have made Whores of all you could,
So, if you durst, you'd say all Women would;
Which words do only argue guilt and spight:
All makes you cheap in ev'ry Mortals sight.
And it doth shew that you have always bin
Only with Women guilty of that Sin.
You ne'er desired, nor were you fit for those,
Whose modest carriage doth their minds disclose,
And, Sir, methinks you do describe so well
The way and manner Bewley enter'd Hell,
As if your love for her had made you go
Down to the black infernal shades below.

But I suppose you never was so near,
Nay, if you had, you scarce would have been here,
For had they seen you, they had kept you there;
Unless they thought, whene'er it was you came,
Your red-hot entrance might encrease the flame
(If burning Hell add to their extreme pain)
And so were glad to turn you off again.

                    .   .   .   .

And that she's all that pious, chast and true,
Heroick, constant, nay and modest too:
The later Vertue is a thing you doubt,
But 'tis cause you ne'er sought to find it out.
You question where there's such a thing or no,
'Tis only 'cause you hope you've lost a foe,
A hated object, yet a stranger too.
I'll speak like you, if such a thing there be,
I'm certain that she doth not dwell with thee.
Thou art Antipodes to that, and all
That's Good, or that we simply Civil call.
From Vertue's yoke thou hast thy self release,
Turn'd Bully, Hector, and a human Beast.
That Beasts do speak, it rarely comes to pass,

Yet you may paralel with Balaam's Ass.
You do describe a Woman so, that one
Would almost think she had the Fiends out-done:
As if at her strange Birth did shine no Star
Or Planet, only Furies in Conjunction were;
And did conspire what mischief they should do,
Each act his part, and her with plagues pursue,
'Tis false in her, yet 'tis summ'd up in you.
You almost would perswade one that you thought
That Providence to a low ebb was brought;
And that to Eve and Jezebel was given
Souls of so great extent, that Heav'n was driven
Into a straight, and liberality
Had made her void of wanting, to supply
These later bodies, she was for'd to take
Their souls asunder, and so numbers make,
And transmigrate them into others, and
Still shift them as she finds the matter stand.
'Tis 'cause they are the worst makes me believe
You must imagine Jezebel and Eve.
But I'm no Pythagorean, to conclude
One Soul could serve for Abraham and Jude:
Or think that Heaven's so bankrupt, or so poor,
But that each body has one soul or more.
I do not find our Sex so near ally'd,
Either in disobedience or in pride,
Unto the 'bove-nam'd Females (for I'm sure
They are refin'd, or else were alwaies pure)
That I must needs conceit their souls the same,
Tho' I confess there's some that merit blame:
But yet their faults only thus much infer,
That we're not made so perfect, but may err;
Which adds much lustre to a vertuous mind,
And 'tis her prudence makes her soul confin'd
Within the bounds of Goodness, for if she
Was all perfection unto that degree,
That 'twas impossible to do amiss,
Then heaven, not she, must have the praise of this.
But she's in such a state as she may fall,
And, without care, her freedom may inthral.
But to keep pure and free in such a case,
Argues each vertue with its proper grace.
And as a Woman's composition is
Most soft and gentle, she has happiness
In that her soul is of that nature too,
And yields to any thing that Heav'n will do;

Takes an impression when 'tis seal'd in heaven,
Turns to a cold refusal, when 'tis given
By any other hand: She's all divine,
And by a splendid lustre doth outshine
All masculine souls, who only seem to be
Made up of pride and their lov'd luxury.

. . . .

Their pride in some small measure I have shown,
But 'tis too great a Task for me alone;
Nor yet more possible I should repeat
The Crimes of Men extravagantly great;
I would not name them, but to let them see
I know they'r bad and odious unto me.
'Tis true, pride makes Men great in their own eyes,
But them proportionable I despise;
And tho' Ambition still aims to be high,
Yet Lust, at best, is but Beastiality;
A Sin with which there's none that can compare,
Not Pride nor Envy, &c. for this doth insnare
Not only those whom it at first inflam'd,
This Sin must have a Part'ner to be sham'd,
And punish'd like himself. Hold, one wont do,
He must have more, for he doth still pursue
The Agents of his Passion; 'tis not Wife,
That mutual Name, can regulate his Life;
And tho' he for his Lust might have a shrow'd,
And there might be Polygamy allow'd,
Yet all his Wives would surely be abhorr'd,
And still some common Lais be ador'd.
Most mortally the Name of Wife they hate,
Yet they will take one as their proper fate,
That they may have a Child legitimate,
To be their Heir, if they have an Estate,
Or else to bear their Names: So for by ends,
They take a Wife, and satisfie their Friends;
Who are desirous that it should be so,
And for that end, perhaps, Estates bestow;

Which, when possess'd, is spent another way;
The spurious Issue do the right betray,
And with their Mother-Strumpets are maintain'd;
The Wife and Children by neglect disdain'd,
Wretched and poor, unto their Friends return,
Having got nothing, unless cause to mourn.
The dire Effects of Lust I cannot tell,

But I suppose they're Catalogu'd in Hell;
And he, perhaps, at last may read it there,
Written in flames, fierce as his own, whilst here.
I could say more, but yet not half that's done
By these strange Creatures, nor is there scarce one
Of these inhumane Beasts that do not die
As bad as Bewley's Pox turns Leprosie,
And Men do catch it by meer phantasie.
Tho' they seem chast and honest, yet it doth
Pursue them, while they swear it with an oath
'Twas only in Company, infected breath
Gave them that Plague, which hastens on their death,
Or else the Scurvy, or some new Disease,
As the base Wretch, or vain Physitian please;
Then a round sum the Surgeon he must have,
To keep Corruption from the threatning grave;
And then 'tis doubled, for to hide the cheat;
(O the sad horrour of debaucht Deceit!)
The Body and Estate together go,
And then the only objects here below,
On which he doth his Charity bestow,
Are Whores and Quacks, and perhaps Pages too
Must have a share, or else they will reveal
What Money doth oblige 'em to conceal.

Sure trusty Stewards of extensive heaven,
When what's for common good is only given
Unto peculiar friends of theirs, who be
Slaves to their lust, friending debauchery;
These are partakers of a great a fate
As those whose boldness turns them reprobate,
And tho' a Hypocrite doth seem to be
A greater sharer of Morality,
And yet methinks they almost seem all one,
One hides, and t'other tells what he hath done;
But if one Devil's better than another,
Then one of these is better than the t'other:
Hypocrisie preheminence should have,
(Tho' it has not the priviledge to save)
Because the Reprobate's example may,
By open Custom, make the rugged way
Seem much more smooth, and a vile common sin
More pardonable look, and so by him
More take example: 'tis he strives to win
Mad Souls, to fill up Hell! But should there be
Nothing e're acted but Hypocrisie,

Yet Man would be as wicked as he is,
And be no nearer to eternal bliss;
For he who's so unsteady, as to take
Example by such Men, should never make
Me to believe, that he was really chast,
And, without pattern, never had imbrac't:
Such kind of force at best, such virtue's weak,
That streight with such a slender stress will break;
And that's no virtue which cannot withstand
A slight temptation at the second hand:
But I believe one might as deeply pry
For't, as the Grecian did for honesty,
And yet find none; and then if Women be
Averse to't too, sure all's iniquity
On this side Heaven, and it with Justice went
Up thither, 'cause here is found no content,
But did regardless and neglected ly,
And with an awful distance was past by.
Instead of hiding their prodigious Acts,
They do reveal, brag of their horrid Facts;
Unless it be some few who hide them, 'cause
They would not seem to violate those laws
Which with their tongues they'r forc'd for to maintain,
Being grave Counsellers or Aldermen,
Or else the Wives Relations are alive,
And then, if known, some other way they'l drive
Their golden wheels, that way doth seem uneven,
Then the Estate most certainly is given
Some other way, or else 'tis setled
As he may never have it to bestow,
Upon his Lusts, and therefore he doth seem
To have a very high and great esteem
For his pretended Joy; but when her friends
Are dead, then he his cursed life defends,
With what they leave; then the unhappy wife,
With her dear children, lead an horrid life,
And the Estate's put to another use,
And their great kindness turn'd to an abuse;
And should I strive their falshood to relate,
Then I should have but Sisiphus his fate,
For Man is so unconstant and untrue,
He's like a shadow which one doth pursue,
Still flies from's word, nay and perfidious too.
An Instance too of Infidelity
We have in Egypt's false King Ptolomy,
Who, tho' he under obligations were,

To secure luckless Pompey from the snare,
Who fled to him for succour, yet base he
Approv'd his Death, and Murderer let go free;
He was inconstant too, or else design'd
The same at first, so alter'd words not mind,
Which is much worse, for when that one doth speak
With a full resolution, for to break
One's word and oath, most surely it must be
A greater crime than an inconstancy,
Which is as great a failing in the soul
As any sin that reason doth controul,
But I designed to be short, so must
Be sure to keep confin'd to what I first
Resolved on, or else I should reprove
These faults which first I ought for to remove;
Therefore, with Brutus, I this point will end,
Who, tho' he ought to have been Caesar's friend,
By being declar'd his Heir, yet it was he
Was the first actor in his tragedy:
Perfidious, and ungrateful, and untrue
He was at once, nay and disloyal too:
A thousand Instances there might be brought,
(Not far fetch'd neither, tho' more dearly bought)
To prove that Man more false than Woman is,
Far more unconstant, nay perfidious:
But these are Crimes which hell, (I'm sure not heaven)
As they pretend, hath in peculiar given
Unto our Sex, but that's as false as they,
And that's more false than any one can say.
All Pride and Lust too to our charge they lay,
As if in sin we all were so sublime
As to monopolize each hainous crime;
Nay, Woman now is made the Scape-goat, and
'Tis she must bear the sins of all the land:
But I believe there's not a Priest that can
Make an atonement for one single man,
Nay, it is well if he himself can bring
An humble, pious heart for th' offering;
A thing which ought to be inseparable
To men o'th' Gown and of the Sacred Table;
Yet it is sometimes wanting, and they be
Too often sharers of Impiety:
But howsoever the strange World now thrives,
I must not look into my Teachers lives,
But now methinks the World doth seem to be
Nought but confusion and degeneracy,

Each Man's so eager of each fatal sin,
As if he fear'd he should not do't agen;
Yet still his soul is black, he is the same
At all times, tho' he doth not act all flame,
Because he opportunity doth want,
And to him always there is not a grant
Of Objects for to exercise his will,
And for to shew his great and mighty skill
In Sciences all diabolical,
But when he meets with those which we do call
Base and unjust, why then his part he acts
Most willingly, and then with hell contracts
To do the next thing that they should require;
And being thus inflam'd with hellish fire,
He yields to any thing it doth desire,
Unless 'twere possible for hell to say,
They should be good, for then they'd disobey.
I am not sorry you do Females hate,
But rather deem ourselves more fortunate,
Because I find, when you'r right understood,
You are at enmity with all that's good,
And should you love them, I should think they were
A growing bad, but still keep as you are:
I need not bid you, for you must I'm sure,
And in your present wretched state indure;
'Tis as impossible you should be true,
As for a Woman to act like to you,
Which I am sure will not accomplish'd be,
Till heaven's turn'd hell, and that's repugnancy;
When vice turns vertue, then 'tis you shall have
A share of that which makes most Females brave;
Which transmutations I am sure can't be;
So thou must lie in vast eternity,
With prospect of thy endless misery,
When Woman, your imagin'd Fiend, shall live
Bless'd with the Joys that Heaven can always give.

FINIS.

FROM
POEMS ON SEVERAL OCCASIONS

The Liberty

Shall I be one, of those obsequious Fools,
    That square there lives, by Customs scanty Rules;
Condemn'd for ever, to the puny Curse,
Of Precepts taught, at Boarding-school, or Nurse,
That all the business of my Life must be,
Foolish, dull Trifling, Formality.
Confin'd to a strict Magick complaisance,
And round a Circle, of nice visits Dance,
Nor for my Life beyond the Chalk advance:
The Devil Censure, stands to guard the same,
One step awry, he tears my ventrous Fame.
So when my Friends, in a facetious Vein,
With Mirth and Wit, a while can entertain;
Tho' ne'er so pleasant, yet I must not stay,
If a commanding Clock, bids me away:
But with a sudden start, as in a Fright,
I must be gone indeed, 'tis after Eight.
Sure these restraints, with such regret we bear,
That dreaded Censure, can't be more severe,
Which has no Terror, if we did not fear;
But let the Bug-bear, timerous Infants fright,
I'll not be scar'd, from Innocent delight:
Whatever is not vicious, I dare do,
I'll never to the Idol Custom bow,
Unless it suits with my own Humour too.
Some boast their Fetters, of Formality,
Fancy they ornamental Bracelets be,
I'm sure their Gyves, and Manacles to me.
To their dull fulsome Rules, I'd not be ty'd,
For all the Flattery that exalts their Pride:
My Sexs forbids, I should my Silence break,
I lose my Jest, cause Women must not speak.
Mysteries must not be, with my search Prophan'd,
My Closet not with books, but Sweat-meats cram'd
A little China, to advance the Show,
My Prayer Book, and seven Champions, or so.
My Pen if ever us'd imploy'd must be,

In lofty Themes of useful Houswifery,
Transcribing old Receipts of Cookery:
And what is necessary 'mongst the rest,
Good Cures for Agues, and a cancer'd Breast,
But I can't here, write my *Probatum est.*
My daring Pen, will bolder Sallies make,
And like my self, an uncheck'd freedom take;
Not chain'd to the nice Order of my Sex,
And with restraints my wishing Soul perplex:
I'll blush at Sin, and not what some call Shame,
Secure my Virtue, slight precarious Fame.
This Courage speaks me, Brave, 'tis surely worse,
To keep those Rules, which privately we Curse:
And I'll appeal, to all the formal Saints,
With what reluctance they indure restraints.

The Emulation.

Say Tyrant Custom, why must we obey,
 The impositions of thy haughty Sway;
From the first dawn of Life, unto the Grave,
Poor Womankind's in every State, a Slave.
The Nurse, the Mistress, Parent and the Swain,
For Love she must, there's none escape that Pain;
Then comes the last, the fatal Slavery,
The Husband with insulting Tyranny
Can have ill Manners justify'd by Law;
For Men all join to keep the Wife in awe.
Moses who first our Freedom did rebuke,
Was Marry'd when he writ the Pentateuch;
They're Wise to keep us Slaves, for well they know,
If we were loose, we soon should make them, so.
We yeild like vanquish'd Kings whom Fetters bind,
When chance of War is to Usurpers kind;
Submit in Form; but they'd our Thoughts controul,
And lay restraints on the impassive Soul:
They fear we should excel their sluggish Parts,
Should we attempt the Sciences and Arts.
Pretend they were design'd for them alone,
So keep us Fools to raise their own Renown;
Thus Priests of old their Grandeur to maintain,
Cry'd vulgar Eyes would sacred Laws Prophane.
So kept the Mysteries behind a Screen,
There Homage and the Name were lost had they been seen:
But in this blessed Age, such Freedom's given,
That every Man explains the Will of Heaven;

And shall we Women now sit tamely by,
Make no excursions in Philosophy,
Or grace our Thoughts in tuneful Poetry?
We will our Rights in Learning's World maintain,
Wits Empire, now, shall know a Female Reign;
Come all ye Fair, the great Attempt improve,
Divinely imitate the Realms above:
There's ten celestial Females govern Wit,
And but two Gods that dare pretend to it;
And shall these finite Males reverse their Rules,
No, we'll be Wits, and then Men must be Fools.

———————————————— • ————————————————

PRIMARY SOURCES
The Female Advocate, or, an Answere to a Late Satyr against the Pride, Lust and Inconstancy, etc., of Woman. London: John Raylor, 1686. 2d ed. London, 1687. Photo-reprint of the 1687 edition with an introduction by Felicity Nussbaum. William Andrews Clark Memorial Library, University of California, Los Angeles, 1976.
Poems on Several Occasions, together with a pastoral. London: J. Nutt, 1703.

RELATED SOURCES
Anderson, Paul Bunyan. "Mistress Delarivière Manley's Biography." *Modern Philology,* November 1934: 271–72.
Architectural and Archaeological Society. *Records of Buckinghamshire.* Aylesbury: G. T. De Fraine, "Bucks Herald" Office, 1903. Vol. 8, p. 34.
Gentleman's Magazine 50 (1780): 562; 51 (1781): 121, 455
H. J. (John Heydon). *The English Physicians Guide: or a Holy Guide. . . .* London J. M. for Samuel Ferris, 1662.
Manley, Delarivière. *The Lady's Pacquet Broke Open.* London, 1707. Letters V– IX concern correspondence between Manley and Egerton.
Medoff, Jeslyn. "New Light on Sarah Fyge (Field, Egerton)." *Tulsa Studies in Women's Literature* 1, 2 (1982): 155–75.

JANE BARKER
fl. 1688 *and* 1723

Jane Barker's father was a Royalist who received an annual grant of eighty pounds from Charles I from 1675 onward. He may have retired to the country after he lost his court position. Her mother, whose brother Colonel William Connock fought for James II, is reputed to have been descended from a Cornish Royalist family. Anticipating the life of a "country gentlewoman" for her daughter, she may have removed Jane Barker from a school in Putney. Jane Barker was subsequently educated by a country clergyman in Wilsthorp village, near Stamford in Lincolnshire.

As a House of Stuart supporter she probably left England for France after James II fled in 1688. According to G. S. Gibbons, "she became a very keen Roman Catholic and retired to the Court of St. Germain where she composed poems until 1701." Between 1685 and 1700 she found herself going blind and while at court may have been obliged to dictate her writings.

By 1715 it is known that she had returned to Lincolnshire, as Gibbons discovered her name in a list of Roman Catholic Non-Jurors as "Jane Barker of Wilsthorp, spinster." She had an estate of under fifty pounds annual value as a result of her father's royal grant. Around 1718 in London she is alleged to have engaged in secret political correspondence with the exiled Jacobite hero, James Butler, Duke of Ormond.

Barker's first literary efforts may have been for a small provincial coterie. In *A Patch-Work Screen for the Ladies* (1723), she talks of her admiration for Katherine Philips, who was celebrated for her Society of Friendship among Commonwealth and Restoration contemporaries. Barker's praise of Philips's poems, "so interwoven with Vertue and Honour, that each line was like a Ladder to climb . . . to Heaven," indicates that she initially took Philips as an unofficial mentor.

Published in 1688, *Poetical Recreations: Consisting of Original Poems, Songs, Odes, etc.,* a collective venture "occasionally written by Mrs. Jane Barker . . . [and] by several gentlemen of the Universities, and others" might have been an attempt to emulate the work of Philips's celebrated circle. The volume's complimentary notes and poems to Barker attest to her popularity. Her second work was *Love's Intrigues; or, the History of the Amours of Bosvil and Galesia* (1713), told as a story from Galesia to a supportive female friend, Lucasia. In this work, with its echo of the Catholic confessional idiom, Galesia's sense of independence and constant self-scrutiny eventually enable her to see through the insincere Bosvil. In "To the Reader," which prefaces *A Patch-Work Screen* (1723), Barker responds to questions by a hypothetical reader about the title of the work by saying that "I ought to say something in Favour of Patch-Work, the better to recommend it to my Female Readers, as well in their Discourse, as their Needle-Work: . . . Whenever one sees a set of Ladies together, their Sentiments are as differently mix'd as the Patches in their Work, . . . this Disunion [is like] . . . the clashing of Atoms, which at last united to compose this glorious Fabrick of the Universe." Frequently she used her seemingly autobiographical narratives to explain her choice of art, study, and the single life over marriage.

Barker also wrote *Exilius; or The Banished Roman* (1715) and *The Lining for the Patch-Work Screen: Design'd for the Farther Entertainment of the Ladies* (1726). In the latter Barker accords primacy to the process of Galesia's consciousness and positively presents, here and elsewhere, a woman's resistance to convention. The extracted story focusses on the ambiguity of the wife's behavior, but readers are left with an unmistakable impression of female friendship. The story overtly challenges patriarchal norms about marriage and employer/employee relationships, as do the poems, which attach emphatic significance to female friendship and the single life. In one of the poems not included, "A Virgin Life," she explicitly proclaims her dislike of patriarchal "Suffer me not to fall into the Pow'rs of Men's almost Omnipotent Amours." Her aim is "To Serve her God, enjoy her Books and Friends."

From *Poetical Recreations*

On the DEATH of my Dear Friend
and Play-fellow, Mrs. E. D. having
Dream'd the night before I heard
thereof, that I had lost a Pearl.

I Dream'd I lost a Pearl, and so it prov'd;
I lost a Friend much above Pearls belov'd:
A Pearl perhaps adorns some outward part,
but Friendship decks each corner of the heart:
Friendship's a Gem, whose Lustre do's out-shine
All that's below the heav'nly Crystaline:
Friendship is that mysterious thing alone,

SOURCE: Selections from *Poetical Recreations* are taken from the printed volume in the Henry E. Huntington Library, no. 446158. The selection from *A Patch-Work Screen* comes from a photo-reprint (facsimile) edition, published by Garland Publishing "from a copy in the possession of the publishers."

Which can unite, and make two Hearts but one;
It purifies our Love, and makes it flow
I'th' clearest stream that's found in Love below;
It sublimates the Soul, and makes it move
Towards Perfection and Celestial Love.
We had no by-designs, nor hop'd to get
Each by the other place amongst the great;
Nor Riches hop'd, nor Poverty we fear'd,
'Twas Innocence in both, which both rever'd.
Witness this truth the Wilsthorp-Fields, where we
So oft enjoy'd a harmless Luxurie;
Where we indulg'd our easie Appetites,
With Pocket-Apples, Plumbs, and such delights.
Then we contriv'd to spend the rest o'th' day,
In making Chaplets, or at Check-stone play;

The Anchorite in Scipina

Ah, happy are we Anchorites that know
Not Women's Ebbs, nor when their love will Flow
We know no storms that rage in women's Breasts,
But here in quiet build our Halcyon Nests;
Where we deceitfull Calm our Faith beguiles,
No cruel frowns, nor yet more cruel smiles;
No rising Wave of Fate our hopes advance;
Nor fear we fathomless despair of Chance;
But our strong Minds, like rocks, their Firmness prove,
Defying both the Storms of Fate and Love.

FROM

A PATCH-WORK SCREEN
FOR THE LADIES;

TO THE READER.

My Two former Volumes of NOVELS having met with a favourable
Reception, (much beyond their Desert) encourages me to
perform my Promise in pursuing The Sequel of Galesia's Story.*

---

* The last NOVEL in Mrs. Barker's 2d. Volume.

But I doubt my Reader will say, Why so long about it? And why a HISTORY reduc'd into Patches? especially since HISTORIES at Large are so Fashionable 'n this Age; viz. Robinson Crusoe, and Moll Flanders; Colonel Jack, and Sally Salisbury; with many other Heroes and Heroines? Why, truly, as to the First, I had lost my GALESIA, she being gone from St. Germains, and I retir'd into an obscure Corner of the World. As to the Second, you'll find in the following Pages, by what Steps and Means it was framed into this Method. And now, having given you this Account, I think I ought to say something in Favour of Patch-Work, the better to recommend it to my Female Readers, as well in their Discourse, as their Needle-Work: Which I might do with Justice, if my Genius were capable: But indeed, I am not much of an Historian; but in the little I have read, I do not remember any thing recorded relating to Patch-Work, since the Patriarch Joseph, (whose Garment was of sundry Colours) by which means it has not been common in all Ages; and 'tis certain, the Uncommonness of any Fashion, renders it acceptable to the Ladies.

And I do not know but this may have been the chief Reason why our Ladies, in this latter Age, have pleas'd themselves with this sort of Entertainment; for, whenever one sees a Set of Ladies together, their Sentiments are as differently mix'd as the Patches in their Work: To wit, Whigs and Tories, High-Church and Low-Church, Jacobites and Williamites, and many more Distinctions, which they divide and sub-divide, 'till at last they make this Dis-union meet in an harmonious Tea-Table Entertainment. This puts me in mind of what I have heard some Philosophers assert, about the Clashing of Atoms, which at last united to compose this glorious Fabrick of the UNIVERSE.

Forgive me, kind Reader, for carrying the Metaphor too high; by which means I am out of my Sphere, and so can say nothing of the Male Patch-Workers; for my high Flight in Favour of the Ladies, made a mere Icarus of me, melted my Wings, and tumbled me Headlong down, I know now where. Nevertheless my Fall was amongst a joyful Throng of People of all Ages, Sexes, and Conditions! who were rejoycing at a wonderful Piece of Patch-Work they had in Hand; the Nature of which was such, as was to compose (as it were) a New Creation, where all Sorts of People were to be Happy, as if they had never been the Off-spring of fallen Adam.

I was greatly rejoyc'd at this my Fall, when I found my self amongst these happy Undertakers, and hop'd to unite my-self in their Confraternity; but they finding some Manuscript Ballads in my Pocket, rejected me as one of that Race of Mortals who live on a certain barren Mountain 'till they are turn'd into Camelions; so I was forc'd to get away, every one hunching and pushing me, with Scorn and Derision. However, as the Sequel prov'd, I had no small Reason to rejoice at being thus used; for soon after, their Patch-Work Scheme, by carrying the Point too high, was blown up about their Ears, and vanish'd into Smoke and Confusion; to the utter Ruin of many Thousands of the Unhappy Creatures therein concern'd.

When I was got out of this Throng into the open Field, I met with the poor Galesia, walking to stretch her Legs, having been long sitting at her Work. With her I renew'd my Old Acquaintance; and so came to know all this Story of her Patch-Work: Which if you like, I will get the remaining Part of the Screen; for they are still at Work: And, upon my Word, I am glad to find the Ladies of This Age, wiser than Those of the Former; when the working of Point and curious Embroidery, was so troublesome, that they cou'd not take Snuff in Repose, for fear of soiling their Work: But in Patch-Work there is no Harm done; a smear'd Finger does not add a Spot to a Patch, or a Shade to a Light-Colour: Besides, those curious Works were pernicious to the Eyes; they cou'd not see the Danger themselves and their Posterity might be in, a Thousand Years hence, about I know not what—But I will inquire against the next Edition; therefore, be sure to buy these Patches up quickly, if you intend to know the Secret; thereby you'll greatly oblige the Bookseller, and, in some degree, the Author. Who is,

Your humble Servant,
Jane Barker.

The Unaccountable Wife.

This Gentleman, said Galesia, had married a young Gentlewoman of Distinction, against the Consent of her Friends; which she accomplish'd by the Help of her Mother's Maid-Servant. To say the Truth, though her Birth was very considerable, yet her Person was not at all agreeable; and her Fortune but indifferent: her Parents, I suppose, thinking, that more than just enough to support her, would but betray her to an unhappy Marriage. In short, married she was to the foresaid young Man, whose Person was truly handsome; and with Part of her Fortune he plac'd himself in the Army, bestow'd another Part in furnishing her a house, and so liv'd very decently; and notwithstanding her indifferent Person, he had Children by her, though they did not live long. Thus they made a pretty handsome Shift in the World, 'till a vile Wretch, her Servant, overturn'd all; as follows. This Servant, whether she was a Creature of her Master's before she came to her Mistress, is not known; but she became very fruitful, and had every Year a Child; pretending that she was privately married to an Apprentice. Whether the Wife knew the whole of the Matter, or was impos'd upon, is uncertain; but which way soever it was, she was extremely kind to this Woman, to a degree unheard of; became a perfect Slave to her, and, as if she was the Servant, instead of the Mistress, did all the Household-Work, made the Bed, clean'd the House, wash'd the Dishes; nay, farther than so, got up in the Morning, scour'd the Irons, made the fire, &c. leaving this vile Strumpet in Bed with her Husband; for they lay all Three together every Night. All this her Friends knew, or at least suspected; but thought it Complaisance, not Choice in her; and that she consider'd her own Imperfections, and Deformity; and therefore, was willing to take no Notice of her Husband's Fancy in the Embraces of this Woman her Servant. But the Sequel opens quite another Scene: And now I come to that Part of the Story, where he came to my Mother. His Business was, to desire her to come to his Wife, and endeavour to persuade her to part with this Woman; For, said he, she has already Three Children living, and God knows how many more she may have: Which indeed, Madam, said he, is a Charge my little Substance is not able to sustain; and I have been using all Endeavours to persuade my Wife to part with her, but cannot prevail: Wherefore I beg you, as a Friend, Relation, and her Senior in Years, to come, and lay before her the Reasonableness of what I desire, and the Ridiculousness of her proceeding. Good Heaven! said my Mother, can you think thus to bore my Nose with a Cushion? Can you imagine me so stupid, as to believe your Wife can persist in such a condition of Nature? It is impossible a Wife should oppose her Husband's Desire in parting with such a Woman. Madam, reply'd he, I beg you once more to be so good as to come to my Wife, and then condemn me if I have advanc'd a Falshood. Well, reply'd my Mother, I will come; though I doubt not but upon due Inspection, the whole, will prove a Farce compos'd amongst you, in which your Wife is to act her Part just as you between you think fit to teach her; which she, out of Fear, or some other Delusion, is to perform. But he averr'd again and again, that, without Fraud or Trick, the Thing was as he said. In short, my Mother went; and there she found the Servant sitting in a handsome Velvet Chair, dress'd up in very good lac'd Linnen, having clean Gloves on her Hands, and the Wife washing the Dishes. This sight put my Mother into such a violent Passion, that she had much ado to refrain from laying Hands on her. However, she most vehemently chid the Mistress; telling her, that she offended God, disgrac'd her Family, scandaliz'd her Neighbours, and was a Shame to Woman-kind. All which she return'd with virulent Words; amongst other Things, she stood Buff in Favour of that Woman; saying, That she had been not only a faithful Servant, but the best of Friends, and those that desir'd to remove such a Friend from her, deserved not the Name of Friends, neither did she desire they should come into her House: All which she utter'd with such an Air of Vehemency, that there was no Room left to doubt of the Sincerity of her Words; but that all proceeded from an Interiour thoroughly degenerated. All which my Mother related to me with great Amazement: But withal, told me, that she would have me go to her on the Morrow; and with calm and friendly Words, endeavour to persuade her to Reason; for, said she, I was in a Passion at the disagreeable View; but you, who have naturally more Patience than my-self, pray put on the best Resolutions you can to keep your Temper, whatsoever Provocations shall occur. This instructed, thus resolved, I went next Day, hoping that a Night's Repose would calm the Storm my Mother's Anger might have rais'd. But when I came, I found it all the same: Though I took her apart, and with the utmost Mildness, persuaded her, and us'd the best Reasons I could think on to inforce those Persuasions, yet all was in vain; and she said, We all join'd with her Husband to make her miseerable, by removing from her, the only Friend she had in the World; and passionately swore by Him that made her, that if we combin'd to send that Woman away, she would go with her. I would try that, reply'd I, were I in your Husband's Place: At which her Passion redoubled; and she, with violent Oaths, repeated her Resolution; desiring, that her Friends would meddle with their own Business, and let her alone, to remain in Quiet in her house, and not come to give her Disturbance. After these uncouth Compliments, I left her, carrying with me the greatest Amazement possible. After this, the Husband came to us, and ask'd, If we did not find true what he had told us? Indeed, replied I, true, and doubly true; such a Truth as I believe never was in the World before, nor never will be again. In this Case, said he, What would you counsel me to do? Truly, said my Mother, it is hard to advise; for to let the Woman live there still, is not proper; nor can your Circumstances undergo the Charge: And if your Wife should do as she says, and go with her; I should in some Degree be accessary to the parting Man and Wife. I would venture, said I, for when it comes to the Push, I warrant her she will not go. Hereupon the Man said he would try; and accordingly, hired a Place in a Waggon to carry the Creature into her own Country; hoping, as I suppose, that his Wife would have rested herself contented with him, when the Woman had been gone; but instead thereof, she acted as she said, and went along with her.

This Transaction was so extraordinary, that every-body was amazed at it; and when they had been gone some time, there arose a Murmuring, amongst Friends, Neighbours and Acquaintance, as if he had made his Wife away; and when he told them the Manner of her Departure, they would not believe him, the thing in itself being so incredible.

But as we will leave him to make his Party good, as well as he can, amidst the Censure of his Neighbours, the Threats of her Friends, and the Ridicule of his Acquaintance; and follow the Travellers, into the Country whither they were gone.

They arrived safe at the Woman's Father's, where they found as kind Reception as a poor Cottage could afford; and a very poor one it was, there being no Light but what came in at the Door, no Food but from the Hands of Charity, nor Fewel but what they pilfer'd from their Neighbours Hedges.

Now what this unaccountable Creature thought of this kind of Being, is unknown, or what Measures she and her Companion thought to take, or what Schemes they form'd to themselves, is not conceivable: But whatever they were, the discreet Neighbourhood put a Period to their Projects; for they got a Warrant to have them before a Justice, in order to prevent a Parish Charge; there being two Children there already, which they had sent some time before; and now two helpless Women being come, they knew not where the Charge might light, and therefore proceeded as aforesaid. It happen'd as the Constable was conducting them to the Justice, with a Mob at their Heels, that they pass'd by the House of a Lady of Quality, who looking out of her Window, saw in the midst of this Throng, this unfortunate Wife, whom she immediately knew to be the Daughter of her Friend; knew to be the Child of an honourable Family. It is impossible to describe what Amazement seiz'd her: She call'd out to the Constable and other Neighbours there, bidding them bring that Gentlewoman to her, which they immediately did. This good Lady, out of Respect to her old Friends, a worthy Family, bid them discharge her, telling them, That her-self would be bound that she should be no Parish Charge; so took her into her house, treated her kindly, and offer'd her all she could do on such an Occasion: For all which she return'd the Lady but cold Thanks, and begg'd her Ladyship's Assistance to convey her to London along with the other Woman, who, she said, was the truest Friend in the World. The Lady knowing nothing of her Story, with much Goodness provided for her Departure, together with her Companion. In this manner, loaden with Disgrace, they came back to London, to her Husband, from whom, no doubt, she found Reproaches suitable to her Folly.

Long it was not, e'er Deth made a true and substantial Separation, by carrying the Husband into the other World. Now was the time to make manifest, whether Promises, Flatteries or Threatnings had made her act the foresaid Scene: But it appear'd all voluntary; for when he was dead, her Friends and Relations invited and persuaded her to leave that Creature and her Children, and come to live with them, suitable to her Birth and Education. But all in vain; she absolutely adher'd to this Woman and her Children, to the last Degree of Folly; insomuch, that being reduc'd to Poverty, she begg'd in the Streets to support them. At last, some Friend of her Family told the Queen of the distressed way she was in; and in some Degree, how it came to pass, that neither her dead Husband nor her Relations might be blameable. The Queen, with much Goodness, told her Friend, That if she would leave that Woman, and go live with some Relation, she would take Care she should not want; and withal sent her Five Guineas, as an Earnest of a Monthly Pension; but notwithstanding, this infatuated Crature refus'd the Queen's Favour, rather than part with this Family: And so, for their Support, begg'd in the Streets, the remainder of her Days.

Sure, said the Lady, This poor Creature was under some Spell or Inchantment, or she could never have persisted, in so strange a manner, to oppose her Husband, and all her nearest Friends, and even her Sovereign. As they were descanting on this Subject, a Servant came and told them, that all was ready in the Arbour; and that the Gentlemen having finish'd their Bowl of Punch, were attending their coming, to share with them in a Dish of Tea, and Welsh Flummery.

Accordingly, the Ladies went thither, where they were saluted with a most pleasant consort of chirping Musicians, whose wild Notes, in different Strains, set forth the Glory of their great Creator, exciting the whole

Company to certain Acts of Joy and Thanksgiving: Amongst which Quire, none seem'd so harmonious as the soft Strains of the delightful Philomel, whose various Notes ingag'd every one's Attention; insomuch that the Lady call'd to her Page, to sing that old Song, the Words of which held due Measure with the Tunes and different changes of the Nightingale.

———————————————— • ————————————————

PRIMARY SOURCES

Poetical Recreations: consisting of Original Poems, Songs, Odes, etc. With Several New Translations. In Two Parts. Part I. Occasionally Written by Mrs. Jane Barker. Part II. By Several Gentlemen of the Universities, and Others. London: printed for Benjamin Crayle, 1688.

A Patch-Work Screen for the Ladies, or, Love and Virtue recommended: in a Collection of Instructive Novels, Related After a Manner Entirely New, and Interspersed with Rural Poems, describing the Innocence of a Country-Life. London, 1723. Reprinted in *Foundations of the Novel,* vol. 39, edited by Josephine Grieder. New York: Garland Publishing, 1973.

RELATED SOURCES

Gibbons, G. S. "Mrs. Jane Barker." *Notes and Queries* 12, s. 11 (1922): 278–79.

McBurney, William H. "Edmund Curll, Mrs. Jane Barker, and the English Novel." *Philological Quarterly* 37 (1958): 385–99.

Richetti, John J. *Popular Fiction Before Richardson: Narrative Patterns 1700–1739.* Oxford: Clarendon Press, 1969.

MARY ASTELL
1666–1731

The daughter of Newcastle coal merchant families on both sides, Mary Astell is said to have been educated by a clergyman uncle, Ralph Astell. Sometime around 1688 she moved to Chelsea, South London.

Her best-known writing remains *A Serious Proposal to the Ladies, . . . By a Lover of Her Sex* (1694), with Part 2 published in 1697. This work stamps Astell as the first self-avowed, sustained feminist polemicist in English. Her authorship, although anonymous, was widely known. When her plan was attacked as "Romanish" because the proposal called for a religious retirement for females somewhat akin to a Roman Catholic nunnery, she defended it by citing the need of females for spiritual and intellectual nourishment outside a male-dominated society. She geared her plan toward wealthy, upper-class women who sought a permanent alternative to life in a patriarchal society. Astell argued that education was the natural right of all thinking people and that marriage prospects should not be treated unthinkingly. While her ideas and their implementation were not intended to train women for a waged occupation in the outside world, Astell's educational proposals theoretically empowered women to reason out their disadvantaged situation in society. Moreover, the establishment by Astell (and some friends) of a girls' charity school in Chelsea suggests that she also believed that laboring women were entitled to receive some instruction.

Astell's tract on marriage, *Some Reflections upon Marriage,* was published in 1700. The appendix (originally the preface to the third edition, 1706), contributes powerfully to the tradition of feminist polemic. All are equal, Astell insists, and cites humanity's descent (including Christ's) through women. Astell explains that she wrote it after reading an "Account of an unhappy Marriage" which turned out to be that of her Chelsea neighbor, the Duchess of Mazarin, niece of Cardinal Mazarin and a victim of forced marriage. Although she suggests that "Devotion is the proper remedy . . . [for] Domestick Troubles," a course the Duchess did not pursue, Astell's sympathy clearly lies with women subjected to unhappy marriages. Since the Duchess died in 1699, it seems likely that Astell was posthumously defending the Duchess's beleaguered reputation, another tribute to her feminist consciousness.

Astell's other writings include *The Christian Religion as Profess'd by a Daughter of the Church* (1705), and *Letters Concerning the Love of God* (1695), a long epistolary debate with her friend John Norris, Anglican divine and Rector of Bemerton, that she dedicated to her friend, Lady Catherine Jones.

An orthodox Anglican and a Tory who never married, moving mostly in female circles, Astell counted Lady Elizabeth Hastings, Elizabeth Elstob, and the younger Lady Mary Wortley Montagu among her friends and acquaintances. Both Lady Mary Chudleigh and Elizabeth Thomas, writers with whom Astell was acquainted, acknowledged her influence in laudatory poems. However once, after feeling snubbed by Astell's "haughty carriage," Thomas did concede that Astell "who has no certain subsistence may be allowed to improve a Friendship with those that have." Thomas's comment indicates not only Astell's stature and recognition by women writers about their collective economic difficulties, but also their connections and overlapping circles. One contemporary, Thomas Birch, records that Astell lived for many years at Chelsea with Lady Catherine Jones.

The excerpts indicate her support for female education, her subtly and deftly argued resistance to the quality of marriage for most women, the necessity for resistance to tyranny, and the strength of female friendships.

A SERIOUS PROPOSAL
TO THE LADIES.

Ladies,
Since the Profitable Adventures that have gone abroad in the World have met with so great Encouragement, tho' the highest advantage they can propose, is an uncertain Lot for such matters as Opinion, not real worth, gives a value to; things which if obtain'd are as flitting and fickle as that Chance which is to dispose of them; I therefore persuade my self, you

SOURCE: The selections from *A Serious Proposal*... come from the Source Book Press reprint of the fourth edition, 1701. This excerpt from a modern republication now out of print may have corrupt readings, it has not been checked against the original. The selection from *Some Reflections* ... is taken from the original in the Henry E. Huntington Library fifth edition, 1730, shelf no. 352787. The appendix of 1730 was originally the preface to the third edition, 1706. (I thank Ruth Perry for suggesting this selection.) The Preface to the Embassy Letters is reprinted in *The Complete Letters to Lady Mary Wortley Montagu*, Vol. 1, and is stated by the modern editor to be a republication of the 1701 edition with new type and, in Part II, corrections based on original errata.

will not be less kind to a Proposition that comes attended with more certain and substantial Gain; whose only design is to improve your Charms and heighten your Value, by suffering you no longer to be cheap and contemptible. Its aim is to fix that Beauty, to make it lasting and permanent, which Nature with all the helps of Art cannot secure, and to place it out of the reach of Sickness and Old Age, by transferring it from a corruptible Body to an immortal Mind. An obliging Design, which wou'd procure them inward Beauty, to whom Nature has unkindly denied the outward, and not permit those Ladies who have comely Bodies, to tarnish their Glory with deformed Souls. Wou'd have you all be Wits, or what is better, Wise. Raise you above the Vulgar by something more truly illustrious, than a sounding Title or a great Estate. Wou'd excite in you a generous Emulation to excel in the best things, and not in such Trifles as every mean person who has but Money enough may purchase as well as you. Not suffer you to take up with the low thought of distinguishing your selves by any thing that is not truly valuable, and procure you such Ornaments as all the Treasures of the Indies are not able to purchase. Wou'd help you to surpass the Men as much in Vertue and Ingenuity, as you do in Beauty, that you may not only be as lovely, but as wise as Angels. Exalt and Establish your Fame, more than the best wrought Poems and loudest Panegyricks, by ennobling your Minds with such Graces as really deserve it. And instead of the Fustian Complements and Fulsome Flatteries of your Admirers, obtain for you the Plaudit of Good Men and Angels, and the approbation of Him who cannot err. In a word, render you the Glory and Blessing of the present Age, and the Admiration and Pattern of the next. And sure, I shall not need many words to persuade you to close with this Proposal. The very offer is a sufficient inducement, nor does it need the set-off's of Rhetorick to recommend it, were I capable, which yet I am not, of applying them with the greatest force. Since you can't be so unkind to your selves, as to refuse you real Interest, I only entreat you to be so wise as to examine wherein it consists; for nothing is of worse consequence than to be deceiv'd in a matter of so great concern. 'Tis as little beneath your Grandeur as your Prudence, to examine curiously what is in this case offer'd you, and to take care that cheating Hucksters don't impose upon you with deceitful Ware. This is a Matter infinitely more worthy your Debates, than what Colours are most agreeable, or what's the Dress becomes you best. Your Glass will not do you half so much service as a serious reflection on your own Minds, which will discover Irregularities more worthy your Correction, and keep you from being either too much elated or depress'd by the Representations of the other. 'Twill not be near so advantageous to consult with your Dancing Master as with your own Thoughts, how you may with greatest exactness tread in the Paths of Vertue, which has certainly the most attractive Air, and Wisdom the most graceful and becoming Mien: Let these attend you, and your Carriage will be always well compos'd, and ev'ry thing you do will carry its Charm with it. No solicitude in the adornation of your selves is discommended, provided you imploy your care about that which is really your self, and do not neglect that particle of Divinity within you, which must survive, and may (if you please) be happy and perfect, when it's unsuitable and much inferiour Companion is mouldring into Dust. Neither will any pleasure be denied you, who are only desir'd not to catch at the Shadow and let the Substance go. You may be as ambitious as you please, so you aspire to the best things, and contend with your Neighbours as much as you can, that they may not out do you in any commendable Quality. Let it never be said, That they to whom pre-eminence is so very agreeable, can be tamely content that others shou'd surpass them in this, and precede them in a better World! Remember, I pray you, the famous Women of former Ages, the Orinda's of late, and the more Modern Heroins, and blush to think how much is now, and will hereafter be said of them, when you your selves (as great a Figure as you make) must be buried in silence and forgetfulness! Shall your Emulation fail there only where 'tis commendable? Why are you so preposterously humble, as not to contend for one of the highest Mansions in the Court of Heav'n? Believe me, Ladies, this is the only Place worth contending for, you are neither better nor worse in your selves for going before, or coming after now, but you are really so much the better, by how much the higher your station is in an Orb of Glory.

When a poor Young Lady is taught to value her self on nothing but her Cloaths, and to think she's very fine when well accoutred; When she hears say, that 'tis Wisdom enough for her to know how to dress her self, that she may become amiable in his eyes, to whom it appertains to be knowing and learned; who can blame her if she lay out her Industry and Money on such Accomplishments, and sometimes extends it farther than her misinformer desires she should? When she sees the vain and the gay, making Parade in the World and attended with the Courtship and admiration of the gazing herd, no wonder that her tender Eyes are dazled with the Pageantry, and wanting Judgment to pass a due Estimate on them and their Admirers, longs to be such a fine and celebrated thing as they? What tho' she be sometimes told of another World, she has however a more lively perception of this, and may well think, that if her Instructors were in earnest when they tell her of hereafter, they would not be so busied and concerned about what happens here. She is it may be, taught the Principles and Duties of Religion, but not Acquainted with the Reasons and Grounds of them; being told 'tis enough for her to believe, to examine why, and wherefore, belongs not to her. And therefore, though her Piety may be tall and spreading, yet because it wants Foundation and Root, the first rude Temptation overthrows and blasts it, or perhaps the short liv'd Gourd decays and withers of its own accord. But why should she be blamed for setting no great value on her Soul, whose noblest Faculty her Understanding is render'd useless to her? Or censur'd for relinquishing a course of Life, whose Prerogatives she was never acquainted with, and tho highly reasonable in it self, was put upon the embracing it with as little reason as she now forsakes it? For if her Religion it self be taken up as the Mode of the Country, 'tis no strange thing that she lays it down again in conformity to the Fashion. Whereas she whose Reason is suffer'd to display it self, to inquire into the grounds and Motives of Religion, to make a disquisition of its Graces and search out its hidden Beauties; who is a Christian out of Choice, not in conformity to those among whom she lives; and cleaves to Piety, because 'tis her Wisdom, her Interest, her Joy, not because she has been accustom'd to it; she who is not only eminently and unmovably good, but able to give a Reason why she is so, is too firm and stable to be mov'd by the pitiful Allurements of sin, too wise and too well bottom'd to be undermin'd and supplanted by the strongest Efforts of Temptation. Doubtless a truly Christian Life requires a clear Understanding as well as regular Affections, that both together may move the Will to a direct choice of Good and a stedfast adherence to it. For tho' the heart may be honest, it is but by chance that the Will is right if the Understanding be Ignorant and Cloudy. And what's the reason that we sometimes see persons unhappily falling off from their Piety, but because 'twas their Affections, not their Judgment, that inclin'd them to be Religious? Reason and Truth are firm and immutable, she who bottoms on them is on sure ground, Humour and Inclination are sandy Foundations, and she who is sway'd by her Affections more than by her Judgment, owes the happiness of her Soul in a great measure to the temper of her Body; her Piety may perhaps blaze high but will not last long. For the Affections are various and changeable, mov'd by every Object, and the last comer easily undoes whatever its Predecessor had done before. Such Persons are always in extreams, they are either violently good or quite cold and indifferent; a perpetual trouble to themselves and others, by indecent Raptures, or unnecessary Scruples; there is no Beauty and order in their lives, all is rapid and unaccountable; they are now very furious in such a course, but they cannot well tell why, and anon as violent in the other extream. Having more Heat than Light, their Zeal outruns their Knowledge, and instead of representing Piety as it is in it self, the most lively and inviting thing imaginable, they expose it to the contempt and ridicule of the censorious World. Their devotion becomes ricketed, starv'd and contracted in some of it's vital parts, and disproportioned and over-grown in less material instances; whilst one Duty is over-done to commute for the neglect of another, and the mistaken person thinks the being often on her knees, attones for all the miscarriages of her Conversation: Not considering that 'tis in vain to petition for those Graces which we take no care to practise, and a mockery to adore those Perfections we run counter to, and that the true end of all our Prayers and external observances is to work our minds into a truly Christian temper, to obtain for us the Empire of our Passions, and to reduce all irregular Inclinations, that so we may be as like GOD in Purity, Charity, and all his imitable excellencies, as is consistent with the imperfection of a Creature.

And now having discovered the Disease and its cause, 'tis proper to apply a Remedy; single Medicines are too weak to cure such complicated Distempers, they require a full Dispensatory; and what wou'd a good Woman refuse to do, could she hope by that to advantage the greatest part of the World, and improve her Sex in Knowledge and true Religion? I doubt not, Ladies, but that the Age, as bad as it is, affords very many of you who will readily embrace whatever has a true tendency to the Glory of GOD and your mutual Edification, to revive the ancient Spirit of Piety in the World and to transmit it to succeeding Generations. I know there are many of you who so ardently love God, as to think no time too much to spend in his service, nor any thing too difficult to do for his sake; and bear such a hearty good will to your Neighbours, as to grudge no Prayers or Pains to reclaim and improve them. I have therefore no more to do but to make the Proposal, to prove that it will answer these great and good Ends, and then 'twill be easy to obviate the Objections that Persons of more Wit than Vertue may happen to raise against it.

Now as to the Proposal, it is to erect a Monastery, or if you will (to avoid giving offence to the scrupulous and injudicious, by names which tho' innocent in themselves, have been abus'd by superstitious Practices), we will call it a Religious Retirement, and such as shall have a double aspect, being not only a Retreat from the World for those who desire that advantage, but likewise, an Institution and previous discipline, to fit us to do the greatest good in it; such an Institution as this (if I do not mightily deceive my self) would be the most probable method to amend the present, and improve the future Age. For here those who are convinc'd of the emptiness of earthly Enjoyments, who are sick of the vanity of the world and its impertinencies, may find more substantial and satisfying entertainments, and need not be confin'd to what they justly loath. Those who are desirous to know and fortify their weak side, first do good to themselves, that hereafter they may be capable of doing more good to others; or for their greater security are willing to avoid Temptation, may get out of that danger which a continual stay in view of the Enemy, and the familiarity and unwearied application of the Temptation may expose them to; and gain an opportunity to look into themselves, to be acquainted at home and no longer the greatest strangers to their own hearts. Such as are willing in a more peculiar and undisturb'd manner, to attend the great business they came into the world about, the service of GOD and improvement of their own Minds, may find a convenient and blissful recess from the noise and hurry of the world. A world so cumbersom, so infectious, that altho' thro' the grace of GOD and their own strict watchfulness, they are kept from sinking down into its corruptions, 'twill however damp their flight to heav'n, hinder them from attaining any eminent pitch of Vertue.

You are therefore Ladies, invited into a place, where you shall suffer no other confinement, but to be kept out of the road of sin: You shall not be depriv'd of your Grandeur but only exchange the vain Pomps and Pageantry of the world, empty Titles and Forms of State, for the true and solid Greatness of being able to despise them. You will only quit the Chat of insignificant people for an ingenious Conversation; the froth of flashy Wit for real Wisdom; idle tales for instructive discourses. The deceitful Flatteries of those who under pretence of loving and admiring you, really served their own base ends, for the seasonable Reproofs and wholsom Counsels of your hearty well-wishers and affectionate Friends, which will procure you those perfections your feigned lovers pretended you had, and kept you from obtaining. No uneasy task will be enjoyn'd you, all your labour being only to prepare for the highest degrees of that Glory, the very lowest of which is more than at present you are able to conceive, and the prospect of it sufficient to outweigh all the Pains of Religion, were there any in it, as really there are none. All that is requir'd of you, is only to be as Happy as possibly you can, and to make sure of a Felicity that will fill all the capacities of your Souls! A happiness, which when once you have tasted, you'll be fully convinc'd you cou'd never do too much to obtain it, nor be too solicitous to adorn your Souls with such tempers and dispositions, as will at present make you in some measure, such holy and Heavenly Creatures as you one day hope to be in a more perfect manner; without which Qualifications you can neither reasonably expect, nor are capable of enjoying the Happiness of the Life to come. Happy Retreat! which will be the introducing you into such a Paradise as your Mother Eve forfeited, where you shall feast on Pleasures, that do not like those of the World, disappoint your expectations, pall your Appetites, and by the disgust they give you put you on the fruitless search after new Delights, which when obtain'd are as empty as the former; but such as will make you truly happy now, and prepare you to be perfectly so hereafter. Here are no Serpents to deceive you, whilst you entertain your selves in these delicious Gardens. No Provocations will be given in this Amicable Society, but to Love and to good Works, which will afford such an entertaining employment, that you'll have as little inclination as leisure to pursue those Follies, which in the time of your ignorance pass'd with you under the name of love, altho' there is not in nature two more different things, than true Love and that brutish Passion, which pretends to ape it. Here will be no Rivalling but for the Love of GOD, no Ambition but to procure his Favour, to which nothing will more effectually recommend you, than a great and dear affection to each other. Envy that Canker, will not here disturb your Breasts; for how can she repine at anothers well-fare, who reckons it the greatest part of her own? No Covetousness will gain admittance in this blest abode, but to amass huge Treasures of good Works, and to procure one of the brightest Crowns of Glory. You will not be solicitous to encrease your Fortunes, but to enlarge your Minds, esteeming no Grandeur like being

conformable to the meek and humble JESUS. So that you only withdraw
from the noise and trouble, the folly and temptation of the world, that you
may more peaceably enjoy your selves, and all the innocent Pleasures it
is able to afford you, and particularly that which is worth all the rest, a
noble, Vertuous and Disinterest'd Friendship. And to compleat all, that
Acme of delight which the devout Seraphic Soul enjoys when dead to the
World, she devotes her self entirely to the Contemplation and Fruition of
her Beloved; when having disengag'd her self from all those Lets which
hindred her from without, she moves in a direct and vigorous motion
towards her true and only Good, whom now she embraces and acqui-
esces in with such an unspeakable pleasure, as is only intelligible to
those who have tried and felt it, which we can no more describe to the
dark and sensual part of Mankind, than we can the beauty of Colours and
harmony of Sounds to the Blind and Deaf. In fine, the place to which you
are invited is a Type and Antepast of Heav'n, where your Employments
will be as there, to magnify GOD, to love one another, and to communicate that useful Knowledge, which by the due improvement of your
time in Study and Contemplation you will obtain, and which when obtain'd will afford you a much sweeter and more durable delight, than all
those pitiful diversions, those revellings and amusements, which now
thro' your ignorance of better, appear the only grateful and relishing
Entertainments.

But because we were not made for our selves, nor can by any means
so effectually glory GOD, and do good to our own Souls, as by doing
Offices of Charity and Beneficence to others; and to the intent that every
Vertue, and the highest degrees of every Vertue may be exercis'd and
promoted the most that may be; your Retreat shall be so manag'd as not
to exclude the good Works of an Active, from the pleasure and serenity
of a Contemplative Life, but by a due mixture of both retain all the
advantages and avoid the inconveniences that attend either. It shall not
so cut you off from the world as to hinder you from bettering and improving it, but rather qualify you to do it the greatest Good, and be a
Seminary to stock the Kingdom with pious and prudent Ladies, whose
good Example it is to be hop'd, will so influence the rest of their Sex, that
Women may no longer pass for those little useless and impertinent
Animals, which the ill conduct of too many has caus'd 'em to be mistaken for.

We have hitherto consider'd our Retirement only in relation to Religion, which is indeed its main, I may say its only design; nor can this be
thought too contracting a word, since Religion is the adequate business
of our lives, and largely consider'd, takes in all we have to do, nothing
being a fit employment for a rational Creature, which has not either a
direct or remote tendency to this great and only end. But because, as we
have all along observ'd, Religion never appears in it's true Beauty, but
when it is accompanied with Wisdom and Discretion; and that without
a good Understanding, we can scarce be truly, but never eminently

Good; being liable to a thousand seductions and mistakes (for even the
men themselves, if they have not a competent degree of Knowledge, are
carried about with every wind of Doctrine). Therefore, one great end of
this Institution shall be, to expel that cloud of Ignorance which Custom
has involv'd us in, to furnish our minds with a stock of solid and useful
Knowledge, that the Souls of Women may no longer be the only un-
adorn'd and neglected things. It is not intended that our Religious shou'd
waste their time, and trouble their heads about such unconcerning
matters, as the vogue of the world has turn'd up for Learning, the imper-
tinency of which has been excellently expos'd by an ingenious Pen, but
busy themselves in a serious enquiry after necessary and perfective
truths, something which it concerns them to know, and which tends to
their real interest and perfection, and what that is the excellent Author
just now mention'd will sufficiently inform them. Such a course of Study
will neither be too troublesome nor out of the reach of a Female Virtu-
oso; for it is not intended she shou'd spend her hours in learning words
but things, and therefore no more Languages than are necessary to
acquaint her with useful Authors. Nor need she trouble her self in turning
over a great number of Books, but take care to understand and digest a
few well chosen and good ones. Let her but obtain right Ideas, and be
truly acquainted with the nature of those Objects that present themselves
to her mind, and then no matter whether or no she be able to tell what
fanciful people have said about them: And thoroughly to understand
Christianity as profess'd by the Church of England, will be sufficient to
confirm her in the truth, tho' she have not a Catalogue of those particular
errors which oppose it. Indeed a Learned Education of the Women will
appear so unfashionable, that I began to startle at the singularity of the
proposition, but was extremely pleas'd when I found a late ingenious
Author (whose Book I met with since the writing of this) agree with me
in my Opinion. For speaking of the Repute that Learning was in about 150
Years ago, It was so very modish (says he) that the fair Sex seem'd to
believe that Greek and Latin added to their Charms: and Plato and
Aristotle untranslated, were frequent Ornaments of their Closets. One
wou'd think by the effects, that it was a proper way of Educating them,
since there are no accounts in History of so many great Women in any
one Age, as are to be found between the years 15 and 1600.

     For since GOD has given Women as well as Men intelligent Souls, why
should they be forbidden to improve them? Since he has not denied us
the faculty of Thinking, why shou'd we not (at least in gratitude to him)
employ our Thoughts on himself their noblest Object, and not unworthily
bestow them on Trifles and Gaities and secular Affairs? Being the Soul
was created for the contemplation of Truth as well as for the fruition of
Good, is it not as cruel and unjust to exclude Women from the knowledge of the one as from the enjoyment of the other? Especially since the
Will is blind, and cannot chuse but by the direction of the Understanding; or to speak more properly, since the Soul always Wills accord-

ing as she Understands, so that if she Understands amiss, she Wills amiss. And as Exercise enlarges and exalts any Faculty, so thro' want of using it becomes crampt and lessened; if therefore we make little or no use of our Understandings, we shall shortly have none to use; and the more contracted and unemploy'd the deliberating and directive Power is, the more liable is the elective to unworthy and mischievous choices. What is it but the want of an ingenious Education, that renders the generality of Feminine Conversations so insipid and foolish and their solitude so insupportable? Learning is therefore necessary to render them more agreeable and useful in company, and to furnish them with becoming entertainments when alone, that so they may not be driven to those miserable shifts, which too many make use of to put off their Time, that precious Talent that never lies on the hands of a judicious Person. And since our Happiness in the next World, depends so far on those dispositions which we carry along with us out of this, that without a right habitude and temper of mind we are not capable of Felicity; and seeing our Beatitude consists in the contemplation of the divine Truth and Beauty, as well as in the fruition of his Goodness, can Ignorance be a fit preparative for Heaven? Is't likely that she whose Understanding has been busied about nothing but froth and trifles, shou'd be capable of delighting her self in noble and sublime Truths? Let such therefore as deny us the improvement of our Intellectuals, either take up his Paradox, who said that Women have no Souls, which at a time when the most contend to have them allow'd to Brutes, wou'd be as unphilosophical as it is unmannerly, or else let them permit us to cultivate and improve them. There is a sort of Learning indeed which is worse than the greatest Ignorance: A Woman may study Plays and Romances all her days, and be a great deal more knowing but never a jot the wiser. Such a knowledge as this serves only to instruct and put her forward in the practice of the greatest Follies, yet how can they justly blame her who forbid, or at least won't afford opportunity of better? A rational mind will be employ'd, it will never be satisfy'd in doing nothing, and if you neglect to furnish it with good materials, 'tis like to take up with such as come to hand.

We pretend not that Women shou'd teach in the Church, or usurp Authority where it is allow'd them; permit us only to understand our own duty, and not be forc'd to take it upon trust from others; to be at least so far learned, as to be able to form in our minds a true Idea of Christianity, it being so very necessary to fence us against the danger of these last and perilous days, in which Deceivers a part of whose Character is to lead captive silly Women, need not creep into Houses since they have Authority to proclaim their Errors on the House top. And let us also acquire a true Practical knowledge, such as will convince us of the absolute necessity of Holy Living as well as of Right Believing, and that no Heresy is more dangerous than that of an ungodly and wicked Life. And since the French Tongue is understood by most Ladies, methinks they may much better improve it by the study of Philosophy (as I hear the French

Ladies do) Des Cartes, Malebranche and others, than by reading idle
Novels and Romances. 'Tis strange we shou'd be so forward to imitate
their Fashions and Fopperies, and have no regard to what really deserves
our Imitation. And why shall it not be thought as genteel to understand
French Philosophy, as to be accoutred in a French Mode? Let therefore
the famous Madam D'acier, Scudery, etc, and our own incomparable
Orinda, excite the Emulation of the English Ladies.

The Ladies, I'm sure, have no reason to dislike this Proposal, but I
know not how the Men will resent it to have their enclosure broke down,
and Women invited to taste of that Tree of knowledge they have so long
unjustly Monopoliz'd. But they must excuse me, if I be as partial to my
own Sex as they are to theirs, and think Women as capable of Learning
as Men are, and that it becomes them as well. For I cannot imagine
wherein the hurt lies, if instead of doing mischief to one another, by an
uncharitable and vain Conversation, Women be enabled to inform and
instruct those of their own Sex at least; the Holy Ghost having left it on
record, that Priscilla as well as her Husband, catechiz'd the eloquent
Apollos and the great Apostle found no fault with her. It will therefore be
very proper for our Ladies to spend part of their time in this Retirement,
in adorning their minds with useful Knowledge.

FROM
SOME REFLECTIONS
UPON MARRIAGE

THE Reflector, who hopes Reflector is not bad English, (now Governor is happily of the Feminine Gender) guarded against Curiosity in
vain: For a certain ingenuous Gentleman, as she is inform'd, had the
Good-nature to own these Reflections, so far, as to affirm that he had the
Original MS. in his Closet, a Proof she is not able to produce; and so to
make himself responsible for all their Faults, for which, she returns him
all due Acknowledgement. However, the Generality being of Opinion,
that a Man would have had more Prudence and Manners than to have
Publish'd such unseasonable Truths, or to have betray'd the *Arcana
Imperii* of his Sex; she humbly confesses, that the Contrivance and
Execution of this Design, which is unfortunately accus'd of being so
destructive to the Government, (of the Men, I mean) is intirely her own.
She neither advis'd with Friends, nor turn'd over antient or modern
Authors, nor prudently submitted to the Correction of such as are, or
such as *think* they are good Judges, but with an *English* Spirit and

Genius, set out upon the Forlorn Hope, meaning no Hurt to any body, nor designing any thing but the publick Good, and to retrieve, if possible, the Native Liberty, the Rights and Privileges of the Subject.

FAR be it from her to stir up Sedition of any sort: none can abhor it more; and she heartily wishes, that our Masters would pay their Civil and Ecclesiastical Governors the same Submission, which they themselves exact from their Domestick Subjects. Nor can she imagine how she any way undermines the Masculine Empire, or blows the Trumpet of Rebellion to the Moiety of Mankind. Is it by exhorting Women, not to expect to have their own Will in any thing, but to be intirely Submissive, when once they have made Choice of a Lord and Master, though he happen not to be so wise, so kind, or even so just a Governor as was expected? She did not, indeed, advise them to think his Folly Wisdom, nor his Brutality, that Love and Worship he promised in his Matrimonial Oath; for this required a Flight of Wit and Sense much above her poor Ability, and proper only to Masculine Understandings. However, she did not in any manner prompt them to Resist, or to Abdicate the Perjur'd spouse, though the Laws of GOD, and the Land, make special Provision for it, in a Case, wherein, as is to be fear'd, few Men can truly plead Not Guilty.

'Tis true, through want of Learning, and that of Superior Genius which Men, as Men, lay claim to, she was ignorant of the Natural Inferiority of our Sex, which our Masters lay down as a Self-evident and Fundamental Truth. She saw nothing in the Reason of Things, to make this either a Principle or a Conclusion, but much to the contrary; it being Sedition at least, if not Treason, to assert it in this Reign. For if by the Natural Superiority of their Sex, they mean, that every Man is by Nature superior to every Woman, which is the obvious Meaning, and that which must be stuck to if they would speak Sense, it would be a Sin in any Woman, to have Dominion over any Man, and the greatest Queen ought not to command, but to obey, her Footman: because no Municipal Laws can supersede or change the Law of Nature: So that if the Dominion of the Men be such, the Salique Law, as unjust as English Men have ever thought it, ought to take Place over all the Earth, and the most glorious Reigns in the English, Danish, Castilian, and other Annals, were wicked Violations of the Law of Nature!

If they mean that some Men are superior to some Women, this is no great Discovery; had they turn'd the Tables, they might have seen that some Women are superior to some Men. Or had they been pleased to remember their Oaths of Allegiance and Supremacy, they might have known, that One Woman is superior to All the Men in these Nations, or else they have sworn to very little Purpose. And it must not be suppos'd, that their Reason and Religion would suffer them to take Oaths, contrary to the Law of Nature and Reason of Things. . . .

BUT what says the Holy Scripture? It speaks of Women as in a State of Subjection, and so it does of the Jews and Christians, when under the

Dominion of the Chaldeans and Romans, requiring of the one as well as of the other, a quiet Submission to them under whose Power they liv'd. But will any one say, that these had a Natural Superiority and Right to Dominion? that they had a superior Understanding, or any Pre-eminence, except what their greater Strength acquir'd? Or, that the other were subjected to their Adversaries for any other Reason but the Punishment of their Sins, and, in order to their Reformation? Or for the Exercise of their Vertue, and because the Order of the World and the Good of Society requir'd it?

If Mankind had never Sinn'd, Reason would always have been obeyed, there would have been no Struggle for Dominion, and Brutal Power would not have prevail'd. But in the lapsed State of Mankind, and now, that Men will not be guided by their Reason but by their Appetites, and do not what they ought but what they can, the Reason, or that which stands for it, the Will and Pleasure of the Governor, is to be the Reason of those who will not be guided by their own, and must take Place for Order's sake, although it should not be conformable to right Reason. Nor can there be any Society great or little, from Empires down to private Families, without a last Resort, to determine the Affairs of that Society by an irresistible Sentence. Now unless this Supremacy be fix'd some-where, there will be a perpetual Contention about it, such is the Love of Dominion, and let the Reason of Things be what it may, those who have least Force or Cunning to supply it, will have the Disadvantage. So that since Women are acknowledged to have least Bodily Strength, their being commanded to Obey is in pure Kindness to them, and for their Quiet and Security, as well as for the Exercise of their Vertue. But does it follow, that Domestick Governors have more Sense than their Subjects, any more than other Governors have? We do not find that any Man thinks the worse of his own Understanding, because another has superior Power; or concludes himself less capable of a Post of Honour and Authority, because he is not prefer'd to it. How much Time would lie on Mens Hands, how empty would the Places of Concourse be, and how silent most Companies, did Men forbear to censure their Governors, that is, in effect, to think themselves wiser. Indeed, Government would be much more desirable than it is, did it invest the Possessor with a superior Understanding as well as Power. And if meer Power gives a Right to Rule, there can be no such Thing as Usurpation; but a Highway-Man, so long as he has Strength to force, has also a Right to require our Obedience.

AGAIN, if absolute Sovereignty be not necessary in a State, how comes it to be so in a Family? Or if in a Family why not in a State; since no Reason can be alledged for the one that will not hold more strongly for the other? If the Authority of the Husband, so far as it extends, is sacred and inalienable, why not that of the Prince? The Domestick Sovereign is without Dispute elected; and the Stipulations and Contract are mutual; is it not then partial in Men to the last Degree, to contend for, and practise that Arbitrary Dominion in their Families, which they abhor and exclaim against in the State? For if Arbitrary Power is evil in it self, and an improper Method of Governing Rational and Free Agents, it ought not to be practis'd any where; nor is it less, but rather more mischievous in Families than in Kingdoms, by how much 100,000 Tyrants are worse than one. What though a Husband can't deprive a Wife of Life without being responsible to the Law, he may, however, do what is much more grievous to a generous Mind, render Life miserable, for which she has no Redress, scarce Pity, which is afforded to every other Complainant, it being thought a Wife's Duty to suffer every thing without Complaint. If all Men are born Free, how is it that all Women are born Slaves? As they must be, if the being subjected to the inconstant, uncertain, unknown, arbitrary Will of Men' be the perfect Condition of Slavery? And, if the Essence of Freedom consists, as our Masters say it does, in having a standing Rule to live by? And why is Slavery so much condemn'd and strove against in one Case, and so highly applauded, and held so necessary and so sacred in another.

'TIS true, that GOD told Eve after the Fall, that her Husband should Rule over her: And so it is, that he told Esau by the Mouth of Isaac his Father, that he should serve his younger Brother, and should in Time, and when he was strong enough to do it, break the Yoke from off his Neck. Now, why one Text should be a Command any more than the other, and not both of them be Predictions only; or why the former should prove Adam's Natural Right to Rule, and much less every Man's, and any more than the latter is a Proof of Jacob's Right to Rule, and of Esau's to Rebel, one is yet to learn? The Text in both Cases foretelling what would be; but neither of them determining what ought to be.

BUT the Scripture commands Wives to submit themselves to their own Husbands. True; for which St. Paul gives a Mystical Reason (Eph. v. 22, &c.) and St. Peter, a Prudential and Charitable one, (I Pet. iii.) but neither of them derive that Subjection from the Law of Nature. Nay, St. Paul, as if he foresaw and meant to prevent this Plea, giving Directions for their Conduct to Women in general, I Tim. ii. when he comes to speak of Subjection, he changes his Phrase from Women, which denotes the whole Sex, to Woman, which in the New Testament is appropriated to a Wife.

As for his not suffering Women to speak in the Church, no sober Person that I know of pretends to it. That learned Paraphrast, indeed, who lays so much Stress on the Natural Subjection, provided this Prerogative be secur'd, is willing to give up the other. For he endeavours to prove, that Inspir'd Women, as well as Men, us'd to speak in the Church, and that St. Paul does not forbid it, but only takes Care that the Women should signify their Subjection by wearing a Veil. But the Apostle is his own best Expositor, let us therefore compare his Precepts with his Practice, for he was all of a Piece, and did not contradict himself. Now by this Comparison we find, that though he forbids Women to teach in the Church, and this for several Prudential Reasons, like those he introduces with an "I give my Opinion, and now speak I, not the Lord," and not because of any Law of Nature, or positive Divine Precept, for that the Words they are commanded (I Cor. xiv. 24.) are not in the Original, appears from the Italick Character, yet he did not found this Prohibition on any suppos'd Want of Understanding in Woman, or of Ability to teach; neither does he confine them at all Times to learn in Silence. For the eloquent Apollos, who was himself a Teacher, was instructed by Priscilla, as well as by her Husband Aquila, and was improv'd by them both in the Christian Faith. Nor does St. Paul blame her for this, or suppose that she usurp'd Authority over that great Man; so far from this, that as she is always honourably mention'd in Holy Scripture, so our Apostle, in his Salutations, Rom. xvi. places her in the Front, even before her Husband, giving to her, as well as to him, the Noble Title of, his Helper in Christ Jesus, and of one to whom all the Churches of the Gentiles had great Obligations. . . .

SOME Men will have it, that the Reason of our LORD's appearing first to the Women, was, their being least able to keep a Secret; a witty and masculine Remark, and wonderfully Reverent! But not to dispute whether those Women were Blabs or no, there are many Instances in Holy Scripture, of Women who did not betray the Confidence repos'd in them. Thus Rahab, though formerly an ill Woman, being converted by the Report of those Miracles, which, though the Israelites saw, yet they believed not in GOD, nor put their Trust in his Word. She acknowledges the GOD in Heaven, and, as a Reward of her faithful Service, in concealing Joshua's Spies, is, with her Family, exempted from the Ruin of her Country, and also, has the Honour of being named in the Messiah's Genealogy. Michal, to save David's Life, exposes her self to the Fury of a Jealous and Tyrannical Prince. A Girl was trusted by David's grave Counsellors to convey him Intelligence in his Son's Rebellion; and when a Lad had found it out, and blab'd it to Absalom, the King's Friends confiding in the Prudence and Fidelity of a Woman, were secur'd by her. When our LORD escaped from the Jews, he trusted Himself in the Hands of Martha and Mary. So does St. Peter with another Mary, when the Angel deliver'd him from Herod, the Damsel Rhoda too, was acquainted with the Secret. More might be said, but one would think here is enough to shew, that whatever other great and wise Reasons Men may have for despising Women, and keeping them in Ignorance and Slavery, it can't be from their having learnt to do so in Holy Scripture. The Bible is for, and not against us, and cannot without great Violence done to it, be urg'd to our Prejudice.

HOWEVER, there are strong and prevalent Reasons which demonstrate the Superiority and Pre-eminence of the Men. For in the first Place, Boys have much Time and Pains, Care and Cost bestow'd on their Education, Girls have little or none. The former are early initiated in the Sciences, are made acquainted with antient and modern Discoveries, they study Books and Men, have all imaginable Encouragement; not only

Fame, a dry Reward now a-days, but also Title, Authority, Power, and Riches themselves, which purchase all Things, are the Reward of their Improvement. The latter are restrain'd, frown'd upon, and beat, nor for, but from the Muses; Laughter and Ridicule, that never-failing Scare-Crow, is set up to drive them from the Tree of Knowledge. But if, in spite of all Difficulties Nature prevails, and they can't be kept so ignorant as their Masters would have them, they are star'd upon as Monsters, censur'd, envied, and every way discouraged, or, at the best, they have the Fate the Proverb assigns them, Vertue is prais'd and starv'd. And therefore, since the coarsest Materials need the most Curing, as every Workman can inform you, and the worst Ground the most elaborate Culture, it undeniably follows, that Mens Understandings are superior to Womens, for, after many Years Study and Experience, they become wise and learned, and Women are not born so!

AGAIN, Men are possessed of all Places of Power, Trust and Profit, they make Laws and exercise the Magistracy, not only the sharpest Sword, but even all the Swords and Blunderbusses are theirs; which by the strongest Logick in the World, gives them the best Title to every Thing they please to claim as their Prerogative: Who shall contend with them? Immemorial Prescription is on their Side in these Parts of the World, antient Tradition and modern Usage! Our Fathers, have all along, both taught and prac-tised Superiority over the weaker Sex, and consequently Women are by Nature inferior to Men, as was to be demonstrated. An Argument which must be acknowledged unanswerable; for, as well as I love my Sex, I will not pretend a Reply to such Demonstration!

ONLY let me beg to be inform'd, to whom we poor Fatherless Maids, and Widows who have lost their Masters, owe Subjection? It can't be to all Men in general, unless all Men were agreed to give the same Com-mands; Do we then fall as Strays, to the first who finds us? by the Maxims of some Men, and the Conduct of some Women one would think so. But whoever he be that thus happens to become our Master, if he allows us to be reasonable Creatures, and does not meerly Compliment us with that Title, since no Man denies our Readiness to use our Tongues, it would tend, I should think, to our Master's Advantage, and therefore he may please to be advis'd to teach us to improve our Reason. But if Reason is only allow'd us by way of Raillery, and the secret Maxim is, that we have none, or little more than Brutes, 'tis the best way to confine us with Chain and Block to the Chimney-Corner, which, probably, might save the Estates of some Families and the Honour of others.

I do not propose this to prevent a Rebellion, for Women are not so well united as to form an Insurrection. They are for the most part wise enough to love their Chains, and to discern how very becomingly they fit. They think as humbly of themselves as their Masters can wish, with respect to the other Sex, but in regard to their own, they have a Spice of Masculine Ambition; every one would Lead, and none would Follow. Both Sexes being too apt to Envy, and too backward in Emulating, and take more

Delight in Detracting from their Neighbour's Vertue, than in Improving
their own. And therefore, as to those Women who find themselves born
for Slavery, and are so sensible of their own Meanness, as to conclude
it impossible to attain to any thing excellent, since they are, or ought to
be best acquainted with their own Strength and Genius, She's a Fool who
would attempt their Deliverance or Improvement. No, let them enjoy the
great Honour and Felicity of their tame, submissive and depending Temper! Let the Men applaud, and let them glory in this wonderful Humility!
Let them receive the Flatteries and Grimaces of the other Sex, live un-
envied by their own, and be as much belov'd as one such Woman can
afford to love another! Let them enjoy the Glory of treading in the Footsteps of their Predecessors, and of having the Prudence to avoid that
audacious Attempt of soaring beyond their Sphere! Let them Huswife or
Play, Dress, and be pretty entertaining Company! Or, which is better,
relieve the Poor to ease their own Compassions, read pious Books, say
their Prayers, and go to Church, because they have been taught and us'd
to do so, without being able to give a better Reason for their Faith and
Practice! Let them not by any Means aspire at being Women of Understanding, because no Man can endure a Woman of Superior Sense, or
would treat a reasonable Woman civilly, but that he thinks he stands on
higher Ground, and, that she is so wise as to make Exceptions in his
Favour, and to take her Measures by his Directions; they may pretend to
Sense, indeed, since meer Pretences only render one the more ridiculous! Let them, in short, be what is call'd very Women, for this is most
acceptable to all sorts of Men; or let them aim at the Title of good devout
Women, since some Men can bear with this; but let them not judge of the
Sex by their own Scantling: For the great Author of Nature and Fountain
of all Perfection, never design'd that the Mean and Imperfect, but that the
most Compleat and Excellent of His Creatures of every Kind, should be
the Standard to the rest.

TO conclude; If that GREAT QUEEN who has subdued the Proud, and
made the pretended Invincible more than once fly before her; who has
Rescued an Empire, Reduced a Kingdom, Conquer'd Provinces in as
little Time almost as one can Travel them, and seems to have chain'd
Victory to her Standard; who disposes of Crowns, gives Laws and Liberty
to Europe, and is the chief Instrument in the Hand of the Almighty, to pull
down and to set up the great Men of the Earth; who conquers every where
for others, and no where for her self but in the Hearts of the Conquer'd,
who are of the Number of those who reap the Benefit of her Triumphs;
whilst she only reaps for her self the Laurels of disinterested Glory, and
the Royal Pleasure of doing Heroically; if this Glory of her own Sex, and
Envy of the other, will not think we need, or does not hold us worthy of,
the Protection of her ever victorious Arms, and Men have not the Gratitude, for her sake at least, to do Justice to her Sex, who has been such
a universal Benefactress to theirs: Adieu to the Liberties, not of this or
that Nation or Reign only, but of the Moiety of Mankind! To all the great

Things that Women might perform, inspir'd by her Example, encouraged by her Smiles, and supported by her Power! To their Discovery of new Worlds for the Exercise of her Goodness, new Sciences to publish her Fame, and reducing Nature it self to a Subjection to her Empire! To their destroying those worst of Tyrants Impiety and Immorality, which dare to stalk about even in her own Dominions, and to devour Souls almost within View of her Throne, leaving a Stench behind them scarce to be corrected even by the Incense of her Devotions! To the Women's tracing a new Path to Honour, in which none shall walk but such as scorn to Cringe in order to Rise, and who are Proof both against giving and receiving Flattery! In a Word, to those Halcyon, or, if you will, Millennium Days, in which the Wolf and the Lamb shall feed together, and a Tyrannous Domination, which Nature never meant, shall no longer render useless, if not hurtful, the Industry and Understandings of half Mankind!

FROM

THE COMPLETE LETTERS OF
LADY MARY WORTLEY MONTAGU,

VOL. 1

APPENDIX III

MARY ASTELL'S PREFACE
TO THE EMBASSY LETTERS

The Travels of an English Lady in Europe, Asia and Affrica

Let the Male-Authors with an envious eye
Praise coldly, that they may the more decry:
Women (at least I speak the Sense of some)
This little Spirit of Rivalship o'recome.
I read with transport, and with Joy I greet ⎫
A Genius so Sublime and so Complete, ⎬
And gladly lay my Laurels at her Feet. ⎭
M[ary] A[stell]

To the Reader.

I was going, like common Editors, to advertise the Reader of the Beautys and Excellencys of the Work laid before him; to tell him that the Illustrious Author had oppertunitys that other Travellers, whatever their Quality or Curiosity may be, cannot obtain, and a Genius capable of making the best Improvement of every oppertunity. But if the Reader, after perusing one Letter only, has not discernment to distinguish that natural Elegance, that delicacy of Sentiment and Observation, that easy gracefulness and lovely Simplicity (which is the Perfection of Writing) in which these Letters exceed all that has appear'd in this kind, or almost in any other, let him lay the Book down and leave it to those who have.

The noble Author had the goodness to lend me her M.S. to satisfy my Curiosity in some enquirys I made concerning her Travels. And when I had it in my hands, how was it possible to part with it! I once had the Vanity to hope I might acquaint the Public that it ow'd this invaluable Treasure to my Importunitys. But alas! The most Ingenious Author has condemn'd it to obscurity during her Life, and Conviction, as well as Deference, obliges me to yeild to her Reasons. However, if these Letters appear hereafter, when I am in my Grave, let this attend them in testimony to Posterity, that among her Contemporarys one Woman, at least, was just to her Merit.

There is not any thing so excellent but some will carp at it, and the rather because of its excellency. But to such Hypercritics, I shall only say, ***

I confess I am malicious enough to desire that the World shou'd see to how much better purpose the LADYS Travel than their LORDS, and that whilst it is surfeited with Male Travels, all in the same Tone and stuft with the same Trifles, a Lady has the skill to strike out a New Path and to embellish a worn-out Subject with variety of fresh and elegant Entertainment. For besides that Vivacity and Spirit which enliven every part and that inimitable Beauty which spreds thro the whole, besides that Purity of Style for which it may justly be accounted the Standard of the English Tongue, the Reader will find a more true and accurate Account of the Customs and Manners of the several Nations with whom the Lady Convers'd than he can in any other Author. But as her Ladyship's penetration discovers the inmost follys of the heart, so the candor of her Temper passes over them with an air of pity rather than reproach, treating with the politeness of a Court and gentleness of a Lady what the severity of her Judgment cannot but Condemn.

In short, let her own Sex at least do her Justice; Lay aside diabolical Envy and its Brother Malice with all their accursed Company, Sly Whispering, cruel backbiting, spiteful detraction, and the rest of that hideous crew, which I hope are very falsely said to attend the Tea Table, being more apt to think they haunt those Public Places where Virtuous Women never come. Let the Men malign one another, if they think fit, and strive

to pul down Merit when they cannot equal it. Let us be better natur'd than to give way to any unkind or disrespectful thought of so bright an Ornament of our Sex, merely because she has better Sense. For I doubt not but our hearts will tell us that this is the Real and unpardonable Offence, whatever may be pretended. Let us be better Christians than to look upon her with an evil eye, only because the Giver of all good Gifts has entrusted and adorn'd her with the most excellent Talents. Rather let us freely own the Superiority of this Sublime Genius as I do in the sincerity of my Soul, pleas'd that a Woman Triumphs, and proud to follow in her Train. Let us offer her the Palm which is justly her due, and if we pretend to any Laurels, lay them willingly at her Feet.
Dec. 18th 1724.

M[ary] A[stell]

Charm'd into Love of what obscures my Fame, ⎫
If I had Wit, I'de celebrate Her Name,   ⎬
And all the Beautys of her Mind proclaim;   ⎭
Till Malice deafned with the mighty sound,
Its ill-concerted Calumnys confound,
Let fall the Mask, and with pale Envy meet
To ask, and find, their Pardon at Her Feet.

You see, Madam, how I lay every thing at your Feet. As the Tautology shews the poverty of my Genius, it likewise shews the extent of your Empire over my Imagination.

May 31. 1725
Text H MS 254

———————————————— • ————————————————

PRIMARY SOURCES

A Serious Proposal to the Ladies, for the advancement of their true and greatest interest. Part 1. 4th ed. London: R. Wilkin, 1694. *A Serious Proposal to the Ladies. Part 2. Wherein a Method is offer'd for the improvement of their minds.* London: R. Wilkin, 1697. Reprint of both parts of the 1701 London edition. New York: Source Book Press, 1970.

Some Reflections upon Marriage, occasion'd by the Duke and Duchess of Mazarine's case; which is also considered. With Additions. 4th ed. London: William Parker, 1730. Reprint. New York: Source Book Press, 1970.

Some Reflections upon Marriage. With Additions. 5th ed. Dublin: printed by and for S. Hyde et al., 1730.

Mary Astell's Preface to *The Embassy Letters of Lady Mary Wortley Montagu.* In *The Complete Letters of Lady Wortley Montagu.* Edited by Robert Halsband, Appendix III, Vol. 1. Oxford: Clarendon Press, 1965.

RELATED SOURCES

Erard, Claude. *The Arguments of M. Hérard, for M. the Duke of Mazarin, against Madam the Dutchesse of Mazarin, his spouse. And the Factum for Madam the Dutchesse of Mazarin, against Mazarin, the Duke of Mazarin, her husband.* By M. de St. Evremont. London: C. Broom, 1699.

Mémoires of the Dutchesse Mazarin written in French by her own hand, and done into English by R. Porter, esq., together with the reasons of her coming into England . . . 2nd impression. London: W. Cadema, 1676.

Perry, Ruth. *The Life and Times of Mary Astell (1666–1731): An Early English Feminist.* Forthcoming.

————. "The Veil of Chastity: Mary Astell's Feminism." *Studies in Eighteenth Century Culture* 9 (1979): 25–63.

Smith, Florence Mary. *Mary Astell.* New York: Columbia University Press, 1916.

Smith, Hilda L. *Reason's Disciples: Seventeenth-Century English Feminists.* Urbana: University of Illinois Press, 1982.

JUDITH DRAKE
fl. 1696

*A*n *Essay in Defence of the Female Sex. In which are inserted the
Characters of a Pedant, a Squire, a Beau, a Vertuoso, a Poetaster,
a City-Critick, etc.* was published anonymously, but was probably written
by Judith Drake, whose name is affixed to the Houghton Library volume's
dedication to Princess Anne of Denmark. (The eminent seventeenth-
century historian, Christopher Hill, it should be noted, remains dubious
about this attribution.) Florence Smith, an early biographer of Mary
Astell, notes that the words "Mrs. Drake" are pencilled after "to a Lady"
on the British Library copy and that a contemporary publisher's catalogue listed the author as "Mrs. Drake, probably a sister of James Drake,
who attended to the publication of the pamphlet." Furthermore, Ruth
Perry discovered Judith Drake's name affixed to the preface of James
Drake's *Anthropologia Nova* in the British Library volume, frequently a
telling sign in determining authorship. Born in Cambridge in 1667,
James Drake, a celebrated Anglican, political activist, occassional poet,
Doctor and Fellow of the College of Physicians, wrote the sixty-four line
commendatory poem that prefaced *An Essay in Defence . . .* Judith Drake
also wrote prefaces to his posthumous works, in one of which, just after
his death, she describes herself as "a Posthumous, humorous Orphan,
of a Person that sincerely Lov'd and Honour'd [James Drake]" and
speaks of her "Melancholy Circumstances." In another posthumous preface she calls herself a "retir'd Disconsolate Woman." These public
testimonies appear to affirm that James and Judith Drake were siblings.
Since James Drake "by the care of an Indulgent Father had a very liberal
Education," Judith Drake may have shared somewhat in that.

Judith Drake's avowed justification for anonymity (assuming her authorship) rests on the contention that some men might assume that her
character sketches were directed at themselves. In these sketches, which
form the substantial mid-section of her defense, she chastised male
scholars for their freedom from "Domestic Affairs" and squires for their
lack of sense and their access to patrimony. This mode of character
writing, which derives from the Greek writer Theophrastus (c. 370–
c. 288 B.C.), enjoyed renewed popularity in the late Renaissance and
during the Restoration. In the first and last sections of her work, Drake
expressed her anger about socially sanctioned sexual inequality (due
partly to male jealousy), the suppression of women's literature, and a

sex-differentiated system of education. She encouraged women to write, talked proudly of distinguished women of the past, and succinctly refuted the notion that women are naturally inferior. Claiming reason and observation as her guides, she indicated an educated familiarity with current ideas.

The popularity of this work is attested to by its numerous additions; the fourth edition, corrected, was published in 1721. In the apparatus to the third edition with additions, published November 15, 1697, appeared a section titled "To Madam—on the Occasion of her Essay . . . ," which is a short eulogy addressed to the author by James Drake. This is followed by "The Lady's Answer to 'To Madam' " dated February 15, 1696. That James Drake had been named as author of the original essay provoked this good-humored exchange. In it, Judith Drake wittily remarked that "most men pronounce it [the *Essay*] a Performance above the ability of a woman, yet none answer the Arguments in it to the contrary. But of all the nice Judges are those that think the Stile too masculine: [who] will no more be able to discern a Man's stile for a woman's than they can tell whether this was written with a Goose Quill, or a Gander's. . . ."

FROM
AN ESSAY
IN DEFENCE OF THE
FEMALE SEX.

TO HER ROYAL HIGHNESS THE

PRINCESS ANNE OF DENMARK.

MADAM,

If in adventuring to lay this little Piece at your Highnesses Feet, and humbly beg your Royal Protection of it, I have presum'd too far, be

---

SOURCE: The dedication at the end of which Judith Drake's name appears, comes from a volume in the Houghton Library, Harvard University. "The Lady's

pleas'd to impute it to your own, most gracious Goodness, the knowledge of which encourag'd me. Our Sex are by Nature tender of their own Offspring, and may be allow'd to have more fondness for those of the Brain, then any other; because they are so few, and meet with so many Enemies at their first appearance in the World. I hope therefore to find pardon, if like an indulgent Parent, I have endeavour'd to advance my first Born, by entering it very early into your Highnesses Service.

I have not presum'd to approach your Highness out of any Confidence in the merits of this Essay, but of the Cause which it pleads, wherein the Honour of the whole Sex seem'd to exact of me no less a Patronage than that of the Best, as well as Greatest among 'em, whom they are all ambitious to see at their head. I have only endeavour'd to reduce the Sexes to a Level, and by Arguments to raise Ours to an Equallity at most with the Men: But your Highness by Illustrious Example daily convinces the World of our Superiority, and we see with wonder, Vertues in you, Madam, greater than your Birth. In this I am peculiarly happy, that I am exempted from the common Task of other Dedicators, who lie under an Obligation of publishing to the World those Excellencies of their Patrons, which perhaps appear no where but in their Epistles. In me it were as great folly, to pretend to make known the Illustrious Quallities of your Highness, as it wou'd be to go about to demonstrate by Argument, that the Sun shin'd, to a Crowd that are warm'd by the Influence of it.

I had attempted the Character of a consummate Woman, could I, tho' but faintly have shaddow'd the inimitable Graces of you Highness; but the impossibility of that Task forc'd me to desist. It were easy here to lanch into those glorious particulars, which affirmed of any other than your Royal Highness, would have been extravagance of Flattery; but to you Injustice, and in me the highest presumption, to attempt with my feeble Hand those Perfections, which the ablest must fall infinitely short of. The lustre of your Royal Vertues, Madam, like the Sun, gives us warmth and light, and while at a modest distance we admire it, improves our sight, which too bold a view confounds, yet the meanest and most ignorant see those Glories, which the most exquisite Artist can never express. The World therefore will rather justify than condemn my conduct, if I do not wrong so bright an Original with a dark obscure Copy.

Madam, Tho' the world may condemn my performance, it must applaud my choice in this Address, and own that had I known as well how to Argue, and to Instance, I must infallibly have Triumph'd over all Opposition. It may be easie to evade, or baffle the force of my Arguments, but it is impossible without the utmost Stupidity, and Injustice to deny the manifest Advantages of those Illustrious Graces, which raise your

---

Answer" comes from a volume in the Henry E. Huntington Library, shelf no. D. A4060 263604 (*An Essay in Defence* . . . The third edition with Additions, London: A. Roper and R. Clavel, 1697). The text comes from a Source Book Press reprint of the 1696 edition.

Highness so far above theirs as well as your own Sex. In this I have imitated the conduct of prudent Generals, who, when they doubt the sufficiency of their strength, retire to some strong Fort, and rest secure under the Protection of it.

There is yet another Reason, *Madam,* which tho' the least justifable, was nevertheless most prevalent with me to devote this Essay to your Highness. My Ambition to shew the profound Respects I have always had for your Highness, would not suffer me to let slip any occasion of expressing it, even tho I blush for the meanes of it. Thus I find my self reduc'd by my Zeal, to the condition of poor Tenants, who must expose their Poverty, to shew their Affection to their Lord in a worthless Present. I am sensible of the rashness of my Ambition in aspiring to the Patronage of Your Highness, and the need I have of an Apology; but were I able to make one as I ought, I should have taken care to have had less occasion for it. Yet I doubt not from Your Goodness that Indulgence, which I cannot expect from Your Justice, nor but that you will (like Heaven, whose more immediate Images Princes are) accept my unprofitable Service, for the sincerity with which it is tender'd. If my unfeign'd Submission may procure pardon for my Presumption, that Your Happiness may equal Your illustrious Vertues, and Your Royal Person be as far out of the reach of Fortune, as your Fame and Honour of Detraction, shall ever be the prayers of

Madam,
Your Royal Highness's
most Humble, most
Obedient, and most
Devoted Servant
JUDITH DRAKE.

THE LADY'S ANSWER.*

However impertinent the unjust Aspersions of those that envie you, may appear to your self, and others; yet methinks, there is a sort of Generosity in it, that makes em deny me Justice with a Complement: If they will not suffer me to own my Triffle, I am at least oblig'd to 'em, that in ascribing it to you, they confess it deserves a better Author. I am far from imagining, that this was intended as a Civility to me, which was indeed design'd as an Injury to you: But it has laid fresh Obligations upon me, since it lessens not their Respect, tho' you suffer in the Imputation, and lets me see that you can with all the Gallantry of a Courtier engage

---

* This is Judith Drake's reply to J.D. (probably her brother, James Drake) who was "accused" of writing *An Essay in Defence.* . . . In his statement "To Madam— on the Occasion of her Essay, in Defence of her Sex," he speaks of himself as being "shin'd by the lustre of another's worth."

in a Friends Cause, and scorn the Court Trick of deserting it, when it grows troublesome, or difficult. 'Tis no small comfort to me, that I have such a Champion against such petty Adversaries; for tho' a Man can't decently draw his Sword upon e'ry yelping little Cur, that barks at him in the street, yet if they snarl too near his heels, he may spurn 'em without offence to his gravity. To oppose such Fellows their own way, were like quarrelling with the common Scavengers, and throwing Filth about to bewray themselves and annoy the Neighhood. Such immoral Swine ought to be submitted to the Ecclestastical Censure, and do Pennance in one clean sheet, for the filthy Rheams they've abus'd the World with.

I send you herewith the Enclos'd, that you may see there are those, that tho' they differ in my Opinion, yet can treat me with good Breeding: The Candour and Ingenuity of this Gentleman, makes me regret his being unknown to me, because it deprives me of the proper means of Acknowledgement:

PREFACE

Prefaces to most Books, are like Prolocutors to Puppet-Shows, they come first to tell you what Figures are to be presented, and what Tricks they are to play. According therefore to ancient and laudable Custom, I have thought fit to let you know by way of Preface, or Advertisement, (call it which you please) that here are many fine Figures within to be seen, as well worth your curiosity, as any in Smithfield at Bartholomew Tide. I will not deny, Reader, but that you may have seen some of 'em there already; to those that have, I have little more to say, than that if they have a mind to see them again in Effigie, they may do it here. What is it you wou'd have? Here are St. George's, Batemans, John Dories, Punchinello's, and the Creation of the World, or what's as good; here's the German Artist too, or one that can show more Tricks than he: If all this will not invite you, y'are grown more squeamish of late, Gentleman, than you us'd to be, and the poor Bookseller will make but an indifferent Market of you. Well, let the worst come to the worst, 'tis but shifting the scene to Smithfield, and making an Interest in half a dozen Vizer-Masks to be sure of your Company: But he, good Man, is desirous to please you at first hand, and therefore has put a fine Picture in the front to invite you in, so like some of you (as he protests) that you ought never look in a Glass again, if it offends you. For my part, I declare, he has acted clear against my Opinion in this case, and so he has been told; for many a poor Man has lost the showing of his Monster, by gratifying the curiosity of the gaping Crowd with too exact a picture without doors. Besides, there's an unlucky Rogue of a left-handed Barber, that looks like an ill Omen in the beginning. He was told too, that if he wou'd please most of you, he ought to take example by your Glasses and flatter you. Yet he continued obstinate and unmoveable to all these weighty Reasons, and is so fondly bent for his Picture, that he resolv'd against all advice to have it. Nay, and he wou'd have Rhimes underneath it too, which, he says, weigh more with you, than all the Reasons in the world. I thought fit to let you know this, that the Bookseller might not lose the credit of his Fancy, if it takes with you, as he is perswaded it will. For you must know, I am a great lover of strict Justice, and therefore would by no means Rob, or Defraud him of the Glory of his Invention, or by any sinister way sullie, or diminish the Honour, or Reputation of his Parts and Ingenuity. For the same Reason likewise I must acquaint you, that the Rhimes are none of mine neither; and now my Hand is in, I don't much care if I tell you, that I am not very good at that ingenious Recreation, called Crambo, from which some rise to be very considerable Rhimers. This now is more then I was oblig'd to tell you, and therefore I hope no body will deny, but that I deal ingenuously at least with you.

This one would think were Preface sufficient; but there are some Men so impertinently curious, that they must needs have a Reason for every thing, that is done in the World, tho' it were in their favour (for which perhaps it were hard to give a good one) when it were their Interest to be satisfied, and thankful without further enquiry. To comply therefore in some measure with the humour of these People, if any such think fit to peruse this Book, I must tell 'em very freely, that I was so far from aiming to oblige, or disoblige 'em by it, that it was never intended for their View. It was occasion'd by a private Conversation, between some Gentlemen and Ladies, and written at the request, and for the Diversion of one Lady more particularly, by whom with my consent it was communicated to two or three more of both Sexes, my Friends likewise.

By them I was with abundance of Complements importun'd to make it publick; now tho' I do with good Reason attribute much more, of what was said to me upon this Occasion, to their good Breeding and Friendship, than to their real Opinions of my Performance; yet I have so much satisfaction in their Sincerity, and Friendship as to be confident they would not suffer, much less perswade me to expose to the world any thing, of which they doubted so far, as to think it would not be tollerably acceptable. Nor have I less assurance of their Judgment and Skill in things of this nature, beside that I have been inform'd by some of 'em, that it has been seen, and favourably receiv'd by some Gentlement, whom the world thinks so incompetent Judges. After all this Encouragement, I suppose, I shall not be thought vain, if, as I pretend not to the applause, so I fear not the contempt of the world: Yet I presume not so far upon the Merits of what I have written, as to make my Name publick with it. I have elsewhere held, that Vanity was almost the universal mover of all our Actions, and consequently of mine, as well as of others; yet it is not strong enough in me, to induce me to bring my Name upon the publick stage of the World.

There are many Reasons, that oblige me to this cautious reserv'd way of procedure; tho' I might otherwise be very ambitious of appearing in the defence of my Sex, cou'd I persuade my self, that I was able to write any thing sutable to the dignity of the Subject, which I am not vain enough to think. This indeed is one Reason, because I am sensible it might have been much better defended by abler Pens, such as many among our own Sex are; though I believe scarce thus much wou'd have been expected from me, by those that know me. There is likewise another Reason, which was yet more prevalent with me, and with those few Friends whom I consulted about it, which is this; There are a sort of Men, that upon all occasions think themselves more concern'd, and more thought of than they are, and that, like Men that are deaf, or have any other notorious Defect, can see no body whisper, or laugh, but they think 'tis at themselves. These Men are apt to think, that every ridiculous description they meet with, was intended more particularly for some one or other of them; as indeed it is hard to paint any thing compleat in their several Kinds, without hitting many of their particular Features, even without drawing from them. The knowledge of this, with the consideration of the tenderness of Reputation in our Sex, (which as our delicatest Fruits and finest Flowers are most obnoxious to the injuries of Weather, is submitted to every infectious Blast of malicious Breath) made me very cautious, how I expos'd mine to such poisonous Vapours. I was not ignorant, how liberal some Men are of their Scandal, whenever provok'd, especially by a Woman; and how ready the same Men are to be so, tho upon never so mistaken Grounds. This made me resolve to keep 'em in Ignorance of my Name, and if they have a mind to find me out, let 'em catch me (if they can) as Children at Blindmans Buff do one another, Hoodwinkt; and I am of Opinion I have room enough to put 'em out of Breath before they come near me.

The Event has in Effect prov'd my suspicions Prophetick; for there are (as I am inform'd) already some, so forward to interest themselves against me, that they take Characters upon themselves, before they see 'em; and, for fear they should want some Body to throw their Dirt at, with equal Ignorance, and Injustice Father this Piece upon the Gentleman, who was so kind as to take care of the Publication of it, only to excuse me from appearing. This made me once resolve to oppose my Innocence to their Clamour, and perfix my Name, which I thought I was bound to do in Justice to him. In this Resolution I had persisted, had not the very same Gentleman generously perswaded, and over-rul'd me to the contrary, representing how weak a defence Innocence is against Calumny, how open the Ears of all the World are, and how greedily they suck in any thing to the prejudice of a Woman; and that (to use his own Expression) the scandal of such Men, was like Dirt thrown by Children, and Fools at random, and without Provocation, it would dawb filthily at first, though it were easily washt off again: Adding, that he desir'd me not to be under any concern for him; for he valued the Malice of such men, as little, as their Friendship, the one was as feeble, as tother false.

I suppose I need make no Apology to my own Sex for the meaness of this defence; the bare intention of serving 'em will I hope be accepted, and of Men, the Candid and Ingenuous I am sure will not quarrel with me for any thing in this little Book; since there is nothing in it, which was not drawn from the strictest Reason I was Mistress of, and the best Observations I was able to make, except a start or two only concerning the Salique Law, and the Amazons, which, if they divert not the Reader, can't offend him.

I shall not trouble the Reader with any account of the Method I have observ'd, he will easily discover that in reading the Piece it self. I shall only take notice to him of one thing, which with a little attention to what he reads he will readily find to be true, that is, that the Characters were not written out of any Wanton Humour, or Malicious Design to characterize any Particular Persons, but to illustrate what I have said upon the several Heads, under which they are rang'd, and represent not single Men, but so many Clans, or Divisions of Men, that play the Fool seriously in the World. If any Individual seem to be more peculiarly markt, it is because he is perhaps more notorious to the World, by some one or more Articles of the General Character here given. I am sure that there is no Man, who is but moderately Accquainted with the World, especially this Town, but may find half a Dozen, or more Originals for every Picture. After all, if any Man have so little Wit, as to appropriate any of these Characters to himself, He takes a liberty I have hitherto never given him, but shall do it now in the Words of a Great Man, If any Fool finds the Cap fit him, let him put it on.

An Essay in Defence

. . . I shall desire those, that hold against us to observe the Country People, I mean the inferiour sort of them, such as not having Stocks to follow Husbandry upon their own Score, subsist upon their daily Labour. For amongst these, though no so equal as that of the Brutes, yet the Condition of the two Sexes is more level, than amongst Gentlemen, City Traders, or rich Yeomen. Examine them in their several Businesses, and their Capacities will appear equal; but talk of them of things indifferent, and out of the Road of their constant Employment, and the Balance will fall on our side, the Women will be found the more ready and polite. Let us look a little further, and view our Sex in a state of more improvement, amongst our Neighbours the Dutch. There we shall find them managing not only the Domestick Affairs of the Family, but making and receiving all Payments as well great as small, keeping the Books, ballancing the

Accounts, and doing all the Business, even the nicest of Merchants, with as much Dexterity and Exactness as their, or our Men can do. And I have often hear'd some of our considerable Merchants blame the conduct of our Country-Men in this point; that they breed our Women so ignorant of Business; whereas were they taught Arithmetick, and other Arts which require not much bodily strength, they might supply the places of abundance of lusty Men now employ'd in sedentary Business; which would be a mighty profit to the Nation by sending those Men to Employments, where hands and Strength are more requir'd, especially at this time when we are in such want of People. Beside that it might prevent the ruine of many Families, which is often occasion'd by the Death of Merchants in full Business, and leaving their Accounts perplex'd, and embroil'd to a Widdow and Orphans, who understanding nothing of the Husband or Father's Business occasions . . . the utter Confounding a fair estate; which might be prevented, did the Wife understand Merchants Accounts. . . .

He asks your Opinion, yet for fear you shou'd not jump with him, tells you his own first. He desires no Favour, yet is disappointed, if he be not Flatter'd, and is offended always at the Truth. His first Education is generally a Shop, or a Counting-House, where his acquaintance commences with the Bell-man upon a new Years day. He puts him upon Intriguing with the Muses, and promises to Pimp for him. From this time forward he hates the name of Mechanick, and resolves to sell all his stock, and purchase a Plantation in Parnassus. He is now a Poetical Haberdasher of Small Wares, and deals very much in Novels, Madrigals, Riddles, Funeral, and Love Odes, and Elegies, and other Toyes from Helicon, which he has a Shop so well furnish'd with, that he can fit you with all sorts and Sizes upon all Occasions in the twinkling of an Eye. He frequents Apollo's Exchange in Covent-Garden, and picks up the freshest Intelligence what Plays are upon the Stocks, or ready to be lauch'd; who have lately made a good Voyage, who a saving one only, and who have suffer'd a Wreck in Lincoln's-Inn-Feilds, or Drury-Lane, and which are brought into the Dock to be Careen'd and fitted for another Voyage. He talks much of Jack Dryden, and Will Wycherley, and the rest of the Set, and protests he can't help having some respect for 'em, because they have so much for him, and his Writings; otherwise he cou'd shew 'em to be meer Sots and Blockheads that understand little of Poetry, in comparison of himself; but he forbears 'em meerly out of Gratitude, and Compassion. Once a Month he fits out a small Poetical Smeck at the charge of his Bookseller, which he lades with French Plunder new Vampt in English, small Ventures of Translated Odes, Elegies and Epigrams of Young Traders, and ballasts with heavy Prose of his own; for which returns are to be made to the several Owners in Testers, or applause from the Prentices and Tyre Women that deal for 'em. He is the Oracle of those that want Wit, and the Plague of those that have it; for he haunts their Lodgings, and is more terrible to 'em, than their Duns. His Pocket is an

Character of a Poetaster

unexhaustible Magazine of Rhime, and Nonsense, and his Tongue like a repeating Clock with Chimes, is ready upon every touch to sound to 'em. Men avoid him for the same Reason, they avoid the Pillory, the security of their Ears; of which he is as merciless a Persecutor. He is the Bane of Society, a Friend to the Stationers, the Plague of the Press, and the Ruine of his Bookseller. He is more profitable to the Grocers and Tabacconists than the Paper Manufacture; for his Works which talk so much of Fire and Flame, commonly expire in their Shops in Vapour and Smoak. If he aspire to Comedy, he intrigues with some experienc'd Damsel of the Town, in order to instruct himself in the humour of it, and is cullied by her into Matrimony, and so is furnish'd at once with a Plot, and two good Characters, himself and his Wife and is paid with a Portion for a Jointure in Parnassus, which I leave him to make his best of.

I shall not trouble you with any more Instances of the foolish vanities of Mankind; because I am afraid I have been too large upon that Head already. Not that I think there is any Order or Degree of Men, which wou'd not afford many and notorious instances for our Purpose. For as I think Vanity almost the Universal mover of all our Actions, whether good or bad; so I think there are scarce any Men so Ingenious, or so Vertuous, but something of it will shine through the greatest Part of what they do, let them cast never so thick a Vail over it. What makes Men so solicitous of Leaving a Reputation behind 'em in the World, though they know they can't be affected with it after Death, but this even to a degree of Folly? What else makes great Men involve themselves in the Fatigues and Hazards of War, and Intricate Intrigues of State, when they have already more than they can enjoy, but an Itch of being talk'd of and remembred to which they sacrifice their present happiness and repose?

But I shall carry these Considerations no farther; because I have already singled out some of those many whose Vanity is more extravagant and ridiculous, than any our Sex is chargeable with, these slight Touches may serve to let 'em see, that even the greatest, and Wisest are not wholly exempt, if they have it not in a higher Degree, tho' they exercise it in things more Popular, and Plausible. I hope therefore the burthen of this good Quality will not hereafter be laid upon us alone, but the Men will be contented to divide the Load with us, and be thankful that they bear less than their Proportion. . . .

PRIMARY SOURCE

An Essay in Defence of the Female Sex. In which are inserted the Characters of a Pedant, a Squire, a Beau, a Vertuoso, a Poetaster, a City-critick, etc., In a letter to a lady. Written by a lady. London: A. Roper and E. Wilkinson, 1696. Reprint. New York: Source Book Press, 1970. (Stated by the modern editor to be a republication of the 1696 London edition with new type and corrections based on original errata.)

RELATED SOURCES

Perry, Ruth. *The Life and Times of Mary Astell (1666–1731): An Early English Feminist,* Chapter one. Forthcoming.

Reynolds, Myra. *The Learned Lady in England, 1650–1760.* Boston: Houghton Mifflin, 1920.

Smith, Florence Mary. *Mary Astell.* New York: Columbia University Press, 1916.

MARY LEE

LADY CHUDLEIGH

1656 – 1710

Mary Lee was the daughter of a gentleman, Richard Lee, of Winslade in Devon. To date, nothing is known of her mother. A Royalist self-educated in literature, she married George Chudleigh of Ashton in Devon who later inherited a baronetcy. She bore two sons and a daughter, Eliza Maria, "who died in the bloom of life."

Angered by a sermon preached at a Dorsetshire wedding in 1699 by the nonconformist minister John Sprint, in which he advocated women's total subjection to their husbands, Lady Chudleigh wrote a verse-debate in response entitled *The Ladies Defence: or, the Bride-Woman's Counsellor answer'd; . . . ,* which was published without her consent in the second edition of her *Poems.*

This work sounds many important notes in turn of the century feminist controversy that followed the varying tenets of Church and Dissenting beliefs: the negative attitude of males and their demeaning expectations of women; the role of the church in propagating pernicious ideas about women, couched as protection of public morals; the duties of a wife to be silent, abjectly obedient, and tolerant of physical and psychological abuse; and the conventional dismissal of female education. Her poem also advances an eloquent defense (by a superficially well-meaning male) of female intellectuality and blames male insecurity about women's potential power on the persistent denial of a worthwhile education. The female protagonist proclaims women's right to knowledge and reason and their necessary and understandable refuge in one another for support, friendship, and understanding.

A deeply pious and frequently melancholic Anglican whose stated purpose in writing was "exercising and enlarging my Thoughts, and of height'ning and refining those ideas . . . of the infinite Goodness, Wisdom, and Power of God," Lady Chudleigh immersed herself in religious, scientific, and philosophical speculations. She was well-attuned to such ideas as the Pythagorean transmigration of souls and the "Cartesian Hypothesis" that "the first stars are suns, and each the center of a Vortex," which she occasionally drew on for literary material and images.

She may have been part of an informal group of women writers. Many of her poems extol friendship and the women friends upon whom she bestowed classical names. In her correspondence with Elizabeth Thomas, for example, she alludes to Mary Astell, whom she apparently found awe-inspiring. In a letter dated October 8, 1703, she tells Thomas that "the greatest Part of my time is spent in my Closet; . . . I find my Books and my Thoughts to be the most agreeable Companions, and had I not betime accustomed my self to their Conversation, perhaps I should have been as unhappy as any of my Sex . . . Life & Death are Things very indifferent to me; I'm neither solicitious for the one or afraid of the Other." One week later she confided that "Life is what I have for many years had no Reason to be fond of, and a Grave has appeared to me the happiest and best Asylum." A volume of her essays was published in 1710, the same year that she died of a painful rheumatism in Ashton, Devon.

THE LADIES DEFENCE

"TO ALL INGENIOUS LADIES."

LADIES,

The Love of Truth, the tender Regard I have for your Honour, joyn'd with a just Indignation to see you so unworthily us'd, makes me assume the Confidence of imploying my Pen in your Service. The Knowledge I had of my Inability for so great a Task, made me for a while stifle my Resentments, as thinking it much better privately to lament the Injuries that were done you, than expose you by a weak Defence to the fresh Insults of a Person, who has not yet learnt to distinguish between Railing and Instruction, and who is so vain as to fancy, that the Dignity of his Function will render everything he thinks fit to say becoming: But when I found that some Men were so far from finding fault with his Sermon, that they rather defended it, and express'd an ill-natur'd sort of Joy to see you ridicul'd, and that those few among 'em who were Pretenders to more Generosity and good Humour, were yet too proud, too much devoted to their Interest, and too indulgent to their Pleasures, to give themselves the Trouble of saying any thing in your Vindication, I had not the Patience to

SOURCE: *The Ladies Defence* and selections from *Poems on Several Occasions* are taken from manuscripts in the Houghton Library, Harvard University. "To all Ingenious Ladies" and "The Preface to the Reader" are prefatory material to *The Ladies Defence* from a manuscript in the Henry E. Huntington Library, shelf no. 58020.

be Silent any longer. Besides it vex'd me to think he should have the Satisfaction of believing, that what by the Malice of some, the Neutrality of others, and the Sacredness of his Character, he was secur'd from all Opposition, and might triumph over you at his Pleasure: it also troubl'd me to find that but one of our own Sex had the Courage to enter the Lists with him:* I know there are several other Ladies, who, if they wou'd be so kind to themselves, and you, as to undertake the Quarrel, wou'd manage it with more Learning, Eloquence and Address, than I dare pretend to, as being infinitely my Superiours in all the Indowments of the Mind; but since they think fit to decline it, I hope they will permit me to enter the Field, and try my Fortune with our mighty Antagonist. I assure 'em I do not do it out of an ambitious desire of being talk'd of, or with hopes of having it said, I can Write well; no, if I know my own Heart, I am far from any such Vanity, as being too well acquainted with my own Insufficiency, to entertain any such unbecoming Thoughts of my mean Performance. The following Poem is intirely the Result of that great Concern and Zeal I have for your Reputation; and if it happens to do you any Service, I have all that I aim at; and the only Favour I have to beg of you is, that you will be so generous as to receive it into your Protection, and so obliging as to let the Affection with which 'twas written, compensate for its Faults. I am sorry Mr. Sprint should have any occasion given him for so severe an Invective, and I heartily wish my Sex wou'd keep a stricter Guard over their Passions, and amidst all the various Occurrences of Life, consult neither their Ease, the Gratification of their Humour, nor the Satisfaction of others, when 'tis in Opposition to their Reason; but having rightly inform'd themselves what ought to be done on each Emergency, go steadily on, without being disturb'd either at Unkindness, Reproaches, Affronts or Disappointments; that all who see 'em may have just cause to conclude, from the Regularity of their Actions, the Calmness of their Tempers, and the Serenity of their Looks, that there are no Uneasinesses within, and that they are infinitely better pleas'd with the secret Plaudits of their own Consciences, than they would be with the flattering Acclamations of a deceitful inconstant World; but such an Evenness, such a Tranquility of Mind, is not attainable without much Study, and the closest Application of Thought; it must be the work of Time, and the Effect of a daily Practice. But perhaps, while I am indeavouring to make you happy, and shewing you the way to transmit your Names with Honour to succeeding Ages, my kindness may be misconstru'd, and I thought guilty of unpardonable Arrogancy, for presuming to prescribe Rules to Persons, who already know much more than I can teach 'em. To free my self from this Imputation, I solemnly declare, That what I write is wholly intended for such as are on the same Level with my self, and have not been blest with a learned and ingenious Education, and cannot boast of such a strength of Resolution, such a constancy of

---

* Eugenia. See Supplementary Readings. (Ed.)

Mlnd, such a depth of Reason and solidity of Judgment, as is requisite, in order to the obtaining that desirable Firmness, and, (if I may be allow'd to call it so) Inflexibility of Soul, which I have been recommending; and not for those who, by the greatness of their Virtue, and the Sublimity of their Wit, are rais'd to a Height above me; on such I content my self to gaze at an awful distance, and am pleas'd to see, notwithstanding what has been said to the contrary by some envious Detractors, still among us Women that are shining Examples of Piety, Prudence, Moderation, Patience, and all other valuable Qualities; by such as these I should take it as a Favour to be instructed; and would they by a generous Condescension give themselves the Trouble of directing us in the management of our Lives, we should be for ever bound to pay 'em the highest Retributions. 'Tis only to such as are in the lowest Form, to the meanest Proficients in the School of Virtue, that I take the Liberty of giving Advice. So well, so intirely well I love my Sex, that if 'twere in my Power they shou'd be all wholly faultless, and as much admir'd for the Comprehensiveness of their Knowledge, as they are now despis'd for their Ignorance, and have Souls as beauteous as their Faces, Thoughts as bright and sparkling as their Eyes: And in what Station so ever Providence thinks fit to place 'em, I would earnestly desire 'em, as a thing exceedingly for their Honour, to be careful to observe a just Decorum, and neither suffer themselves to be transported with Joy when they are Happy, or dispirited when they are Miserable; but to be humble, kind, sincere, and easie of Access, when Great, Liberal when Rich, Sedate, Chearful and Contented when Poor, free from Revenge, and ready to forgive when injur'd, the same when reproach'd or applauded, when caress'd, or neglected: And if it is their hard Fortune to be marry'd to Men of brutish unsociable Tempers, to Monsters in Humane Shape, to Persons who are at open defiance with their Reason, and fond of nothing but their Folly, and under no other Government but that of their irregular Passions, I would perswade them to struggle with their Afflictions, and never leave contending, 'till they have gain'd an absolute Victory over every repining Thought, every uneasie Reflection: And tho' 'tis extreamly difficult, yet I wou'd advise 'em to pay 'em as much Respect, and to obey their Commands with as much readiness, as if they were the best and most indearing Husbands in the World; this, will not only put a stop to the invidious Censures of their spightful Enemies, but give 'em the possession of that inward Joy, that unspeakable Satisfaction, which naturally arises from the apprehension of having done good and laudable Actions: In order to the gaining such a happy disposition of Mind, I would desire 'em seriously to consider what those things are which they can properly call their own, and of which Fortune cannot deprive 'em, and on these alone they ought to terminate their Desires, and not vainly extend 'em to those things which are not within their Power, as Honours, Riches, Reputation, Health, and Beauty; for they being Goods which they cannot bestow on themselves, and of which they may have but a very

transient possession, they ought to enjoy 'em with indifferency, and
look on 'em only as Gifts, which the Almighty Donor freely and liberally
gives, and which he may, when he thinks fit, resume without the least
injustice: . . .

LADIES,
Your most Humble
and Devoted Servant.

M---y C-------

THE LADIES DEFENCE

"THE PREFACE TO THE READER."

THE BOOK, which has been the occasion of the insuing Poem, was
presented to me by its Author, of whom, notwithstanding he has
been pleas'd to treat us with the utmost Severity and Neglect, I think my
self oblig'd in Justice to say, that he is a Person of Learning. What his
Reasons were for using us so roughly, I know not; perhaps he did it to
let us see his Wit, who has had the ill Fortune to converse with Women
of ungovernable Tempers, whose Passions have got the Ascendant of
their Reason; such I think cannot be too harshly treated, and the greatest
kindness that can be done 'em, is to bring 'em (if 'tis possible) to the
Knowledge of themselves, and their Duty, and by shewing them their
Faults, indeavour to depress those towring Imaginations. But 'tis hard
that all should suffer for the Failures and Indiscretions of some; that
those who are willing to give up themselves intirely to the Conduct of
Reason, who make it their Study to live according to the strictest Rules
of Vertue, and are so far from indulging themselves in their Follies, that
they esteem Reproofs as the greatest Favours that can be shown 'em, and
are contented that all Mankind should be Judges of their Actions; whom
Passions cannot byass, nor Interest tempt, nor Ill Usage provoke to do or
say any thing unworthy of themselves, should be rank'd with Criminals,
and have no Deference pay'd em: 'Tis for their Sakes alone I have made
the following Remarks. I have done it by way of Dialogue, and those
Expressions which I thought would be indecent in the Mouth of a Reverend Divine, are spoken by Sir *John Brute*, who has all the extraordinary
Qualifications of an accomplish'd Husband; and to render his Character
compleat, I have given him the Religion of a Wit, and the good Humour
of a Critick. I am afraid the Clergy will accuse me of Atheism for making
Sir John speak so irreverently of them; but before they condemn me, I
beg 'em to be so just as to consider, that I do not speak my own Thoughts,

but what one might rationally suppose a Man of his Character will say on such Occasions: And to prevent their having any misapprehensions of me, I do assure 'em, that for all such of their Order as are pious and ingenuous Men, whose Conversations are instructive, and whose Lives are conformable to those holy Truths they teach, none can have a higher Veneration than I: And if such as these find any thing in my Poem that they dislike, they will oblige me in letting me know it, and I promise 'em I will retract it. Had he treated us with a little more Respect, and instead of the surly Sourness of a Cynick, express'd himself with the good Humour of an English Man, and the soft and indearing Mildness of a Christian, I should have thought my self oblig'd to have return'd him Thanks for his Instructions. That we are generally less Knowing, and less Rational than the Men, I cannot but acknowledge; but I think 'tis oftener owing to the illness of our Education, than the weakness of our Capacities. The learned F. Malebranch says, *'Tis in a certain Temperature of the Largeness and Agitation of the Animal Spirits, and conformity with the Fibres of the Brain, that the Strength of Parts consists;* and he tells us, That Women are sometimes blest with that just Temperature, and are Learned, Couragious, and capable of every thing; and instead of that nauseous Jargon, and those impertinent Stories with which our Maids usually entertain us in our younger Years, taught the Languages of the Schools, and accustom'd to the reading of Histories, and Books of Morality; and did our Husbands treat us with that Kindness, that Sincerity, I will not say with that Respect, for fear that should be thought too much for a Wife, but only with that common Civility which is due to Strangers, they would meet with a grateful return, and have much less reason to complain. Would the Men do me the honour to take my Advice, I am confident they would for the future have less occasion to complain. First; I would have them be more judicious in their Choice, and prefer Virtue and good Sense, before either Riches, Beauty or Quality; these, joyn'd with an agreeable Humour, will make them happier than the greatest Affluence of Wealth, or than all the Charms of a lovely Face; and if 'tis their good Fortune to meet with such, I would in the second Place perswade 'em to treat them with all that Affection and Tenderness which they deserve, and leave intirely to their management the Affairs of the Kitchen, and those other little Concerns of the Family which seem to be below their inspection. And Lastly, I would have them look upon them as Friends, as Persons fit to be confided in, and trusted with their Designs, as such whose Interest is inseparably united with theirs: by such Methods as these, they would not only win their Love, but preserve it, and engage 'em to a reciprocal Esteem; and when once they have secur'd their Affection, they need not doubt of their Obedience; the desire to please will render the most difficult Commands easie.

There is one thing which I think does more contribute to the Unhappiness of the married State, than any of those which he has mention'd, and that is, Parents forcing their Children to Marry contrary to their Inclinations; Men believe they have a right to dispose of their Children as they please; and they think it below them to consult their Satisfaction: 'Tis no matter what their Thoughts are, if the Fathers like, 'tis enough: And is it rational to suppose, that such Matches can ever be fortunate? If the Men are prudent, they will carry it civilly to their Wives; and the Women if they are discreet, will be obsequious and respectful to their Husbands, but there cannot be that Friendship, that Tenderness, that Unity of Affection which ought to be in that sacred State. I could say much more on so copious a Subject, but I fear I have already weary'd my Reader, to whose Trouble I will not add, by making trifling Apologies for what I have written: The liberty I take, I am willing to give, and the ingenious Author may, if he pleases, Animadvert as freely on my Book, as I have done on his; if he finds any thing in it that can justly give him any Offence, I beg his Pardon for it; and I do assure him, that what I have writ is wholly the Result of that great Concern and Kindness I have for my Sex, and is so far from proceeding from the least Disrespect to him, that I am ready to own to the whole World, that I think for his Piety he deserves an universal Esteem.

THE LADIES DEFENCE:

OR

A DIALOGUE BETWEEN SIR JOHN BRUTE, SIR WILLIAM LOVEALL, MELISSA, AND A PARSON.

Sir JOHN. WElcome, thou brave Defender of our Right;
'Till now, I thought you knew not how to write:
Dull heavy Morals did your Pen employ;
And all your Business was to pall our Joy:
With frightful Tales our Ears you still did grate,
And we with awful Reverence heard you prate;
Heard you declaim on Vice, and blame the Times,
Because we impudently shar'd your Crimes;
Those darling Sins you wholly wou'd ingross:
And when disturb'd, and fretting at your Loss
With whining Tones, and a pretended Zeal,
Saw you the Rancour of your Minds reveal:

'Till now, none of your Tribe were ever kind,
Good Humour is alone to you confin'd;
You, who against those Terrors of our Lives,
Those worst of Plagues, those Furies call'd our Wives,
Have shew'd your Anger in a Strain divine,
Resentment sparkles in each poignant Line.
Sure you've the Fate of wretched Husbands met,
And 'tis your own Misfortune you regret;
You cou'd not else with such a feeling Sense
Expatiate on each Fault, and blazon each Offence.
How happy, O Sir William, is your Life!
You have not known the Trouble of a Wife:
Your rural Cares you undisturb'd can mind,
And 'midst your brutal Subjects Pleasure find:
Your snowy Flocks you with Delight can view,
They are both innocent, and pretty too:
And when from Business you your Thoughts unbend,
You can with Joy the noble Chase attend,
Or when you please drink freely with a Friend.
No frowning Female stands observing by,
No Children fright you with their hideous Cry;
None dare contend; none your Commands dispute;
You, like the great Mogul, are Absolute:
Supream in all Things; from our Slavery free,
And taste the Sweets of envy'd Liberty.

Sir WILLIAM. The beauteous Sex I ever did revere,
And can't with Patience these Reflections hear:
To them I've long a constant Homage pay'd,
And with Delight each charming Face survey'd.
I've had of Mistresses a numerous Store,
The fam'd Anacreon could not boast of more;
Yet each was good, each with Perfections blest,
And each by turns has triumph'd in my Breast.
That I'm unmarry'd, is my Fate, not Choice:
I in a happy Bondage should rejoyce;
And thank my Stars, if they wou'd yet incline
Some lovely She to be for ever mine:
Then wonder not to hear me take their Part,
And plead for the dear Idols of my Heart.
Spightful Invectives shou'd no Patrons find,
They are the Shame, and Venom of the Mind.

PARSON. Not led by Passion, but by Zeal inspir'd,
I've told the Women what's of them requir'd:
Shew'd them their Duty in the clearest Light,

Adorn'd with all the Charms that cou'd invite:
Taught them their Husbands to obey and please,
And to their Humours sacrifice their Ease:
Give up their Reason, and their Wills resign,
And ev'ry Look, and ev'ry Thought confine.
Sure, this Detraction you can't justly call?
'Tis kindly meant, and 'tis address'd to All.

   MELISSA. Must Men command, and we alone obey,
As if design'd for arbitrary Sway:
Born petty Monarchs, and, like Homer's Gods,
See all subjected to their haughty Nods?
Narcissus like, you your own Graces view,
Think none deserve to be admir'd but you:
Your own Perfections always you adore,
And think of others despicably poor:
We have our Faults, but you are all divine,
Wisdom does in your meanest Actions shine:
Just, Pious, Chast, from ev'ry Passion free,
By Learning rais'd above Humanity;
For every Failure you a Covering find:
Rage is a noble Bravery of Mind;
Revenge, a Tribute due to injur'd Fame;
And Pride, but what transcendant Worth does claim:
Cowards are wary, and the Dull are grave,
Fops are genteel, and hectoring Bullies brave:
Such as live high, regardless of Expence,
Are generous Men, and ever bless'd with Sense:
Base Avarice, Frugality you call,
And he's a prudent Man who grasps at all:
Who to be Rich, does labour, cheat, and lie;
Does to himself the Sweets of Life deny,
And wretched lives, that he may wealthy dye.
Thus to each Vice you give some specious Name,
And with bright Colours varnish o'er your Shame.
But unto us is there no Deference due?
Must we pay all, and look for none from you?
Why are not Husbands taught, as well as we;
Must they from all Restraints, all Laws be free?
Passive Obedience you've to us transferr'd,
And we must drudge in Paths where you have err'd:
That antiquated Doctrine you disown;
'Tis now your Scorn, and fit for us alone.

   PARSON. Love and Respect, are, I must own, your due;
But not 'till there's Obedience paid by you:

Submission, and a studious Care to please,
May give a Right to Favours great as these:
But if Subjection is by you deny'd,
You'll fall th' unpity'd Victims of your Pride:
We then all Husband justly may appear,
And talk, and frown, 'till we have taught you Fear.

Sir JOHN. Yes, as we please, we may our Wives chastise,
'Tis the Prerogative of being Wise:
They are but Fools, and must as such be us'd:
Heaven! how I blush to see our Pow'r abus'd:
To see Men doat upon a Female Face,
And all the Manly Roughness of their Sex disgrace!

MELISSA. Not thus you talk'd when you Lenera lov'd;
By softer Passion, sure, your Soul was mov'd:
Then at her Feet, false Man, you flatt'ring lay,
And pray'd, and vow'd, and sigh'd your Hours away;
Admir'd her Face, her Shape, her Mein, her Air,
And swore that none was so divinely fair;
None had such Charms, none else the wond'rous Art
To gain th' entire Possession of your Heart.
Having expended your whole Stock of Sense,
And quite exhausted all your Eloquence,
When not one Phrase was left of all your Store,
Asham'd to have it known you were so poor,
You made your Silence want of Words supply,
And look'd, as if your Love wou'd make you die;
Shew'd all your Art, your Native Guile display'd,
And gaz'd till you had won the thoughtless Maid.

Sir JOHN. I lov'd her, 'till to her I was confin'd:
But who can long to what's his own be kind?
Plagues seize the Wretch who ty'd the cursed Knot,
Let him be damn'd: Eternally forgot.

MELISSA. There spoke the Husband; all the Fiend reveal'd:
Your Passion utters what's by most conceal'd.
O that my Sex safe Infidels would live,
And no more Credit to your Flatt'ries give.
Mistrust your Vows, despise your little Arts,
And keep a constant Guard upon their Hearts.
Unhappy they, who by their Duty led,
Are made the Partners of a hated Bed;
And by their Fathers Avarice or Pride,
To Empty Fops, or nauseous Clowns are ty'd;

Or else constrain'd to give up all their Charms
Into an old ill-humour'd Husband's Arms,
Who hugs his Bags, and never was inclin'd
To be to ought besides his Money kind,
On that he dotes, and to increase his Wealth,
Wou'd sacrifice his Conscience, Ease and Health,
Give up his Children, and divorce his Wife,
And live a Stranger to the Joys of Life.
Who's always positive in what is Ill,
And still a Slave to his imperious Will:
Averse to any Thing he thinks will please,
Still sick, and still in love with his Disease:
With Fears, with Discontent, with Envy curst,
To all uneasy, and himself the worst:
A spightful Censor of the present Age,
Or dully jesting, or deform'd with Rage.
These call for Pity, since it is their Fate;
Their Friends, not they, their Miseries create:
They are like Victims to the Alter led,
Born for Destruction, and for Ruin bred;
Forc'd to sigh out each long revolving Year,
And see their Lives all spent in Toil and Care.
But such as may be from this Bondage free,
Who've no Abridgers of their Liberty;
No cruel Parents, no imposing Friends,
To make 'em wretched for their private Ends;
From me shall no Commiseration have,
If they themselves to barbarous Men enslave.
They'd better wed among the savage Kind,
And be to generous Lyons still confin'd;
Or match'd to Tygers, who would gentler prove
Than you, who talk of Piety and Love,
Words, whose true Sense you never understood,
And for that Reason, are not kind, nor good.

PARSON. Why all this Rage? we merit not your Hate;
'Tis you alone disturb the Marriage State:
If to your Lords you strict Allegiance pay'd,
And their Commands submissively obey'd,
If like wise Eastern Slaves with trembling Awe
You watch'd their Looks, and made their Will your Law,
You wou'd both Kindness and Protection gain,
And find your duteous Care was not in vain.
This I advis'd, this, I your Sex have taught;
And ought Instruction to be call'd a Fault?
Your Duty was, I knew, the harder part;

Obedience being a harsh, uneasy Art:
The Skill to Govern, Men with Ease can learn;
We're soon instructed in our own Concern.
But you need all the Aid that I can give,
To make you unrepining Vassals live.
Heav'n, you must own, to you has been less kind,
You cannot boast our Steadiness of Mind,
Nor is your Knowledge half so unconfin'd;
We can beyond the Bounds of Nature see,
And dare to fathom vast Infinity.
Then soar aloft, and view the Worlds on high,

   Sir JOHN. That is a Task exceeds your utmost Skill;
Spite of your Rules, they will be Women still:
Wives are the common Nusance of the State;
They all our Troubles, all our Cares create,
And, more than Taxes, ruin an Estate.
Wou'd they, like Lucifer, were doom'd to Hell,
That we might here without Disturbance dwell;
Then we should, uncontroul'd, our Wealth employ,
Drink high, and take a full Repast of Joy:
Damn Care, and bravely roar away our Time,
And still be busied in some noble Crime.
Like to the happier Brutes, live unconfin'd,
And freely chuse among the Female kind.
So liv'd the mighty Thunderer of old,
Lov'd as he pleas'd, and scorn'd to be controul'd:
No Kindred Names his Passion cou'd restrain:
Like him I'll think all Nice Distinctions vain;
And tir'd with one, to a new Mistress fly,
Blest with the Sweets of dear Variety.

   MELISSA. To live at large, a Punishment wou'd prove,
To one acquainted with the Joys of Love.
Sincere Affection centers but in one,
And cannot be to various Objects shown.
Wou'd Men prove kind, respectful, just and true,
And unto us their former Vows renew,
They wou'd have then no Reason to complain;
But 'till that time Reproofs will be in vain.
Some few perhaps, whom Virtue has refin'd,
Who in themselves no vicious Habits find,
Who sway'd by Reason, and by Honour led,
May in the Thorney Paths of Duty tread;
And still unweary'd with your utmost Spight,
In the blest Euges [approval]of their Minds delight:

But still the most will their Resentment show,
And by deplor'd Effects let you their Anger know.

    Sir WILLIAM. She's in the right. They still wou'd virtuous prove,
Were they but treated with Respect and Love:
Your barbarous Usage does Revenge produce,
It makes 'em bad, and is their just Excuse.
You've set 'em Copies, and dare you repine,
If they transcribe each black, detested Line?

    PARSON. I dare affirm, those Husbands that are ill,
Were they unmarry'd, wou'd be faultless still.
If we are cruel, they have made us so;
Whate'er they suffer, to themselves they owe:
Our Love on their Obedience does depend,
We will be kind, when they no more Offend.

    MELISSA. Of our Offences who shall Judges be?

    PARSON. For that great Work, Heav'n has commission'd me.
I'm made one of his Substitutes below,
And from my Mouth unerring Precepts flow;
I'll prove your Duty from the Law Divine,
Celestial Truth in my Discourse shall shine;
Truth drest in all the Gaieties of Art,
In all that Wit can give, or Eloquence impart.
Attend, attend, the August Message hear,
Let it imprint a reverential Fear,
'Twill on your Mind a vital Influence have,
If while I speak, you're Silent as the Grave.
The sacred Oracles for Deference call,
When from my Oily Tongue they smoothly fall.
First, I'll by Reason prove you should obey,
Next, point you out the most compendious way,
And then th' important Doctrine I'll improve;
These are the Steps by which I mean to move.
And first, because you were by Heav'n design'd
To be the Comforts of our Nobler Kind;
For us alone with tempting Graces blest,
And for our Sakes by bounteous Nature drest
With all the choicest Beauties of her Store,
And made so fine, that she cou'd add no more.
And dare you now, as if it were in Spight,
Become our Plagues, when form'd for our Delight?
Consider next, we are for you accurst;

We sinn'd, but you, alas! were guilty first.
Unhappy Eve unto her Ruin led,
Tempted by Pride, on the bright Poyson fed;
Then to her thoughtless Husband gave a Part,
He eat, seduc'd by her bewitching Art.
And 'twas but just that for so great a Fault
She shou'd be to a strict Subjection brought;
So strict, her Thoughts shou'd be no more her own,
But all Subservient made to him alone.
Had she not err'd, her Task had easie been,
He ow'd his Change of Humour to her Sin.
From that unhappy Hour he Peevish grew;
And she no more of solid Pleasure knew.
His Looks a sullen Haughtiness did wear,
And all his Words were Scornful, or Severe:
His Mind so rough, Love cou'd not harbour there.
The Gentle God in haste forsook his Seat,
And frighted fled to some more soft Retreat:
His Place was by a thousand Ills possest,
The crouding Daemons throng'd into his Breast,
And left no Room for tender Passions there:
His Sons with him in the sad Change did share.
His Sourness soon Hereditary grew;
And its Effects are still perceiv'd by you.
With all your Patience, all your Toil and Art,
You scarce can keep the surly Husband's Heart.
Your Kindness hardly can Esteem create;
Yet do not blame him, since it is his Fate:
But on your Mother Eve alone reflect;
Thank her for his Moroseness and Neglect:
Who with a fond indulgent Spouse being blest,
And like a Mistress Courted, and Carest,
Was not contented with her present State,
But must her own Unhappiness create;
And by ill Practices his Temper spoil,
And make what once was easie, prove a Toil.
If you wou'd live as it becomes a Wife,
And raise the Honour of a marry'd Life,
You must the useful Art of wheedling try,
And with his various Humours still comply:
Admire his Wit, praise all that he does do,
And when he's vex'd, do you be pettish to:
When he is sad, a clouded Aspect wear,
And talk to him with a dejected Air:
When Rage transports him, be as mad as he,

And when he's pleas'd, be easie, gay and free.
You'll find this Method will effectual prove,
Inhance your Merit, and secure his Love.

    Sir JOHN. It wou'd: But Women will be Cross and Proud;
When we are Merry, Passionate and Loud:
When we are angry, then they frolick grow,
And Laugh, and Sing, and no Compliance show.
In Contradictions they alone delight,
Are still a-curst, and never in the Right.
By Heav'n, I'd rather be an Ape, or Bear,
Or live with Beggars in the open Air,
Expos'd to Thunder, Lightning, Want or Cold,
Than be a Prince, and haunted with a Scold.
Those noisy Monsters much more dreadful are,
Than threatning Comets, Plagues or bloody War.
Grant Providence (if such a thing there be)
They never may from Hoarsenesses be free;
May on their Tongues as many Blisters grow
As they have Teeth; and to increase their Woe,
Let their Desires by Signs be still convey'd,
And talking be for ever Penal made.

    PARSON. Hold, hold: I can't these Interruptions bear;
If you don't me, these sacred Truths revere.
Now, Madam, I'll instruct you to obey,
And as I promis'd point you out the way
First, to your Husband you your Heart must give,
He must, alone, in your Affection live.
Whate'er he is, you still must think him best,
And boast to all that you are truly blest;
If Fools shou'd Laugh, and cry 'tis but a Jest,
Yet still look Grave, and vow you are Sincere,
And undisturb'd their ill-bred Censures bear.
Do what you can his Kindness to ingage,
Wink at his Vices, and indulge his Rage.
How vain are Women in their youthful Days,
How fond of Courtship, and how proud of Praise,
What Arts they use, what Methods they devise,
To be thought Fair, Obliging, Neat and Wise.
But when they're marry'd, they soon careless grow,
Neglect their Dress, and no more Neatness show.
Their Charms are lost, their Kindness laid aside,
Smiles turn'd to Frowns, their Wisdom into Pride,
And they or Sullen are, or always Chide.
Are these the Ways a Husband's Love to gain?

Or won't they rather heighten his Disdain?
Make him turn Sot, be troublesome and sad,
Or if he's Fiery, Cholerick and Mad?
Thus they their Peace industriously destroy,
And rob themselves of all their promis'd Joy.
Next, unto him you must due Honour pay;
And at his Feet your Top-knot Glories lay;
The Persian Ladies chalk you out the way:
They humbly on their Heads a Foot do wear,
As I have Read, but yet the Lord knows where.
That Badge of Homage graceful does appear;
Wou'd the good Custom were in Fashion here.
Also to him you inward Reverence owe;
If he's a Fool. you must not think him so;
Nor yet indulge one mean contemptuous Thought,
Or fancy he can e'er commit a Fault.
Nor must your Deference be alone confin'd
Unto the hid Recesses of your Mind,
But must in all your Actions be display'd,
And visible to each Spectator made.
With him, well pleas'd, and always chearful live,
And to him still respectful Titles give,
Call him your Lord, and your good Breeding show,
And do not rudely too familiar grow:
Nor like some Country Matrons call him Names,
As John, or Jeffrey, William, George or James;
Or what's much worse, and ne'er to be forgot,
Those courser Terms of Sloven, Clown, or Sot;
For tho' perhaps they may be justly due,
Yet must not, Madam, once be spoke by you:
Soft winning Language will become you best;
Ladies ought not to Rail, tho' but in Jest.
Lastly, to him you Fealty must pay,
And his Commands without Dispute obey.
A blind Obedience you from Guilt secures,
And if you err, the Fault is his, not yours.
What I have taught you, will not tiresom prove,
If as you ought, you can but truly love:
Honour and Homage then no Task will be;
And we shall, sure, as few ill Husbands see,
As now good Wives: They'll Prodigies appear,
Like Whales and Comets, shew some Danger near.
Now to Improvement I with haste will run,
Be short in that, and then my Work is done.
To you, Sir, First, I will my self apply,
To you, who are more fortunate than I,

And yet are free from the dire Gordian Tye;
You that Religion ought to love, and praise,
Which does you thus above the Females raise;
Next me admire, who can such Comments make,
And kindly wrest the Scripture for your Sake:
And now if you dare try a marry'd State,
You'll have no Reason to accuse your Fate,
Since I have told 'em, if they be good Wives,
They must Submit and flatter all their Lives.
You, who already drag the Nuptial Chain,
Will now have no occasion to complain,
Since they beyond their Sphere no more will tow'r,
But for the future own your Sov'reign Pow'r,
And being induc'd by this Advice of mine,
To you their Sense and Liberty resign:
Turn Fools and Slaves, that they the more may please.
Now it is fit for Gifts so vast as these,
We shou'd some little Gratitude express,
And be more Complaisant in our Address:
Bear with their Faults, their Weaknesses of Mind,
When they are Penitent, we shou'd be kind.
And that their Faith we may the more secure,
For them some Inconveniencies indure;
When they're in Danger, their Defenders prove;
'Twill shew at once, our Valour, and our Love.
But let it be our more immediate Care
To make 'em these unerring Rules revere.
Bid 'em attentively each Precept read:
And tell 'em, they're as holy as their Creed:
Be sure each Morning, ere they Eat or Pray,
That they with Care the sacred Lesson say:
This, will our Quiet, and their Souls secure,
And both our Happiness, and theirs ensure.
I on their Duty cou'd with ease inlarge,
But I wou'd not too much their Mem'ries charge:
They're weak, and shou'd they over-loaden be,
They'll soon forget what has been said by me;
Which Heav'n avert! since it much Thought has cost:
And who wou'd have such wond'rous Rhet'rick lost?

    MELISSA. A Mouse the lab'ring Mountain does disclose;
What rais'd my Wonder, my Derision grows.
With mighty Pomp you your Harangue begun,
And with big Words my fixt Attention won.
Each studied Period was with Labour wrought,
But destitute of Reason and of Thought.

What you meant Praise, upon your selves reflects;
Each Sentence is a Satyr on your Sex.
If we on you such Obloquies had thrown,
We had not, sure, one peaceful Minute known.
But you are Wise, and still know what is best,
And with your selves may be allow'd to Jest.

PARSON. How dare you treat me with so much Neglect?
My sacred Function calls for more Respect.

MELISSA. I've still rever'd your Order as Divine;
And when I see unblemish'd Virtue shine,
When solid Learning, and substantial Sense,
Are joyn'd with unaffected Eloquence;
When Lives and Doctrices of a Piece are made,
And holy Truths with humble Zeal convey'd;
When free from Passion, Bigottry and Pride,
Not sway'd by Int'rest, nor to Parties ty'd,
Contemning Riches, and abhorring Strife,
And shunning all the noisy Pomps of Life,
You live the aweful Wonders of your Time,
Without the least Suspicion of a Crime:
I shall with Joy the highest Deference pay,
And heedfully attend to all you say.
From such, Reproofs shall always welcome prove,
As being th' Effects of Piety and Love.
But those from me can challenge no Respect,
Who on us all without just Cause reflect:
Who without Mercy all the Sex decry,
And into open Defamations fly:
Who think us Creatures for Derision made,
And the Creator with his Works upbraid:
What he call'd Good, they proudly think not so,
And with their Malice, their Prophaneness show.
'Tis hard we shou'd be by the Men despis'd,
Yet kept from knowing what wou'd make us priz'd:
Debarr'd from Knowledge, banish'd from the Schools,
And with the utmost Industry bred Fools.
Laugh'd out of Reason, jested out of Sense,
And nothing left but Native Innocence:
Then told we are incapable of Wit,
And only for the meanest Drudgeries fit:
Made Slaves to serve their Luxury and Pride,
And with innumerable Hardships try'd,
'Till Pitying Heav'n release us from our Pain,
Kind Heav'n to whom alone we dare complain.

Th' ill-natur 'd World will no Compassion show;
Such as are wretched, it wou'd still have so:
It gratifies its Envy and its Spight;
The most in others Miseries take Delight.
While we are present they some Pity spare,
And feast us on a thin Repast of Air:
Look Grave and Sigh, when we our Wrongs relate,
An in a Compliment accuse our Fate:
Blame those to whom we our Misfortunes owe,
And all the Signs of real Friendship show.
But when we're absent, we their Sport are made,
They fan the Flame, and our Oppressors aid;
Joyn with the Stronger, the Victorious Side,
And all our Suff'rings, all our Griefs deride.
Those gen'rous few, whom kinder Thoughts inspire,
And who the Happiness of all desire;
Who wish we were from barb'rous Usage free,
Exempt from Toils, and shameful Slavery,
Yet let us, unreprov'd, mis. spend our Hours,
And to mean Purposes imploy our nobler Pow'rs.
They think, if we our Thoughts can but express,
And know but how to Work, to Dance and Dress,
It is enough, as much as we shou'd mind,
As if we were for nothing else design'd,
But made, like Puppets, to divert Mankind.
O that my Sex wou'd all such Toys despise;
And only study to be Good, and Wise;
Inspect themselves, and every Blemish find,
Search all the close Recesses of the Mind,
And leave no Vice, no ruling Passion there,
Nothing to raise a Blush, or cause a Fear:
Their Memories with solid Notions fill,
And let their Reason dictate to their Will,
Instead of Novels, Histories peruse,
And for their Guides the wiser Ancients chuse,
Thro' all the Labyrinths of Learning go,
And grow more humble, as they more do know.
By doing this, they will Respect procure,
Silence the Men, and lasting Fame secure;
And to themselves the best Companions prove,
And neither fear their Malice, nor desire their Love.

  Sir WILLIAM. Had you the Learning you so much desire,
You, sure, wou'd nothing, but your selves admire:
All our Addresses wou'd be then in vain,
And we no longer in your Hearts shou'd reign:

Sighs wou'd be lost, and Ogles cast away,
You'd laugh at all we do, and all we say.
No Courtship then durst by the Beaux be made
To any Thing above a Chamber-Maid.
Gay Cloaths, and Periwigs wou'd useless prove;
None but the Men of Sense wou'd dare to love:
With such, Heav'n knows, this Isle does not abound,
For one wise Man, ten thousand Fools are found;
Who all must at an awful Distance wait,
And vainly curse the Rigour of their Fate.
Then blame us not if we our Int'rest mind,
And would have Knowledge to our selves confin'd,
Since that alone Pre-eminence does give,
And robb'd of it we should unvalu'd live.
While You are ignorant, we are secure,
A little Pain will your Esteem procure.
Nonsense well cloath'd will pass for solid Sense,
And well pronounc'd, for matchless Eloquence:
Boldness for Learning, and a foreign Air
For nicest Breeding, with th' admiring Fair.

Sir JOHN. By Heav'n, I wish 'twere by the Laws decreed
They never more should be allow'd to read.
Books are the Bane of States, the Plagues of Life,
But both conjoyn'd, when studied by a Wife:
They nourish Factions, and increase Debate,
Teach needless Things, and causeless Fears create.
From Plays and Novels they learn how to plot,
And from your Sermons all their Cant is got:
From Those they learn the damn'd intreiguing Way,
How to attract, and how their Snares to lay:
How to delude the Jealous Husband's Care,
Silence his Doubts, and lull asleep his Fear:
And when discover'd, by the Last they're taught
With Shews of Zeal to palliate their Fault;
To look demure, and talk in such a Strain,
You'd swear they never would be ill again.

PARSON. You're in the right: Good Things they misapply;
Yet not in Books, but them, the Fault does lie:
Plays are of use to cultivate our Parts,
They teach us how to win our Hearers Hearts:
Soft moving Language for the Pulpit's fit,
'Tis there we consecrate the Poet's Wit:
But Women were not for this Province made,
And shou'd not our Prerogative invade;

Whate'er they know shou'd be from us convey'd:
We their Preceptors and their Guides shou'd prove,
And teach them what to hate, and what to love.
But from our Sermons they no Ill can learn,
They're there instructed in their true Concern;
Told what they must, and what they must not be;
And shew'd the utmost Bounds of Liberty.

    Sir WILLIAM. Madam, since we none of your Beauty share,
You shou'd content your selves with being Fair:
That is a Blessing, much more Great, than all
That we can Wisdom, or can Science call:
Such beauteous Faces, such bewitching Eyes,
Who wou'd not more than musty Authors prize?
'Such wond'rous Charms will much more Glory yield,
Than all the Honours of the dusty Field;
Or all those Ivy Wreaths that Wit can give,
And make you more admir'd, more rev'renc'd live.
To you, the knowing World their Vows do pay,
And at your Feet their learned Trophies lay;
And your Commands with eager Haste obey.
By all my Hopes, by all that's Good I swear,
I'd rather be some celebrated Fair,
Than wise as Solon, or than Croesus' Heir,
Or have my Memory well stuff'd with all
Those Whimseys which they high-rais'd Notions call.

    MELISSA. Beauty's a Trifle merits not my Care,
I'd rather Aesop's ugly Visage wear,
Joyn'd with his Mind, than be a Fool, and Fair.
Brightness of Thought, and an extensive View
Of all the Wonders Nature has to shew;
So clear, so strong, and so enlarg'd a Sight
As can pierce thro' the gloomy Shades of Night,
Trace the first Heroes to their dark Abodes,
And find the Origin of Men and Gods:
See Empires rise, and Monarchies decay,
And all the Changes of the World survey:
The ancient and the modern Fate of Kings,
From whence their Glory, or Misfortunes springs;
Wou'd please me more, than if in one combin'd,
I'd all the Graces of the Female Kind.
But do not think 'tis an ambitious Heat;
To you I'll leave the being Rich and Great:
Yours be the Fame, the Profit, and the Praise;
We'll neither rob you of your Vines, nor Bays:

Nor will we to Dominion once aspire;
You shall be Chief, and still your selves admire:
The Tyrant Man may still possess the Throne;
'Tis in our Minds that we wou'd Rule alone:
Those unseen Empires give us leave to sway,
And to our Reason private Homage pay:
Our struggling Passions within Bounds confine,
And to our Thoughts their proper Tasks assign.
This is the Use we wou'd of Knowledge make;
You quickly wou'd the good Effects partake.
Our Conversations it wou'd soon refine,
And in our Words, and in our Actions shine:
Any by a pow'rful Influence on our Lives,
Make us good Friends, good Neighbours, and good Wives.
Of this, some great Examples have been shown,
Women remarkable for Virtue known:
Jealous of Honour, and upright of Life,
Serene in Dangers, and averse to Strife:
Patient when wrong'd, from Pride and Envy free,
Strangers to Falsehood and to Calumny;
Of every noble Quality possest:
Well skill'd in Science, and with Wisdom [sic] blest.
In ancient Greece, where Merit still was crown'd,
Some such as these in her Records were found.
Rome her Lucretia, and her Porcia show,
And we to her the fam'd Cornelia owe:
A Place with them does Great Zenobia claim;
With these I cou'd some modern Ladies name,
Who help to fill the bulky Lists of Fame:
Women renown'd for Knowledge, and for Sense,
For sparkling Wit, and charming Eloquence.
But they're enough; at least to make you own,
If we less wise and rational are grown,
'Tis owing to your Management alone.
If like the Ancients you wou'd gen'rous prove,
And in our Education shew your Love;
Into our Souls wou'd noble Thoughts instill,
Our Infant-Minds with bright Ideas fill:
Teach us our Time in Learning to employ,
And place in solid Knowledge all our Joy:
Perswade us trifling Authors to refuse,
And when we think, the useful'st Subjects chuse:
Inform us how a prosperous State to bear,
And how to Act when Fortune is severe:
We shou'd be wiser, and more blameless live,
And less Occasion for your Censures give:

At least in us less Failings you wou'd see,
And our Discourses wou'd less tiresom be:
Tho' Wit, like yours, we never hope to gain,
Yet from Impertinence we should refrain,
And learn to be less Talkative and Vain.
Unto the strictest Rules we should submit,
And what we ought to do, think always fit.
Never dispute, when Duty leads the Way,
But its Commands without a Sigh obey.
To Reason, not to Humour, give the Reins,
And be the same in Palaces and Chains.
But you our humble Suit will still decline;
To have us wise was never your Design:
You'll keep us Fools, that we may be your Jest;
They who know least are ever treated best.
If we do well, with Care it is conceal'd;
But every Error, every Fault's reveal'd:
While to each other you still partial prove,
Can see no Failures, and even Vices love.
The Bloody Masters of the martial Trade,
Are prais'd for Mischiefs, and for Murders pay'd.
The noisy Lawyers, if they can but bawl,
Soon grace the Wool-sacks, and adorn the Hall.
The envy'd Great, those darling Sons of Fame,
Who carry a Majestick Terrour in their Name;
Who like the Demy Gods are plac'd on High,
And seem th' exalted Natives of the Sky:
Who sway'd by Pride, and by Self-love betray'd,
Are Slaves to their imperious Passions made,
Are with a Servile Awe by you rever'd:
Prais'd for their Follies, for their Vices fear'd.
The Courtier, who with every Wind can veer,
And 'midst the Mounting Waves can safely steer;
Who all can flatter; and with wond'rous Grace,
Low cringing Bows, and a designing Face,
A smiling Look, and a dissembl'd Hate,
Can hug a Friend, and hasten on his Fate,
Has your Applause; his Policy you praise;
And to the Skies his prudent Conduct raise.
The Scholar, if he can a Verb decline,
And has the Skill to reckon Nine times Nine,
Or but the Nature of a Fly define;
Can Mouth some Greek, and knows where Athens stood,
Tho' he perhaps is neither Wise, nor Good,
Is fit for Oxford; where when he has been,
Each College view'd, and each grave Doctor seen,

He mounts a Pulpit, and th' exhalted Height
Makes Vapours dance before his troubl'd Sight,
And he no more can see, nor think aright.
Yet such as these your Consciences do guide,
And o'er your Actions and your Words preside;
Blame you for Faults which they themselves commit,
Arraign your Judgment, and condemn your Wit;
Instill their Notions with the greatest Ease,
And hood-wink'd lead you wheresoe'er they please.
The formal Justice, and the Jolly Knight,
Who in their Money place their chief Delight;
Who watch the Kitchin, and survey the Field,
To see what each will to their Luxury yield;
Who Eat and Pun, then Quarrel, Rail and Drink,
But never are at leisure once to Think,
Who weary of Domestick Cares being grown,
And yet, like Children, frighted when alone,
(Detesting Books) still Hunt, or Hawk, or Play,
And in laborious Trifles waste the Day,
Are lik'd by you, their Actions still approv'd,
And if they're Rich, are sure to be belov'd.
These are the Props, the Glory of the State,
And on their Nod depends the nation's Fate:
These weave the Nets, where little Flies betray'd,
Are Victims to relentless Justice made;
While they themselves contemn the Snares that they have laid;
As Bonds too weak such mighty Men to hold,
As scorn to be by any Laws controul'd.
Physicians, with hard Words and haughty Looks,
And promis'd Health, bait their close-cover'd Hooks:
Like Birds of Prey, while they your Gold can scent,
You are their Care, their utmost Help is lent:
But when your Guineas cease, you to the Spaw [spa] are sent.
Yet still you court 'em, think you cannot die
If you've a Son of Aesculapius by.
The Tradesmen you caress, altho' you know
They wealthy by their Cheats and Flatt'ries grow;
You seem to credit ev'ry Word they say,
And as they sell, with the same Conscience pay.
Nay to the Mob, those Dregs of human kind,
Those Animals you slight, you're wond'rous kind;
To them you cringe; and tho' they are your Sport,
Yet still you fawn, and still their Favour court.
Thus on each other daily you impose,
And all for Wit, and dext'rous Cunning goes.
'Tis we alone hard Measure still must find;

But spite of you, we'll to our selves be kind;
Your Censures slight, your little Tricks despite,
And make it our whole Business to be wise:
The mean low trivial Cares of Life disdain,
And read and think, and think and read again,
And on our Minds bestow the utmost Pain.
Our Souls with strictest Morals we'll adorn,
And all your little Arts of wheedling Scorn;
Be humble, mild, forgiving, just and true,
Sincere to all, respectful unto you,
While, as becomes you, sacred Truths you teach,
And live those Sermons you to others preach.
With Want of Duty none shall us upbraid;
Where-e'er 'tis due, it shall be nicely pay'd.
Honour and Love we'll to our Husbands give,
And ever Constant and Obedient live:
If they are Ill, we'll try by gentle Ways
To lay those Tempests which their Passions raise:
But if our soft Submissions are in vain,
We'll bear our Fate, and never once complain.
Unto our Friends the tend'rest Kindness show,
Be wholly theirs, no sep'rate Interest know:
With them their Dangers and their Suff'rings share,
And make their Persons and their Fame our Care.
The Poor we'll feed, to the Distress'd be kind,
And strive to comfort each afflicted Mind:
Visit the Sick, and try their Pains to ease;
Not without Grief the meanest Wretch displease:
Any by a Goodness as diffus'd as Light,
To the Pursuit of Virtue all invite.
Thus will we live, regardless of your Hate,
'Till re-admitted to our former State;
Where, free from the Confinement of our Clay,
In glorious Bodies we shall bask in Day,
And with inlight'ned Minds new Scenes survey;
Scenes, much more bright than any here below,
And we shall then the whole of Nature know;
See all her Springs, her secret Turnings view,
And be as knowing, and as wise, as you.
With generous Spirits, of a Make divine,
In whose blest Minds Celestial Virtues shine,
Whose Reason, like their Station, is sublime,
And who see clearly, thro' the Mists of Time,
Those puzzl'ing Glooms where busy Mortals stray,
And still grope on, but never find their Way,

We shall, well-pleas'd, eternally converse,
And all the Sweets of sacred Love possess:
Love, freed from all the gross Allays of Sense,
So pure, so strong, so constant, so intense,
That it shall all our Faculties employ,
And leave no Room for any Thing but Joy.

FINIS.

---·---

FROM

POEMS ON SEVERAL OCCASIONS . . . PARAPHRAS'D

To The Ladies.

Wife and servant are the same,
But only differ in the name:
For when that fatal knot is ty'd,
Which nothIng, nothing can divide:
When she the word *obey* has said,
And man by law supreme has made,
Then all that's kind is laid aside,
And nothing left but state and pride:
Fierce as an eastern prince he grows
And all his innate rigor shows:
Then but to look, to laugh, or speak,
Will the nuptual contract break.
Like mutes, she signs alone must make,
And never any freedom take:
But still be govern'd by a nod,
And fear her husband as a God:
Him still must serve, him still obey,
And nothing act, and nothing say,
But what her haughty lord thinks fit,
Who with the power, has all the wit.
Then shun, oh! shun that wretched state,
And all the fawning flatt'rers hate:
Value yourselves, and Men despise:
You must be proud, if you'll be wise.

SONG.

To Lerinda.

Cease, Dear Lerinda, cease admiring
   Why Crouds and Noise I disapprove;
What e'er I see abroad is tiring;
   O let us to some Cell remove;
Where all alone our selves enjoying,
   Enrich'd with Innocence and Peace,
On noblest Themes our Thoughts employing,
   Let us our inward Joys increase:
And still the happy Taste pursuing,
   Raise our Love and Friendship higher,
And thus the sacred Flames renewing,
   In Extasies of Bliss expire.

PRIMARY SOURCES

The Ladies Defence; or, "The Bride-Womans, Counsellor" answer'd: a poem. In a Dialogue between Sir John Brute, Sir William Loveall, Melissa and a Parson. London: for John Deeve, 1701.

Poems, on Several Occasions, Together with The Song of the Three Children, paraphras'd. London: Bernard Lintot, 1703.

Essays upon Several Subjects in Prose and Verse. London: R. Bonwicke, W. Freeman et al., 1710.

RELATED SOURCES

Ballard, George. *Memoirs of several Ladies of Great Britain who have been celebrated for their writings or skill in the learned languages, arts and sciences.* Oxford: W. Jackson, 1752. Reprint. Edited by Ruth Perry. Detroit: AMS Press, forthcoming.

Sprint, John. *The Bride-Womans Counsellor, Being a Sermon Preach'd at a Wedding, May the 11th, 1699, at Sherbourn, in Dorsetshire.* London: H. Hills, 1699.

ELIZABETH ELSTOB
1683 – 1756

Elizabeth Elstob was born September 29, 1683 in Newcastle-on-Tyne, the daughter of Ralph Elstob, a member of the company of Merchant Adventurers and onetime Sheriff of Foxton, County Durham, and Jane Elstob, the daughter of a Newcastle merchant William Hall, and sister of William Elstob. Her father died in 1688 and her mother, who had evidently encouraged her daughter's educational pursuits, in about 1691. At that point she and her brother were placed under the guardianship of Charles Elstob, who considered that "one tongue was enough for a woman" and opposed female education. Undeterred, she eventually went to Oxford with her brother who, according to Elstob, encouraged her propensity to study languages. (Women were formally excluded from universities.) The noted Anglo-Saxon scholar, George Hickes, also fostered these scholarly pursuits, and she was soon acclaimed as a leading Anglo-Saxon scholar in the reign of Queen Anne. She and her brother were members of an informal group of antiquarian scholars who researched in the Cottonian and Harleian library collections.

In 1709 she published *An English-Saxon Homily, on the birth-day of St. Gregory,* with an English translation and preface, in which she stressed the need for women to be among her readers. Her Anglo-Saxon grammar, *The Rudiments of Grammar for the English-Saxon Tongue, first given in English, with an apology for the study of northern antiquities* (1715), an underestimated scholarly work praised by Thomas Jefferson, was the first grammar of its kind. In presenting her case in *The Rudiments* for the elegance of English monosyllables, Elstob illustrated a wide literary knowledge of male writers and of the works of Katherine Philips, Lady Wharton, and Lady Winchilsea. Dr. Hicks helped her to publish this grammar after her brother's death on March 3, 1714 or 1715, when she fell into dire economic straits.

Of independent mind and possibly fearful of incurring debts, she moved to Evesham in Worcestershire, but unluckily, to compound her difficulties, she lost all her books and manuscripts that had been entrusted to a friend prior to her departure. In Evesham she seems to have established a day school, receiving one groat (fourpence) per pupil per week. She states in a letter to George Ballard, Anglo-Saxon scholar and memoir-writer of learned women, about these exigent years: "I must tell you that mine may be termed a life of disappointment from my cradle till now. . . . Nor do I repine, for I am so inured to disappointments." Sarah Chapone (or Capon) visited Elstob in 1733 and helped raise an annuity for her of twenty guineas; Ballard also assisted her financially. Bluestocking Mary Granville Pendarves Delaney used her influence with Queen Caroline to settle a five-year renewable annuity on Elstob that unfortunately ceased in 1737 when the Queen died. Again with Mary Delaney's aid—a tribute to Bluestocking gynocentricity—Elstob was hired in 1739 as a governess in the Duchess Dowager of Portland's household, and received room and board and £30 per year until she died. She was buried in St. Margaret, Westminster.

Elstob's preferred view of herself, as she wrote to Ballard, was as "the first woman that has studied that language since it was Spoke," a self-confident yet poignant statement from a learned woman excluded from a life of scholarship by a male-centered society.

An English-Saxon Homily

from

The Preface.

I am very apprehensive of the Expectation of some, and the Censure of others, who shall take this Treatise into their Hands: Those whose good Nature has inclined them towards any favourable Expectation from it, I should be very glad to find them, any way gratifyed with the Endeavours I have used to please them. In which I have employ'd much of my Desires: And as the more candid sort of Readers will, perhaps, be so generous as to think, I have also taken some Pains. Those who are more addicted to Censure, will not be so easily satisfyed. For in dealing with this sort of People, there are these great Obstacles to be conquer'd, Ignorance on one Hand, or an affection of Wit and Knowledge on the other, Both of which have their share in condemning and despising all that does not immediately tend, as they imagine, to their own Honour or Advantage. Those who set up for Censurers under the former of these Characters, are obliged to declare universally against all kinds of Learning, that Ignorance may seem not to be an inconsiderable thing. And yet I cannot help thinking all such, not to deserve to be consider'd. Those

SOURCE: This selection comes from the 1709 edition in Special Collections at the University of Nebraska-Lincoln, no. 829.6, Ae 43e.

who please themselves with an Opinion of their own extraordinary Wit or Learning, usually think themselves obliged to overlook all that they do not know themselves, as useless, and impertinent. So that it is not a difficult Matter to foresee, what kind of reception a Work of this Nature will meet with, from this kind of Persons.

For first, I know it will be said, What has a Woman to do with Learning? This I have known urged by some Men, with an Envy unbecoming that greatness of Soul, which is said to dignify their Sex. For if Women may be said to have Souls, and that their Souls are their better part, and that what is Best deserves our greatest Care for its Improvement; furthermore, if good Learning be one of the Soul's greatest Improvements; we must retort the Question. Where is the Fault in Womens seeking after Learning? why are they not to be valu'd for acquiring to themselves the noblest Ornaments? what hurt can this be to themselves? what Disadvantage to others? But there are two things usually opposed against Womens Learning. That it makes them impertinent, and neglect their houshold Affairs. Where this happens it is a Fault. But it is not the Fault of Learning, which rather polishes and refines our Nature, and teaches us that Method and Regularity, which disposes us to greater Readiness and Dexterity in all kinds of Business. I do not observe it so frequently objected against Womens Diversions, that They take them off from Houshold Affairs. Why therefore should those few among us, who are Lovers of Learning, altho' no better account cou'd be given of it than its being a Diversion, be deny'd the Benefit and Pleasure of it, which is both so innocent and improving. But perhaps most of these Persons mean no more than that it makes them neglect the Theatre, and long sittings at Play, or tedious Dressings, and visiting Days, and other Diversions, which steal away more time than are spent at Study.

I shall not enter into any more of the Reasons why[a] some Gentlemen are so eager to deny us this Privilege: I am more surpriz'd, and even asham'd, to find any of the Ladies even more violent than they, in carrying on the same Charge. Who despairing to arrive at any eminent or laudable degree of Knowledge, seem totally to abandon themselves to Ignorance, contenting themselves to sit down in Darkness, as if they either had not Reason, or it were not capable by being rightly cultivated, of bringing them into the Light; but these Persons have in themselves an answer to all their Cavils against Learning, and their Punishment. *viz.* The Punishment of their Ignorance, for which they are to be pityed, tho' they are not sensible of it: and a being in love with their Ignorance, which justly renders them contemptible. I have often thought it very strange

---

[a] The usual Objections that are made by Gentlemen to Womens Learning, are fully answer'd in a Scholastick way, and in very elegant Latin, by that Glory of her Sex, Mrs. Anna Maria a Schurman, who hath also writ several Latin Epistles, to Andreas Rivetus on the same Subject. See her Opuscula Hebraea, Graeca, Latina, Gallica, Prosaica, & Metrica. Printed by Elzevir Lugd. Batav. M DC XLVIII.

Incogitancy in some Persons, when with an air of Wit, as they imagin'd, they would declare openly they hated any Woman that knew more than themselves. But so they may hate any one that's better dress'd than themselves, or richer, or in a degree of Power or Authority superior to them: and yet what the Consequence of such Hatred would be, if it were not fantastical, rather than real, might justly be feared; and I think the rash Wit, and thoughtless Expressions of such Persons ought not to pass for any thing else but Folly, with those who have any real taste of good Sense, or Christian Prudence.

But I shall not give my self, or the Reader, any farther trouble with these Admirers of Ignorance, whether real, or pretended. I shall chuse rather to converse a little with those who have some degrees of Learning, and know how to value it in themselves: but are not so favourable to any degree or Portion of it when found in others, of which they are not possess'd themselves. They admire a Play, a Romance, a Novel, perhaps entertain themselves a little with History, they read a Poem gracefully, and make Verses prettily, they rally and repartee with abundance of Wit and readiness; and with these Embellishments imagine themselves perfectly accomplish'd. They ought not indeed to be disturbed in this good Opinion of themselves, and of such Attainments. And this good Humour of Self-Love, which produces such Improvement, might deserve both Praise and Encouragement: were it innocently good natur'd to it self, without being injurious to others. For my part, I could never think any part of Learning either useless, or contemptible, because I knew not the Advantages of it; I have rather thought my self obliged to reverence those who are skilful in any Art or Profession, and can gladly subscribe to the Praise of any liberal Accomplishment, be it in any Person, of any Sex; justly valuing those which adorn even the Persons above mention'd, when they confine them not to themselves, and are not attended with Envy.

Plato, if we may lay any stress upon Heathen Authorities, makes it a mark of Ingenuity to despise no kind of Learning;[a] and one of the most elegant Apologies for Learning, that perhaps has ever been made, informs us, that the Arts have a mutual connexion and dependence between themselves, mutually illustrate and assist each other; which Testimonies must not be refused by those, who have any Esteem for politer Learning, and I hope they may prepare a way for me to obviate those Objections to which this Work may be thought liable.

And the next probably will be this. Admit a Woman may have Learning, is there no other kind of Learning to employ her time?[b] What is this Saxon? what has she to do with this barbarous antiquated Stuff? so

---

[a] Cicer. Orat. pro Archia Poeta.

[b] See Dr. Hickes's Apology for the Saxon Learning, both in his lesser Grammar, and his larger Thesaurus, as also that learned Defence made for it by Mr. Lisle, in the Preface to his Saxon Monuments.

useless, so altogether out of the way? But how came they to know that it is out of the way, and useless, who know nothing of it? and they seem to have forgot the Sentiments of their polite Masters, who judg'd not any part of Learning to be out of the way. I fear, if things were rightly consider'd, that the charge of Barbarity would rather fall upon those who, while they fancy themselves adorn'd with the Embellishments of foreign Learning, are ignorant, even to barbarity, of the Faith, Religion, the Laws and Customs, and Language of their Ancestors. I assure you, these are Considerations which have afforded me no small Encouragement in the Prosecution of these Studies.

But to leave these Censurers to please themselves with their own Humours and Discourse. For the Satisfaction of more candid Readers, I shall give some short Account of the Motives that urged me to this Undertaking, and of the Performance it self.

Having accidentally met with a Specimen of K. Alfred's Version of Orosius into Saxon, design'd to be publish'd by a near Relation and Friend, I was very desirous to understand it, and having gain'd the Alphabet, I found it so easy, and in it so much of the grounds of our present Language, and of a more particular Agreement with some Words which I had heard when very young in the North, as drew me in to be more inquisitive after Books written in that Language. With this the kind Encourager of my Studies being very well pleased, recommended to me the Saxon Heptateuch, most accurately publish'd by Mr. Thwaites. The Matter of that Book being well known and familiar to me, made the reading of it very easy and agreeable: and led me on to the reading of several other Treatises, and to divert my self in taking Transcripts from such ancient Manuscripts as I could meet with. Among these was one I made of the Athanasian Creed, which the great Instaurator [restorer] of Northern Literature was pleased to accept from me: and to think not unworthy of being publish'd with the Conspectus, or account in *Latin*, which the learned Mr. *Wotton* has given us of his ample and learned *Thesaurus Linguarum Vett. Septentrionalium.* This great Patron of the Septentrional Studies, hath ever since persevered to encourage my Proceeding in them, and to urge me: that by publishing somewhat in Saxon, I wou'd invite the Ladies to be acquainted with the Language of their Predecessors, and the Original of their Mother Tongue. Particularly he recommended to me the Publication of this Homily. And here I cannot but observe, how great an Argument Women have, for engaging in Learning, even Saxon Learning, from so great an Authority. Of how great importance he thinks the having a due Care for Female Education, may be understood by his so earnestly recommending those excellent Instructions for the Education of a Daughter, ascribed to the *Author of Telemachus.* And it is no wonder that he, who is so well skill'd in Primitive Antiquity, shou'd in this likewise imitate the Practice of the Primitive Fathers, who were very zealous to encourage good Learning amongst the Ladies: as may be seen by the Epistles of St. Jerom, St.

Augustin, St. Chrysostom, and our St. Gregory, to the learned and virtuous Ladies of their times. A Catalogue of such Epistles to excellent
Women, by the Holy Fathers, was made and presented to Mr. *Astley*, by
Mr. *Roger Ascham*, Tutor to the most *Illustrious Queen Elizabeth*, and
born in the same Place that gave Birth to my most learned Friend: as if
there were something peculiar in the genius of that Place, not only for
the Production of great and learned Men, but such also as have been
remarkable for encouraging Learning in our Sex. Mr.[a] Ascham, in recommending this Catalogue, makes this Observation. That by his Enquiry
into Matters of that kind, he perceived that Age to have been both most
learned, and most happy: in which there were more Women, than there
are now Men, celebrated for their Learning.

---------------- • ----------------

The Transcript of this Homily I compared with that antient Parchment
Book of Homilies in the Bodleian Library amongst Junius's Books N E.F.
4. being the second of those Volumes that had formerly belong'd to the
Hattonian Library, an Account of which we have in that most elaborate
Catalogue of Saxon Manuscripts by Mr. Wanley, which makes the second
Volume of Dr. Hickes's Thesaurus p. 43. I had access to this Book, by the
singular Courtesy of Dr. Hudson, a Person of so much Learning; that as
he needs not envy it in any other, so has he that generous Quality to
be found only in those great and generous Minds that are inform'd
with a truly Scholar-like Genius; of not discouraging Learning, even in
our Sex.

Having given an Account of the Homilist, some will expect, somewhat
shou'd be said of the Translator. I have been askt the Question, more than
once, whether this Performance was all my own? How properly such a
Question may be ask'd by those who know with whom I live, I shall not
dispute: But since some there are who may have a Curiosity to know the
same thing, who yet suspect the Decency of such a Question: that they
may be under no Uneasiness on this account, they may be pleas'd to
understand that I have a kind Brother, who is always ready to assist and
encourage me in my Studies. I might say much of my Obligations on this
account: wou'd he permit me to express my self at large on that Subject.
But as I think it no shame to me to take any Advice where it may be so
easily obtain'd: so I should think it unpardonable to be guilty of such a
Silence, as might make me seem averse to all Acknowledgment.

---

[a] Tandem, clarissime Astlaee, Catalogum Epistolarum ad claras feminas ex
Hieronymo, & Augustino tibi mitto. In quibus rebus investigandis animadverti,
felicissimum illud, & doctissimum seculum fuisse: in quo plures feminae, quam
nunc viri, literarum laude floruerunt Rogeri Aschami Epist. Fam. lib. secund.
Epist. 37.

I have little more to add, than my Thanks to all my Encouragers, which have far exceeded the Number I cou'd have expected to a first Attempt: the greatest Part whereof have done me a great deal of Honour by the Countenance both of their Quality and Learning, and to all I am one way or other obliged for their Kindnesses and good Esteem. I am very glad to find so many of the Ladies, and those, several of them, of the best Rank: favouring these Endeavours of a Beginner, and one of their Sex. It may be some Excuse for me to them, to justify this Undertaking, and with which they will not probably be displeas'd: That the Conversion of the English here celebrated in this Homily, was affected by the Endeavours of a Pious Lady; Berhta the first Christian Queen of England: as the Conversion of the whole Roman Empire before had been by Helena Mother of Constantine the Great, by most affirm'd to have been a Native of this Island. That as the Southern Parts of England were first converted by Berhta's Endeavours, who engaged her Husband King Ethelbert to receive the Faith: so the Northern Parts beyond Humber, received the same blessed Influence, by the means of her Daughter Edelburga: who was highly instrumental in the Conversion of her glorious Consort, King Edwin the first Monarch of the English, and the greatest of all the Saxon Princes of those times. I might give many more Instances of this kind, Chlodesuinda Daughter of King Chlotharius persuaded her Husband, Alboinus, King of the Lombards, to become Christian. And Hermenegildus, by the sollicitation of his Wife Ingundis, Daughter of Sigibert, and Sister to King Childebert, of an Arrian, become Orthodox. It were endless to repeat all the Instances of illustrious Women, that might be enumerated, as contributing to the Advancement of Religion, in their several Ages. But we may content our selves with late, and domestick, Examples, of two of the greatest Monarchs that the World has known: for Wisdom and Piety, and constant Success in their Affairs, QUEEN ELIZABETH, and ANNE QUEEN OF GREAT BRITAIN. And I think it some farther Apology for me, to the Ladies of Great Britain; that this is publish'd in the Reign of so highly Excellent a Lady: who, as She surpasses all her Royal Predecessors, in all noble and royal Accomplishments; so is She peculiarly eminent, in being both an Example, and Encourager, of all Virtues, and laudable Qualities in those of Her Sex.

PRIMARY SOURCES

Translation of and "The Preface" to *An English-Saxon Homily, on the birth-day of St. Gregory: Anciently used in the English Saxon Church Giving an Account of the Conversion of the English from Paganism to Christianity, Translated into Modern English, with Notes, etc.* London: W. Bowyer, 1709.

The Rudiments of Grammar for the English-Saxon Tongue, first given in English, with an apology for the study of northern antiquities. London: W. Bowyer and C. King, 1715.

RELATED SOURCES

Collins, Sarah Huff. "Elizabeth Elstob: A Biography." Ph.D. dissertation, Indiana University, 1970.

Hughes, S. F. D. "The Anglo-Saxon Grammars of George Hickes and Elizabeth Elstob." In *Essays on Early Anglo-Saxon Studies.* Edited by Carl Berkhout and M. McGatch. Boston: G. K. Hall, 1979.

————. "Mrs. Elstob's Defense of Antiquarian Learning in her Rudiments of Grammar for the English-Saxon Tongue (1715)." *Harvard Library Bulletin* 27, 2 (1970):172–91.

Perry, Ruth. "George Ballard's Biographies of Learned Ladies." In *Biography in the 18th Century.* Edited by J. D. Browning. New York: Garland Publishing, 1980.

White, Caroline A. "Elizabeth Elstob, the Saxonist." *Sharpe's London Magazine* 50, n.s. 35 (1869): 180ff; 51, n.s. 36 (1869–70): 26 ff.

ANNE KINGSMILL FINCH

COUNTESS OF WINCHILSEA

1661 – 1720

Born in Southampton, the daughter of Sir William Kingsmill, Anne Kingsmill was orphaned at three years of age. In 1688 she married the Royalist Heneage Finch, who would become the fourth Earl of Winchilsea. They met at court where they were both attendants to James, Duke of York, later James II, and his wife Mary of Modena. After James was deposed in 1689, Finch and her husband, still loyal to the former king, were forced to retire to the country. In 1691 they took up residence at the Kentish estate of Heneage Finch's nephew, the Earl of Winchilsea. That same year Finch first published her poems, although the subject matter suggests they were written earlier. (She began writing at Court as a lady-in-waiting.) On his nephew's death in 1712, Heneage Finch succeeded to the title and estate; Anne Finch became the Countess of Winchilsea. Heneage Finch's family ties also brought them as frequent visitors to the Longleat community (which included Elizabeth Rowe and Frances Thynne), as Lady Winchelsea's poem "A Description of one of the Pieces of Tapestry at Longleat" confirms. The couple also knew Henry Fielding and probably Sarah Fielding, the latter of whom was attached both to Samuel Richardson's predominantly female circle and to the loose network of writers in and around Bath.

Inspired by her personal connections and the difficulties she experienced as a woman writer, Lady Winchilsea frequently favored themes of love and friendship and the besieged female condition in her poems. The poems she wrote to her friend, Catherine Cavendish, illustrate particularly well her view of female friendship. Critic Ann Messenger persuasively argues that she reserved her most controversial ideas for unpublished works, several of which appear as excerpts. Moreover, her exile from court due to her Jacobite beliefs introduced her to a form of oppression at first hand. Lady Winchilsea's poem entitled "The Unequal Fetters" displays a feminist concern for the lot of women in general; her own marriage was happy and secure. She also wrote on the theme of melancholy, or spleen, which absorbingly engaged female writers from the Duchess of Newcastle and Elizabeth Rowe to Elizabeth Carter and Mary Wollstonecraft. Like the Duchess, Lady Winchilsea was a retired

Royalist, well-supported financially and emotionally by her husband,
with no call to earn a living by writing poetry and no incentive to think
about the difficulty of that undertaking.

Her collected works appeared anonymously in 1713; her more intimate and political poems prefaced by a feminist "introduction" were
published posthumously. The excerpted poems testify to her feminist
philosophy.

FROM
MISCELLANY POEMS,
ON SEVERAL OCCASIONS
AND
THE POEMS OF ANNE,
COUNTESS OF WINCHILSEA

THE INTRODUCTION

Did I, my lines intend for publick view,
   How many censures, wou'd their faults persue,
Some wou'd, because such words they do affect,
Cry they're insipid, empty, uncorrect.
And many, have attain'd, dull and untaught
The name of Witt, only by finding fault.
True judges, might condemn their want of witt,
And all might say, they're by a Woman writt.
Alas! a woman that attempts the pen,
Such an intruder on the rights of men,
Such a presumptuous Creature, is esteem'd,
The fault, can by no vertue be redeem'd.
They tell us, we mistake our sex and way;
Good breeding, fassion, dancing, dressing, play
Are the accomplishments we shou'd desire;
To write, or read, or think, or to enquire
Wou'd cloud our beauty, and exaust our time,

SOURCE: These selections come from *Miscellany Poems . . . 1713 edition*, and
The Poems of Anne, Countess of Winchilsea, 1903 edition.

And interrupt the Conquests of our prime;
Whilst the dull mannage, of a servile house
Is held by some, our outmost art, and use.
   Sure 'twas not ever thus, nor are we told
Fables, of Women that excell'd of old;
To whom, by the diffusive hand of Heaven
Some share of witt, and poetry was given.
On that glad day, on which the Ark return'd,
The holy pledge, for which the Land had mourn'd,
The joyfull Tribes, attend itt on the way,
The Levites do the sacred Charge convey,
Whilst various Instruments, before itt play;
Here, holy Virgins in the Concert joyn,
The louder notes, to soften, and refine,
And with alternate verse, compleat the Hymn Devine.
Loe! the yong Poet, after Gods own heart,
By Him inspired, and taught the Muses Art,
Return'd from Conquest, a bright Chorus meets,
That sing his slayn ten thousand in the streets.
In such loud numbers they his acts declare,
Proclaim the wonders, of his early war,
That Saul upon the vast applause does frown,
And feels, itts mighty thunder shake the Crown.
What, can the threat'n'd Judgment now prolong?
Half of the Kingdom is already gone;
The fairest half, whose influence guides the rest,
Have David's Empire, o're their hearts confess't.
   A Woman here, leads fainting Israel on,
She fights, she wins, she tryumphs with a song,
Devout, Majestick, for the subject fitt,
And far above her arms, exalts her witt,
Then, to the peacefull, shady Palm withdraws,
And rules the rescu'd Nation, with her Laws.
How are we fal'n, fal'n by mistaken rules?
And Education's, more then Nature's fools,
Debarr'd from all improve-ments of the mind,
And to be dull, expected and dessigned;
And if some one, wou'd Soar above the rest,
With warmer fancy, and ambition press't,
So strong, th' opposing faction still appears,
The hopes to thrive, can ne're outweigh the fears,
Be caution'd then my Muse, and still retir'd;
Nor be dispis'd, aiming to be admir'd;
Conscious of wants, still with contracted wing,
To some few friends, and to thy sorrows sing;
For groves of Lawrell, thou wert never meant;
Be dark enough thy shades, and be thou there content.

FRIENDSHIP BETWEEN EPHELIA AND ARDELIA

Eph. What Friendship is, ARDELIA shew.
Ard. 'Tis to love, as I love You.
Eph. This Account, so short (tho' kind)
      Suits not my enquiring Mind.
      Therefore farther now repeat;
      What is Friendship when compleat?
Ard. 'Tis to share all Joy and Grief;
      'Tis to lend all due Relief
      From the Tongue, the Heart, the Hand;
      'Tis to mortgage House and Land;
      For a Friend be sold a Slave;
      'Tis to die upon a Grave,
      If a Friend therein do lie.
Eph. This indeed, tho' carry'd high.
      This, tho' more than e'er was done
      Underneath the rolling Sun,
      This has all been said before.
      Can ARDELIA say no more?
Ard. Words indeed no more can shew:
      But 'tis to love, as I love you.

THE CIRCUIT OF APPOLLO

Appollo as lately a Circuit he made,
Throo' the lands of the Muses when Kent he survey'd
And saw there that Poets were not very common,
But most that pretended to Verse, were the Women
Resolv'd to encourage, the few that he found,
And she that writt best, with a wreath shou'd be crown'd.
A summons sent out, was obey'd but by four,
When Phebus, afflicted, to meet with no more,
And standing, where sadly, he now might descry,
From the banks of the Stoure the desolate Wye,
He lamented for Behn o're that place of her birth,
And said amongst Femens was not on the earth
Her superiour in fancy, in language, or witt,
Yett own'd that a little too loosly she writt;
Since the art of the Muse is to stirr up soft thoughts,
Yett to make all hearts beat, without blushes, or faults.
But now to proceed, and their merritts to know,
Before he on any, the Bay's wou'd bestow,
He order'd them each in their several way,
To show him their papers, to sing, or to say,
What 'ere they thought best, their pretention's might
   prove,

When Alinda, began, with a song upon Love.
So easy the Verse, yett compos'd with such art,
That not one expression fell short of the heart;
Apollo himself, did their influence obey,
He catch'd up his Lyre, and a part he wou'd play,
Declaring, no harmony else, cou'd be found,
Fitt to wait upon words, of so moving a sound.
The Wreath, he reach'd out, to have plac'd on her head,
If Laura not quickly a paper had read,
Wherein She Orinda has praised so high,
He own'd itt had reach'd him, while yett in the sky,
That he thought with himself, when itt first struck his
   ear,
Who e're cou'd write that, ought the Laurel to wear.
Betwixt them he stood, in a musing suspence,
Till Valeria withdrew him a little from thence,
And told him, as soon as she'd gott him aside,
Her works, by no other, but him shou'd be try'd;
Which so often he read, and with still new delight,
That Iudgment t'was thought wou'd not passe till twas
   'night;
Yet at length, he restor'd them, but told her withall
If she kept itt still close, he'd the Talent recall.
Ardelia, came last as expecting least praise,
Who writt for her pleasure and not for the Bays,
But yett, as occasion, or fancy should sway,
Wou'd sometimes endeavour to passe a dull day,
In composing a song, or a Scene of a Play
Not seeking for Fame, which so little does last,
That e're we can taste itt, the Pleasure is Past.
But Appollo reply'd, tho' so carelesse she seemed,
Yett the Bays, if her share, wou'd be highly esteem'd.
And now, he was going to make an Oration,
Had thrown by one lock, with a delicate fassion,
Upon the left foot, most genteely did stand,
Had drawn back the other, and wav'd his white hand,
When calling to mind, how the Prize alltho' given
By Paris, to her, who was fairest in Heaven,
Had pull'd on the rash, inconsiderate Boy,
The fall of his House, with the ruine of Troy,
Since in Witt, or in Beauty, itt never was heard,
One female cou'd yield t'have another preferr'd,
He changed his dessign, and devided his praise,
And said that they all had a right to the Bay's,
And that t'were injustice, one brow to adorn,
With a wreath, which so fittly by each might be worn.
Then smil'd to himself, and applauded his art,

Who thus nicely has acted so suttle a part,
Four Women to wheedle, but found 'em too many,
For who wou'd please all, can never please any.
In vain then, he thought itt, there longer to stay,
But told them, he now must go drive on the day,
Yett the case to Parnassus, shou'd soon be referr'd,
And there in a councill of Muses, be heard,
Who of their own sex, best the title might try,
Since no man upon earth, nor Himself in the sky,
Wou'd be so imprudent, so dull, or so blind,
To loose three parts in four from amongst woman kind.

THE UNEQUAL FETTERS

Cou'd we stop the time that's flying
    Or recall itt when 'tis past
Put far off the day of Dying
    Or make Youth for ever last
To Love wou'd then be worth our cost.

But since we must loose those Graces
    Which at first your hearts have wonne
And you seek for in new Faces
    When our Spring of Life is done
It wou'd but urdge our ruine on

Free as Nature's first intention
    Was to make us, I'll be found
Nor by subtle Man's invention
    Yeild to be in Fetters bound
By one that walks a freer round.

Mariage does but slightly tye Men
    Whil'st close Pris'ners we remain
They the larger Slaves of Hymen
    Still are begging Love again
At the full length of all their chain.

THE SPLEEN

A Pindarik Poem

What art thou, SPLEEN which ev'ry thing dost ape?
    Thou Proteus to abus'd Mankind,
    Who never yet thy real Cause cou'd find,

Or fix thee to remain in one continued Shape.
  Still varying thy perplexing Form,
  Now a Dead Sea thou'lt represent,
  A Calm of stupid Discontent,
Then, dashing on the Rocks wilt rage into a Storm.
  Trembling sometimes thou dost appear,
  Dissolved into a Panick Fear;
  On Sleep intruding dost thy Shadows spread,
  Thy gloomy Terrours round the silent Bed,
And croud with boading Dreams the Melancholy
    Head;
  Or, when the Midnight Hour is told,
  And drooping Lids thou still dost waking hold,
  Thy fond Delusions cheat the Eyes,
  Before them antick Spectres dance,
Unusual Fires their pointed Heads advance,
  And airy Phantoms rise.
  Such was the monstrous Vision seen,
When Brutus (now beneath his Cares opprest,
And all Rome's Fortunes rolling in his Breast,
  Before Philippi's latest Field,
Before his Fate did to Octavius lead)
  Was vanquish'd by the Spleen.
  Falsly, the Mortal Part we blame
  Of our deprest, and pond'rous Frame,
  Which, till the First degrading Sin
  Let Thee, its dull Attendant, in,
  Still with the Other did comply,
Nor clogg'd the Active Soul, dispos'd to fly,
And range the Mansions of it's native Sky.
  Nor, whilst in his own Heaven he dwelt,
  Whilst Man his Paradice possest,
His fertile Garden in the fragrant East,
  And all united Odours smelt,
  No armed Sweets, until thy Reign,
  Cou'd shock the Sense, or in the Face
  A flusht, unhandsom Colour place.
Now the Jonquille o'ercomes the feeble Brain;
We faint beneath the Aromatick Pain,
Till some offensive Scent thy Pow'rs appease,
And Pleasure we resign for short, and nauseous Ease.
  In ev'ry One thou dost possess,
  New are thy Motions, and thy Dress:
  Now in some Grove a list'ning Friend
  Thy false Suggestions must attend,
Thy whisper'd Griefs, thy fancy'd Sorrows hear,

Breath'd in a Sigh, and witness'd by a Tear;
　　Whilst in the light, and vulgar Croud,
　　Thy Slaves, more clamorous and loud,
By Laughters unprovok'd, thy Influence too confess.
In the Imperious Wife thou Vapours art,
　　Which from o'erheated Passions rise
　　In Clouds to the attractive Brain,
　　Until descending thence again,
　　Thro' the o'er-cast, and show'ring Eyes,
　　Upon her Husband's soften'd Heart,
　　He the disputed Point must yield,
Something resign of the contested Field;
Till Lordly Man, born to Imperial Sway,
Compounds for Peace, to make that Right away,
And Woman, arm'd with Spleen, do's servilely Obey.

　　The Fool, to imitate the Wits,
　　Complains of thy pretended Fits,
　　And Dulness, born with him, wou'd lay
　　Upon thy accidental Sway;
　　Because, sometimes, thou dost presume
　　Into the ablest Heads to come:
　　That, often, Men of Thoughts refin'd,
　　Impatient of unequal Sence,
Such slow Returns, where they so much dispense,
Retiring from the Croud, are to thy Shades inclin'd.
　　O'er me alas! thou dost too much prevail:
　　I feel thy Force, whilst I against thee rail;
I feel my Verse decay, and my crampt Numbers fail.
Thro' thy black Jaundice I all Objects see,
　　As Dark, and Terrible as Thee,
My Lines decry'd, and my Employment thought
An useless Folly, or presumptuous Fault:
　　Whilst in the Muses Paths I stray,
Whilst in their Groves, and by their secret Springs
My Hand delights to trace unusual Things,
And deviates from the known, and common way;
　　Nor will in fading Silks compose
　　Faintly th' inimitable Rose,
Fill up an ill-drawn Bird, or paint on Glass
The Sov'reign's blurr'd and undistinguish'd Face,
The threatning Angel, and the speaking Ass.

　　Patron thou art to ev'ry gross Abuse,
　　　The sullen Husband's feign'd Excuse,
When the ill Humour with his Wife he spends,

And bears recruited Wit, and Spirits to his Friends.
   The Son of Bacchus pleads thy Pow'r,
   As to the Glass he still repairs,
   Pretends but to remove thy Cares,
Snatch from thy Shades one gay, and smiling Hour,
And drown thy Kingdom in a purple Show'r.
When the Coquette, whom ev'ry Fool admires,
   Wou'd in Variety be Fair,
   And, changing hastily the Scene
   From Light, Impertinent, and Vain,
   Assumes a soft, a melancholy Air,
   And of her Eyes rebates the wand'ring Fires,
   The careless Posture, and the Head reclin'd,
   The thoughtful, and composed Face,
Proclaiming the withdrawn, the absent Mind,
   Allows the Fop more liberty to gaze,
   Who gently for the tender Cause inquires;
   The Cause, indeed, is a Defect in Sense,
Yet is the Spleen alledg'd, and still the dull Pretence.
   But these are thy fantastic Harms,
   The Tricks of thy pernicious Stage,
   Which do the weaker Sort engage;
Worse are the dire Effects of thy more pow'rful Charms.
   By Thee Religion, all we know,
   That shou'd enlighten here below,
   Is veil'd in Darkness, and perplext
With anxious Doubts, with endless Scruples vext,
And some Restraint imply'd from each perverted Text.
   Whilst Touch not, Taste not, what is freely giv'n,
Is but thy niggard Voice, disgracing bounteous Heav'n.
   From Speech restrain'd, by thy Deceits abus'd,
   To Deserts banish'd, or in Cells reclus'd,
   Mistaken Vot'ries to the Pow'rs Divine,
   Whilst they a purer Sacrifice design,
Do but the Spleen obey, and worship at thy Shrine.
   In vain to chase thee ev'ry Art we try,
     In vain all Remedies apply,
     In vain the Indian Leaf infuse,
     Or the parch'd Eastern Berry Bruise;
Some pass, in vain, those Bounds, and nobler Liquors use.
   Now Harmony, in vain, we bring,
   Inspire the Flute, and touch the String.
   From Harmony no help is had;
Musick but soothes thee, if too sweetly sad,
And if too light, but turns thee gayly Mad.
   Tho' the Physicians greatest Gains,

Altho' his growing Wealth he sees
Daily increas'd by Ladies Fees,
Yet dost thou baffle as his studious Pains.
Not skilful Lower thy Source cou'd find,
Or thro' the well-dissected Body trace
The secret, the mysterious ways,
By which thou dost surprise, and prey upon the Mind.
Tho' in the Search, too deep for Humane Thought,
With unsuccessful Toil he wrought,
'Till thinking Thee to've catch'd, Himself by thee
was caught,
Retain'd thy Pris'ner, thy acknowledg'd Slave,
And sunk beneath thy Chain to a lamented Grave.

PRIMARY SOURCES

Miscellany Poems, on Several Occasions, Written by a Lady. London: printed for
J. B., 1713.

The Poems of Anne, Countess of Winchilsea. Edited by Myra Reynolds. Chicago:
The University of Chicago Press, 1903. (Note that this text is incomplete
and sometimes inaccurate.)

Selected Poems of Anne Finch, Countess of Winchilsea. Edited by Katharine M.
Rogers. New York: Frederick Ungar, 1979.

Neill, D. G. "Studies for an Edition of the Poems of Anne, Countess of Winchilsea,
Consisting of a Bibliography of her Poems and a Study of All Available
Mss." Ph.D. dissertation, Oxford, 1954. (Not seen.)

RELATED SOURCES

Hampsten, Elizabeth. "Petticoat Authors: 1660–1720." *Women's Studies* 5, 1/2
(1980):21–38.

Messenger, Ann. "Publishing Without Perishing: Lady Winchilsea's *Miscellany
Poems* of 1713." *Restoration* 5, 1 (1981):27–37.

Rogers, Katharine. "Anne Finch, Countess of Winchilsea: An Augustan Woman
Poet." In *Shakespeare's Sisters: Feminist Essays on Woman Poets.* Edited
by Sandra M. Gilbert and Susan Gubar. Bloomington: Indiana University
Press, 1979.

See also introductions to volumes edited by Myra Reynolds and Katharine M.
Rogers, cited in primary sources, for further information.

MARY COLLIER
1689/90 – *after* 1759

Mary Collier wrote *The Woman's Labour* in 1739 in angry response to *The Thresher's Labour* (1736) by Stephen Duck. In the autobiographical preface to the expanded 1762 edition of *The Woman's Labour,* Mary Collier explained that Stephen Duck's poem infuriated her in its relegation of women field-workers to the status of dilatory, feckless characters. Her decision to repudiate Duck's dismissal of women was prompted by the encouragement of a family who had temporarily employed her.

Without this kind of patronage and encouragement, however slight, Collier's poems had barely a chance of publication, and even with patronage, she remained an unknown. Stephen Duck, by contrast, was patronized by the Queen, received various minor court appointments, and became a national literary celebrity. As the first known rural laboring woman to publish creative work, Collier told of her life in the 1762 preface: She was born, she stated, "near Midhurst in Sussex of poor, but honest Parents by whom I was taught to read when very Young." Sent out "to such labour as the Country afforded" when her mother died, she "lost" her education, but kept up her "Recreation" in reading, living with her father until he died. At this juncture she moved to Petersfield, where her chances of employment were probably enhanced. She worked in Petersfield as a washerwoman until the age of sixty-three, then took over the management of a farmhouse in nearby Alton for the next seven years, until she was incapacitated. In 1762 she "retired to a Garret (The poor Poets Fate) in Alton where I am endeavouring," she concluded, "to pass the Relict of my days in Piety, Purity, Peace, and an Old Maid."

Collier's narrative of a woman worker's year-round industry in *The Woman's Labour,* included here, spelled out the difficulties experienced by laboring women who tried to earn a decent living. As lack of employment, changing conditions, and the rise of prices began to affect women day laborers, jobs became more poorly paid and even harder to obtain. In the poem, Collier described the tribulations of domestic service with which she was probably well acquainted. (She may also have been a seasonal agricultural laborer.)

Very little else is known about Mary Collier. In her 1762 volume she wrote "An Elegy upon Stephen Duck" after his suicide, which offers a glimpse of a Collier who endured something of Duck's dark nights of the soul, due in part (it seems) to personal loneliness and the rigors of an overworked life.

The Woman's Labour

IMMORTAL Bard! thou Fav'rite of the Nine!
Enrich'd by Peers, advanc'd by CAROLINE!
   Deign to look down on one that's poor and low,
Remembring you yourself was lately so;
Accept these Lines: Alas! what can you have
From her, who ever was, and's still a Slave?
No Learning ever was bestow'd on me;
My Life was always spent in Drudgery:
And not alone; alas! with Grief I find,
It is the Portion of poor Woman-kind.
Oft have I thought as on my Bed I lay,
Eas'd from the tiresome Labours of the Day,
Our first Extraction from a Mass refin'd,
Could never be for Slavery design'd;
Till Time and Custom by Degrees destroy'd
That happy State our Sex at first enjoy'd.
When Men had us'd their utmost Care and Toil,
Their Recompence was but a Female Smile;
When they by Arts or Arms were render'd Great,
They laid their Trophies at a Woman's Feet;
They, in those Days, unto our Sex did bring
Their Hearts, their All, a Free-will Offering;
And as from us their Being they derive,
They back again should all due Homage give.

   JOVE once descending from the Clouds, did drop
In showers of Gold on lovely Danae's Lap;
The sweet-tongu'd Poets, in those generous Days,
Unto our Shrine still offer'd up their Lays:
But now, alas! that Golden Age is past,
We are the Objects of your Scorn at last.
And you, great DUCK, upon whose happy Brow

SOURCE: Both selections come from the British Library. *The Woman's Labour* is shelf no. 1346.f.17; *Poems, on Several Occasions* (the title page missing) is shelf no. 11632.f.12.

The Muses seem to fix their Garland now,
In your late Poem boldly did declare
Alcides' Labours cant with yours compare;
And of your annual Task have much to say,
Of Threshing, Reaping, Mowing Corn and Hay;
Boasting your daily Toil, and nightly Dream,
But cant conclude your never-dying Theme,
And let our hapless Sex in Silence lie.
Forgotten, and in dark Oblivion die;
But on our abject State you throw your Scorn,
And Women wrong, your Verses to adorn.
You of Hay-making speak a Word or two,
As if our Sex but little Work could do:
This makes the honest Farmer smiling say,
He'll seek for Women still to make his Hay;
For if his Back be turn'd the Work they mind
As well as Men, as far as he can find.
For my own Part, I many a Summer's Day
Have spent in throwing, turning, making Hay;
But ne'er could see, what you have lately found,
Our Wages paid for sitting on the Ground.
'Tis true, that when our Morning's Work is done,
And all our Grass expos'd unto the Sun,
While that his scorching Beams do on it shine,
As well as you we have a Time to dine:
I hope, that since we freely toil and sweat
To earn our Bread, you'll give us Time to eat;
That over, soon we must get up again,
And nimbly turn our Hay upon the plain:
Nay, rake and row it in, the Case is clear;
Or how should Cocks in equal Rows appear?
But if you'd have what you have wrote believ'd,
I find, that you to hear us talk are griev'd:
In this, I hope, you do not speak your Mind,
For none but Turks, that ever I could find,
Have Mutes to serve them, or did e'er deny
Their Slaves, at Work, to chat it merrily.
Since you have Liberty to speak your Mind,
And are to talk, as well as we, inclin'd,
Why should you thus repine, because that we,
Like you, enjoy that pleasing Liberty?
What! would you Lord it quite, and take away
The only Privilege our Sex enjoy?

WHEN Ev'ning does approach, we homeward hi
And our domestick Toils incessant ply:

Against your coming Home prepare to get
Our Work all done, Our House in order set;
Bacon and Dumpling in the Pot we boil,
Our Beds we make, our Swine we feed the while;
Then wait at Door to see you coming Home,
And set the Table out against you come:
Early next Morning we on you attend,
Our Children dress and feed, their Cloaths we mend;
And in the Field our daily Task renew;
Soon as the rising Sun has dry'd the dew.

   WHEN Harvest comes, into the Field we go,
And help to reap the Wheat as well as you;
Or else we go the Ears of Corn to glean;
No Labour scorning, be it e'er so mean;
But in the Work we freely bear a Part,
And what we can, perform with all our Heart.
To get a Living we so willing are,
Our tender Babes unto the Field we bear,
And wrap them in our Cloaths to keep them warm,
While round about we gather up the Corn;
And often unto them our Course do bend,
To keep them save, that nothing them offend:
Our Children that are able bear a share,
In gleaning Corn, such is our frugal Care.
When Night comes on, unto our Home we go,
Our Corn we carry, and our Infant too;
Weary indeed! but 'tis not worth our while
Once to complain, or rest at ev'ry Stile;
We must make haste, for when we home are come,
We find again our Work but just begun;
So many Things for our Attendance call,
Had we ten Hands, we could employ them all.
Our Children put to Bed, with greatest Care
We all Things for your coming home prepare:
You sup, and go to Bed without Delay,
And rest yourselves till the ensuing Day;
While we, alas! but little Sleep can have,
Because our froward Children cry and rave;
Yet, without fail, soon as Day-light doth spring,
We in the Field again our work begin,
And there, with all our Strength, our Toil renew,
Till Titan's golden Rays have dry'd the Dew;
Then home we go unto our Children dear,
Dress, feed, and bring them to the Field with Care.

Were this your Case, you justly might complain
That Day or Night you are secure from Pain;
Those mighty Troubles which perplex your Mind,
(Thistles before, and Females come behind)
Would vanish soon, and quickly disappear,
Were you, like us, encumber'd thus with Care.
What you would have of us we do not know:
We oft take up the Corn that you do mow;
We cut the Peas, and always ready are
In every Work to take our proper Share;
And from the Time that Harvest doth begin,
Until the Corn be cut and carry'd in,
Our Toil and Labour's daily so extreme,
That we have hardly ever Time to Dream.

THE Harvest ended, Respite none we find;
The hardest of our Toil is still behind:
Hard Labour we most chearfully pursue,
And out, abroad, a Chairing often go:
Of which I now will briefly tell in part,
What fully to describe is past my Art;
So many Hardships daily we go through,
I boldly say, the like you never knew.

WHEN bright Orion glitters in the Skies
In Winter Nights, then early we must rise;
The Weather ne'er so bad, Wind, Rain, or Snow,
Our Work appointed, we must rise and go;
While you on easy Beds may lie and sleep,
Till Light does thro' your Chamber Windows peep:
When to the House we come where we should go,
How to get in, alas! we do not know:
The Maid quite tir'd with Work the day before,
O'ercome with Sleep; we standing at the Door
Oppress'd with Cold, and often call in vain,
E'er to our Work we can admittance gain:
But when from Wind and Weather we get in,
Briskly with Courage we our Work begin;
Heaps of fine Linnen we before us view,
Whereon to lay our Strength and Patience too;
Cambricks and Muslins which our Ladies wear,
Laces and Edgings, costly, fine, and rare,
Which must be wash'd with utmost Skill and Care;
With Holland Shirts, Ruffles and Fringes too,
Fashions, which our Fore-fathers never knew.

For several Hours here we work and slave,
Before we can one Glimpse of Day-light have;
We labour hard before the Morning's past,
Because we fear the Time runs on too fast.

AT length bright Sol illuminates the Skies,
And summons drowsy Mortals to arise;
Then comes our Mistress to us without fail,
And in her Hand, perhaps, a Mug of Ale
To cheer our Hearts, and also to inform
Herself what Work is done that very Morn;
Lays her Commands upon us, that we mind
Her Linnen well, nor leave the Dirt behind:
Nor this alone, but also to take Care
We don't her Cambricks nor her Ruffles tear;
And these most strictly does of us require,
To save her Soap, and sparing be of Fire;
Tells us her Charge is great, nay furthermore,
Her Cloaths are fewer than the Time before:
Now we drive on, resolv'd our Strength to try,
And what we can we do most willingly;
Untill with Heat and Work, 'tis often known,
Not only Sweat, but Blood runs trickling down
Our Wrists and Fingers; still our Work demands
The constant Action of our lab'ring Hands.

NOW Night comes on, from whence you have Relief,
But that, alas! does but increase our Grief;
With heavy Hearts we often view the Sun,
Fearing he'll set before our Work is done;
For either in the Morning, or at Night,
We peice the Summers Day with Candle-light.
Tho' we all Day with Care our Work attend,
Such is our Fate, we know not when 'twill end:
When Evening's come, you homeward take your Way,
We, till our Work is done, are forc'd to stay;
And after all our Toil and Labour past,
Six-pence or Eight-pence pays us off at last;
For all our Pains, no Prospect can we see
Attend us, but Old Age and Poverty.

THE Washing is not all we have to do:
We oft change Work for Work as well as you.
Our Mistress of her Pewter doth complain,
And 'tis our part to make it clean again.

This Work, tho very hard and tiresome too,
Is not the worst we hapless Females do:
When Night comes on, and we quite weary are,
We scarce can count what falls unto our Share;
Pots, Kettles, Sauce-pans, Skillets, we may see,
Skimmers, and Ladles, and such Trumpery,
Brought in to make compleat our Slavery.
Tho' early in the Morning 'tis begun,
'Tis often very late before we've done;
Alas! our Labours never know no End,
On Brass and Iron we our Strength must spend;
Our tender Hands and Fingers scratch and tear:
All this, and more, with Patience we must bear.
Colour'd with Dirt and Filth we now appear;
Your threshing sooty Peas will not come near.
All the Perfections Woman once could boast,
Are quite obscur'd, and altogether lost.

ONCE more our Mistress sends to let us know
She wants our Help, because the Beer runs low:
Then in much haste for Brewing we prepare,
The Vessels clean, and scald with greatest Care;
Often at Midnight from our Bed we rise
At other Times ev'n that will not suffice;
Our Work at Ev'ning oft we do begin,
And e'er we've done, the Night comes on again.
Water we pump, the Copper we must fill,
Or tend the Fire; for if we e'er stand still,
Like you, when Threshing, we a Watch must keep,
Our Wort [?] boils over, if we dare to sleep.

    BUT to rehearse all Labour is in vain,
Of which we very justly might complain:
For us, you see, but little Rest is found;
Our Toil increases as the Year runs round.
While you to Sysiphus yourselves compare,
With Danaus' Daughters we may claim a Share;
For while he labours hard against the Hill,
Bottomless Tubs of Water they must fill.

    So the industrious Bees do hourly strive
To bring their Loads of Honey to the Hive;
Their sordid Owners always reap the Gains,
And poorly recompense their Toil and Pains.

FROM

POEMS ON
SEVERAL OCCASIONS

Some Remarks of the Author's Life
Drawn by Herself.

I WHO am the Author of these Poems was Born near Midhurst in Sussex of poor, but honest Parents, by whom I was taught to read when very Young, and took great delight in it; but my Mother dying, I lost my Education, Never being put to School: As I grew up, I was set to such labour as the Country afforded. My Recreation was reading, I bought and borrow'd many Books, any foolish History highly delighted me; but as I grew Older I read Speed and Bakers Chronicles, Fox's Acts and Monuments of the Church, Josephus, and others. Continuing with my Father, who before his Death was long sickly and infirm, after his Death being left alone, I came to Petersfield, where my chief Employment was, Washing, Brewing and such labour, still devoting what leisure time I had to Books. After several Years thus Spent, Duck's Poems came abroad, which I soon got by heart, fancying he had been too Severe on the Female Sex in his Thresher's Labour brought me to a Strong propensity to call an Army of Amazons to vindicate the injured Sex: Therefore I answer'd him to please my own humour, little thinking to make it Public it lay by me several Years and by now and then repeating a few lines to amuse myself and entertain my Company, it got Air.

I happen'd to attend a Gentlewoman in a fit of Illness, and she and her Friends persuaded me to make Verses on the Wife Sentences, which I did on such Nights as I waited on her. I had learn'd to write to assist my memory, and her Spouse transcrib'd it with a promise to keep it private, but he exposed it to so many, that it soon Became a Town Talk, which made many advise me to have it printed and at length I comply'd to have it done

PRIMARY SOURCES

Poems, on Several Occasions, by M. Collier, . . . With some remarks on her life. Winchester: printed for the author, 1762.

The Woman's Labour: an epistle to Mr. Stephen Duck; in answer to his late poem, called "The Thresher's Labour." To which are added, The Three Wise Sentences, Taken From The First Book of Esdras, Ch. III and IV. London: printed for the author, 1739.

RELATED SOURCES

Collier, Mary, *The Woman's Labour: an epistle to Mr. Stephen Duck* . . . London: Printed for the author, 1739, and Stephen Duck, *The Thresher's Labour* in *Poems on Several Occasions*. London: W. Bickerton, 1736. Photo-reprint of both poems with an introduction by Moira Ferguson. William Andrew Clark Memorial Library, Univ. of California, Los Angeles, forthcoming.

SOPHIA
fl. 1739–1741

Nothing is known about Sophia that is not speculation, but clearly she was well-educated, for the Sophia tracts, *Woman not Inferior to Man* (1739) and *Woman's Superior Excellence over Man* (1740) are rearranged semi-translations, with substantial additions of her own, of François Poulain de la Barre's *De L'Egalité des deux Sexes* (1673). Poulain de la Barre was a French Roman Catholic cleric who, eventually renouncing his religion for Protestantism, left France and settled in Geneva after the revocation of the Edict of Nantes in 1685.

In 1677 an English translation by "A.L." was published. Sophia may have reshaped the translation and interspersed such additional material as references to Alexander Pope, Lady Winchilsea (see biography of Anne Kingsmill Finch, Countess of Winchilsea), and John Gay, all of whom are absent from Poulain de la Barre's work and A.L.'s translation. Introducing a moralistic note, Sophia expressed regret that "a Manley, a Behn, or a Saphira, have shamefully misapplied their talents."

In 1740 a "Gentleman" responded to *Woman not Inferior* with *Man Superior to Woman.* This format follows that of Poulain de la Barre. Once again, the author was probably Sophia, who employed traditional misogynous arguments including Theophrastian-based, antifeminist character sketches. *Woman's Superior Excellence* answered the "Gentleman."

According to C.A. Moore, for Sophia's first work "[she] appropriated most of the First Part of Poullain's [*sic*] work and a good deal of the Second Part." Moore goes on to suggest that for *Woman's Superior Excellence* (twice the length of the first tract) Sophia is more indebted to William Walsh's *Dialogue Concerning Women,* 1691. After several reprintings of each individual tract, *Beauty's Triumph,* a volume containing all three—*Woman not Inferior; Man Superior to Woman; and Woman's Superior Excellence*—was published in 1751 and reprinted in the 1790s. Under other titles, the individual tracts were reprinted at least twice in the 1750s and once in the 1780s.

Sophia's tracts appeared in the same year as three other important feminist declarations: *The Woman's Labour* by Mary Collier; the sixth essay (particularly) in Lady Mary Wortley Montagu's periodical, *The Nonsense of Common-Sense;* and an article in *The Gentleman's Magazine* on male usurpation of female occupations. Taken as a feminist quartet, these works indicate a stronger, growing resistance to male domination after the lean feminist years of the previous decades.

---------------------- • ----------------------

FROM

WOMAN NOT INFERIOR TO MAN.

SECTION I.

The Introduction.

IF a celebrated Author had not already told us, that there is nothing in nature so much to be wonder'd at, as THAT WE CAN WONDER AT ALL; it must appear to every one, who has but a degree of understanding above the idiot, a matter of the greatest surprize, to observe the universal prevalence of prejudice and custom in the minds of Men. One might naturally expect to see those lordly creatures, as they modestly stile themselves, every where jealous of superiority, and watchful to maintain it. Instead of which, if we except the tyrannical usurpation of authority they exert over us Women, we shall find them industrious in nothing but courting the meanest servitude. Was their ambition laudable and just, it would be consistent in itself, and this consistency would render them alike imperious in every circumstance, where authority is requisite and justifiable. And if their brutal strength of body entitled them to lord it over our nicer frame; the rightful superiority of reason to passion might suffice to make them ashamed of submitting that noble principle to baser passion, prejudice, and groundless custom. If this haughty sex would have us believe, they have a natural right of superiority over us, why don't they prove their charter from nature, by making use of reason to subdue themselves. We know we have reason, and are sensible that it is the only prerogative nature has bestow'd upon us, to lift us above the sphere of sensitive Animals. And the same reason, which points us out our equality with them, would enable us to discern the superiority of *Men* over us; if we could discover in them the least degree of sense above what we ourselves possess. But it will be impossible for us, without forfeiting that reason, ever to acknowledge ourselves inferior to creatures, who make no other use of the sense they boast of, than meanly to

SOURCE: The selection for *Woman not Inferior to Man* comes from the Newberry Library, Chicago. The selection for *Woman's Superior Excellence over Man* comes from the Humanities Research Center, University of Texas, Austin.

subject it to the passions they have in common with Brutes. Were we to see the Men every where, and at all times, masters of themselves, and their animal appetites in a perfect subordination to their rational faculties, we should have some colour to think that nature design'd them for masters to us, who cannot perhaps always boast of so complete a command over ourselves. But how is it possible for us to give into such a notion; while we see those very men, whose ambition of ascendancy over us nothing less than absolute dominion can satiate, court the most abject slavery, by prostituting reason to their groveling passions, suffering sense to be led away captive by prejudice, and sacrificing justice, truth, and honour to inconsiderate custom?

How many things do these mighty wise creatures hold for undoubted truths, without being able to assign a reason for any one of their opinions? The cause of which is, that they suffer themselves to be hurried away by appearances. With them, what seems true must be so; because the light, in which they eye things, stands them in the stead of conviction, Where they want evidence in the principles, fallacy helps them to fill up the vacancy with chimeras in their inference. In a word, as they suppose without reason, so they discourse without grounds; and therefore would have as strongly maintain'd the negative of what they assert, if custom and the impression of the senses had determin'd them to it after the same manner. . . .

I should never have done, was I to reckon up the many groundless notions the Men are led into by custom: of which there in none more absurd than that of the great difference they make between their own sex and ours. Yet it must be own'd, that there is not any vulgar error more antient or universal. For the learned and illiterate alike are prepossest with the opinion, that Men are really superior to Women, and that the dependence we now are in is the very state which nature pointed out for us.

> Self-prais'd, and grasping at despotick Power,
> They look on Slav'ry as the female Dow'r;
> To Nature's Boon ascribe what Force has given,
> And Usurpation deem the Gift of Heaven.

So that to advance the contrary doctrine, after so long a prepossession, must appear as great a paradox as it did some years ago to assert, that on the nether surface of the globe there were men who walk'd with their heads downwards to us; and whether the one be not as agreeable to truth as the other, will best be found on a fair trial. But what judge shall we have recourse to, or what evidence can be admitted in an affair of so delicate a nature as this, whereon depends the right of one half the creation, which ever side prevails?

All the witness we desire to be allow'd, is plain undisguised truth; and if the Men have but generosity enough left to admit this evidence, we shall have no room to fear any they can bring in Contradiction to it. We are willing, for charity's sake, to hope, that, however they may be disposed, they will at least blush to make any exceptions against a witness so unquestionably impartial.

But who shall the matter be tried by? We ourselves are too nearly concern'd in the decision, to be admitted even as witnesses in the trial, much less as judges of the cause; and the same consideration equally excludes the Men from acting in it in either capacity. And yet so far are we from having any thing to apprehend from the defect of justice in our pretensions, that if the Men were ever so little more candid and less corrupted in their judgments than they really are, we would readily subscribe to their own sentence. But as the case now stands, we must appeal to a more impartial arbitrator.

Hitherto the difference between the sexes has been but very slightly touch'd upon. Nevertheless, the Men, bias'd by custom, prejudice, and interest, have heretofore presumed boldly to pronounce sentence in their own favour, because possession empower'd them to make violence take place of justice. And the Men of our times, without trial or examination, have taken the same liberty from the report of other Men. Whereas to judge soundly whether their sex has received from nature any real supereminence beyond ours, they should entirely divest themselves of all interest and partiality, and suffer no bare reports to fill the place of argument, especially if the reporter be a party immediately concern'd.

If a Man could thus put off the partiality attach'd to self, and put on for a minute a state of neutrality, he would be able to see, and forced to acknowledge, that prejudice and precipitance are the chief causes of setting less value upon Women than Men, and giving so much greater excellence and nobility to the latter than to the former. In a word, were the Men Philosophers, in the strict sense of the term, they would be able to see, that nature invincibly proves (at least) an equality in our sex with their own.

But as there are extremely few among them capable of such an abstracted way of thinking, they have no more right to act the judges in this matter than ourselves; and therefore, we must be obliged to appeal to a more impartial judge, one incapable of inclining to either side, and consequently unsuspected on both. This I apprehend to be rectified reason, as it is a pure intellectual faculty, elevated above the consideration of any sex, and equally concern'd in the welfare of the whole rational species. To this Judge we leave our cause; by the decision of this we are prepared to stand or fall; and if, upon the evidence of truth, reason should declare us inferior to Men, we will chearfully acquiesce in the sentence.

But what if we obtain a decree in our favour, upon impartial examination? Why then all the authority, which the Men have exerted over us hitherto, will appear an unjust usurpation on their side; for which nothing can make a tolerable atonement, but their restoring us to the state of equality nature first placed us in. And till they do that, the fancied wrongs they charge upon our whole sex, tho' but applicable (if at all) to a very small number among us, whom I don't pretend to justify, can only be looked upon as very moderate reprisals upon theirs.

To set this whole matter then in as clear a light as possible, it will be necessary to clear our ideas, by separating the fictitious from the real, the obscure from the evident, supposition from matter of fact, seemings from entities, practice from principle, belief from knowledge, doubt from certainty,—and interest and prejudice from justice and sound judgment.

> Here let us fix our foot, hence take our view,
> And learn to try false merit by the true.

To this end therefore we must examine, in order, what are the general notions which the Men entertain of our sex, on what grounds they build their opinions, and what are the effects to us and to themselves of the treatment we receive from them, in consequence of their present opinion. In the course of this little treatise, I shall also occasionally examine, whether there be any essential difference between the sexes which can authorize the superiority the Men claim over the Women; and what are the causes of, and who are accountable for, the seeming difference which makes the sum of their plea. And if, upon mature consideration, it appears, that there is no other difference between Men and Us than what their tyranny has created, it will then be evident how unjust they are in excluding us from that power and dignity we have a right to share with them, how ungenerous in denying us the equality of esteem which is our due, and, how little reason they have to triumph in the base possession of an authority which unnatural violence and lawless usurpation put into their hands. Then let them justify, if they can, the little meannesses, not to mention the grosser barbarities, which they daily practise towards that part of the creation whose happiness is so inseparably link'd with their own. (End of Chapter 1)

SECT. VIII.

Conclusion.

WHAT I have hitherto said, has not been with an intention to stir up any of my own sex to revolt against the Men, or to invert the present order of things with regard to government and authority. No, let them stand as they are. I only mean to shew my sex that they are not so despicable as the Men wou'd have them believe themselves, and that we are capable of as much greatness of soul as the best of that haughty species. And I am fully convinc'd, it wou'd be to the joint interest of both to think so.

This is plain from the ill consequences attending the opposite error. The Men, by thinking us incapable of improving our intellects, have entirely thrown us out of all the advantages of education; and thereby contributed as much as possible to make us the senseless creatures they represent us. So that, for want of education, we are render'd subject to all the follies they dislike in us, and are loaded with their ill treatment for faults of their own creating.

And what is the consequence of this tyrannic treatment? Why, it finally reverts on themselves: The same want of learning and education, which hurries Women into what displeases the Men, debars them of the virtues requisite to support them under the ill treatment they are loaded with by the Men, on that account; and for want of those virtues they often run very unjustifiable lengths to be revenged on their tyrants. Thus does it arrive, generally speaking, that both Men and Women hold one-another in sovereign contempt, and therefore vie with each-other which shall treat the other the worst. Whereas, how happy might they be, wou'd both sexes but resolve to give one another that just esteem which is their due.

However, if truth may be spoken, it is undeniable that the blame lies chiefly and originally in the Men. Since if they wou'd but allow Women the advantages of education and literature, the latter wou'd learn to despise those follies and trifles for which they are at present unjustly despised. Our sex wou'd be enabled to give the Men a better opinion of our capacity of head and disposition of heart: And the Men, in proportion to the encrease of their esteem for us, wou'd lessen, and by degrees reform, their ill-treatment of us. Women wou'd make it their study to improve their parts, and with encrease of knowledge would grow in every useful accomplishment. Their pleasure and study wou'd be to entertain the *Men* with sense, and to add solidity to their charms. By which means both sexes wou'd be happy, and neither have cause to blame the other. But while they lock up from us all the avenues to knowledge, they cannot, without reproach to themselves, blame us for any misconduct which ignorance may be the occasion of: and we cannot but accuse them of the most cruel injustice in disesteeming and mis-using us for faults they deprive us of the power of correcting. . . .

Thus then does it hitherto fully appear, how falsely we are deem'd, by the Men, wanting in that solidity of sense which they so vainly value themselves upon. Our right is the same with theirs to all public employ-ments; we are endow'd, by nature, with geniuses at least as capable of filling them as theirs can be; and our hearts are as susceptible of virtue as our heads are of the sciences. We neither want spirit, strength, nor courage, to defend a country, nor prudence to rule it. Our souls are as perfect as theirs, and the organs they depend on are generally more refined. However, if the bodies be compared to decide the right of excellence in either sex; we need not contend: The Men themselves I presume will give it up. They cannot deny but that we have the advantage of them in the internal mechanism of our frames: Since in us is produced the most beautiful and wonderful of all creatures: And how much have we not the advantage of them in outside? What beauty, comeliness, and graces, has not heaven attach'd to our sex above theirs? I shou'd blush with scorn to mention this, if I did not think it an indication of our souls being also in a state of greater delicacy: For I cannot help thinking that the wise author of nature suited our frames to the souls he gave us. And surely then the acuteness of our minds, with what passes in the inside of our heads, ought to render us at least EQUALS to Men, since the outside seldom fails to make us their absolute mistresses.

And yet I wou'd have none of my sex build their authority barely on so slight a foundation. No: Good sense will out-last a handsome face: And the dominion gain'd over hearts by reason is lasting. I wou'd therefore exhort all my sex to throw aside idle amusements, and to betake themselves to the improvement of their minds, that we may be able to act with that becoming dignity our nature has fitted us to; and, without claiming or valuing it, shew our selves worthy something from them, as much above their bare esteem, as they conceit themselves above us. In a word, let us shew them, by what little we do without aid of education, the much we might do if they did us justice; that we may force a blush from them, if possible, and compel them to confess their own baseness to us, and that the worst of us deserve much better treatment than the best of us receive.

FINIS.

——————————————— · ———————————————

FROM

WOMAN'S SUPERIOR EXCELLENCE
OVER MAN

WHEN first I began to examin into the real talents of my sex in general, it was purely from a desire of improving them in myself, to the full extent of the capacity I might possibly find myself gifted with by heaven. And tho' the prejudice I had imbibed from vulgar error falsly convinced me, that I should find the sphere which Women are capable of acting in extremely narrow; I thought it, nevertheless, a duty in us all to make ourselves perfectly acquainted with all our obligations, by a full discovery of the province of our abilities. In reality I don't yet see how any Woman (or Man either) can answer the end of their creation in the faithful discharge of all they ought to do, without first being perfectly apprised of all they can do. Upon these principles I began my enquiry; and as I can with utmost veracity aver, that I enter'd into it without the least pride, or partiality to my own sex, so I can with equal safety say, that all the prejudice I set out with was in favour of the Men: Tho' the honesty of my intentions soon help'd to undeceive me. I was not long in my pursuit before I discover'd a much wider fairer field of female glory to expatiate in than I expected; and upon the nicest, most unpassionate comparison of my own sex with the opposit, to my great astonishment, I found Woman by nature form'd no less capable of all that is good and great than Man.

Once I got the better of pre-possession, I was thoroughly sensible of the prodigious advantage which education gives that arrogant sex over us, and cou'd not help being provoked to scorn and indignation at the little mean artifices which most of them practice to deprive us of the same benefit: But what incensed me the most was to consider the immense fund of knowledge, and useful discoveries, which their groveling jealousy has by such means rob'd the world of. If two heads are better than one; two thousand enquiries must in course be better than one thousand, and in all probability make at least double the discoveries. So that, if it be but allow'd that the Women are equal in numbers to the Men; we may very modestly conclude that, at the lowest computation, one half the profitable knowledge which human species might by this time have been possest of is irreparably lost, through the indolence of some Women in not exerting their talents, and the mean tyranny of most Men, in putting it out of their power to improve those talents.

The impossibility of concealing with any honour such reflections as these, which so nearly concern the whole human species, and more particularly my own injured sex, was the grand motive which set me on writing the little piece I lately communicated to the public, under the title of WOMAN not inferior to MAN. When I had finish'd, examin'd and measured it by all the rules of unbias'd truth and rectified reason, I resolved to publish it; not from any ambition of commencing an author, as the writer of MAN superior to WOMAN wou'd ungenerously insinuate; but from a disinterested desire of contributing to the benefit of others, at the same time that I was seeking information myself in an affair, in which I was not vain enough to think it impossible for me to be mistaken. I was not insensible that such an undertaking must meet with some opposition, this however I was fully persuaded of, that whether what I advanced was right or wrong, I had but two sorts of adversaries to apprehend, Wise Men and Fools: The approbation of the Latter wou'd be an infamy to possess; and the Former, to act like such, must either at least tacitly give me their approbation, or confute me with such instructive arguments as wou'd largely over-ballance to me the mortification of having exposed my own ignorance.

But it seems I have been grosly mistaken, and in consequence of my mistake find myself unawares attack'd from a quarter I the least expected opposition from: It is one of your amphibious things between both, which I think they call a WIT. Every one will guess from these outlines, than I am speaking of the anonymous author of the above-mention'd Treatise, entitled MAN superior to WOMAN, who has taken abundance of pains to give us under his hand that he is none of your rigid sticklers for truth and sense call'd Wisemen, and yet, to do him all the justice he deserves, sufficiently appears to be no Fool.

It must be own'd indeed that this gentleman wou'd have been a very formidable adversary, had his strength been equal to his courage. For my own part, I no sooner saw his first solemn strut towards the lists than I dreaded all for my self and Sex, apprehended nothing less than destruction to all our pretensions, and was upon the point of surrendering at discretion, with a submissive address As you are big be merciful. But how great was my surprise, when I beheld at his approach the giant dwindle to a dwarf, the Achilles to a Hector, nay, the Hector to a Thersites! He has omitted nothing to shew himself a zealous champion of his own sex, and as implacable an adversary to ours; but then his attacks are as void of generosity as his Zeal is without Knowledge. What thanks his good-will to serve them may deserve from the Men, I shall leave to them to determin; but I am very sure they owe him none for the manner of expressing it: And for my own sex I dare answer, that, however incensed those few may be whom he has painted in so odious (and perhaps native) colours, much the major part of us must be indebted to him for the eminent service he has effectually, tho' undesignedly, done us in his impotent endeavours to wound us. Had he, like the rest of his sex, remain'd silent, all the harm he could have done them, and all the service he could have render'd us, would have been merely negative, and amounted to no more than a tacit confirmation of all I advanced, according to the common received notion that Silence is a plea of consent. And the vainer part of the Men might have still triumph'd in the trivial bravado, that their silence was the effect of their contempt for their adversary. Whereas by attempting to support their pretensions, without proper materials, he could not fail of corroborating ours, since a weak defence is ever the surest way to make a bad cause worse. How excessively weak is the answer he has endeavour'd to make to my former piece I shall find no difficulty to make appear; and every one who but reads that answer will be able to see that if he has not been able to make a better, it was not for want of inclination or genius, it must then be for want of materials. But where is the honesty, or generosity, in endeavouring to crush innocence and equity to palliate palpable fraud and falshood? As where is the wit in labouring to stifle truth with fallacious witticism, merely to countenance bare-faced oppression and tyranny? Does he imagin all the Men to be so perverse as not to be reason'd into justice and generosity, while they may make use of the mean methods of fallacy and evasion? Or does he take all the Women for such easy ideots that they are to be coax'd out of their natural right by every fawning sycophant, sneer'd out of it by every word-retailing witling, or braved out of it by every wife-beating bully? No, I hope, he is mistaken; at least I would believe there are some among that corrupted sex capable of soaring above prejudice and passion, to discern truth and honesty from fiction and fraud, and to give justice and reason the right hand of usurpation and fallacy. And for my own part I am resolved to shew my adversary, and all his sex, that there is at least one Woman capable of preferring truth to flattery, sense to sound, and who dares assert her right in the face of usurpation, tho' harden'd by custom into tyranny: And if one is so, why may not all, or at least as many of them as of the Men, be so too? They have under-standings capable of proving that right which the generality of Men want the heart to acknowledge; and they have hearts capable of resolution enough to assert that right against such of the opposit sex as want the sense to do them justice.

But these are truths I have already made sufficiently appear in my first Essay upon this subject; and experience has made them so trite that I should blush to repeat them, was it not to answer the much triter reflec-tions on our sex, which my adversary blushes not to make use of: Tho' frequent repetition has made those reflections so rank, and reason has render'd them so obsolete, that the little modesty which still subsists among the more sensible part of his sex has shamed them out of such stale meannesses.

However the gentleman I have to oppose is not so easily put out of countenance, I find; resolved to omit nothing which cou'd possibly answer his purpose of decrying the Women, he has ransack'd all the rubbish of antiquity, and plunder'd all the Men of note, who have in any ages distinguish'd themselves by their mannish spleen against us, of all the ribaldry they have so liberally bestow'd upon us. But of what use can all this be to raise the merit of his sex, or depress that of ours, unless he can produce better reasons to justify the repetition of their scurrilities than they cou'd bring to vindicate their advancing them? To make them of any weight, he should have shewn the reasonableness of them; for till he does, they can have no other weight than that of voluntary assertions. And with me, nay with every one who will be at the pains of thinking justly, every man, whether ancient or modern is a Cato, and every Cato a fool, as often as he advances more than he can prove, or believes more than he has sufficient grounds for believing. And no assertions unback'd with reason can be sufficient motives of credibility to any one in posses-sion of common-sense. Now I wou'd fain ask any one of my impartial readers who has perused the answer of my antagonist, what one solid reason, which can justify belief, has he given throughout that piece, for all the voluntary assertions of his own, or any of the authors he has quoted? And lest I shou'd seem upon the catch; I will even entreat them to persue it a second time and till they can satisfy me, all I desire is that they suspend their belief of any thing they find there merely asserted.

However the better to guard the candid part of my judges from every surprise of fallacy, let me beg leave to attend them in the perusal of that extravagant piece, a favour which no polite man can with any decency refuse a young lady when ask'd.

The first method then which our author makes use of to prove the superiority of his sex over ours, is to overthrow what I have so fully proved in the introduction to my former Treatise, that all their pretended superiority is only the blind effect of prejudice built on inconsiderate custom. And how does he go about this? Why truly, to prove that custom not to be groundless, he is reduced to the humble shift of pleading it's antiquity; as if any thing was more ancient than prejudice and error: But it seems that prejudice can have no share in this custom, according to my adversary, because, forsooth, it is universal, and I am challeng'd to name any one custom as universal, as to place and time, in which mankind have confessedly found themselves in an error: As if too Man must needs be so besotted an animal that he cannot be grosly mistaken in one considerable point without being so in others. . . .

The pacific disposition of Woman-kind and the universal ease with which they support their subject condition he brings as a plea to authorize the Men's unjust usurpation of superiority over them, and to prove that superiority to be the dictate of nature and reason. So ungenerous is that assuming sex! And so dangerous is it for us to stoop to their weakness in any thing! Our complaisance but serves to make them more arrogant; our tenderness more savage; and every favour we bestow upon them adds fresh fuel to their ingratitude.

To vindicate their engrossing the advantages of education and learning to themselves, they must be able to prove that monopoly grounded on reason; and to warrant them to say it is so, they must be in a condition to prove that they have never communicated among themselves those advantages but to such as were susceptible of them; never admitted any to study but such as had talents for them; and never raised to a publick charge but such as had a capacity for it. In a word, they must never have set any one upon any thing to which his genius, as well as inclination, did not render him equal: Whereas we see nothing more common than the contrary practice, chance, necessity, or avarice, engaging the major part of the Men in the different states of civil society. Children are put to the trades which please their friends the most, tho' they suit themselves least; one is hurry'd into the gown, and his merit strangled with a scarf, who wou'd have made an incomparable beef-eater; another is dubb'd a physician, who might have excell'd in a Clare-market slaughter-house or Oratory; a third is buried in contempt beneath the character of a statesman, whose native genius for making breeches for the public sufficiently appears from his unwearied assiduity in pulling up his own; and had not a fourth been made a politician what credit might he have acquired in making ragouts, who has but a sorry hand at cooking Conventions.

Wherefore do the Men fancy that we Women are less fit for such employs than they themselves are? Surely it is not nature, but mannish injustice, which debars us from playing our parts. I do not pretend to say that all Women are capable of all employments; neither can the Men, forward as they are, have the confidence to make any such pretension. No, all I intended in my first Essay was to shew that, considering both sexes in a fair light, it must be own'd that we have an equal aptitude to sense and virtue with the Men, and consequently an equal right to dignity, power and esteem with any of them. But since the Men are so ungenerous, as to disallow us this modest pretension, and the gentleman, my antagonist, is so weak as to dispute our equality with the Men, till we can shew a superiority over them; I think it but a justice due to my injured sex to accept of his challenge, and to prove, what is matter of fact, that Woman-kind are not only by nature equal, but far superior to the Men; which I shall not only make appear from rational theory, but even, to stoop to my adversary's method of arguing, consider in a practical light.

Our adversary seems to triumph mightily in the scriptural texts he has produced to authorize his tyrannic usurpation of authority over us. But surely he did not sufficiently weigh them, or he wou'd have found how little they are to his purpose. Unable to justify their subjecting us from any laws of nature, he has recourse to divine laws; but happily for us these are as little favourable to his purpose as the others, which we shall see upon a fair examination. The first law he pretends to quote against us is from the words which GOD spoke to Eve, in Gen. iii. Thy desire shall be to thy husband, and he shall rule over thee, as our English translators have render'd this passage; tho' I think the Latin is *Et ipse dominabitur tui,* which may be equally translated, and he shall domineer over thee. But let the text be translated which way best pleases my antagonist: Who does not see plainly from the whole chapter, that these words were not utter'd by GOD in form of precept, any more than those to Adam, In the sweat of thy face shalt thou eat bread till thou return to the ground. And if this had been a precept it must bind all Men to eat bread at the sweat of their brows, whether rich or poor, noble or ignoble. All then these passages can import is the curse which the ALMIGHTY declared our first parents to have entail'd on themselves and their posterity, in consequence of their joint disobedience: Which curse to the Men was perpetual drudgery, and to us Women that we shou'd stoop our easy tempers to the savages our husbands, till we taught those ungenerous creatures to take advantage from our meekness to enslave domineer and play the hectors over us. . . .

The pretty whimsical slight of imagination, with which our adversary diverts himself, concerning the creation of both sexes, may for ought I know supply the place of demonstration with the witlings of his own sex, who seldom think any thing so convincing an argument as prophanity.

If I had less compassion than I have for the gentleman's weakness; I cou'd laugh along with him: Or if I cou'd think it lawful to be merry with scripture subjects; I wou'd make bold to retort his joke upon himself. I cou'd easily shew him how very forced is the jest he labours to divert us with, and how much more natural it is to conjecture that Man being form'd a mere rough draught of that finish'd creature Woman, God snatch'd from the lumpish thing the few graces and perfections he found in it, to add them to the many he design'd to enrich her with. And if he did entail upon her a rib of that stupified mortal, it was out of pure pity to him, that Woman bias'd by the sympathetic tye might with less repugnance stoop her exalted soul to some regard for him. I will not, however, carry the jest so far as my adversary thinks proper to do. I am not so weak to think the Creator, in order to make Woman the compleat being she is, had any need to produce that rude sketch of her, Man: Neither do I trouble my head whether the production of him can be justly deem'd a compleat creation in the strict sense of the word or not. This I know, there need but five senses to compare them together, to perceive that Man among the works of nature is as much beneath the perfection of Woman as those rude half-shapen blocks, which the first Egyptians erected into deities, were short of the beauties of those masterpieces of art which the ablest statuaries have since produced. And why heaven has been pleased to place so wide a difference between creatures of the same species, I can best answer by retorting the text quoted by this gentleman, and recurring to that unsearchable wisdom of him who had it in his power of the same lump to make one vessel to honour, and the other to dishonour.

It is a very poor shift then our adversary is reduced to, to overthrow the proof taken from her after-production, of man's being rather created for woman's use than she for his. What tho' St. Paul seems to say the direct opposit; yet it is plain from his own words a very little lower, that he was too divinely inspired to think, Man as he was himself, that Woman was in any other sense made for Man than to be his glory, if he copied after her, as she is his shame while he does not. It is still true then, that the only argument Man has for his being created superior to the rest of his brother brutes, and their being created for his use, is that of his not being created till they were all in readiness for him: And it is as true what I observed in my former Essay, that if this argument has any weight it must equally prove that the Man was made for the Woman's use and not she for his. This appears sufficiently from the miserable come-off which that gentleman is reduced to of denying the Women to be created; tho' without being able to give any better proof than that of horse-jest: An argument which, did I not scorn to retort it, might sufficiently shew what wretched poor creatures they must be, who are glad to lay hold on any evasion capable of screening them from the truths their injustice dare not face.

Our adversary, however, is honest enough to own: "that the Women

deserve some regards from the public, in consideration of the part they have in the propagation of human nature." But then lest those very generous creatures the Men shou'd exceed in their regards for us, he adds, "that there is no reason why we shou'd be consider'd on a level with those of his own sex whom we bring forth." Nay, we are all to be vilified, and ill-treated, because some few among us are so little like Women as to forfeit their native modesty and continence. But if I may ask a fair question; upon a just and unbias'd computation, which of the two sexes is the most notorious for lewdness and libertinage? If there are among our sex, as it cannot be denied but there are, some few wretches (tho' too many by all) who are as infamous as this gentleman paints them; are they not more the abomination of the generality of us, than they are of the *Men?* Are not we ourselves the first to condemn and give them up? On the contrary, how few among the *Men* prescribe any bounds to their lust and brutality! Do they not openly glory in their iniquity? Where is there one among them who, if he is not himself a profligate letcher, scruples to keep company with another *Man* who is so? Nay, so little are they ashamed of the vice they so unjustly and basely ascribe to us, that the wretch who either wants spirit, money, or parts to gratify his libidinous appetites to their utmost extent, is forced to add to his real vicious practices the borrow'd guilt of feign'd adventures, merely to recommend himself to the rest of his sex as a *polite Man.* Whereas the most notorious rakes are so convinced of the natural love which our sex in general have to modesty and continence, that, spite of all the vehemence of their corrupt inclinations, they are forced to put on the reserve of decency, to recommend themselves to our esteem and to save themselves from being shamefully banish'd from our presence. What horror, foulness, and confusion, must not the world be over-run with; were not *Women* in general infinitely more chaste than the *Men* are!
[After having given numerous examples of celebrated women:]

It is more than plain then, that whenever the *Women* have been upon any degree of equal advantage with the *Men,* they have always run at least parallel with them in most things, and even outstrip them in some particulars; and that there are almost an infinity of our sex, who had they had the like advantages would have made an equal progress with them in useful knowledge.

And yet tho' from the cradle the softest sex given the fairest hopes, such is the unjust partiality of the *Men* to the blockheads of their own, that all the advantages of education are wholly reserved for them. The greatest care is taken to form and improve their minds; and the poor Women are left to loiter away life in indolence and ignorance, or at best are employ'd in such offices only as the *Men* think the lowest and most servile.

In fact nothing is omitted to give our sex a degenerate way of thinking, and to reduce them to as narrow a way of acting. All their science is confined to the needle; and the looking-glass is the great oracle they are taught to consult for their deportment. The industry with which the business of dress is inculcated to a young girl makes her give up her favourite hours to it. The ogles, the sighs, the love-tales, the encomiums on her beauty, and the fulsome compliments she is eternally pester'd with, decoy her unawares into placing all her happiness in being admired, and contribute to fill her mind with vanity and impertinence. Dancing, reading, writing, and playing a soft tune, are the sum of her compleatest education; the books her *Father* or *Guardian* stocks her study with are at best a treatise or two of devotion, a few playbooks, and set of romances; and all her entertainments are limited to balls, operas and fashions. Such of our sex as distinguish themselves by useful and instructive books they have seized with utmost difficulty, and often by stealth, are frequently forced to hide them from the eyes of the *Men,* whose envy is ever ready to sneer them out of the true knowledge of themselves and the world: Nay, they are forced to hide them even from such of their own jealous companions as have earlily lost a relish for the like entertainments, thro' the crafty practices of the *Men* they have been ruled by. . . .

Neither am I ignorant that some ladies will be angry with me for what I have said, however conscious they are of the truths I have advanced. That modesty which leads them into the mistake of concealing their own superior merit, and the fear they are in of incensing the irrational tyrants of the other sex to redouble their ferocity will make them look upon this as a rash attempt, which instead of healing their wounds will only be a pretext for their Butchers to gall them with fresh ones. But let them reflect that if the *Men* of sense and spirit can but be reason'd out of following the example of the fools and cowards they have to deal with; these will easily be shamed and scared into using *Women* better, to cloke that baseness which actuates them. For it is very remarkable that nothing is more subject to fear and shame than that bullying race who ill-treat their wives; as nothing could spirit a *Man* to lord it over a *Woman,* but that heartless cowardice which makes him fond of insulting the only creature he has a power over, from the single consideration of his having more brutal strength, and legal authority to exert it. Besides let such of my fair readers, as may be disposed to think I have carried some things too far, reflect that I have no where gone beyond the strictest rules of truth; and if I have too strongly proved our right to an equal share of power, dignity and esteem with the *Men,* and our natural capacity of surpassing them, I have notwithstanding never aim'd at wresting the power they are in possession of out of their hands. On the contrary, let all I have advanced be candidly consider'd, it will be found that I have declared openly against it. I have indeed in my former treatise, and again in this, endeavour'd to spirit my sex to have that just esteem for themselves which is requisit to force the *Men* to pay them that esteem which is their due. If any blame me for this let them reflect on the advice of *Pythagoras: Above all things be sure to have a due respect for yourself.* If we think meanly of ourselves; how can we be surprised if that ungenerous sex should lay hold of it to load us with the contempt we seem conscious of deserving. No, the only way to force those unjust creatures to do us justice is to be just to ourselves, by the improvement of our minds, the enrichment of our hearts, and such a conduct as may convince them that if we are content to be subject to them it is not for want of talents to command them. I am for shewing them that our submitting to act in a more confined sphere is only owing to the superiority of our virtue, and the want of that avarice, arrogance, and ambition which are the great inspirers of the best actions of most of them.

The only indulgence then I have to crave from my fair partners in oppression is, that such of them as modesty, humility, or contracted timidity, may have induced to be displeased with some strokes of mine, would favour the whole of what I have written with a second perusal; in order to qualify themselves for judging justly and unprejudicedly. If they do this, whatever faults they may find with the method or expression, for being so short of the delicacy of their own talent and taste, I am confident they cannot disapprove of the reasoning and design. I have no where been for the *Women's* departing from their character: But have aim'd wholly at giving it it's true lustre, by shewing that the modesty, meekness, humility and reserve, which are so inseparably blended with it, are no arguments of their wanting sense, courage, conduct, and spirit, to act in a much superior sphere than they chuse to do. If I have not treated this subject in so compleat a manner as some of my sex now in being are capable of doing, I frankly own It to be more owing to want of genius than of matter. I was conscious indeed from my first setting out, that among the infinite arguments I could produce of the superior talents of *Woman* the visible littleness of my own would appear a perplexing argument against me. Still an irresistible love of truth, spite of all disadvantages, made me resolve to do the rest of my sex all the justice I was capable of, however I might suffer by having it done to myself. If there be any rashness in this, I am content that such of my sex as are capable of excelling me in such an undertaking should blame my forwardness, provided they will give me leave to blame them in turn for their remissness, in not exerting their abilities in so just a cause. For the rest I shall regret no freedoms which any ladies may think proper to take with my slender productions, if they will but indulge me the innocent liberty of exhorting them to apply themselves to the sciences, without regarding the little reasons of the *Men,* whose jealousy is so industrious to divert them from the improvement they might thence gather. Truth and knowledge are the only objects worthy their being sollicitous after; and these they have a mind capable of reaching in the most perfect manner. It is therefore an indispensable duty in them to put themselves in a condition to avoid that reproach, which the stifling truth and knowledge in ignorance and indolence would justly bring upon them. Neither have they any other way to guard themselves from the error and surprise to which they are perpetually exposed, whose knowledge is but a kind of collection of oral traditions, for the truth of which they have little better than *Gazetteer* authority. In a word they have no other certain means to secure happiness to themselves through life by a steady pursuit of virtue and prudence. . . .

. . . In a word, if it was not for the narrow limits this little Treatise confines me to, I could from the single evidence of History, which is so much perverted to debase us, throw such a dazzling glory round my whole sex, as would suffice to render their honour inaccessible by the most presumptuous and daring of the *Men*. However what I omit at present I may possibly make up hereafter, by giving a parallel History of the most eminent persons of both sexes in past ages, for virtue or vice. In the mean time what I have here barely hinted will to suffice to convince the most obstinate of that sex who have any sense left, that if the MEN have by fraud and violence gain'd a superiority of power over us; we still retain our original superiority of sense and virtue over them: And if they are not ashamed of truth they must own that the best qualities they are masters of give them no more title to an equality with us in the perfections of soul, than their homely aukward figures can justify their vyeing with us in the charm of personal beauty and graces.

FINIS.

PRIMARY SOURCES

Woman not Inferior to Man: or, a short and modest vindication of the natural right of the fair sex to a perfect equality of power, dignity and esteem, with the Men. London: John Hawkins 1739. Reprinted in *Beauty's Triumph.* London: J. Robinson, 1751.

Women's Superior Excellence over Man: or, a reply to the author of a late treatise, entitled, Man Superior to Woman. In which, the excessive weakness of that gentleman's answer to woman not inferior to man is exposed; with a plain demonstration of woman's natural right even to superiority over the men in head and heart; proving their minds as much more beautiful than the men's as their bodies are, and that, had they the same advantages of education, they would excel them as much in sense as they do in virtue. The whole interspersed with a variety of mannish characters, which some of the most noted heroes of the present age had the goodness to fight for. London, 1740. Reprinted in *Beauty's Triumph.* London: J. Robinson, 1751.

RELATED SOURCES

Moore, C. A. "The First of the Militants in English Literature." *The Nation* 102, no. 2642 (1926):194–96.

Poulain de la Barre, François. *De l'Egalité des deux Sexes, discours physique et moral on l'on voit l'importance de se défaire des préjugéz.* Paris: 1673. Translated by "A.L." *The Woman as Good as The Man, or, The Equality of Both Sexes.* London: 1677.

Seidel, Michael. "Poulain de la Barre's *The Woman as Good as the Man.*" *Journal of the History of Ideas* 35, 3 (1974): 499–508.

Women, the Family and Freedom, ed. Susan Groag Bell and Karen M. Offen, Vol. 1, 1750–1880. Stanford Univ. Press, Stanford, CA, 1983 (especially pp. 24–27).

CHARLOTTE CIBBER CHARKE
?–1760

Charlotte Cibber was the tenth child of Colly Cibber and the forty-five-year-old former Katherine Shore. Cibber, an actor, dramatist, theater manager, and poet laureate, regarded Charlotte disapprovingly because of her independent nature. Even at the age of four, attired in her father's clothing, she paraded boldly in public on a donkey.

She was well-educated for two years at Mrs. Draper's school in Westminster and then liberally at home. In her teens, her family became concerned about her over-indulgence in such "masculine" activities as hunting, shooting, and riding. Later, for medical and practical reasons, they sent her to relatives in Hertfordshire where she dressed in male clothing, dispensed drugs, and travelled on horseback to visit the sick as did her relation Dr. Hales. In further defiance of traditional female behavior, she acquired skill in gardening, grooming, and blacksmithing. Around 1729 she married a minor actor-violinist and librettist, the philandering Richard Charke, who seems to have been more enamoured of being Colley Cibber's son-in-law than a husband, and the marriage ended quickly with the birth of a daughter and her husband's retreat to and probable eventual death in Jamaica. Forced to support herself and the child, Charke turned to the stage. In 1730, she made her Drury Lane debut in *The Provoked Wife*.

Charke then acted in several plays in the Haymarket and Drury Lane, but was eventually fired by Charles Fleetwood in 1735 for stubborn opposition and some kind of unspecified "immorality." After writing a farce and being rehired in the theater due to her father's influence, she seems to have fallen out of favor again, whereupon she left the stage for the business world, first as an oil-seller and a grocer, then in 1737 as a puppet-mistress. All these enterprises collapsed. Apparently in this period she contracted "an honourable though very secret alliance," possibly to John Sacheverell, who died soon afterward.

Having developed "a natural propensity for a hat and wig," Charke found herself involved in several complicated situations with women who mistook her for a man. When she was arrested for a debt she was dressed in a silverlaced hat. Numerous female friends and acquaintances contributed to her release. Casting failure behind her, she became a strolling player for nine years and teamed up with a Mrs. Brown who tended Charke during a three-year illness.

On April 19, 1755, the first of eight installments of her boisterous and popular autobiography appeared. The preface to herself is a good example of Charke's zesty self-confidence. Having gone into the second edition by the end of that year, the autobiography mentioned that Charke had completed another work, a novel, that attracted to Charke's abode two would-be entrepreneurs—a future editor, Samuel Whyte and H. Slater, Jr., a bookseller. She was living, they said, in "a wretched thatched hovel where it was usual at that time for the scavengers to deposit the sweepings of the streets." The two men published *The History of Henry Dumont Esq; and Miss Charlotte Evelyn* the following year, a mixed novel that makes fun of a homosexual, attacks the condition of slaves, and appears to recommend a life of virtue.

The circumstances of Charke's life, coupled with her narrative (whether authentic to the last detail or not), point to the near impossibility of decent survival for an eighteenth-century woman who flamboyantly rejected society's restricted, ascribed roles. Her last known words, on a playbill in 1759, the year before she died, speak to that near impossibility: "As I am entirely dependant upon chance for subsistence and desirous of settling into business, I humbly trust the town will favour me on the occasion."

FROM

A NARRATIVE OF THE LIFE OF MRS. CHARLOTTE CHARKE.

The Author to Herself

Madam,—

THO' Flattery is universally known to be the Spring from which Dedications frequently flow, I hope I shall escape that Odium so justly thrown on poetical Petitioners, notwithstanding my Attempt to illustrate those WONDERFUL QUALIFICATIONS by which you have so EMINENTLY DISTINGUISH'D YOURSELF, and gives you a just Claim to the Title of a NONPAREIL OF THE AGE.

That thoughtless Ease (so peculiar to yourself) with which you have run thro' many strange and unaccountable Vicissitudes of Fortune, is an

---

SOURCE: This selection is taken from the reprint edition (facsimile) of the second edition, 1755, of *A Narrative. . . .*

undeniable Proof of the native indolent Sweetness of your Temper. With
what Fortitude of Mind have you vanquish'd Sorrow, with the fond Imagination and promissary Hopes (ONLY FROM YOURSELF) of a Succession
of Happiness, neither WITHIN YOUR POWER OR VIEW?

Your exquisite Taste in Building must not be omitted: The magnificent
airy Castles, for which you daily drew out Plans without Foundation,
must, could they have been distinguishable to Sight, long ere this have
darken'd all the lower World; nor can you be match'd, in Oddity of Fame,
by any but that celebrated Knight-Errant of the Moon, G———E
A———R ST———S: whose Memoirs, and yours conjoin'd, would make
great Figures in History, and might justly claim a Right to be transmitted
to Posterity; as you are, without Exception, two of the greatest Curiosities
that ever were the Incentives to the most profound Astonishment.

My Choice of you, Madam, to patronize my Works, is an evidential
Proof that I am not disinterested in that Point; as the World will easily be
convinc'd, from your natural Partiality to all I have hitherto produc'd, that
you will tenderly overlook their Errors, and, to the utmost of your Power,
endeavour to magnify their Merits. If, by your Approbation, the World
may be perswaded into a tolerable Opinion of my Labours, I shall, for the
Novelty-sake, venture for once to call you, FRIEND; a Name, I own, I
never as yet have known you by.

I hope, dear Madam, as MANLY says in The Provok'd Husband, that
"LAST REPROACH HAS STRUCK YOU", and that you and I may ripen our
Acquaintance into a perfect Knowledge of each other, that may establish
a lasting and social Friendship between us.

Your two friends, PRUDENCE and REFLECTION, I am inform'd, have
lately ventur'd to pay you a visit; for which I heartily congratulate you, as
nothing can possibly be more joyous to the Heart than the Return of
absent Friends, after a long and painful Peregrination.

Permit me, Madam, to subscribe myself for the future, what I ought to
have been some years ago,

> Your real Friend,
> And humble Servant,
> Charlotte Charke.

A NARRATIVE

As the following History is the Product of a Female Pen, I tremble for
the terrible Hazard it must run in venturing into the World, as it may very
possibly suffer, in many Opinions, without perusing it; I therefore humbly move for its having the common Chance of a Criminal, at least to be
properly examin'd, before it is condemn'd: And should it be found guilty
of Nonsense and Inconsistencies, I must consequently resign it to its
deserved Punishment; instead of being honour'd with the last Row of a
Library, undergo the Indignancy of preserving the Syrup of many a choice
Tart; which, when purchas'd, even the hasty Child will soon give an
Instance of its Contempt of my Muse, by committing to the Flames, or

perhaps cast it to the Ground, to be trampled to Death by some Thread-bare Poet, whose Works might possibly have undergone the same Malev-olence of Fate.

However, I must beg Leave to inform those Ladies and Gentlemen, whose Tenderness and Compassion may excite 'em to make this little Brat of my Brain the Companion of an idle Hour, that I have paid all due Regard to Decency wherever I have introduc'd the Passion of Love; and have only suffer'd it to take its Course in its proper and necessary Time, without fulsomely inflaming the Minds of my young Readers, or shame-fully offending those of riper Years; a Fault I have often condemn'd, when I was myself but a Girl, in some Female Poets. I shall not descant on their Imprudence, only wish that their Works had been less confined to that Theme, which too often led 'em into Errors, Reason and Modesty equally forbid.

In Regard to the various Subjects of my Story, I have, I think, taken Care to make 'em so interesting, that every Person who reads my Volume may bear a Part in some Circumstance or other in the Perusal, as there is nothing inserted but what may daily happen to every Mortal breathing.

Not that I would have the Publick conceive, tho' I am endeavouring to recommend it to their Protection, that my Vanity can so far overcome my small Share of Reason, as to impute the Success it should meet with to any other Motive, than a kind Condescension in my Readers to pity and encourage one, who has used her utmost Endeavours to entertain 'em.

As I have promis'd to give some Account of my UNACCOUNTABLE LIFE, I shall no longer detain my Readers in respect to my Book, but satisfy a Curiosity which has long subsisted in the Minds of many: And, I believe, they will own, when they know my History, if Oddity can plead any Right to Surpize and Astonishment, I may positively claim a Title to be shewn among the Wonders of Ages past, and those to come. Nor will I, to escape a Laugh, even at my own Expence, deprive my Readers of that pleasing Satisfaction, or conceal any Error, which I now rather sigh to reflect on; but formerly, thro' too much Vacancy of Thought, might be idle enough rather to justify than condemn.

I shall now begin my Detail of the several Stages I have pass'd thro' since my Birth, which made me the last-born of Mr. *Colley Cibber*, at a Time my Mother began to think, without this additional Blessing (mean-ing my sweet Self) she had fully answer'd the End of her Creation, being just Forty-five Years of Age when she produc'd her last, "THO' NOT LEAST IN LOVE." Nor was I exempted from an equal Share in my Father's Heart; yet, partly thro' my own Indiscretion (and, I am too well convinc'd, from the cruel Censure of false and evil Tongues) since my Maturity, I lost that Blessing: Which, if strongest Compunction and uninterrupted Hours of Anguish, blended with Self-conviction and filial Love, can move his Heart to Pity and Forgiveness, I shall, with Pride and unutterable Trans-port, throw myself at his Feet, to implore the only Benefit I desire or expect, his BLESSING, and his PARDON.

But of that, more hereafter—And I hope, ere this small Treatise is finish'd, to have it in my Power to inform my Readers, my painful Separation from my once tender Father will be more than amply repaid, by a happy Interview; as I am certain neither my present or future Conduct, shall ever give him Cause to blush at what I should esteem a justifiable and necessary Reconciliation, as 'tis the absolute Ordination of the Supreme that we should forgive, when the Offender becomes a sincere and hearty Penitent. And I positively declare, were I to expire this Instant, I have no self-interested Views, in regard to worldly Matters; but confess myself a Miser in my Wishes so far, as having the transcendant Joy of knowing that I am restor'd to a Happiness, which not only will clear my Reputation to the World, in Regard to a former Want of Duty, but, at the same Time, give a convincing Proof that there are yet some Sparks of Tenderness remaining in my Father's Bosom, for his REPENTANT CHILD.

I confess, I believe I came not only an unexpected, but an unwelcome Guest into the Family, (exclusive of my Parents,) as my Mother had borne no Children for some few Years before; so that I was rather regarded as an impertinent Intruder, than one who had a natural Right to make up the circular Number of my Father's Fire-Side: Yet, be it as it may, the Jealousy of me, from her other Children, laid no Restraint on her Fondness for me, which my Father and she both testified in their tender Care of my Education. His paternal Love omitted nothing that could improve any natural Talents Heaven had been pleased to endow me with; the Mention of which, I hope, won't be imputed to me as a vain Self-conceit, of knowing more, or thinking better, than any other of my Sister Females. No! far be it from me; for as all Advantages from Nature are the favourable Gifts of the Power Divine, consequently no Praise can be arrogated to ourselves, for that which is not in ourselves POSSIBLE TO BESTOW.

I should not have made this Remark, but, as 'tis likely my Works may fall into the Hands of People of disproportion'd Understandings, I was willing to prevent an Error a weak Judgment might have run into, by inconsiderately throwing an Odium upon me, I could not possibly deserve—FOR, ALAS! ALL CANNOT JUDGE ALIKE.

As I have instanc'd, that my Education was not only a genteel, but in Fact a liberal one, and such indeed as might have been sufficient for a Son instead of a Daughter; I must beg Leave to add, that I was never made much acquainted with that necessary Utensil which forms the housewifely Part of a young Lady's Education, call'd a Needle; which I handle with the same clumsey Awkwardness a Monkey does a Kitten, and am equally capable of using the one, as Pug is of nursing the other.

This is not much to be wondered at, as my Education consisted chiefly in Studies of various Kinds, and gave me a different Turn of Mind than what I might have had, if my Time had been employ'd in ornamenting a Piece of Canvas with Beasts, Birds and the Alphabet; the latter of which I understood in *French,* rather before I was able to speak *English.*

As I have promised to conceal nothing that might raise a Laugh, I shall begin with a small Specimen of my former Madness, when I was but four Years of Age. Having, even then, a passionate Fondness for a Perriwig, I crawl'd out of Bed one Summer's Morning at *Twickenham*, where my Father had Part of a House and Gardens for the Season, and, taking it into my small Pate, that by Dint of a Wig and a Waistcoat, I should be the perfect Representative of my Sire, I crept softly into the Servants-Hall, where I had the Night before espied all Things in Order, to perpetrate the happy Design I had framed for the next Morning's Expedition. Accordingly I paddled down Stairs, taking with me my Shoes, Stockings, and little Dimity Coat; which I artfully contrived to pin up, as well as I could, to supply the Want of a Pair of Breeches. By the Help of a long Broom, I took down a Waistcoat of my Brother's, and an enormous bushy Tie-wig of my Father's, which entirely enclos'd my Head and Body, with the Knots of the Ties thumping my little Heels as I marched along, with slow and solemn Pace. The Covert of Hair in which I was concealed, with the Weight of a monstrous Belt and large Silver-hilted Sword, that I could scarce drag along, was a vast Impediment in my Procession: And, what still added to the other Inconveniences I laboured under, was whelming myself under one of my Father's large Beaver-hats, laden with Lace, as thick and broad as a Brickbat.

Being thus accoutred, I began to consider that 'twould be impossible for me to pass for Mr. Cibber in Girl's Shoes, therefore took an Opportunity to slip out of Doors after the Gardener, who went to his Work, and roll'd myself into a dry Ditch, which was as deep as I was high; and, in this Grotesque Pigmy-State, walked up and down the Ditch bowing to all who came by me. But, behold, the Oddity of my Appearance soon assembled a Croud about me; which yielded me no small Joy, as I conceived their Risibility on this Occasion to be Marks of Approbation, and walked myself into a Fever, in the happy Thought of being taken for the 'Squire.

When the Family arose, 'till which Time I had employ'd myself in this regular March in my Ditch, I was the first Thing enquir'd after, and miss'd; 'till Mrs. *Heron*, the Mother of the late celebrated Actress of that Name, happily espied me, and directly call'd forth the whole Family to be Witness of my State and Dignity.

The Drollery of my Figure rendered it impossible, assisted by the Fondness of both Father and Mother, to be angry with me; but, alas! I was borne off on the Footman's Shoulders, to my Shame and Disgrace, and forc'd into my proper Habiliments.

The Summer following our Family resided at *Hampton-Town*, near the Court. My Mother being indisposed, at her first coming there, drank every Morning and Night Asses Milk. I observed one of those little health-restoring Animals was attended by its Fole, which was about the Height of a sizeable Greyhound.

I immediately formed a Resolution of following the Fashion of taking the Air early next Morning, and fix'd upon this young Ass for a Pad-nag;

and, in order to bring this Matter to bear, I communicated my Design to a small Troop of young Gentlemen and Ladies, whose low Births and adverse States rendered it entirely convenient for them to come into any Scheme, Miss *Charlotte Cibber* could possibly propose. Accordingly my Mother's Bridle and Saddle were secretly procured, but the riper Judgments of some of my Followers soon convinced me of the unnecessary Trouble of carrying the Saddle, as the little destin'd Beast was too small, and indeed too weak, to bear the Burden; upon which 'twas concluded to take the Bridle only, and away went Miss and her Attendants, who soon arrived at the happy Field where the poor harmless Creature was sucking. We soon seiz'd, and endeavour'd to bridle it; but, I remember, 'twas impossible to bring that Point to bear, the Head of the Fole being so very small, the Trappings fell off as fast as they strove to put them on. One of the small Crew, who was wiser than the rest, propos'd their Garters being converted to that Use; which was soon effected, and I rode triumphantly into Town astride, with a numerous Retinue, whose Huzzas were drown'd by the dreadful Braying of the tender Dam, who pursued us with agonizing Sounds of Sorrow, for her oppress'd young one.

Upon making this Grand-Entry into the Town, I remember my Father, from the violent Acclamations of Joy on so glorious an Occasion, was excited to enquire into the Meaning, of what he perhaps imagin'd to be an Insurrection; when, to his Amazement, he beheld his Daughter mounted as before described, preceded by a Lad, who scrap'd upon a Twelve-penny Fiddle of my own, to add to the Dignity and Grandeur of this extraordinary Enterprize.

I perfectly remember, young as I was then, the strong Mixture of Surprize, Pleasure, Pain and Shame in his Countenance, on his viewing me seated on my infantical Rosinante; which, tho' I had not then Sense enough to distinguish, my Memory has since afforded me the Power to describe, and also to repeat his very Words, at his looking out of Window, *Gad demme! An Ass upon an Ass!*

But, alas! how momentary are sometimes the Transports of the most Happy? My Mother was not quite so passive in this Adventure, as in that before related; but rather was, as I thought, too active: For I was no sooner dismounted then I underwent the Discipline of Birch, was most shamefully taken Prisoner, in the Sight of my Attendants, and with a small Packthread my Leg was made the sad Companion with that of a large Table.

"O! Fall of Honour!"

'Tis not to be conceived, the violent Indignation and Contempt my Disgrace rais'd in my Infant-Breast; nor did I forgive my Mother, in my Heart, for six Months after, tho' I was oblig'd to ask Pardon in a few Moments of her, who, at that Time, I conceiv'd to be most in Fault.

Were I to insert one quarter Part of the strange, mad Pranks I play'd, even in Infancy, I might venture to affirm, I could swell my Account of 'em to a Folio, and perhaps my whimsical Head may compile such a Work; but I own I should be loth, upon Reflection, to publish it, lest the Contagion should spread itself, and make other young Folks as ridiculous and mischievous as myself. Tho' I can't charge my Memory with suffering other People to feel the ill Effects of my unaccountable Vagaries; except once, I remember, a cross, old Woman at *Richmond* having beat me, I revenged myself, by getting some of my Playfellows to take as many as they could of her Caps, and other small Linnen that hung in the Garden to dry, and who sent 'em sailing down a Brook that forc'd its Current to the *Thames,* whilst I walk'd into the Parlour, secretly pleas'd with the Thoughts of my Revenge.

. . . I shall now proceed in my Account. At eight Years of Age I was placed at a famous School in Park-Street, Westminster, governed by one Mrs. Draper, a Woman of great Sense and Abilities, who employed a Gentleman, call'd Monsieur Flahaut, an excellent Master of Languages, to instruct her Boarders. Among the Number of his Pupils, I had the Happiness of being one; and, as he discovered in me a tolerable Genius, and an earnest Desire of Improvement, he advised my Mother, in a Visit to me at School, to let him teach me Latin and Italian, which she, proud of hearing me capable of receiving, readily consented to.

Nor was my Tutor satisfied with those Branches of Learning alone, for he got Leave of my Parents to instruct me in Geography; which, by the Bye, tho' I know it to be a most useful and pleasing Science, I cannot think it was altogether necessary for a Female: But I was delighted at being thought a learned Person, therefore readily acquiesced with my Precepter's Proposal.

Accordingly I was furnish'd with proper Books, and two Globes, caelestial and terrestrial, borrow'd of my Mother's own Brother, the late John Shore, Esq; Serjeant–Trumpet of England, and pored over 'em, 'till I had like to have been as mad as my Uncle, who has given a most demonstrative Proof of his being so for many Years, which I shall hereafter mention.

The vast Application to my Study almost distracted me, from a violent Desire I had to make myself perfect Mistress of it. Mr. Flahaut, perceiving that I was too close in the Pursuit of Knowledge not absolutely needful, shorten'd the various Tasks I had daily set me; thinking that one mad Mortal in a Family was rather too much, without farther Addition.

After I had received, in two Years schooling, a considerable Share of my Education (in which Musick and Singing bore their Parts) I was, thro' my indulgent Parents Fondness, allow'd Masters at Home to finish my Studies.

Mr. Flahaut, my Master of Languages, was continued. Mr. Young, late Organist of St. Clement's Danes, instructed me in Musick; tho' I was originally taught by the famous Dr. King, who was so old, when I learnt of him, he was scarce able to give the most trifling Instructions. The celebrated Mr. Grosconet was my Dancing-Master; and, to do Justice to his Memory, I have never met with any that exceeded him in the easy sublime Taste in Dancing, which is the most reasonable Entertainment can be afforded to the Spectators, who wish only to be delighted with the genteel Movement of a Singular, or Plurality of Figures, with becoming Gracefulness; in which no Performer ever so eminently distinguished themselves as Mrs. Booth, Widow of the late incomparable and deservedly-esteemed Barton Booth, Esq; one of the Patentees of Drury-Lane Theatre, conjunctive with my Father and Mr. Wilks.

The present Taste in Dancing is so opposite to the former, that I conceive the high-flown Caprioles, which distinguish the first Performers, to be the Result of violent Strength, and unaccountable Flights of Spirits, that rather convey an Idea of so many Horses a la Menage, than any Design form'd to please an Audience with the more modest and graceful Deportment, with which Mrs. Booth attracted and charmed the Hearts of every Gazer.

When 'twas judged that I had made a necessary Progression in my Learning and other Accomplishments, I went to Hillingdon, within one Mile of Uxbridge; where my Mother, who was afflicted with the Asthma, chose to retire for the Preservation of her Health.

This was an agreeable Retreat my Father had taken a Lease of for some Years, but a Winter Residence in the Country was not altogether so pleasing to me as that of the Summer; I therefore began to frame different Schemes, for rendering my Solitude as agreeable to myself as possible. The first Project I had, was in the frosty Mornings to set out upon the Common, and divert myself with Shooting; and grew so great a Proficient in that notable Exercise, that I was like the Person described in The Recruiting Officer, capable of destroying all the Venison and Wild Fowl about the Country.

In this Manner I employed several Days from Morn to Eve, and seldom failed of coming Home laden with feather'd Spoil; which raised my Conceit to such a Pitch, I really imagined myself equal to the best Fowler or Marksman in the Universe.

At length, unfortunately for me, one of my Mother's strait-lac'd, old-fashion'd Neighbours paying her a Visit, perswaded her to put a Stop to this Proceeding, as she really thought it inconsistent with the Character of a young Gentlewoman to follow such Diversions; which my Youth, had I been a Male, she thought would scarce render me excusable for, being but Fourteen. Upon this sober Lady's Hint, I was deprived of my Gun; and, with a half-broken Heart on the Occasion, resolved to revenge myself, by getting a Muscatoon that hung over the Kitchen Mantlepiece, and use my utmost Endeavours towards shooting down her Chimnies. After having wasted a considerable Quantity of Powder and Shot to no

Purpose, I was obliged to desist, and give up what I had, though wish-fully, vainly attempted.

I remember upon my having a Fit of Illness, my Mother, who was apprehensive of my Death, and consequently, thro' exessive Fondness, us'd all Means to prevent it that lay within her Power, sent me to Thorly, in Hertfordshire, the Seat of Dr. Hales, an eminent Physician and Re-lation, with a Design not only to restore and establish my Health, but with the Hopes of my being made a good Houswife; in which needful Accom-plishment, I have before hinted, my Mind was entirely uncultivated. But, alas! she ENDED where, poor dear Soul, she ought to have BEGAN; for by that Time, from her Desire of making me too wise, I had imbibed such mistaken, pedantick Notions of a Superiority of Schollarship and Sense, that my utmost Wisdom centered in proclaiming myself a Fool! by a stupid Contempt of such Qualifications as would have rendered me less troublesome in a Family, and more useful to myself, and those about me.

. . . While I staid at Thorly, though I had the nicest Examples of housewifely Perfections daily before me, I had no Notion of entertaining the least Thought of those necessary Offices, by which the young Ladies of the Family so eminently distinguished themselves, in ornamenting a well-dispos'd, elegant Table, decently graced with the Toil of their Morn-ing's Industry; nor could I bear to pass a Train of melancholly Hours in pouring over a Piece of Embroidery, or a well-wrought Chair, in which the young Females of the Family (exclusive of my mad-cap Self) were equally and industriously employed; and have often, with inward Contempt of 'em, pitied their Misfortunes, who were, I was well assured, incapable of currying a Horse, or riding a Race with me.

Many and vain Attempts were used, to bring me into their Working-Community; but I had so great a Veneration for Cattle and Husbandry, 'twas impossible for 'em, either by Threats or tender Advice, to bring me into their SOBER SCHEME.

If any Thing was amiss in the Stable, I was sure to be the First and Head of the Mob; but if all the Fine-Works in the Family had been in the Fire, I should not have forsook the Curry-comb, to have endeavoured to save 'em from the utmost Destruction.

During my Residence in the Family, I grew passionately fond of the Study of Physick; and was never so truly happy, as when the Doctor employed me in some little Offices in which he durst intrust me, without Prejudice to his Patients.

As I was indulged in having a little Horse of my own, I was frequently desired to call upon one or other of the neighbouring Invalids, to enquire how they did; which gave me a most pleasing Opportunity of fancying myself a Physician, and affected the Solemnity and Gravity which I had often observed in the good Doctor: Nor am I absolutely assured, from the significant Air which I assumed, whether some of the weaker Sort of People might not have been persuaded into as high an Opinion of my

Skill as my Cousin's, whose Talents chiefly were adapted to the Study of Physick. To do him Justice, he was a very able Proficient; and, I dare say, the Loss of him in Hertfordshire, and some Part of Essex, is not a little regretted, as he was necessary to the Rich, and tenderly beneficent to the Poor.

At the Expiration of two Years his Lady died, and I was remanded Home, and once again sent to our Country-House at Hillingdon; where I was no sooner arrived, than I persuaded my fond Mother to let me have a little Closet, built in an Apartment seldom used, by Way of Dispensatory. This I easily obtained, and summoned all the old Women in the Parish to repair to me, whenever they found themselves indisposed. I was indeed of the Opinion of Leander in *The Mock Doctor*, that a few physical hard Words would be necessary to establish my Reputation; and accordingly had recourse to a Latin Dictionary, and soon gathered up many Fragments as served to confound their Senses, and bring 'em into a high Opinion of my Skill in the medicinal Science.

As my Advice and Remedies for all Disorders were designed as Acts of Charity, 'tis not to be imagined what a Concourse of both Sexes were my constant Attendants; though I own, I have been often obliged to refer myself to Salmon, Culpepper, and other Books I had for that Purpose, before I was able to make a proper Application, or indeed arrive at any Knowledge of their Maladies. But this Defect was not discovered by my Patients, as I put on Significancy of Countenance that rather served to convince them of my incomparable Skill and Abilities.

Fond as I was of this learned Office, I did not chuse to give up that of being Lady of the Horse, which delicate Employment took up some Part of my Time every Day; and I generally served myself in that Capacity, when I thought proper to pay my Attendance on the believing Mortals, who entrusted their Lives in my Hands. But Providence was extreamly kind in that Point; for though, perhaps, I did no actual Good, I never had the least Misfortune happen to any of the unthinking, credulous Souls who relied on me for the Restoration of their Healths, which was ten to one I had endangered as long as they lived.

When I had signified my Intention of becoming a young Lady *Bountiful*, I thought it highly necessary to furnish myself with Drugs, etc. to carry on this notable Design; accordingly I went to Uxbridge, where was then living an Apothecary's Widow, whose Shop was an Emblem of that described in Romeo and Juliet. She, good Woman, knowing my Family, entrusted me with a Cargo of Combustibles, which were sufficient to have set up a Mountebank for a Twelve-month; but my Stock was soon exhausted, for the silly Devils began to fancy themselves ill, because they knew they could have Physick for nothing, such as it was. But, Oh! woeful Day! the Widow sent in her Bill to my Father, who was intirely ignorant of the curious Expence I had put him to; which he directly paid, with a strict Order never to let Doctor Charlotte have any farther Credit, on Pain of losing the Money so by me contracted.

Was not this sufficient to murder the Fame of the ablest Physician in the Universe? However, I was resolved not to give up my Profession; and, as I was deprived of the Use of Drugs, I took it into my Head, to conceal my Disgrace, to have recourse to Herbs: But one Day a poor old Woman coming to me, with a violent Complaint of rheumatick Pains and a terrible Disorder in her Stomach, I was at a dreadful Loss what Remedies to apply, and dismissed her with an Assurance of sending her something to ease her, by an inward and outward Application, before she went to Bed.

It happened that Day proved very rainy, which put it into my strange Pate to gather up all the Snails in the Garden; of which, from the heavy Shower that had fallen, there was a superabundant Quantity. I immediately fell to work; and, of some Part of 'em, with coarse brown Sugar, made a Syrup, to be taken a Spoonful once in two Hours. Boiling the rest to a Consistence, with some green Herbs and Mutton Fat, I made an Ointment; and, clapping conceited Labels upon the Phial and Callipot, sent my Preparation, with a joyous Bottle of Hartshorn and Sal Volatile I purloined from my Mother, to add a Grace to my Prescriptions.

In about three Days Time the good Woman came hopping along, to return me Thanks for the extream Benefit she had received; intreating my Goodness to repeat the Medicines, as she had found such wonderful Effects from their Virtues.

But Fortune was not quite kind enough to afford me the Means of granting her Request at that Time; for the friendly Rain, which had enabled me to work this wonderful Cure, was succeeded by an extream Drought, and I thought it highly necessary to suspend any further Attempts to establish my great Reputation, 'till another watry Opportunity offered to furnish me with those Ingredients, whose sanative Qualities had been so useful to her Limbs and my Fame: I therefore dismissed her with a Word of Advice, not to tamper too much; that as she was so well recovered, to wait 'till a Return of her Pains; otherwise a too frequent Use of the Remedy might possibly lose its Effect, by being applied without any absolute Necessity. With as significant an Air as I could assume, I bid her besure to keep herself warm, and DRINK NO MALT LIQUOR; and, that if she found any Alteration, to send to me.

Glad was I when the poor Creature was gone, as her harmless credulity had rais'd such an invincible Fit of Laughter in me, I must have died on the Spot by the Suppression, had she staid a few Minutes longer.

This Relation is an Instance of what I have often conceived to be the happy Motive for that Success, which Travelling-Physicians frequently meet with; as it is rather founded on the Faith of the Patient, than any real Merit in the Doctor or his Prescriptions. But the Happiness I enjoyed, and still continue to do, in the pleasing Reflection of not having, through Inexperience, done any Harm by my Applications, I thank the Great Creator for, who (notwithstanding my extream Desire of being distinguished as an able Proficient) knew my Design was equally founded on a charitable Inclination; which, I conceive, was a strong Guard against any Evils that might have accrued, from merely a wild Notion of pleasing myself.

My being unfortunately deprived of the Assistance of the Widow's Shop to carry on this grand Affair, made me soon tire in the Pursuit, and put me upon some other Expedient for my Amusement; I therefore framed the tenderest Excuses I could possibly invent to drop my Practice, that those who had before thought themselves indispensibly obliged to me, might not conceive I had lost that charitable Disposition which they had so often blessed me for; and which, indeed, I heartily regretted the not having Power still to preserve and maintain.

My next Flight was Gardening, a very pleasing and healthful Exercise, in which I past the most Part of my Time every Day. I thought it always proper to imitate the Actions of those Persons, whose Characters I chose to represent; and, indeed, was as changeable as Proteus.

When I had blended the Groom and Gardener, I conceived, after having worked two or three Hours in the Morning, a broiled Rasher of Bacon upon a Luncheon of Bread in one Hand, and a Pruning-Knife in the other, (walking, instead of sitting to this elegant Meal) making Seeds and Plants the general Subject of my Discourse, was the true Characteristick of the Gardener; as, at other Times, a Halter and Horse-cloth brought into the House, and aukwardly thrown down on a Chair, were Emblems of my Stable-profession; with now and then a Shrug of the Shoulders and a Scratch of the Head, with a hasty Demand for Small-Beer, and a ———— God bless you make haste, I have not a single Horse dressed or watered, and here 'tis almost Eight o'Clock, the poor Cattle will think I've forgot 'em; and Tomorrow they go a Journey, I'm sure I'd need take Care of 'em. Perhaps this great Journey was an Afternoon's Jaunt to Windsor, within seven Miles of our House; however, it served me to give myself as many Airs, as if it had been a Progress of five hundred Miles.

It luckily happened for me that my Father was gone to France, and the Servant who was in the Capacity of Groom and Gardener, having the Misfortune one Afternoon to be violently inebriated, took it in his Head to abuse the rest of his Fellow-Servants; which my Mother hearing, interfered, and shared equally the Insolence of his opprobrious Tongue: Upon which, at a Minute's Warning, he was dismissed, to the inexpressible Transport, my gentle Reader, of your humble Servant, having then the full Possession of the Garden and Stables.

But what Imagination can paint the Extravagance of Joy I felt on this happy Acquisition! I was so bewildered with the pleasing Ideas I had framed, in being actually a proper Successor to the deposed Fellow, I was entirely lost in a Forgetfulness of my real Self; and went each Day with that orderly Care to my separate Employments, that is generally the recommendatory Virtue for the FIRST MONTH ONLY of a new-hired Servant.

The Rumour of the Man's Dismission was soon spread, and reached, to my great Uneasiness, to Uxbridge, and every little adjacent Village; upon which I soon found it necessary to change my Post of Gardener, and became, for very near a Week, Porter at the Gate, lest some lucky Mortal might have been introduced, and deprived me of the happy Situation I enjoyed.

I began to be tired with giving Denials, and, in order to put an End to their fruitless Expectations, gave out that we had received Letters from France, to assure us, that my Papa had positively hired a Man at Paris to serve in that Office, and therefore all future Attempts would be needless on that Account.

I kept so strict a Watch at the Gate, during the Apprehensions I had of being turned out of my Places, the Maids wondered what made me so constantly traversing the Court-Yard, for near eight Days successively: But,

"Alas! they knew but little of Calista!"

'Twas really to secure my Seat of Empire; which, at that Time, I would not have exchanged for a Monarchy; and I conceived so high an Opinion of myself, I thought the Family greatly indebted to me for my Skill and Industry.

One Day, upon my Mother's paying me a Visit in the Garden, and approving something I had done there, I rested on my Spade, and, with a significant Wink and a Nod, ask'd, Whether she imagined any of the rest of her Children would have done as much at my Age? adding, very shrewdly, Come, come, Madam; let me tell you, a Pound saved is a 'Pound got: Then proceeded in my Office of Digging, in which I was at that Time most happily employed, and with double Labour pursued, to make the strongest Impression I could on my admiring Mother's Mind, and convince her of the Utility of so industrious a Child.

I must not forget to inform the Reader, that my Mother had no extraordinary Opinion of the Fellow's Honesty whom she had turned away; and, what confirmed it, was tracing his Footsteps under the Chamber-Windows the Night after his Dismission, and the Neighbours had observed him to have been hovering round the House several Hours that very Evening.

As we had a considerable Quantity of Plate, my Mother was a good deal alarmed with an Apprehension of the Man's attempting to break in at Midnight; which might render us not only liable to be robbed, but murdered. She communicated her Fears to me, who most heroically promised to protect her Life, at the utmost Hazard of my own. Accordingly I desired all the Plate might be gathered up, and had it placed in a large Flasket by my Bedside. This was no small Addition to my Happiness, as it gave me an Opportunity of raising my Reputation as a courageous Person, which I was extream fond of being deemed; and, in Order to establish that Character, I stripp'd the Hall and Kitchen of their Fire-Arms, which consisted of my own little Carbine (I had, through the old Maid's Perswasion, been barbarously divested of not long before) a heavy Blunderbuss, a Muscatoon, and two Brace of Pistols, all which I loaded with a Couple of Bullets each before I went to Bed; not with any Design, on my Word, to yield to my Repose, but absolutely kept awake three long and tedious Hours, which was from Twelve to Three, the Time I thought most likely for an Invasion.

But no such Thing happened, for not a Mortal approached, on which I thought myself undone; 'till a friendly Dog, who barked at the Moon, gave a happy Signal, and I bounc'd from my Repository with infinite Obligations to the Cur, and fir'd out of the Window Piece after Piece, re-charging as fast as possible, 'till I had consumed about a Pound of Powder, and a proportionable Quantity of Shot and Balls.

'Tis not to be supposed but the Family was, on my first Onset in this singular Battle (having nothing to combat but the Air) soon alarm'd. The frequent Reports and violent Explosions encouraged my kind Prompter to this Farce, to change his lucky Bark into an Absolute Howl, which strongly corroborated with all that had been thought or said, in Regard to an Attempt upon the House. My trembling Mother, who lay Half expiring with dreadful Imaginations, rang her Bell; which Summons I instantly obey'd, firmly assuring her, that all Danger was over, for that I heard the Villain decamp on the first Firing; which Decampment was neither more nor less than the Rustling of the Trees, occasioned by a windy Night, for the Fellow was absolutely gone to London the very Morning I declared War against him, as was afterwards proved.

Notwithstanding I was fully convinced I had nothing to conquer, but my unconquerable Fondness and Resolution to acquire the Character of a couragious Person, I settled that Point with the whole Family, in begging 'em not to be under the least Apprehension of Danger; urging, that my constant firing would be the Means of preventing any: And bid 'em consider, that the Loss of Sleep, was not to be put in Competition with the Hazard of their Lives.

This Reflection made them perfectly easy, and me entirely happy; as I had an unlimitted Power, without Interruption, once in ten Minutes to waste my Ammunition to no Purpose: And retiring to my Rest, as soon as my Stock was exhausted, enjoy'd in Dreams a second Idea of my glorious Exploits.

'Tis certain, nothing but my Mother's excessive Fondness could have blinded her Reason, to give in to my unpresidented, ridiculous Follies; as she was, in all other Points, a Woman of real good Sense: But where the Heart is PARTIALLY ENGAGED, we have frequent Instances of its clouding the Understanding, and MAKING DUPES OF THE WISEST. . . .

. . . It happened, not long after, that I was applied to by a strange, unaccountable Mortal, call'd Jockey Adams; famous for dancing the Jockey Dance, to the Tune of, Horse to New-Market. As I was gaping for a Crust, I readily snap'd at the first that offered, and went with this Person to a Town within four Miles of London, where a very extraordinary Occurrence happened; and which, had I been really what I represented, might have rid in my own Coach, in the Rear of six Horses.

Notwithstanding my Distresses, the Want of Cloaths was not amongst the Number. I appeared as Mr. Brown (A NAME MOST HATEFUL TO ME NOW, FOR REASONS THE TOWN SHALL HAVE SHORTLY LEAVE TO GUESS AT) in a very genteel Manner; and, not making the least Discovery of my Sex by my Behaviour, ever endeavouring to keep up to the well-bred Gentleman, I became, as I may most properly term it, the unhappy Object of Love in a young Lady, whose Fortune was beyond all earthly Power to deprive her of, had it been possible for me to have been, what she designed me, nothing less than her Husband. She was an Orphan Heiress, and under Age; but so near it, that, at the Expiration of eight Months, her Guardian resigned his Trust, and I might have been at once possessed of the Lady, and forty thousand Pounds in the Bank of England: Besides Effects in the Indies, that were worth about twenty Thousand more.

This was a most horrible Disappointment on both Sides; the Lady of the Husband, and I of the Money; which would have been thought an excellent Remedy for Ills, by those less surrounded with Misery than I was. I, who was the Principal in this Tragedy, was the last acquainted with it: But it got Wind from the Servants, to some of the Players; who, as Hamlet says, Can't keep a Secret, and they immediately communicated it to me.

Contrary to their Expectation, I received the Information with infinite Concern; not more in regard to myself, than from the poor Lady's Misfortune, in placing her Affection on an improper Object; and whom, by Letters I afterwards received, confirmed me, "She was too fond of her mistaken Bargain".

The Means by which I came by her Letters, was through the Perswasion of her Maid; who, like most Persons of her Function, are too often ready to carry on Intrigues. 'Twas no difficult Matter to perswade an amorous Heart to follow its own Inclination; and accordingly a Letter came to invite me to drink Tea, at a Place a little distant from the House where she lived.

The Reason given for this Interview was, the Desire some young Ladies of her Acquaintance had to hear me sing; and, as they never went to Plays in the Country, 'twould be a great Obligation to her if I would oblige her Friends, by complying with her Request.

The Maid who brought this Epistle, informed of the real Occasion of its being wrote; and told me, if I pleased, I might be the happiest Man in the Kingdom, before I was eight and forty Hours older. This frank Declaration from the Servant, gave me but an odd Opinion of the Mistress; and I sometimes conceived being conscious how unfit I was to embrace so favourable an Opportunity, that it was all a Joke.

However, be it as it might, I resolved to go and know the Reality. The Maid too insisted that I should, and protested her Lady had suffered much on my Account, from the first Hour she saw me; and, but for her, the Secret had never been disclosed. She farther added, I was the first Person who had ever made that Impression on her Mind. I own I felt a tender Concern, and resolved within myself to wait on her; and, by honestly confessing who I was, kill or cure her Hopes of me for ever.

In Obedience to the Lady's Command I waited on her, and found her with two more much of her own Age, who were her Confidents, and entrusted to contrive a Method to bring this Business to an End, by a private Marriage. When I went into the Room I made a general Bow to all, and was for seating myself nearest the Door; but was soon lugg'd out of my Chair by a young Mad-cap of Fashion; and, to both the Lady's Confusion and mine, aukwardly seated by her.

We were exactly in the Condition of Lord Hardy and Lady Charlotte, in the Funeral; and I sat with as much Fear in my Countenance, as if I had stole her Watch from her Side. She, on her Part, often attempted to speak; but had such a Tremor on her Voice, she ended only in broken Sentences. 'Tis true, I have undergone the dreadful Apprehensions of a Bomb-Bailiff; but I should have thought one at that Time a seasonable Relief, and without repining have gone with him.

The before-mention'd Mad-cap, after putting us more out of Countenance by bursting into a violent Fit of Laughing, took the other by the Sleeve and withdrew, as she thought, to give me a favourable Opportunity of paying my Address; but she was deceived, for, when we were alone, I was ten thousand Times in worse Plight than before: And what added to my Confusion was, seeing the poor Soul dissolve into Tears, which she endeavoured to conceal.

This gave me Freedom of Speech, by a gentle Enquiry into the Cause; and, by tenderly trying to sooth her into a Calm, I unhappily encreased, rather than asswaged, the dreadful Conflict of Love and Shame which labour'd in her Bosom.

With much Difficulty, I mustered up Courage sufficient to open a Discourse, by which I began to make a Discovery of my Name and Family, which struck the poor Creature into Astonishment; but how much greater was her Surprize, when I positively assured her that I was actually the youngest Daughter of Mr. Cibber, and not the Person she conceived me! She was absolutely struck speechless for some little Time; but, when she regained the Power of Utterance, entreated me not to urge a Falshood of that Nature, which she looked upon only as an Evasion, occasioned, she supposed, through a Dislike of her Person: Adding, that her Maid had plainly told her I was no Stranger to her miserable Fate, as she was pleased to term it; and, indeed, as I really thought it.

I still insisted on the Truth of my Assertion; and desired her to consider, whether 'twas likely an indigent young Fellow must not have thought it an unbounded Happiness, to possess at once so agreeable a Lady and immense a Fortune, both which many a Nobleman in this Kingdom would have thought it worth while to take Pains to atchieve.

Notwithstanding all my Arguments, she was hard to be brought into a Belief of what I told her; and conceived that I had taken a Dislike to her, from her too readily consenting to her Servant's making that Declaration of her Passion for me; and, for that Reason, she supposed I had but a light Opinion of her. I assured her of the contrary, and that I was sorry for us both, that Providence had not ordained me to be the happy Person she designed me; that I was much obliged for the Honour she conferr'd on me, and sincerely grieved it with [was] not in my Power to make a suitable Return.

With many Sighs and Tears on her Side, we took a melancholly Leave; and, in a few Days, the Lady retir'd into the Country, where I have never heard from, or of her since; but hope she is made happy in some worthy Husband, that might deserve her.

She was not the most Beautiful I have beheld, but quite the Agreeable; sung finely, and play'd the Harpsichord as well; understood Languages, and was a Woman of real good Sense: But she was, poor Thing! an Instance, in regard to me, *that the Wisest may sometimes err.*

On my Return Home, the Itinerant-Troop all assembled round me, to hear what had passed between the Lady and me—when we were to celebrate the Nuptials?—Besides many other impertinent, stupid Questions; some offering, agreeable to their villainous Dispositions, as the Marriage they suppos'd would be a Secret, to supply my Place in the Dark, to conceal the Fraud: Upon which I look'd at them very sternly, and, with the Contempt they deserved, demanded to know what Action of my Life had been so very monstrous, to excite them to think me capable of one so cruel and infamous?

For the Lady's sake, whose Name I would not for the Universe have had banded about by the Mouths of low Scurrility, I not only told them I had revealed to her who I was, but made it no longer a Secret in the Town; that, in Case it was spoke of, it might be regarded as an Impossibility, or, at worst, a trump'd-up Tale by some ridiculous Blockhead, who was fond of hearing himself prate, as there are indeed too many such: . . .

The Day following I entered into my new Office, which made me the superior Domestick in the Family. I had my own Table, with a Bottle of Wine, and any single Dish I chose for myself, extra of what came from my Lord's, and a Guinea paid me every Wednesday Morning, that being the Day of the Week on which I entered into his Lordship's Service.

At this Time, my Lord kept in the House with him a Fille de Joye. Though no great Beauty, yet infinitely agreeable, (a Native of Ireland) remarkably genteel and finely shaped; and a sensible Woman, whose Understanding was embellished by a Fund of good Nature.

When there was any extraordinary Company, I had the Favour of the Lady's at my Table; but, when there was no Company at all, his Lordship permitted me to make a third Person at his, and very good-naturedly obliged me to throw off the Restraint of Behaviour incidental to the Servant, and assume that of the humble Friend and chearful Companion. Many agreeable Evenings I passed in this Manner; and, when Bed-time approached, I took Leave and went Home to my own Lodgings; attending the next Morning at Nine, my appointed Hour.

I marched every Day through the Streets with Ease and Security, having his Lordship's Protection, and proud to cock my Hat in the Face of the best of the Bailiffs, and shake Hands with them into the Bargain. In this State of Tranquility I remained for about five Weeks; when, as the Devil would have it, there came two supercilious Coxcombs, who, wanting Discourse and Humanity, hearing that I was his Lordship's Gentleman, made me their unhappy Theme, and took the Liberty to arraign his Understanding for entertaining one of an improper Sex in a Post of that Sort. His Lordship's Argument was, for a considerable Time, supported by the Strength of his Pity for an unfortunate Wretch, who had never given him the least Offence: But the pragmatical Blockheads teized him at last into a Resolution of discharging me the next Day, and I was once again reduced to my Scenes of Sorrow and Desolation.

I must do Justice to the Peer, to confess he did not send me away empty handed; but so small a Pittance as he was pleased to bestow, was little more than a momentary Support for myself and Child. When my small Stock was exhausted, I was most terribly puzzled for a Recruit.

Friendship began to cool! Shame encompassed me! that where I had the smallest Hope of Redress remaining, I had not Courage sufficient to make an Attack. In short, Life became a Burden to me, and I began to think it no Sin not only to WISH, but even DESIRE to die. When Poverty throws us beyond the Reach of Pity, I can compare our Beings to nothing so adaptly, as the comfortless Array of tattered Garments in a frosty Morning.

But Providence, who has ever been my Friend and kind Director, as I was in one of my Fits of Despondency, suddenly gave a Check to that Error of my Mind, and wrought in me a Resolution of making a bold Push; which had but two Chances, either for my Happiness or Destruction— Which is as follows.

I took a neat Lodging in a Street facing Red-Lyon-Square, and wrote a Letter to Mr. Beard, intimating to him the sorrowful Plight I was in; and, in a Quarter of an Hour after, my Request was most obligingly complied with by that worthy Gentleman, whose Bounty enabled me to set forward to Newgate-Market, and bought a considerable Quantity of Pork at the best Hand, which I converted into Sausages, and with my Daughter set out, laden with each a Burden as weighty as we could well bear; which, not having been used to Luggages of that Nature, we found extreamly troublesome: But Necessitas non habeat Leges—We were bound to that, or starve.

Thank Heaven, our Loads were like AEsop's when he chose to carry the Bread, which was the weightiest Burden, to the Astonishment of his Fellow-Travellers; not considering that his Wisdom preferred it, because he was sure it would lighten as it went: So did ours, for as I went only where I was known, I soon disposed, among my Friends, of my whole Cargo; and was happy in the Thought, that the utmost Excesses of my Misfortunes had no worse Effect on me, than an industrious and honest

Inclination to get a small Livelihood, without Shame or Reproach: Though the Arch-Dutchess of our Family, who would not have relieved me with a Half-penny Roll or a Draught of Small-Beer, imputed this to me as a Crime.

I suppose she was possessed with the same dignified Sentiments Mrs. Peachum is endowed with, and THOUGHT THE HONOUR OF THEIR FAMILY WAS CONCERNED: If so, she knew the way to have prevented the Disgrace, and in a humane, justifiable Manner, have preserved her own from that Taint of Cruelty I doubt she will never overcome.

My being in Breeches was alledged to me as a very great Error, but the original Motive proceeded from a particular Cause; and I rather chuse to undergo the worst Imputation that can be laid on me on that Account, than unravel the Secret, which is an Appendix to one I am bound, as I before hinted, by all the Vows of Truth and Honour everlastingly to conceal.

For some Time I subsisted as a Higgler, with tolerable Success; and, instead of being despised by those who had served me in my utmost Exigencies, I was rather applauded. Some were tender enough to mingle their pitying Tears, with their Approbation of my endeavouring at an honest Livelihood, as I did not prostitute my Person, or use any other indirect Means for Support, that might have brought me to Contempt and Disgrace.

Misfortunes, to which all are liable, are too often the Parents of Forgetfulness and Disregard in those we have, in happier Times, obliged. Too sure I found it so! for I could name many Persons, who are still in Being, that I have both clothed and fed, who have since met with Success; but when strong Necessity reduced me to an Attempt of using their Friendship, scarce afforded me a civil Answer, which closed in an absolute Denial, and consequently the Sting of Disappointment on such Occasions struck the deeper to my Heart: Though none so poignant, as the Rebuffs I met with from those who ought, in regard to themselves, to have prevented my being under such universal Obligations; but, instead of acting agreeable to the needful Sentiments of Compassion and sorrowful Regret, for the Sufferings of a near Relation, where a villainous Odium could not be thrown a ridiculous one was sure to be cast, even on the innocent Actions of my Life.

Upon being met with a Hare in my Hand, carried by Order to the Peer I had then lately lived with, this single Creature was enumerated into a long Pole of Rabbits; and 'twas affirmed as a Truth, that I made it my daily Practice to cry them about the Streets.

This Falshood was succeeded by another, that of my selling Fish, an Article I never thought of dealing in; but notwithstanding, the wicked Forger of this Story positively declared, that I was selling some Flounders one Day, and, seeing my Father, stept most audaciously up to him, and slapt one of the largest I had full in his Face. Who, that has common Senses, could be so credulous to receive the least Impression from so inconsistent a Tale; or that, if it had been true, if I had escaped my Father's Rage, the Mob would not, with strictest Justice, have prevented my surviving such an unparallel'd Villainy one Moment?

I always thought myself unaccountable enough in Reality, to excite the various Passions of Grief and Anger, Pity or Contempt, without unnecessary additional Falshoods to aggravate my Misdeeds. I own I was obliged, 'till seiz'd with a Fever, to trudge from one Acquaintance to another with Pork and Poultry, but never had the Honour of being a Travelling fishmonger, nor the Villainy of being guilty of that infamous Crime I was inhumanly charged with.

When I was brought so low, by my Illness, as to be disempowered to carry on my Business myself, I was forced to depend upon the infant Industry of my poor Child; whose Strength was not able to bear an equal Share of Fatigue, so that I consequently was obliged to suffer a considerable Deficiency, by the Neglect of my Customers: And though I could scarce afford myself the least Indulgence, in regard to my Illness, I found, though in a trifling Degree, it largely incroached upon my slender Finances, so that I was reduced to my last three Pounds of Pork, nicely prepared for Sausages, and left it on the Table covered up. As I was upon Recovery, I took it in my Head a little fresh Air would not be amiss, and set forth into Red-Lyon-Fields: But, on my Return, OH! DISASTROUS CHANCE! a hungry Cur had most savagely entered my Apartment, confounded my Cookery, and most inconsiderately devoured my remaining Stock, and, from that Hour, a Bankruptcy ensued! the Certificate of which was signed, by the Woefulness of my Countenance at the horrid View.

The Child and I gap'd and star'd at each other; and, with a Despondency in our Faces, very natural on so deplorable an Occasion, we sat down and silently conceived that starving must be the sad Event of this shocking Accident, having at that Time neither Meat, Money, nor Friends. My Week's Lodging was up the next Day, and I was very sure of a constant Visit from my careful Landlord, but how to answer him was a puzzling Debate between me and myself; and I was very well assured, could only be answered but by an Affirmative in that Point.

After having sighed away my Senses for my departed Pork, I began to consider that Sorrow would not retrieve my Loss, or pay my Landlord; and without really knowing where to go, or to whom I should apply, I walked out 'till I should either meet an Acquaintance, or be inspired with some Thought that might happily draw off the Scene of Distress I was then immers'd in.

Luckily, I met with an old Gentlewoman whom I had not seen many Years, and who knew me when I was a Child. She, perceiving Sadness in my Aspect, enquired into the Cause of that, and my being in Mens Cloaths; which, as far as I thought proper, I informed her. When we parted, she slipt Five Shillings into my Hand; on which I thankfully took Leave, went Home with a chearful Heart, paid my Lodging off next Morning, and quitted it.

The next Vexation that arose, was how to get another; for the Child was too young to be sent on such an Errand, and I did not dare to make my Appearance too openly: However, that Grief was soon solved by the good Nature of a young Woman, who gave a friendly Invitation to us both; and, though not in the highest Affluence, supported myself and Child for some Time, without any View or Hopes of a Return, which has since established a lasting Friendship between us, as I received more Humanity from her Indigence, than I could obtain even a Glimpse of from those, whose FORTUNES I had a more ample Right to expect a Relief from.

I had not been many Days with my Friend before I relapsed, my Fever encreasing to that Degree my Death was hourly expected; and, being deprived of my Senses, was left without Means of Help in this unhappy Situation, and, had it not been for the extensive Goodness of the Person before-mentioned, my Child must have either begged her Bread, or perished for the Want of it.

When I was capable of giving a rational Answer, she was my first Care; and I had, in the Midst of this Extremity, the pleasing Relief of being informed, my Friend's Humanity had protected her from that Distress I apprehended she must have otherwise suffered, from the Severity of my Illness. I was incapable of writing, and therefore sent a verbal Message, by my good Friend, to my Lord A———a; who sent me a Piece of Gold, and expressed a tender Concern for my Misfortunes and violent Indisposition.

As soon as I was able to crawl, I went to pay my Duty there, and was again relieved through his Bounty; and might have returned to my Place, 'till something else had fallen out, but that his Lordship was obliged to go suddenly out of England, which, as I had a Child, was not suitable to either him or me.

Mr. Yeates's New Wells being open, and he having Occasion for a Singer in the Serious Part of an Entertainment, called, Jupiter and Alcmena, I was sent for to be his Mercury; and, by the Time that was ready for Exhibition, I began to be tolerably recovered: And a Miracle indeed it was, that I overcame a dreadful Spotted-Fever, without the Help of Advice. Nor had I any Remedy applied, except an Emetick, prescribed and sent me by my Sister Marples, who was the only Relation I had that took any Notice of me.

As I have no Power of making her Amends, equal to my Inclinations, I can only entreat the Favour of my Acquaintance in general, and those whom I have not the Pleasure of knowing, whenever 'tis convenient and agreeable for them to use a neat, well-accommodated House of Entertainment, they will fix a lasting Obligation on me by going to her's, which she opened last Thursday, the 20th Instant, in Fullwood's-Rent, near Gray's-Inn: Where they will be certain of Flesh, Fish and Poultry, dressed in an elegant Manner, at reasonable Rates; good Wines, etc. and a Politeness of Behaviour agreeable to the Gentlewoman; whose hard Struggles, through Seas of undeserved Misfortunes, will, I hope, be a

Claim to that Regard I am certain she deserves, and will, wherever she finds it, most gratefully acknowledge.

For some few Months I was employed, as before-mentioned, 'till Bartholomew Fair; and, as I thought 'twould be more advantageous to me to be there, obtained Leave of Mr. Yeates to quit the Wells for the four Days, and returned to him at the Expiration thereof.

The Rumour of my being in Business having spread itself among my Creditors, I was obliged to decamp; being too well assured my small Revenue, which was but just sufficient to buy Bread and Cheese, would not protect me from a Jail, or satisfy their Demands. Had not my Necessities been pressing, my Service would not have been purchased at so cheap a Rate; but thought I must have been everlastingly condemned, had I, through Pride, been so repugnant to the Laws of Nature, Reason and maternal Love, as to have rejected, with insolent Scorn, this scanty Maintainance, when I was conscious I had not Sixpence in the World to purchase a Loaf. I therefore found it highly necessary to set apart the Remembrance of what I had been,

> "I THEN WAS WHAT I HAD MADE
> "MYSELF;"
> N

And, consequently, obliged to submit to every Inconvenience of Life my Misfortunes could possibly involve me in.

The Amount of all I owed in the World did not arise to Five and Twenty Pounds, but I was as much perplexed for that Sum as if it had been as many Thousands. In order to secure my Person and defend myself from Want, I joined with a Man who was a Master of Legerdemain; but, on my entering on an Agreement with him, he commenced Manager, and we tragedized in a Place called Petticoat-Lane, near White-Chapel; I then taking on me THAT DARLING NAME OF BROWN, which was a very great Help to my Concealment, and indeed the only ADVANTAGE I EVER RECEIVED FROM IT, OR THOSE WHO HAVE A BETTER CLAIM TO IT.

. . . I must beg Pardon of the Reader for omitting a Circumstance, that happened about a Year before I was thus intendedly settled by my Uncle. Being, as I frequently was, in great Distress, I went to see a Person who knew me from my Childhood, and though not in a Capacity of serving me beyond their good Wishes and Advice, did their utmost to convince me, as far as that extended, how much they had it at Heart to serve me; and, upon Enquiry into what Means I proposed for a Subsistance, I gave the good Woman to understand there was nothing, which did not exceed the Bounds of Honestly, that I should think unworthy of my undertaking: That I had been so innur'd to Hardships of the Mind, I should think those of the Body rather a kind Relief, if they would afford but daily Bread for my poor Child and Self.

The Woman herself knew who I was, but her Husband was an entire Stranger, to whom she introduced me as a young Gentleman of a decay'd Fortune; and, after apologizing for Half an Hour, proposed to her Spouse to get me the Waiter's Place, which was just vacant, at one Mrs. Dorr's, who formerly kept the King's-Head, at Mary-la-Bonne.

I thankfully accepted the Offer, and went the next Morning to wait on the Gentlewoman, introduced by my Friend's Husband, and neither he or Mrs. Dorr in the least suspected who I was. She was pleased to tell me, she liked me on my first Appearance; but was fearful, as she understood I was well born and bred, that her Service would be too hard for me. Perceiving me to wear a melancholly Aspect, tenderly admonished me to seek out for some less robust Employment, as she conjectur'd that I should naturally lay to Heart the Impertinence I must frequently be liable to, from the lower Class of People; who, when in their Cups, pay no Regard either to Humanity or good Manners.

I began to be Half afraid, her Concern would make her talk me from my Purpose; and, not knowing which Way to dispose of myself, begg'd her not to be under the least Apprehensions of my receiving any Shock on that Account: That notwithstanding I was not born to Servitude, since Misfortunes had reduced me to it, I thought it a Degree of Happiness, that a mistaken Pride had not foolishly possessed me with a Contempt of getting an honest Livelihood, and chusing rather to perish by haughty Penury, than prudently endeavour to forget what I had been, and patiently submit to the Severities of Fortune; which, at that Time, was not in my Power to amend.

To be short, the Gentlewoman bore so large a Share in my Affliction, she manifested her Concern by a hearty Shower of Tears; and, as she found I was anxious for a Provision with her, we agreed, and the next Day I went to my Place: But when I informed her I had a Daughter about ten Years of Age, she was doubly amazed; and the more so, to hear a young Fellow speak so feelingly of a Child.

She ask'd me, if my Wife was living? I told her no; that she died in Child-Bed of that Girl; whom she insisted should be brought to see her next Day, and entertained the poor Thing in a very genteel Manner, and greatly compassionated her's, and her supposed Father's Unhappiness.

I was the first Waiter that was ever permitted to sit at Table with her; but, she was pleased to compliment me, that she thought my Behavior gave me a Claim to that Respect, and that 'twas with the utmost Pain she obliged herself to call me any Thing but, Sir.

To her great Surprize, she found me quite a handy Creature; and being light and nimble, trip'd up and down Stairs with that Alacrity of Spirit and Agility of Body, that is natural to those Gentlemen of the Order of the Tap-tub; though, as Hob says, we sold all Sorts of Wine and Punch, etc.

At length Sunday came, and I began to shake in my Shoes, for fear of a Discovery, well knowing our House to be one of very great Resort, as I found it; for I waited that Day upon twenty different Companies, there being no other Appearance of a Male, except myself, throughout the House, exclusive of the Customers; and, to my violent Astonishment, not one Soul among 'em all that knew me.

Another Recommendation of me to my good Mistress, was my being able to converse with the Foreigners, who frequented her Ordinary every Sabbath-Day, and to whom she was unable to talk, but by Signs; which I observing, prevented her future Trouble, by signifying in the French Tongue, I perfectly well understood it. This was a universal Joy round the Table, which was encompassed by German Peruke-Makers and French Taylors, not one of whom could utter one single Syllable of English.

As soon as Mrs. Dorr heard me speak French, away she run with her Plate in her Hand, and, laughing, left the Room to go down and eat an English Dinner; having, as she afterwards told me, been obliged once a Week to dine pantomimically, for neither she or her Company were able to converse by any other Means.

When I came down with the Dishes, I thought the poor Soul would have eat me up; and sent as many thankful Prayers to Heaven as would have furnished a Saint for a Twelvemonth, in Behalf of the Man who brought me to her. Her over Joy of her Deliverance from her foreign Companions, wrought a generous Effect on her Mind; which I had a convincing Proof of, by her presenting me with Half a Crown, and made many Encomiums I thought impossible for me ever, in such a Sphere of Life, to be capable of deserving.

In regard to my Child, I begg'd not to be obliged to lie in the House, but constantly came to my Time in a Morning, and staid 'till about Ten or Eleven at Night; and have often wondered I have escaped, without Wounds or Blows, from the Gentlemen of the Pad, who are numerous and frequent in their Evening Patroles through them Fields, and my March extended as far as Long-Acre, by which Means I was obliged to pass through the thickest of 'em. But Heaven everlastingly be praised! I never had any Encounter with 'em; and used to jog along with the Air of a raw, unthinking, pennyless 'Prentice, which I suppose, rendered me not worthy their Observation.

In the Week Days, Business (though good,) was not so very brisk as on Sundays, so that when I had any leisure Hours I employed 'em in working in the Garden, which I was then capable of doing with some small Judgment; but that, and every Thing else, created fresh Surprize in my Mistress, who behaved to me as if I had been rather her Son than her Servant.

One Day, as I was setting some Windsor Beans, the Maid came to me, and told me she had a very great Secret to unfold, but that I must promise never to tell that she had discovered it. As I had no extraordinary Opinion of her Understanding, or her Honesty, I was not over anxious to hear this mighty Secret, lest it should draw me into some Premunire; but she insisted upon disclosing it, assuring me 'twas something that might turn to my Advantage, if I would make a proper Use of it. This last Assertion raised in me a little Curiosity, and I began to grow more attentive to her Discourse; which ended in assuring me, to her certain Knowledge, I might marry her Mistres's Kinswoman, if I would pay my Addresses; and that she should like me for a Master extreamly, advising me to it by all Means.

I asked her what Grounds she had for such a Supposition? To which she answer'd, she had Reasons sufficient for what she had said, and I was the greatest Fool in the World if I did not follow her Advice. I positively assured her I would not, for I would not put it in the Power of a Mother-in-Law to use my Child ill; and that I had so much Regard, as I pretended, to the Memory of her Mother, I resolved never to enter into Matrimony a second Time.

Whatever was the Motive, I am entirely ignorant of, but this insensible Mortal had told the young Woman, that I intended to make Love to her; which, had I really been a Man, would have never entered in my Imagination, for she had no one Qualification to recommend her to the Regard of any Thing beyond a Porter or a Hackney-Coachman. Whether she was angry at what I said to the Wench, in regard to my Resolution against marrying, or whether it was a Forgery of the Maid's, of and to us both, I cannot positively say; but a Strangeness ensued, and I began to grow sick of my Place, and stay'd but a few Days after.

In the Interim Somebody happened to come, who hinted that I was a Woman; upon which, Madam, to my great Surprize, attacked me with insolently presuming to say she was in Love with me, which I assured her I never had the least Conception of. No, truly; I believe, said she, I should hardly be 'namour'd WITH ONE OF MY OWN SECT: Upon which I burst into a Laugh, and took the Liberty to ask her, if she understood what she said? This threw the offended Fair into an absolute Rage, and our Controversy lasted for some Time; but, in the End I brought, in Vindication of my own Innocence, the Maid to Disgrace, who had uncalled for trumped up so ridiculous a Story.

Mrs. Door still remained incredulous, in regard to my being a Female; and though she afterwards paid me a Visit, with my worthy Friend (at my House in Drury-Lane) who brought my unsuccessful Letter back from my Father, she was not to be convinced, I happening that Day to be in the Male-Habit, on Account of playing a Part for a poor Man, and obliged to find my own Cloaths.

She told me, she wished she had known me better when I lived with her, she would, on no Terms, have parted with her Man Charles, as she had been informed I was capable of being Master of the Ceremonies, in managing and conducting the Musical Gardens; for she had a very fine Spot of Ground, calculated entirely for that Purpose, and would have trusted the Care of it to my Government. But t'was then too late; which I am sorry for, on the Gentlewoman's Account, who might have been by such a Scheme preserved in her House; from which, through ill Usage, in a short Time after she was drove out, and reduced to very great Extremities, even by those most nearly related to her: But I find 'tis become a fashionable Vice, to proclaim War against those we ought to be most tender of; and the surest and only Way to find a Friend, is to make a Contract with the greatest Stranger.

After I left my unfortunate Mistress, I was obliged to look out for Acting-Jobbs, and luckily one soon presented itself.

PRIMARY SOURCE

A Narrative of the Life of Mrs. Charlotte Charke, youngest daughter of Colley Cibber. 2d ed. London, 1755. Reprint. Edited by Leonard R. N. Ashley, Gainesville, Fla.: Scholars' Facsimiles and Reprints, 1969.

RELATED SOURCES

"Account of a Visit to Mrs. Charlotte Charke by Mr. Samuel Whyte of Dublin; Taken from Barker's *Biographica/Dramatica*" (I, p. 106), 1812." Reprinted as Preface to *A Narrative*. London: W. Reeve, 1855.

Ashley, Leonard R. N. *Colley Cibber.* New York: Twayne, 1965.

Cotton, Nancy. *Women Playwrights in England, c. 1363–1750.* Lewisberg, Penn.: Bucknell University Press, 1980.

Strange, Sallie Minter. "Charlotte Charke: Transvestite or Conjuror." *Restoration and 18th-Century Theatre Research* 15, 2 (1976):54–59.

Waddell, Helen. "Eccentric Englishwoman: viii Mrs. Charke." *Spectator,* 4 June 1937: 1,047–48.

Sarah Robinson Scott
1723 – 1795

Sarah Robinson was born the sixth child and eldest daughter to the well-connected (but not wealthy, as customarily believed) Matthew Robinson of West Layton and Elizabeth Drake, daughter of Counsellor Robert Drake of Cambridge and Sarah Morris. Together with her sister, Elizabeth, who later flowered as an outstanding Bluestocking, Sarah Robinson read the best literature of the times, but lacked a formal education. Both sisters received informal instruction from Conyers Middleton, a classics professor at Cambridge who was married to their maternal grandmother. When three older brothers were students at Cambridge, the sisters felt the effects indirectly. Most important, their mother, who had probably been educated at Bathsua Makin's school, sent her daughters to a similar establishment.

Since Sarah Robinson Scott decreed that all her private papers be destroyed after her death, many facts about her life remain veiled. Among the know facts is her marriage to George Lewis Scott in 1751. He had been appointed that year as tutor to the Prince of Wales. One year later, however, "taken from her house and husband by her father and brothers" (Walter Crittenden, Preface to the reprint edition of *Millenium Hall*), she left him for good. Sarah Scott's close friend Lady Barbara (Bab) Montagu, who inherited only a modest fortune because of her spendthrift father, the Earl of Halifax, had accompanied the Scotts on their honeymoon (a contemporary custom) and had lived with them during their brief marriage. In 1754, the two women took up residence in Batheaston where they began a charity project for females. The unavailability of productive and creative social roles for women must in part have helped to stimulate this venture. That project became one of the subjects of Scott's novel *Millenium Hall* (1762). In addition, she wrote several historical, moral, and fictional works: *The History of Cornelia* (1750); *A Journey through every stage of Life* (1754); and *A Test of Filial Duty, in a Series of Letters between Emilia Fernand and Charlotte Arlington* (1772). *The History of Sir George Ellison* (1766) includes substantial commentary on the maltreatment of slaves and argues against arranged marriages. Both *The History of Sir George Ellison* and a condensed later version contain glowing references to the *Millenium Hall* project, which nicely exemplifies the connectiveness of Scott's philanthropic vision.

After Lady Barbara died in 1765, Scott lived in several residences around the country until her own death thirty years later at Catton. The lives of Sarah Scott and Lady Barbara Montagu offer another fine example of "romantic friendship," while Scott's novel is a literary rendition of several "romantic friendships" and also shows one way that Mary Astell's "Serious Proposal" was executed three-quarters of a century later. The same stress on a life of virtue and usefulness continues.

FROM

A Description of
Millenium Hall

[During a storm, male travellers seek shelter]
. . . The house to which we had so nearly approached was a very large, old mansion, and its inhabitants so numerous, that I was curious to know how so many became assembled together. Mrs. Maynard said, that "if she did not satisfy my inquiries, I was in great danger of remaining ignorant of the nature of that society, as her friends would not be easily prevailed with to break silence on that subject.

"These ladies," she said, "long beheld with compassion the wretched fate of those women, who from scantiness of fortune, and pride of family, are reduced to become dependent, and to bear all the insolence of wealth, from such as will receive them into their families; these, though in some measure voluntary slaves, yet suffer all the evils of the severest servitude, and are, I believe, the most unhappy part of the creation. Sometimes they are unqualified to gain a maintenance, educated as it is called, genteelly, or, in other words idly, they are ignorant of every thing that might give them superior abilities to the lower rank of people, and their birth renders them less acceptable servants to many, who have not generosity enough to treat them as they ought, and yet do not choose while they are acting the mistress, perhaps too haughtily, to feel the secret reproaches of their own hearts. Possibly pride may still oftener reduce these indigent gentlewomen into this wretched state of dependance, and therefore the world is less inclined to pity them; but my friends see human weakness in another light.

"They imagine themselves too far from perfection to have any title to expect it in others, and think that there are none in whom pride is so

SOURCE: This selection comes from the 1955 reprint edition (facsimile) of the 1762 edition of *Millenium Hall*.

excusable as in the poor; for if there is the smallest spark of it in their compositions, (and who is entirely free from it?) the frequent neglects and indignities they meet with must keep it continually alive. If we are despised for casual deficiencies, we naturally seek in ourselves for some merit, to restore us to that dignity in our own eyes, which those humiliating mortifications would otherwise debase. Thus we learn to set too great a value on what we still possess, whether advantages of birth, education, or natural talents; any thing will serve for a resource to mortified pride; and as every thing grows by opposition, and persecution, we cannot wonder, if the opinion of ourselves increases by the same means.

"To persons in this way of thinking, the pride which reduces many to be, what is called with too little humanity, toad-eaters, does not render them unworthy of compassion. Therefore for the relief of this race they bought that large mansion.

"They drew up several regulations, to secure the peace and good order of the society they designed to form, and sending a copy of it to all their acquaintance, told them, that any gentleman's daughter, whose character was unblemished, might, if she desired it, on those terms be received into that society."

I begged, if it was not too much trouble, to know what the regulations were.

"The first rule," continued Mrs. Maynard, "was, that whoever chose to take the benefit of this asylum, for such I justly call it, should deposit, in the hands of a person appointed for that purpose, whatever fortune she was mistress of, the security being approved by her and her friends, and remaining in her possession. Whenever she leaves the society, her fortune should be repaid to her, the interest in the mean time being appropriated to the use of the community. The great design of this was to preserve an exact equality between them; for it was not expected, that the interest of any of their fortunes should pay the allowance they were to have for their cloaths. If any appeared to have secreted part of her fortune, she should be expelled from the society.

"Secondly, Each person to have a bed-chamber to herself, but the eating-parlour and drawing-room in common.

"Thirdly, All things for rational amusement shall be provided for the society; musical instruments, of whatever sort they shall chuse; books; tents for work; and, in short, conveniences for every kind of employment.

"Fourthly, They must conform to very regular hours.

"Fifthly, An house-keeper will be appointed to manage household affairs, and a sufficient number of servants provided.

"Sixthly, Each person shall alternately, a week at a time, preside at the table, and give what family orders may be requisite.

"Seventhly, Twenty-five pounds a year shall be allowed to each person for her cloaths and pocket expences.

"Eighthly, Their dress shall be quite plain and neat, but not particular nor uniform.

"Ninthly, The expences of sickness shall be discharged by the patronesses of the society.

"Tenthly, If any one of the ladies behaves with imprudence, she shall be dismissed, and her fortune returned; likewise if any should, by turbulence or pettishness of temper, disturb the society, it shall be in the power of the rest of them to expel her; a majority of three parts of the community being for the expulsion, and this to be performed by ballotting.

"Eleventhly, A good table, and every thing suitable to the convenience of a gentlewoman, shall be provided.

"These were the principal articles; and in less than two months a dozen persons of different ages were established in the house, who seemed thoroughly delighted with their situation. At the request of one of them, who had a friend that wished to be admitted, an order was soon added, by the consent of all, that gave leave for any person who would conform exactly to the rules of the house, to board there for such length of time, as should be agreeable to herself and the society, for the price of an hundred pounds a year, fifty for any child she might have, twenty for a maid-servant, and thirty for a man.

"The number of this society is now increased to thirty, four ladies board there, one of whom had two children, and there are five young ladies, the eldest not above twelve years old, whose mothers being dead, and their families related to some of the society, their kinswomen have undertaken their education; these likewise pay an hundred pounds a year each. It has frequently happened, that widow ladies have come into this society, till their year of deep mourning was expired.

"With these assistances the society now subsists with the utmost plenty and convenience, without any additional expence to my good friends, except a communication of what this park affords; as our steward provides them with every thing, and has the entire direction of the household affairs, which he executes with the most sensible economy."

"I should imagine," said I, "it were very difficult to preserve a comfortable harmony among so many persons, and consequently such variety of tempers."

"Certainly," answered Mrs. Maynard, "it is not without its difficulties. For the first year of this establishment my friends dedicated most of their time and attention to this new community, who were every day either at the hall, or these ladies with them, endeavouring to cultivate in this sisterhood that sort of disposition which is most productive of peace. By their example and suggestions, (for it is difficult to give unreserved advice where you may be suspected of a design to dictate) by their examples and suggestions therefore, they led them to industry, and shewed it to be necessary to all stations, as the basis of almost every virtue. An idle mind, like fallow ground, is the soil for every weed to grow in; in it vice strengthens, the seed of every vanity flourishes unmolested and luxuriant; discontent, malignity, ill humour, spread far and wide, and the mind becomes a chaos, which it is beyond human power to call into order and beauty. This therefore my good friends laboured to expel from their infant establishment. They taught them that it was the duty of every person to be of service to others. That those whose hands and minds were by the favours of fortune exempt from the necessity of labouring for their own support, ought to be employed for such as are destitute of these advantages. They got this sisterhood to join with them in working for the poor people, in visiting, in admonishing, in teaching them wherever their situations required these services. Where they found that any of these ladies had a taste for gardening, drawing, music, reading, or any manual or mental art, they cultivated it, assisted them in the pleasantest means, and by various little schemes have kept up these inclinations with all the spirit of pursuit, which is requisite to preserve most minds from that state of languidness and inactivity, whereby life is rendered wearisome to those who have never found it unfortunate.

"By some regulations made as occasions occurred, all burdensome forms are expelled. The whole society indeed must assemble at morning and evening prayers, and at meals, if sickness does not prevent, but every other ceremonious dependence is banished; they form into different parties of amusement as best suit their inclinations, and sometimes when we go to spend the afternoon there, we shall find a party at cards in one room, in another some at work, while one is reading aloud, and in a separate chamber a set joining in a little concert, though none of them are great proficients in music; while two or three shall be retired into their rooms, some go out to take the air, for it has seldom happened to them to have less than two boarders at a time who each keep an equipage; while others shall be amusing themselves in the garden, or walking in the very pleasant meadows which surround their house.

"As no one is obliged to stay a minute longer in company than she chuses, she naturally retires as soon as it grows displeasant to her, and does not return till she is prompted by inclination, and consequently well disposed to amuse and be amused. They live in the very strict practice of all religious duties; and it is not to be imagined how much good they have done in the neighbourhood; how much by their care the manners of the poorer people are reformed, and their necessities relieved, though without the distribution of much money; I say much, because, small as their incomes are, there are many who impart out of that little to those who have much less.

"Their visits to us are frequent, and we are on such footing, that they never impede any of our employments. My friends always insisted when they waited on the community, that not one of the sisterhood should discontinue whatever they found her engaged in; this gave them the hint to do the same by us, and it is a rule, that no book is thrown aside, no pen laid down, at their entrance. There are always some of us manually employed, who are at leisure to converse, and if the visit is not very short, part of it is generally spent in hearing one of the girls read aloud, who take it by turns through a great part of the day; the only difference made for this addition to the company is the change of books, that they may not hear only part of a subject, and begin by a broken thread. Thus they give no interruption, and therefore neither trouble us, nor are themselves scrupulous about coming, so that few days pass without our seeing some of them, though frequently only time enough to accompany us in our walks, or partake of our music."

"Have you not," said Lamont, "been obliged to expel many from the community? Since you do not allow petulancy of temper, nor any lightness of conduct, I should expect a continual revolution."

"By no means," answered Mrs. Maynard, "since the establishment of the community, there has been but one expelled; and one finding she was in danger of incurring the same sentence, and I believe inwardly disgusted with a country life, retired of her own free choice. Some more have rendered themselves so disagreeable, that the question has been put to the ballot; but the fear of being dismissed made them so diligent to get the majority on their side, before the hour appointed for decision arrived, that it has been determined in their favour, and the earnest desire not to be brought into the same hazard again, has induced them to mend their tempers, and some of these are now the most amiable people in the whole community.

"As for levity of conduct, they are pretty well secured from it, by being exposed to few temptations in this retired country.

"Some, as in the course of nature must happen, have died, and most of them bequeathed what little they had towards constituting a fund for the continuation of the community. More of them have married; some to persons who knew them before, others to gentlemen in the neighbourhood, or such as happened to come into it; to whom their admirable conduct recommended them."

I could not help exclaiming, "In what a heaven do you live, thus surrounded by people who owe all their happiness to your goodness! This is, indeed, imitating your Creator, and in such proportion as your faculties will admit, partaking of His felicity, since you can no where cast your eyes, without beholding numbers who derive every earthly good from your bounty, and are indebted to your care and example for a reasonable hope of eternal happiness."

"I will not," said Mrs. Maynard, "give up my share of the felicity you so justly imagine these ladies must enjoy, though I have no part in what occasions it. When I reflect on all the blessings they impart, and see how happiness flows, as it were, in an uninterrupted current from their hands and lips, I am overwhelmed with gratitude to the Almighty disposer of my fate, for having so mercifully thrown me into such a scene of felicity, where every hour yields true heartfelt joy, and fills me with thanksgiving to Him, who enables them thus to dispense innumerable blessings, and so greatly rewards them already by the joyful consciousness of having obeyed Him."

The Ladies at this time were at too great a distance to hear our conversation; for not chusing to be present while their actions were the subjects of discourse, they had gradually strayed from us. Upon enquiring of my cousin, whether the persons in the large community we had been talking of brought any fortunes with them, she told me that "most of them had a trifle, some not more than an hundred pounds. That in general the ladies chose to admit those who had least, as their necessities were greatest, except where some particular circumstances rendered protection more requisite to others. That the house not being large enough to contain more than were already in it, they have been obliged to refuse admission to many, and especially some young women of near two thousand pounds fortune, the expensive turn of the world now being such. . . .

. . . In this condition Mr. Morgan lay for three months, when death released him from this world; and brought a seasonable relief to Mrs. Morgan, whose health was so impaired by long confinement, and want of quiet rest, that she could not much longer have supported it; and vexation had before so far impaired her constitution, that nothing could have enabled her to undergo so long a fatigue, but the infinite joy she received from Miss Mancel's company.

When Mr. Morgan's will was opened, it appeared, that he had left his wife an estate which fell to him about a month before the commencement of his illness, where we now live. The income of it is a thousand pounds a year; the land was thoroughly stocked, and the house in good repair. Mr. Morgan had at his marriage settled a jointure on his wife of four hundred pounds a year rent charge, and in a codicil made just after his sister's wedding, he bequeathed her two thousand pounds in ready money.

After Mrs. Morgan had settled all her affairs, it was judged necessary, that, for the recovery of her health, she should go to Tunbridge, to which place Miss Mancel accompanied her. As Mrs. Morgan's dress confined her entirely at home, they were not in the way of making many acquaintance; but Lady Mary Jones being in the house, and having long been known to Miss Mancel, though no intimacy had subsisted between them, they now became much connected. The two friends had agreed to retire into the country, and though both of an age and fortune to enjoy all the pleasure which most people so eagerly pursue, they were desirous of fixing in a way of life where all their satisfactions might be rational, and as conducive to eternal, as to temporal happiness. They had laid the plan of many things, which they have since put into execution, and engaged Mr. d'Avora to live with them, both as a valuable friend, and an useful assistant, in the management of their affairs.

Lady Mary was at that time so much in the same disposition, and so charmed with such part of their scheme as they communicated to her,

that she begged to live with them for half a year, by which time they would
be able to see whether they chose her continuance there, and she should
have experienced how far their way of life was agreeable to her. Lady
Mary's merit was too apparent not to obtain their ready consent to her
proposal, and when they had the satisfaction of seeing Mrs. Morgan
much recovered by the waters, and no farther benefit was expected, they
came to this house.

They found it sufficiently furnished, and in such good order, that they
settled in it without trouble. The condition of the poor soon drew their
attention, and they instituted schools for the young, and alms-houses for
the old. As they ordered every thing in their own family with great
oeconomy, and thought themselves entitled only to a part of their fortunes, their large incomes allowed them full power to assist many,
whose situations differed very essentially from theirs. The next expence
they undertook, after the establishment of schools and alms-houses, was
that of furnishing a house for every young couple that married in their
neighbourhood, and providing them with some sort of stock, which by
industry would prove very conducive towards their living in a comfortable degree of plenty. They have always paid nurses for the sick, sent
them every proper refreshment, and allow the same sum weekly which
the sick person could have gained, that the rest of the family may not lose
any part of their support, by the incapacity of one.

When they found their fortunes would still afford a larger communication, they began to receive the daughters of persons in office, or
other life-incomes, who, by their parent's deaths, were left destitute of
provision; and when, among the lower sort, they meet with an uncommon genius, they will admit her among the number. The girls you see sit
in the room with us are all they have at present in that way; they are
educated in such a manner as will render them acceptable, where accomplished women of an humble rank and behaviour are wanted, either
for the care of a house or children. These girls are never out of the room
with us, except at breakfast and dinner, and after eight o'clock in the
evening, at which times they are under the immediate care of the house-
keeper, with whom they are allowed to walk out for an hour or two every
fine day; lest their being always in our company should make them think
their situation above a menial state; they attend us while we are dressing,
and we endeavour that the time they are thus employed shall not pass
without improvement. They are clad in coarse and plain for the same
reason, as nothing has a stronger influence on vanity than dress.

Each of us takes our week alternately of more particular inspection
over the performances of these girls, and they all read by turns aloud to
such of us, as are employed about any thing that renders it not incon-
venient to listen to them. By this sort of education my friends hope to do
extensive good, for they will not only serve these poor orphans, but
confer a great benefit on all who shall be committed to their care, or have
occasion for their service; and one can set no bounds to the advantages

that may arise from persons of excellent principles, and enlarged understandings, in the situations wherein they are to be placed. In every thing
their view is to be as beneficial to society as possible, and they are such
oeconomists even in their charities, as to order them in a manner, that
as large a part of mankind as possible should feel the happy influence
of their bounty.

In this place, and in this way of life, the three ladies already mentioned
have lived upwards of twenty years; for Lady Mary Jones joined her
fortune to those of the two friends, never chusing to quit them, and is too
agreeable not to be very desirable in the society. Miss Mancel has often
declared, that she plainly sees the merciful hand of Providence bringing
good out of evil, in an event, which she, at the time it happened, thought
her greatest misfortune; for had she married Sir Edward Lambton, her
sincere affection for him would have led her to conform implicitly to all
his inclinations, her views would have been confined to this earth, and
too strongly attached to human objects, to have properly obeyed the
giver of the blessings she so much valued, who is generally less thought
of, in proportion as He is more particularly bountiful. Her age, her
fortune, and compliant temper, might have seduced her into dissipation,
and have made her lose all the heart-felt joys she now daily experiences,
both when she reflects on the past, contemplates the present, or antici-
pates the future.

I think I ought to mention Mrs. Morgan's behaviour to her half sisters.
Sir Charles died about five years ago, and through his wife's extravagance, left his estate over-charged with debts, and two daughters and a
son unprovided for. Lady Melvyn's jointure was not great; Sir George, her
eldest son, received but just sufficient out of his estate to maintain
himself genteelly. By the first Lady Melvyn's marriage-settlements, six
thousand pounds were settled on her children, which, as Mrs. Morgan
was her only child, became her property; this she divided between her
mother-in-law's three younger children, and has besides conferred
several favours on that family, and frequently makes them valuable
presents. The young gentleman and ladies often pass some time here;
Lady Melvyn made us a visit in the first year of her widowhood, but our
way of life is so ill suited to her taste, that, except during that dull period
of confinement, she has never favoured us with her company.

My cousin, I believe, was going to mention some other of the actions
of these ladies, which seemed a favourite topic with her, when the rest
of the company came into the garden, and we thought ourselves obliged
to join them.

The afternoons, in this family, generally concluded with one of their
delightful concerts; but as soon as the visitors were departed, the ladies
said, they would amuse us that evening with an entertainment, which
might possibly be more new to us, a rustic ball. The occasion of it was
the marriage of a young woman, who had been brought up by them, and
had for three years been in service, but having for that whole time been

courted by a young farmer of good character, she had been married in the morning, and that evening was dedicated to the celebration of their wedding.

We removed into the servants hall, a neat room, and well lighted, where we found a very numerous assembly; sixteen couple were preparing to dance; the rest were only spectators. The bride was a pretty genteel girl, dressed in a white callico gown, white ribbons, and in every particular neat to an excess. The bridegroom was a well-looking young man, as clean and sprucely dressed as his bride, though not with such emblematic purity. This couple, contrary to the custom of finer people on such occasions, were to begin the ball together; but Lamont asked leave to be the bride's partner for two or three dances, a compliment not disagreeable to the ladies, and highly pleasing to the rest of the company, except the bride, whose vanity one might plainly see did not find gratification enough in having so genteel a partner, to recompence her for the loss of her Colin; he, however, seemed well satisfied with the honour conferred on his wife.

That the bridgroom might not be without his share of civility, the ladies gave him leave to dance with the eldest of the young girls more particularly under their care, till his wife was restored to him.

We sat about above an hour with this joyous company, whose mirth seemed as pure as it was sincere, and I never saw a ball managed with greater decorum. There is a coquettry and gallantry appropriated to all conditions; and to see the different manner in which it was expressed in this little set, from what one is accustomed to behold in higher life, afforded me great amusement; and the little arts used among these young people to captivate each other, were accompanied with so much innocence, as made it excessively pleasing. We staid about an hour and half in this company, and then went to supper.

My cousin told me that Mrs. Mancel gave the young bride a fortune, and that she might have her share of employment, and contribute to the provision of her family, had stocked her dairy, and furnished her with poultry. This, Mrs. Maynard added, was what they did for all the young women they brought up, if they proved deserving; shewing, likewise, the same favour to any other girls in the parish, who, during their single state, behaved with remarkable industry and sobriety. By this mark of distinction they were incited to a proper behaviour, and appeared more anxious for this benevolence, on account of the honour that arose from it, than for the pecuniary advantage.

As the ladies conduct in this particular was uncommon, I could not forbear telling them, that "I was surprised to find so great encouragement given to matrimony by persons, whose choice shewed them little inclined in its favour."

"Does it surprise you," answered Mrs. Morgan smiling, "to see people promote that in others, which they themselves do not chuse to practice? We consider matrimony as absolutely necessary to the good of society;

it is a general duty; but as, according to all antient tenures, those obliged to perform knight's service, might, if they chose to enjoy their own fire-sides, be excused by sending deputies to supply their places; so we, using the same privilege, substitute many others, and certainly much more promote wedlock, than we could do by entering into it ourselves. This may wear the appearance of some devout persons of a certain religion, who equally indolent and timorous, when they do not chuse to say so many prayers as they think their duty, pay others for supplying their deficiencies."

"In this case;" said I, "your example is somewhat contradictory, and should it be entirely followed, it would confine matrimony to the lower rank of people, among whom it seems going out of fashion, as well as with their superiors; nor indeed can we wonder at it, for dissipation and extravagance are now become such universal vices, that it requires great courage in any to enter into an indissoluble society. Instead of being surprised at the common disinclination to marriage, I am rather disposed to wonder when I see a man venture to render himself liable to the expences of a woman, who lavishes both her time and money on every fashionable folly; and still more, when one of your sex subjects herself to be reduced to poverty, by a husband's love for gaming, and to neglect by his inconstancy."

"I am of your opinion," said Mrs. Trentham, "to face the enemy's cannon appears to me a less effort of courage, than to put our happiness into hands of a person, who perhaps will not once reflect on the importance of the trust committed to his or her care. For the case is pretty equal as to both sexes, each can destroy the other's peace. Ours seems to have found out the means of being on an equality with yours. Few fortunes are sufficient to stand a double expence. The husband must attend the gaming-table and horseraces; the wife must have a profusion of ornaments for her person, and cards for her entertainment. The care of the estate and family are left in the hands of servants, who, in imitation of their masters and mistresses, will have their pleasures, and these must be supplied out of the fortunes of those they serve. Man and wife are often nothing better than assistants in each others ruin; domestic virtues are exploded, and social happiness despised, as dull and insipid.

"The example of the great infects the whole community. The honest tradesman, who wishes for a wife to assist him in his business, and to take care of his family, dare not marry, when every woman of his rank, emulating her superiors, runs into such fashions of dress, as require great part of his gains to supply, and the income which would have been thought sufficient some years ago for the wife of a gentleman of large estate, will now scarcely serve to enable a tradesman's wife to appear like her neighbours. They too must have their evening parties, they must attend the places of public diversion, and must be allowed perpetual dissipation without controul. The poor man sighs after the day when his father married; then cleanliness was a woman's chief personal ornament, half the quantity of silk sufficed for her cloaths, variety of trumpery ornaments were not thought of, her husband's business employed her attention, and her children were the object of her care. When he came home, wearied with the employment of the day, he found her ready to receive him, and was not afraid of being told she was gone to the play or opera, or of finding her engaged in a party at cards, while he was reduced to spend his evening alone. But, in a world so changed, a man dare not venture on marriage which promises him no comfort, and may occasion his ruin; nor wishes for children, whose mother's neglect may expose them to destruction.

"It is common to blame the lower sort of people for imitating their superiors; but it is equally the fault of every station, and therefore those of higher rank should consider it their duty to set no examples that may hurt others. A degree of subordination is always acquiesced in, but while the nobleman lives like a prince, the gentleman will rise to the proper expences of a nobleman, and the tradesman take that vacant rank which the gentleman has quitted; nor will he be ashamed of becoming a bankrupt, when he sees the fortunes of his superiors mouldering away, and knows them to be oppressed with debt. Whatever right people may have to make free with their own happiness, a beneficial example is a duty which they indispensibly owe to society, and the profuse have the extravagance of their inferiors to answer for. The same may be said for those who contribute to the dissipation of others, by being dissipated themselves."

"But, madam," interrupted Lamont, "do you think it incumbent on people of fashion to relinquish their pleasures, lest their example should lead others to neglect their business?"

"I should certainly," replied Mrs. Trentham, "answer you in the affirmative, were the case as you put it, but much more so in the light I see it. Every station has its duties, those of the great are more various than those of their inferiors. They are not so confined to oeconomical attentions, nor ought they to be totally without them; but their more extensive influence, their greater leisure to serve their Creator with all the powers of their minds, constitute many duties on their part, to which, dissipation is as great an enemy, as it can be to those more entirely domestic; therefore on each side there is an equal neglect; and why should we expect that such as we imagine have fewer advantages of education, should be more capable of resisting temptations, and dedicating themselves solely to the performance of their duties, than persons whose minds are more improved?"

"I cannot deny," answered Lamont, "but what you say is just, yet I fear you have uttered truths that must continue entirely speculative; though, if any people have a right to turn reformers, you ladies are the best qualified, since you begin by reforming yourselves; you practice more than you preach, and therefore must always be listened to with attention."

"We do not set up for reformers," said Mrs. Mancel, "we wish to regulate ourselves by the laws laid down to us, and, as far as our influence can extend, endeavour to enforce them; beyond that small circle all is foreign to us; we have sufficient employment in improving ourselves; to mend the world requires much abler hands. . . ."

"You observed, Sir," said Mrs. Trentham, "that we live for others, without any regard to our own pleasure, therefore I imagine you think our way of life inconsistent with it; but give me leave to say you are mistaken. What is there worth enjoying in this world that we do not possess? We have all the conveniences of life, nay, all the luxuries that can be included among them. We might indeed keep a large retinue; but do you think the sight of a number of useless attendants could afford us half the real satisfaction, that we feel from seeing the money, which must be lavished on them, expended in supporting the old and decrepid, or nourishing the helpless infant? We might dress with so much expence, that we could scarcely move under the burden of our apparel; but is that more eligible, than to see the shivering wretch clad in warm and comfortable attire? Can the greatest luxury of the table afford so true a pleasure, as the reflection, that instead of its being overcharged with superfluities, the homely board of the cottager is blessed with plenty? We might spend our time in going from place to place, where none wish to see us except they find a deficiency at the card table, perpetually living among those, whose vacant minds are ever seeking after pleasures foreign to their own tastes, and pursue joys which vanish as soon as possessed; for these would you have us leave the infinite satisfaction of being beheld with gratitude and love, and the successive enjoyments of rational delights, which here fill up every hour? Should we do wisely in quitting a scene where every object exalts our mind to the great Creator, to mix among all the folly of depraved nature?

"If we take it in a more serious light still, we shall perceive a great difference in the comforts arising from the reflexions on a life spent in an endeavour to obey our Maker, and to correct our own defects, in a constant sense of our offences, and an earnest desire to avoid the commission of them for the future, from a course of hurry and dissipation, which will not afford us leisure to recollect our errors, nor attention to attempt amending them."

"The difference is indeed striking," said Lamont, "and there can be no doubt which is most eligible; but are you not too rigid in your censures of dissipation? You seem to be inclined to forbid all innocent pleasures."

"By no means," replied Mrs. Trentham, "but things are not always innocent because they are trifling. Can any thing be more innocent than picking of straws, or playing at push-pin; but if a man employs himself so continually in either, that he neglects to serve a friend, or to inspect his affairs, does it not cease to be innocent? Should a school-boy be found whipping a top during school hours, would his master forbear correction because it is an innocent amusement? And yet thus we plead for things as trifling, tho' they obstruct the exercise of the greatest duties in life. Whatever renders us forgetful of our Creator, and of the purposes for which He called us into being, or leads us to be inattentive to His commands, or neglectful in the performance of them, becomes criminal, however innocent in its own nature. While we pursue these things with a moderation which prevents such effects, they are always innocent, and often desireable; the excess only is to be avoided."

"I have nothing left to say," answered Lamont, "than that your doctrine *must* be true, and your lives *are* happy; but may I without impertinence observe, that I should imagine your extensive charities require an immense fortune."

"Not so much, perhaps," said Mrs. Morgan, "as you suppose. We keep a very regular account, and at an average, the total stands thus. The girls school four hundred pounds a year, the boys an hundred and fifty, apprenticing some and equipping others for service one hundred. The cloathing of the girls in the house forty. The alms houses two hundred. The maintenance of the monsters an hundred and twenty. Fortunes and furniture, for such young persons as marry in this and the adjoining parishes, two hundred. All this together amounts only to twelve hundred and ten pounds a year, and yet afford all reasonable comforts. The expenses of ourselves and household, in our advantageous situation, come within eight hundred a year. Finding so great a balance in our favour, we agreed to appropriate a thousand a year for the society of gentlewomen with small or no fortunes; but it has turned out in such a manner that they cost us a trifle. We then dedicated that sum to the establishment of a manufacture, but since the fourth year it has much more than paid its expences, though in some respect we do not act, with the oeconomy usual in such cases, but give very high wages; for our design being to serve a multitude of poor desitute of work, we have no nice regard to profit. As we did not mean to drive a trade, we have been at a loss what to do with the profits. We have out of it made a fund for the sick and disabled, from which they may receive a comfortable support, and intend to secure it to them to perpetuity in the best manner we can."

"How few people of fortune are there," said Lamont, "who could not afford £1200 a year, with only retrenching superfluous and burdensome expences? But if they would only imitate you in any one branch, how much greater pleasure would they then receive from their fortunes than they now enjoy?"

While he was engaged in discourse with the ladies, I observed to Mrs. Maynard, that by the account she had given me of their income, their expences fell far short of it. She whispered me, that "their accidental charities were innumerable, all the rest being employed in that way. Their acquaintance know they cannot so much oblige, as by giving them an opportunity of relieving distress. They receive continual applications, and though they give to none indiscriminately, yet they never refuse any who really want. Their donations sometimes are in great sums, where the case requires such extraordinary assistance. If they hear of any gentleman's family oppressed by too many children, or impoverished by sickness, they contrive to convey an adequate present privately, or will sometimes ask permission to put some of their children into business, or buy them places or commissions."

We acquainted the ladies that we should trouble them no longer than that night, and with regret saw it so ended. The next morning, upon going into Lamont's room, I found him reading the New Testament; I could not forbear expressing some pleasure and surprize, at seeing him thus uncommonly employed.

He told me, "he was convinced by the conduct of the ladies of this house, that their religion must be the true one. When he had before considered the lives of Christians, their doctrines seemed to have so little influence on their actions, that he imagined there was no sufficient effect produced by Christianity, to warrant a belief, that it was established by a means so very extraordinary; but he now saw what that religion in reality was, and by the purity of its precepts, was convinced its original must be divine. It now appeared evidently to be worthy of its miraculous institution. He was resolved to examine, whether the moral evidences concurred with that divine stamp, which was so strongly impressed upon it, and he had risen at day break to get a Bible out of the parlour, that he might study precepts, which could thus exalt human nature almost to divine."

It was with great joy I found him so seriously affected; and when we went to breakfast, could not forbear communicating my satisfaction to my cousin, who sincerely shared it. As soon as breakfast was over we took leave of the ladies, though not till they had made us promise a second visit, to which we very gladly agreed, for could we with decency have prolonged this, I know not when we should have departed.

You, perhaps, wish we had done it sooner, and may think I have been too prolix in my account of this society; but the pleasure I find in recollecting is such, that I could not restrain my pen within moderate bounds. If what I have described, may tempt any one to go and do likewise, I shall think myself fortunate in communicating it. For my part, my thoughts are all engaged in a scheme to imitate them on a smaller scale.

I am, Sir.

FINIS

---•---

PRIMARY SOURCES

A Description of Millenium Hall and the Country Adjacent: together with the Characters of the Inhabitants, and such historical anecdotes and Reflections, as may excite in the reader Proper Sentiments of Humanity, and lead the Mind to the Love of Virtue. By a Gentleman on his Travels. London: for T. Carnan, 1762. Reprint. Edited and Introduction by Walter M. Crittenden. New York: Bookman Associates, 1955.

The History of Sir George Ellison. London: A Millar, 1766.

RELATED SOURCES

Crittenden, Walter M. *The Life and Writings of Mrs. Sarah Scott—Novelist (1723–1795).* Philadelphia: University of Pennsylvania, 1932.

Faderman, Lillian. *Surpassing the Love of Men: Romantic Friendship and Love Between Women from the Renaissance to the Present.* New York: William Morrow & Co., 1981.

Larsen, Edith. *Early Eighteenth-Century English Women Writers: Their Lives and Fiction.* Ph.D. dissertation, Brandeis University, 1980.

Todd, Janet. *Women's Friendship in Literature.* New York: Columbia University Press, 1980.

ELIZABETH CARTER
1717–1806

Born in 1717 in Deal—her permanent home except for occasional visits—Elizabeth Carter was the eldest daughter of the Reverend Nicholas Carter, perpetual curate of Deal Chapel and one of the six preachers at Canterbury Cathedral. Her mother was the only daughter and heiress of Richard Swayne, but the fortune was lost in unlucky investments. Carter lived with her father until he died. A learned man, he taught her Latin, Greek, and Hebrew; she learned French from a Huguenot minister. With an admirable perseverance, she taught herself Italian, Spanish, and German, with some Portugese and Arabic. She also wrote music for the flute and spinet and studied mathematics, geography, history, and astronomy. To accomplish this regimen of study she took snuff, wrapped a wet towel round her head, and chewed green tea to stay awake. A small collection of her poems appeared in 1738 published by her father's friend, Edward Cave.

Acclaimed as an outstanding Greek scholar, Carter earned one thousand pounds for her translation of Epictetus in 1758, which Samuel Richardson published by subscription. (Others' translations had appeared earlier.) She lived off these earnings. She also published poems in 1762 that went through four editions, and contributed to the *Gentleman's Magazine* and *The Rambler.* According to a respectful convention of the time toward unmarried women, she was known as Mrs. Carter.

Carter enjoyed a preeminent reputation as the intellectual paragon of the Bluestockings, whose literary gatherings, unlike the earlier French salons, were frequented largely by women. Political conservatives, the Bluestockings strove for higher standards in moral, cultural, and intellectual life. They scorned female "accomplishments," abhorred card-playing and inconsequential frivolities, and favored the single life over an unhappy married one. They particularly disparaged forced marriages and many of them opposed slavery, including Elizabeth Carter, who was an original subscriber to the committee to abolish the slave trade. Carter supported social change, but with reservations, once lamenting in a letter to Hannah More that, barring miraculous intervention, "reformations must be brought about by bad men." With Elizabeth Robinson Montagu, honorary Queen of the Bluestockings and a close friend, Carter visited Bath in 1763 and Paris in 1776. When her husband died, Montagu gave Carter a £100 annuity.

For several decades, Carter corresponded with her beloved friend, Catherine Talbot, whom she termed in her last letter before Talbot died, "one of the dearest and most distinguished blessings of my life." In these letters, they discussed a variety of interests and preoccupations, from their personal feelings and concerns about friends' health and comfort and their intellectual, literary, and religious opinions, to Carter's agonizingly painful headaches and their mutual preference for an unmarried life. The extracts, including several by Talbot, help to indicate how such a correspondence could play an essential and extensive part in women's emotional and intellectual lives.

Consistent with the lives of other early feminists, Carter lived as self-determindedly as she reasonably could and moved in predominantly feminocentric circles.

FROM

A SERIES OF LETTERS

BETWEEN MRS. ELIZABETH CARTER AND MISS CATHERINE TALBOT (vol. 1)

MRS. CARTER TO MR. WRIGHT.

Jan. 28, 1741.

SIR,

I DO not know whether you ought to congratulate me upon my good success last Sunday, for what have I gained by it? only a new addition to my impatience, which really was very strong before, but is now out of all bounds of moderation. Miss Talbot is absolutely my passion; I think of her all day, dream of her all night, and one way or other introduce her into every subject I talk of. You say she has a quarrel against my fan sticks; give me the pleasure, if you can, of knowing she had no objection to the paper. You will see her to-morrow (a happiness I envy you much more than all your possessions in the skies.) Pray make her a thousand compliments and apologies for my haunting her in the manner I have done, and still intend to do, though I am afraid she will think me as

---

SOURCE: These selections come from the 1809 edition of *A Series of Letters.* [Please note that, according to Lucy Ewart, this is a corrupt text, but there is none other available.]

troublesome as an evil genius, a species of beings she never could be acquainted with before.

Is there no possibility of my conversing with Miss Talbot except in dumb show through my fan sticks? Is she absolutely inaccessible? I cannot long support this playing Pyramus and Thisbe. Must I never hope for a nearer view till I meet her glittering among the stars in a future state of being?

I could dwell on this subject for ever, but must descend from the stars and Miss Talbot, wretch as you are, to you, in the language of mere mortals acquaint you that I left my name at your door this evening. If your conjurorship's worship is not engaged to-morrow in the afternoon, Mrs. Rooke bids me tell you, she desires your company

---

Miss Talbot to Mrs. Carter.

Cuddesden, Sept. 15, 1741.

IF it cost even Miss Carter herself half an hour's study to frame the Introduction to one who she might be sure would receive any thing of her writing with a great deal of pleasure, I will give her leave to imagine that I have been racking my brains for an answer ever since I received it, and then I need make no further excuse for not acknowledging the favor sooner. This really ought to have been the case, and would sound much better than to tell you that I have been engaged at a horse race, or in working a short apron; employments so idle that I am afraid if your expedition to the Goodwin sands had led you to those coral groves you talk of, you would scarce have thought the person who could be pleased with them, worthy your leaving the sea nymphs to come and pay her a visit.

I am sorry to hear you are forgetting your alphabet, and it was something cruel to accompany this bad news with a proof what agreeable use you could make of it, that I might know how to regret it the more. It is certain however, that as you have already made more and better use of it, than most people do in a whole lifetime, you have acquired the privilege to lay it aside whenever you please. Do not think though that this way of reasoning will hold in every thing; the pleasure your acquaintance gave me last winter, was more than my utmost vanity could expect, but this is so far from satisfying me, that I am only more desirous of having it repeated this year, and begin to wish that Kent may not afford you even your favourite amusement of push pin, but force you from mere dullness to return to London, where indeed I greatly want your interest to make up a quarrel which a whole Summer's idleness will give Mr.

Wright too great handle for. To my shame be it spoken, his Letter too is still unanswered, and may probably remain so a good while longer, which is this case I must own to be the height of ingratitude, since it is that poor unanswered Letter of his, which procured me the pleasure of hearing from you, and the opportunity I so gladly lay hold of subscribing myself, dear Miss Carter, &c.

— · —

Mrs. Carter to Miss Talbot.

Deal, Nov. 5, 1741.

INSTEAD of making any apology, Madam, for not sooner acknowledging the favor of your letter, I may with great justice boast of that omission, as a real merit, and a singular instance of mortification and self-denial, but I do not design to enter into a panegyric of my own fortitude, as I think that rather incumbent upon you, as it has so long reprieved you from the trouble of a very insignificant Epistle.

Your wishes have succeeded but too well, for a constant run of success has made me take an utter distate to push pin. I need not tell you after this, that I have one after another quarrelled with all my playthings. My ball and battledores are quite thrown aside, and even my favourite toy a pen has so long lain undisturbed, that it now becomes a novelty to me; and may perhaps divert me for a week, which I dare say you are very sorry to hear, and heartily petition the stars that I may not employ it all that time in tormenting you. But really, Madam, however agreeable this might be to my own inhuman inclinations, you would be under no dread could you guess how extremely I must be puzzled for a subject in these regions of obscurity and uninterrupted dullness; a place where nothing remarkable ever happened since the landing of Julius Caesar, and all that passes ten miles distant, is as absolutely unknown as if it fell out in the country of Prester John; and to sum up all in one word, a place where the name of Miss Talbot is a stranger, and her character would be looked upon as a fiction. *On voit par là, Mademoiselle que la Rennommée (même la votre) a ses bornes, et qu'il y a au monde des coeurs et des esprits qui ne reconnoissent pas votre pouvoir.* People here are not in the least danger of losing their wits about you, but proceed as quietly and as regularly in their affairs as if there was no such person in being. Nobody has been observed to lose their way, run against a door, or sit silent and staring in a room full of company in thinking upon you, except my solitary self, who (as you may perceive in the description) have the advantage of looking half mad when I do not see you, and (as you know by many ocular proofs) extremely silly when I do.

It was quite unnecessary for you to make an apology for your employments, to a person who cannot boast of any thing half so useful; however I cannot help thinking myself mistress of some resolution in observing the advice of my physician, and riding out between four and five every morning, and thus I have very idly passed the whole summer in the care of my health, and the utter neglect of my intellects. The season now confines my exercise to a solitary moonlight walk along the sea shore, which is at present a favourite entertainment with me, as it helps to indulge the melancholy turn of my thoughts by a view of that element which has separated me for ever, from a brother extremely dear to me.

I believe you will have no objection to my returning as soon as possible to these silent amusements; but will be very rejoiced to find that I am going to subscribe myself, dear Miss Talbot, &c.

MRS. CARTER TO MISS TALBOT.

Deal, May 24, four in the morning. [1744]

I HAVE a strong inclination, dear Miss Talbot, to visit you like an apparition at this unseasonable hour, which I may safely indulge as it will do you no harm, for I may talk to you as long as I please, without any danger of disturbing your slumbers, or depriving you of an agreeable dream.

I thought myself infinitely obliged to you for your Letter, though I feel some little scruples about answering one part of it, for as there are but very few people in the world to whom I would so unwillingly appear in a ridiculous light, 'tis very odd I should acquaint you with a folly, which I have had prudence enough to conceal from all the world besides. However if you can have any curiosity about so insignificant a person as I, it will give me pleasure to gratify it, and laugh at me as much as you think proper, if you will laugh by yourself.

The splenetic fit of which you enquire the cause, was occasioned by some apprehensions, that a person for whom I have a great love was going to be married; and as I have read in a book, that people when they marry are dead and buried to all former attachments; I could not think of resigning a friendship which constitutes some of the brightest intervals of my life, without a very severe uneasiness; for to converse with her in the dull, formal, indifferent way of a common acquaintance, was a change I could not think of with any degree of temper. Now you have set me upon the history of my own nonsense, arm yourself with patience, for you must hear it out in all its instances, one of which was, that I might have been freed in a minute from the pain which this groundless suspicion gave me, if I had told her of it; but a certain vile obstinacy which I endeavoured to persuade myself was a laudable pride, prevented my asking her any questions, and I detested the thoughts of getting information by any more indirect means, so unless she had penetration enough to discover my uneasiness, and so much good-nature as to deliver me from it, I should have wrought myself into a firm belief that the affair was quite certain; and by this time you might have heard of my being run wild into a wood, and hopping about from tree to tree like a squirrel, and feeding on nuts and acorns. Whether you will laugh at, or pity me most for this strange delicacy of friendship I cannot tell, but as I have so honestly confessed all my weakness, I hope you will have the charity to give me your advice how to conquer it, against the calamity should, as it will in all probability some time or other, befal me in good earnest.

As I imagine you are by this time in the country, I congratulate you on the fine weather, which is so necessary to make it agreeable. I hope you are perfectly sensible to all the charms of a South West wind, which surely blows from Paradise, and brings with it all the sweets of the garden of Eden. I shall long to hear some account of your rural amusements; for my own part I am at present engaged in a very eager, and I may add a violent pursuit of health. I get up at four, read for an hour, then set forth a walking, and without vanity I may pretend to be one of the best walkers of the age. I had at first engaged three or four poor souls to their sorrow in this ambulatory scheme, and 'tis not to be told the tracts of land we rambled over; but I happen to be much too volatile for my suffering fellow-travellers, who come panting and grumbling at a considerable distance, and labor along like *Christian* climbing up the hill *difficulty,* till at length they quite sink into the *slough of despond.* (Have you ever read "Pilgrim's Progress?") I often divert myself by proposing in the midst of my walk to call at places a dozen miles off, to hear the universal squall they set up, that I intend to be the death of them. Terrible are the descriptions that they give at our return, of the mischiefs occasioned by my impetuous rapidity, though I protest I do not know of any harm I have done, except pulling up a few trees by the roots, carrying off the sails of a windmill, and over-setting half a dozen straggling cottages that stood in my way.

My sister has desired to be excused going with me any more, till she has learnt to fly, and another of our troop sent me word last night she could not possibly venture, as our last walk had absolutely dislocated all her bones; so I have nobody to depend on now but my youngest sister, who is as strong as a little Welch horse; so she trudges after me with great alacrity, and promises never to forsake me if I should walk to the North pole. As we daily improve in the peripatetic way of living, I propose to do myself the pleasure of breakfasting with you some morning in Oxfordshire, from whence I shall proceed to dine with Miss Ward in London, drink tea with Miss Lynch in Canterbury, and dream of you all the same night at Deal.

I don't know what to say to you next, for I am quite weary of talking of myself, unless I entertain you with the sweetly flowing syllables of *Kietlenski, Wilkousti, Lawoyski,* &c. a set of Polish officers who were taken by an English man of war, and brought prisoners here. I have often seen them, for they can find nobody to understand, or converse with them here but my father. 'Tis quite diverting to hear what a confusion of languages there is among them. One talks Latin, another French, a third Polish, a fourth high Dutch, and a fifth something that sounds like no language at all. But what entertained me most, was to hear one of them who is a great disputant, talk for a considerable time about religion in French, to a person who understood not one word of the language, and she making replies and quotations in English, which he understood just as little; so no doubt the discourse tended much to the edification of both. I was going to say a great deal more to you, but luckily my sister came in and told me, whoever I was writing such an unmerciful Letter to, would never have patience to read it; so I e'en follow her admonition, and conclude, &c.

MISS TALBOT TO MRS. CARTER.

Cuddesden, June 27, 1744.

I HOPE you are sensible, my dear Miss Carter, that I have taken due time to consider what consolatory advice I can give you, in case the calamity you seem so apprehensive of should happen, and your un-faithful friend forsake the society of us spinsters. I really know no better expedient than that you should be beforehand with her, since I have always observed that the people who set out upon a journey, are much less affected at parting, than those who stay on in the same situation without any variety of new objects to dispel their melancholy. By this means you will make sure of an inseparable friend, since I have read in a book (David Simple by name) that a real friend is only to be found in that state. If you do not like this scheme, you must turn Roman catholic, and go into a convent, where you may have a whole sisterhood of friends secluded from the rest of the world.

If that project does not suit you, why then, my dear Miss Carter, we must e'en lower our ideas of friendship to the pitch of common life, and be content with loving and esteeming people constantly and affection-ately amid a variety of thwarting, awkward circumstances, that forbid all possibility of spending our lives together. Let people in such a situation be glad that they have known enough of one another to make affection mutual, and then let them resign the complete enjoyment of it, as inconsistent with such a world as this, and accommodate themselves to the perverse changes of a varying life, with as much calmness and philosophy as those changes were perhaps meant to perfect us in.

I have not preached out my thirty minutes yet, have I? Alas! Alas! does not my entering so very deeply and seriously into this subject, look as if I had been a good deal touched with it myself? One of my most favourite, most amiable friends has been married for several years, and I experience that the difference of circumstances make an alteration in the ease and frequency of our seeing one another, which robs me of the gayest, happiest moments I ever enjoyed. But our affection for one another continues the same it ever was; and indeed if ever so many people instead of one had a right to share it with me, I should feel not the least jealousy, as I have no notion of monopolies in friendship; and provided people love me with sincerity, in the moderate degree I deserve, they are welcome to love as many more as they please, and only furnish me with so many more objects of affection. I see her happy, I see her act becomingly in her station, we sometimes lament the distance that it puts between us, but are upon the whole mighty reasonable people, and very well satisfied that every thing should be as it is.

Well but all this while you have never walked over to breakfast with me in your seven league boots that you seem to have borrowed out of the Fairy Tales. As for your sister I'll put a force on my inclinations if she comes along with you, and not admit her; for it would be having no spirit at all not to resent such an injury as she did me, in putting an end to your Letter when you was so well inclined to prolong my entertainment. However upon your intercession I may probably relent, if you promise not to root up any of my beloved elms in your way hither. They furnish me this hot summer with such an agreeable shade, that I should be unpardonable to part with them so easily, even for an hour spent in your company. Beneath their shelter I converse with a variety of authors, and pass away the time in an amusing indolence, beginning my day some two hours later than you do, and living through the whole of it with a dullness of temper, ill suited to those inspiring beauties which summer diffuses all around.

There are times when even the magnificence of the sky, the fair extensions of a flowery lawn, the verdure of the groves, the harmony of rural sounds, and the universal fragrance of the balmy air, strike us with no agreeable sensations,

> "What does of their sweetness those blossoms beguile,
> That meadow, those daisies why do they not smile?"

nothing surely but the ungrateful perverseness of one's own humour. This reflection throws human happiness in a most mortifying light. If these most beautiful, most innocent enjoyments, are so very imperfect, so sadly unsatisfactory, where shall the fugitive be found? There only where it shall no longer be fugitive or uncertain. You see I am in a sermonizing humour, and do what I will I fall into the style every moment. Adieu! I will no longer trust myself with the pen, &c.

MRS. CARTER TO MISS TALBOT.

Deal, Aug. 12, 1752.

MANY thanks, dear Miss Talbot, for that fifth side, which assured me you was quite well. Poor soul, that you should ever be shut up in a room with such racketting people as Con. Philips, and Jack Connor. It was quite inhuman to confine you to such company; and I can never give my consent to your spending another week in Surry, unless you are suffered to walk quietly and soberly through the world with John Bunyan.

You laugh at me for my charity to all kind of people, as some folks laugh at me for my charity to all kind of books, and indeed when people tell me they are not wicked, it is with much difficulty I can believe them so. However I do not look upon this said Teresa Constantia as absolutely a saint, nor even, as a Scotch captain to the great scandal of a friend of mine affirmed to be, *an honour to her sex,* for seriously I think her own account proves her a very bad woman, in more instances than one. Such as she is, I hear she at present keeps a boarding school at Jamaica. An excellent academy for young ladies!

Miss Mulso's* visit was really most delightful, only too short. She has an uncommon exactness of understanding and lively agreeable turn of conversation, and her conduct seems to be governed by the best and noblest principles. You have often heard her described by her friend and your friend, and I am sorry I have no pretensions to say my friend, though we are upon mighty civil terms, and write very handsome postscripts about each other. How truly do you judge of my follies! That doubtful paragraph of your's did really, though I know not why or wherefore, put me into a fright. I had for a moment absolutely forgot that some folks were married, that other folks were galloped away ready to break their necks to look for a wife in some distant country, and there are upon the whole no folks in the world that trouble their heads about me. And it was not till I saw the quiet harmless name of Richardson, that all these comfortable considerations occurred to my thoughts.

I cannot sufficiently thank you for the manner in which you speak of those trifling Letters, which have no other merit than having procured me such a treasure of excellent answers. I have often wondered by what

---

* Later known as Hester Chapone, a well-known Bluestocking. [Ed.]

happy assurance I could venture at first to trouble you with an impertinent Letter. And what obligations have I not to you for the manner in which you treated that Letter, by giving so kind an encouragement as made it a means of introducing me to the acquaintance of a family whose regard I consider as one of the principal advantages of my life; to whose friendship I have been so much obliged; and from whose superior talents and excellent example I have had the means of so much improvement. I always think with gratitude of the obligation I owe Mr. Wright. It was he who first excited my curiosity about you, and kindly contributed all in his power to gratify it, All the expectations which he had raised fell below my own experience: and that realities may sometimes exceed our most lively imagination, is a useful and very pleasing truth on which you so civilly congratulate me, indeed I never have found, nor desire to find any such thing. I know you have been angry with me for this minute or more, but your extreme perverseness drives me to say all this, for why will you not suffer me to enjoy my own opinion about you, considering how dear it is to me, and how harmless to you. All the grave arguments you make use of to prove your own insignificancy, are thrown away upon me, nor is it possible they should convince yourself; but there is perhaps in every human mind some one peculiar whim, some strange oddity by which in some instance or other it contradicts the judgement of all the world besides.

Though I could talk by the hour of Miss Lynch, I know not what intelligence to give you about Mrs. Bargrave, except what I mention with great pleasure, that by all accounts she is very happy. Though I seldom have any information of it from herself; she was never very fond of writing, and is now much more negligent than ever, I do not hear from her once in a half a year.

And now, dear Miss Talbot, I will talk to you about my own happinesses, because I know you will be pleased to hear of them. My father I thank God is in better health and spirits since his return from London than I have known him for years. He has taken a curate, a point we had long been endeavouring to gain, but his great tenderness for the interests of his family made him defer it. My uncle has made him a present of £1000 to enable him to do it without feeling the expence. I could not resist telling you this trait of generosity because I know you will be particularly pleased with it. My uncle has declared he has further intentions for the advantage of the family, for these we feel obliged, but they cannot make any of us half so happy as what he has done for my father's present ease and comfort.

You are very good to warn me about my foolish panics for my pupil, and to prove I endeavour to mend, I shall leave him to go to the races, though I think it more than probable in the midst of the assembly, I shall wish the music over, and be longing to hear him stunning my ears with Greek and Latin.

Miss Talbot to Mrs. Carter.

Lambeth, June 9, 1761.

How good-humoured it was of the weather to change so prettily just for the King's birthday! A fair, cool, mild, cheerful-looking day was just what one wished for. The crowd was without example both at noon and night. I am told that at the ball there was much difficulty in making room even for the King himself, and at noon many of the Royal Family were forced to wait an hour in the street. The finery was prodigious; but, as my mother observes, when one has said gold, silver, and diamonds, one has said all that the subject affords. My own share in the gaieties of the day was painting flowers all the morning, appointing a dance for our folks below stairs, looking in upon them for five minutes, and afterwards watching the blaze of bonfires and the starry rain of rockets from the gallery windows.

The next remarkable of the week was the transit of Venus, to which the day was remarkably favourable. Having no better help than a bit of smoked glass, two or three minutes blinded me sufficiently, nor did I envy Mr. Ford, who had watched it from four o'clock from the roof of his house; however, he came at noon, and insulted me extremely. He made me amends by chusing two *gowns* for me, I assure you! Your pretty butter-cup yellow for a night-gown, and a pretty checked blue and white for a negligée, and they are actually at the mantuamaker's; so that grand point is at last decided, which gives me hopes that in time the Augsburg preliminaries may be settled too.

I have never seen Mrs. Montagu since you went; however, I have heard of her from Emin and Dr. Monsey, who speak well of her looks, and also of her wisdom, for she kept out of the birth-day crowd. By the help of these two worthies I supplied Mrs. Mackenzie with gallery tickets for the ball. Did you ever chance to see Orinda's Letters? They are rather stiff, but seem to have an air of genuineness—and were not printed for Curl, but Lintot. Tell me any thing you recollect of Mrs. Catherine Phillips. I have a notion that for a romantic women she was a good woman. But my dear Mr. Hanway has published two volumes at last, which you saw, and only told me you had seen them, but for which I love and honour him (and so far as spending thirty hours upon them I believe I shall also *obey* him) as much as the worlds, and the wits, and the critics will, I suppose, despise him. Indeed *that is* a good man. Not that I would have licensed every word in his book neither, but the whole delights me.

Emin is happy in having been introduced to Lord Bath. Will you take a trip with him into Russia if he should chance to go that way this year? He is admirable this year. I wish you had staid to have seen more of him.

---------------------·---------------------

MRS. CARTER TO MISS TALBOT

Deal, June 13, 1761.

I AM glad you were so prettily entertained on the birth-day. We had squibs and rockets, bonfires and sociables, and music parties here too, which I meant to have shared in, but found the task too much for me, so quietly slunk to my pillow.

It was well for you astronomers in London and Lambeth that the day was less cloudy on the 6th than it was with us, for the sun never once shewed his face till Venus had finished her journey over him, and we concluded that the honour of seeing this fine phenomenon was still reserved entire to Mr. Horrox and his friend Mr. Crabtree, but it seems you and Mr. Ford have robbed them of this exclusive privilege.

I find by the news, that Mrs. Talbot was mistaken in reducing all the finery of the birth-day to gold, silver, and diamonds, as some of the gentlemen—pretty creatures! were trimmed with point and blond lace. Pray had any of the ladies swords and bag wigs?

I never had the least doubt but Mrs. Phillip's Letters to Sir Charles Cotterel were genuine; it is so long since I met with them that I remember very little what they were. All that I recollect of her poetry is, that it is very moral and sentimental; and all that I know of herself is, that her genius and character are mentioned with the highest respect, admiration, and reverence by the writers of that time. I believe her Poems are very scarce; I have two or three little pieces in a miscellany, which if you have any curiosity to see I will send you. I never saw Mr. Hanway's two volumes but in an advertisement, nor do I know what they are about, but am glad they have afforded you an agreeable amusement.

We have been in some bustle here since I writ last. Sir P. Brett is gone on board of ship, the Captains are ordered not to lie on shore, and Lady Brett is gone from here pretty suddenly. It is certain the French have drawn soldiers together at Boulogne, &c. but the wise people seem to think it is rather from an apprehension about their own coast than any design of invading our's; however, it is perfectly right to watch their motions.

I have just now received a parcel of Sermons, which I imagine his Grace would have me disperse. I wish they may be of use, but if either preaching or example in this particular could have influenced the people of this place, they have not wanted either. It is strange Mr. Franklyn should have said nothing to the purchasers of things gotten by this wicked rapine. They seem to be at least equally guilty with the first robbers; perhaps more so, if one considers that the last have often the temptation of extreme poverty, and the others most commonly have not.

MISS TALBOT TO MRS. CARTER.
(Vol. III)

Lambeth, Aug. 11, 1763.

I fear, dear Miss Carter, you will be gone from Spa before this Letter arrives there; however, it will overtake you in some part of your tour. When I received your last paquet I had the satisfaction of knowing I had a Letter and Note on the road to you, besides a million of remembrances sent by Mr. Arden. But after all, could you find in your heart to leave l'amiable Baronne Allemande? I wish sincerely you could find out that Bath waters were better for her nerves than Spa, (I had still rather you could in conscience recommend the Dog and Duck, just by us,) and bring her over to England with you. The description you give of her has had such effects as would make Mrs. Montagu,* amid all her flaunting with Altesses, pale with envy. Such a conquest has Madame la Baronne made at so many hundred miles distance, as even her own humility would be proud of. We shall scarce forgive you if you leave Spa before she does, and not even then, if you do not settle a Correspondence with her; nay, I do not know whether I shall be quite satisfied with your taste, if you do not espouse some German Baron, in order to pass the remainder of your days in her neighbourhood. Do tell me what part of Germany she adorns. I have but two German friends, and for their sakes, because they are good girls, I wish them acquainted with her. You have not so much told me her name, nor whether she has a Baron or is an *aimable veuve.* I am impatient for another Letter—and how peevish shall I be if you are gone away from Spa, and write to me only about fine houses and prospects. But write about what you will, your Letters make me vastly important, *et c'est a qui les aura le premier.* As for Mrs. Montagu's, it would have heightened my importance beyond imagination, but in this point I was extremely honourable, resisted an almost irresistible temptation (for I actually did not shew it to Lord Hardwicke, who came hither just as I had received the paquet, and would have been peculiarly worthy of the confidence) and by the very next Post sent it away to Mrs. Vesey.

---

* Elizabeth Robinson Montagu, Queen of the Bluestockings [Ed.]

Aug. 10. What heads and hearts folks have at Spa! I have just received your's of the 31st, in which you talk to me of a belle Hollandoise and a Chanoinesse angelique, for neither of whom do I care, and say no more of la Baronne than if no such amiable being existed. I begin to suspect this is really the case, and that she is only *un etre d'imagination,* whom you dreamt of on the inspiring brink of the Geronstere spring. The Archbishop says, No, you are only fallen in love with another woman, and the first is forgot. A pretty gentleman you will come home indeed, *fi volage!* But my mother, who loves variety, applauds you extremely for writing no more on one subject. 'Tis surely impossible that with so many French airs fresh imported (for Germany being by your account frenchified, I know nothing that can sober you, except you return through Holland,) 'tis impossible you can think of rusticating for some months on the Kentish coast. Take my advice, come directly to London, and play off all your coquetteries and minauderies for one week that we may see them in perfection; then go to Deal, and grow domestic again, and return in spring just such as you used to be. That being beyond sea, and having once trod on French ground, you should come back without seeing Paris, is to me astonishing; or that being so apparelled as Mrs. Montagu describes, you should bear the thoughts of not being seen at Paris, is most exemplary. Too many English are there already, and French hotels are actually advertised in our newspapers.

If Princess Esterhasi saw two ladies I have in my head at this minute as samples of English women, I do not wonder at her impatience to be introduced to the rest; but let her never come over, that she may never be undeceived. Dr. Monsey has twice exhibited himself here, and seems tolerably well. If newspapers reach Spa, you will have been hurt at seeing the Archbishop mentioned in them as confined with a fit of the gravel. It was, I thank God, tolerably short and favourable, and he was quite well and riding out again before the newspapers made him ill. Two days' anxiety disagreed both with my mother and myself, but we are quite well again. No other event has varied our quiet life here, but the agreeable one of having had Mr. Berkeley with us for a few days; a friend that, whether in cheerful or melancholy hours, is always welcome, always useful; indeed I know no one of his years that is in any degree comparable with him; yet, formed for the most important stations, he seems fated to live in a cottage, which makes me peculiarly peevish just now, for that cottage is surrounded by the small-pox, so much to be apprehended for his wife and son. Pray thank Mrs. Montagu very much for permitting me to see your true character. I hope for a second part, as she who has so exquisitely described your preparations ought also to inform us what conquests they have made. I long also for a Letter from Cologne, because I have no notion what to expect or what motive carries you thither. May good angels guard you through all your Journeys!

Miss Talbot to Mrs. Carter.

Lambeth, Nov. 28, 1763.

I HAVE long owed you my thanks, dear Miss Carter, for enclosing to me that sweet melancholy sonnet,* which as you kindly sent me in confidence I have shewn to no one but my mother. I wish you would grant me an exception for Lady Margaret, as I know it would please her, and she peculiarly at present needs every little help. I have not seen her this long long while, for she is still at Northend, and comes to Grosvenor Square every morning. The Dean of Lincoln and her beloved sister in law are still with her, but I fear this long anxious suspence will do away all the good effects of Tunbridge. For several days past Lord Hardwicke has had few alarming symptoms, but every day diminishes his strength, and gives more fears than hopes: those who attend him hope still, and I sometimes flatter myself that so valuable a life will still be spared to a country which so much wants such a true friend as he has always been to it. All you say of him is most perfectly just. Had he been taken off by a sudden stroke, one should have felt the shock severely; yet there is something peculiarly painful in the thought of such a one lying ill and inactive so long; though as I hope and dare say he makes the right and best improvement of these first tedious hours he ever knew, this is probably best for him, as well as for those nearest friends who by alternate hopes and fears are thus gradually weaned from the happiness to which they have been so long accustomed.

Thank God my spirits and my health are so good that I can now take a solitary walk in the long gallery with a single candle, and be almost as much pleased with my reveries as I used to be in a walk of the same kind at Cuddesden; only from the various avocations of this house I have not time to indulge it near so long. This *capability*, however, of being pleased again with a lonely winter evening walk I reckon a very good sign, as I could never attain to it here till this year. I propose still more pleasure in walking there with you early in spring, during the time that (remember you are engaged) you spend with us in your way to town. I believe I shall never find the time to put on your ornaments; for I do not foresee one dinner or one evening party, but I will dress *a quatre epingles* to receive you.

I have been often in town but seen very few persons, except Lady Grey,

---

* Probably those verses first printed in the quarto edition of Mrs. Carter's Poems, which begin, "While pensive memory." They were on the death of Miss Louisa Poyntz.

Mrs. J. Yorke who is a very amiable woman, and Mrs. Mackenzie. Lady Robert lies in, and Lord Robert is just getting out of a fit of the gout. My mother and I were much pleased the other day with a new and volunteer visitor whom it seems you knew somewhat of at the Hague. I know not what was her name, but you saw her at Count Bentinck's whose youngest son she has since married, and is come over with him. The message you was so good as to leave with her for Mademoiselle Bercel has produced for me from her the kindest of all polite Letters, which indeed gave me great pleasure, as I had quite taken an affection for her, and took it for granted she had quite forgot me, as well she might. The only thing I dislike in this Letter is the necessity of answering it, for my aversion to writing (except to you and one or two more) continues as strong as ever.

This morning I have been much delighted with hearing the praises of your friend Miss Bouverie: it makes one feel quite rich to know that there are such characters in the world, and that they have a power of doing good in some degree proportionable to their will. One had need have some comfort of this sort, considering how frequently one has occasion to groan over characters that disgrace a country which as yet calls itself Christian.—How long it will do so I know not, since I find the author of the most exercrable performance that ever saw the sun is still popular, not only amongst the mob, but even amongst the sober citizens. I have been reading French books lately that represent us as a nation of infidels. The specimens we most commonly send abroad, and the books they most commonly get from hence, give too much colour to this most injurious and abominable opinion.

Charles Poyntz dined here yesterday, he is quite plump. He has been at Bruxelles where Mrs. Poyntz, who, he says, is excessively well, spends the winter with her grand-daughter. He says it is a very agreeable place to live in, though merely passing through it appeared to you so uncomfortable. Miss Bishop the maid of honour is to marry Sir George (Lovelace) Warren. Shall I send your subscription copy of the *Messiah*, or keep it till you come? I admire many things in it extremely, but am grievously hurt and disappointed at many more. I wish Dr. Young had been the translator, and I the correctress. Nancy Richardson is not married nor likely to be—The paragraph in the news belonged to some other Miss Richardson.

MRS. CARTER TO MISS TALBOT.

Deal, Dec. 5, 1763.

I HAVE not the least objection, my dear Miss Talbot, to your shewing the verses* to Lady Margaret, as she will not be likely to talk about them, which I believe you would think not to be proper, as Mrs. Poyntz would not venture to shew them to Lady Spencer: and yet if they are capable of producing any effect, I think it is not such a one as would have done her hurt. I am obliged to you for mentioning my Lord Hardwicke's health, about which nobody I believe who has the honour of being personally acquainted with him is more solicitious, and I watch every newspaper for an account of him. That diminution of strength does not denote a recovering state: but we will hope a good constitution will at last bring him well through this attack. Never indeed did the blessing of such a life appear to be more necessary to the public than at present.

I shall be happy in your admitting me to partake your walks in the long gallery; your reveries you will then I hope communicate. Indeed I do remember I am engaged to you in my way to town, and should have been exceedingly mortified if you had forgot it. I hope to be there early in next month, but cannot exactly fix the day, as my sister is from home, and does not return till Friday.

I think you will be pleased with Madame Bentinck; she was married before we were at the Hague. I shall wait on her as soon as I get to town, and if you should see her, I beg you will be so good as to make my compliments to her: upon condition, however, that no such evil consequences may arise therefrom as followed my exact discharge of your commission to Mademoiselle Bercel. To be sure in all equity I ought to take the burden of one half of your answer to her Letter, as one half of my diligence arose from the vanity of talking about you.

As you love great objects, I think you must have taken a view of the river last Friday, as I did of the sea which was extremely sublime. The tide was amazingly high here, especially as it was not arrived to the spring. If it had, I know not whether all the buildings on the beach might not have been utterly demolished. The damage even now is computed at about £500; several ships were driven from their anchors, but I don't hear that any were lost. The house in which we lived last year has been greatly damaged: this in which we are at present is farther from the sea, and has

---

* The verses were probably those first printed in the quarto edition of Mrs. Carter's poems, beginning "While pensive memory—," on the death of Miss Louisa Poyntz.

suffered no other inconvenience than having every thing set a swimming about the cellar. The violence of the tide was the more remarkable, as the wind, though pretty high, could not be called a storm. I believe it must have been much stronger in London, for I have not heard of any mischief done here by land. My sister was on her journey home that day, and as she came through Stroud, boats were rowing along the streets. She longed exceedingly to get into one of them, as a safer voiture than the coach. She was in more danger in walking from my uncle's to the machine, from the falling of tiles and chimneys; and it was happy for me that I knew nothing of the storm there, till after I saw her, thank God, safely arrived through it.

I will not trouble you to send me Klopstock's poem,* as I hope so soon to come and fetch it; I enquired the character of it amongst the Germans, and they talked of it, as in general absolutely unintelligible. Did not I subscribe for two copies? Be so good as to pay the second for me, and trust me till I see you.

Your French books, which represent us as a nation of infidels, ought at the same time to own how much theirs contribute to make us so; I am told that whenever any of our young men go to Paris, the pert halfthinkers there, who are dignified with the title of Philosophers (helas la pauvre philosophie) seize on them, and stuff their poor empty heads with their detestable notions.

Have you read Mrs. Macauley's history? I have seen only some extracts from it, which seemed to be writ with strength and spirit. As Sir George Lovelace is provided with one maid of honour, it is to be hoped Captain Grosvenor's merits will entitle him to another.

Mrs. Carter to Miss Talbot.

Clarges Street, Feb. 3, 1764.

TWO days of sunshine were particularly chearing to me, my dear Miss Talbot, from the hope that they enlivened your journey to Canterbury, where I long to hear that you were safely arrived before the return of disheartening weather last night. I hope the Kentish roads afforded Mrs. Talbot no opportunity of walking into the middle of the coach. As I trust all your apprehensions and fatigues of the journey are by this time happily over, I rejoice to think on the cordial which I am sure your arrival must convey to his Grace, and which notwithstanding all your scruples, I am persuaded he took without making one wry face.

---

* The Messiah, mentioned before.

I dined yesterday with Mrs. Montagu, with Lord Bath, Lord Lyttelton and Sir James Macdonald. I know not whether I ever mentioned to you this very extraordinary young man.—He is not twenty-one, yet has an understanding so formed, and such variety of knowledge as is really astonishing. His manners are pleasing, and he does not discover the least degree of pertness or presumption. He is sovereign of the Isle of Skey, which he has formed a scheme to improve and civilize. That he may the better carry his point, he has set himself to learn the Erse language, which he understands perfectly well. This gave me an opportunity of asking some questions about the translation of Ossian, which Sir James affirmed to be inferior to the original. I asked if Mr. Macpherson had not made some embellishments in the epithets; but this he absolutely denied. . . .

Mrs. Carter to Miss Talbot.

Clarges Street, Feb. 6, 1764.

I AM delighted, my dear Miss Talbot, to find you arrived so safe and well at Canterbury, and that his Grace is better. I think I have not picked up any intelligence for you in my travels through the cities of London and Westminster, since I wrote last. I would fain take advantage of your absence and be very civil to the rest of the world, but it rains so perpetually, and the streets are so impracticable that I cannot walk. However my comfort is, that I shall not long be under the necessity of either staying at home, or being draggled to the neck in dirty streets. The bon ton at Paris is *furieusement* to have every thing *a la Grecque.* It must necessarily be the ton in London too, and as no fine gentlemen can be happy without a wife a la Grecque, I expect soon to have my choice of the most splendid parties; for though I am not Minerva, I may make my fortune very prettily as her owl. Only think what a number of duels will be fought about me, and how many targets battered into cullenders! When I have enjoyed the triumph of a few dozens of these rencontres, I propose before the fashion varies to take the richest survivor, flourish down to breakfast with you in a post chaise and six, and return to town time enough for the opera.

Mr. Wilkes's post chaise and two servants landed at Deal last week; one of his servants said that his master's wound was perfectly healed. I lately heard that Churchill, within two years, has got £3500. by his ribbald scribbling. Happy age of virtue and genius, in which Wilkes is a patriot, and Churchill a poet! I have just heard that there was a squabble yesterday in the House of Commons. Sir Wm. Meredith made a motion, that the warrants for apprehending Wilkes should be laid before the House. He was seconded by Sir G. Saville: opposed by Mr. Grenville and the Attorney General. Mr. Conway and Lord G. Sackville spoke particularly well. In some minority motion which was unexpected, your Bristol friend *l'amiable scelerat,* sent in all haste to a neighbouring tavern to enquire whether there were any members, and to desire they would come to the House. There did happen to be two who came immediately, and they were both of the minority.

Feb. 9.

Two days head-ache must account for the delay of this, and for not having yet heard that the yatches are arrived any where. During the supper at Witham the Princess appeared out of spirits, on which the Prince said, "Eh qu'avez vous dont ma chére princesse? est ce que vous manquez vos *gardes.* Nous sommes tous egaux ici. Mais consolez vous, quand vous serez a B. vous en aurez." The Princess laughed and grew very cheerful. I think I have repeated the words exactly as I heard them: and I have some reason to think they were really spoken. Various and very ingenious have been the political inventions of every day. The minority to have a fair pretence for hanging the ministry, have sunk the yatch and drowned the Prince and Princess. The majority on their side, have choaked the Duke of C. by fat and a dropsy. I hope it is as certain that the Prince, &c. are safely landed in spite of being drowned, as that the Duke rode out after he was killed. From the H. of C. to the basket women in St. James's market is no such fall as will hazard one's neck. These ladies have been most intemperately vociferous in their wishes, that all who sent the Prince and Princess away in such weather were in their places. The Marriage Act is to be examined by a Committee of the whole House on Wednesday. I have this moment heard the good news that the yatches are arrived at Helvoet, one of them sprung a mast. I have now told you all the news of every sort I can collect, so adieu. I go on piano piano with my history of the Incas.

MRS. CARTER TO MRS. VESEY.

Clarges Street, Jan. 15, 1770.

YOU will be so kindly solicitous about me, my dear Mrs. Vesey, when you see in the papers a confirmation of the reality of my apprehensions about my dear Miss Talbot, that I cannot forbear writing you some account of myself. I am tolerably well, and my spirits, though low, are very composed. With the deepest feeling of my own unspeakable loss of one of the dearest and most invaluable blessings of my life, I am to the highest degree thankful to the Divine goodness for removing her from the multiplied and aggravated sufferings, which in a longer struggle with such a distemper, must probably have been unavoidable. The calm and peaceful sorrow of tenderness and affection, sweetly alleviated by the joyful assurance of her happiness, is a delightful sentiment compared with what I have suffered for these last two or three months.

Two or three days before her death she was seized with a sudden hoarseness and cough, which seemed the effect of a cold, and from which bleeding relieved her; but there remained an oppression from phlegm which was extremely troublesome to her. On the ninth this symptom increased, and she appeared heavy and sleepy, which was attributed to an opiate the night before. I staid with her till she went to bed, with an intention of going afterwards into her room, but was told she was asleep. I went away about nine, and in less than an hour afterwards she waked; and after the struggle of scarcely a minute, it pleased God to remove her spotless soul from its mortal sufferings to that heaven for which her whole life had been an uninterrupted preparation. Never surely was there a more perfect pattern of evangelical goodness, decorated by all the ornaments of a highly improved understanding, and recommended by a sweetness of temper, and an elegance and politeness of manners, of a peculiar and more engaging kind than in any other character I ever knew.

I am just returned from seeing all that was mortal of my angelic friend deposited in the earth. I do not mean that I went in ceremony, which, had it been proper, would have been too strong a trial for my spirits, but privately with two other of her intimate friends. I felt it would be a comfort to me, on that most solemn occasion, to thank Almighty God for delivering her from her sufferings, and to implore his assistance to prepare me to follow her. Little, alas! infinitely too little, have I yet profited by the blessing of such an example. God grant that her memory, which I hope will ever survive in my heart, may produce a happier effect.

Adieu, my dear friend, God bless you, and conduct us both to that happy assembly, where the spirits of the just shall dread no future separation! And may we both remember that awful truth, that we can hope to die the death of the righteous only by resembling their lives.

PRIMARY SOURCES

Letters from Mrs. Elizabeth Carter, to Mrs. Montagu, between the Years 1755 and 1800, Chiefly upon Literary and Moral Subjects. Edited by Montagu Pennington. 3 vols. London: F. C. and J. Rivington, 1817.

Memoirs of the Life of Mrs. Elizabeth Carter. Edited by Montagu Pennington. London, 1807.

A Series of Letters between Mrs. Elizabeth Carter and Miss Catherine Talbot from the year 1741 to 1770, to which are added, letters from Mrs. Elizabeth Carter to Mrs. Vesey, between the years 1763 and 1787. Edited by Montagu Pennington. 4 vols. London: F. C. and J. Rivington, 1809.

RELATED SOURCES

Doran, Dr. *A Lady of the Last Century (Mrs. Elizabeth Montagu).* London: Richard Bentley & Sons, 1873.

Faderman, Lillian. *Surpassing the Love of Men: Romantic Friendship and Love Between Women from The Renaissance to the Present.* New York: William Morrow & Co., 1981.

Johnson, Reginald Brimley, ed. *Bluestocking Letters.* London and New York: John Lane, 1926.

Scott, Walter Sidney. *The Bluestocking Ladies.* London: John Green, 1947.

Williamson, Marilyn L. "Who's Afraid of Mrs. Barbauld? The Bluestocking and Feminism." *International Journal of Women's Studies* 3, 1 (1980): 89–102.

Mary Scott (Taylor)
1752?–1793

Mary Scott was born around 1752 and lived for some time at Milborne Port in Somerset, West England, where her father was a linen merchant. Her mother's participation in charitable enterprises is attested to by her obituary in *The Gentleman's Magazine* (1787). The Scotts also had a son Russell, who was the Unitarian Minister at Portsmouth from 1788 to 1833.

Around 1774 Mary Scott met John Taylor when he was a student at Daventry Academy, a Unitarian establishment, in Coventry, North England. Their courtship lasted for fourteen years because Scott "would not marry during the life of her aged mother." The reason for her mother's objection is unknown. It seems unlikely that Mary Scott's parents disapproved of the match for religious reasons since their son was also a Unitarian.

According to a later letter (February 1789), Mary Scott's mother expired in October 1787 in her daughter's arms. Another letter dated two months later tells of Scott's father's death on April 13, 1788. The writer Anna Seward sympathizes with her old friend Mary Scott in her loss. The year after the death of Scott's mother, John Taylor "migrated to the south, and became Minister of the chapel of Ilminster in Somersetshire." The couple married that year.

Seward's letter before the impending marriage—she referred to Scott as about to "resign that name"—expressed regret that Scott's "health has doubtless suffered much from the conflicts you endured." The letter also suggested that John Taylor's anger apparently raised doubts in Scott's mind about her future happiness. Seward further mentioned that Scott has been writing *The Messiah,* a religious poem which was shortly to be published. On February 3, 1789, Seward responded to Scott's worries about the early part of her difficult confinement. She attempted to cheer her friend by complimenting her on her luck in "living in the mansion in which that dear fascinating enthusiastic saint, Mrs. Rowe, once inhabited" [Elizabeth Singer Rowe, the Dissenter Poet]. Scott gave birth to a daughter, Mary Ann, on the 25th of February, 1789, in the town of Milborne Port, Somerset. From this it appears that the couple temporarily lived in the town (perhaps in the home) where Scott had lived with her parents. By January 1790, Mary Scott described "the sweetness of material happiness" to Seward. She praised Seward's sonnet in *The Gentleman's Magazine* and disagreed with Helen Maria Williams's choice of meter in her poem on the slave trade. At the end of this particularly long letter, Seward referred to the length of their friendship, intimating that it probably began in Lichfield where Seward lived in 1770: "Through twenty summers ripening in my heart."

By the following year, the Scott Taylor family of three had moved to Ilminster, Somerset, for the birth of a son, John Edward Taylor, was recorded in the Bristol and Somerset Registers on the 11th of January, 1791. No occupations were entered in the register for either parent.

An ominous letter of July 29, 1792, from Anna Seward in response to one from Mary Scott hinted at the misfortunes that precipitated Scott's death the following year: "We have each had long and painful experience of sickness and of sorrow," confided Seward, "since the year commenced; but you are at present blest with two fine children. I trust they will live to repay you yet more and more for the increase of pain and debility which their birth and infant nurture cost you." She went on in a new paragraph to respond to Scott's anxieties about her husband, who apparently had renounced "rationality as the guide of faith and allowed no test of truth but inward feeling and imaginary inspiration." Equating poetry with vice, he disapproved of creativity, causing Mary Scott severe emotional and psychological deprivation in addition to her physical ailments.

The Bristol and Somerset Register of Burials records that Mary Taylor died June 5, 1793, aged 41, that she had been resident at Somerset and James's Parish, Bristol, that she was buried on the 19th of June 1793, at Fryars.

Very little else is known of Mary Scott (Taylor). In the Huntington-Library edition of *The Female Advocate,* someone has inserted in the preface and poem the name of Anna Steele, the poet and daughter of a dissenting Baptist minister from Broughton, Hants, from which it appears that Steele was the dedicatee to *The Female Advocate* and a close friend of Mary Scott.

This poem confirms that Mary Scott is one of the first female writers in English in any genre to attempt a female-lauding poem, which constructs, with the aid of copious, factually informative footnotes and an attack on women's cultural exclusion, a somewhat systematic history of notable women. She saw her work as a response or complement to mid-century pro-women works by John Duncombe and George Ballard. Scott also displayed her affiliations with the nonconformist tradition and abolitionist sentiment, not simply by selecting women connected exclusively to the Protestant tradition, but also by including Phillis Wheatley, of African birth, who wrote poems in Boston after being bought, shipped, and sold by slavetraders, and by her discussing approvingly with Anna

Seward an antislavery poem by Seward's friend, the radical Helen Maria Williams. Although she remains something of a mystery, Scott's importance as a feminist polemicist in *The Female Advocate* is becoming more fully recognized and respected.

FROM

THE FEMALE ADVOCATE

Now, big with storms, rough winter issues forth
From the cold bosom of his parent North;
Now, scarce a flow'ret rears its beauteous head
Above the surface of its native bed;
Stripp'd of its foliage, the late verdant grove,
No more invites my devious feet to rove:
How shall I soothe the anguish of a heart,
Yet bleeding from affliction's poignant dart?
A heart that long, alas, hath ceas'd to glow,
Dead to each hope of happiness below!
Propitious come, ye fair AONIAN maids,
And guide a wanderer to your hallow'd shades;
O, wrap me in your solitary cells
Where Silence reigns, and Inspiration dwells!
For once this tasteless apathy controul,
And wake each sprightly passion of my soul.

But say what theme shall sportive Fancy chuse,
Since nature's charms no more delight the Muse?
What theme! and can it then a doubt remain
What theme demands the tributary strain,
Whilst LORDLY MAN asserts his right divine,
Alone to bow at wisdom's sacred shrine;
With tyrant sway would keep the female mind
In error's cheerless dark abyss confin'd?
Tell what bright daughters *Britain* once could boast,
What daughters now adorn *Her* happy coast.

In ages past, when learning's feeble ray
First shone prophetic of a brighter day,
The female bosom caught the sacred flame,
And on her eagle-pinion soar'd to fame.

Emerging from the gloom of mental night,
Illustrious PARR* first rose divinely bright,
An instrument in Heav'n's o'er-ruling hand,
To succour truth, and bless a guilty land,
The rage of superstition to controul,
And chase the mists of error from the soul.

    Next beauteous *Dudley*† rose to grace the stage,
The pride and wonder of her sex and age!
Low bending at the radiant shrine of truth,
Her soul renounc'd the idle toys of youth:
Impell'd by nobler fires, she boldly soar'd,
And every science, every art explor'd:
Religion in its purest form array'd,
Her tongue, her manners, and her pen‡ display'd.
Rais'd to the splendid burden of a crown,
But soon compell'd to lay that burden down,
Torn sudden from a husband, from a throne,
'Twas then the heroine, then the Christian shone!
Her steady soul fate's fiercest frown could brave,
Secure of lasting bliss beyond the grave!

    O Faith, whose sacred transports never cloy,
Sweet prelibation of immortal joy!

---

    * Catherine Parr, daughter of Sir Thomas Parr of Kendall, and the sixth and last wife of King Henry VIII. She enjoyed the advantages of a liberal education, and was a woman of great sense, singular prudence, and a most strenuous friend to the reformation; which she studied to promote to the extent of her power. She frequently argued with the King on the subject of Religion, and urged him, as he had already separated from the See of Rome, to accomplish the glorious work he had begun; and thoroughly to refine the Church from the remains of superstition that still contaminated it. Impatient as Henry was of controul, such was his opinion of her worth, and such the affection he bore to her person, that he seldom betrayed the least indications of disgust at her freedom. She was very assiduous in studying the Sacred Writings, and books of Divinity, and occasionally had Sermons preached to herself, and such of the ladies of her bedchamber as chose to be present, by several eminent Protestant divines, whom she retained in the character of Chaplains: for she dared to be the patroness of truth at a time when its professors were exposed to the utmost danger: After her death a discourse of her's, found amongst her papers, was published, intituled, Queen Catharine Parr's Lamentations of a Sinner, bewailing the Ignorance of her blind Life.

    † Lady Jane Grey, wife to Lord Guildford Dudley. Her virtues, learning, and sufferings, are so well known, that it would be impertinent to particularize them.

    ‡ See her letter to Mr. Harding, her Father's Chaplain, after his renunciation of the Protestant faith; and letters to her father and sister, in the 3d vol. of Fox's Ecclesiastical History.

What proud Philosophy but aims to preach,
'Tis thine with energy divine to teach:
Inspir'd by thee, we learn to smile at pain,
And all the vanities of life disdain;
Can calmly meet the sudden stroke of fate,
Or wait, if Heav'n approves, a longer date;
Convinc'd, howe'er Eternal Truth decides,
A parent's love still o'er our weal presides.
And THOU, with nature's noblest gifts endu'd,
(Whom rival Kings with eyes of envy view'd,)
ELIZA!* Britain's ever-fav'rite name,
How vain the Muse's wish to speak thy fame!

Long, hid beneath the specious mask of zeal,
Had bigot rage destroy'd the public weal;
Red with the blood of martyr'd saints, the land
Implor'd relief from Heav'ns' benignant hand:
Heav'n heard her cries, beheld her flowing tears,
And sent ELIZA to avert her fears;
Again, Religion rear'd her radiant head,
And all around her sacred influence spread.
To wisdom early train'd by adverse fate,
ELIZA knew to guide the helm of state;
'TWAS HER'S to check the haughty power of Spain,
And faction strove against her life in vain.
Studious by each endearing art to prove,
HER conduct worthy of HER peoples' love,
Yet would SHE from those glorious cares descend,
And with the Muse* HER vacant moments spend:
Well spoke HER verse HER great undaunted soul,
Which, form'd for empire, scorn'd to brook controul.

MORES, SEYMOURS, COKES,† a bright assemblage shone,
And shar'd the palm man fondly thought his own.

---

* Queen Elizabeth

† The ingenious Dr. Percy, in his Reliques of antient English Poetry, hath obliged the world with two or three Poems written by Queen Elizabeth.

‡ Three daughters of Sir Thomas More, Margaret, Elizabeth and Cicely; all women of great talents and learning: But Margaret (wife to Mr. Roper of Eltham in Kent) seems to have been the most distinguished. She was a perfect mistress of the Greek and Latin tongues. She wrote two Latin Orations; and a Treatise of the Four Last Things, with so much fervor of devotion, and strength of reasoning, that her father declared it to be a better performance, than a discourse of the same nature written by himself. She also well understood Musick and Mathe-

See, bending o'er *Newcastle's** sacred urn,
The Muses sigh, and drooping Fancy mourn!
For well *She* knew on vent'rous wing to soar,
And trace her fair ideal regions o'er.
Oh, had *She* liv'd in this more polish'd age,
And judgment rein'd imagination's rage,
What magic songs our raptur'd ears had blest!
Our passions rouz'd, or sooth'd them all to rest.

In thee, illustrious *Killegrew,*† we find
The Poet's and the Painter's arts combin'd:

---

matics, and was complimented by the greatest men of the age, on account of her learning and accomplishments. She had a daughter little inferior to herself in Genius and Learning, who translated into English part of a Latin work of her grandfather; and also Eusebius's Ecclesiastical History, out of Greek into Latin. See the Life of Sir Thomas More in the second Vol. of British Biography.

Three daughters of Edward Seymour Duke of Somerset; uncle, and Protector of King Edward VI. who were also greatly celebrated for their learning and genius.

Five daughters of Sir Anthony Coke, tutor to King Edward VI. who were famous for their knowledge in the learned languages. Ann the eldest was married to Sir Nicholas, and mother of the great Lord Bacon. She translated Bishop Jewel's Apology for the Church of England out of Latin into English; and sent a copy of her translation to the Bishop for his perusal accompanied with a letter written in Greek; who returned her an answer in the same language, and declared it was so correct, that it needed not the least amendment. It was published in 1564, by the particular direction of Archbishop Parker. See the life of Sir Nicholas Bacon in the third Vol. of British Biography.

Among the above-mentioned illustrious ornaments of that age, may be ranked Lady Catharine Grey, sister of Lady Jane Grey, who is also said to have been a woman of considerable learning; and the Countess of Pembroke sister to the famous Sir Philip Sidney: A woman of fine accomplishments, and a great patroness of polite literature.

How unfashionable soever such a maxim may be in our days, it seems to have been a received one by the ladies in that aera, that virtue and learning were the greatest ornaments of a woman!

* Margaret Dutchess of Newcastle was the youngest daughter of Sir Charles Lucas, and born in the reign of King James I. She is said to have uncovered even from her infancy a very strong propensity to poetry and every kind of polite literature. The uncommon turn of many of her compositions, shews her to have been possessed of a luxuriant imagination. In 1643, she was made one of the Maids of Honour to Henrietta, consort to King Charles I. And when that Princess left England, this Lady attended her to France; where she met with the Marquis of Newcastle, to whom she was married during her residence there. She died in 1673.

† Mrs. Ann Killegrew, daughter of Henry Killegrew (one of the Prebendaries of Westminster) was born a short time before the restoration of King Charles II. Her naturally fine genius being improved by a polite education, she made a great

'Twas thine, O all-accomplish'd maid, to charm
Each breast that Virtue, or that Wit could warm:
Though early lost to earth, thy favor'd name
In *Dryden's* verse shall boast immortal fame.
O dire disease! what havock hast thou made!
What crouds convey'd to death's impervious shade!
By thee our fair *Orinda* * too expir'd,
Lov'd by the Muses, by the world admir'd!
(And thou, my *Celia,* in life's gayest bloom
Felt'st its dread stroke, and met an early tomb:
Listless I touch the long-neglected lyre,
Now thy dear name has ceas'd my songs t'inspire.
No more shall Fancy's glowing page delight,
Or Art's proud trophies charm my aching sight,
Still the keen pangs of parting rend my breast,
And rob my days of peace, my nights of rest!)
Yet still convinc'd that providence is just,
She made its arm her unabating trust;
Saw lenient mercy blend her cup of woe,
And deal out all her portion here below:
Forever conscious of her Heav'nly birth,
And dead to all the vanities of earth,
Impatient to attain a purer clime,
With pain her soul sustain'd the load of time.
Yet Heav'n long spar'd her life to bless the age,
And now she charms another by her page.
O, may that page, where all the virtues shine
And faith's strong ardors breathe in every line,
Rouze the lethargic, animate the weak
The sordid ties of sense and time to break;
Since ev'ry wish that centers here below,
Must end in disappointment, pain, or woe!
Yet is not man unblest, nor Heav'n unkind,
True pleasure dwells with ev'ry virtuous mind!
How false the toy that oft assumes its name,
For which we hazard honour, health and fame!
Like the coquette, she on each wooer smiles,
And charms his fancy by her soothing wiles;
His love obtain'd, his fond embrace she flies,
And meets with cold disdain his longing eyes.

---

proficiency in the kindred-arts of Poetry and Painting; especially in the latter, in
which she probably might have rivalled the greatest masters of her time, had not
death arrested her in the bloom of youth and genius. She died of the small-pox,
in the 25th year of her age. Her death was lamented in a long Ode by Mr. Dryden.

* The celebrated Mrs. Catharine Phillips, who also died of the small-pox.

Eternal wisdom, with benignant zeal,
Closely unites our duty and our weal:
Hence, when we quit the Heav'n-directed way,
And through the beaten paths of folly stray,
Peace and contentment wing their hasty flight,
And leave the mind a stranger to delight;
Wild anarchy prevails; and dire despair,
With tyrant sway, the ruffled breast shall tear.

Well do *Miranda's** all-harmonious lays
Demand the Poet's tributary bays,
Who trod through learning's arduous paths alone,
And made the wit of foreign climes our own;
Blest by the Muse in life, nor left in death,
Her panting bosom felt th'inspiring breath;
Love nerv'd her hand (still to its object true)
To bid the partner of her cares adieu,
To bid him dry his sorrow-streaming eyes,
And gratulate her journey to the skies!
    'Twas thine O *Chudleigh*† (name for ever dear
Whilst wit and virtue claim the lay sincere!)
Boldly t'assert great Nature's equal laws,
And plead thy helpless injur'd sex's cause:
For that, thy fame shall undecaying bloom,
And flow'rs unfading grow around thy tomb.

---

* The honourable Mrs. Monk, daughter of Lord Molesworth, and wife to George Monk Esquire. So great was her capacity, that she acquired, without the assistance of a teacher, a perfect knowledge of the Latin, Italian and Spanish tongues: she translated several Poems of the best authors in those languages, and wrote many original pieces. She died about the year 1715; and on her death-bed at Bath, wrote a very pathetic epistle in verse to her husband in London. Soon after her decease her Poems were published under the Title of, "Miranda, or Poems by a Lady."

† Lady Chudleigh was the daughter of Richard Lee Esquire, of Winslade in the County of Devon, and wife to Sir George Chudleigh. She seems to hint in some of her writings that she had not enjoyed the advantages of a liberal education; but her application to study, and great capacity, enabled her to make a considerable figure amongst her contemporary writers. She wrote many poetical pieces which were then highly approved of, and was a zealous asserter of the female right to literature. In 1710, she published a volume of Essays in Prose and Verse dedicated to the Princess Sophia of Hanover, Mother of King George I, who was so well pleased with her Ladyship's compliments, that in return she sent her a letter in her own hand-writing; a copy of which is inserted in Lady Chudleigh's Life in the Biographical Dictionary.

But say, *Hibernia,* can this humble verse
Thy own *Constantia's** various praise rehearse?
What though her fortune low, her birth obscure,
Sprung from a race illiterate, rude and poor:
To all th' emoluments of art unknown,
Yet Wit and Learning mark'd her for their own.
With wond'rous ease, her comprehensive mind
The various stores of knowledge all combin'd:
A mind by nature form'd with strictest care
To teach us what superior beings are.
Of ev'ry virtue, ev'ry grace possest,
Weary of earth, impatient to be blest,
Soon her glad spirit broke each feeble tye
That held her here an exile from the sky;
For there, there only, could her soul improve;
Such her exalted piety and love!

Thrice glorious hour, when truth's unclouded ray
Bursts on the mind in all the blaze of day!
For O, what more than pompous trifles, all
Those things we purblind mortals science call!
In youth, when new-born spirits fire the breast,
Of health, and hope, and vanity possess'd,
With vigorous steps the arduous road we trace,
But soon are wearied in the dubious chace:
Errors, on ev'ry side, beset us round,
And soon our anxious, searching minds confound.
Thrice glorious hour, when truth's unclouded ray
Bursts on the mind in all the blaze of day!
Thrice glorious hour, her ardent vot'ries cry,
And pant for life and immortality!

---

* Mrs. Constantine Grierson was born in the county of Kilkenny in Ireland. She was a perfect mistress of the Hebrew, Greek, Latin, and French languages; and was equally well acquainted with History, Divinity, Philosophy, and Mathematics. She wrote a Dedication of the Dublin Edition of Tacitus to Lord Carteret: to his son she wrote a Greek Epigram. She also wrote many Poems in English, but on those she set so little value, that there are none of them extant, except a few interspersed amongst Mrs. Barber's Poems; and two Epistles to Mrs. Pilkington, published by that Lady, in her Memoirs of her own Life. To her great accomplishments Mrs. Grierson united the most fervent piety, and extensive benevolence. Her wit was not tinctured with ill-nature, nor her learning sullied with pride: nor did her attainments in literature, render her neglectful of the humbler duties of domestic life. What makes her character the more remarkable is, that she had no assistance in acquiring the great fund of knowledge which

And *Thou,** *Hibernia's* other fav'rite name,
Shall'st with *Constantia's* ever join thy fame.
Thy merit well the charming angel knew,
And plac'd it in the fairest point of view.
Immortaliz'd by her, say, can the Muse
The well-meant tribute of her praise refuse?
Thy verse for noblest ends was still design'd;
To form aright the tender infant mind;
Vice to disrobe of ev'ry fair disguise,
And paint bright virtue to our raptur'd eyes.
Thee *Swift,* and noble *Orrery* approv'd,
And ev'ry friend to modest merit lov'd.

Whate'er, in beauty, nature had deny'd
To thee, O *Chandler,*† she in wit supply'd.
No rosy cheek, no lip of Tyrian dye,
No polish'd forehead, nor the sparkling eye,
Taught senseless beaus to prostrate at thy shrine,
And hail their blooming idol all-divine:
But virtue reign'd triumphant in thy heart,
And thine was Poetry's delightful art.

To *Oxford* next the Muse transported turns,
Where Jones‡ with all a Poet's ardour burns;
Jones, in whose strains another *Pope* we view,
Her wit so keen, her sentiments so true.
Like him the charming maid, with skill refin'd,
Hath pierc'd the deep recesses of the mind;

---

she possessed, besides a few accidental instructions from a Clergyman, who resided in the Parish in which she lived. Her parents were in too low a station of life to be capable of affording her any advantages of education. Previous to her marriage she was obliged to submit to the drudgery of the needle, to procure herself a subsistence. Her short intervals of leisure, were the only opportunities she enjoyed for study. She died at the age of 27.

* Mrs. Barber, the wife of a reputable tradesman in Dublin: a very ingenious Poetess, a woman of the most distinguished virtue, and a particular friend of Mrs. Grierson's.

† Mrs. Chandler, sister to the celebrated dissenting clergyman of that name. Her Poems, the principal of which is "A description of Bath, inscribed to her Royal Highness the Princess Amelia," have passed through several editions.

‡ See Essays in prose and verse by Miss Jones. A reader of taste and candour will not, perhaps, scruple to acknowledge, that her Epistle on Patience, addressed to Lord Masham, and that on Desire, to the honorable Miss Lovelace, are worthy the pen of our celebrated ethic Poet.

The latent principles of action trac'd,
And Truth with Art's enchanting beauties grac'd.

Ingenious *Masters*,* well thy tuneful lays
May claim the tribute of the Muse's praise;
Whose soaring mind a parent's frown depress'd,
A mind with virtue, and with genius bless'd!
And yet, how sweetly-soothing in thy strains,
The Royal Bard of Palestine complains!
Well too thou paint'st those envious critics pride
Who, fond to cavil, merit's charms would hide.
Superior to the labour'd songs of Art
The verse that flows spontaneous from the heart!
But yet more sweet, more finish'd far the line,
Where Art, and Nature, in fair union shine.

Thou† who did'st pierce the shades of gothic night,
And bring the first faint dawn of wit to light;
Who did'st the rude essays of genius save,
From dark oblivion's all-devouring grave;
To thee, fair patron of the Muses songs,
To thee each grateful Poet's praise belongs:
Praise, the sole boon a poet can bestow,
And the sole meed his arduous labours know.
Precarious meed! for oft alas, the bard
Finds Envy rob him of that sweet reward:
Her baneful touch his laurels soon destroys,
And blasts the harvest of his promis'd joys.

O, then, ye favor'd few! whom wit inspires,
Whom taste refines, or thirst of glory fires,
To nobler objects turn the dazzled eye,
Than Honour, Fame, or Fortune can supply:
For sure alone in Virtue can ye find,
Enjoyments suited to th'immortal mind.

---

* Mrs. Mary Masters, a native of Otley near Leeds in Yorkshire. She herself informs us, that "her genius for poetry was always discountenanced by her parents; that her education rose no higher than the Spelling-book, and the Writing Master; and that, till her merit got the better of her fortune, she was shut out from all commerce with the more knowing and polite part of the world." The first volume of her Poems and Letters was published 1733; the second came out in 1755.

† See the Muses Library, a collection of antient English Poetry, from the times of Edward the Confessor, to the reign of James I; with an account of the Lives and Characters of the Writers; by Mrs. Cooper.

With ardour then her sacred paths pursue;
There still new pleasures strike the raptur'd view:
Give to ambition there its utmost scope:
Thus shall your bliss surpass your brighest hope.

T'was *Fielding's** talent, with ingenuous Art,
To trace the secret mazes of the Heart.
In language tun'd to please its infant thought,
The tender breast with prudent care *She* taught.
Nature to *Her,* her boldest pencil lent,
And blest *Her* with a mind of vast extent;
A mind, that nobly scorn'd each low desire,
And glow'd with pure Religion's warmest fire.

High in the records of immortal fame
Stands, charming *Tollett!*† thy illustrious name:
Thee Science led to her sequester'd bow'rs,
And deck'd thy mind with all her fairest flow'rs:
The charms of verse, of rapt'rous sounds, are thine,
The pencil's magic, and the lore divine.
O *Lenox,*‡ thou "in various nature wise!"
Proceed to paint our follies as they rise;
Bid the coquette in blushes hide her face,
Which affectation robs of every grace:
Bid virtue, to her generous purpose true,
Press on, and keep perfection still in view.

---

* Mrs. Fielding, sister to the late Henry Fielding Esquire, and author of "The Adventures of David Simple;" "Letters between the principal Character's in David Simple;" "The Governess, or, the Female Academy;" "The Lives of Cleopatra and Octavia;" and "of a translation, from the Greek, of Xenophon's Memorabilia of Socrates."

† Mrs. Elizabeth Tollett, daughter of George Tollett Esquire, Commissioner of the Navy in the reigns of King William and Queen Ann. Her father observing her uncommon genius, gave her so excellent an education, that, besides making a great proficiency in the fine Arts, she spoke fluently and correctly the Latin, Italian, and French languages; and well understood History, Astronomy, and Mathematics. These attainments were crowned with the most fervent piety, and every moral virtue. The former part of her life was spent in the Tower of London, (but under what circumstances her Biographer has not informed us); the latter at Stratford and Westham. She died in February 1754. Her Poems were published in 1755.

‡ Mrs. Charlotte Lenox, author of "Shakespear illustrated, with critical Remarks;" of "The Sister, a Comedy;" and of, "The Female Quixote." She has also translated (from the French) Brumoy's Greek Theatre.

Thus may success thy great designs attend,
And fame, and fortune, smile on virtue's friend!

For love, for wit, and sentiments refin'd,
(Another *Sappho* with a purer mind!)
Endu'd with ev'ry charm that boasts to please,
Good-nature, softness, sprightliness, and ease;
Long may'st thou, tuneful *Frances*,* be renown'd;
Thy life with honour, as with virtue crown'd.

When *Theodosia*† tunes her Heav'n-taught lyre,
What bosom burns not with seraphic fire?
Sweet harmonist! in thy extatic lines
Virtue in all her native graces shines:
There, each bright hope in tuneful numbers flows,
And there, fair faith! thy sacred ardour glows:
There, resignation smiles on care and pain,
And rapt'rous joy attunes the grateful strain.
O yet may Heav'n its healing aid extend,
And yet to health restore my valued friend:
Long be it ere her gentle spirit rise,
To fill some glorious mansion in the skies.

But hark! what softly-plaintive strains I hear!
How sweet they vibrate on my list'ning ear!
Sure *Greville's*‡ Muse must ev'ry bosom please
That finds a charm in elegance or ease:
Hers were those nice sensations of the heart,
Whose magic pow'r can pain to joy impart;
A feeling "heart, that like the needle true,
"Turn'd at each touch, and turning trembled too!"

Daughter of *Shenstone*§ hail! hail charming maid,
Well hath thy pen fair nature's charms display'd!
The hill, the grove, the flow'r-enamell'd lawn,
Shine in thy lays in brightest colours drawn:

---

* See Letters between Henry and Frances. Frances (otherwise Mrs. Griffiths) besides her share in those ingenious and entertaining Letters, has translated from the French the writings of Ninon de L'Enclos, and written Amana a Dramatic Poem, and A Wife in the Right, a Comedy.

† See Poems on subjects chiefly devotional, by Theodosia, in two volumes.

‡ See Mrs. Greville's beautiful Ode to Indifference.

§ See original Poems by Miss Wheately.

Nor be thy praise confin'd to rural themes,
Or idly-musing Fancy's pleasing dreams;
But still may contemplation* (guest divine!)
Expand thy breast, and prompt the flowing line.

But thou *Macaulay,*† say, canst thou excuse
The fond presumption of a youthful Muse?
A Muse, that, raptur'd with thy growing fame,
Wishes (at least) to celebrate thy name;
A name, to ev'ry son of freedom dear,
Which patriots yet unborn shall long revere.

O Liberty! Heav'n's noblest gift below,
Without thee life were but one scene of woe:
Beneath thy sway, in these auspicious isles,
Science erects her laurell'd head, and smiles;
Our great *Augustus* lives the friend of Arts,
And reigns unrivall'd in their vot'ries Hearts.

A softer theme now claims the Muse's praise,
She feels the pow'r of *Anna's*‡ tuneful lays:
Nor fortune's frowns, nor blindness could controul
The noble rage of her aspiring soul.
When pensive o'er the tomb of *Grey*§ she mourns,
Each heart the sympathetic sigh returns.
In poor *Florilla's* varying fate we view,
How vain the toys our eager hopes pursue:
Nor wealth, nor wit, nor beauty can impart
One tranquil moment to the anxious heart.
Virtue! thou only smooth'st the brow of woe,
And thou alone can'st lasting bliss bestow!
Whilst o'er life's various sea my bark shall glide,
Do thou a pilot at the helm preside:
When gathering clouds the changing skies o'ercast,
When rough the surge, and loud the furious blast;
Or when the Heav'ns shall smile serenely fair,
Each wave roll smooth, and mild each breath of air;

---

* This couplet alludes to a fine Poem of that Lady's, intituled, "The Pleasures of Contemplation."

† Mrs. Macaulay the Historian.

‡ See Miscellanies in Prose and Verse by Anna Williams.

§ Stephen Grey, F.R.S. and author of the present doctrine of electricity. Mrs. Williams informs us, that she was the person who first discover'd the emission of the electrical spark from the human body, as she was assisting Mr. Grey in some of his experiments. She has since suffered a total loss of sight.

Teach her one steady, glorious course to steer,
Not rashly bold, nor yet restrain'd by fear;
And may thy faithful compass guide her way,
To the bright regions of Eternal Day!

What various pow'rs in Pennington* we find!
Taste, spirit, learning, elegance combin'd. . . .
　　Say *Montagu*† can this unartful verse
Thy Genius, Learning, or thy Worth rehearse?
To paint thy talents justly should conspire
Thy taste, thy judgment, and thy *Shakespeare's* fire.
Well hath thy Pen with nice discernment trac'd
What various pow'rs the Matchless poet grac'd;
Well hath thy Pen his various beauties shown,
And prov'd thy soul congenial to his own.
Charm'd with those splendid honours of thy Name,
Fain would the Muse relate thy nobler Fame;
Dear to Religion, as to Learning dear,
Candid, obliging, modest, mild, sincere,
Still prone to soften at another's woe,
Still fond to bless, still ready to bestow.

O, sweet Philanthropy! thou guest divine!
What permanent, what heart-felt joys are thine!
Supremely blest the maid, whose generous soul
Bends all-obedient to thy soft controul:
Nature's vast theatre her eye surveys,
Studious to trace Eternal Wisdom's ways;
Marks what dependencies, what different ties,
Throughout the spacious scale of beings rise;
Sees Providence's oft-mysterious plan,
Form'd to promote the general good of man.
With noble warmth thence her expanded mind
Feels for the welfare of all human-kind:
Thence flows each lenient art that sooths distress,
And thence the unremitting wish to bless!

Th' aspiring Muse now droops her trembling wings,
Whilst, *Indolence,*‡ thy tranquil pow'r she sings;

---

* See letters on different subjects by the Author of "The Unfortunate Mother's Advice to her absent Daughters." (Lady Pennington.)

† Mrs. Montagu, Author of the "Essay on the Genius and Writings of Shakespeare, compared with the Greek and French Dramatic Poets."

‡ See Indolence a Poem, by the Author of Almida a Tragedy. (Mrs. Celesia, daughter of the late Mr. Mallett.)

"Not sordid sloth," the low-born mind's disease,
But calm retirement, and poetic ease.
Ah! let me ever live with *Thee* immur'd,
From Folly's laugh, from envy's rage secur'd,
In ev'ry scene of changeful life the same,
Not fondly courting, nor despising Fame.

   *Talbot,** did e'er mortality enshrine
A mind more gen'rous, meek, or kind, than thine?
Delightful moralist! thy well-wrote page
Shall please, correct, and mend the rising age;
Point out the road the thoughtless many miss,
That leads through virtue to the realms of bliss.
Fain would my soul thy sentiments imbibe,
And fain thy manners in my own transcribe:
Genius and Wit were but thy second praise,
Thou knew'st to win by still sublimer ways;
Thy Angel-goodness, all who knew approv'd,
Honour'd, admir'd, applauded too, and lov'd!
Fair shall thy fame to latest ages bloom,
And ev'ry Muse with tears bedew thy tomb. . . .

   Nor shalt *Thou*† be forgot whose tuneful tongue
So well the charms of *Strawberry-Hill* hath sung;
Long shall thy wit in *Walpole's* numbers live,
When dead the little honours mine can give.

   Fir'd with the Music, *Aikin,*‡ of thy lays,
To thee the Muse a joyful tribute pays;
Transported dwells on that harmonious line,
Where taste, and spirit, wit, and learning shine;
Where Fancy's hand her richest colourings lends,

---

   * Mrs. Catherine Talbot, only daughter of the Reverend Edward Talbot, Archdeacon of Berks, and Preacher at the Rolls; (younger son of Dr. Talbot Bishop of Durham.) This truly excellent Lady was blest with the happiest natural talents: her understanding was vigorous, her imagination lively, and her taste refined. Her virtues were equal to her genius, and rendered her at once the object of universal love and admiration. She was the Author of "Reflections on the Seven Days of the Week;" and of "Essays on various Subjects," 2 volumes. Her writings breathe the noblest spirit of Christian benevolence; and discover a more than common acquaintance with human nature.
   † See Poems by A Lady, printed for Walter in 1771.
   ‡ See Poems and Miscellaneous Pieces in Prose, by Miss Aikin, (daughter of the Reverend Mr. Aikin, one of the tutors to the Academy at Warrington) lately married to the Reverend Mr. Rochemont Barbauld.

And ev'ry shade in just proportion blends.
How fair, how beauteous to our gazing eyes
Thy vivid intellectual paintings rise!
We feel thy feelings, glow with all thy fires,
Adopt thy thoughts, and pant with thy desires.
Proceed, bright maid! and may thy polish'd page
Refine the manners of a trifling age:
Thy sex apprize of pleasure's treach'rous charms,
And woo them from the Syren's fatal arms;
Teach them with thee on Fancy's wing to soar,
With thee, the paths of science to explore;
With thee, the open book of Nature scan,
Yet nobly scorn the little pride of Man.

Man, seated high on Learning's awful throne,
Thinks the fair realms of knowledge his alone;
But you, ye fair, his Salic Law disclaim:
Supreme in Science shall the Tyrant reign!
When every talent all-indulgent Heav'n
In lavish bounty to your share hath giv'n?

With joy ineffable the Muse surveys
The orient beams of more resplendent days:
As on she raptur'd looks to future years,
What a bright throng to Fancy's view appears!
To them see Genius her best gifts impart,
And Science raise a throne in ev'ry heart!
One turns the moral, one th' historic page;
Another glows with all a *Shakespeare's* rage!
With matchless *Newton* now one soars on high,
Lost in the boundless wonders of the sky;
Another now, of curious mind, reveals
What treasures in her bowels Earth conceals;
Nature's minuter works attract her eyes;
Their laws, their pow'rs, her deep research descries.

Yet now there sure are some of nobler kind,
From all their sex's narrow views refin'd,
Who, truly wise, attempt not to controul
The generous ardor of th' aspiring soul:
Such, tuneful *Duncombe,** thou, whose Attic lays
Demand the warmest strains of grateful praise:

---

* The Reverend John Duncombe M. A. Fellow of Corpus Christi College
Cambridge, Rector of St. Andrew's and St. Mary Bredman's, one of the Six
Preachers at the Cathedral at Canterbury, and Author of the Feminead, or Female

Fearless of censure, boldly thou stood'st forth
An able Advocate for Female Worth!
For that! may the far-sounding Voice of Fame,
To latest Ages bear thy honour'd Name;
For that! may Fancy still her aid impart,
And still the Muse's smile dilate thy heart;
For that! may Hope still strew thy path with flow'rs,
And ev'ry blessing crown thy circling hours!

   Such *He** who dared "against a World decide,
And stem the rage of Custom's rapid tide;"
Who kindly bade *Athenia's* "growing mind,
Take ev'ry knowledge in of ev'ry kind."

   And such art *Thou,* my ever-valued friend;
Ah! still thy candour to the Muse extend:
Permit that honour'd Name to grace her page,
Which shames the manners of a selfish age!
(That name, whose merit still this heart must feel,
Yet vainly strive that merit to reveal!)
Philander! generous, affable, sincere,
His taste as polish'd as his judgment clear,
Blest with the tenderest feelings of the Heart,
Wise without Stiffness, prudent without Art,
Form'd with like ease t' enjoy a prosp'rous state
Or bear the storms of unpropitious fate.

   Such *He,* who, when I first attun'd the lay,
With his own candour view'd the faint essay;
Enjoin'd me still to court the Muse's smile,
The tiresome hours of languor to beguile.
O could this pen, which gratitude impells,
But tell how ——— in each scene excels!
O could she but some glowing colours find,
To paint each feature of his finish'd mind!
A mind, unstain'd with vanity, or art,

Genius, A Poem. "The Ladies there celebrated are Mrs. Catherine Philips, Anne Countess of Winchelsea, Mrs. Cockburn, Mrs. Rowe, Frances Dutchess Dowager of Somerset, Anne Viscountess Irwin, Mrs. Wright, Mrs. Madan, Mrs. Leapor, Mrs. Carter, Mrs. Brooke, Miss Ferrar, (now Mrs. Peckard); Miss Pennington, (since dead); Miss Mulso, (now Mrs. Chapone); and Miss Highmore (since married to the Author)."

   * See a Poem in Dodsley's Miscellanies, intituled, "The Female Right to Literature, in a Letter to a Young Lady from Florence," written by the Reverend Mr. Seward, Canon of Litchfield.

The gentlest manners, and the kindest heart!
A mind where prudence, judgement, taste unite,
Though learn'd yet humble, though sincere polite;
His passions calm'd, his wishes all subdu'd,
But these (the noblest!) to be wise and good.

Ye generous pleaders of the female cause,
Ye friends to Nature's (her's are Reason's laws)
For you the Muse shall raise her drooping wing,
And Peans echo from each trembling string.

Though sunk with languor, and unceasing pains,
Life's purple current stagnates in my veins;
Though Fancy mourns her fairy visions fled,
And all the fond, fond hopes of youth are dead!
Still next to virtue, science charms my eye,
And frequent prompts the unavailing sigh.

But O would Heav'n my faded health renew,
Unwearied I'd the glorious toils pursue;
Well-pleas'd in sweet retirement's shady bow'rs,
In studious ease, to spend my remnant hours.

FINIS

PRIMARY SOURCES:

The Female Advocate: a poem occasioned by reading Mr. Duncombe's Femi-
    nead. London: Joseph Johnson, 1774.
Messiah: a poem, in two parts. Published for the benefit of the general hospital
    at Bath. London: Joseph Johnson, 1788.

RELATED SOURCES:

Constable, A. ed. Letters of Anna Seward. 6 vols. Edinburgh: George Ramsey,
    1811.
Davis, Natalie Zemon. "Gender and Genre: Women as Historical Writers,
    1400–1820." In Beyond Their Sex: Learned Women of the European Past,
    edited by Patricia Labalme, 153–82. New York: New York University Press,
    1980.
Duncombe, John. The Feminiad. A Poem. London: M. Cooper, 1754; reprint ed.,
    Los Angeles: William Andrews Clark Memorial Library, University of Cali-
    fornia at Los Angeles, 1981, no. 207.
Graham, J. W. "The Father of the Founder of the 'Manchester Guardian.' " In The
    Journal of the Friends Historical Society 18, edited by Norman Penney
    (1921):81–87.

ELEANOR BUTLER
1737 – 1829

Eleanor Butler was descended from an ancient English family who settled in Ireland during Henry II's reign and ended up with a large family estate as part of the Irish Roman Catholic aristocracy. She was the youngest daughter of Walter Butler, the only lineal representative of James Butler, second Duke of Ormonde, a popular Jacobite leader, in exile after Queen Anne died in 1714. Her mother was Ellen Morris, daughter of Nicholas Morris of Latargh, Tipperary, and Susannah Talbot, of Malahide Castle. In 1791, as a result of action in the House of Irish Lords, her brother John was restored to the Ormonde peerage and reclaimed the family title, becoming the seventeenth Earl of Ormonde. He bestowed the rank of Earl's daughter upon Eleanor, who then became known as Lady Eleanor Butler. She was educated at the English Benedictine Convent of Our Blessed Lady of Consolation at Cambrai in France.

In 1768, at thirty years of age, Butler was invited to become companion to the aristocratic thirteen-year-old Honorable Sarah Ponsonby. Much later, inspired largely by personal inclination in conjunction with a prevailing fashion for rural retreat, the two women planned a joint retirement from the world. Although Lady Eleanor's family attempted to send her to a convent to prevent her departure, Lady Eleanor and the Honorable Sarah did finally elope after one unsuccessful effort and ten years of friendship and correspondence. They were accompanied by Mary Carryl (Carrol), a faithful attendant, who lived with them until her death in 1809. After a successful escape from their families, they lived together in the Vale of Llangollen, North Wales, in a manner appropriate to their elegant tastes and somewhat restricted budget, which nonetheless included servants for the house and grounds. In this renowned retirement, they read aloud, studied languages, corresponded, gardened, made additions to their home and alterations to their land, and entertained local and illustrious visitors including distinguished French émigrés and Anna Seward, who celebrated their relationship in verse. On a visit to their home, Plas Newydd, Lady Leighton painted them sitting indoors at a table. (The more celebrated drawing of the Ladies of the Vale or the Ladies of Llangollen, as they were referred to, is probably fraudulent.)

Unfortunately, Sarah Ponsonby's journals are lost except for her daybook of 1785 which recounts their first tour of North Wales in 1778 and is dedicated to "her most tenderly beloved Companion." An account book for 1791 to 1800 records their exceedingly careful management of accounts. Lady Eleanor Butler's journals cover their life intermittently from 1785–1821. Nine journals remain. They tell the story of a tender intimate lesbian relationship of remarkable depth. The excerpts give some indication of the quality of their love and offer a particularly fine example of polemic of the heart, writings which by their very existence and in their essence countermand historical patriarchal authority. Recognition that their relationship posed a threat to established order is testified to by a sensational article in the *General Evening Post* of 1790, which greatly distressed Lady Eleanor and the Honourable Sarah Ponsonby because of the aspersions it cast.

With infrequent visits to the outside world, the couple lived long lives devoted to self-education and good works in the Welsh countryside, their peace occasionally disturbed by Lady Eleanor's migraines and their worries about finances. Their lives embodied the intrinsic nature of what was termed in the eighteenth century "romantic friendship." Colette incorporated a version of their relationship into her novel, *Ces Plaisirs.*

---·---

FROM

THE HAMWOOD PAPERS
OF THE LADIES OF LLANGOLLEN

"Friday, October 7th. (1785)—Reading Rousseau to my Sally. She drawing her map upon Vellum, made a great mistake in one of the tropics which spoil'd her morning's Work. . . . Incessant rain the entire evening. Shut the shutters, made a good fire, lighted the Candles. . . . A day of strict retirement, sentiment, and delight.

"Monday, October 10th.—A very sentimental message from Lady Charlotte Fitzgerald. Answered it. . . . This day our Landlord, Richard Griffiths, and the Clerk began to plough the land before our Cottage for Wheat.

"Wednesday, October 12th.—An excellent fire in the Library, candles lighted and an appearance of Content and cheerfulness never to be found but in a Cottage.

"Monday, October 17th.—My Love and I spent from Five till Seven in the shrubbery and in the Field endeavouring to talk and walk away our little Sorrows. Sent the woman of Pen-y-coed to Ruabon for our Winter

---

SOURCE: This selection comes from the 1930 printed volume of *The Hamwood Papers.*

provision of groceries. At seven walked to the Hand to see Mrs. Myddelton. The Company Col. and Mrs. Myddelton, Mr. and Mrs. and Miss Carter, Mr. Robert Myddelton (little Mrs. Jones' elder brother), Miss Lloydde. Declined supping with them.

. . . *"Thursday, Janury 31st.* (1788)—. . . My beloved and I went to the new garden. Reading. Drawing. Read 'Davila'. Then my beloved read 'La Morte d'Abel'. Nine till twelve in the bedchamber reading. Old Parkes of the Lyon came up to inform us that Mr. Palmer, my brother's chaplain, had been at their House for a moment on his way to Ireland. Had sent his compliments to us and Butler's Love and Duty, who was settled at Maudlin College, liked it very much and was to dine in the Hall yesterday. Very impertinent in them not to Deliver this message yesterday morning. A day of sweet and delicious retirement.

"February 1st.—Three o'clock dinner. Boiled Pork. Peas pudding. Half-past three my beloved and I went to the new garden. Freezing hard. I am much mistaken if there be not a quantity of snow in the sky. I read to my beloved No. 97 of the Rambler written by Richardson,[1] author of those inimitable Books 'Pamela,' 'Clarissa,' and 'Sir Charles Grandison.'

"Sunday, February 3rd.—Post bag from Wrexham. Letter from Miss Davies of Brighton enclosing a very remarkable account given by the Rev. Mr. Whitby of Creswell in Staffordshire to Doctor T. of Mr. E.'s relation of her Mother's appearing to him after her death on Tuesday, March 29th, 1785.

"Monday, February 4th.—Rose at eight. Celestial blue and silver morning . . . Compliments from Mr. Owen of Porkington with a present of 4 sticks of black sealing wax. What a whimsical pleasant mortal he is! Compliments from Col. Mansergh St. George. Just arrived at the Hand, if we are disengaged will wait on us and receive our commands for Ireland. Our Compliments. Shall be glad to see him. He came at six. Stayed till nine. One of the most pleasing men I ever conversed with. Very pretty, slight figure, pale genteel Face. Animated interesting countenance. He was dressed in the deepest mourning, a black silk cap on his head which entirely concealed his hair. He had worn it these many years in consequence of a wound he received in America which has baffled the skill of the most eminent surgeons and Physicians in Europe. He gave us the most satisfying account and the most perfect idea of the Herculaneum and Pompeia. . . . Related many curious anecdotes of Rousseau, and as he draws admirably we requested he would give us some idea of the face and Person of this unfortunate and inimitable genius. He very obligingly took out his pencil and drew two figures (I am persuaded striking likenesses) of Poor Rousseau in a dress lined and trim'd with Fur, and a large muff. . . . Anecdotes of Dr. John Hunter[2] engaged in a

---

[1] Samuel Richardson (1689–1761), novelist. He was the son of a joiner, and published *Pamela* in 1740.

[2] John Hunter, 1728–93, anatomist and surgeon. His museum in Leicester Square, London, was bought by the nation in 1813.

great work, 'The Economy of the Human Frame.' Horrid story of Doctor Radcliffe. Anecdotes of the Prince of Wales, Duchess of Parme. Emperor. Queen of France. We were quite sorry when this agreeable man made his Bow. Howling wind. Sharp keen night.

"Saturday, February 9th. —Rose at eight. The mountains and valley thinly covered with snow. Heavy whitish sky. Sharp air. . . . Present of a hare from Mr. Crowe, followed by himself. The Hare sent by the Dean of St. Asaph. Mr. Crowe dined, drank coffee and sat till ten. Very sensible and agreeable. Gave us an account of his travels with Mr. Marwood of Devonshire. Beautiful description of the journey from Lyons to Geneva. Description of the window in New College, Oxford. Shabby behaviour of Sir J. R.[1] on that occasion. Original cartoon purchased by the late Duke of Rutland[2] for £800 now at Belvoir Castle, falling to pieces, a napkin under it to receive the flakes which continually break off. Anecdotes of the present D. of B.[3] astonishing avarice, meanness and suspicion. Account of Harris, Author of 'Hermes' etc. Of Dr. Young of Salisbury the original of Parson Adams,[4] Story of Boswell, the mock Court of Judicature in which they swore him to secrecy during the Northern circuit. The Duties of a Tutor. Sir John Hawkins' life of Johnson. Wretched performance. The Globes made by Long[5] for Pembroke College, Cambridge. Of the ancient architecture; how infinitely superior in point of magnificence to the present. The multitude of Castles and Churches erected by different Kings in the Course of their Reigns, which could not now be accomplished in a century, accounted for by the Various Manufactures (then unknown) which employ such a number of hands at present. Smith, the great architect in Shropshire and Staffordshire, built all his houses on one Plan. . . . Mr. Crowe sent us two copies of his 'Lewesden Hill.'[6]

"Sunday, February 10th. —Rose at light. Ground thinly covered with snow: Blue sky. Flakes of snow gently descending and mixing with the foliage of the evergreens. Very cold. . . . In the Library, waiting. Forgot to mention yesterday that Mr. Crowe gave us an account how Penrudock Wyndham became Possessed of Lord Melcombe's[7] Diary. The Dodding-

---

[1] Sir Joshua Reynolds.

[2] Charles, 4th Duke of Rutland, died 24th October 1787.

[3] Francis, 5th Duke of Bedford, died 1802. Charles James Fox was one of his greatest friends.

[4] Parson Adams, a poor curate in Fielding's novel, *Joseph Andrews.*

[5] Roger Long, 1680–1770, divine and astronomer.

[6] Issued anonymously. Published at the Clarendon Press, 1788. Its author William Crowe, D.D. (1745–1829), was the son of a carpenter. Sometime a chorister in Winchester Cathedral. Elected a "poor scholar" at the College. Fellow of New College, 1767. Friend of Samuel Rogers. His son killed in action, 1815. The poem is said to contain "noble passages," which fills me with misgivings.—Ed.

[7] Formerly Bubb Dodington.

ton estates fell to the Marquess of Buckingham[1] as next heir but the personal fortune Lord Melcombe bequeathed to his friend Mr. Wyndham,[2] who at his death left it to Col. Wyndham, second brother to P. Wyndham, to whom he left the papers with a strict injunction that nothing injurious to the memory of Lord Melcombe should be published, which injunction was violated as whoever reads the Diary will immediately perceive.

Ten. My beloved and I drank a dish of tea.

Our Mrs. Bunbury is a charming woman in mind and person, Mr. Bunbury is a singular genius, but I think the pleasure of their company may be too dearly purchased by so many tedious hours of expectation; but it is his fault not hers. At half-past one this really charming woman came, blooming and beautiful as an angel. Mr. Bunbury was obliged to go to Chester about poor Mrs. Lee's will. She told us she proposed passing the day and night here but must go to Oswestry to-morrow after breakfast. A delightful day we spent in her sweet society. We dined at three, sup'd at ten, retired at one. . . .

"*Tuesday, February 19th.* —Rose at seven. Misty soft morning. Went in the Hand Chaise to Oswestry, on Chester Hill overtook General Pitt and his sister, passed them and flew on. Breakfasted with our Barretts, walked round their grounds with Mrs. Barrett. Mrs. Disbrone made what she calls coverlet but I know by the name of Lancashire Toughy (toffee). Miss Maddock dressed our hair. We wore our new habits. At three went (Mrs. Barrett in the Chaise with us) to Halston.

Mrs. Lloydd of Aston[3] and her pretty children came soon after. Just before dinner *Miss* Webb made her appearance. I never before beheld anything half so handsome. After dinner Miss Mytton played divinely on the Harpsicord, after tea Miss Webb spoke an epilogue in Percy, another in Douglas,[4] and another in Jane Shore[5] so finely, such a Voice, such gesticulation, a countenance so animated and lovely, every movement so graceful, that every person in company burst into tears. Mrs. Lloydde went away before supper. At eleven we took leave, conducted Mrs. Barrett home. Steped in while the carriage was turning about and at half-past one arrived at our delicious abode. The library, parlour and kitchen chimneys swept in our absence, a disagreeable job well escaped.

"*Saturday, February 23rd.* —Rose at light. Soft rain. Cloudy but not

---

[1] George, 2nd Earl Temple, 1st Marquess of Buckingham, Lord-Lieutenant of Ireland, 1782 and 1787.

[2] Dodington left his property to Thomas Wyndham of Hammersmith, who left it all to Henry Penruddocke Wyndham (1736–1819). He published the *Diary of the late George Bubb Dodington, Baron of Melcombe Regis.*

[3] Rev. John Lloyd of Aston, married (1779) Martha, daughter of William Shakespeare, Esq., of London.

[4] *Douglas,* a play by John Home (1756).

[5] *Jane Shore,* a play by Nicholas Rowe (1714). Dramatist and Poet Laureate.

gloomy. Tim Price, Lady Dungannon's footman, arrived. Letter from her. Answered it. Letter from our Barretts. Lady Th—— gone off with her Priest. A month's warning to Edward. I am sorry. Letter from Mr. Chambre with our account most admirably drawn up. Saucy letter from that old doating garden Woman at Shrewsbury. Wrote to Mrs. Goddard, Charles St. Bath.

State of our correspondence. Letter due from Lady Anne Butler, from Lady Mornington, from Miss Davies, from Page, from Mrs. Lowther.[1] Letter due from us to Miss Bridgeman. The same length of time which these ladies take to answer our Letters shall we take to answer theirs.

"Sunday, February 24th. — . . . Young Downes brought from our Barretts Sheridan's Life of Swift. . . . Post-bag from Wrexham. Letter from the Bishop of St Asaph dated London 22nd, written in the handsomest most flattering terms and promising to do something for poor Mrs. Jones in whose favour we wrote. Reading Sheridan's Life of Swift. A day of most delicious and exquisite retirement . . .

. . . *"Thursday, April 3rd.* —Letter from Lady Dungannon. It is at length determined that she leaves this country. She is to have an apartment at Hampton Court. Poor woman, we shall miss our old very good friend and neighbour, but 'thus the wheel goes round.' Wrote to express our great regret. Its late in life to move, but she will perhaps find it pleasanter than the uninterrupted solitude of that old and lonely mansion.

"Thursday, April 10th. —Fine evening. Gentle wandering light on the mountains. . . . My beloved and I took a delightful walk, ascended the Hill then descended into the narrow deep valley which leads to Llansantffraid. Steep hills on either side clothed to the summit with wood. The Cyflymen gushing rapidly over the Rocks and hastening to the little Mill of Pengwern. That mill, a wooden bridge, our Landlord's cottage closing the scene at one end, the other terminated by the small hamlet of Blaen Bache, the Berwyn Mountains rising behind. Walked by the brook side to Pengwern. Our Landlady came out with great expectation of joy in her countenance, said she was rejoiced to see us, that she thought it a long while since she had that satisfaction. When we had returned her greeting crossed the large wheatfield, then the Miller's field of Peas, the meadow, crossed the lane, returned hence by our own field. Met besides our Landlady the Hand Husbandman with his Team, the old man of Pengwern our Landlord's eldest brother, and a civil modest young woman who removed a great stone which closed a gate we were going to climb over. . . .

. . . *"Sunday, July 28th.* —Note from Col. Mansergh St. George (who it seems arrived last night at the Town) pleading indisposition for not having been to wait on us this morning and desiring to know whether we had heard from Fueselé. This is a very modest way of signifying his arrival in our neighbourhood. We returned a very civil and cool answer.

---

[1] Sarah Ponsonby's step-sister.

. . . We walked to the new waterfall by the Mill, sat on the wall beside it and then returned to Pengwern. Our Landlady brought us cherries. Sat beside the great ash tree and made our Landlady sit with us and relate her Courtship and Marriage with our Landlord. . . . My Beloved and I walked on the Lawn. Saw two Ladies (one in a black capotte, the other one in white muslin, short dress, Each with large straw bonnet) coming up the lane, guessed them to be our neighbours Mrs. St. George and Miss Stepney, noticed they walked round the clump before the pales, stared[1] into the windows, and behaved with a degree of vulgarity peculiar to the stile and line of Life those Ladies have wilfully adopted.

"*Wednesday, July 30th.* —Writing. Drawing. My beloved and I went the home circuit then visited the waterfall. . . . Met a child gathering wild flowers on a bank. Looked[1] in a Cottage by the brook side. A young woman winding thread, a little boy beside her rocking a Cradle.

Three dinner, boiled mutton. Cauliflowers, mushrooms. Potatoes. Just as we had dined the Letters were brought by Mrs. Kynaston's servant from Mrs. Kynaston, dated The Lyon, to say she and Mr. Kynaston would wait on us this evening, and desiring permission to introduce their friends Mr. and Mrs. Smith. Letter from Mrs. Mytton to say that she and Miss Mytton would dine here to-morrow. Returned our Compliments to Mr. and Mrs. Kynaston. Shall be happy to see them and any of their friends. Evening delicious. While we were expecting them, note from Mr. Lewis of Shrewsbury, acquaintance of the Pigotts, desiring permission for himself and a friend to see this place. Permitted on condition they came immediately. They came. Saw them through the window. One a clergyman, the other a shabby dirty officer. My beloved and I went to meet the Kynastons. They were coming down the street as we were coming up. They introduced Mr. and Mrs. Smith of Havering at Bower in Essex. Conducted them by the Vicar's to Cottage. Lewis and his drunken friend still in the shrubbery. Sat in the Library till this ill-behaved couple were gone. . . . Mrs. Smith delightfully pleasant, agreeable and careless. He elderly, sensible, grave. An Asiatic complexion. Came from Buxton, whither they return to-morrow for her health. Caught cold at a Ball a year ago, never from that time been free from the rheumatism . . .

. . . "*Friday, January 1st 1790.* —My beloved and I woke at seven. Found by our bed side Petticoats and Pockets, a new year's gift from our *truest* Friends.

"*Sunday, January 3rd.* —Mrs. Blachford with her son and daughter came in. Staid an hour. Declined dining with us as her Daughter's extraordinary malady always seizes her at two and continues without interruption till nine. Pity, for she is a sweet girl.

"*Wednesday, January 6th.* —The corn just springing up in the furrowed land. Cocks crowing in the different cottages.

"*Thursday, January 7th.* —The field before our cottage quite green.

---

[1] Well, well!—Ed.

Hum of bees and flies in the air. Birds preparing their future nurseries. Threw open the Library window. My beloved and I went over all our grounds, visited Margaret's stables, our pretty yards, admired our new Hedge. Then returned to the Library and our evening occupation of writing, working. Interrupted by E—— and his son. The civilest, best sort of man that can be. Went away not only civilly but cheerfully when we told him to how little purpose he called on us.

"*Thursday, January 21st.* —Letter from Thomas Moore, a pretty letter like the writer.

"*Saturday, January 23rd.* —Met our good Landlord, good man. He said he never remembered so sweet a season, that the Birds' song is loud as in summer and this morning early he called his wife and daughter-in-law to listen to them. His daughter-in-law, after attending some time, said 'they would cry in May', but I trust she is mistaken.

"*Friday, February 5th.* —The Woman of this Village who supplies Halston with Beesoms returned from thence this evening, brought a letter from Mrs. Mytton and a present of the first quarter of Lamb she killed this year.

"*Saturday, February 13th.* —A parcel for me which I should have received by the Bala Carrier last Wednesday. It contained Irish newspapers.

"*Saturday, February 20th.* —Sent the Irish woman to Halston with mushroom spawn, Periwinkle of sorts, American Saxifrage.

"*Wednesday, February 24th.* —My beloved and I went a delightful walk through our cow's field, up the lane, passed Edward Evans' field, the Lane to the Mill, the entire round of Edward Evans' field, returned by the lane. The richest glowing purple tint spread over the Mountain. Brilliant sun. Met in the course of our walk an old grey-headed man leading to the water a horse as ancient as himself. Edward Evans' son, with a dray full of thorns and Hollies from the Mountains to repair the Hedges. A good-looking clean woman with three little children clinging about her, and a fourth in her arms. Told us she had eleven children. Edward Evans' clean and notable wife. A very old woman with pictures to sell. Told us she was from Carnarvonshire, had a blind Daughter whom she supported by the sale of these pictures which she purchased at Chester and Vended about the Country. The miller of Pengwern's son returning from school. Observed the Honeysuckle in the hedges in full leaf.

"*Monday, March 8th.* —At five Lady Bridgeman's footman arrived to tell us she was coming. In a quarter of an Hour that divine woman and her sweet daughter. After an interval of three years how delightful to embrace this charming couple!

"*Tuesday, March 16th.* —Splendid evening. Reading. Writing. My beloved and I walked by the Mill, the Pengwern lane and the beautiful fields near Pengwern wood. Bull bellowing fearfully at some distance. Met three innocent boys, one with a Spinning Wheel on his head. . . .

. . ."*Tuesday, August 3rd.* —Storm. Gloom. Heavy rain. What weather! Writing to the Right Honble. Ed. Burke, Beaconsfield, Bucks. A Rabbit in the Shrubbery. Sent to the village for hounds to hunt it. No Noses. Nor indeed Eyes. Could neither smell nor see the Rabbit which sat before them by the Library window.

"*Sunday, August 8th.* —Just as we sat down to Dinner a rap at the Door announced Visitors, who to our unspeakable satisfaction proved to be our excellent friend Peter Latouche, Mrs. Latouche, and her sister Miss Vicars.[1] They were last at Buxton and kindly came here from Chester on purpose to see us. They stayed till seven, then proceeded on their journey to Ireland. They have been all over England. Among other places at Harewood where they saw a new species of fruit which Mr. Latouche called Fruit bearing Passion Flower. The Fruit is of the melon kind, shaped like a cucumber. The pulp is scooped out and it is eaten with Madeira and sugar. Mr. Latouche also mentioned the flame coloured Tokay as the finest grape in England.

"*Monday, August 9th.* —Note from Mr. Walmsley,[2] an artist from London, desiring to see this place. Desired to be excused. We have appeared in the Newspapers. Will take care not wilfully to be exhibited in the Magazines.

"*Tuesday, August 10th.* —My beloved and I set out in the Lyon Chaise and four. The village of Montford very neat and picturesque on the banks of the Severn, with gardens before the houses. Stop'd at the Talbot. Got a Hair Dresser. At one set out for Berwick. That charming woman Mrs. Powys and her daughter in the drawing-room, an apartment fitted up with perfect elegance and taste. They went with us through the grounds, the Severn winding through them. Finely wooded. Clumps and single Trees of an immense size, beautifully scattered on the lawn, terminated in the front by the Town of Shrewsbury with all its towers and Spires. At our return found Mrs. Mytton, Miss Mytton, Miss Pigott, Miss Fanny Pigott, Miss Webb, Mrs. Powys' Mother. At eight our carriage came. Stop'd at Whittington. Sat in a very neat Parlour by a Pair of Candles. Grew tired of it. Went for a walk. The woman of the house followed us with a candle. She showed us the house of Doctor H——. Walked to it. Examined it. Heard somebody sneeze. Went to the Castle. Examined that. Horses harnessed, proceeded on our way.

"*Tuesday, August 17th.* —My beloved and I went the Home Circuit. Walked to the Gate. Met the Vicar. Invited him to coffee. The good man more stupid than ever, incredible and impossible as that appeared to us that last time we saw him.

---

[1] Lord Loughborough writing to Mr. Eden (later Lord Auckland), 1782, says of Miss Vickars, "She is much handsomer than any Miss I saw here (Buxton) and if she had not left this place when she did I don't know what might have become of me."

[2] Thomas Walmsley, 1763–1805. Chiefly noted as a landscape painter. He painted views of the Dee, North Wales, and Killarney. He studied scene painting and was employed at Covent Garden theatre and the Crow Street theatre, Dublin. He began to exhibit in London, 1790.

"*Saturday, August 21st.* —Rose at four. Turner dress'd our Hair. Morning delicious. My beloved and I set out in the Lyon Chaise and four. At the Hand door a chaise standing with two frightful men in it. One in a nightcap as if he were sick, the other ferocious and like a madman. Windy and misty before we got to the Turnpike. Lime carts without end from there to Whittington. Did not get out of the Carriage. Sent our compliments to Mr. Lloydde of Aston by the man of the White Lyon who is a schoolmaster and goes every Saturday to Aston to teach the little girls to write. From Whittington to Ness wind and rain. One carriage—a dull couple in it—standing at the door of a public House near the Road. Gave the Horses water at Ness Cliff. In the parlour of the Inn a Dancing Master teaching all the Farmers' sons and daughters French Dances. I think a melancholy sight. We were directed to go to Boreatton by the Hostler who told us to turn up the Right by the next House. We did so, got on a wild Heath under the Wood and cliff. Prospect beautiful. Drove through a farmyard, then got into a cornfield, from thence to a field of French wheat. Found it almost impassable. Alighted. A prattling old woman directed us to the village of Ruyton thro' a narrow lane, so very narrow we were under a necessity of taking off a pair of Horses. With the utmost difficulty got to the end of it. From thence got into a narrow Road under a wood. An old woman directed us to Ruyton thro' the wood, a little Boy to Boreatton thro' the field. Followed the latter. Came to three gates. A little girl then appeared and conducted us through meadows, cornfields, ploughed fields to a Bridge and Mill, from whence the Road was direct to Boreatton. Received most hospitably by Mr. and Mrs. Hunt and five of the very Loveliest children I ever beheld. We Breakfasted in the Tent. Mr. and Mrs. Hunt accompanied us, horseback, to the Park. Beautiful. Herds of Deer. Several fine views of the Breidden, Wrekin, Ness Cliff, the Mill, Miller's House, garden so plentifully cropt. At our return went all over the House. Saw the dear little children at dinner in the nursery. Found Mr. and Mrs. Edward Powys of the Council House, Shrewsbury. Brother to Mr. Powys of Berwick. They dined with us. At eight Mr. and Mrs. Powys and we went away. Mr. Hunt sent his coachman to show us the way from the village of Ruyton to the Shrewsbury road. Returned by a splendid moon to Whittington. Fed the horses. My beloved and I did not get out of the carriage. Being Saturday all the neighbouring Farmers had assembled there to pay their Reapers and spend the evening, or rather night, in mirth and conviviality. They sang many Songs all applicable to their Situation, in praise of a Farmer's Life, some Hunting songs, and one on Lord Hawke.[1] We are quite delighted at the Excellence of their Voices. Returned home by a delicious Moon. Arrived at one.

"*Monday, August 23rd.* —Compliments from Mr. Fielden and the Miss

---

[1] Baron Hawke of Towton, Co. York, died 1781. Achieved a notable victory over the French Fleet in the West Indies, 1747, and received the thanks of Parliament for a victory off the French coast in 1759. Vice-Admiral of Great Britain. First Lord of the Admiralty.

Shepherds desiring to see this place. Permitted. They came; one of them so affected by a fearful accident in this village that she was obliged to get a glass of water. The Accident was a Child, son to the Blacksmith, aged six years, killed on the Spot by the Stage Coach going over it.

"*Friday, October 1st.* —Saw a pretty young woman habited in close mourning coming towards us. Mrs. Rogers, the Friend and Ally of Mrs. Goddard, whom we had expected some days and hoped to have for our guest but she travelled in the Stage Coach and therefore could not stay above three minutes to our great regret. Her manners and engaging appearance having captivated as much as her History had formerly interested us. She undertook the charge of the Bond, having first witnessed our signing it. We conducted her down the Lane where two hideous men, her companions in the Stage Coach, were waiting for her. One of them a formal wretch, like one of the Holy Brotherhood of the Inquisition, the other flat faced and vulgar. Returned to the Library, began to write when that most excellent and faithful creature Jenny Cooke came with the kindest message from Mrs. Latouche, who had not resolution to come up. That last time she was here her beloved daughter Lady Lanesborough was with her. This good creature staid half an hour. Brewed Four Swipes, the second time, of J. Williams' Malt.

"*Monday, October 4th.* —Mr. Edwards of the Hand brought a note from Mr. Wilberforce written in the most Polite and flattering terms. We shall carefully preserve it, proud of this distinction from a character we so highly respect. Mrs. Walsh, whom my Beloved knew at Bath came for an hour. Miss Howard, Lord Wicklow's[1] daughter, with whom she was going to Ireland, called on us. . . .

. . . "Thursday, October 21st 1807—My Better half and I rose at five. Went at six to Oswestry. Stopped at the Cross Keys. Sent a messenger to Porkington. Mrs. R. Wingfield came and we three went off. Arrived at the Hall before ten. Were kindly received in the handsome and ancient mansion. Breakfast. Then a tour of the House, office, gardens. Saw the Canary Birds. My Better half and I set out and met Mrs. Powys near the Bridge. Got into her Carriage. Went to Vaughans, then to Eddowes, then to two other filthy Booksellers shops. Then drove to the Council House. Did not alight. Went on to Berwick. Lady Feilding,[2] Miss Powys, Miss Mytton. Luncheon. Mr. Jones powdered and dressed our hair. Mr., Mrs., Miss, Mr. R. and Mr. Charles Wingfield came. Dinner. At twelve Mrs. R. Wingfield and we set out in darkness and rain. One wheel flew off near Aston. Called to the Lodge near the gate. Terrified by the noise, and we made amends. Wheel right, we got to Oswestry. Sat in the parlour of the Cross Keys till the chaise which was to convey Mrs. Wingfield to Porkington was ready. Got home at five in the morning.

---

[1] Ralph Howard, Esq., created Viscount Wicklow 1785, married, 1755, Alice, daughter of William Forward, Esq. She was raised to the peerage as Countess of Wicklow, 1793. They had four daughters.

[2] Daughter of Mrs. Powys and wife of Viscount Feilding.

"*Monday, October 26th.* —From Salop. Boswell's Life of Johnson.

"*Sunday, November 1st.* —My Better half and I set out at half-past eight. Morning soft and spring like. Roads dirty and deep. Met the stage coach on the road. Opened the post bag. Letter from Lady Louisa Harvey.[1] At half-past ten arrived at Miss Mytton's. Lady Feilding there. Walked to church. Sat in Mrs. Barrett's seat. Vile preaching. . . . Volunteers are quartered at Oswestry. My better half and I went to Aston. Long time before we could find any one. After ringing a long time the good civil Butler came to say that Mrs. Lloyd had a premature and very very little girl at 5 in the morning. Lady Louisa Harvey, who had been up all night, was in the room with her. Sat in the antechamber of the Library till church was over. Harriet Pigott, the Miss Harveys, Mr. Kenyon, Mr. Lloyd came. The Lady Louisa came and she and the Miss Harveys walked with us to the carriage. Went on to Oswestry. Very delightfully comfortable in Miss Mytton's little room conversing over the fire till dinner. Delicious heavenly music by Lady Feilding. At half-past nine rain and darkness. Got a boy with a lantern from the Green to sit upon the front seat and open the gates to Porkington. Got there at ten. Miss Ormsby and Miss Gore in the dining-room ready for us. Supper; at twelve set out. Home at four.

PRIMARY SOURCE

The Hamwood Papers of the Ladies of Llangollen and Caroline Hamilton. Edited by Eva Mary Bell. London: Macmillan & Co., 1930.

RELATED SOURCES

Faderman, Lillian. *Surpassing the Love of Men: Romantic Friendship and Love Between Women from the Renaissance to the Present.* New York: William Morrow & Co., 1981.

Less, Sidney. "Butler, Lady Eleanor." *Dictionary of National Biography 1937–1938.* Vol. III:500–01.

Lucas, Edward V. *A Swan and Her Friends.* London: Methuen, 1907.

Mavor, Elizabeth, *The Ladies of Llangollen, A Study in Romantic Friendship.* London: Michael Joseph, 1971.

Penruddocke, Charles. *The Ladies of Llangollen.* Llangollen: Hugh Jones, 1897.

Todd, Janet. *Women's Friendship in Literature.* New York: Columbia University Press, 1980.

---

[1] Lady Louisa Harvey, daughter of Earl Nugent, married Admiral Sir Eliab Harvey, K.C.B., and had six daughters. Sir Eliab (1758–1830) represented Essex 1803–1812 in Parliament. He commissioned the "*Fighting Temeraire*" and she was second ship of the weather line at the Battle of Trafalgar, "closely following the *Victory*." A great fighter but quarrelsome, he was court-martialled May 1809 for an outburst of indignation on the quarter-deck when Lord Cochrane was appointed to a special command.

ANN CROMARTIE YEARSLEY
1756–1806

Born to laboring-class parents on Clifton Hill, just outside Bristol, where her mother Ann, a dairywoman, sold milk door-to-door, Ann Cromartie received little education, beyond help from her brother William in learning to write, a conspicuous skill for a child of that class at that time. Married to "honest and sober" John Yearsley in 1774, she bore six children in six years, one of whom died. She poignantly describes the compulsion of her creativity which made her a poet, and her insatiable thirst for learning.

After the particularly harsh winter of 1783–84, pregnant with her sixth child, she was found with her family and her mother, all on the verge of death by starvation, by a Mr. Vaughan, who managed to save all but her mother, Ann Cromartie.

For Ann Yearsley, the road to becoming a writer and receiving patronage was linked to these tragic events. Some time later Hannah More's cook showed her philanthropic employer some of Yearsley's verses. (Both Yearsley and More lived in Bristol.) More responded admirably, visited Yearsley on Clifton Hill, and despite misgivings about setting Yearsley "above her station," arranged the publication of Yearsley's poems by subscription in June 1785. Later, however, More decided to administer Yearsley's money, and solicited the agreement of Elizabeth Montagu. When the proceeds from Yearsley's poems were placed in a trust fund that she could not touch, Yearsley responded with anger and indignation. Yearsley was enraged that More had extracted a reluctant signature from her, by which Yearsley renounced all claims to the profits of her poetry. Yearsley's subsequent attempt at compromise—she would be a joint trustee and only the children at emancipation would receive the principal—was unacceptable to the intransigent More. Their rift never healed. In correspondence and in the apparatus to poems, More and Yearsley respectively offered their accounts of their quarrel.

Undeterred, Yearsley continued to write. She mounted a pointed yet moving attack on slavery in 1788, not long after Hannah More's poem *The Slave Trade* appeared. Yearsley's reputation as a controversialist intensified with the publication of *Stanzas of Woe* in 1790. The footman of the Mayor of Bristol savagely horsewhipped Yearsley's children for playing on the Mayor's property. In response, Yearsley sued and backed up this action by assailing the footman and the mayor and corrupt power in general in her poem. No matter the cost, Yearsley believed that injustice must be made public. In 1791, her play *Earl Goodwin,* that had been performed in 1789, was published. It portrayed the power struggle between callous church and state dignitaries and the defenders of peasants' rights.

By 1793 Yearsley implemented her long-standing wish to open a circulating library. Possibly the proceeds from the publication of *Earl Goodwin* helped. In 1795 a novel entitled *The Royal Captives* was published, based on the story of the man in the iron mask, and in 1796 *The Rural Lyre,* her third and last collection of poetry. Her last years, when two of her sons died, sent her into seclusion in Melksham in Wiltshire.

The extracts show two significant elements in Yearsley's writing: first, her refusal to be personally coerced or intimidated; and second, her ability to generalize beyond her own subjection to the subjection of others—her condemnation of slavery is one example. Throughout her writings she opposed historical and contemporary tyranny, her ability to identify with the struggles of subjugated men, women and children directly resulting from her own experiences.

———————————— . ————————————

FROM

POEMS ON VARIOUS SUBJECTS

AUTOBIOGRAPHICAL NARRATIVE

TO THE

NOBLE AND GENEROUS SUBSCRIBERS,

WHO SO LIBERALLY PATRONIZED

A BOOK OF POEMS,

PUBLISHED UNDER THE AUSPICES OF

MISS H. MORE,

OF PARK-STREET, BRISTOL,

The following NARRATIVE is most humbly addressed.

I AM said to have proved ungrateful to my patroness.—The charge I disclaim. Every return that powerless gratitude could make, I have offered; but have fatally experienced, that simple expression only was inadequate to Miss More's extensive and superior mind. To exculpate myself from the monstrous charge of ingratitude falls to my lot. Most irksome the talk! yet, with the most humble deference to the noble patronage I am honoured with, I will pursue it.

Highly meritorious would it have been in Miss H. MORE, not to have urged me to the task, by injuring my character, after chaining me down by obligations. And, great as those obligations are, which that Lady has *conditionally* laid on me, I would *gladly* resign every advantage resulting from them; for that untainted and happy obscurity I once possessed.

SOURCE: The "Autobiographical Narrative" was first published in 1786 as a preface to the fourth edition of *Poems on Several Occasions,* her first volume. It appears here, abridged, from a microfilm of *Poems on Various Subjects* at the Suzzallo Library, University of Washington, Seattle.

When the first edition of my book came out, and the balance was paid by the bookseller to Miss H. MORE, she ordered her Attorney to prepare a deed of trust, appointing Mrs. Montagu (for whom I will ever retain the highest veneration and respect) with herself, the trustees. It was sent to Bristol the day my books came here, with an order for it to be signed by my husband and me immediately, and returned to London the next morning—I had no time to peruse it, nor take a copy; and from the rapidity with which this circumstance was conducted, I feared to ask it. The eldest Miss More read the deed, who, in a conversation some time before, had told me, "that if her sister chose to say she had but two-pence of mine, she might, for the *world* could not get it out of her hands."—My feelings were all struck at—I felt as a mother deemed unworthy the tuition or care of her family; and imagined my conduct and principles must of necessity be falsely represented to a generous public, in order to justify the present measure.—Even the interest was not allowed me, but on the capricious terms, that she should lay it out as she thought proper; without any condition in the deed whereby my children might have an undeniable claim in future. In short, every circumstance was calculated to depress a mind naturally despairing; and in despair I signed this incomplete and unsatisfactory deed; and I vainly imagined, by this submission, I had secured my character from the imputation of ingratitude, as I relinquished all, even the rights of a mother, at Miss H. More's request. When that lady came to Bristol, we had several interviews, in one of which her sister mentioned my owing a little money. Miss H. More said she was sorry I owed any money; adding, "If it is much, I cannot pay it—Will you give me an account, to a shilling, what you owe?"—I told her, I believed it was about ten pounds. She said it should be paid. I was invited to sup with her a few nights after, and she then gave me the above sum; addressing me, after supper, in the following words: "Mrs. Yearsley, now you know what you have to trust to. I can do no more, if any thing should happen; the money lodged in the funds is three hundred and fifty pounds, which nobody but myself or Mrs. Montagu can ever call out. You have complained much of being in debt—we hear it from every quarter."—"Madam," said I, "I* complain of nothing, but for the want of a declaration of the deed for the future security of my children; therefore shall be much obliged to you for it, and a copy of the deed itself." Miss H. More explained, "Are you *mad,* Mrs. Yearsley? or have you drank a glass too much? Who are your advisers? I am certain you have drank, or you would not talk to me in this manner."

---

* From this time, I became very obnoxious to Miss H. More, on account of a very trifling additional circumstance, the discovery of my buying what is called the hogwash of her kitchen; and I am charged with the publication of it. I told her, when she charged me with it, that I could not see how it could offend her, as it was the perquisite of her Cook, and had been paid for by the person who had it before I had the honour of knowing her.

I replied, "*Madam,* you are very wrong to think I have drank. I am only anxious on my children's account. Circumstances may change, ten or twenty years hence, when perhaps I am no more; and I only wish for a copy of the deed, as a little memorandum for my children; nor do I think the requisition unreasonable."

Miss Betty More said, "I don't think you unreasonable, Mrs. Yearsley; but there is a manner of speaking."—I told her, "As to the manner of speaking, I fear I shall always err in that, as I have not been accustomed to your rules of polished life."—Miss H. More said, "I wonder you can suspect Mrs. Montagu, if you suspect me."—I answered, "Far be it from me to suspect either; nor do I think I have acted as if I was suspicious."—Miss H. More replied, "How would you have acted if you were?"—"Different from what I have, Madam," said I.—[My answer here alluded to my confidence in giving Miss More all the presents I had received, from time to time, from those generous friends who visited me while I was writing my poems; often leaving myself without a shilling. My motive was, that no person's generosity might be concealed.]

Miss H. More then said, "Why it is your openness of heart, Mrs. Yearsley, that has always charmed us."

I felt more emotion from this trifling commendation, than from all she had haughtily expressed; and, finding I could not conceal it, hastily withdrew, only wishing the ladies a good night.

Three weeks elapsed before I again saw Miss H. More, though I went daily to the house for the dish-washings.*

Miss More, from that period, intirely altered her conduct to me. Though, after the most diligent enquiry, she had given me the most flattering character, in her letter to Mrs. Montagu, informing that lady, "That it has been denied this poor recluse to drink at the pure well-head of pagan poesy; yet, from the true fountain of divine inspiration, her mind has been wonderfully cherished and enriched; nor has the retailing a few fine maxims of virtue cheated her of the most exact probity of heart: industrious in no common degree, pious, unambitious, simple and unaffected in her manners, of which I have received incontestable proofs."

These, with many more perfections, are the ornaments with which this very consistent lady has thought fit to adorn the Milkwoman of Clifton! But, alas! how fallacious is eloquence! how inconstant capricious affection, when steady principle is not the basis!—From elaborate commendation, the elevated Stella descends to low scurrility, charging me with

---

* I am greatly hurt in obliging my readers to descend to this poor circumstance; but the explanation will further elucidate Stella's friendly letter to a lady in London, wherein she says, "At the time this wretch is arraigning my conduct, she is fetching the wash every day from my house." It was in the course of these three weeks her letter was wrote, and, in this interval, the servant offered me the money which I had paid for the year past, which I did not accept.

"drunkenness," "gambling," "extravagance," and terming me "wretched," "base," "ungrateful," "spendthrift;" boasting, in the same letter, of her charity to a *departed mother,* whom, I solemnly declare, Miss More never saw, nor ever relieved. My mother quitted this life in March; the first time I saw Miss More was in September following, when she presented me with a guinea, from the worthy Mrs. Montagu, which was afterwards charged to the subscription, and added to the money which Miss More allowed me while I was writing my poems.

The last and final interview between Miss More and me, took place in July, when three gentlemen were present, and all took a part in the conversation. I spoke but little, my spirits were depressed, but I carefully concealed my emotion.—Miss More appeared to be greatly moved, and told me imperiously, that I was "a savage"—that "my veracity agreed with my other virtues"—that I had "a reprobate mind, and was a bad woman."—I replied, "that her accusations could never make me a bad woman—that she descended in calling me a savage, nor would she have had the temerity to do it, had I not given myself that name!"

Miss More then gave me her account of the money she had advanced me since her friendship first commenced, which was twenty-eight pounds fourteen shillings, and offered me the dividend from the first half-year; which, with so much insult, I could not accept*; but told her calmly, that she had rendered obligation insupportable already, and I never would make it more oppressive; but should be obliged to her if she would return my MS. copies.

Miss More replied, "They are left at the Printer's, Mrs. Yearsley—Don't think I shall make any use of them—They are burnt."—"Burnt!" said I!!—She seemed confused—my heart felt for her;—those short pauses convinced me that she was hurt, and from that consideration I was silent; but am still concerned that she would not return those poems which are not published.—Miss More gave me a copy of the deed. I told her I desired no more, and took my leave.

Shielded by popular opinion, the ungenerous Stella aims at a defenceless breast—her arrows are of the most malignant kind—yet her endeavours to crush an insignificant wretch need not [be] so amazingly strenuous; for I should have sunk into obscurity again, had not my reputation been so cruelly wounded.—I have to lament, that it does not require one short hour for this expeditious lady to make her wonderful transit from the zenith of praise to the center of malicious detraction.— For all the perfection, fame, or virtues she can boast of possessing, I would not be so much a Proteus!

It having been represented that my last work received great ornament and addition from a learned and superior genius, and my manuscripts

---

* Stella wrote to London, that I dashed the money in her face, and that I was otherwise very violent. I declare those charges to be totally without foundation: the money lay on the table, but was not touched by me.

not existing to contradict it, I have ventured, without a guide, on a second volume of poems, and will complete them with as much expedition as the more important duties of my family will permit.

Here let me close this true but unpleasant narrative, with the humble hope of your forgiveness, for obtruding on your attention so insignificant a tale: but, as character is more precious than life itself, the protection of that alone compelled me to the task.—And, in order to wipe away the suggestion of having been aided by other assistance, I will lose as little time as possible in laying before you and the public the promised work, and rest in full confidence of your future protection and support.

I am,

With the utmost respect and gratitude,

Your devoted and faithful servant,

ANN YEARSLEY

Clifton Hill, October 12th, 1786.

A Poem on the Inhumanity of the Slave-Trade.

BRISTOL, thine heart hath throbb'd to glory.—Slaves,
E'en Christian slaves, have shook their chains, and gaz'd
With wonder and amazement on thee. Hence
Ye grov'ling souls, who think the term I give,
Of Christian slave, a paradox! to you
I do not turn, but leave you to conception
Narrow; with that be blest, nor dare to stretch
Your shackled souls along the course of Freedom.

Yet, Bristol, list! nor deem Lactilla's soul
Lessen'd by distance; snatch her rustic thought,
Her crude ideas, from their panting state,
And let them fly in wide expansion; lend
Thine energy, so little understood
By the rude million, and I'll dare the strain
Of Heav'n-born Liberty till Nature moves
Obedient to her voice. Alas! my friend,
Strong rapture dies within the soul, while Pow'r
Drags on his bleeding victims. Custom, Law,
Ye blessings, and ye curses of mankind,
What evils do ye cause? We feel enslav'd,
Yet move in your direction. Custom, thou

Wilt preach up filial piety; thy sons
Will groan, and stare with impudence at Heav'n,
As if they did abjure the act, where Sin
Sits full on Inhumanity; the church
They fill with mouthing, vap'rous sighs and tears,
Which, like the guileful crocodile's, oft fall,
Nor fall, but at the cost of human bliss.

Custom, thou hast undone us! led us far
From God-like probity, from truth, and heaven.

But come, ye souls who feel for human woe,
Tho' drest in savage guise! Approach, thou son,
Whose heart would shudder at a father's chains,
And melt o'er thy lov'd brother as he lies
Gasping in torment undeserv'd. Oh, sight
Horrid and insupportable! far worse
Than an immediate, an heroic death;
Yet to this sight I summon thee. Approach,
Thou slave of avarice, that canst see the maid
Weep o'er her inky fire! Spare me, thou God
Of all-indulgent Mercy, if I scorn
This gloomy wretch, and turn my tearful eye
To more enlighten'd beings. Yes, my tear
Shall hang on the green furze, like pearly dew
Upon the blossom of the morn. My song
Shall teach sad Philomel a louder note,
When Nature swells her woe. O'er suff'ring man
My soul with sorrow bends! Then come, ye few
Who feel a more than cold, material essence;
Here ye may vent your sighs, till the bleak North
Find its adherents aided.—Ah, no more!
The dingy youth comes on, sullen in chains;
He smiles on the rough sailor, who aloud
Strikes at the spacious heav'n, the earth, the sea,
In breath too blasphemous; yet not to him
Blasphemous, for he dreads not either:—lost
In dear internal imag'ry, the soul
Of Indian Luco rises to his eyes.
Silent, not inexpressive: the strong beams
With eager wildness yet drink in the view
Of his too humble home, where he had left
His mourning father, and his Incilanda.

Curse on the toils spread by a Christian hand
To rob the Indian of his freedom! Curse

On him who from a bending parent steals
His dear support of age, his darling child;
Perhaps a son, or a more tender daughter,
Who might have clos'd his eyelids, as the spark
Of life gently retired. Oh, thou poor world!
Thou fleeting good to individuals! see
How much for thee they care, how wide they ope
Their helpless arms to clasp thee; vapour thou!
More swift than passing wind! thou leav'st them nought
Amid th' unreal scene, but a scant grave.

    I know the crafty merchant will oppose
The plea of nature to my strain, and urge
His toils are for his children: the soft plea
Dissolves my soul—but when I sell a son,
Thou God of nature, let it be my own!

    Behold that Christian! see what horrid joy
Lights up his moody features, while he grasps
The wish'd-for gold, purchase of human blood!
Away, thou seller of mankind! Bring on
Thy daughter to this market! bring thy wife!
Thine aged mother, though of little worth,
With all thy ruddy boys! Sell them, thou wretch,
And swell the price of Luco! Why that start?
Why gaze as thou wouldst fright me from my challenge
With look of anguish? Is it Nature strains
Thine heart-strings at the image? Yes, my charge
Is full against her, and she rends thy soul,
While I but strike upon thy pityless ear,
Fearing her rights are violated.—Speak,
Astound the voice of Justice! bid thy tears
Melt the unpitying pow'r, while thus she claims
The pledges of thy love. Oh, throw thine arm
Around thy little ones, and loudly plead
Thou canst not sell thy children.—Yet, beware
Lest Luco's groan be heard; should that prevail,
Justice will scorn thee in her turn, and hold
Thine act against thy pray'r. Why clasp, she cries,
That blooming youth? Is it because thou lov'st him?
Why Luco was belov'd: then wilt thou feel,
Thou selfish Christian, for thy private woe,
Yet cause such pangs to him that is a father?
Whence comes thy right to barter for thy fellows?
Where are thy statutes? Whose the iron pen
That gave thee precedent? Give me the seal

Of virtue, or religion, for thy trade,
And I will ne'er upbraid thee; but if force
Superior, hard brutality alone
Become thy boast, hence to some savage haunt,
Nor claim protection from my social laws.

Luco is gone; his little brothers weep,
While his fond mother climbs the hoary rock
Whose point o'er-hangs the main. No Luco there,
No sound, save the hoarse billows. On she roves,
With love, fear, hope, holding alternate rage
in her too anxious bosom. Dreary main!
Thy murmurs now are riot, while she stands
List'ning to ev'ry breeze, waiting the step
Of gentle Luco. An, return! return!
Too hapless mother, thy indulgent arms
Shall never clasp thy fetter'd Luco more.
See Incilanda! artless maid, my soul
Keeps pace with thee, and mourns. Now o'er the hill
She creeps, with timid foot, while Sol embrowns
The bosom of the isle, to where she left
Her faithful lover: here the well-known cave,
By Nature form'd amid the rock, endears
The image of her Luco; here his pipe,
Form'd of the polish'd cane, neglected lies,
No more to vibrate; here the useless dart,
The twanging bow, and the fierce panther's skin,
Salute the virgin's eye. But where is Luco?
He comes not down the steep, tho' he had vow'd,
When the sun's beams at noon should sidelong gild
The cave's wide entrance, he would swift descend
To bless his Incilanda. Ten pale moons
Had glided by, since to his generous breast
He clasp'd the tender maid, and whisper'd love.

Oh, mutual sentiment! thou dang'rous bliss!
So exquisite, that Heav'n had been unjust
Had it bestow'd less exquisite of ill;
When thou art held no more, thy pangs are deep,
Thy joys convulsive to the soul; yet all
Are meant to smooth th' uneven road of life.

For Incilanda, Luco rang'd the wild,
Holding her image to his panting heart;
For her he strain'd the bow, for her he stript
The bird of beauteous plumage; happy hour,

When with these guiltless trophies he adorn'd
The brow of her he lov'd. Her gentle breast
With gratitude was fill'd, nor knew she aught
Of language strong enough to paint her soul,
Or ease the great emotion; whilst her eye
Pursued the gen'rous Loco to the field,
And glow'd with rapture at his wish'd return.

Ah, sweet suspense! betwixt the mingled cares
Of friendship, love, and gratitude, so mix'd,
That ev'n the soul may cheat herself.—Down, down,
Intruding Memory! bid thy struggles cease,
At this soft scene of innate war. What sounds
Break on her ear? She, starting, whispers "Luco."
Be still, fond maid; list to the tardy step
Of leaden-footed woe. A father comes,
But not to seek his son, who from the deck
Had breath'd a last adieu: no, he shuts out
The soft, fallacious gleam of hope, and turns
Within upon the mind: horrid and dark
Are his wild, unenlighten'd pow'rs: no ray
Of forc'd philosophy to calm his soul,
But all the anarchy of wounded nature.

Now he arraigns his country's gods, who sit,
In his bright fancy, far beyond the hills,
Unriveting the chains of slaves: his heart
Beats quick with stubborn fury, while he doubts
Their justice to his child. Weeping old man,
Hate not a Christian's God, whose record holds
Thine injured Luco's name. Frighted he starts,
Blasphemes the Deity, whose altars rise
Upon the Indian's helpless neck, and sinks,
Despising comfort, till by grief and age
His angry spirit is forced out. Oh, guide,
Ye angel-forms, this joyless shade to worlds
Where the poor Indian, with the sage, is prov'd
The work of a Creator. Pause not here,
Distracted maid! ah, leave the breathless form,
On whose cold cheek thy tears so swiftly fall,
Too unavailing! On this stone, she cries,
My Luco sat, and to the wand'ring stars
Pointed my eye, while from his gentle tongue
Fell old traditions of his country's woe.
Where now shall Incilanda seek him? Hence,
Defenceless mourner, ere the dreary night

Wrap thee in added horror. Oh, Despair,
How eagerly thou rend'st the heart! She pines
In anguish deep, and sullen: Luco's form
Pursues her, lives in restless thought, and chides
Soft consolation. Banish'd from his arms,
She seeks the cold embrace of death; her soul
Escapes in one sad sigh. Too hapless maid!
Yet happier far than he thou lov'dst; his tear,
His sigh, his groan avail not, for they plead
Most weakly with a Christian. Sink, thou wretch,
Whose act shall on the cheek of Albion's sons
Throw Shame's red blush: thou, who hast frighted far
Those simple wretches from thy God, and taught
Their erring minds to mourn his* partial love,
Profusely pour'd on thee, while they are left
Neglected to thy mercy. Thus deceiv'd,
How doubly dark must be their road to death!

Luco is borne around the neighb'ring isles,
Losing the knowledge of his native shore
Amid the pathless wave; destin'd to plant
The sweet luxuriant cane. He strives to please,
Nor once complains, but greatly smothers grief.
His hands are blister'd, and his feet are worn,
Till ev'ry stroke dealt by his mattock gives
Keen agony to life; while from his breast
The sigh arises, burthen'd with the name
Of Incilanda. Time inures the youth,
His limbs grow nervous, strain'd by willing toil:
And resignation, or a calm despair,
(Most useful either) lulls him to repose.

A Christian renegade, that from his soul
Abjures the tenets of our schools, nor dreads
A future punishment, nor hopes for mercy,
Had fled from England, to avoid those laws
Which must have made his life a retribution
To violated justice, and had gain'd,
By fawning guile, the confidence (ill placed)
Of Luco's master. O'er the slave he stands
With knotted whip, lest fainting nature shun

---

* Indians have been often heard to say, in their complaining moments, "God Almighty no love us well; he be good to †buckera; he bid buckera burn us; he no burn buckera."

† White man.

The talk too arduous, while his cruel soul,
Unnat'ral, ever feeds, with gross delight,
Upon his suff'rings. Many slaves there were,
But none who could supress the sigh, and bend,
So quietly as Luco: long he bore
The stripes, that from his manly bosom drew
The sanguine stream (too little priz'd); at length
Hope fled his soul, giving her struggles o'er,
And he resolv'd to die. The sun had reach'd
His zenith—pausing faintly, Luco stood,
Leaning upon his hoe, while mem'ry brought,
In piteous imag'ry, his aged father,
His poor fond mother, and his faithful maid:
The mental group in wildest motion set
Fruitless imagination; fury, grief,
Alternate shame, the sense of insult, all
Conspire to aid the inward storm; yet words
Were no relief, he stood in silent woe.

    Gorgon, remorseless Christian, saw the slave
Stand musing, 'mid the ranks, and, stealing soft
Behind the studious Luco, struck his cheek
With a too-heavy whip, that reach'd his eye,
Making it dark for ever. Luco turn'd,
In strongest agony, and with his hoe
Struck the rude Christian on the forehead. Pride,
With hateful malice, seize on Gorgon's soul,
By nature fierce; while Luco sought the beach,
And plung'd beneath the wave; but near him lay
A planter's barge, whose seamen grasp'd his hair;
Dragging to life a wretch who wish'd to die.

    Rumour now spreads the tale, while Gorgon's breath
Envenom'd, aids her blast: imputed crimes
Oppose the plea of Luco, till he scorns
Even a just defence, and stands prepared.
The planters, conscious that to fear alone
They owe their cruel pow'r, resolve to blend
New torment with the pangs of death, and hold
Their victims high in dreadful view, to fright
The wretched number left. Luco is chain'd
To a huge tree, his fellow-slaves are ranged
To share the horrid sight; fuel is plac'd
In an increasing train, some paces back,
To kindle slowly, and approach the youth,
With more than native terror. See, it burns!

He gazes on the growing flame, and calls
For "water, water!" The small boon's deny'd.
E'en Christians throng each other, to behold
The different alterations of his face,
As the hot death approaches. (Oh, shame, shame
Upon the followers of Jesus! shame
On him that dares avow a God!) He writhes,
While down his breast glide the unpity'd tears,
And in their sockets strain their scorched balls.
"Burn, burn me quick! I cannot die!" he cries:
"Bring fire more close!" The planters heed him not,
But still prolonging Luco's torture, threat
Their trembling slaves around. His lips are dry,
His senses seem to quiver, e'er they quit
His frame for ever, rallying strong, then driv'n
From the tremendous conflict. Sight no more
Is Luco's, his parch'd tongue is ever mute;
Yet in his soul his Incilanda stays,
Till both escape together. Turn, my muse,
From this sad scene; lead Bristol's milder soul
To where the solitary spirit roves,
Wrapt in the robe of innocence, to shades
Where pity breathing in the gale, dissolves
The mind, when fancy paints such real woe.

Now speak, ye Christians (who for gain enslave
A soul like Luco's, tearing her from joy
In life's short vale; and if there be a hell,
As ye believe, to that ye thrust her down,
A blind, involuntary victim), where
Is your true essence of religion? where
Your proofs of righteousness, when ye conceal
The knowledge of the Deity from those
Who would adore him fervently? Your God
Ye rob of worshippers, his altars keep
Unhail'd, while driving from the sacred font
The eager slave, lest he should hope in Jesus.

Is this your piety? Are these your laws,
Whereby the glory of the Godhead spreads
O'er barb'rous climes? Ye hypocrites, disown
The Christian name, nor shame its cause: yet where
Shall souls like yours find welcome? Would the Turk,
Pagan, or wildest Arab, ope their arms
To gain such proselytes? No; he that owns

The name of *Mussulman would start, and shun
Your worse than serpent touch; he frees his slave
Who turns to Mahomet. The †Spaniard stands
Your brighter contrast; he condemns the youth
For ever to the mine; but ere the wretch
Sinks to the deep domain, the hand of Faith
Bathes his faint temples in the sacred stream,
Bidding his spirit hope. Briton, dost thou
Act up to this? If so, bring on thy slaves
to Calv'ry's mount, raise high their kindred souls
To him who died to save them: this alone
Will teach them calmly to obey thy rage,
And deem a life of misery but a day,
To long eternity. Ah, think how soon
Thine head shall on earth's dreary pillow lie,
With thy poor slaves, each silent, and unknown
To his once furious neighbour. Think how swift
The sands of time ebb out, for him and thee.
Why groans that Indian youth, in burning chains
Suspended o'er the beach? The lab'ring sun
Strikes from his full meridian on the slave
Whose arms are blister'd by the heated iron,
Which still corroding, seeks the bone. What crime
Merits so dire a death?‡ Another gasps
With strongest agony, while life declines
From recent amputation. Gracious God!
Why thus in mercy let thy whirlwinds sleep
O'er a vile race of Christians, who profane
Thy glorious attributes? Sweep them from earth,
Or check their cruel pow'r: the savage tribes
Are angels when compared to brutes like these.

---

* The Turk gives freedom to his slave on condition that he embraces Mahometism.

† The Spaniard, immediately on purchasing an Indian, gives him baptism.

‡ A Coromantin slave in Jamaica (who had frequently escaped to the mountains) was, a few years since, doomed to have his leg cut off. A young practitioner from England (after the surgeon of the estate had refused to be an executioner) undertook the operation, but after the removal of the limb, on the slave's exclaiming, You buckera! God Almighty made dat leg; you cut it off! You put it on again? was so shocked, that the other surgeon was obliged to take up the vessels, apply the dressings, &c. The Negro suffered without a groan, called for his pipe, and calmly smoaked, till the absence of his attendant gave him an opportunity of tearing off his bandages, when he bled to death in an instant. Many will call this act of the Negro's stubbornness; under *such* circumstances, I dare give it a more *glorious* epithet, and that is *fortitude*.

Advance, ye Christians, and oppose my strain:
Who dares condemn it? Prove from laws divine,
From deep philosophy, or social love,
That ye derive your privilege. I scorn
The cry of Av'rice, or the trade that drains
A fellow-creature's blood: bid Commerce plead
Her publick good, her nation's many wants,
Her sons thrown idly on the beach, forbade
To seize the image of their God and sell it:—
I'll hear her voice, and Virtue's hundred tongues
Shall sound against her. Hath our public good
Fell rapine for its basis? Must our wants
Find their supply in murder? Shall the sons
Of Commerce shiv'ring stand, if not employ'd
Worse than the midnight robber? Curses fall
On the destructive system that shall need
Such base supports! Doth England need them? No;
Her laws, with prudence, hang the meagre thief
That from his neighbour steals a slender sum,
Tho' famine drove him on. O'er him the priest,
Beneath the fatal tree, laments the crime,
Approves the law, and bids him calmly die.
Say, doth this law, that dooms the thief, protect
The wretch who makes another's life his prey,
By hellish force to take it at his will?
Is this an English law, whose guidance fails
When crimes are swell'd to magnitude so vast,
That Justice dare not scan them? Or does Law
Bid Justice an eternal distance keep
From England's great tribunal, when the slave
Calls loud on Justice only? Speak, ye few
Who fill Britannia's senate, and are deem'd
The fathers of your country! Boast your laws,
Defend the honour of a land so fall'n,
That Fame from ev'ry battlement is flown,
And Heathens start, e'en at a Christian's name.

Hail, social love! true soul of *order*, hail!
Thy softest emanations, pity, grief,
Lively emotion, sudden joy, and pangs,
Too deep for language, are thy own: then rise,
Thou gentle angel! spread thy silken wings
O'er drowsy man, breathe in his soul, and give
Her God-like pow'rs thy animating force,
To banish Inhumanity. Oh, loose
The fetters of his mind, enlarge his views,

Break down for him the bound of avarice, lift
His feeble faculties beyond a world
To which he soon must prove a stranger! Spread
Before his ravish'd eye the varied tints
Of future glory; bid them live to Fame,
Whose banners wave for ever. Thus inspired,
All that is great and good, and sweetly mild,
Shall fill his noble bosom. He shall melt,
Yea, by thy sympathy unseen, shall feel
Another's pang: for the lamenting maid
His heart shall heave a sigh; with the old slave
(Whose head is bent with sorrow) he shall cast
His eye back on the joys of youth, and say,
"Thou once couldst feel, as I do, love's pure bliss;
"Parental fondness, and the dear returns
"Of filial tenderness were thine, till torn
"From the dissolving scene."—Oh, social love,
Thou universal good, thou that canst fill
The vacuum of immensity, and live
In endless void! thou that in motion first
Set'st the long lazy atoms, by thy force
Quickly assimilating, and restrain'd
By strong attraction; touch the soul of man;
Subdue him; make a fellow-creature's woe
His own by heart-felt sympathy, whilst wealth
Is made subservient to his soft disease.

And when thou hast to high perfection wrought
This mighty work, say, "such is Bristhol's soul."

FINIS

---•---

PRIMARY SOURCES

Poems on Several Occasions. London: T. Cadell, 1785.

Poems on Several Occasions. 4th ed. "Autobiographical Narrative" added. London: T. Cadell, 1786.

Poems on Various Subjects. "Autobiographical Narrative" again printed; "The Deed of Trust" added. London: G.G.J. and J. Robinson, 1787.

A Poem on the Inhumanity of the Slave-Trade. London: G. G. J. and J. Robinson, 1788.

RELATED SOURCES

Ferguson, Moira. "Resistance and Power in the Life and Writings of Ann Yearsley, 1785–1791." Forthcoming.

Roberts, William. *Memoirs of the Life and Correspondence of Mrs. Hannah More.* 4 vols. London: R. B. Seeley and W. Burnside, 1834. (See particularly Chap. IV, pp. 361–75 and 383–91 for the altercation.)

Southey, Robert. *The Lives and Works of the Uneducated Poets.* London: Humphrey Milford, 1925.

Tompkins, Joyce Marjorie Sanxter. "The Bristol Milkwoman." In *The Polite Marriage.* Cambridge: University Press, 1938.

CATHERINE SAWBRIDGE MACAULAY GRAHAM 1731–1791

Catherine Sawbridge's family on her father's side were Whigs with financial ties in the City. Her paternal grandfather was a director of the ill-fated South Sea Company. Her mother was the daughter of George Wanley, a wealthy London banker who left her a large inheritance. Of Catherine Sawbridge's three siblings, John became Alderman, Sheriff, then Lord Mayor of London and was one of the Members of Parliament who seceded from the Society of Supporters of the Bill of Rights. She grew up in a Kentish country house, which had been in the Sawbridge family for generations. How she was educated remains unclear but it was probably private and she had the run of her reclusive father's well-stocked library.

When she was twenty-nine, she married a distinguished Scottish physician, George Macaulay, who was also treasurer of the Lying-in-Hospital on Brownlow Street. He seems to have been very supportive of Catherine Sawbridge Macaulay's intellectual pursuits, for she published the first volume of her eight-volume *History* three years after her marriage. They had one daughter. George Macaulay died six years later, in 1766. By the early 1770s, Catherine Sawbridge Macaulay's health had so declined that in 1774 she had taken up permanent residence in Bath. The following year she visited France and met colonial American and French radicals in Paris. In 1777, before a grand assembly at Alfred House in Bath on the occasion of her forty-sixth birthday, six odes were presented to Macaulay, "that justly-celebrated Historian," as announced on the title page. Her physician, James Graham, also presented her with a copy of his works that honored her in a glowing dedication. By 1779, however, Macaulay's defiance of convention in marrying James Graham's twenty-one-year-old brother William, a surgeon's mate and later a cleric, prompted scurrilous attacks and the removal of her statue in Bath. In one of these attacks, "A Bridal Ode on the Marriage of Catherine and Petruchio," the writer seems particularly obsessed with the couple's sexual relationship and exemplifies a particularly crude and virulent strain of late eighteenth-century misogyny. (It is worth noting, and predictable, that two of the toughest-minded women of the revolutionary era, Macaulay and Wollstonecraft, suffered traditional, sexually-based misogynous abuse.) After this second marriage, she lived and wrote in Berkshire, visiting America in 1785 and staying at Mount Vernon for ten days with George and Martha Washington.

Throughout her adult life Catherine Macaulay (as she is most often referred to) was well known as an outspoken radical Whig. Possibly her best known and certainly her longest work, "the first comprehensive anti-royalist history of its time," was *The History of England, from the Accession of James I to that of the Brunswick Line.* The first volume appeared in 1763, and the next four before 1771. Of the remaining three, two appeared in 1781 and the last in 1783. Her responses to Thomas Hobbes's *Philosophical Rudiments . . .* in 1767 and to Edmund Burke in 1770, after which the latter dubbed her "our republican Virago," further enhanced her reputation. She took issue with Burke again, in reply this time to his *Reflections on the Revolution in France* (1790). Mary Wollstonecraft and Thomas Paine also responded. Wollstonecraft, moreover, admired and was influenced in her second *Vindication* by Macaulay's *Letters on Education,* which appeared the year before Macaulay's death. Denying that innate differences between the sexes existed, Macaulay advocated coeducation and condemned the discriminatory treatment of women throughout society. Elsewhere in the *Letters* applauding the idea of benevolence and sympathy, Macaulay deplored cruelty to animals and expressed reservations about meat-eating. She scoffed at the view of beauty that favored the light-complexioned. She also castigated "the savage barbarism which is now displayed on the sultry shores of Africa"—a reference to slavery.

In her day Macaulay was a celebrated radical and the most prominent spokeswoman for the radical Whig cause. Such notable American patriots as John Adams and Benjamin Franklin knew and corresponded with her, while Madame Roland hoped to be "la Macaulay de son pays." Mary Wollstonecraft proudly described her as "the woman of the greatest abilities, undoubtedly, that this country has ever produced."

FROM

LETTERS ON EDUCATION.

LETTER XXI.

Morals must be taught on immutable Principles.

IT is one thing, Hortensia, to educate a citizen, and another to educate a philosopher. The mere citizen will have learnt to obey the laws of his country, but he will never understand those principles on which all laws ought to be established; and without such an understanding, he can never be religious on rational principles, or truly moral; nor will he ever have any of that active wisdom which is necessary for co-operating in any plan of reformation. But to teach morals on an immutable fitness, has never been the practice in any system of education yet extant. Hence all our notions of right and wrong are loose, unconnected, and inconsistent. Hence the murderer, in one situation, is extolled to the skies; and, in another, is followed with reproach even beyond the grave. For it is not only the man of the world who idolises power, though in the garb of villainy, and persecutes dishonesty when united to weakness, but even those who bear the specious title of philosophers are apt to be dazzled with the brilliancy of success, and to treat qualities and characters differently, according to the smiles or frowns of fortune.

As an instance, to illustrate this observation, I will select out of the huge mass of human inconsistencies, the praises bestowed by Xenophon on Cyrus; who, whether a real or fictitious character, is set up by this philosopher as a model of princely perfection.

Cyrus, it is true, is represented as moderate in the gratification of his appetites, liberal to his followers, and just, when he found justice correspond with his interest; but, as himself confesses, he never practiced any virtue on other principles but those of personal utility; and he animates his countrymen to exertions, which he dignifies with this title, on motives of obtaining means, by the spoils of others, for future enjoyment. In short, Cyrus was neither liberal from generosity, just from honesty, nor merciful from benevolence; and the address he made use of to enslave the minds of his subjects, is of the same kind as that used by a courtezan to extend and preserve her influence over the hearts of those she has trepanned into her snares. Cyrus was master of all those arts which are

---

SOURCE: Selections are taken from a reprint (facsimile) of the 1790 edition of *Letters on Education* from the British Library, no. 1030.q.9.

necessary to obtain and preserve to himself and successors an unjust measure of power; he enflamed with this lust all his warlike followers, in order to eradicate from their minds the love of freedom and independence. His system of policy, of which many parts are atrocious outrages on the rights of Nature, established the firmest and the most extensive despotism that was ever established in the East, and has, on these reasons, prevailed more or less in the Persian dynasty, and in all the governments which have been built on its ruins; yet Xenophon and Cicero, who were both republicans and philosophers, extol Cyrus to the skies. But had these men understood rectitude on the principles of truth, they must have perceived, that power never can be justly obtained but by conquest over those by whom we are first unlawfully attacked, or by such a fair influence over the mind as shall convince men that they will be safe and happy under our authority.

Cyrus is one of those plausible knaves who have been set up as models for example; and, on these reasons, he imposes on all those who do not reflect deeply. But I am convinced, that a Caesar Borgia, or a Cataline, had their characters been united with a brilliant success, would have equally imposed on the vulgar; for as Helvetius very justly observes, it is only the weakness of the poor rogue which men despise, not his dishonesty.

In order to take from public sentiment a reproach which leaves a deep stain on the human character, and to correct many irregularities, and even enormities, which arise from incorrect systems of ethics, it ought to be the first care of education to teach virtue on immutable principles, and to avoid that confusion which must arise from confounding the laws and customs of society with those obligations which are founded on correct principles of equity. But as you have had patience to go through my whole plan of education, from infancy to manhood, it is but fair that I should attend to your objections, and examine whether my plan is founded on error, or on the principles of reason and truth. Know then, good Hortensia, that I have given similar rules for male and female enducation [sic], on the following grounds of reasoning.

First, That there is but one rule of right for the conduct of all rational beings; consequently that true virtue in one sex must be equally so in the other, whenever a proper opportunity calls for its exertion; and, vice versa, what is vice in one sex, cannot have a different property when found in the other.

Secondly, That true wisdom, which is never found at variance with rectitude, is as useful to women as to men; because it is necessary to the highest degree of happiness, which can never exist with ignorance.

Lastly, That as on our first entrance into another world, our state of happiness may possibly depend on the degree of perfection we have attained in this, we cannot justly lessen, in one sex or the other, the means by which perfection, that is another word for wisdom, is acquired.

It would be paying you a bad compliment, Hortensia, were I to answer all the frivolous objections which prejudice has framed against the giving a learned education to women; for I know of no learning, worth having, that does not tend to free the mind from error, and enlarge our stock of useful knowledge. Thus much it may be proper to observe, that those hours which are spent in studious retirement by learned women, will not in all probability intrude so much on the time for useful avocation, as the wild and spreading dissipations of the present day; that levity and ignorance will always be found in opposition to what is useful and graceful in life; and that the contrary may be expected from a truly enlightened understanding. However, Hortensia, to throw some illustration on what I have advanced on this subject, it may be necessary to shew you, that all those vices and imperfections which have been generally regarded as inseparable from the female character, do not in any manner proceed from sexual causes, but are entirely the effects of situation and education. But these observations must be left to farther discussion.

LETTER XXII.

No characteristic Difference in Sex.

THE great difference that is observable in the characters of the sexes, Hortensia, as they display themselves in the scenes of social life, has given rise to much false speculation on the natural qualities of the female mind.—For though the doctrine of innate ideas, and innate affections, are in a great measure exploded by the learned, yet few persons reason so closely and so accurately on abstract subjects as, through a long chain of deductions, to bring forth a conclusion which in no respect militates with their premises.

It is a long time before the crowd give up opinions they have been taught to look upon with respect; and I know many persons who will follow you willingly through the course of your argument, till they perceive it tends to the overthrow of some fond prejudice; and then they will either sound a retreat, or begin a contest in which the contender for truth, though he cannot be overcome, is effectually silenced, from the mere weariness of answering positive assertions, reiterated without end. It is from such causes that the notion of a sexual difference in the human character has, with a very few exceptions, universally prevailed from the earliest times, and the pride of one sex, and the ignorance and vanity of the other, have helped to support an opinion which a close observation of Nature, and a more accurate way of reasoning, would disprove.

It must be confessed, that the virtues of the males among the human species, though mixed and blended with a variety of vices and errors, have displayed a bolder and a more consistent picture of excellence than female nature has hitherto done. It is on these reasons that, when we compliment the appearance of a more than ordinary energy in the female mind, we call it masculine; and hence it is, that Pope has elegantly said a perfect woman's but a softer man. And if we take in the consideration, that there can be but one rule of moral excellence for beings made of the same materials, organized after the same manner, and subjected to similar laws of Nature, we must either agree with Mr. Pope, or we must reverse the proposition, and say, that a perfect man is a woman formed after a coarser mold. The difference that actually does subsist between the sexes, is too flattering for men to be willingly imputed to accident; for what accident occasions, wisdom might correct; and it is better, says Pride, to give up the advantages we might derive from the perfection of our fellow associates, than to own that Nature has been just in the equal distribution of her favours. These are the sentiments of the men; but mark how readily they are yielded to by the women; not from humility I assure you, but merely to preserve with character those fond vanities on which they set their hearts. No; suffer them to idolize their persons, to throw away their life in the pursuit of trifles, and to indulge in the gratification of the meaner passions, and they will heartily join in the sentence of their degradation.

Among the most strenuous asserters of a sexual difference in character, Rousseau is the most conspicuous, both on account of that warmth of sentiment which distinguishes all his writings, and the eloquence of his compositions: but never did enthusiasm and the love of paradox, those enemies to philosophical disquisition, appear in more strong opposition to plain sense than in Rousseau's definition of this difference. He sets out with a supposition, that Nature intended the subjection of the one sex to the other; that consequently there must be an inferiority of intellect in the subjected party; but as man is a very imperfect being, and apt to play the capricious tyrant, Nature, to bring things nearer to an equality, bestowed on the woman such attractive graces, and such an insinuating address, as to turn the balance on the other scale. Thus Nature, in a giddy mood, recedes from her purposes, and subjects prerogative to an influence which must produce confusion and disorder in the system of human affairs. Rousseau saw this objection; and in order to obviate it, he has made up a moral person of the union of the two sexes, which, for contradiction and absurdity, outdoes every metaphysical riddle that was ever formed in the schools. In short, it is not reason, it is not wit; it is pride and sensuality that speak in Rousseau, and, in this instance, has lowered the man of genius to the licentious pedant.

But whatever might be the wise purpose intended by Providence in such a disposition of things, certain it is, that some degree of inferiority, in point of corporal strength, seems always to have existed between the two sexes; and this advantage, in the barbarous ages of mankind, was abused to such a degree, as to destroy all the natural rights of the female species, and reduce them to a state of abject slavery. What accidents have contributed in Europe to better their condition, would not be to my purpose to relate; for I do not intend to give you a history of women; I mean only to trace the sources of their peculiar foibles and vices; and these I firmly believe to originate in situation and education only: for so little did a wise and just Providence intend to make the condition of slavery an unalterable law of female nature, that in the same proportion as the male sex have consulted the interest of their own happiness, they have relaxed in their tyranny over women; and such is their use in the system of mundane creation, and such their natural influence over the male mind, that were these advantages properly exerted, they might carry every point of any importance to their honour and happiness. However, till that period arrives in which women will act wisely, we will amuse ourselves in talking of their follies.

The situation and education of women, Hortensia, is precisely that which must necessarily tend to corrupt and debilitate both the powers of mind and body. From a false notion of beauty and delicacy, their system of nerves is depraved before they come out of their nursery; and this kind of depravity has more influence over the mind, and consequently over morals, than is commonly apprehended. But it would be well if such causes only acted towards the debasement of the sex; their moral education is, if possible, more absurd than their physical. The principles and nature of virtue, which is never properly explained to boys, is kept quite a mystery to girls. They are told indeed, that they must abstain from those vices which are contrary to their personal happiness, or they will be regarded as criminals, both by God and man; but all the higher parts of rectitude, every thing that ennobles our being, and that renders us both innoxious and useful, is either not taught, or is taught in such a manner as to leave no proper impression on the mind. This is so obvious a truth, that the defects of female education have ever been a fruitful topic of declamation for the moralist; but not one of this class of writers have laid down any judicious rules for amendment. Whilst we still retain the absurd notion of a sexual excellence, it will militate against the perfecting a plan of education for either sex. The judicious Addison animadverts on the absurdity of bringing a young lady up with no higher idea of the end of education than to make her agreeable to a husband, and confining the necessary excellence for this happy acquisition to the mere graces of person.

Every parent and tutor may not express himself in the same manner as is marked out by Addison: yet certain it is, that the admiration of the other sex is held out to women as the highest honour they can attain; and whilst this is considered as their *summum bonum,* and the beauty of their persons the chief *desideratum* of men, Vanity, and its companion Envy, must taint, in their characters, every native and every acquired excellence. Nor can you, Hortensia, deny, that these qualities, when united to ignorance, are fully equal to the engendering and rivetting all those vices and foibles which are peculiar to the female sex; vices and foibles which have caused them to be considered, in ancient times, as beneath cultivation, and in modern days have subjected them to the censure and ridicule of writers of all descriptions, from the deep thinking philosopher to the man of ton and gallantry, who, by the bye, sometimes distinguishes himself by qualities which are not greatly superior to those he despises in women. Nor can I better illustrate the truth of this observation than by the following picture, to be found in the polite and gallant Chesterfield. "Women," says his Lordship, "are only children of a larger growth. They have an entertaining tattle, sometimes wit; but for solid reasoning, and good sense, I never in my life knew one that had it, or who acted or reasoned in consequence of it for four and twenty hours together. A man of sense only trifles with them, plays with them, humours and flatters them, as he does an engaging child; but he neither consults them, nor trusts them in serious matters."

LETTER XXIII.

Coquettry.

THOUGH the situation of women in modern Europe, Hortensia, when compared with that condition of abject slavery in which they have always been held in the east, may be considered as brilliant; yet if we withhold comparison, and take the matter in a positive sense, we shall have no great reason to boast of our privileges, or of the candour and indulgence of the men towards us. For with a total and absolute exclusion of every political right to the sex in general, married women, whose situation demand a particular indulgence, have hardly a civil right to save them from the grossest injuries; and though the gallantry of some of the European societies have necessarily produced indulgence, yet in others the faults of women are treated with a severity and rancour which militates against every principle of religion and common sense. Faults, my friend, I hear you say; you take the matter in too general a sense; you know there is but one fault which a woman of honour may not commit with impunity; let her only take care that she is not caught in a love intrigue, and she may lie, she may deceive, she may defame, she may ruin her own family with gaming, and the peace of twenty others with her coquettry, and yet preserve both her reputation and her peace. These are glorious privileges indeed, Hortensia; but whilst plays and novels are the favourite study of the fair, whilst the admiration of men continues to be set forth as the chief honour of woman, whilst power is only acquired by personal charms, whilst continual dissipation banishes the hour of reflection, Nature and flattery will too often prevail; and when this is the case, self preservation will suggest to conscious weakness those methods which are the most likely to conceal the ruinous trespass, however safe and criminal they may be in their nature. The crimes that women have committed, both to conceal and to indulge their natural failings, shock the feelings of moral sense; but indeed every love intrigue, though it does not terminate in such horrid catastrophes, must naturally tend to debase the female mind, from its violence to educational impressions, from the secrecy with which it must be conducted, and the debasing dependancy to which the intriguer, if she is a woman of reputation, is subjected. Lying, flattery, hypocrisy, bribery, and a long catalogue of the meanest of the human vices, must all be employed to preserve necessary appearances. Hence delicacy of sentiment gradually decreases; the warnings of virtue are no longer felt; the mind becomes corrupted, and lies open to every solicitation which appetite or passion presents. This must be the natural course of things in every being formed after the human plan; but it gives rise to the trite and foolish observation, that the first fault against chastity in woman has a radical power to deprave the character. But no such frail beings come out of the hands of Nature. The human mind is built of nobler materials than to be so easily corrupted; and with all the disadvantages of situation and education, women seldom become entirely abandoned till they are thrown into a state of desperation by the venomous rancour of their own sex.

The superiority of address peculiar to the female sex, says Rousseau, is a very equitable indemnification for their inferiority in point of strength. Without this, woman would not be the companion of man, but his slave; it is by her superior art and ingenuity that she preserves her equality, and governs him, whilst she affects to obey. Woman has every thing against her; as well our faults, as her own timidity and weakness. She has nothing in her favor but her subtlety and her beauty; is it not very reasonable therefore that she should cultivate both?

I am persuaded that Rousseau's understanding was too good to have led him into this error, had he not been blinded by his pride and his sensuality. The first was soothed by the opinion of superiority, lulled into acquiescence by cajolement; and the second was attracted by the idea of women playing off all the arts of coquettry to raise the passions of the sex. Indeed the author fully avows his sentiments, by acknowledging that he would have a young French woman cultivate her agreeable talents, in order to please her future husband, with as much care and assiduity as a young Circassian cultivates her's to fit her for the harem of an eastern bashaw.

These agreeable talents, as the author expresses it, are played off to great advantage by women in all the courts of Europe; who, for the arts of female allurement, do not give place to the Circassian. But it is the practice of these very arts, directed to enthral the man, which act in a peculiar manner to corrupting the female mind. Envy, malice, jealousy, a cruel delight in inspiring sentiments which at first perhaps were never intended to be reciprocal, are leading features in the character of the coquet, whose aim is to subject the whole world to her own humour; but in this vain attempt she commonly sacrifices both her decency and her virtue.

By the intrigues of women, and their rage for personal power and importance, the whole world has been filled with violence and injury; and their levity and influence have proved so hostile to the existence or permanence of rational manners, that it fully justifies the keeness of Mr. Pope's satire on the sex.

But I hear my Hortensia say, whither will this fit of moral anger carry you? I expected an apology, instead of a libel, on women; according to your description of the sex, the philosopher has more reason to regret the indulgence, than what you have sometimes termed the injustice of the men; and to look with greater complacency on the surly manners of the ancient Greeks, and the selfishness of Asiatic luxury, than on the gallantry of modern Europe.

Though you have often heard me express myself with warmth in the vindication of female nature, Hortensia, yet I never was an apologist for the conduct of women. But I cannot think the surliness of the Greek manners, or the selfishness of Asiatic luxury, a proper remedy to apply to the evil. If we could inspect narrowly into the domestic concerns of ancient and modern Asia, I dare say we should perceive that the first springs of the vast machine of society were set a going by women; and as to the Greeks, though it might be supposed that the peculiarity of their manners would have rendered them indifferent to the sex, yet they were avowedly governed by them. They only transferred that confidence which they ought to have given their wives, to their courtezans, in the same manner as our English husbands do their tenderness and their complaisance. They will sacrifice a wife of fortune and family to resentment, or the love of change, provided she give them opportunity, and bear with much Christian patience to be supplanted by their footman in the person of their mistress.

No; as Rousseau observes, it was ordained by Providence that women should govern some way or another; and all that reformation can do, is to take power out of the hands of vice and folly, and place it where it will not be liable to be abused.

To do the sex justice, it must be confessed that history does not set forth more instances of positive power abused by women, than by men; and when the sex have been taught wisdom by education, they will be glad to give up indirect influence for rational privileges; and the precarious sovereignty of an hour enjoyed with the meanest and most infamous of the species, for those established rights which, independent of accidental circumstances, may afford protection to the whole sex.

LETTER XXIV.

Flattery—Chastity—Male Rakes.

AFTER all that has been advanced, Hortensia, the happiness and perfection of the two sexes are so reciprocally dependant on one another that, till both are reformed, there is no expecting excellence in either. The candid Addison has confessed, that in order to embellish the mistress, you must give a new education to the lover, and teach the men not to be any longer dazzled by false charms and unreal beauty. Till this is the case, we must endeavour to palliate the evil we cannot remedy; and, in the education of our females, raise as many barriers to the corruptions of the world, as our understanding and sense of things will permit.

As I give no credit to the opinion of a sexual excellence, I have made no variation in the fundamental principles of the education of the two sexes; but it will be necessary to admit of such a difference in the plan as shall in some degree form the female mind to the particularity of its situation.

The fruits of true philosophy are modesty and humility; for as we advance in knowledge, our deficiencies become more conspicuous; and by learning to (form?) a just estimate on what we possess, we find little gratification for the passion of pride. This is so just an observation, that we may venture to pronounce, without any exception to the rule, that a vain or proud man is, in a positive sense, an ignorant man. However if it should be our lot to have one of the fair sex, distinguished for any eminent degree of personal charms, committed to our care, we must not attempt by a premature cultivation to gather the fruits of philosophy before their season, nor expect to find the qualities of true modesty and humility make their appearance till the blaze of beauty has in some measure been subdued by time. For should we exhaust all the powers of oratory, and all the strength of sound argument, in the endeavour to convince our pupil that beauty is of small weight in the scale of real excellence, the enflamed praises she will continually hear bestowed on this quality will fix her in the opinion, that we mean to keep her in ignorance of her true worth. She will think herself deceived, and she will resent the injury by giving little credit to our precepts, and placing her confidence in those who tickle her ears with lavish panegyric on the captivating graces of her person.

Thus vanity steals on the mind, and thus a daughter, kept under by the ill exerted power of parental authority, gives a full ear to the flattery of a coxcomb. Happy would it be for the sex did the mischief end here; but the soothings of flattery never fail to operate on the affections of the heart; and when love creeps into the bosom, the empire of reason is at an end. To prevent our fair pupils therefore from becoming the prey of coxcombs, and serving either to swell their triumph, or repair their ruined fortunes, it will be necessary to give them a full idea of the magnitude of their beauty, and the power this quality has over the frail mind of man. Nor have we in this case so much to fear from the intimations of a judicious friend, as from the insiduous adulation of a designing admirer. The haughty beauty is too proud to regard the admiration of fops and triflers; she will never condescend to the base, the treacherous, the dangerous arts of coquettry; and by keeping her heart free from the snares of love, she will have time to cultivate that philosophy which, if well understood, is a never failing remedy to human pride.

But the most difficult part of female education, is to give girls such an idea of chastity, as shall arm their reason and their sentiments on the side of this useful virtue. For I believe there are more women of understanding led into acts of imprudence by the ignorance, the prejudices, and the false craft of those by whom they are educated, than from any other cause founded either in nature or in chance. You may train up a docile idiot to any mode of thinking or acting, as may best suit the intended purpose; but a reasoning being will scan over your propositions, and if they find them grounded in falsehood, they will reject them with disdain. When you tell a girl of spirit and reflection that chastity is a sexual virtue, and the want of it a sexual vice, she will be apt to examine into the principles of religion, morals, and the reason of things, in order to satisfy herself on the truth of your proposition. And when, after the strictest enquiries, she finds nothing that will warrant the confining the propositions to a particular sense, she will entertain doubts either of your wisdom or your sincerity; and regarding you either as a deceiver or a fool, she will transfer her confidence to the companion of the easy vacant hour, whose compliance with her opinions can flatter her vanity. Thus left to Nature, with an unfortunate biass on her mind, she will fall a victim to the first plausible being who has formed a design on her person. Rousseau is so sensible of this truth, that he quarrels with human reason, and would put her out of the question in all considerations of duty. But this is being as great a fanatic in morals, as some are in religion; and I should much doubt the reality of that duty which would not stand the test of fair enquiry; beside, as I intend to breed my pupils up to act a rational part in the world, and not to fill up a niche in the seraglio of a sultan, I shall certainly give them leave to use their reason in all matters which concern their duty and happiness, and shall spare no pains in the cultivation of this only sure guide to virtue. I shall inform them of the great utility of chastity and continence; that the one preserves the body in health and vigor, and the other, the purity and independence of the mind, without which it is impossible to possess virtue or happiness. I shall intimate, that the great difference now beheld in the external consequences which follow the deviations from chastity in the two sexes, did in all probability arise from women having been considered as the mere property of the men; and, on this account had no right to dispose of their own persons: that policy adopted this difference, when the plea of property had been given up; and it was still preserved in society from the unruly licentiousness of the men, who, finding no obstacles in the delicacy of the other sex, continue to set at defiance both divine and moral law, and by mutual support and general opinion to use their natural freedom with impunity. I shall observe, that this state of things renders the situation of females, in their individual capacity very precarious; for the strength which Nature has given to the passion of love, in order to serve her purposes, has made it the most ungovernal propensity of any which attends us. The snares therefore, that are continually laid for women, by persons who run no risk in compassing their seduction, exposes them to continual danger; whilst the implacability of their own sex, who fear to give up any advantages which a superior prudence, or even its appearances, give them, renders one false step an irretrievable misfortune. That, for these reasons, coquettry in women is as dangerous as it is dishonorable. That a coquet commonly finds her own perdition, in the very flames which she raises to consume others; and that if any thing can excuse the baseness of female seduction, it is the baits which are flung out by women to entangle the affections, and excite the passions of men.

I know not what you may think of my method, Hortensia, which I must acknowledge to carry the stamp of singularity; but for my part, I am sanguine enough to expect to turn out of my hands a careless, modest beauty, grave, manly, noble, full of strength and majesty; and carrying about her an aegis sufficiently powerful to defend her against the sharpest arrow that ever was shot from Cupid's bow. A woman, whose virtue will not be of the kind to wrankle into an inveterate malignity against her own sex for faults which she even encourages in the men, but who, understanding the principles of true religion and morality, will regard chastity and truth as indispensible qualities in virtuous characters of either sex; whose justice will incline her to extend her benevolence to the frailties of the fair as circumstances invite, and to manifest her resentment against the underminers of female happiness; in short, a woman who will not take a male rake either for a husband or a friend. And let me tell you, Hortensia, if women had as much regard for the virtue of chastity as in some cases they pretend to have, a reformation would long since have taken place in the world; but whilst they continue to cherish immodesty in the men, their bitter persecution of their own sex will not save them from the imputation of those concealed propensities with which they are accused by Pope, and other severe satirists on the sex.

PRIMARY SOURCES

History of England, from the Accession of James I to that of the Brunswick Line.
8 vols. London: J. Nourse, 1763–1783.

Letters on Education, with observations on religious and metaphysical subjects.
London, 1790. Reprinted in *Feminist Controversy in England, 1788–1810.*
Edited by Gina Luria. New York: Garland Publishing, 1974.

Observations on the Reflections of the Right Hon. Edmund Burke on the Revolution in France, in a letter to the Right Hon. the Earl of Stanhope. London, 1790.

RELATED SOURCES

Boos, Florence, and William Boos. "Catherine Macaulay: Historian and Political Reformer." *International Journal of Women's Studies* 3, 1 (January–February 1980): 49–65.

Davis, Natalie Zemon. "Gender and Genre: Women as Historical Writers, 1400–1820." In *Beyond Their Sex: Learned Women of the European Past,* edited by Patricia Labalme, 153–82. New York: New York University Press, 1980.

Kamm, Josephine. "Theorists and Reformers of the Eighteenth Century." In *Hope Deferred: Girls' Education in English History.* London: Methuen, 1965.

Schnorrenberg, Barbara Brandon. "Catharine Macaulay Graham: The Rise and Fall of a Female Intellectual." Paper read at the annual meeting of the American Society for Eighteenth-Century Studies, University of Pennsylvania, Philadelphia, 1975.

————. "The Brood Hen of Faction: Mrs. Macaulay and Radical Politics, 1765–1775." *Albion* 2, 1 (Spring 1979): 33–43.

MARY HAYS
1759/60 – 1843

Mary Hays was born in the London borough of Southwark to a middle-class family of Rational Dissenters who encouraged her literary inclinations. Little is known of her early life apart from an exchange of letters between Hays and another Dissenter, John Eccles, written from 1779–1780. After a successful struggle to obtain permission to marry her, Eccles died just weeks before the ceremony was to have taken place. She never married.

During the 1780s Hays read widely in fiction, philosophical tracts, poetry, and religious treatises. *La Nouvelle Héloïse* by Jean-Jacques Rousseau particularly affected her. In 1788, Robert Robinson, a radical Baptist preacher who helped her emerge from mourning and became an informal mentor, introduced her to other influential Dissenters such as Joseph Priestly, Theophilus Lindsey (founder of the Unitarian Church), and Lindsey's successor, John Disney.

Under the pseudonym "Eusebia," Hays published her *Cursory Remarks on an Inquiry into the Expediency and Propriety of Public or Social Worships* (1791), in response to Gilbert Wakefield's attack on nonconformist modes of worship. The success of this pamphlet brought Hays into closer contact with other Dissenters, including William Frend, a mathematician to whom Hays was strongly attracted, and Mary Wollstonecraft, with whom she became friends. In fact, Wollstonecraft's *A Vindication of the Rights of Woman,* (1792), strongly induced Hays to agitate for equality, educational opportunity, and personal independence for females. Wollstonecraft also critiqued Hays's second work, *Letters and Essays, Moral and Miscellaneous,* in 1793. Hays left her mother's home for her own abode at this time—a traumatic experience—and not long after she began a voluminous correspondence with William Godwin, the anarchist philosopher and novelist, to which he responded in long conversations over tea. He encouraged her to use fiction as a vehicle for her ideas. The autobiographically-based *Memoirs of Emma Courtney* resulted, with her by now one-sided passion for Frend a major theme.

Having established a reputation as a contemporary novelist, Hays reviewed fiction for the *Analytical Review* and other journals. From February 1796 until February 1797 she frequently contributed to the *Monthly Magazine* on the subject of women's rights and education.

Excerpts here illustrate her concerns with notions about "sexual charac-
ter" (now known as "gender distinctions") and her bold, direct style.
In the September volume for 1797, she wrote a heartfelt obituary to
Wollstonecraft.

Despite the dangerous political situation in England, Hays remained
a staunch Jacobin and feminist. Her second novel, *The Victim of Prejudice* (1799), was vehemently criticized. The Reverend Richard Polwhele
described her as one of "the blasphemous band of Wollstonecraftians"
in his misogynous poem, *The Unsex'd Females*. Her feminist tract, *Appeal to the Men of Great Britain in Behalf of Women* was published
anonymously by Joseph Johnson in 1798. In *Female Biography* (1803),
she argued persuasively for the superiority of women—a "female worthies" update—and followed this with *Harry Clinton; or a Tale of Youth*
(1804); *Historical Dialogues for Young Persons* (1808); *The Brothers*
(1815); and *Family Annals; or the Sisters* (1817). She associated in her
last thirty years with such notable writers as William Wordsworth,
Samuel Taylor Coleridge, and Robert Southey.

FROM
Monthly Magazine

Remarks on A. B.'s Strictures on the Talents of Women. To the Editor
of the Monthly Magazine, July 2, 1796.

Sir,
The petty and unphilosophical contest respecting sexual superiority,
has, in this advanced age of reason and science, become frivolous and
uninteresting. Of all exclusive pretensions, there is none more absurd
and mischievous, in its operation and consequences, than that of mind.
That one half of the human species, on a self-erected throne, should
prescribe bounds to, and impose intellectual fetters on, the other half;
and dictate to them to what purposes they are to apply, and how far they
are to be allowed to exercise, their common faculties, is not more
intolerable than vain. How long, with sectarian inconsistency, will man
refuse the liberty he claims; how long will he cherish, with narrow policy
and superstitious veneration, and maxims of tyranny, and the institutions of barbarism? These idle disputes were entirely superseded, the
moment that an enlightened philosophy demonstrated, "That man (in-

SOURCE: Selections are taken from *Monthly Magazine* on microfilm at Love
Library, University of Nebraska-Lincoln.

cluding the species, without distinction of sex) was simply a perceptive being, incapable of receiving knowledge through any other medium than that of the senses: that the actions and dispositions of men are not the offspring of any original bias that they bring into the world in favour of one sentiment or character rather than another, but flow entirely from the operation of circumstances, and events acting upon a faculty of receiving sensible impressions: that all our knowledge, all our ideas, every thing we possess as intelligent beings, comes from impression. All the minds that exist set out from absolute ignorance. They received first one impression and then a second. As the impressions became more numerous, and more stored by the help of memory, and combined by the faculty of association, so the experience increased, and with the experience, the knowledge, the wisdom, every thing that distinguishes man from what we understand by a "clod of the valley."* This, adds our author, is a simple and incontrovertible history of intellectual being. Allowing this statement to be just, from whence is derived the fanciful distinction between creatures similarly organized, endowed with a like number of senses or inlets to perception?

Assuredly, your correspondent is wonderfully generous in granting, that women have "a right to the enjoyment of intellectual pleasures"—though this, he seems to imply, is to be subject to some limitations. The existence of the right is proved by capacity, and not to be yielded as a favour. The argument upon which the superiority of man is grounded, is both novel and curious.

"There have certainly been female writers, of very considerable merit; but no evidence has yet appeared that they possess powers equal to those of men. We have never yet seen a female Homer, or Virgil, or Bacon, or Newton. Great numbers of women have received a much better education than Shakspeare ever enjoyed; and yet, I believe, we may venture to ask, whether the works of all the female authors who ever existed, taken collectively, are equal in value to the works of Shakspeare, an uneducated man?" Admitting, for the sake of the hypothesis, these observations to be just, is the superiority of a whole species to be deduced from the example of a few individuals formed by extraordinary circumstances? But we are willing to grant still more to A. B. and yet deny the conclusion which he has so sagaciously and triumphantly inferred.

We will allow that, upon the aggregate, from a fair calculation, the balance of intellectual attainment would, probably, be found on the side of the men. And why? Not from any occult and original difference in their conformation, but because the education of women has been uniformly more perverted, as well as neglected, than that of men. Their general inferiority then, follows as a consequence from the principles already stated: nor is it necessary to refer to remote and mysterious causes what may be traced, with much greater facility, to sources obviously existing

---

* Godwin's *Political Justice.*

and daily observed. Many women, it is said, have been better educated than Shakpeare. This would be difficult to prove, when education is comprehensively considered, as consisting of precept, accident, social intercourse, and political institution. In all these branches, by which the human character is wholly modified, women suffer great and peculiar disadvantages. Till it can be demonstrated, that man has a sixth sense, or some method of acquiring, combining, and associating his ideas, from which nature has precluded woman, these arrogant claims must be referred to the same source with every other proud and exclusive pretension.

In the early ages, and in the infancy of reason, every appeal was decided, and every dispute settled, by brute force. Man having, for physical purposes, a *small* degree of superior bodily strength (for the difference, as present observable, is the systematic result of education and habit) subjugated woman. As civilization advanced, the slavery of the female was meliorated, and in an exact ratio with rational and philosophical improvement, became less and less apparent. But, so intoxicating is the nature of power, endeavours were still made to sophisticate and entangle the truths which could no longer be suppressed: and woman, beginning so to feel her own dignity, and to assert the glorious privilege of thinking and reasoning, was to be flattered into the feeble imbecile creature which (excepting a few individuals, whose number, we perceive with pride and pleasure, is daily and rapidly increasing) has, in every age, corrupted, degraded, and, in her turn, tyrannized over her oppressor. Rousseau, whose genius and vanity led him to adopt and defend eccentric and erroneous opinions, which he so well knew how to render alluring by the charms of a captivating eloquence, set the example, and reared, on fanciful principles, a dazzling and beautiful hypothesis, involving in itself contradictions, and demonstrably false. Woman herself, cajoled by these artifices, has, not unfrequently, been induced pertinaciously to contend for "the sentiment that brutalizes her," and to relinquish the only valuable and noble purpose of existence, mental and moral improvement, which are inseparably connected, because she is told, in the fauning accents of a designing courtier—"That it would be an unjust monopoly to pretend to be at once the most lovely and the wisest part of the human species." Amidst the disadvantages under which women have hitherto laboured, the heroines of antiquity, Semiramis, Zenobia, and Boadicea—the Catherines of the North, and Elizabeth of England; the Lesbian Sappho, the Grecian Hypatia, Madame de Chatelet, the commentator upon Newton; Dacier, the translator of Homer; and Macauley, the English historian, with many others, who have rendered their names illustrious, have afforded proofs of powers and capacities, perhaps, little less extraordinary than either those of Homer, Newton, or Shakspeare. How have arts, sciences, literature, morals, and happiness been impeded in their progress by jealous and paltry contentions for pre-eminence, whether monarchical, aristocratical, feudal, professional, or sexual? When will the mists of prejudice be dispelled by the light of reason? When will a generous policy take place of partial institution? When shall we cease to be disgusted with unmeaning and ostentatious pretentions to liberality of sentiment; liberality which has hitherto been little more than a name?

A WOMAN.

July 2, 1796

---•---

MONTHLY MAGAZINE

To the Editor of the Monthly Magazine, March 2, 1797.

Sir,

I AM encouraged by your insertion of my defence of the talents of women, in reply to the structures of A. B. and C. to address you upon a subject, which if not entirely depending upon the principle in question, is yet intimately connected with it. An eloquent advocate for the rights of her sex, and of humanity, waving the controverted, though not unimportant, question, respecting sexual equality, contends, that our virtues and acquirements should be the same in nature, if differing in degree. In establishing this important truth, the deplorable consequences resulting from the distinctions hitherto adhered to in the education of the sexes, are painted with glowing colouring, and insisted upon in energetic language.

Female education, as at present conducted, is a complete system of artifice and despotism; all the little luxuriances and exuberances of character, which individualise the being, which give promise of, and lay the foundation for, future powers, are carefully lopped and pruned away; sincerity and candour are repressed with solicitude; the terrors of opinion are set in array, and suspended over the victim, till the enfeebled and broken spirit submits to the trammels, and passive, tame, and docile, is stretched or shortened (as on the frame of the tyrant Procrustes) to the universal standard. From woman, thus rendered systematically weak and powerless, to whom truth and morals have been confounded, inconsistent and contrary qualities are absurdly expected: for principle, it is attempted to substitute rule and dogma, while prejudice is combated only by other prejudices, equally, if not still more pernicious. The majority of human beings have yet to learn, notwithstanding a daily and melancholy experience, the dangerous tendency of every species of imposition and falsehood: one erroneous idea, entangling itself with others, from the nature of association and mind, is sufficient to destroy the whole character, nay more, to poison a community. Not an action nor a thought can be entirely unconsequential; nothing is stationary; truth or error rapidly and incessantly propagates itself.

Sexual distinctions respecting chastity, an important branch of temperance, have served but to increase the tide of profligacy, and have been the fruitful source of the great part of the infelicity and corruption of society. "Destroy love and friendship," says Hume, "what remains in the world worth accepting?" To insist upon the tendency which libertinisn and gross sensuality must have to blunt the finer sensibilities, and vitiate the delicacy of taste, which is favourable to the production of these affections, would be unnecessary. One of the principal causes which seems to have given rise to the present dissolute and venal motives by which the intercourse of the sexes is influenced, is perhaps the dependence for which women are uniformly educated. Upon the general enfeebling effects of this system I shall not insist; its obvious consequences are sufficient for my present purpose. The greater proportion of young women are trained up by thoughtless parents, in ease and luxury, with no other dependence for their future support than the precarious chance of establishing themselves by marriage: for this purpose (the men best know why) elaborate attention is paid to external attractions and accomplishments, to the neglect of more useful and solid acquirements. "A young girl," says Rousseau, "must be trained up for a husband, like an Eastern beauty for a harem:" and he was right; while they have but one means (every rule admits of individual exceptions) not merely of gratifying the heart (sensibility and nature will here always exert their honest arts) but of satisfying their pride, their ambition, the laudable desire of distinction, even of procuring a subsistence, or barely the means of existing. If, thus situated, women marry from mercenary and venal motives (the worst kind of prostitution) with little delicacy or selection, is it reasonable to condemn them? If misery, disgust, or infidelity result from such connections, ought it to be matter of surprise? Supposing they fail in this sole method of procuring for themselves an establishment, and such failures are frequent in this expensive and profligate age, what is the consequence? Must we rigidly pursue and censure these innocent and helpless victims to barbarous prejudice, should they prefer the flowery paths of pleasure, for which their education has been in a great measure preparatory, to the almost equally degrading alternative of servile occupation, or the more specious, but not less galling situation of companion, or humble martyr to the caprice of a fellow-being, not unfrequently rendered callous and despotic by prosperity and indulgence? One of the world's maxims, with a view to counteract other notions, equally false and pernicious, is, that a woman having once deviated from chastity is to be considered as irreclaimable.

To demonstrate the truth of this philosophic and merciful adage, great care is taken to bar up every avenue against the return of this frail, unfortunate being, who, driven from the society and countenance of the virtuous and respectable, is reduced to associate with those whose habitual vices render them little calculated to assist her in regaining the path from which she has wandered. By these wise and humane methods, the tender, affectionate heart, betrayed, perhaps, by its own amiable susceptibility, and artless credulity, is precipitated by despair into real depravity. The numbers of women who are thus thrown into a state of abandoned profligacy are almost incalculable and incredible; while the universal contagion spreads through every rank, strikes at the root not only of the sweetest and most affecting felicities of life; but the order and well-being of society. Men, satiated with beauty, marry merely for wealth and convenience; while domestic happiness, and the tender confidence, and affecting endearments, of virtuous love, are almost as obsolete as the maxims of chivalry. In their stead, a heartless, mindless intercourse is substituted, the insipidity of which is its least evil.

I am aware, that the absurd distinction alluded to, is deeply entangled with the system of property, and is one of those evils flowing from feudal institutions; the baneful effects of which can only cease with the reno-vation of civil society. Yet, in the mean time, its deplorable con-sequences might be ameliorated, by an alteration of the system of female education. Might not a part of the time wasted in the acquisition of beliefs and frivolous accomplishments, be devoted to the attainment of some ingenious art of useful trade by which a young woman might hope to gain an honest and honourable independence, and be freed from the disgraceful necessity of bartering her person to procure a maintenance? Every parent having a family of daughters, for whom it is not in his power to make a suitable provision, is guilty of cruelty and vice, when he hazards their being exposed, helpless and unprotected, to the world. There are a variety of trades and professions, by their nature peculiarly appropriate to women, exercised, with very few exceptions, at present, entirely by men; to these many of the liberal arts might be added, also the knowledge and practice of arithmetic and book-keeping. A woman enabled to support herself, and to acquire property by her industry, would gain by regular occupation, and the healthful exertion of her faculties, more firmness of mind and greater vigour of body. Marriages would be contracted from motives of affection, rather than of interest; and entered into with less apprehensions, when the whole burden of providing for a family rested not upon the efforts of the man, but was cheerfully shared between the parties. It may be objected, that the weak-ness and cares of a mother, in bearing and nursing her offspring, must incapacitate her for farther exertion. This objection, with but few excep-tions, might be proved futile, by the example of whole towns and com-munities; not to insist on the number of poor hard-labouring women, with large families (the support of which is thrown by a profligate hus-band wholly upon them) in this and in almost every other country. The constitution, strengthened by labour or wholesome exercise, would like-wise acquire greater vigour, and many of those physical evils which afflict the female frame, in an enervated and artificial state of society, would be greatly alleviated, if not wholly removed. Those women whom disappointed affection, or personal disadvantages, consigned to celebacy, in the exercise of body and mind, in occupations that promised competence or distinction, would be preserved from the numerous evils and follies, I might add, cruel insults, to which they are at present exposed.

The only happy life, it is justly observed, by Mr. Hume, is that which is equally divided between action and rest (or relaxation). Duties will never be properly performed unless softened by pleasures; nor can pleasures deserve the title, unless earned by business.

Inequality, in the present state of things, is not confined to property; while one part of the community, worn down by toil, sacrifice the end to the means, the remainder are sunk in a still more destructive incapacity or intolerable latitude, from which there is no escape but by mischievous and dangerous experiments and exertions.

The prosperous or declining state of a nation might, perhaps, be more accurately deduced from the possession or want of private virtue and happiness, than from the condition of its revenue or its foreign connections. Government is valuable only as a mean of which individual happiness is the end: should this not be produced, the institution becomes vain or pernicious. Till one moral and mental standard is established for every rational agent, every member of a community, and a free scope afforded for the exertion of their faculties and talents, without distinction of rank or sex, virtue will be an empty name, and happiness elude our most anxious research.

M.H.

March 2, 1797

——————————————— • ———————————————

PRIMARY SOURCES

Appeal to the Men of Great Britain in Behalf of Women. London, 1798. Reprinted in *Feminist Controversy in England, 1788–1810.* Edited by Gina Luria. New York: Garland Publishing, 1974.

Female Biography; or Memoirs of illustrious and celebrated women, of all Ages and Countries. 6 vols. London: R. Phillips. 1803.

Memoirs of Emma Courtney. 2 vols. London, 1796. Reprinted in *Feminist Controversy.*

Monthly Magazine. July 2, 1796.

Monthly Magazine. March 2, 1797.

RELATED SOURCES

Luria, Gina M. "Mary Hays's Letters and Manuscripts." *Signs: Journal of Women in Culture and Society* 3, 2 (Winter 1977):524–30.

Pollin, Burton R. "Mary Hays on Woman's Rights in the *Monthly Magazine.*" *Etudes Anglaises* 24, 3 (1971):271–82.

Tompkins, Joyce Marjorie Sanxter. "Mary Hays, Philosophess." In *The Polite Marriage.* Cambridge: University Press, 1938.

MARY WOLLSTONECRAFT
1759–1797

Mary Wollstonecraft's father Edward tried unsuccessfully to be a gentleman-farmer after investing an inheritance from Wollstone-craft senior, a financially shrewd master-weaver. Her mother Elizabeth (née Dixon) bore seven children and had to endure drunken abuse as her husband's fortune dwindled and he became frustrated. In an early bid for independence from this turbulent, unhappy domestic life, Woll-stonecraft tried her hand at the limited occupations open to females of the petty-bourgeois class, first as a chaperone, then as a teacher, a private tutor, a governess to aristocratic children, and finally as an edito-rial assistant, a journalist, and an independent writer. During this period she became firm friends with Frances (Fanny) Blood, with whose family and Fanny herself she lived for a time. Her first novel, *Mary, a Fiction* (1788), is a fictive semi-autobiographical elegy to her beloved friend who died in Portugal following childbirth, with Mary Wollstonecraft at her side.

She associated for a period with the North London Rational Dissenters who included Richard Price and Sarah Burgh, and wrote *Thoughts on the Education of Daughters* in 1786, loosely based on her North London teaching experiences, her readings, and her recent exposure to non-conformist thought. After a stint in Ireland as a governess, she returned to London where she wrote and worked for Joseph Johnson, the radi-cal publisher. Her social circle included Thomas Paine, Anna Laetitia Barbauld, Henry Fuseli, William Blake, and William Godwin, and for a time, she was enamored of Fuseli. Intrepidly, she left London alone for Paris at the height of revolutionary tumult in December 1792. An involved relationship in France with a New Jersey author and entrepreneur, Gil-bert Imlay, resulted in the birth of a daughter, Fanny. With Imlay, she displayed the same passion and insecurity in her letters and relationship that had been evident earlier with friends and relatives.

Thoughts addressed the right of females to be educated and the power of education to promote virtue and improve the quality of human life, a recurring issue in Wollstonecraft's works. She also wrote *Original Sto-ries* for children, advocating a pious, morally pure life. She included antislavery extracts in her educational anthology and teaching hand-book entitled *The Female Reader*, and in her translation of *Elements of Morality* (1790) she appealed for a more humanitarian approach toward

Native American Indians. *A Vindication of the Rights of Men* (which also attacked slavery) and *A Vindication of the Rights of Woman* appeared in 1791 and 1792 respectively, after the outbreak and partly because of the French Revolution; they displayed the growing sophistication of her ideas, influenced both by her rich experiences and by circles she frequented. The second *Vindication* has secured her a reputation as the most significant and influential British feminist thinker of the century. To recuperate from a suicide attempt over her benighted affair with Imlay, she travelled to Scandinavia as his business executor. Her epistolary narrative of these Scandinavian travels, *Letters from Sweden,* remains one of her most popular works. William Godwin, the philosophical anarchist whom she married in 1796, dated his love for her from his reading of that work.

Wollstonecraft died ten days after giving birth to a daughter, Mary, who later married Percy Bysshe Shelley and wrote *Frankenstein.* At the end of her life, Wollstonecraft was working on a manuscript on pediatrics and female pedagogy, and on an exciting novel of propaganda entitled *Maria, or the Wrongs of Woman.* Godwin's frank memoirs of her life, which he published posthumously to assuage his grief and vindicate her memory, had an adverse effect on her reputation. The public was scandalized at an unmarried woman who bore a child, ventured into public life successfully on her own, ignored notoriety, attempted suicide twice, supported revolutions, and as an avowed feminist wrote persuasively and passionately for human justice. The counterpoint to this public censure was the steady enhancement of her reputation among such radical thinkers as Percy Bysshe Shelley and Virginia Woolf, from Wollstonecraft's time to the present. These excerpts from the second *Vindication* and her unfinished posthumous novel, *Maria,* indicate her commitment, her range of concerns, and the appropriate forcefulness of her style.

FROM

A Vindication of the Rights of Woman

CHAP. IX.

OF THE PERNICIOUS EFFECTS WHICH ARISE FROM THE UNNATURAL DISTINCTIONS ESTABLISHED IN SOCIETY.

From the respect paid to property flow, as from a poisoned fountain, most of the evils and vices which render this world such a dreary scene to the contemplative mind. For it is in the most polished society that noisesome reptiles and venomous serpents lurk under the rank herbage; and there is voluptuousness pampered by the still sultry air, which relaxes every good disposition before it ripens into virtue.

One class presses on another; for all are aiming to procure respect on account of their property: and property, once gained, will procure the respect due only to talents and virtue. Men neglect the duties incumbent on man, yet are treated like demi-gods; religion is also separated from morality by a ceremonial veil, yet men wonder that the world is almost, literally speaking, a den of sharpers or oppressors.

There is a homely proverb, which speaks a shrewd truth, that whoever the devil finds idle he will employ. And what but habitual idleness can hereditary wealth and titles produce? For man is so constituted that he can only attain a proper use of his faculties by exercising them, and will not exercise them unless necessity of some kind first set the wheels in motion. Virtue likewise can only be acquired by the discharge of relative duties; but the importance of these sacred duties will scarcely be felt by the being who is cajoled out of his humanity by the flattery of syco-phants. There must be more equality established in society, or morality will never gain ground, and this virtuous equality will not rest firmly even when founded on a rock, if one half of mankind be chained to its bottom by fate, for they will be continually undermining it through ignorance or pride.

SOURCE: The selections are taken from these editions: *A Vindication of the Rights of Woman* from the 1975 reprint by W. W. Norton & Co. of the 1792 edition. *Maria, or The Wrongs of Woman* from the 1975 reprint by W. W. Norton & Co. of the 1798 edition.

It is vain to expect virtue from women till they are in some degree, independent of men; nay, it is vain to expect that strength of natural affection which would make them good wives and mothers. Whilst they are absolutely dependent on their husbands they will be cunning, mean, and selfish, and the men who can be gratified by the fawning fondness of spaniel-like affection have not much delicacy, for love is not to be bought, in any sense of the words, its silken wings are instantly shrivelled up when anything beside a return in kind is sought. Yet whilst wealth enervates men, and women live, as it were, by their personal charms, how can we expect them to discharge those ennobling duties which equally require exertion and self-denial? Hereditary property sophisticates[1] the mind, and the unfortunate victims to it, if I may so express myself, swathed from their birth, seldom exert the locomotive faculty of body or mind; and, thus viewing everything through one medium, and that a false one, they are unable to discern in what true merit and happiness consist. False, indeed, must be the light when the drapery of situation hides the man, and makes him stalk in masquerade, dragging from one scene of dissipation to another the nerveless limbs that hang with stupid listlessness, and rolling round the vacant eye which plainly tells us that there is no mind at home.

I mean, therefore, to infer that the society is not properly organized which does not compel men and women to discharge their respective duties, by making it the only way to acquire that countenance from their fellow-creatures which every human being wishes some way to attain. The respect, consequently, which is paid to wealth and mere personal charms, is a true north-east blast that blights the tender blossoms of affection and virtue. Nature has wisely attached affections to duties to sweeten toil, and to give that vigour to the exertions of reason which only the heart can give. But the affection which is put on merely because it is the appropriated insignia of a certain character, when its duties are not fulfilled, is one of the empty compliments which vice and folly are obliged to pay to virtue and the real nature of things.

To illustrate my opinion, I need only observe that when a woman is admired for her beauty, and suffers herself to be so far intoxicated by the admiration she receives as to neglect to discharge the indispensable duty of a mother, she sins against herself by neglecting to cultivate an affection that would equally tend to make her useful and happy. True happiness, I mean all the contentment and virtuous satisfaction that can be snatched in this imperfect state, must arise from well regulated affections; and an affection includes a duty. Men are not aware of the misery they cause and the vicious weakness they cherish by only inciting women to render themselves pleasing; they do not consider that they thus make natural and artificial duties clash by sacrificing the comfort

---

[1] Corrupts.

and respectability of a woman's life to voluptuous notions of beauty when in nature they all harmonize.

Cold would be the heart of a husband, were he not rendered unnatural by early debauchery, who did not feel more delight at seeing his child suckled by its mother, than the most artful wanton tricks could ever raise; yet this natural way of cementing the matrimonial tie and twisting esteem with fonder recollections, wealth leads women to spurn. To preserve their beauty and wear the flowery crown of the day, which gives them a kind of right to reign for a short time over the sex, they neglect to stamp impressions on their husbands' hearts that would be remembered with more tenderness when the snow on the head began to chill the bosom than even their virgin charms. The maternal solicitude of a reasonable affectionate woman is very interesting, and the chastened dignity with which a mother returns the caresses that she and her child receive from a father who has been fulfilling the serious duties of his station, is not only a respectable but a beautiful sight. So singular indeed are my feelings, and I have endeavoured not to catch factitious ones, that after having been fatigued with the sight of insipid grandeur and the slavish ceremonies that with cumbrous pomp supplied the place of domestic affections, I have turned to some other scene to relieve my eye by resting it on the refreshing green everywhere scattered by nature. I have then viewed with pleasure a woman nursing her children, and discharging the duties of her station with, perhaps, merely a servant maid to take off her hands the servile part of the household business. I have seen her prepare herself and children, with only the luxury of cleanliness, to receive her husband, who returning weary home in the evening found smiling babes and a clean hearth. My heart has loitered in the midst of the group, and has even throbbed with sympathetic emotion, when the scraping of the well known foot has raised a pleasing tumult.

Whilst my benevolence has been gratified by contemplating this artless picture, I have thought that a couple of this description, equally necessary and independent of each other, because each fulfilled the respective duties of their station, possessed all that life could give.— Raised sufficiently above abject poverty not to be obliged to weigh the consequence of every farthing they spend, and having sufficient to prevent their attending to a frigid system of economy, which narrows both heart and mind. I declare, so vulgar are my conceptions, that I know not what is wanted to render this the happiest as well as the most respectable situation in the world, but a taste for literature, to throw a little variety and interest into social converse, and some superfluous money to give to the needy and to buy books. For it is not pleasant when the heart is opened by compassion and the head active in arranging plans of usefulness, to have a prim urchin continually twitching back the elbow to prevent the hand from drawing out an almost empty purse, whispering at the same time some prudential maxim about the priority of justice.

Destructive, however, as riches and inherited honours are to the human character, women are more debased and cramped, if possible, by them than men, because men may still, in some degree, unfold their faculties by becoming soldiers and statesmen.

As soldiers, I grant, they can now only gather, for the most part, vain glorious laurels, whilst they adjust to a hair the European balance, taking especial care that no bleak northern nook or sound incline the beam. But the days of true heroism are over, when a citizen fought for his country like a Fabricius[1] or a Washington, and then returned to his farm to let his virtuous fervour run in a more placid, but not a less salutary, stream. No, our British heroes are oftener sent from the gaming table than from the plough;[2] and their passions have been rather inflamed by hanging with dumb suspense on the turn of a die, than sublimated by panting after the adventurous march of virtue in the historic page.

The statesman, it is true, might with more propriety quit the faro bank,[3] or card-table, to guide the helm, for he has still but to shuffle and trick. The whole system of British politics, if system it may courteously be called, consisting in multiplying dependents and contriving taxes which grind the poor to pamper the rich; thus a war, or any wild goose chase, is, as the vulgar use the phrase, a lucky turn-up of patronage for the minister, whose chief merit is the art of keeping himself in place. It is not necessary then that he should have bowels for[4] the poor, so he can secure for his family the odd trick. Or should some show of respect, for what is termed with ignorant ostentation an Englishman's birthright, be expedient to bubble[5] the gruff mastiff that he has to lead by the nose, he can make an empty show very safely by giving his single voice and suffering his light squadron to file off to the other side. And when a question of humanity is agitated he may dip a sop in the milk of human kindness to silence Cerberus,[6] and talk of the interest which his heart takes in an attempt to make the earth no longer cry for vengeance as it sucks in its children's blood, though his cold hand may at the very moment rivet their chains by sanctioning the abominable traffic. A minister is no longer a minister than while he can carry a point which he is

---

[1] A Roman general (3rd century B.C.) renowned for his incorruptibility; on one occasion when he was sent to ransom prisoners from the enemy, the foe sent back both ransom and the freed prisoners, so impressed were they with Fabricius.

[2] Cincinnatus was supposedly called from his plow on his humble farm to defend Rome.

[3] Card game in which players bet on which card will chance to appear at the top of the deck.

[4] Compassion for.

[5] Delude.

[6] In Greek myth the dog, usually represented as having three heads, who guarded the entrance to Hades.

determined to carry. Yet it is not necessary that a minister should feel like a man, when a bold push might shake his seat.

But, to have done with these episodical observations, let me return to the more specious slavery which chains the very soul of woman, keeping her for ever under the bondage of ignorance.

The preposterous distinctions of rank, which render civilization a curse by dividing the world between voluptuous tyrants, and cunning envious dependents, corrupt, almost equally, every class of people, because respectability is not attached to the discharge of the relative duties of life, but to the station, and when the duties are not fulfilled the affections cannot gain sufficient strength to fortify the virtue of which they are the natural reward. Still there are some loopholes out of which a man may creep, and dare to think and act for himself; but for a woman it is a herculean task, because she has difficulties peculiar to her sex to overcome which require almost superhuman powers.

A truly benevolent legislator always endeavours to make it the interest of each individual to be virtuous; and thus private virtue becoming the cement of public happiness, an orderly whole is consolidated by the tendency of all the parts towards a common centre. But, the private or public virtue of woman is very problematical; for Rousseau, and a numerous list of male writers, insist that she should all her life be subjected to a severe restraint, that of propriety. Why subject her to propriety—blind propriety, if she be capable of acting from a nobler spring, if she be an heir of immortality? Is sugar always to be produced by vital blood? Is one half of the human species, like the poor African slaves, to be subject to prejudices that brutalize them, when principles would be a surer guard, only to sweeten the cup of man? Is not this indirectly to deny woman reason? for a gift is a mockery, if it be unfit for use.

Women are, in common with men, rendered weak and luxurious by the relaxing pleasures which wealth procures; but added to this they are made slaves to their persons, and must render them alluring that man may lend them his reason to guide their tottering steps aright. Or should they be ambitious, they must govern their tyrants by sinister tricks, for without rights there cannot be any incumbent duties. The laws respecting woman, which I mean to discuss in a future part, make an absurd unit of a man and his wife;[1] and then, by the easy transition of only considering him as responsible, she is reduced to a mere cypher.

The being who discharges the duties of its station is independent; and, speaking of women at large, their first duty is to themselves as rational creatures, and the next in point of importance, as citizens, is that which includes so many, of a mother. The rank in life which dispenses with their fulfilling this duty necessarily degrades them by making them mere

---

[1] According to the concept of *couverture* in English common law of the period, a husband and wife were one legal unit, and the responsible legal person was the husband.

dolls. Or, should they turn to something more important than merely fitting drapery upon a smooth block, their minds are only occupied by some soft platonic attachment; or, the actual management of an intrigue may keep their thoughts in motion; for when they neglect domestic duties, they have it not in their own power to take the field and march and counter-march like soldiers, or wrangle in the senate to keep their faculties from rusting.

I know that, as a proof of the inferiority of the sex, Rousseau has exultingly exclaimed, How can they leave the nursery for the camp![1] And the camp has by some moralists been termed the school of the most heroic virtues; though, I think, it would puzzle a keen casuist to prove the reasonableness of the greater number of wars that have dubbed heroes. I do not mean to consider this question critically; because, having frequently viewed these freaks of ambition as the first natural mode of civilization, when the ground must be torn up, and the woods cleared by fire and sword, I do not choose to call them pests; but surely the present system of war has little connection with virtue of any denomination, being rather the school of *finesse* and effeminacy, than of fortitude.

Yet, if defensive war, the only justifiable war, in the present advanced state of society, where virtue can show its face and ripen amidst the rigours which purify the air on the mountain's top, were alone to be adopted as just and glorious, the true heroism of antiquity might again animate female bosoms. But fair and softly, gentle reader, male or female, do not alarm thyself, for though I have compared the character of a modern soldier with that of a civilized woman, I am not going to advise them to turn their distaff into a musket, though I sincerely wish to see the bayonet converted into a pruning-hook. I only recreated an imagination, fatigued by contemplating the vices and follies which all proceed from a feculent stream of wealth that has muddied the pure rills of natural affection, by supposing that society will some time or other be so constituted, that man must necessarily fulfil the duties of a citizen or be despised, and that while he was employed in any of the departments of civil life, his wife, also an active citizen, should be equally intent to manage her family, educate her children, and assist her neighbours.

But, to render her really virtuous and useful, she must not, if she discharge her civil duties, want, individually, the protection of civil laws; she must not be dependent on her husband's bounty for her subsistence during his life or support after his death—for how can a being be generous who has nothing of its own? or virtuous, who is not free? The wife, in the present state of things, who is faithful to her husband, and neither suckles nor educates her children, scarcely deserves the name of a wife, and has no right to that of a citizen. But take away natural rights, and duties become null.

---

[1] *Émile*, p. 325: "Can [a woman] be a nursing mother today and a soldier tomorrow?"

Women then must be considered as only the wanton solace of men when they become so weak in mind and body that they cannot exert themselves, unless to pursue some frothy pleasure or to invent some frivolous fashion. What can be a more melancholy sight to a thinking mind than to look into the numerous carriages that drive helter-skelter about this metropolis in a morning full of pale-faced creatures who are flying from themselves. I have often wished, with Dr. Johnson, to place some of them in a little shop with half a dozen children looking up to their languid countenances for support.[1] I am much mistaken, if some latent vigour would not soon give health and spirit to their eyes, and some lines drawn by the exercise of reason on the blank cheeks, which before were only undulated by dimples, might restore lost dignity to the character, or rather enable it to attain the true dignity of its nature. Virtue is not to be acquired even by speculation, much less by the negative supineness that wealth naturally generates.

Besides, when poverty is more disgraceful than even vice, is not morality cut to the quick? Still to avoid misconstruction, though I consider that women in the common walks of life are called to fulfil the duties of wives and mothers, by religion and reason, I cannot help lamenting that women of a superiour cast have not a road open by which they can pursue more extensive plans of usefulness and independence. I may excite laughter by dropping a hint which I mean to pursue some future time, for I really think that women ought to have representatives, instead of being arbitrarily governed without having any direct share allowed them in the deliberations of government.

But, as the whole system of representation is now in this country only a convenient handle for despotism, they need not complain, for they are as well represented as a numerous class of hard-working mechanics, who pay for the support of royalty when they can scarcely stop their children's mouths with bread. How are they represented whose very sweat supports the splendid stud of an heir apparent, or varnishes the chariot of some female favourite who looks down on shame? Taxes on the very necessaries of life, enable an endless tribe of idle princes and princesses to pass with stupid pomp before a gaping crowd, who almost worship the very parade which costs them so dear. This is mere gothic grandeur, something like the barbarous useless parade of having sentinels on horseback at Whitehall,[2] which I could never view without a mixture of contempt and indignation.

How strangely must the mind be sophisticated when this sort of state impresses it! But, till these monuments of folly are levelled by virtue, similar follies will leaven the whole mass. For the same character, in

---

[1] Wollstonecraft may be referring to the *Rambler* Essay No. 85 (January 8, 1751), "The Mischiefs of Total Idleness."

[2] The famous Horse Guards who daily post guard on Whitehall, the hub of the British government.

some degree, will prevail in the aggregate of society; and the refinements of luxury, or the vicious repinings of envious poverty, will equally banish virtue from society, considered as the characteristic of that society, or only allow it to appear as one of the stripes of the harlequin coat, worn by the civilized man.

In the superior ranks of life every duty is done by deputies, as if duties could ever be waived, and the vain pleasures which consequent idleness forces the rich to pursue appear so enticing to the next rank that the numerous scramblers for wealth sacrifice everything to tread on their heels. The most sacred trusts are then considered as sinecures, because they were procured by interest, and only sought to enable a man to keep *good company.* Women, in particular, all want to be ladies. Which is simply to have nothing to do, but listlessly to go they scarcely care where, for they cannot tell what.

But what have women to do in society? I may be asked, but to loiter with easy grace; surely you would not condemn them all to suckle fools and chronicle small beer![1] No. Women might certainly study the art of healing, and be physicians as well as nurses. And midwifery, decency seems to allot to them, though I am afraid the word midwife, in our dictionaries will soon give place to *accoucheur,*[2] and one proof of the former delicacy of the sex be effaced from the language.

They might also study politics, and settle their benevolence on the broadest basis; for the reading of history will scarcely be more useful than the perusal of romances, if read as mere biography; if the character of the times, the political improvements, arts, &c., be not observed. In short, if it be not considered as the history of man; and not of particular men, who filled a niche in the temple of fame, and dropped into the black rolling stream of time, that silently sweeps all before it, into the shapeless void called—eternity.—For shape, can it be called, 'that shape hath none?'[3]

Business of various kinds they might likewise pursue, if they were educated in a more orderly manner, which might save many from common and legal prostitution. Women would not then marry for a support, as men accept of places under government, and neglect the implied duties; nor would an attempt to earn their own subsistence—a most laudable one!—sink them almost to the level of those poor abandoned creatures who live by prostitution. For are not milliners and mantua-makers[4] reckoned the next class? The few employments open to women, so far from being liberal, are menial; and when a superior education enables them to take charge of the education of children as governesses,

---

[1] *Othello* II. i. 160.

[2] A male physician who presides at childbirth.

[3] *Paradise Lost* II. 666–67.

[4] Dressmakers.

they are not treated like the tutors of sons, though even clerical tutors are not always treated in a manner calculated to render them respectable in the eyes of their pupils, to say nothing of the private comfort of the individual. But as women educated like gentlewomen are never designed for the humiliating situation which necessity sometimes forces them to fill, these situations are considered in the light of a degradation; and they know little of the human heart, who need to be told, that nothing so painfully sharpens sensibility as such a fall in life.[1]

Some of these women might be restrained from marrying by a proper spirit or delicacy, and others may not have had it in their power to escape in this pitiful way from servitude; is not that government then very defective, and very unmindful of the happiness of one half of its members, that does not provide for honest, independent women, by encouraging them to fill respectable stations? But in order to render their private virtue a public benefit, they must have a civil existence in the state, married or single; else we shall continually see some worthy woman, whose sensibility has been rendered painfully acute by undeserved contempt, droop like 'the lily broken down by a plow-share.'[2]

It is a melancholy truth—yet such is the blessed effect of civilization!—the most respectable women are the most oppressed; and, unless they have understandings far superior to the common run of understandings, taking in both sexes, they must, from being treated like contemptible beings, become contemptible. How many women thus waste life away the prey of discontent, who might have practised as physicians, regulated a farm, managed a shop, and stood erect, supported by their own industry, instead of hanging their heads surcharged with the dew of sensibility, that consumes the beauty to which it at first gave lustre; nay, I doubt whether pity and love are so near akin as poets feign, for I have seldom seen much compassion excited by the helplessness of females, unless they were fair; then, perhaps, pity was the soft handmaid of love, or the harbinger of lust.

How much more respectable is the woman who earns her own bread by fulfilling any duty, than the most accomplished beauty!—beauty did I say?—so sensible am I of the beauty of moral loveliness, or the harmonious propriety that attunes the passions of a well-regulated mind, that I blush at making the comparison; yet I sigh to think how few women aim at attaining this respectability by withdrawing from the giddy whirl

---

[1] Wollstonecraft had spent one year as governess to the older daughters of the Viscount Kingsborough, County Cork, Ireland.

[2] In Fenelon's *Telemachus,* see the story of Ideomeneus who, to obey the gods, must kill his own son; the lad dies "as a beautiful lily of the fields, that is wounded in its root by the plough-share, droops" (*The Adventures of Telemachus* [Boston, 1797], p. 68). See also Robert Burns's "To a Mountain Daisy," lines 49–54.

of pleasure, or the indolent calm that stupifies the good sort of women it sucks in.

Proud of their weakness, however, they must always be protected, guarded from care, and all the rough toils that dignify the mind. If this be the fiat of fate, if they will make themselves insignificant and contemptible, sweetly to waste 'life away,' let them not expect to be valued when their beauty fades, for it is the fate of the fairest flowers to be admired and pulled to pieces by the careless hand that plucked them. In how many ways do I wish, from the purest benevolence, to impress this truth on my sex; yet I fear that they will not listen to a truth that dearbought experience has brought home to many an agitated bosom, nor willingly resign the privileges of rank and sex for the privileges of humanity, to which those have no claim who do not discharge its duties.

Those writers are particularly useful, in my opinion, who make man feel for man, independent of the station he fills, or the drapery of factitious sentiments. I then would fain convince reasonable men of the importance of some of my remarks; and prevail on them to weigh dispassionately the whole tenor of my observations. I appeal to their understandings; and, as a fellow-creature, claim, in the name of my sex, some interest in their hearts. I entreat them to assist to emancipate their companion, to make her a *help meet* for them!

Would men but generously snap our chains, and be content with rational fellowship instead of slavish obedience, they would find us more observant daughters, more affectionate sisters, more faithful wives, more reasonable mothers—in a word, better citizens. We should then love them with true affection, because we should learn to respect ourselves; and the peace of mind of a worthy man would not be interrupted by the idle vanity of his wife, nor the babes sent to nestle in a strange bosom,[1] having never found a home in their mother's.

---

[1] It was common practice for babies to be fed by wet-nurses rather than their own mothers.

Maria,

or

The Wrongs of Woman

CHAPTER 17

SUCH was her state of mind when the dogs of law were let loose on her. Maria took the task of conducting Darnford's defence upon herself. She instructed his counsel to plead guilty to the charge of adultery; but to deny that of seduction.

The counsel for the plaintiff opened the cause, by observing, "that his client had ever been an indulgent husband, and had borne with several defects of temper, while he had nothing criminal to lay to the charge of his wife. But that she left his house without assigning any cause. He could not assert that she was then acquainted with the defendant; yet, when he was once endeavouring to bring her back to her home, this man put the peace-officers to flight, and took her he knew not whither. After the birth of her child, her conduct was so strange, and a melancholy malady having afflicted one of the family, which delicacy forbade the dwelling on, it was necessary to confine her. By some means the defendant enabled her to make her escape, and they had lived together, in despite of all sense of order and decorum. The adultery was allowed, it was not necessary to bring any witnesses to prove it; but the seduction, though highly probable from the circumstances which he had the honour to state, could not be so clearly proved.—It was of the most atrocious kind, as decency was set at defiance, and respect for reputation, which shows internal compunction, utterly disregarded."

A strong sense of injustice had silenced every motion, which a mixture of true and false delicacy might otherwise have excited in Maria's bosom. She only felt in earnest to insist on the privilege of her nature. The sarcasms of society, and the condemnations of a mistaken world, were nothing to her, compared with acting contrary to those feelings which were the foundation of her principles. [She therefore eagerly put herself forward, instead of desiring to be absent, on this memorable occasion.]

Convinced that the subterfuges of the law were disgraceful, she wrote a paper, which she expressly desired might be read in court:

"Married when scarcely able to distinguish the nature of the engagement, I yet submitted to the rigid laws which enslave women, and obeyed the man whom I could no longer love. Whether the duties of the state are reciprocal, I mean not to discuss; but I can prove repeated infidelities which I overlooked or pardoned. Witnesses are not wanting to establish these facts. I at present maintain the child of a maid servant, sworn to him, and born after our marriage. I am ready to allow, that education and circumstances lead men to think and act with less delicacy, than the preservation of order in society demands from women; but surely I may without assumption declare, that, though I could excuse the birth, I could not the desertion of this unfortunate babe:—and, while I despised the man, it was not easy to venerate the husband. With proper restrictions however, I revere the institution which fraternizes the world. I exclaim against the laws which throw the whole weight of the yoke on the weaker shoulders, and force women, when they claim protectorship as mothers, to sign a contract, which renders them dependent on the caprice of the tyrant, whom choice or necessity has appointed to reign over them. Various are the cases, in which a woman ought to separate herself from her husband; and mine, I may be allowed emphatically to insist, comes under the description of the most aggravated.

"I will not enlarge on those provocations which only the individual can estimate; but will bring forward such charges only, the truth of which is an insult upon humanity. In order to promote certain destructive speculations, Mr. Venables prevailed on me to borrow certain sums of a wealthy relation; and, when I refused further compliance, he thought of bartering my person; and not only allowed opportunities to, but urged, a friend from whom he borrowed money, to seduce me. On the discovery of this act of atrocity, I determined to leave him, and in the most decided manner, for ever. I consider all obligations as made void by his conduct; and hold, that schisms which proceed from want of principles, can never be healed.

"He received a fortune with me to the amount of five thousand pounds. On the death of my uncle, convinced that I could provide for my child, I destroyed the settlement of that fortune. I required none of my property to be returned to me, nor shall enumerate the sums extorted from me during six years that we lived together.

"After leaving, what the law considers as my home, I was hunted like a criminal from place to place, though I contracted no debts, and demanded no maintenance—yet, as the laws sanction such proceeding, and make women the property of their husbands, I forbear to animadvert. After the birth of my daughter, and the death of my uncle, who left a very considerable property to myself and child, I was exposed to new persecution; and, because I had, before arriving at what is termed years of discretion, pledged my faith, I was treated by the world, as bound for ever to a man whose vices were notorious. Yet what are the vices generally known, to the various miseries that a woman may be subject to, which, though deeply felt, eating into the soul, elude description, and may be glossed over! A false morality is even established, which makes all the virtue of women consist in chastity, submission, and the forgiveness of injuries.

"I pardon my oppressor—bitterly as I lament the loss of my child, torn from me in the most violent manner. But nature revolts, and my soul sickens at the bare supposition, that it could ever be a duty to pretend affection, when a separation is necessary to prevent my feeling hourly aversion.

"To force me to give my fortune, I was imprisoned—yes; in a private madhouse.—There, in the heart of misery, I met the man charged with seducing me. We became attached—I deemed, and ever shall deem, myself free. The death of my babe dissolved the only tie which subsisted between me and my, what is termed, lawful husband.

"To this person, thus encountered, I voluntarily gave myself, never considering myself as any more bound to transgress the laws of moral purity, because the will of my husband might be pleaded in my excuse, than to transgress those laws to which [the policy of artificial society has] annexed [positive] punishments.—While no command of a husband can prevent a woman from suffering for certain crimes, she must be allowed to consult her conscience, and regulate her conduct, in some degree, by her own sense of right. The respect I owe to myself, demanded my strict adherence to my determination of never viewing Mr. Venables in the light of a husband, nor could it forbid me from encouraging another. If I am unfortunately united to an unprincipled man, am I for ever to be shut out from fulfilling the duties of a wife and mother?—I wish my country to approve of my conduct; but, if laws exist, made by the strong to oppress the weak, I appeal to my own sense of justice, and declare that I will not live with the individual, who has violated every moral obligation which binds man to man.

"I protest equally against any charge being brought to criminate the man, whom I consider as my husband. I was six-and-twenty when I left Mr. Venables' roof; if ever I am to be supposed to arrive at an age to direct my own actions, I must by that time have arrived at it.—I acted with deliberation.—Mr. Darnford found me a forlorn and oppressed woman, and promised the protection women in the present state of society want.—But the man who now claims me—was he deprived of my society by this conduct? The question is an insult to common sense, considering where Mr. Darnford met me.—Mr. Venables' door was indeed open to me—nay, threats and intreaties were used to induce me to return; but why? Was affection or honour the motive?—I cannot, it is true, dive into the recesses of the human heart—yet I presume to assert, [borne out as I am by a variety of circumstances,] that he was merely influenced by the most rapacious avarice.

"I claim then a divorce, and the liberty of enjoying, free from molestation, the fortune left to me by a relation, who was well aware of the character of the man with whom I had to contend.—I appeal to the justice and humanity of the jury—a body of men, whose private judgment must be allowed to modify laws, that must be unjust, because definite rules can never apply to indefinite circumstances—and I deprecate punishment upon the man of my choice, freeing him, as I solemnly do, from the charge of seduction.

"I did not put myself into a situation to justify a charge of adultery, till I had, from conviction, shaken off the fetters which bound me to Mr. Venables.—While I lived with him, I defy the voice of calumny to sully what is termed the fair fame of woman.—Neglected by my husband, I never encouraged a lover; and preserved with scrupulous care, what is termed my honour, at the expence of my peace, till he, who should have been its guardian, laid traps to ensnare me. From that moment I believed myself, in the sight of heaven, free—and no power on earth shall force me to renounce my resolution."

The judge, in summing up the evidence, alluded to "the fallacy of letting women plead their feelings, as an excuse for the violation of the marriage-vow. For his part, he had always determined to oppose all innovation, and the newfangled notions which incroached on the good old rules of conduct. We did not want French principles in public or private life—and, if women were allowed to plead their feelings, as an excuse or palliation of infidelity, it was opening a flood-gate for immorality. What virtuous woman thought of her feelings?—It was her duty to love and obey the man chosen by her parents and relations, who were qualified by their experience to judge better for her, than she could for herself. As to the charges brought against the husband, they were vague, supported by no witnesses, excepting that of imprisonment in a private madhouse. The proofs of an insanity in the family, might render that however a prudent measure; and indeed the conduct of the lady did not appear that of a person of sane mind. Still such a mode of proceeding could not be justified, and might perhaps entitle the lady [in another court] to a sentence of separation from bed and board, during the joint lives of the parties; but he hoped that no Englishman would legalize adultery, by enabling the adulteress to enrich her seducer. Too many restrictions could not be thrown in the way of divorces, if we wished to maintain the sanctity of marriage; and, though they might bear a little hard on a few, very few individuals, it was evidently for the good of the whole."

———————————— • ————————————

PRIMARY SOURCES
Collected Letters of Mary Wollstonecraft. Edited by Ralph M. Wardle. Ithaca and London: Cornell University Press, 1979.

Mary, a Fiction. London: Joseph Johnson, 1788. Reprinted in *Feminist Contro-
    versy in England, 1788–1810.* Edited by Gina Luria. New York: Garland
    Publishing, 1974. Reprinted with *The Wrongs of Woman: or Maria.* Edited
    by Gary Kelly. Oxford, 1976. Reprint ed. New York: Schocken Books, 1977.
*A Vindication of the Rights of Woman: With Scriptures on Political and Moral
    Subjects.* London, 1792. Reprint. Edited by Carol Poston. New York: W. W.
    Norton, 1967, 1975; Edited by Miriam Brody Kramnick. New York: Penguin
    Books, 1975.
The Wrongs of Woman; or, Maria (part of *Posthumous Works*). London, 1798.
    Reprinted with *Mary, A Fiction.* Edited by Gary Kelly. Oxford: Oxford Uni-
    versity Press, 1976. Reprinted as *Maria, or the Wrongs of Woman.* New
    York: W. W. Norton, 1975.
Posthumous Works of the Author of A Vindication of the Rights of Woman. In Four
    Volumes. London, 1798. Reprint. Clifton, N.Y.: Augustus M. Kelley, 1972.
    (Four volumes in two.) Note: *The Wrongs of Woman; or, Maria* is Volumes
    1 and 2 of the original edition and Volume 1 of the reprint edition.

RELATED SOURCES
Ferguson, Moira, and Janet Todd. *Mary Wollstonecraft.* Boston: Twayne, 1984.
Flexner, Eleanor. *Mary Wollstonecraft: A Biography.* New York: Coward, McCann
    & Geoghegan, 1972.
Godwin, William. *Memoirs of the Author of a Vindication of the Rights of
    Woman.* London, 1798. Reprinted in *Feminist Controversy in England,
    1788–1810.* Edited by Gina Luria. New York: Garland Publishing, 1974.
George, Margaret. *One Woman's "Situation": A Study of Mary Wollstonecraft.*
    Urbana: University of Illinois Press, 1970.
Sunstein, Emily W. *A Different Face: The Life of Mary Wollstonecraft.* New York:
    Harper & Row, 1975.
Tomalin, Claire. *The Life and Death of Mary Wollstonecraft.* London: Weidenfeld
    and Nicholson, 1974.
Wardle, Ralph M. *Mary Wollstonecraft: A Critical Biography.* Lincoln: University
    of Nebraska Press, 1966.

MARY ANNE RADCLIFFE
1746?— *after* 1810

Born to a seventy-year-old Protestant father and a thirty-year-old Roman Catholic mother, Mary Anne Radcliffe inherited a considerable fortune from her father and on his death had two guardians appointed to supervise her patrimony. (Her parents' surname is not yet known.) Secretly courted by a Roman Catholic friend of her mother and clandestinely married, Radcliffe indicated in her *Memoirs* (1810) that she regretted this impetuous move much of her married life.

After a long, painful confinement she gave birth to a daughter and had six subsequent children in close succession, the last two of whom died. Her husband, supposedly descended from the Earl of Derwentwater, was a kind-hearted but inactive man, reckless with money, partial to alcohol, and disinclined to work. His debts and ill-conceived schemes caused Mary Anne Radcliffe's patrimony to dwindle. After selling personal effects, opening an ill-fated coffee-shop, attempting an exchange of land with the Duke of R., and taking in lodgers—living first with his parents and then with her mother—she eventually sent her sons off to school, left her daughters with her mother, and set off alone for London. There she collapsed when she made a bid to sell the family silver, and by the time she advertised for work—ignominy for a landed heiress—she was fully apprised of the difficulties faced by women seeking employment.

Through friends, she found a post in Scotland as governess to aristocratic children, an appointment to which her husband agreed on condition that their own sons attend a Roman Catholic school. Their youngest daughter was apprenticed to learn dressmaking while the other two stayed with Radcliffe's mother. Still separated from her, in time her husband took up a position as a steward. They never lived together for any substantial period after her London adventures.

Family problems continued to beset her. Nervous collapses followed. While she recuperated from one, she tells in muted prose in her *Memoirs* about an attempted rape or abuse of some sort by a "friend," an event that forced her to leave Edinburgh. She describes the loneliness and depression that motivated her poems, also incorporated in her *Memoirs*. Similarly, personal experiences engendered her best known work, *The Female Advocate; or, an attempt to recover the rights of woman from male usurpation* (1799), which rails against beggary and prostitution as the economically coerced lot of women forced to fend for

themselves and their families. Radcliffe's experiences seeking employment and observing the destitution of other women motivated her, as did
writing as a means of economic support. She wrote the tract in 1792, it
was published in 1799, and then incorporated with the *Memoirs*. Radcliffe wove together many different strands from earlier feminist writings, such as the right of women to legitimate employment and attacks
on male usurpation of female occupations. Radcliffe's circumstances
generated a deep concern for the lives and work of laboring women, and
showed how only unusual circumstances or unusual vision made the
problems of impoverished women the concern of middle-class feminists. Eventually crippled with rheumatism, reduced, unemployed, her
family dispersed, and her mother dead, she penned her *Memoirs* in the
form of letters to a beloved female friend. The *Memoirs* stop in July 1810
and no information is currently known about Radcliffe's last years, possibly spent in penury in or near Edinburgh.

FROM
THE FEMALE ADVOCATE
TO
THE READER

So various and complicated are the scenes of this life, that seven
years have elapsed since the following pages were written, a period,
perhaps, more favourable for publishing than the present; but timidity,
or other hinderances, have repeatedly prevented their appearing before
the public, during which time, the author hoped some more able advocate would have taken up the cause, to do justice to a subject of such
importance to society at large, and particularly a much injured part
thereof. For, alas! it is too well known, that female education in general
is confined within very narrow limits, and seldom permitted to extend to
classical accomplishments.

The writer of this volume being a female, with only a female's education, is sufficiently aware of her inadequacy to the undertaking, but
trusts the importance of the subject will claim some attention; at the
same time, reposing a full confidence in the candour and unbounded

---

SOURCE: This selection of *The Female Advocate* is from the British Library
volume of the *Memoirs*, shelf no. 1203.1.18, reprinted in 1974. (These pages
occupy pages 392–471 in the British Library volume.

goodness of some part of her readers at least, she is once more encouraged to resume the pen, to add or amend such remarks as the nature of
the times and circumstances require, and at length has so far sur-
mounted her timidity, as to submit the following sheets, with all their
imperfections, to the inspection of a generous public, who are more
ready to appreciate the works of individuals from the rectitude of intention, than the beauty of composition. The attempt, she must acknowledge, has cost her many a painful emotion; for surrounded by all the
disadvantages peculiar to the sex, seems to her to require no small share
of courage, and which, indeed, nothing but the importance of the subject
should have induced her to encounter.

The subject of the following pages, is an attempt to delineate the
situation of those poor helpless females, whose sufferings, from a variety of causes, are too grievous to be borne; the sources and dire consequences of which, the exalted in life cannot form the least conception,
unless they condescend to examine for themselves, when it is to be
hoped their grievances will be sought into and redressed.

For the munificence of the people of Great Britain, being ever ready
and adequate to support, aid and comfort the afflicted, when their
troubles are fully investigated, and the great number of unfortunate
women, who doubtless would rejoice to become virtuous and useful
members of society, in some lawful employment,—have encouraged the
author to offer this feeble representation. Nor can she despair of eventual
success to the cause she has engaged in, if she is but so happy as to
excite the attention of those whose souls are enlarged with the exalted
ideas of Christian charity.

Indeed it is a work which, as a duty to our fellow creatures, she has
long, very long, wished to see executed by a more able pen; but, not
having met with this desirable effort, the silence of others, the liberality
of a generous public, and with an ardent wish to see misery alleviated,
and virtuous industry crowned with success, have been the motives for
the author engaging in so arduous an undertaking. Conscious, however,
that whatever good may be the result, the praise alone is due to the
benevolent principles of humanity.

But these advantages, in Britain, being monopolised by the male sex,
permit me to ask, if it is not their duty, at least to afford protection in their
stead; for, surely, if they refuse to protect, they have no right whatever to
govern.

> "Britons, attend! be worth like this approv'd,
> "And show you have the virtue to be mov'd."

Therefore I am led to keep firmly to the assertion, that it is not power, but
protection, which is required; for the generality of women, (natives of
this country,) are so perfectly tamed, either through custom or compul-
sive submission, that let but the lenient hand of protection be stretched

out to their aid, and, doubtless, content and happiness will resume their seat, and cheerfulness form the leading feature to bespeak the tranquillity of those souls which have been so long depressed.

All women possess not the Amazonian spirit of a Wolstonecraft; but, indeed, unremitted oppression is sometimes a sufficient apology for their throwing off the gentle garb of a female, and assuming some more masculine appearance; yet, when the curtain of misrepresentation is once withdrawn, it is to be hoped (not doubted) that the cause of complaint will quickly be removed.

It seems, however, very necessary to call in some able assistants; and, consequently, I make my appeal to reason, justice, and truth, which, in checking the spirit of malevolence, should it rear its hydra head to the prejudice of the cause, will also be the means of shielding the writer from the common censure which the narrow-minded in general bestow on a first production.

PART FIRST.

THE FATAL CONSEQUENCES OF MEN TRADERS ENGROSSING WOMENS' OCCUPATIONS.

To detail human misery in all its various shapes is not in the power of any individual: so complicated and numerous are the ills of this life, and so various its misfortunes, that we need not have recourse to the airy regions of fiction or romance, to find out objects of distress, to pourtray the woes of our fellow creatures; yet, from motives of delicacy, beg leave to withhold names, lest the suffering objects should feel hurt at the melancholy recital of their tale of woe; and shall therefore only select a few instances, and leave the candid moralist to take a comparative view of the rest, through all the wonderful mazes and wide tracts, to which a part of our fellow mortals have been condemned. And by what? Not by divine law, which is, or ought to be, the standing rule of all our actions, but by an evil precedent, which happens to fall with all its force upon that part of the community, whose feeble powers of resistance, joined to an habitual passive submission, are the least able to defend them. Consequently it has never yet been thought a business worth investigation, although so many others, of much less moment, have been sought out and redressed.

When we look around us, nothing is more conspicuous in the eyes of the world, than the distresses of women; I do not say those whom a kind Providence hath placed under the immediate care of a tender father, or an affectionate and kind husband; or, *by chance,* a friend, or brother. But these, alas! comprise only one part of the community. Notwithstanding all are of the same nature, and were formed by the same Divine Power, yet their comforts differ very widely indeed. Still, as women seem formed by nature to seek protection from man, why, in the name of justice, refuse the boon? Does it not become highly worthy the attention of men in general, to consider in what manner to redress the grievances *already within their notice?*

Perhaps it may be said, and very justly, that, considering human frailty, there is amongst women, as well as men, a vast number of vicious and undeserving. Granted; still, is it not better to pass over a hundred guilty, than let punishment fall upon one innocent person?—Besides, IS THERE NOT A POSSIBILITY OF FORMING A PLAN OF DISCRIMINATION, FOR THE BENEFIT OF THOSE ONLY WHO MERIT SUCH HUMANE AND FRIENDLY INTERFERENCE?

Some years ago, who would have been made believe, so many persons could be restored to life, as the Royal Humane Society, for the recovering of drowned persons, has effected? Yet so it is; which proves to a demonstration, the practicability of this design. But before I proceed with my Hint for erecting any established plan, for the restoration of peace and happiness to the, perhaps, once happy, but now most miserable of beings, I cannot help making a remark, that, in order to lay a good foundation, every builder must find it necessary, first, to remove the rubbish out of the way—therefore let us proceed to the ground-work of the design; and, before any further steps are taken, ask, What can be said of men-milliners, men-mantua-makers, and men stay-makers? besides all the numerous train of other professions, such as hair-dressers, &c. &c.; all of which occupations are much more calculated for women than men. But, thanks to the fashions of the times, (which have nearly exploded that disgraceful custom of men dressing ladies' heads), by the introduction of all the brutuses and chignons, of so many demoninations [denominations], which have found their way to the toilets of all descriptions of females.—Where is there a Stevens now? was there ever a wider field for the display of his talents? Yet, if perukes are the fashion of the day, what is to prevent a woman from displaying her taste upon a lady's head as well as a man, who is much better calculated for a more masculine employment.

"Look," says an observer, "to the shops of perfumers, toymen, and others of a similar situation; and, above all, look to the haberdashery magazines, where from ten to twenty fellows, six feet high, may be counted in each, to the utter exclusion of poor females, who could sell a tooth-pick, or a few ribbons, just as well."

A tax upon these fellows would be very salutary *so say I;* yet, for a poor female individual to attack so numerous a body of men, however insignificant by custom, is a bold stroke, no doubt; yet, having thrown these sentiments together, in defence of the oppressed, even the censure of malevolence itself *will* not prevent the truth, which, like a huntsman's whip, cannot give pain to any *but* those it touches: for, as no rule can be established without exceptions, so, in this case, more than one must be granted, which shall be treated of in a subsequent part of these pages. For to class the innocent with the guilty, would be doing injustice to the cause.

But, in the mean time, where are those fathers, husbands, brothers, and professed friends to virtue and happiness, who step not forward in the business? No doubt but there are many men of great probity and humanity, and yet, through the progressive course of custom, have not adverted *either* to the cause or its fatal consequences; or, in fine, are not aware of the real distresses of our fellow creatures; from which idea it is so frequently wished a reference to facts may take place, since neither the sufferings of these poor women, nor the cause of their sufferings, can possibly be known, but by investigation.

It is not to be supposed but all, in some degree, share the common misfortunes in life; and few there are, however wretched their situations, who cannot single out other beings as bad, if not in a more deplorable state.

But, in the case of these poor women, where is there a state nearly equal to theirs? borne down by fate's afflicting hand, they are not able to act, or seek redress; and this, by the unfeeling part of the world, we have too great reason to fear, is termed idleness and profligacy.

What a littleness of mind! what an unfeeling and despicable meanness must lurk in the breasts of those, who can, with impunity, insult over distress! Into what fits of desperation have numbers of helpless females fallen through these contemptible insults and revilings, and even neglects! for, it is in those dark moments of distress, when the senses are all alive to the fine feelings of nature, that every nerve is relaxed and ready to receive the fatal dart.

Then indeed it is, that she stands exposed in the field of adversity, surrounded by every disadvantage, without the aid of education, or the guardian hand of protection; that is to say, without either weapon or shield of defence: a situation which, it is natural to suppose, would draw pity from the most obdurate hearts. Yet how many are the instances of the censorious part of the creation, dastardly and cruelly assassinating and murdering the character of these poor unfortunate victims, and those, of all murderers, are the worst under heaven. The common and detected murderer stands exposed to the laws of his country; but the assassin, who, under a cloak of hypocrisy, can persecute and defame the characters of oppressed females, are no longer worthy the invaluable title of Christian.

That there should be a mixture of characters in the world is, beyond a doubt, for wise and good reasons; which we poor short-sighted mortals know not, more than that it is a principle in which all reflecting persons have agreed, that our present state, on this side the grave, is certainly designed for improvement, in order to fit us for a better. Thus being admitted, where can the well-disposed find a better opportunity, than by defending the innocent and unprotected, selecting them from the noxious part of mankind, with whom they are, through keen adversity, obliged to associate; and placing them in such situations, as will enable them to pursue the paths of virtue, by means of some honest employment?

But to accomplish so laudable a design rests both with the humane and the opulent, by whose investigation, there is not a doubt, but it will be found a work of the utmost importance, not only in the present state of things, but in looking forward to a succession. For, in times like the present, is not the aid and assistance of men required in the military and naval departments? And in more peaceable times, which we have to look forward to, are not, or ought not, the manufactories of the country to be the first object considered? In either of these cases, it evidently appears, that men may be much better employed than in filling women's occupations. For, in the words of St. Luke, these poor females may very justly say, "to dig I cannot, to beg I am ashamed." For from this evil precedent, there is no other alternative for these poor women, but beggary or vice!

Let us then, if you please, select one of these distressed females, out of the prodigious multitude, and pursue her through the humiliating scene of beggary: I believe it is granted, that pride is well known to be the predominant passion of the human breast, and consequently any comments on that head are needless; but certain it must be, that after, perhaps, a life of ease and affluence, to be compelled to such a mortifying situation, requires more than a common share of fortitude to support. Still this prevailing passion, with all its train of attendants, must be subdued, in the dreadful situation of beggary, which cannot fail to bring down the spirits of these unhappy victims, with more oppressive force than it is in the power of words to express, or pen to paint, and can only be conceived, *in part*, by the silent sensations of those who can adopt another's woes, and trace the passions of the human mind. For what must not be the purturbation of a mind like this, when dire necessity compels the poor, neglected victim to pursue such degrading steps, in order to support a miserable existence! See her trembling limbs, which are scarcely able to support her load of wretchedness, whilst she asks an alms from the casual passenger. She who, perhaps, a short time since, charmed her acquaintance with her sprightly conversation and virtuous example, by one adverse stroke, is nevertheless so soon become the contempt, the scorn, and the outcast of mortals! Nor is this wretched doom confined to youth alone; but, by the cruel hand of fate, the poor, dejected mother, as well as daughter, is condemned to share the same direful misfortunes, and be reduced to the same low state of wretchedness, from which their characters are stigmatized with infamy, and to which they unavoidably fall a sacrifice. And in this miserable state they must for ever remain, until the spirit of oppression and mistaken prejudice is eradicated, and the heavy cloud of misrepresentation cleared away, through a proper investigation of the cause, which, doubtless, will lead to a conviction, that the distress and wretchedness of these poor, abandoned creatures originate chiefly from the avaricious and mercenary views of that set of beings, who are "Eating the bread of the hungry, and drinking the drink of the thirsty." Nor are these poor women allowed "to pick up the crumbs," which will appear in the sequel.

In the mean time, let us, if you please, take another view of this poor mother and her miserable daughter, in this forlorn and distressing state of beggary, and there see what relief they obtain, from their piercing accents and broken sighs—little more, it is to be feared, than contempt or insults. For even the hand of charity, accustomed to bestow upon the needy, no sooner observes the appearance of youth, or a capability of industry, than it is instantly withdrawn, and the few pence is kept in reserve (as it is thought) for some more proper object.

Good heavens, what a scene of woe! where the poor mother and her helpless daughter are turned adrift, to the mercy of an unfeeling world; which neither their genteel education, or delicate constitutions, broken down by poverty and hardships, can prevent. O! what distress, in a situation like this! The mother, the fond mother, in the full bitterness of maternal affection, takes another, and another view of darling child; perhaps the only remaining pledge of a late kind partner! she sees her still laden with the fruits of a pious education; and views her with unutterable fondness, "whilst all the soft passions of her tender soul throb through her breast with unavailing grief," at the near approach of their destruction! In vain do they supplicate their former friends, for the voice of censure has pointed them out as infamous! Good God! what grief can equal this? Abandoned by friends, and left to the reproach, contempt, and censure of a cruel world, without a provision, or any probable means of gaining a subsistence, or even the smallest glimpse of distant hope.

And, though shocking to relate, yet such is the miserable situation of thousands of defenceless women.

Nor let the unfeeling and censorious part of mankind refute the assertion, until provision is made for the relief of all those who would be both industrious and virtuous, had they the means. After which, the remaining few may justly be reckoned in the class of incorrigible sinners, and be a sufficient mode of forming a discrimination.

But until that provision is made, it is inhuman, base, and cruel, and beneath the dignity of a Christian, to load with infamy the poor, neglected female, who suffers through misfortunes, and the continuation of an evil precedent; and whose passive virtue is, perhaps, at the very instant of calumny, offering up the divine petition of, "Father, forgive them, they know not what they do;" and endeavouring to arm with Christian fortitude herself and beloved child, according to the advice of the wise man, who says, "Hast thou children, instruct them from their youth." She remonstrates with the child of her bosom, notwithstanding she is her partner in wretchedness, and still encourages her to persevere in virtue, and live in joyful hope.

"Let us, my dear child," says she, "form our estimation of the world and its objects as they deserve; remembering we are pilgrims and strangers here. Let us keep in view the glorious prize; and let us soar above the crowd of human difficulties, and rejoice that the hand which made us is divine. Then, let not our feet tread in the muddy paths of vice, nor suffer the purity of our good intentions to be stained with a single act of disobedience to a Supreme Power."

And under these and such like reviving comforts, the effects of a religious and pious education, she still endeavours to persevere in virtue, though in the midst of poverty; a state which, without the interference of the humane, not any thing can hide them from but the silent grave. Oh! let not then our ears be polluted by the envenomed breath of censure, but endeavour to remove the cause, as well as stigma, which, like the pendulum to a clock, sets every wheel of wretchedness in motion; and, by seriously investigating the cause, searching deeply into the state of facts, and the origin of this tribulation, let the censure rest where it is due. For, is it not enough, enough indeed! for the innocent to struggle with the hardships of penury and want, without the double load of malevolence? Alas! even in this despicable state, they are still liable to sorrows they never yet felt, nor are even aware of; for the very means they are driven to use, to obtain the trifling pittance which they sue for, renders them exposed to the merciless hand of any avaricious ruffian, who may be base enough to drag these poor victims they know not where.

What says the Vagrant Act?—"Persons who beg in the street are idle and disorderly; and any person who apprehends and carries such a beggar before a justice, shall receive five shillings, when the said justice may commit them to a house of correction."

However shocking the sentence, what numbers of these poor objects have been dragged away by the ruthless hand of the unfeeling savage, to some loathsome prison, without regard to the more refined or delicate sensations of one or another? Good heavens? [sic] there surely needs no Siddonian powers to heighten such a tragic scene. She who, perhaps, was reared with all the gentle softness and maternal care of a fond parent; she, who so lately was looked upon as an ornament to her sex, until the pressure of misfortunes compelled her to seek for bread, to be at once confined in a dark prison, there to be obliged to hear all the opprobrious language of the very lowest set of beings, and that under a storm of oaths and imprecations, which, of itself, must pierce her very soul. There to have her ears grated with the rattling of bolts and bars, and all the adamantine fetters of misery. Good God! is it possible we can see our fellow creatures debased so low! Can we see the tender and delicate frame, which was formerly accustomed to ease and tranquillity, and which was formed by nature to participate in others misfortunes! can we let these innocent and helpless beings pass unnoticed, and not commiserate their distress, and ask, from whence the cause?—No! it is impossible the eyes can any longer be shut to their sufferings, or the ears to their piercing cries of, "Have pity on me! Oh! ye, my friends, have pity on me!"

Is not this real distress? Surely there cannot be any thing more wretchedly miserable than the situation of these poor women, who are prohibited from sharing in industry, or the common necessaries of life, or even tasting the very dregs of comfort. For let us but figure to ourselves this wretched pair upon their bed of straw, with all their innocence, with all their tenderness, and quick sensations of distress, still laden with the fruits of a pious education,

> "They shriek, start up, the same sad prospect find,
> "And wake to all the ills they left behind."

And thus they linger out a wretched exile in this miserable dungeon, until the law hath had its course, and they again are liberated. When see, the fond mother, the poor mother, taking another, and another review of her wretched offspring, groaning out a miserable existence on the narrow verge of life! her sorrow surrounds her like the stern winter's blast, and she feels her worn-out senses just bordering upon desponding madness; for, when Hope no longer offers her consolation, despondency must take place; and with all the bitter pangs of distress, she, like the poor widow in sacred writ, sets about to prepare her last handful of meal, that "they may eat it and die." A release they most ardently wish for, whilst in a state of innocence, rather than keep life upon such wretched terms as are now presented: for, alas! by this time, they see that period near at hand, which must determine the great and shocking alternative between vice or death. And what must be the conflict at this long-dreaded moment, to a heart which, in early youth, was taught to serve its Creator, and still retains an ardent wish to be virtuous! Can any state under heaven be more distressing to a delicate and susceptible mind, than that between good and evil? And how shocking it must be, at length, to hear these poor victims of wretchedness defend themselves, by exclaiming, "I sought not redress in vice, till urged to it by self-defence, in order to support an existence, which, though I no longer covet, it is my duty to preserve: nor is there any other remedy for ills like mine; for, as the wise man Solomon says, "extreme oppression maketh us desperate!"

What a horrid and shocking state! to be driven, by absolute necessity, to support a wretched existence by the forfeiture of every thing she holds most dear in this life, and at the hazard of what is still more precious, her immortal soul!

Besides, what must not be the agonies of her soul in this wretched state, on the dreadful approach of death! a death which, though so much desired in innocence, is dreaded with so great horror in guilt, when all her crimes appear at once to her distracted view. Worn out with intemperance and disease, she feels the dreadful period near at hand, when she must appear before the grand tribunal!

How many are her penitential tears in such a horrid situation? She calls, and calls again, upon her great Creator, "O Lord, rebuke me not in thy fury, nor chastise me in thy wrath; for who can stand before the face of thy indignation?" And thus surrounded with all these dismal and heart-piercing sensations, without a friend to comfort, or the still more invaluable consolation of a dying Christian; her every sense is racked with horror, and little unlike the infernal regions is her wretched situation.

Whilst her associates in vice are revelling in drunkeness, in order to banish from their reflections all ideas of the horrid scene, and thus she lies, "Groaning out the poor remains of life," her limbs bathed in sweat, and struggling with convulsive throws, pains insupportable throbbing in every pulse, and innumerable darts of agony transfixing her conscience.

> "In that dread moment, how the frantic soul
> "Raves round the walls of her clay tenement,
> "Runs to each avenue and shrieks for help,
> "But shrieks in vain. How wishfully she looks
> "On all she's leaving, now no longer her's.
> "A little longer, yet a little longer."

Thus her exhausted breath expires, and she dies in all the bitterness of woe. And this alike must continue to be the fate (as it has been so long to numbers) of both parents and children, unless the kind hand of interference shall sever the chain of misery, by which they have so long been held down.

But will not a serious investigation into these scenes of horror be sufficient to arouse the most callous of mankind? for who would not use their utmost endeavours to relieve such unheard of distress? Or, what is still better, prevent such dire calamities, and all such complicated scenes of misery and wretchedness: for, is it not always granted, that prevention is better than cure?

It is said, the city of London alone pays upwards of twenty thousand pounds annually to patrols, beadles, and watchmen; and it may be a much greater sum; yet, that of itself seems a vast sum indeed, to be raised by levy, in which the honest trader must unavoidably contribute a large share. Would not that contribution answer a much better purpose in providing for the necessitous poor, such as we have just been treating of, and who are judged unfit objects to be received into a parish work-house; being, *as it is termed,* able enough to earn their own bread out of the house?

Yet, so long as there continues a prohibition against women having an employment, it is to be feared, double the sum already raised by the inhabitants will be found inefficatious. But such is the link of progression, arising from this dreadful usurpation; which shews the necessity of entering into the origin of these melancholy truths, that so the chain of connection may be found whole; otherways, far be it from me to entertain a wish to offer the generous part of my readers a work fraught with so many tragic representations; but, least the want of a full narrative should leave the subject dark to comprehend, I still pursue my plan; and even should my zeal in the cause of happiness lead into an eccentric mode of writing, be it remembered it is an eccentric cause, but with a most sanguine wish to see all the inhabitants of this favoured isle become useful and happy members of society, instead of being the harpies of destruction.

That political and private happiness are invariably connected, is beyond a doubt; and that the morals of this nation are very corrupt, is but too visible, from the vast numbers of disgraceful women who infest the face of the country. As for the number of these miserable beings, it cannot be an easy matter to ascertain: but suppose, from the prodigious numbers, that are seen scattered about, like sheep having no shepherd, that in London, for example, there are five or six thousand: Nay; I have either read, or heard it said, ten thousand! but how that calculation can be made, I shall not take upon me to say; yet, suppose we call it half that number; are not five thousand destitute females too many to suffer through so poor a cause, and will not a much less number suffice to contaminate the morals of more than half the youths in town, and prove a source of destructive oppression to a vast number of inhabitants? for, without morals, how can we expect happiness, or what is to support the public good?

Then, what sort of beings are they, who can, with impunity, oppress these unfortunate women, to the entire destruction of all happiness, both national and domestic? Or where is the breast, truly warm in the cause of virtue and a country's good, who will suffer the continuance of a precedent so destructively oppressive, without exerting themselves in the cause? for granting it is a great part of the Christian religion, to assist our neighbours as far as we are empowered. For to neglect an investigation of these grievances admits of no excuse; and when once the clouds of obscurity are dispersed, by enquiry is the great foundation of knowledge.

From the holy scriptures we learn, that "Wisdom is justified in all her children;" and from what but wisdom and justice is derived the support of our common weal, by investigating which, will not the judicious quickly discover a numerous train of oppressive grievances not yet told. Let him but enquire the cause of such vast numbers of convicts having been sent abroad, to the great expence of the nation; and see if their connection with these necessitous women has not been a great means of their misfortunes: for, alas! young men, upon their first entrance into the world, are too often inebriated with the pleasing, but baneful, draught of pleasures, till their senses are so much intoxicated, that they run they know not where, and at length find themselves ensnared in the net which these poor abandoned women, or rather the instigators of their misery, have so artfully set to ensnare the unwary.

Yet a serious consideration, no doubt, will prompt an enquiry, and a perseverance in the pursuit; and surely we may hope, an undertaking, founded on such a basis as the laws of humanity, and a general good, can never fail of success. Nor will the more generous part of men-traders, such as are before described, delay to resign a privilege, maintained upon such unjust principles; for far, very far, be it from me to suppose, or entertain a wish to insinuate a supposition, that all effeminate tradesmen are equally guilty of a known violation. Nor is any individual accused for involuntary crimes: yet, does it not behove every member of society to inform themselves, especially when the object of enquiry is of such great magnitude, as to extend beyond the interest of individuals, and affect a whole community?

It is beyond a doubt, that many men, through the force of custom, are ignorant of the injury they are doing their neighbour, and mankind in general, the details of which I have very scrupulously collected, and may say with Shakespeare, I have "nothing extenuated, nor set down aught in malice."

. . . Then, give me leave to ask, what provision there is for unfortunate women, who are turned of that period, amongst whom are great numbers of widows, but just in the meridian of their days, who, after a life of affluence, and, perhaps, every ease and comfort, are now wandering about through this vale of tears, in the abject and forlorn condition just described; possibly driven from their homes by keen adversity, naked and destitute, in the most inclement season of the year, without a prospect, or means of any sort, for providing the common necessaries of life, since every branch of trade is occupied by these usurpers of a female's right, till, at length, quite weary with fatigue and pining with hunger, the dreaded period arrives, "when, like a hunted bird, she becomes quite exhausted with fatigue," and weariness obliges her to fall to the ground, and become the prey or sport of every school-boy.

Poor, helpless creatures! will no one fly to their relief? They assuredly have a claim on the assistance and compassion of every one: and, I flatter myself, the generous feelings of the humane will no sooner be sensible of their sufferings, than all, who wish well to the cause of virtue, will lend their assistance towards abolishing so destructive a precedent; and every lady, that has a wish to support the general character of her sex, will retire with indignation, when offered to be served by any of these authors of female destruction.

The efficacy of these reflections to a feeling and generous mind, that can participate in another's woes, cannot be doubted; yet what will all that pity or all that sympathy avail, unless some exertions are used towards effecting a redress?

Suppose no lady would suffer herself to be served, in the shops of these effeminate traders, by any of the short clothed gentry, would it not be a means of compelling all those who chuse to carry on the tragi-comic farce, to effect the business under the disguise of gown and petticoat?

But joking apart: believe me, ladies, it is past a joke, when poor, unfortunate females are compelled to go without clothing, in order to support an army of Herculian figures at the back of a counter, displaying the beauties of a lady's bandeau, or commenting upon the device of a fan.

Fie upon such conduct! let men act like men, and, as men of honour, support the dignity of their character. To hear them talk, they profess the finest feelings; but what do all these professions tend to? is it not an apparent solecism, that the same person, in the very moment they profess to be friends to civil society, should be loading the defenceless with unheard of oppression? But let us, if you please, develope these assertions in the full light of impartial truth. . . .

What is life? a bare existence, when compared with a life of civil security and freedom, neither of which do these unfortunate women experience: for, notwithstanding, sometimes even difficulties are instructive, and, in many cases, may prevent a number of unforeseen troubles; they cannot even profit by their knowledge, from their not being empowered to exercise their talents. It is truly shocking to see such numbers of miserable wretches wandering about without employment, or any human comfort, either dressed up at the cost of their virtue and peace of mind, or in so wretched, forlorn, and abject a state, that they scarcely retain an appearance of their sex; thus dragging on a miserable existence, which nothing but the effects of a religious education can induce them to preserve. For, what is life without hope? and where is there the smallest glimpse of hope for them? they cannot fly from the frowns of the world, which on all sides attack them. Yet how astonishing is it, that the oppressions of these men, who are the authors of so much mischief, should so long have been passed unnoticed!

Did every one candidly deliver their sentiments without restraint, would it not be a means of affording a light to the discerning eye of impartiality to examine into these heinous grievances? for where no less than private interest is the foundation of so much misery, dragging after it the most dreadful consequences, the origin, may we not suppose, proceeds from one of the three following causes, viz. A want of reflection, from its being a precedent of long standing; a wilful blindness, through avaricious views; or a downright want of understanding. The latter of which we hope is the case, that it may rest in their favour; for, where little is given, little may be required.

But ye of the world, whose understandings have so long been carried down the stream of misrepresentation, suffer not yourselves to be any longer led away by false and mistaken prejudice, nor let the innocent suffer with the guilty; for pity's sake, spare the innocent, although it be at the risk of suffering the guilty to go unpunished; mercy is Heaven's distinguished attribute, and contains a greatness next to celestial.

In searching for a date to the era of this destructive precedent, wherein men have been made substitutes in women's occupations, it will be found to be of very long standing; and in its infancy might not, nor, perhaps, was not attended with the evils it has since produced; for, in those days, when manufactures and commerce were not so extensive, every situation and scene in life were in a more contracted state, and while the father and the brother were employed in trade, the mother and daughters were employed in the domestic concerns of the household. In fact, they were then the manufacturers also, and consequently were never at a loss for employment; they found enough to do in spinning, knitting, and preparing necessaries for the use of the family, which, being common, was not looked upon as any degradation.

But were the tradesman, in this refined age, to employ his wife or daughters in any such low capacity, what would the world suppose, or where would be his credit! Therefore, in exploring the case and its consequences, shall we not be well convinced, it is not custom alone which ought to constitute a right; for what precedent or practice ought to be supported upon unjust principles? Doubtless there have been various precedents, which seemed good at the beginning, and yet have been productive of much evil in the end, as the one in question; at the commencement of which, as I before observed, it might be, and was, a very laudable pursuit; for in those days, when all things were in a more contracted state, and trade not so universally extended, the father of a family was glad to dispose of his sons to such mechanical branches of trade as first presented, that his son might be empowered to improve or increase his little fund, and be able to make a provision, not only for himself, but for a wife which, in primitive times, he was obliged to endow.

Alas! how much unlike our modern days, when women endow their husbands, and, with large portions, frequently purchase a very heavy bondage.

In fact, the generality of things appear to be diametrically opposite to what they were in former times.

We need but look back about three centuries, and see the vast change; for example: What would be the consequence, were a labourer, in the present times, to receive no better wages than a penny a day, which used to be the standard even in the reign of Henry VII.* and in the reign of Henry VIII. it did not exceed three halfpence? Must not every one allow, so small a recompence, in the present times, insufficient to exist upon, and much less to support a family? Still, in those days, it was found a sufficient provision, and they could live comfortably upon it; but the reason is evident; every article of provision at that time bore a very inferior price to what it does now. Wheat, for example, which we may call the first grand article of provision, sold in King Henry VII's reign† at so low a price as three shillings per quarter, and every other article equally cheap; which enforces a conviction, that through time all things alter. Therefore, to come to the point in view, whilst all things change according to the state of times and contingencies, why exclude poor females from a small share in the improvements? it is well known they cannot defend themselves.

Were a body of miserable women, be they really virtuous or not, to assemble with a petition to parliament, where is the person who would be persuaded to present it, particularly when they are all considered as worthless wretches?

But were a body of men artificers (be their conduct or morals as they may) to offer a representation of grievances, doubtless their case would be heard, and considered, in every sense of the word, both political and humane.

Yet I would gladly believe, these differences must alone proceed from the defect of not knowing the true state of grievances; for, in every other case of oppression, except the one in question, do we not always find a protection from the police of the country? consequently, there is no fear, but a serious investigation will throw open the iron gates of misrepresentation, and lead to the avenues of happiness, both for these poor women and the community in general.

The very poor, who are born in an abject state, are taught from their infancy to struggle through life in the same manner they see their needy connections: bread must be had, and all the instructions they can possibly get, is in what way to obtain it. Consequently, if by labour and industry they can acquire a sufficiency to exist upon, they are perfectly at ease, without bestowing a single thought upon to-morrow.

But the poor unfortunate woman, who has seen better days, and been reared and educated with tenderness and care, she it is that feels her broken slumbers can no longer give relief to her weary limbs. Her inability to wrestle with difficulties are great indeed; especially when she finds her whole endeavours fruitless: and, what is still as bad, by running to and fro, in pursuit of some means for bread, (which she is not able to obtain) the shrill voice of censure, or the destructive whisper of calumny,

---

* Vide stat. 11th of Henry VII. and stat. 6 of Henry VIII. concerning artificers.

† Vide Baker's Chronicle.

have breathed such a poisonous vapour over her character, she is despised by all, in the manner described in the foregoing pages, and irremediably doomed to sink, never more to rise; for who will admit a woman of lost reputation into their house? O, cruel censure! what must be the sensations of oppressed innocence, under the censure of guilt! Even what is it they do not feel, on the bare appellation of idle and disorderly, when they have tried every expedient to obtain employment, though without effect?

Under such a pressure of misfortunes, they must bear their sorrows in silence, unknown and unpitied! and must frequently put on a face of cheerful serenity, when their hearts are torn with secret grief. Thus they pass their time in sorrow, till they meet the fatal alternative, either to be passive under the horrors of a prison, or compound for their preservation, by entering under the infernal roof of vice for protection.

When such an alternative is presented, what is to be expected? Should they evade the latter by conforming to the former, what is to be the advantage? I believe, it is generally allowed, that all prisons, or places of confinement, are but poor schools for virtue; and that youth and inexperience, or even those of a more advanced age, seldom return to the world without being, in some degree, contaminated; for it is not to be supposed that these poor miserable mortals are invulnerable. Indeed, should they even pass through these tracts unpolluted, it is next to impossible they should still escape destruction. After the death of kindred, faithlessness of friends, misfortunes and disgrace, where are they to find a plank to save them from the wreck, where they see so many tossing up and down before them? and may very applicably say, with Pope's Sappho,

> "Shall fortune still in one sad tenor run,
> "And still increase the woes so soon begun?"

Part Second.

Let us then commence with a gentleman of small, independent fortune; for, as it is the general maxim through life, that every one should endeavour to outvy his neighbour, the gentleman also must keep up appearances for the benefit of his family (as he is pleased to term it); and, in the present day, where do we see the father or mother of a family, with an independent fortune, be it ever so small, who would not be shocked at the bare idea of placing their daughter in the world in such situations as would enable them to rise, through their own industry and merit, or fit them for becoming wives to some honest and industrious tradesman?—No: that would be a degradation which must not take place. It is the etiquette of the times for the daughters to be bred fine ladies, although it be without a fortune, either dependent or independent, to support it. As for trade, that is out of the question. The sons, indeed, are differently provided: the eldest, in course, inherits the paternal estate, and the younger ones are placed in the church, the army, the navy, or at the bar; and others, again, are genteelly situated in the mercantile world: the whole of which are fit professions for a gentleman, and by which, if they have merit and success, they may acquire a competency.

But for the female part of the family, what appears in their favour? what prospects have they in life?—The parents die, and leave them, without a provision, a burden upon their connections; which forms the first step to deprive them of friends as well as subsistence. A miserable inheritance, to be their best and only portion! What can be said in behalf of such parents? can their easy compliance with the fashion of the times form any apology for such a mistaken conduct?—This surely cannot be called true paternal affection, to entail upon these helpless young creatures such a succession of misery as must eventually ensue . . .

. . . What was it brought ruin upon the first distressed female, who was admitted into the Magdalen charity; and what but a miracle led her to taste comfort?*

What numbers of helpless and destitute young women there are, who, seeing themselves neglected and despised by their connections, notwithstanding all the refined and delicate ideas which their education and mode of bringing up have possessed them with, would gladly endeavour, through necessity, to make up the deficiency of their parents' neglect, by putting themselves forward in the world, in order to obtain a support. But, alas! to their sorrow, they quickly see it is not in their power; for, under their present circumstances, "the world is not their friend, nor the world's laws;" and what was not effected by their parents, cannot possibly be obtained by an inexperienced young woman.

. . . How far the wife was intended to be the slave to her husband, I know not; but certain we are, she was designed to be his friend, his companion, and united part; or, according to the gentlemen's phrase, his better part; and yet how often do we see her sinking under the burden of a household load, whilst the unfeeling husband is lavishing away the substance which ought to be the comfort and support of a family? Yet such unnatural beings there are, who, by giving way to some unlawful passion, can, without scruple or remorse, trample under foot all laws, divine and human, and with impunity bring wretchedness upon those he is bound to support: notwithstanding St. Paul tells us, "if any one provide

---

* See a book, entitled, *The Magdalen, or, a History of the First received into that charitable Asylum.*

not for his own, and especially those of his own house, he hath denied the faith, and is worse than an infidel."

Let us but look at the many unhappy females, who come to ruin through mercenary marriages. How many are the instances of young women, who have been brought up in affluence, and reared with all the tender care and attention, which are in the power of maternal affection to bestow; yet, perhaps, through her youthful follies and credulity, she is led away by the artifice and false pretensions of those mercenary men, on whom she cheerfully bestows her patrimony, whether acquired by inheritance, or the smiles of fortune upon the honest industry of her deceased parents, avails not, for her expected happiness is vanished in empty air, and she is quickly exposed to all the ills of fate.

> "O thoughtless mortals! ever blind to fate,
> "Too soon dejected, and too soon elate.
> "Sudden their honours shall be snatch'd away,
> "And doom'd for ever this victorious day."
>
> POPE.

But the justice of retribution taking place, shall we not see these poor, helpless, and forlorn women set on a level with their fellow creatures, and not be under the shocking and cruel necessity of starving in a land of plenty? And when the face of sorrow is enlivened with the smile of happiness and content, and the weary tradesman can lye down in peace, without fear or danger of being annoyed by the lawless plunderer; when all are united in the bands of mutual benefit and preservation, and the memory of former woes is lost in the blessings of a future age; it is then we may reasonably expect, that less than half the immense sums which are now required, will be sufficient to encourage honest industry.

---·---

PRIMARY SOURCES

The Female Advocate; or, an attempt to recover the rights of women from male usurpation. London, 1799. Reprinted in Feminist Controversy in England, 1788–1810. Edited by Gina Luria. New York: Garland Publishing, 1974.

The Memoirs of Mrs. Mary Anne Radcliffe in Familiar Letters to her Female Friend. Edinburgh and London: Manners and Miller, 1810.

Supplementary Readings Works Not Excerpted

The following works, written between 1605 and 1799, address a range of women's issues throughout or in part. The suggested excerpts from each work contain particularly striking examples of the struggle of women for rights or recognition and include works of love and friendship among women as well as works that condemn slavery and the slave trade.

Although the full name of each author as cited here may not appear on the title page of the cited work, I have included the full names (and birth and death dates where known) for reference purposes. In most cases, I cite an edition from the year of publication, or a reprint edition, or a modern edition where that was more accessible. This list, which is not to be viewed as exhaustive, is meant only to indicate the many women who protested or chose alternatives to their situation.

Cary, Elizabeth Tanfield, Viscountess Falkland. 1585–1639. *The Tragedie of Mariam, the Faire Queene of Jewry.* London: printed by Thomas Creede for Richard Hawkins, 1613. (Probably written around 1605).

Lanier, Aemelia Bassanio. 1569–1645. "To the Vertuous Reader" and "Eve's Apology" to *Salve Deus Rex Judaeorum.* London: Valentine Simmes, 1611.

Speght, Rachael. *fl.* 1617–21. *Mortalities Memorandum, with a Dreame Prefixed, imaginarie in manner; reall in matter.* London: by Edward G   ffin for Jacob Bloome, 1621. (Speght was also one of Swetnam's respondents. See biography of Ester Sowernam.)

Munda, Constantia. *fl.* 1617. *The Worming of a Mad Dogge: Or, a soppe for Cerberus, The Jayler of Hell. No confutation but a sharpe Redargution of the bayter of Women.* London: printed for Laurence Hayes, 1617. (Another response to Joseph Swetnam.)

Chidley, Katherine. *fl.* 1641–45. *The Justification of the Independent Churches of Christ. Being an answer to Mr. Edwards his booke, which hee hath written against the government of Christs Church, and the toleration of Christs publicke worship; briefly declaring that the congregations of the Saints ought not to have dependence in government upon any other, or direction in worship from any other than Christ their head and law giver.* London: William Lahrner, 1641.

Sharp, Jane. *fl.* 1671. Prefatory material and chaps. 10 and 18 to *The Compleat Midwife's Companion; or, the art of midwifry improv'd. Directing childbearing women how to order themselves in their conception, breeding, bearing, and nursing of children . . . with physical prescriptions for each disease incident to the female sex whether virgins, wives, or widows;* *adapted chiefly for their use.* London: for Simon Miller, 1725. (Illustrated 4th ed. of *The Complete Midwives Companion . . .*, 1671.)

Ephelia. [Pseud.] *fl.* 1679. *Female Poems on Several Occasions.* London: William Downing for James Courtney 1679.

Cellier, Elizabeth Dormer. *fl.* 1680. *A Scheme for the Foundation of a Royal Hospital, and raising a revenue of five or six-thousand pounds a year, by, and for the maintenance of a corporation of skilful midwives, and such foundlings or exposed children, as shall be admitted therein, etc.* London: T. Osborne, 1687. Reprinted in *Harleian Miscellany,* 4, 1745: 142–47.

Anon: "The Emulation: A Pindarick Ode." In *Triumphs of Female Wit, in Some Pindarick Odes. Or, The Emulation.* Together with an Answer to an Objector against Female Ingenuity, and Capacity of Learning. Also, a Preface to the Masculine Sex, by a Young Lady. London: T. Malthus and J. Waltho, 1683. ("Written by a Young Lady" is subscribed after the last stanza (p. 5) of "The Emulation."

Fiennes, Celia. 1662–1741. *Through England on a Side Saddle in the Time of William and Mary.* London, 1888. Republished as *The Illustrated Journey of Celia Fiennes 1685–1712,* edited by Christopher Morris. London: MacDonald & Co., 1982. (Probably written 1685–1703.)

Rowe, Elizabeth Singer. [Philomela]. 1674–1737. From *Poems on several occasions.* London: John Dunton, 1696.

Johnson, Elizabeth. *fl.* 1696. "Preface to the Reader," to *Poems on Several Occasions* by Philomela [Elizabeth Singer Rowe.] 1674–1737. London: John Dunton, 1696.

Manley, Delarivière. 1663–1724. Preface to *The Royal Mischief, A tragedy.* London: R. Bentley, 1696.

———. Preface to *The Lost Lover; or, the Jealous Husband, A comedy.* London: R. Bentley, 1696.

———. "To the Author of Agnes de Castro." Prefatory address to *Agnes de Castro, a tragedy* by Catherine Trotter. London: H. Rhodes, 1696.

———. *Almyna, or The Arabian Vow.* London: for William Turner, 1707.

———. *The New Atalantis.* London, 1709. Reprinted in *The Novels of Mary Delarivière Manley.* Edited by Patricia Koster. 2 vols. Gainesville, Fla.: Scholars Facsimiles and Reprints, 1971, vol. 2. (See particularly the controversial lesbian section on the Cabal.)

Trotter, Catherine Cockburn. 1679–1749. *A Poem occasioned by the busts set up in the Queen's Hermitage; designed to be presented with a book in vindication of Mr. Locke, which was to have been inscribed to her Majesty,* 1732. In *The Works of Mrs. Catherine Cockburn, Theological, Moral, Dramatic, and Poetical.* Edited by Thomas Birch. 2 vols. London: J. & P. Knapton, 1751, pp. 572–76.

Pix, Mary Griffith. 1666–1720. *The Royal Mischief, A tragedy.* London: R. Bentley, 1696. Commendatory verse to Delarivière Manley. (This verse and other interlocking materials written by the female wits, Trotter, Pix, and Manley indicate their solidarity against public attack.)

Eugenia. [Pseud.] *fl.* 1700. *The Female Advocate; or a Plea for the just Liberty of the Tender Sex, and particularly of Married Women. Being Reflections on a late Rude and Disingenuous Discourse, Delivered by Mr. John Sprint, in a Sermon at a Wedding, May 11th, at Sherburn, in Dorsetshire, 1699. By a Lady of Quality.* London: for Andrew Bell, 1700. Also printed as *The Female Preacher. Being an Answer to a late Rude and Scandalous Wedding-Sermon, Preach'd by Mr. John Sprint, May 11th at Sherburn, in Dorsetshire: wherein that Levite is Expos'd as he deserves.* By a Lady of Quality. London: for H. Hills, n.d. (noted as 1699 in Huntington Library catalogue, shelf-mark 289255.)

Masham, Damaris Cudworth. 1658–1708. *Occasional thoughts in reference to a vertuous or Christian life.* London: A. & F. Churchill, 1705.

Centlivre, Susanna Freeman. 1667?–1723. *Poems on Several Occasions.* London: J. Nutt, 1706. Commendatory verse to Sarah Fyge Field Egerton.

————. Preface to *The Platonick Lady. A Comedy.* London, 1707.

————. *A Woman's Case, in an Epistle to Charles Joye, Esq.; Deputy-Governor of the South-Sea.* London: E. Curll, 1720.

Thomas, Elizabeth. 1677–1731. *The Metamorphosis of the Town: Or, a view of the present fashions.* A tale: After the Manner of Fontaine. London: for J. Wilford, 1730.

————. *Miscellany Poems on Several Subjects.* London: T. Combs, 1722. (Also published as *Poems on Several Occasions,* by a Lady. London: T. Combs, 1726).

Davys, Mary. 1674–1732. Prologue to *The Self-Rival; a Comedy.* In vol. 1 of *The Works of Mrs. Davys: Consisting of Plays, Novels, Poems, and Familiar Letters.* 2 vols. London: printed by H. Woodfall for the Author, and sold by J. Stevens, 1725.

————. Preface to *The Works of Mrs. Davys.* (Note also this is a reprint in the now out-of-print *Eighteenth-Century British Novelists and the Novel.* Edited by George L. Barnett. New York: Appleton-Century-Crofts, 1968.)

Anon. *The Gentlemen's Magazine* 9 (1739):525–26.

Montagu, Lady Mary Wortley. 1689–1762. From *The Complete Letters of Lady Mary Wortley Montagu.* Edited by Robert Halsband. 3 vols. Oxford: Clarendon Press, 1965–67. To Gilbert Burnet, July 20, 1710; to Wortley, July 20, 1710; to Philippa Mundy, December 12, 1711; to Philippa Mundy, February 6, 1712; to Philippa Mundy, February 27, 1712; to Lady Pomfret, March, 1739; to Lady Bute, October 1, 1752; to Lady Bute, January 28, 1753; to Lady Bute, March 6, 1753; to Lady Bute, March 1, 1754.

————. *The Nonsense of Common-Sense,* Number VI. In *Essays and Poems and Simplicity, A Comedy.* Edited by Robert Halsband and Isobel Grundy. Oxford: Clarendon Press, 1977.

Dixon, Sarah. *fl.* 1740. *Poems on Several Occasions.* Canterbury: J. Abree, 1740.

Howard, Anne, Viscountess Irwin, (later Douglas). 1696?–1764. "A Defence of her sex in answer to Pope's *Characters of Women.*" London, n.d. Reprinted in Bethune, George. *The British Female Poets: with Biographical and Critical Notices.* Philadelphia, 1848. Reprint. Freeport, N.Y.: Books for Libraries Press, 1972.

Haywood, Eliza Fowler 1689/90–1756. *The Female Spectator.* Edited by E. Haywood. Vols. 1–4. London: T. Gardner, April 1744– May 1746. For an attack on prejudice, see "The Jaundice of the Mind," in *The Female Spectator* 21:133–34.

Fielding, Sarah. 1710–1768. Preface to the first edition of *The Adventures of David Simple in Search of a Faithful Friend.* 3 vols. London: A. Millar, 1744. Reprint. London: Oxford University Press, 1969.

Leapor, Mary. 1722–1746. *Poems upon several occasions.* 2 vols. London: J. Roberts, 1748, 1751.

Jones, Mary. *fl.* 1750. *Miscellanies in prose and verse.* Oxford: R. and J. Dodsley, 1750.

Chapone, Hester Mulso. 1727–1801. *The Posthumous Works of Mrs. Chapone containing her correspondence with Mr. Richardson . . .* 2 vols. London: John Murray, 1807. (See especially first and third letters on *"Filial Obedience,"* 1750–51.)

Tollet, Elizabeth. 1694–1754. *Poems on Several Occasions. With Anne Boleyn to King Henry VIII. An Epistle.* London: John Clarke, 1755. (See especially "Hypatia.")

Montagu, Elizabeth Robinson, 1720–1800. In *Dialogues of the Dead* by George Lyttelton. London: W. Sandy, 1760. (The last three dialogues are by Montagu.)

Anon. "Preface" and Address "To the World" to *The Works of the Celebrated Mrs. Centlivre.* London: J. Knapton et al., 1761.

Seward, Anna. 1747–1809. *The Poetical Works of Anna Seward; with Excerpts from her Literary Correspondence.* Vol. 3. Edited by Walter Scott. Edinburgh and London: James Ballantyne and Longman et al., 1810.

Ponsonby, Sarah. 1755–1831. *The Hamwood Papers of the Ladies of Llangollen and Caroline Hamilton.* Edited and introduction by Eva Mary Bell. London: Macmillan & Co., 1730. (Written between 1785 and 1821.)

Williams, Helen Maria. 1762–1827. *A Poem on the Bill lately passed for regulating the Slave Trade.* London: T. Cadell, 1788.

———. *Peru, a poem.* London, 1784.

———. *Julia, A Novel: interspersed with some Poetical Pieces.* London: T. Cadell, 1790.

More, Hannah. 1745–1833. *Slavery, a poem.* London: T. Cadell, 1788.

———. *Strictures on the Modern System of Female Education with a view of the principles and conduct prevalent among women of rank and fortune.* 2 vols. London: T. Cadell & W. Davies, 1799.

Lennox, Charlotte Ramsey. 1730?–1804. *Euphemia.* 4 vols. London: T. Cadell, 1790. (Novel is the correspondence of two female friends.)

Benger, Elizabeth. *The Female Geniad; A Poem.* London: T. Hookham and J. Carpenter, C & G Kearsley, 1791 (Title page states "written at the age of thirteen".)

Smith, Charlotte Turner. 1769–1806. Preface to and *Desmond, a novel.* 3 vols. London: G. G. G. and J. Robinson, 1792. (Novel attacks slavery.)

Wakefield, Priscilla Bell. 1751–1832. *Reflections on the Present Conditions of the Female Sex; with suggestions for its improvement.* London: Joseph Johnson, 1798.

———. *Excursions in North America, described in Letters from a gentleman and his young companion, to their friends in England.* London: Darton & Harvey, 1806. (Includes a condemnation of slavery.)

Hanway, Mary Ann. *fl.* 1798. *Ellinor. Or, the World As It Is.* London, 1798.

Robinson, Mary Darby 1758–1800. *Thoughts on the Condition of Women.* London, 1799.

———. *A Letter to the Women of England on the Injustice of Mental Subordination, with Anecdotes by Anne Frances Randall.* London, 1799.

Burney, D'Arblay, Frances (Fanny). 1752 – 1840. *The Wanderer; or, Female difficulties. By the author of Evelina.* 5 vols. London: Longman & Co., 1814.
(Written later than the period under discussion by a writer of that period,
but interesting for its depiction of feminist character, Elinor Joddrell).

MOIRA FERGUSON is Associate Professor of English and former Chairwoman of Women's Studies at the University of Nebraska, Lincoln. She
is coauthor of *Mary Wollstonecraft.*

MOIRA FERGUSON is Associate Professor of English and former Chairwoman of Women's Studies at the University of Nebraska, Lincoln. She is coauthor of *Mary Wollstonecraft* and a contributing editor to *Feminist Studies*.